WIRELESS AND CELLULAR TELECOMMUNICATIONS

WIRELESS AND CELLULAR TELECOMMUNICATIONS

William C. Y. Lee, Ph.D.

Chairman, Treyspan, Inc.
(Formerly Vice President and Chief Scientist of
Vodafone AirTouch PLC, and Chairman of
LinkAir Communications, Inc.)

Third Edition

McGRAW-HILL

New York   Chicago   San Francisco   Lisbon   London
Madrid   Mexico City   Milan   New Delhi   San Juan
Seoul   Singapore   Sydney   Toronto

The McGraw·Hill Companies

Library of Congress Cataloging-in-Publication Data

Lee, William C. Y.
   Wireless and cellular telecommunications / William C.Y. Lee.—3rd ed.
      p.   cm.
   Includes index.
   ISBN 0-07-143686-3
   1. Mobile communication systems.   2. Wireless communication systems.
   3. Cellular telephone systems.   I. Title.
   TK6570.M6L375   2005
   621.3845′6—dc22

                                            2005052256

2 3 4 5 6 7 8 9 0   DOC/DOC   0 1 0 9 8 7 6 5

ISBN 0-07-143686-3

The sponsoring editor for this book was Stephen S. Chapman and the production supervisor was Richard Ruzycka. It was set in Times Roman by TechBooks. The art director for the cover was Anthony Landi.

Printed and bound by RR Donnelley.

This book is printed on recycled, acid-free paper containing a minimum of 50% recycled, de-inked fiber.

McGraw-Hill books are available at special quantity discounts to use as premiums and sales promotions, or for use in corporate training programs. For more information, please write to the Director of Special Sales, McGraw-Hill Professional, Two Penn Plaza, New York, NY 10121-2298. Or contact your local bookstore.

CONTENTS

Chapter 3. Specifications of Analog Systems   59

Chapter 4. Digital Cellular Systems (2G Systems)   85

Chapter 5. B2G Systems   187

Chapter 6. 3G Systems

Chapter 7. B3G Systems

Chapter 8. Cell Coverage and Antennas

Chapter 9. Cochannel and Code-Channel Interference Reductions 425

Chapter 10. Types of Non-Cochannel Interference 455

Chapter 11. Handoffs and Dropped Calls

485

Chapter 12. Operational Techniques and Technologies 509

Chapter 13. Switching and Traffic   549

Chapter 14. Data Links and Microwaves   573

Chapter 15. System Evaluations   603

Chapter 16. Intelligent Cell Concept and Applications 647

Chapter 17. Intelligent Network for Wireless Communications 697

Chapter 18. Perspective Systems of 4G and Related Topics   731

PREFACE

When I started revising the second edition of *Wireless Telecommunication* to create the current edition, I faced some difficulties. First, I did not know which parts of the book should be saved if dictated by reader preferences over the past ten years.

Second, during the last ten years, so many new technologies and systems were developed that it became difficult to decide what new information to include and how to include it in a succinct fashion; I have therefore tried to present the best of both worlds: to cover as much as I can while, keeping the size of the book as manageable as I feel the second edition was.

It took me almost two years to revise this book, and from those two years' work emerged a book that I feel can be useful to readers on the following fronts:

- as a textbook as well as a handbook, since it covers new systems and technologies.
- as a guide to broadband wireless access and cellular systems.
- as a reference book for executives.
- as a textbook for college seniors and graduate students.

There are many new chapters (Chapter 1, Chapters 5–7, and most of Chapter 18), and I have added a great deal of new material to existing chapters concerning current topics such as MIMO, AdHoc/Mesh Networks, LDPC codes, RFID, etc.

For reference sake, the chapters of this books can be divided into the following areas:

Chapter 1 Introduction to wireless communications
Chapter 2 Basic principles
Chapters 3–6 Cellular systems from first generation to third generation
Chapter 7 Broadband wireless access
Chapters 8–15 System design and deployment
Chapters 16–18 New ways of achieving broadband wireless access

Also, there are so many wireless communication acronyms that it is hard to expect readers memorize them. To make it simpler, this book divides the acronyms into three parts: general terms of telecommunications, cellular communication terms, and, broadband wireless access terms.

The Internet is obviously a good place to gather a great deal of information. However, technical books such as *Wireless Telecommunication* pull many pieces of information together and provide a range of general topics that readers can then understand as a whole. This is why the Internet cannot replace textbooks and why I believe textbooks will remain a valuable source of information in the future.

As I recall, I finished writing the first edition of *Wireless Telecommunication* in 1986, but the manuscript was evaluated by McGraw-Hill for almost a year before it entered production. The reason for the delay was that McGraw wondered if readers would actually be interested in learning about cellular systems. I'm happy to say that with the publication of this third edition, the answer was clearly yes.

When the first edition was published in late 1988, it was still the only book available worldwide on the topic of cellular communications. Before long, I was receiving compliments on the book—how one reader read the book to prepare for an industry job (in this brand-new industry) and landed the position, how informative another reader found the book, etc. But I also receive other compliments as "I always carry this book because the book fits well in my briefcase", or "I like to read the book because it is light and easy to carry." I know those readers really spoke from their heart. I thanked them from my heart.

The third edition, while a bit longer, a bit heavier, can still be pocketed, yet containing even more updated information on wireless telecommunication technology—and can be glanced at just before a job interview to another brand new field today named broadband wireless access (BWA) which will create its new and growing market and probably will evolve toward 4G era in the future. Good luck to those readers.

William C. Y. Lee

PREFACE TO THE FIRST EDITION

As the number of cellular subscribers increases, the interference that will be experienced by the systems will also increase. This means that many large cellular systems will, sooner or later, have to handle interference problems. This is a lucrative field that is ripe for research and that will soon be begging for more advanced applications.

This all-inclusive and self-contained work, consisting of fifteen chapters, is a basic textbook that supports further exploration in a new communications field, cellular communications. Since it is the first in its field, this book may be considered a handbook or building block for future research.

For years it has been my desire to write a book on the technical aspects of cellular systems. Since it is a new field, the theory has to be developed and then verified by experiment. I am seeking to adhere to the progression of learning that I described in *Who's Who in America:*

1. Use mathematics to solve problems.
2. Use physics to interpret results.
3. Use experiments and counterexamples to check outcomes.
4. Use pictures to emphasize important points.

Since I have accumulated many pictures in my mind, I would like to share them with my readers. In this field many new applications and theories have been discovered. Thus, my findings will help the reader to assimilate this new knowledge and accelerate learning time. The many mistakes that have been made in the past in designing cellular systems can now be avoided. Engineers who work in other communication systems will appreciate the many diverse concepts used in cellular systems. The reader should be aware that it is possible to apply the various theories improperly and thereby create many serious problems. I would like to hear from readers about their cellular systems experiences, both successful and unsuccessful.

Overall, I have written this book for technical engineers who would like to explore options in the cellular industry. However, Chapters 1 and 2 are for *executives* and for anyone who would like to familiarize himself or herself with key concepts of the field. Chapter 3 describes the specification of cellular systems. The North American specification works in Canada, the United States, and Mexico, so a cellular phone will work anywhere in this territory because of the standardized specification.

Chapter 4 introduces the point-to-point model I developed over the last 15 years. It can be used as a core to develop many design tools. Chapters 5 and 6 deal with cochannel interference problems, and Chapter 7 deals with noncochannel interference problems. Chapters 8 through 13 offer detailed material for engineers to solve problems concerning improved system performance. Chapter 14 describes the digital systems which may become the next-generation cellular systems, and presents many key issues in order to alert readers to possible future developments. Chapter 15 highlights some miscellaneous topics related to cellular systems.

Much of my unpublished work is included in these 15 chapters. I welcome feedback from readers about how I can better meet their needs in the second edition of the book.

I have always felt that cellular technology should be openly shared by cellular operators. Competition only occurs in a saturated market, and the cellular market is almost unlimited. Therefore, competition is not to be feared in this early stage of the cellular industry. We need to promote this industry as much as possible by involving more interested engineers and investors.

In the last six years, I have taught 3-day seminars sponsored by George Washington University. I am trying to convince the cellular industry that if we have narrow-minded attitudes and do not share our experiments or knowledge, the whole industry will not advance fast enough and could be replaced by other new industries, such as wireless communications or in-building communications.

Let us join together to allow the cellular industry its optimum potential and set our goal that one day a pocket cellular phone will carry our calls to any place in the world.

William C. Y. Lee

ACKNOWLEDGMENTS

Over the last ten years, the workday as we know it has changed dramatically for everyone. With so much international travel, conference calls, and cell phone calls, we're seemingly at work 24 hours a day. This endless schedule makes it difficult to work on "peripheral" projects, such as the revision of my book, and I finished this book only because of much encouragement and help.

First, I have to thank my mentor, Chap Cutler, who gave me valuable guidance throughout my career and who advised me to revise this book. Unfortunately, I could not finish it before he passed away. I owe him a great deal.

I am deeply thankful to my colleagues at Vodafone-AirTouch, and LinkAir Communications who helped me in the past, especially Ting Zheng, who has given me full support to work on my book. I am also thankful to David J. Y. Lee, my first Ph.D. student, who helped me draft Chapter 7 and reviewed several chapters.

I am also obliged to my dear assistant, Kathy Gardner, who has been so patient in reading and editing my sloppy writing, written on paper pads, while I was traveling or out of my office. This book could not have been completed without her help.

I have to thank Steve Chapman of McGraw-Hill, who constantly encouraged me, and Stephanie Lentz of TechBooks, for the tedious proofreading and schedule keeping and for doing what I requested of her with great patience.

Finally, I have to thank my lovely wife Margaret for her understanding over these years in giving me the time to write books. I hope this book can inspire my grandson, Alex, although he is only one year old now.

WIRELESS AND CELLULAR TELECOMMUNICATIONS

CHAPTER 1
TREND OF MOBILE WIRELESS

1.1 HISTORY OF MOBILE CELLULAR

In order to classify in this book the generations for mobile cellular development, it may be logical to use the multiple access schemes. The analog frequency division multiple access (FDMA) systems are 1G systems. The digital time division multiple access (TDMA) systems with circui switching are 2G systems. The code division multiple access (CDMA) systems with packet/circuit switching are 3G systems, and some different advanced mobile access technology used with an all Internet protocol (IP) network will be called 4G. However, because each technology itself is advanced with time, we use time periods to classify the generations. Those, analog systems are 1G, digital voice systems are 2G, digital voice/data systems are B2G, and broadband digital systems are 3G. Wireless local area network/wireless metropolitan area network (WLAN/WMAN) are B3G systems, and very-high-speed data-rate systems are 4G systems.

1.1.1 AMPS System (First-Generation System)

In 1964, Bell Laboratories formed a mobile communication department after the U.S. Congress took away the satellite communications business from AT&T. The early wireless networks only concentrated on voice communication. In the beginning, the analog systems named HCMTS (high-capacity mobile telephone system) were developed at Bell Labs in the period 1964–1974. The HCMTS used an FM modulation with a bandwidth of 30 kHz for both signaling and voice channels. The FM modulation index for voice is 4 which is the ratio of the frequency deviation (12 kHz) and the voice frequency (3 kHz). The signaling rate is 10 kbps. The system also migrated new handoff features. At that time, there was no standard organization for wireless mobile systems. AT&T made its standard for HCMTS[1] the first-generation cellular system. Later, the standard EIA (Electronic Industrial Association) named the system IS-3 (Interim Standard 3). EIA merged with TIA (Telecommunication Industrial Association) and was then called TIA-EIA. The new name for the system, AMPS (Advanced Mobile Phone Service),[2–5] was used since 1976, and the system was deployed in 1984. Bell Labs in 1975 awarded OKI a contract to manufacture the first 200 mobile phones (car phones), as AT&T could not be permitted to manufacture the car phones according to the FCC's ruling. Then next year, a total of 1800 car phones were awarded to OKI, E.F. Johnson, and Motorola—each manufactured 600 car phones. Bell Labs built car phone testing equipment. All the phones made by the three companies had to pass the test, which none passed the first time. The world's first 2000 car phones were used in the Chicago Trial in 1977. The system specification was finalized after the trial. The U.S. cellular system could not commercialize until the FCC divided the allocated 20-MHz cellular spectrums into two: one 10 MHz went to telephone companies (wirelines) called Band B and the other 10 MHz went to paging/dispatch companies (non-wireline) called Band A, and the Band B system began deployment in 1984. The specification of AMPS is described in Chapter 3.

Therefore, Japan NTT (Nippon Telephone and Telegraph Co.) deployed its version of AMPS in Tokyo in 1979, which was the first commercial system in the world. The NTT systems had no diversity scheme at the base, and the signaling used was multitone signaling at a rate of 300 tones/s. The service cost was high, and the voice quality was unsatisfactory. After AMPS deployed in the United States, the voice quality was outstanding, and the service cost was much lower than the NTT system. Then, the United Kingdom modified the AMPS system with a channel bandwidth of 25 kHz, called Total Access Communication System (TACS). Besides, the Nordic Mobile Telephone (NMT) majority deployed in four Nordic countries; the system C450 in Germany and cordless phone 2 (CT2) in the United Kingdom were also served in the market, but they were not cellular systems. Because the technology in the 1980s could not make a handset phone, the analog AMPS systems were designed and used as car phones, and the car battery supplied the power. The coverage for each cell was around an area of 8 miles radius.

1.1.2   Second-Generation System

In 1983, Europe started to develop GSM[6-9] (the original name was called Group of Special Mobile, then was changed to Global System for Mobile). GSM is a digital TDMA system and was first deployed in Germany in 1991. It was the first digital mobile cellular system in the world. The specification of GSM is described in Section 4.2.

In 1987, due to the fast-growing number of subscribers, the capacity of AMPS became an issue. Then, the North American TDMA (NA-TDMA) was voted as a digital standard in 1988 for trying to solve the capacity issue. The specification of NA-TDMA is appeared in Section 4.3. However, TDMA technology might not be the right choice for future needs.

In 1989, Qualcomm was starting to develop CDMA with great assistance from PacTel in financial, technical, and spectrum issues; the CDMA system could have a capacity that was 10 times more than AMPS according to theoretical analysis at that time. To prove the technology, PacTel in 1990 migrated its 1.25 MHz (40 AMPS channels) from 12.5-MHz spectrum bandwidth in 800 MHz for trialing a CDMA system in the San Diego market. At that time, performance of the analog systems in San Diego suffered because of the CDMA trial. Nevertheless, PacTel believed that a new technology was needed for the future. In 1993, after the U.S. market reached 1 million analog mobile subscribers, this high-capacity CDMA digital system[10-12] was born. The system is described in Section 4.4. In 1994, PacTel's name was changed to AirTouch. AirTouch pursued the deployment of its commercial CDMA systems.

In 1989, the United Kingdom had released the PCN (Personal Communications Networks) licensed band in 1900 MHz and awarded four licenses through a beauty contest. Later, PCN adopted the GSM system. Also, the 900-MHz spectrum of the TACS band was migrated to GSM as well. In 2000, GSM had a data transmission enhancement called GPRS (General Packet Radio Service), which could use any number of time slots among the total eight slots for sending data. The data rate is from 14.4 kbps to 64 kbps. There is another high-speed data enhancement called EDGE (Enhanced Data Rates for GSM Evolution), which modulations are changed from GMSK (Gaussian minimum shift keying) to 8 PSK (phase shift keying). The transmission data rate can be up to 500 kbps. The EDGE is described in Sec. 5.2. In 1990, Japan had developed its PDC (Personal Digital Cellular).[13] The 12.5-kHz offset the 25-kHz channels, thus the number of channels were increased in the system. It is a TDMA cellular system operating at 800 MHz and 1.5 GHz. The structure of PDC is very similar to that of NA-TDMA, and is described in section 4.5.2.

In 1995, the CDMA IS-95 was the first CDMA system (later called cdmaOne in 1998) using 1.25-MHz bandwidth. It was suggested by PacTel that the operator could give up one tenth of the spectrum from analog spectrum to create a CDMA channel and generate at least twice the capacity of the entire analog system for voice. The CDMA systems were commercialized in Hong Kong, Los Angeles, and Seattle almost at the same time in early 1995. However, those systems themselves were not fully developed at that time.

In 1996, the Korean market demonstrated the merit of the CDMA system. From January 1996 to September 1996, the number of subscribers went from zero to 1 million in 9 months. The Korean CDMA systems observed their expected high capacity. In 1999, cdma1X was developed. It can have a data rate up to 64 kbps (see Section 5.6). In 2000, cdma1X created an EVDO (Enhanced Version of Data Only) option[14–15]. It was using a 1.25-MHz channel dedicated for data only. It can transmit 2 Mbps while the terminal is nomadical and 384 kbps while in motion. The TDM scheme is used in the EVDO. Then, in 2004, EVDV (Enhanced Version for Data and Voice) became another option to implement on a 1.25-MHz channel to have 2 Mbps data plus voice. EVDO and EVDV are sometimes called CDMA2000 1X systems. Both EVDO and EVDV are described in Section 6.8.

1.1.3 3G Systems

In 1997, 3G (third generation) had been suggested mainly by DoCoMo and Ericsson and cdmaOne was called 2.5G. At that time, all the system providers around the world did not ask for 3G but were told by the vendors to prepare for the future.

In 1998, there were 13 proposals submitted to ITU. Three of them were chosen by OHG (Operator Harmonization Group) for ITU. Wideband CDMA WCDMA,[14] CDMA2000,[15] and UTRA-TDD (UMTS Terrestrial Radio Access -TDD TD-SCDMA (Time Division-Synchrous CDMA) are all 5-MHz bandwidth channels. Ericsson and DoCoMo mainly developed WCDMA. The carrier bandwidth is 5 MHz and the chip rate is 3.84 Mcps. One version of 3G systems, called FOMA (Freedom of Mobile Multimedia Access), has been deployed in Japan. FOMA's handsets can have a higher data rate and be operated in the WCDMA system but not the other way around. CDMA2000[15] has been developed from cdma1X with a channel bandwidth of 1.25 MHz and a chip rate of 1.2288 Mcps and becomes cdma3X with a bandwidth of 3.75 MHz and a chip rate of 3.68 Mcps. cdma3X is a multicarrier CDMA system. Its downlink is 3×1.25 MHz, and its uplink is a wideband 3.75 MHz. WCDMA and CDMA2000 are using frequency division duplexing (FDD) spectrum. The 3G systems, UTRA-TDD/TD-SCDMA, are using time division duplexing (TDD) spectrum implementing multicode, multislot, and orthogonal variable spreading factor (OVSF) technologies. UTRA-TDD developed in Europe with its bandwidth of 5 MHz and carrier chip rate of 3.84 Mcps. TD-SCDMA, developed in China, had a channel bandwidth of 1.6 MHz and a carrier chip rate of 1.2288 Mcps. TD-SCDMA can be used as a multicarrier $(3 \times)$ CDMA system. All 36 systems are described in chapter 6.

To choose a channel bandwidth of 5 MHz for WCDMA creates difficulty in designing a CDMA radio channel. First, the bandwidth of 5 MHz had not been studied in-depth to determine whether it was an optimum bandwidth for mobile cellular before choosing it. Second, many multipaths were unexpectedly received in a 5-MHz bandwidth than that received by the conventional CDMA system with a bandwidth of 1.25 MHz. Thus, more studies were needed to understand the multipath phenomenon in a bandwidth of 5 MHz. Therefore, the delay in developing the WCDMA system was not avoidable. Since 2000, the postponement of deploying the WCDMA system continued year after year. In the United Kingdom, the 3G spectrum licenses were auctioned in 1999 and awarded in 2000 to four system providers. Vodafone was one of the four system providers. Vodafone bet US 10 billion in order to win the license for a 30-MHz $(2 \times 15$ MHz) nationwide

FDD system in the United Kingdom. Vodafone has already waited for 5 years and is very concerned about the 3G developments not only in Europe, but worldwide.

1.1.4 4G Systems

In the past 20 years, wireless networks have evolved from an analog, single medium (voice), and low data rate (a few kilobits per second) system to the digital, multimedia, and high data rate (ten to hundreds of megabits per second) system of today. Future systems will be based on user's demands as the fourth-generation (4G) cellular system. Many rich applications need high-speed data rates to achieve them.

ITU in July 2003, had made a requirement for 4G system as follows:[16]

1. At a standstill condition, the transmission data rate should be 1 Gbps.

2. At a moving condition, the transmission data rate should be 100 Mbps.

Any proposed system that can meet these requirements with less bandwidth and higher mobile speed will be considered. It is a beauty contest. With this high-speed data system, many advanced applications for the users can be realized. A potential 4G system could be used in the family of OFDM (Orthogonal Frequency Division Multiplexing), because the WMAN described in Section 7.4.2 using OFDM can have a transmission data rate of 54–70 Mbps, which is much higher than the CDMA system can provide. The 4G perspective systems using OFDM are described in Chapter 18.

1.1.5 Other Cellular–Like Systems

In 1989, the United Kingdom had developed a cordless phone called CT-2 system.[17] It was the first digital mobile radio system to use handsets. The total spectrum bandwidth is 4 MHz in 800 MHz. The channel access is FDMA/TDD. The channel bandwidth is 100-kHz spacing, thus there are 40 channels. The two-way conversation can be sent out but cannot be received, just like a portable telephone booth. The United Kingdom has issued the CT-2 system to four operators for the reason of fair competition. Each operator can provide many phone zones, and each one has 10 channels to serve its subsidiaries. Because there was no coordination in radio operation among the operators and, also because the phone zones of each operator were not properly located, the radio interference problem among the four operators could not be solved. Ericsson had developed an upgrade system from the CT-2 version, originally called DCT900, and then changed to CT-3.[18] Its channel bandwidth was 1 MHz with 64 time slots. Overall data rate was 640 kbps. CT3 did not really deploy into mobile markets but was used for fixed wireless application with PBX (Private Branch Exchange).

DECT (Digital European Cordless Telecommunication System)[19] is a European standard system. It is also a CT2-like system operating at 1.8 GHz and its channel bandwidth is 1.728 MHz. It is a TDD system with 12 slots; 6 time slots for downlink and 6 for uplink. It used the public network to have mobile communication within the home or to provide business communication locally and mainly provide wireless local loops. DECT was deployed in regional areas in Europe as described in Section 4.5.

PHS (Personal Handy Phone)[20] is a TDD system operating at 1.9 GHz and supporting personal communication services; the channel bandwidth is 300 kHz. There are eight time slots in each channel. Among all the PHS channels, some slots are sending, some slots receiving at the same time. In 1995, there were four PHS operators in Japan. The number of subscribers reached 7 million, but none of them were making profit. Finally, DoCoMo consolidated with the other three, using the wireline switches instead of mobile phone switches, and started to survive the PHS business. In 1999, PHS went to China, called by the nickname "Little Smarter," used by two wireline companies to serve customers for cellular-like systems. In 2003, the PHS subscribers already reached 20 million in China and became a threat to the cellular system providers. PHS is described in Section 5.5.

In the 1980s, the specialized mobile radio (SMR) bands were issued to the trunking radio. Every license is allowed have 200 kHz in 900-MHz bands and needs to have 100 subscribers in 2 years to continue the license. Motorola acquired most SMR bands in the 1990s and developed its proprietary system called MIRS (Mobile Integrated Radio System), and then changed the name to iDEN (Integrated Digital Enhanced Network) described in Section 5.4. It is a TDMA/FDD system with a channel bandwidth of 25 kHz at 850 MHz. The number of time slots is six; usually, three time slots are always inactive. The modulation is 16 QAM (Quadrature amplitude modulation). Its digital system is a cellular-like system mainly for voice. At the beginning, its voice quality was not as good as cellular systems. The system started to provide many good features by using Nortel's switch and was the first one in year 2001 to have a push-to-talk feature. The push-to-talk can have a virtual connection in real-time to connect a group of party members online after pushing the buttons. Thus, the caller doesn't need to dial the phone number of every party member. It can be treated as a conference call to a group of people. Other cellular system providers adopted this attractive feature. Nextel is using nonauction spectrum. Therefore, the system is a nonstandard system.

1.2 WIRELESS DATA NETWORKS

1.2.1 General Description

The wireless data networks[21-24] can be classified according to their coverage areas. The smallest coverage area, where the network is called wireless personal area network (PAN), is limited to an office. A cell of such a small size would enable connecting computers or electronic input devices. A wireless local area network (LAN) connects users on a particular floor of a building. A community area network serves an industrial or university campus, where the network can roam throughout the campus. A wireless metropolitan area network (WMAN) connects the residents and visitors to a city. And finally, the most extensive network is a wireless wide area network (WWAN), which connects the entire country.

A wireless PAN network can use Bluetooth, developed by Ericsson in 1978. Bluetooth was named after a pirate king in the Nordic countries. It is used for short distances up to 10 feet. The channel bandwidth is 200 kHz using QAM modulation. The data rate can be 1 Mbps. It is a short wire replacement for wireless. Today, most cell phones are equipped with Bluetooth. The Zigbee was developed from the IEEE 802.15 standard in the United States. It can have a range of 30 m, but the data rate is about 144 kbps. It can be used as a networking video. Devices used in PAN are described in Section 14.11.

In the 1990s, WLANs was divided into the radio-frequency (RF) systems and infrared (IR) systems specified by the FCC. The RF systems are subdivided into the licensed non-spread-spectrum (NSS) and the unlicensed spread spectrum (SS). In the unlicensed SS, it requires a minimum of 50 and 75 hopping frequency at 910 MHz and 2.5 GHz, respectively, or achieved by a spread-spectrum modulation exceeding a spreading factor of 10 in direct sequence systems.

The wavelength of IR is slightly longer than the wavelength of visible light. It is used for data communications in wireless LANs; to download data among PCs, PDAs, and cell phones. IR links are limited to distances under 15 m. There is a diffuse IR, that does not require a line-of-sight path between transmitter and receiver. But it is suitable for fixed links, not for nomadic. A standard point-to-point infrared at a 1–2 m range can have up to 4 Mbps. Infrared can download data fast and have little or no interference.

1.2.2   Wireless LAN Standards

Standardization activities on wireless LAN are the key to spread the use of its application. They are concentrated mostly on the unlicensed bands. Two major approaches are used to regulate the unlicensed bands: one is an interoperable rule among all equipment, the other is spectrum etiquette (i.e., enables wireless LAN equipment manufactured by different vendors to fairly share the wireless resources).

The European Telecommunications Standards Institute (ETSI) has defined a wireless standard called HIPERLAN to provide 23.5 Mbps in the 5-MHz band, and the FCC allocated 2.4 GHz and 5.8 GHz for IEEE 802.11 a/b/g:

Standards	Carrier Frequency	Data Rates
IEEE 802.11 b	2.4 GHz	10 Mbps
IEEE 802.11 a	5.8 GHz	20 Mbps
IEEE 802.11 g	2.4 GHz	20 Mbps

The HIPERLAN can be used as a wireless MAN (called HIPERMAN), so HIPERMAN is very similar to IEEE 802.11 a/b/g. The IEEE 802.11 a/b/g will be described in Chapter 7.

1.2.3   Wireless WAN Evolution

As the data rate of using the broadband medium becomes popular, a user can use any wireless LAN device whether in a building, in an airport, or at a hot spot. In the 1980s, existing wireless wide area networks (WWAN) were Mobitex's RAM mobile data, providing 8 kbps, and Motorola's ARDIS (Advanced Radio Data Information Services), providing 19.2 kbps. IBM has used ARDIS since 1983 to keep in touch with its field servicemen; ARDIS opened for public use in 1990. Also, Ricochet wireless WAN service was introduced by Metricom in 1994 using unlicensed (ISM) band over a typical range of 0.25 km to 0.75 km. Ricochet access points also can be used as a repeater to send data back to a central point via access points as relays. This system can serve 14.4 kbps, but the ratio of the number of subscribers and the number of access points is around 3:1. The traffic congestion was the problem. There were 30,000 subscribers of Metricom in San Francisco. Metricom also deployed a new Ricochet system in New York with a data rate of 28.8 kbps. Again, the system was not intelligent enough to resolve the traffic congestion problems.

The CDPD (Cellular Digital Packet Data)[22] was designed to provide packet data services as an overlay to the existing analog cellular AMPS network. The CDPD will use one of the AMPS channels when it is idle and will hop out to another channel when AMPS is starting to use it. Each 30-kHz channel supports 19.2 kbps. CDPD used GMSK modulation and frequency hopping techniques. Because most cellular systems had foreign interference detectors installed at base stations, as soon as a CDPD channel occupied one cellular channel, the cellular system would not assign that channel for a new call. Thus, CDPD channels reduced the cellular capacity. Also, CDPD took too long to develop its system to be deployed and missed the window of business opportunity.

Because the GSM system's primary purpose was voice service system, the European ETSI in 1992 had developed a public standard for trunked radio and mobile data systems called TETRA (Trans European Trunked Radio) using $\pi/4$-DQPSK (differential binary phase shift keying) modulation operating at a channel rate of 3G kbps in each 25-kHz channel. Since GSM became a worldwide system and it needed not only voice but also data service. Thus a GPRS packet data add-on system was developed, then TETRA has become less valid.

For wireless WAN, IEEE 802.16 is developed for LMDS (local multipoint distribution system) (23–40 GHz), and IEEE 802.16 a/d/e for MMDS (multichannel multipoint distribution service) (2.4–7 GHz). IEEE 802.16 and IEEE 802.16 a/d are for the fixed link condition, and 802.16e is for the mobile condition. The range for 802.16 is around 100 m and for 802.16 a/d/e is 5–30 km. The IEEE 802.16 is not active because the LMDS markets were not ready in 1990. All the 802.11 and 802.16 are using OFDM modulations with frequency hopping as an option in TDD band. IEEE 802.16e can become an OFDMA (Orthogonal Frequency Division Multiple Access) system with an all IP network. IEEE 802.16e has five proposed technologies, and one of them is OFDM. In 2004, the companies who endorsed OFDM technology formed an appliance called WiMAX, with this effort led by Intel. WiMAX system can use VoIP (Voice over IP) for voice and transmit 54 Mbps over a bandwidth of 20 MHz. The frequency spectrum is at the unlicensed band of 5.8 GHz. The WiMAX chip will be embedded in all notebooks or PCs by the year 2006, and a WiMAX phone will be made by the year 2007 as predicted. There is another standard wireless WAN system called IEEE 802.20, led by Flarion. Flarion's system is using OFDMA in FDD bands with frequency hopping called Flash OFDM system. It can implement handoffs for mobile units while crossing the cells as a cellular-like system. However, Flarion's system has not yet been a standard system in IEEE 802.20. The description of IEEE 802.20 is appeared in Section 7.4.4.

1.3 COMMUNICATION SATELLITE SYSTEMS

1.3.1 History

In 1945, A.C. Clarke suggested that if a satellite were at a height of 35,880 km above the Equator, it would orbit Earth every 24 hours and appear stationary over a fixed point above the Equator. Three satellites could cover the whole Earth's surface except at the areas near the poles.[25] A passive balloon called Echo, developed by Bell Labs in conjunction with JPL, was launched in 1960 in a low orbit of 500 km. It was a passive satellite. In July 1962, Telstar was launched into an elliptical orbit with its altitude varying between 950 and 5700 km. Telstar, an active satellite, receives the earth signal at 6390 MHz and retransmits at 4170 MHz with a power of 2 W. The Relay satellite was launched in December 1962 into an inclined orbit. The uplink frequency is 2000 MHz, and the downlink frequency is 4170 MHz. The first experimental Syncom satellite was launched in 1963 and was the first near-synchronous-orbit satellite. In August 1962, the U.S. Congress expressed willingness to establish a global communication satellite system and thereby created INTELSAT[26] (International Telecommunication Satellite Consortium). Early Bird, known as Intelsat I, was launched in 1965. The four Intelsat series launched in different years with increasing channel capacity are listed in Table 1.1. The uplink frequency and downlink frequency are 6 and 4 GHz, respectively, in all four Intelsat series. The Russian communication satellite Molniya I was launched in 1965 into an elliptical orbit in which the orbit time is 12 hours. The orbit was inclined so that the satellite would appear over a point on Earth at the same local time each day in Russia. Then, a number of Molniya satellites provided a television distribution system known as the Orbital system, covering the whole Soviet Union. Global communications are often based on the satellite systems to establish global coverage.

TABLE 1.1 Communication Satellite Characteristics

Satellite	Weight in Orbit (kg)	Diameter (cm)	Length* (cm)	Direct-Current Power (W)	Effective Radiated Power (dB Relative to 1 W)	Bandwidth (MHz)	Channel Capacity (Number of Voice Channel)	Year of Launching
Intelsat I	34	71	59	45	15	50	240	1965
Intelsat II	73	142	74	81	17	250	240	1967
Intelsat III	114	142	102	106	22	450	1200	1969
Intelsat IV	766	240	280	—	23[†]	500	3000–9000	1973
					34.7[‡]			

*Excluding antenna.

[†] Global-coverage antenna.

[‡] Spot-beam antenna.

1.3.2 Attributes

In the satellite communication systems, by choosing the satellite orbit, the communication between any two points, "visible" from the satellite over a planned area, observes different transmission delays because receiving a call from a stationary satellite is 250 ms. round trip. The low earth orbit (LEO) satellites are close to the earth, and can shorten the transmission delay to 50 ms, but the LEO satellites travel around the earth every 2 hours or less. The time for a ground user to last a call from a LEO satellite is only a few minutes. In order to keep the call continue, the call needs to be passed from one satellite to another. Any particular LEO only carries a piece of data or call segments from the sender to the receiver. In satellite communications, a near-zero Doppler effect in the receiving signal is a significant advantage. The choice of frequency is important: When the frequency is below 5 GHz, the signal is affected by galactic noise and disturbed Sun noise. In satellite communications, using two linear polarized waves to send two different pieces of data can increase the spectral efficiency. However, Faraday rotation effects occur between two linear polarized waves and degrade the signal quality. Faraday rotation effects are negligible above 10 GHz. Also, ionosphere scintillations are caused by the fluctuations of the electron density in the sporadic E layer and F layer due to geographical location and season of the year. The ionosphere scintillations are negligible also at gigahertz frequencies. Above 10 GHz, the signal attenuation due to water vapor or rain clouds, in the space can increase in sky noise temperature. In most cases, the diversity schemes and depolarization solution are applied to reduce the undesired natural phenomenon effect on the received signal.

1.3.3 Satellites in Different Orbits

The satellite systems, because of the high altitude, can establish global coverage. The first public communication by satellite took place in 1962, after Echo and Telstar experiments were successfully done by AT&T Bell Labs. Comsat Communication, Inc., was formed, and the early work was based on the National Aeronautics and Space Administration (NASA) applications technology satellite program (ATS). Satellite systems can provide wireless mobile communications. The actual footprint size on Earth depends on the orbit of the satellite above Earth.

1. A geostationary earth orbit (GEO) satellite is in orbit 36,000 km above Earth and moves along the orbit with the same speed as the rotation of Earth. Thus, the GEO satellite stays at one spot as seen from Earth. GEO has a field-of-view (FOV) diameter of approximately 13,000 km. It can cover most of one country. GEO is a regional satellite. It can have multiple spot beams and can have frequency reuse through small spot beams. GEO has an advantage of being able to maintain a connection with a node but a disadvantage of a signal's round trip delay of approximately 250 ms. Users will notice a delay when making phone calls or using real-time video.

2. A medium earth orbit (MEO) satellite is in orbit at approximately 10,000 km above Earth and has a FOV diameter of approximately 7000 km. It is used in a group of MEO satellites to have the footprints cover the important regions around the world, as the MEO satellite orbits the world every 12 hours, such as Global Positioning System (GPS) satellites. There are 24 GPS satellites among them, 18 are active and 6 for spares. GPS covers the entire world. At any one time, one spot on Earth can see three GPS satellites above Earth to determine the location of that spot. There are two kinds of codes: P code for U.S. military use and C code for commercial use worldwide. Since 2003, GPS navigation systems have been installed in many cars and in cell phones. Its location accuracy is within 3 m. However, GPS can be used only outside of buildings. If assisted by other technologies, GPS can also be used inside buildings.

Odyssey is a MEO satellite system.[25] It has only 16 satellites and covers the entire world. The cost of this system should be less expensive. The life span of the satellites can be 10 years or longer.

Inmarsat's ICO (Intermedia Circular Orbit)[26] is also an MEO. It has 8 satellites and serves for data transmission only.

3. A low earth orbit (LEO) satellite is a low-altitude-orbit satellite and is in orbit at approximately 800 km above Earth. It has a FOV diameter of about 1500 km. The FOV area of each LEO satellite travels around Earth about every 2 hours. The concept of deploying a cellular communication system using LEO satellites is different from the terrestrial cellular systems. The cells are moving and the ground mobile (terminal) sees a satellite only for a few minutes; then, the connection must be handed over to the next satellite. The short coverage area changing in time results in frequent handovers in a LEO system. Handovers do introduce inefficiencies in system capacity and may drop connections. From LEO satellite to Earth, a delay time of only 5 ms round trip is obtained as compared with the delay time of 250 ms round trip from GEO satellites.

The LEO has many advantages:

(a) A delay time of 5 ms can be achieved;

(b) A smaller path loss is obtained due to the line-of-sight condition, so that Earth antennas can be smaller and lighter;

(c) Broader coverage is provided than terrestrial systems. LEO also uses spot beams for frequency reuse like terrestrial cellular systems;

(d) Fewer base stations (i.e., satellites) are needed; and

(e) Land, sea, and air can be covered.

However, the LEO has several disadvantages:

(a) The satellite signal is too weak to penetrate the walls of buildings; the wired or wireless LANs can help extend the satellite's coverage indoors.

(b) The LEO operates at above 10 GHz, and rain attenuation effects on the signal is another big concern.

LEO satellite systems are Motorola's Iridium,[27] Loral and Qualcomm's GlobalStar,[28] and Teledesic Corporation's Teledesic

• Iridium:[27] a global satellite phone system for voice and data traffic with a 2400 bps data modem. It was a constellation of 77 LEO satellites and decreased its number to 66 in order to reduce the construction cost. Launched in 1997, it entered commercial service in 1998 at an altitude of 778 km. It uses switches on the satellites; the signal can pass from one satellite to another in space and come down to Earth after reaching a proper satellite for its destination. Because the Iridium system is more expensive to use than the cellular systems, it could not compete with them. It will become a backup system in areas of the world, such as oceans or mountains, where cellular can hardly be deployed. Iridium satellites are interconnected via microwave links and interface via gateways with PSTN (Public Switched Telephone Network). Because of the networking in the sky is through switches in the satellites, fewer ground gateways are needed.

• GlobalStar[28] is also a LEO satellite system. It is a simple and low-cost system. It has 48 satellites at an altitude of 648 km. All the satellites are repeaters (transponders). The signal received by a certain satellite from a ground terminal has to send back down to a ground gateway. Therefore, more ground gateways are needed. Furthermore the life span of LEO satellites in orbit is about only 5 years on average.

- Teledesic Corporation's Teledesic satellites were used to build a satellite PSTN network. Originally, 960 satellites were planned, which number was dropped down to 240 due to the high investment cost. This system was never deployed and does not exist.
- The LEO satellite systems such as Iridium, GlobalStar, and Teledesics did not have a sound business strategy to either compete with or enhance cellular as they originally planned and as they were struggling to survive. Because the cellular service charge had dropped drastically year after year, the LEO system's service charge was too high compared to cellular. None of the LEO satellite systems were served to the commercial.

1.4 PAGING SYSTEMS

Paging system[29] is a one-way personal wireless alerting and messaging system. Paging was started in the 1960s. The receiver is a tone page (beeper) with a dedicated telephone number to receive the message. The message primarily is the caller's phone number. In some tone paging systems, a voice message may be transmitted after the beep. Also, the pager can be an alphanumeric pager, which has a fairly large screen to display several text strings. It was introduced in the late 1970s and became popular in the mid-1990s. The bandwidth of the paging channel is 25 kHz. Each paging channel can serve 50,000 pagers. Each paging tower can be 100 m high and can cover an area of 16-km radius. Therefore, the paging system is the most spectrally efficient system. Also, the paging frequencies operate at around 35 MHz, 150 MHz, 450 MHz, and 900 MHz. In these low-frequency ranges, the propagation loss is minimal compared to the operation system with frequencies above 1 GHz. There are several kinds of paging systems based on their air interfaces.[29] The British Post Office initiated one signal format called the Post Office Code Standardization Advisory Group (POCSAG) during 1970. In early 1990, a high-speed protocol called European Radio Message System (ERMES) was approved by ETSI. Motorola developed FLEX, and Philips Telecom developed Advanced Paging Operations Code (APOC). Therefore, different types of pagers receive different signal formats.

The POCSAG coding format can be operated at 2400 bps and can accommodate 2 million pagers. The FLEX coding format also can be operated at 2400 bps. The ERMES can have an effective transmission rate of 3750 bps.

In the 1990s, the paging system was very popular, especially in the Asian region. Many people carried pagers because of its low service charge. Also, the pagers were smaller in size and lighter in weight as compared with cellular phones. Motorola was developing ReFLEX two-way paging systems but could not find a market. In the year 2000s, the size, weight, and service charge of cellular phones were drastically reduced, and the need of a paging system did not exist. The paging systems disappeared.

1.5 STANDARDS BODIES

1.5.1 International Standard Bodies

The International Telecommunication Union (ITU), formerly known as the Consultative Committee for International Telephone and Telegraph (CCITT), has developed standards for modem over voice lines. The standards association of the Institute of Electrical and Electronics Engineers (IEEE-SA) and International Standards Organization (ISO), two international standards organizations, have developed local area network (LAN).

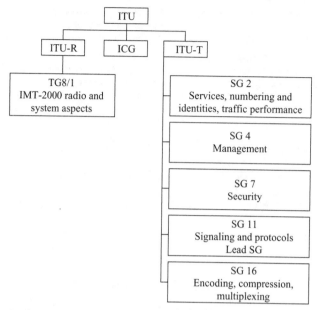

FIGURE 1.1 IMT-2000 standardization structure in ITU.

Some organizations are not standards bodies but are promoting their interested standards and influence the standards bodies.

- ITU was formed in 1865, with its headquarters in Geneva, Switzerland. It establishes regulations on international use of telegraph, telephone, and radio and satellite communication services. In the past, the mobile cellular systems were not standardized by ITU until 3G, which were then called IMT-2000. Also, ITU has its functions in managing radio transmission technology (RTT) evaluation process and 3G spectrum allocations. The telecommunication standardization in ITU is divided into two sectors: Radio communication section (ITU-R) and Telecommunication Standardization Section (ITU-T) as shown in Fig. 1.1. In ITU-R, the task group TG8/1 is responsible for 3G. The Intersector Coordination Group (ICG) is coordinating the IMT-2000 radio and network standards.

- IEEE standard association (IEEE-SA) is a leading developer of global industry standards in a broad range of industries; one area is in telecommunications.

IEEE-802 is a program to work on local and metropolitan networks. The working groups related to wireless local and metropolitan area networks are

802.11–Wireless LAN working group: WiFi alliance is a nonprofit international association formed in 1999 to certify interoperability of wireless local area network products based on IEEE 802.11 a/b/g specifications. IEEE 802.11n is working on a high-speed data rate at 130 Mbps, a fixed wireless network.

802.15–Wireless Personal Area Network (WPAN) working group: There are eight working groups among them; six are TGs (Task Groups). 802.15.1 is Bluetooth standard. 802.15.3a is WPAN alternate high rate (20 Mbps or higher) standard for UWB (Ultra Wideband). 802.15.4 is investigating a low data rate solution with multiyear battery life and a simple device. Zigbee alliance is manufacturing products based on 802.15.4

standard. Bluetooth, UWB and Zigbee are also named as wire replacement apparatus described in Section 14.11.

802.16–Broadband Wireless Access working group: WiMax is an industry-led, nonprofit corporation formed to promote and certify compatibility and interoperability of broadband wireless products based on 802.16d and 802.16e.

802.20–Mobile Broadband Wireless Access (MBWA) working group. The purpose of this group is to enable worldwide deployment of affordable, ubiquitous, always on and interoperable multivendor mobile broadband wireless access networks. It will operate in licensed bands below 3.5 GHz, 1 Mbps per user at a vehicle speed up to 250 kmph. Flarion's Flash-OFDMA is one of the candidate systems.

1.5.2 Standards Bodies in Different Areas

- **The United States:** In the 1970s, Bell Labs developed the AMPS system; no standard body was involved. Later, AMPS became IS-3 of TIA. Also NTT, NMT, and C450 were developed as the standards in their respective countries. The North American TDMA had been TIA's standard called IS-54, then changed to IS-136. cdmaOne is another TIA's standard called IS-95.

   American National Standards Institute (ANSI) can set standards from two standardization bodies for mobile radio systems: Telecom Industry Association (TIA) and the Committee T1. Within TIA, the wireless communication division is responsible for standardization of wireless technologies. The two main committees are TR45 (Public Mobile) and TR46 (Personal Communications). In TR45, there are six permanent subcommittees as shown in Fig. 1.2. Among them, TR45.4, TR45.5, and TR45.6 are active on cdma2000 as 3G standard. In TR45.5, four subcommittees are listed to standardize the digital technology for cdma2000. Within T1, subcommittee T1P1 is responsible for the management and coordination activities of PCS (Personal Communications System) regarding PCS1900/GSM technology.

- **Europe:** Telecommunication standards were developed by the Europe Telecommunication Standard Institute (ETSI). Under ETSI, there is a group called SMG (Spread Mobile Group, or Group of Special Mobile [GSM]) devoted to developing GSM systems as

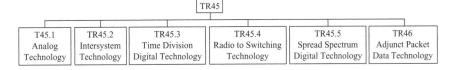

TR45					
T45.1	TR45.2	TR45.3	TR45.4	TR45.5	TR46
Analog Technology	Intersystem Technology	Time Division Digital Technology	Radio to Switching Technology	Spread Spectrum Digital Technology	Adjunct Packet Data Technology

- TR45.1 is responsible for the AMPS standardization.
- TR45.2 is responsible of the development of the IS-41 standard.
- TR45.3 is responsible for IS-136, the U.S. TDMA system, and its evolution to UWC-136.
- TR45.4 is responsible for the IS-634 standard (i.e., the A-interface standard between BS and MSC). For the third generation, TR45.4 will most likely develop the interface between the access and core networks.
- TR45.5 is responsible for IS-95 technology and its evolution to cdma2000.
- TR45.6 work items include support for packet data and Internet access. TR45.6 coordinates its activities with TR45.2 to define network architecture for IMT-2000 that complies with packet data requirements.

FIGURE 1.2   Structure of TIA TR45.

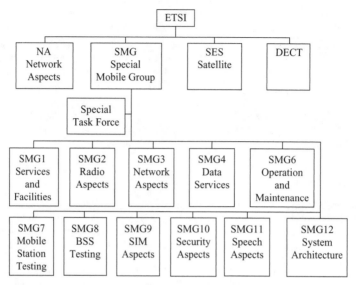

FIGURE 1.3 Partial view of the ETSI organization relevant to UMTS.

shown in Fig. 1.3. Under SMG, there are 12 subgroups; each of them is responsible for a specified technical area. SMG started in 1983. The GSM system was ready to deploy in 1991. GSM MOU (Memorandum of Understand) Association in Europe is the operator's organization for promoting GSM worldwide. Most major vendors in Europe were the members. In GSM, they shared their IPRs (intellectual property rights). Thus, the cost of the GSM system and its handsets became very inexpensive later. v

- **Japan:** In Japan, IMT-2000 standardization is divided between two organizations, ARIB (Association of Radio Industries and Business) and TTC (Telecommunication Technology Committee). The former is responsible for radio standardization and the latter for network standardization. The organization and functions of ARIB are shown in Fig. 1.4(a). The coordination group of standard subcommittee is responsible for international coordination. Application G is responsible for study requirement and objectives. Three subgroups of the radio control working group are SWG1, responsible for system description; SWG2, responsible for specification of an interface Layer 1; and SWG3, responsible for specification of Layers 2 and 3. TTC is responsible for the development of system architecture, information flow, and requirements for network control as shown in Fig. 1.4(b).

- **Korea:** Korean MIC (Ministry of Information and Communications) established TTA (Telecommunication Technology Association) in 1988 to develop Korean Information Communication Standard (KICS). The organization of TTA is shown in Fig. 1.5. A network synchronous wideband CDMA scheme was adopted by U.S. TR45.5 (cdma2000) and by Korea TTA (TTAI). There are two asynchronous wideband CDMA schemes, WCDMA in ETSI and in ARIB and TTAII in Korea. The difference in TTAII is the uplink pilot symbols, time-multiplexed containing the power control bits.

- **China:** The old standardization organization called CWTS (China Wireless Telecommunications Standard) was driven by the MII (Ministry of Information and Industry). In December 2002, a new standardization organization called CCSA (China Communications Standard Association) was formed. It united all the standards organizations and

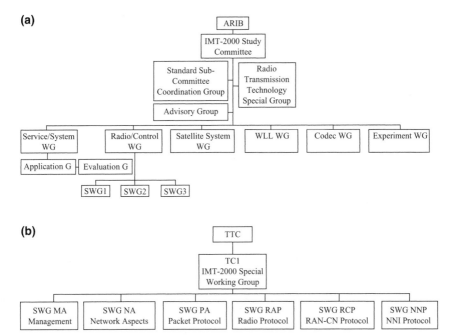

FIGURE 1.4 Standards organizations in Japan. (*a*) IMT-2000 standard in ARIB organization. (*b*) IMT-2000 standard in TTC organization.

is independent from MII. The organization chart is shown in Fig. 1.6. There are eight technical committees; one of them is a wireless communication technical committee that retains the same functions as CWTS.

1.6 SPECTRUM ALLOCATION

The spectrum is a limited natural resource. Wireless communication equipment depends on the appropriate and available frequency bands. The signal propagation characteristics are different with different frequency bands. Also, the scope of the service

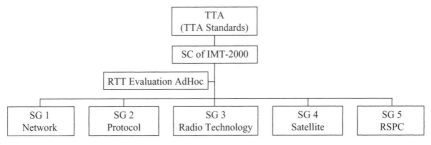

FIGURE 1.5 Structure of TTA standards organization in Korea.

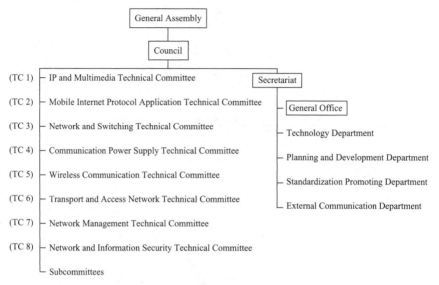

FIGURE 1.6   China CCSA organization structure.

for the new system used in that band determines the bandwidth of that band. The higher the data rate, the wider bandwidth is needed. Manufacturers want to allocate a desired spectrum band and have an investment leverage of economic scale.

The task of authorizing the allocation and licensing of the available spectrum to different systems (allocation band) and to different service operators (licenses) falls to different frequency administrative bodies throughout the world. It is a process of restructuring of frequency band allocations and allows the new systems and services to migrate toward higher frequency bands. Many issues are surrounded by major controversies among segments of the communication industry and are brought to Congress to resolve. In the past, satellite communications needed a global plan of spectrum allocation. The spectrum allocation of terrestrial communication systems has only come from the regional authorities. As of today, the global roaming of terrestrial communication systems forces the spectrum allocations of the systems to be planned globally as well; the GSM system is an example. As of today, there is a need to have three spectral bands for GSM to roam in most areas of the world: 900 MHz and 1800 MHz operates in Europe and Asia, 1900 MHz in North and South America. Therefore, a triple-band handset is a solution today for international roaming.

1.6.1   Spectrum Allocation in the United States

In the United States, the FCC is the authority that allocates the spectrum for different services and licenses to the operators in each service and in each market. Mobile radio (with a one-way dispatch system) was first operated in 1921 by the Detroit Police Department. The FCC granted 11 frequency channels in 1934 at 54 MHz and granted 29 new channels in 1936 and 1937 to 58 state police stations. In 1946, the FCC granted AT&T a license for mobile telephone services in St. Louis operating at 450 MHz (VHF) with a channel bandwidth of 120 kHz. In 1947, the service was being offered in more than 25 cities in the United States. In 1950, the channel bandwidth was reduced to 60 kHz. In 1956, the FCC authorized new channels in the UHF band, around 450 MHz with a channel bandwidth of 50 kHz. In 1960,

FM receiver design had been significantly improved. VHF channels were split from 60 kHz to 30 kHz, called MJ system, and UHF channels were split from 50 kHz to 25 kHz, called MK system. MJ and MK were the mobile telephones with 12 channels operating in the United States prior to AMPS.

From the end of World War II to 1970, besides the 14 VHF TV channels, the FCC had established 70 new channels to UHF TV channels. The proposal by AT&T to have new mobile channels in the UHF band was rejected by the FCC in 1949 and 1964, respectively.

In the 1960s, trunked radio systems such as SMR (Special Mobile Radio) operating at 800 MHz were introduced and could automatically tune to the mobile radio and establish the calls. Thus, the existing spectrum allocations for mobile radio were not adequate in the spectrum of the 800 MHz band.

In 1975, the cable TV industry was introduced. There was no need to allocate a huge spectrum to TV channels. The FCC allocated 115 MHz (806–947 MHz) to land mobile communication: 40 MHz for cellular mobile, 30 MHz for conventional and trunked dispatch service, and 45 MHz to be held in reserve. This 115 MHz of spectrum, previously allocated for education TV channels, was now dedicated to the cellular mobile band. In 1981, because of the duopoly policy won, the FCC decided to establish two 20-MHz systems per market; one system operated by a local telephone company (wireline company) and one operated by a non-wireline company. In 1986, each system received an additional 5 MHz of spectrum, totaling 25 MHz for each system. It was a frequency division duplexing (FDD) system; that is, 12.5 MHz one way, called advanced mobile phone service (AMPS), an analog system, now referred to as first-generation mobile telephone system. There were 416 FM channels with 30-kHz channel bandwidth.

The Land Mobile Radio (LMR) bands are at 150, 450, and 850 MHz with 25 kHz channels or 12.5-Hz channels. It is mostly used for law enforcement, public safety, taxicabs, truck fleets, as well as for military services.

Mobile data systems, such as ARDIS and Ram Mobile, operate in the 800–900 MHz region.

After the United Kingdom introduced PCN in 1989, operated at 1800 MHz, the FCC released PCS (Personal Communication Services) in 1993, with seven frequency blocks (A, B, C, D, E, F and an unlicensed block in two GHz spectrums as follows:

- Wideband PCS spectrum for cellular-like systems (120 MHz)

    From 1850 MHz to 1990 MHz

    A, B, C blocks have 30 MHz (a pair of 15 MHz for FDD)

    D, E, F blocks have 10 MHz (a pair of 5 MHz for FDD)

    Unlicensed block has 20 MHz

      UV (unlicensed voice) (a pair of 5 MHz)

      UD (unlicensed data) (a single block of 10 MHz)

- Narrowband PCS spectrum for two-way paging systems in 901-940.90 MHz

    Five channels (50 kHz paired channels)

    Three channels (three 50 kHz channels paired with three
      12.5-kHz channels)

    Three channels (50 kHz unpaired channels)

- Unlicensed band

    1. Data equipment: 1890–1930 MHz bands for wireless telephones, PBX's wireless data networks, and the low unlicensed equipment.

    2. ISM (industrial, scientific and medical) bands at 900 MHz, 2.4 GHz, and 5.7 GHz based on FCC Part-15 regulations. Sometimes it is also called part 15 bands. WLAN

uses ISM bands, which allow low-power transmission and provide transmission rates as high as 20 Mbps.

3. MMDS band: in 5 GHz region.

4. LMDS band: in 16–30 GHz region.

- 3G Spectrum: 2 × 45 MHz is allocated and will divide into 5 to 7 blocks upon FCC's ruling.

1710–1755 MHz   Mobile Transmit

2110–2155 MHz   Base Transmit

1.6.2   ITU: Spectrum for 3G (IMT-2000)

For IMT-2000, a total of 230 MHz was determined at WARC'92 (World Administrative Radio Conference). This was the first time ITU started to manage spectrum for the terrestrial mobile communication as shown in Table 1.2.

The IMT-2000 FDD spectrum overlapping with the existing PHS band is also shown in Table 1.2. Also, the U.S. PCS band is overlapped with IMT-2000's uplink (lower) band. The spectrum of 2010–2025 MHz is assigned for TDD in IMT-2000.

The functions of ITU related to spectrum management and standardization are described as follows:

- ITU is a Geneva-based United Nations organization that consists of more than 170 member nations and is responsible for two functions: (1) communications standards and (2) treaty-based agreements.

TABLE 1.2   Diagram of Global Spectrum Allocation

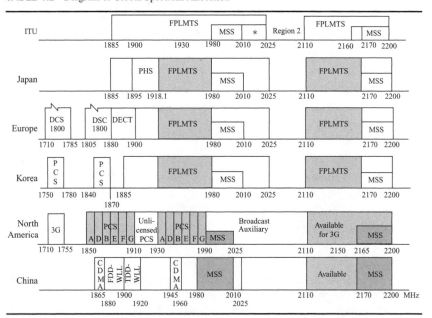

* TDD bands

- The responsibility of ITU'S spectrum management is to minimize radio interference by establishing international rules. It is different from the United States in that two functions are handled by two different entities: communication system standards by industrial standard bodies, and spectrum allocations by FCC. ITU underwent a major structural change on March 1, 1993. There are three sectors, one council, and WARC (World Administrative Radio Conference). The three sectors are

1. Radio communications sector (assigning the spectrum), which combined with IFRB (International Frequency Registration Board) and CCIR (Consultative Committee on International Radio) is sometimes called ITU-R.

    IFRB has two responsibilities: first, it assigns international frequency applications and services. WARC is to update the radio regulations and review international frequency activities. All the interested countries participate and contribute their views.

    CCIR is (a) concerned with technical aspects of radio spectrum usage and (b) concerned with performance criteria and system characteristics for compatible networking.

    Study Group 8 is a special international group in CCIR to identify the requirements for globally compatible FPLMTS (Future Public Land Mobile Telecommunications Systems), and it recommended to WARC '92 that 227 MHz in 1–3 GHz bands would be required for FPLMTS.

2. The telecommunications standardization sector, called ITU-T, is responsible for both radio and wired telecommunication standardization. The former CCITT (Consultative Committee on International Telegraph and Telephone) only made recommendations for devices in wired telecommunication networks.

3. Telecommunication Development Sector: takes all the nonstandardization responsibilities.

1.6.3   The Other Areas of the World

Europe

- CEPT (Conference of European Posts and Telecommunications Administration): Brings together the posts and telecommunications administration of most European countries for coordination of their telecommunication networks in radio means spectrum. In the early 1990s, the European Community (EC) took over the CEPT responsibilities for standardization.
- ETSI (European Telecommunications Standards Institute): Technical committees, such as GSM, PCN, do its work.

China

- Wireless Spectrum Control Bureau, a state government institution, is managing the spectrum nationwide. Also, each province has its wireless spectrum control bureau to manage the spectrum within the province. In principle, the province bureau has to coordinate with the state bureau.

North and South America

- The Inter-American Telecommunications Commission (CITEL) is making recommendations on spectrum issues for North and South America.

Japan and Korea

- Japan and Korea have their own national institutes to manage spectrum utilization within their countries.

1.7 SPECTRUM EFFICIENCY CONSIDERATIONS

A major problem facing the radio communication industry is the limitation of the available radio-frequency spectrum. In setting allocation policy, the FCC seeks systems that need minimal bandwidth but provide high usage and consumer satisfaction. It often sends out NPRM (Notice of Proposed Rule Making) and asks for feedback from the industry.

The ideal mobile telephone system would operate within a limited assigned frequency band and would serve an almost unlimited number of users in unlimited areas. Three major approaches to achieve the ideal are[30-31]

- **Modulation schemes**
  - **A.** *Apply to analog systems*
    1. Single-sideband (SSB), which divides the allocated frequency band into maximum numbers of channels.
    2. Frequency modulation (FM), which uses frequency deviation (an early application of spread spectrum) to reduce the noise.
    3. Cellular, which reuses the allocated frequency band in different geographic locations.
  - **B.** *Apply to digital systems*
    1. Frequency shift keying (FSK), Gaussian FSK (GFSK), minimum FSK (MSK): an abrupt frequency changes at the symbol transitions.
    2. Phase shift keying (PSK), Quadrature PSK (QPSK): an abrupt phase change at the symbol transitions.
    3. Quadrature amplitude modulation (QAM): a combination of amplitude (ASK) and phase shift keying.
    4. Orthogonal frequency division multiplexing (OFDM): consists of a sum of subcarriers that are modulated by using PSK or QAM.
    5. Spread spectrum or frequency-hopped, which generates many codes over a wide frequency band.

In 1971, the cellular approach was shown to be a spectrally efficient system based on the frequency reuse scheme.

- **Antenna configurations: smart antennas**
  - **A.** Diverse antennas at base station
    1. Receiving diversity antennas: does not cause any interference in the air.
    2. Transmit diversity antennas: gain the diversity without diversity antennas at the mobile station.
  - **B.** Adaptive antenna array
    1. Beam forming
    2. Beam steering
  - **C.** Space-Time code antenna systems
  - **D.** MIMO (multiple in and multiple out) antenna systems

- **System planning**
  - **A.** Intelligent base station

1. Assign resources to mobile stations intelligently

2. Power control and power adjustment

3. Smart handoffs

B. Intelligent network

1. Ad hoc network

2. Mesh network

3. Sensor network

The consideration of spectrum efficiency will always be the key topic for developing future wireless communication systems. The modulation schemes will be described in Chapter 4, smart antennas in Chapter 8, intelligent base station in Chapter 16, and intelligent network in Chapter 17.

REFERENCES

1. Bell Laboratories, "High-Capacity Mobile Telephone System Technical Report," December 1971, submitted to FCC.

2. F. H. Blecher, "Advanced Mobile Phone Service," *IEEE Transactions on Vehicular Technology*, Vol. VT-29, May 1980, pp. 238–244.

3. V. H. MacDonald, "The Cellular Concept," *Bell System Technical Journal*, Vol. 58, January 1979, pp. 15–42.

4. W. C. Y. Lee, *Mobile Communications Engineering*, McGraw-Hill Book Co., 1998, Introduction to Part I and Part II.

5. W. C. Y. Lee, *Lee's Essentials of Wireless Communications*, McGraw-Hill Book Co., 2000, Chapters 1 and 2.

6. Bernard J. T. Mallinder, "An Overview of the GSM System," *Conference Proceedings*, Digital Cellular Radio Conference, Hagen FRG, October 1988.

7. M. Mouly, M. B. Pautet, "The GSM System Mobile Communications," M. Mouly et M. B. Pautet, 49, vue Louis Bruneau, F-91120 Palaisea, France, 1992.

8. S. M. Redl, M. K. Weber, M. W. Oliphant, *An Introduction GSM*, Artech House Publishers, 1995.

9. A. Mehrotra, *GSM System Engineering*, Artech House, 1996.

10. A. J. Viterbi, *CDMA, Principles of Spread Spectrum Communication*, Addison-Wesley, 1995.

11. W. C. Y. Lee, *Mobile Communications Design Fundamentals*, John Wiley & Sons, 1993, Chapter 9.

12. H. Harte, K. McLaughin, *CDMA IS-95 for Cellular and PCS*, McGraw-Hill Book Co., 1996.

13. Nippon Ericsson K.K. Research & Development Center for Radio System (RCR), "PDC-Digital Cellular Telecommunication System, RCR STF-27A Version," January 1992.

14. C. Smith, D. Collins, *3G Wireless Networks*, McGraw-Hill Book Co., 2002.

15. S. C. Yang, *3G CDMA 2000*, Artech House, 2004.

16. ITU "Radio Requirements of 4G Systems," issued July 2003.

17. Cordless Telephone 2/Common Air Interface (CT2/CAI), "Management of International Telecommunications, MIT 12-850-201, McGraw-Hill, Inc. DataPro Information Service Group, Delran, N.J., February 1994.

18. *Digital European Cordless Telecommunications*, Part I, "Overview," DE/RES 3001-1, Common Interface, Radio Equipment and Systems, ETS 300 175-1, ETSI, B.P. 152, F-06561 Valbonne Cedex, France, August 1991.

19. Sybo Dijkstra, Frank Owen, "The Case for DECT," *Mobile Communications International*, pp. 60–65, September–November 1993.

20. PHS-Personal Handy Phone Standard, Research Development Center for Radio System (RCR), "Personal Handy Phone Standard (PHS)," CRC STD-28, December 20, 1993.

21. E. K. Wesel, "Wireless Multimedia Communications," Addison-Wesley, 1998, Chapter 1.

22. "CDPD–Cellular Digital Packet Data, Cell Plan II Specification," prepared by PCSI, San Diego, CA 92121, January 1992.

23. L. Goldberg, "Wireless LANs: Mobile Computing's Second Wave," *Electronic Design*, June 25, 1995.

24. W. C. Y. Lee, *Lee's Essentials of Wireless Communications*, McGraw-Hill, 2001, Chapter 8.

25. O. G. Williams, "Communications satellite systems" Ed by B. J. Halliwell in Advanced Communications Systems, Buttworth & Co. 1974.

26. N. Hart, H. Haugli, P. Poskett, and K. Smith, "Immarsat's Personal Communications System," *Proc. Third International Mobile Satellite Conference*, Pasadena, pp. 303–304, June 16–18, 1993.

27. J. E. Hatlelid and L. Casey, "The Iridium System: Personal Communications Anytime, Anyplace," *Proc. Third International Mobile Satellite Conference*, Pasadena, pp. 285–290, June 16–18, 1993.

28. R. A. Wiedeman, "The Globalstar Mobile Satellite System for Worldwide Personal Communications," *Proc. Third International Mobile Satellite Conference*, Pasadena, pp. 291–296, June 16–18, 1993.

29. Y. B. Lin, I. Chlamtac, *Wireless and Mobile Network Architectures*, John Wiley & Sons, 2001, Chapter 22.

30. W. C. Y. Lee, "Spectrum Efficiency Digital Cellular," *38th IEEE Vehicular Technology Conference Record*, Philadelphia, PA, January 15–17, 1988, pp. 643–646.

31. W. C. Y. Lee, *Mobile Communication Engineering, Theory and Applications*, 2nd Ed., McGraw-Hill, 1998, p. 305.

CHAPTER 2
INTRODUCTION TO CELLULAR SYSTEMS

To describe cellular systems in general, it is necessary to include discussion of the basic cellular systems, their performance criteria, the uniqueness of the mobile radio environment, the operation of the cellular systems, reduction of cochannel interference, handoffs, and so forth.

2.1 BASIC CELLULAR SYSTEMS

There are two basic cellular systems; one is the circuit-switched system and the other is the packet-switched system.

2.1.1 Circuit-Switched Systems

In a circuit-switched system, each traffic channel is dedicated to a user until its cell is terminated. We can further distinguish two circuit-switched systems: one for an analog system and one for a digital system.

A. Analog System

A basic analog cellular system[1–3] consists of three subsystems: a mobile unit, a cell site, and a mobile telephone switching office (MTSO), as Fig. 2.1 shows, with connections to link the three subsystems.

1. *Mobile units.* A mobile telephone unit contains a control unit, a transceiver, and an antenna system.

2. *Cell site.* The cell site provides interface between the MTSO and the mobile units. It has a control unit, radio cabinets, antennas, a power plant, and data terminals.

3. *MTSO.* The switching office, the central coordinating element for all cell sites, contains the cellular processor and cellular switch. It interfaces with telephone company zone offices, controls call processing, provides operation and maintenance, and handles billing activities.

4. *Connections.* The radio and high-speed data links connect the three subsystems. Each mobile unit can only use one channel at a time for its communication link. But the channel is not fixed; it can be any one in the entire band assigned by the serving area, with each site having multichannel capabilities that can connect simultaneously to many mobile units.

23

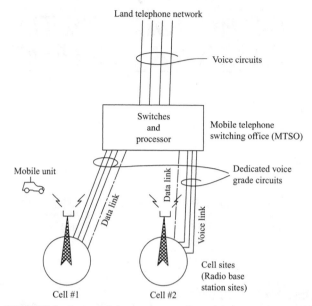

Land telephone network

Voice circuits

Switches and processor

Mobile telephone switching office (MTSO)

Mobile unit

Data link

Dedicated voice grade circuits

Data link

Voice link

Cell sites (Radio base station sites)

Cell #1   Cell #2

FIGURE 2.1   Analog cellular system.

The MTSO is the heart of the analog cellular mobile system. Its processor provides central coordination and cellular administration.

The cellular switch, which can be either analog or digital, switches calls to connect mobile subscribers to other mobile subscribers and to the nationwide telephone network. It uses voice trunks similar to telephone company interoffice voice trunks. It also contains data links providing supervision links between the processor and the switch and between the cell sites and the processor. The radio link carries the voice and signaling between the mobile unit and the cell site. The high-speed data links cannot be transmitted over the standard telephone trunks and therefore must use either microwave links or T-carriers (wire lines). Microwave radio links or T-carriers carry both voice and data between cell site and the MTSO.

B. Digital Systems

A basic digital system consists of four elements: mobile station, base transceiver station (BTS), base station controller (BSC), and switching subsystems, as shown in Fig. 2.2.

- *MS:* It consists of two parts, mobile equipment (ME) and subscriber identify module (SIM). SIM contains all subscriber-specific data stored on the MS side.

- *BTS:* Besides having the same function as the analog BTS, it has the Transcoder/Rate Adapter Unit (TRAU), which carries out coding and decoding as well as rate adaptation in case data rate varies.

- *BSC:* A new element in digital systems that performs the Radio Resource (RR) management for the cells under its control. BSC also handles handovers, power management time and frequency synchronization, and frequency reallocation among BTSs.

- Switching subsystems:

  a. MSC: The main function of MSC is to coordinate the setup of calls between MS and PSTN users.

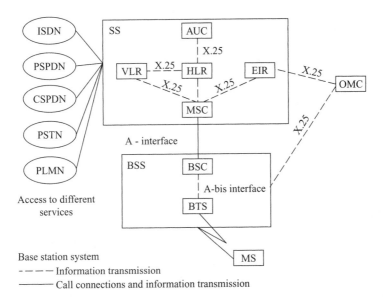

FIGURE 2.2 Digital cellular system.

b. VLR (Visitor Location Register): A database of all mobiles roaming in the MSC's area of control.

c. HLR (Home Location Register): A centralized database of all subscribers registered in a Public Land Mobile Network (PLMN).

d. AUC (Authentication Center): Provides HLR with authentication parameters and ciphering keys that are used for security purposes.

e. EIR (Equipment Identity Register): A database for storing all registered mobile equipment numbers.

f. IWF: Provides the subscriber with data services that can acess data rate and protocol conversion facilities and interfaces with public and private data networks.

g. EC (Echo Canceller): Used on the PSTN side of the MSC for all voice circuits.

h. XC (Transcoder): Usually installs in each BTS. But for the cost reason, it can be installed in BSC or MSC.

i. OMC (Operational and Maintenance Center): This function resided in analog MSC but became a separated entity in digital systems.

The specifications of different digital systems will be shown in Chapters 4 and 5.

2.1.2 Packet-Switched System

A cellular packet-switched system is shown in Fig. 2.3.
There are six elements: MS, Node B, RNC, SGSN, GGSN, and GF as shown in Fig. 2.3.

MS: Provides the voice and packet data services. It is also called UE (User Equipment).

Node B: The name for base station in GSM.

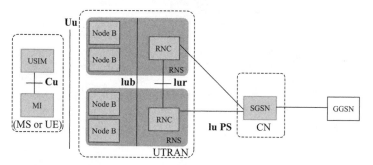

FIGURE 2.3 Cellular packet system.

RNC (Radio Network Controller): Controls the radio resources of the Node Bs that are connected to it. Its function is similar to BSC. A device PCU (Packet Control Unit) converts the data stream into packet format.

SGSN (Service GPRS Support Node): Analogous to MSC/VLR in the circuit-switched system. This includes mobility management, security, and access control functions. It interfaces to HLR.

GGSN (Gateway GPRS Support Node): The point of interface with external packet data networks such as the Internet.

CGF (Changing Gateway Function): Mainly for billing.

RNS (Radio Network Subsystem): It consists of RNC and Node B. UTRAN consists of two or more RNS. The specifications of different packet switched systems will be described in Chapters 6 and 7.

2.2 PERFORMANCE CRITERIA

There are three categories for specifying performance criteria.

2.2.1 Voice Quality

Voice quality is very hard to judge without subjective tests for users' opinions. In this technical area, engineers cannot decide how to build a system without knowing the voice quality that will satisfy the users. In military communications, the situation differs: armed forces personnel must use the assigned equipment.

CM: For any given commercial communications system, the voice quality will be based on the following criterion: a set value x at which y percent of customers rate the system voice quality (from transmitter to receiver) as good or excellent; the top two circuit merits (CM) of the five listed below.

CM	Score	Quality Scale
CM5	5	Excellent (speech perfectly understandable)
CM4	4	Good (speech easily understandable, some noise)
CM3	3	Fair (speech understandable with a slight effort, occasional repetitions needed)
CM2	2	Poor (speech understandable only with considerable effort, frequent repetitions needed)
CM1	1	Unsatisfactory (speech not understandable)

MOS: As the percentage of customers choosing CM4 and CM5 increases, the cost of building the system rises.

The average of the CM scores obtained from all the listeners is called mean opinion score (MOS). Usually, the toll-quality voice is around MOS ≥4.

DRT (Diagnostic Rhyme Test): An ANSI standardized method used for evaluation of intelligibility. It is a subjective test method. Listeners are required to choose which word of a rhyming pair they perceived. The words differ only in their leading consonant. The word pairs have been chosen such that six binary attributes of speech intelligibility are measured in their present and absent states. This attribute profile provides a diagnostic capability to the test. For details on the attributes evaluated by the DRT check http://www.arcon.com/tests.htm and follow this link: ATTRIBUTES. To perform a sample DRT follows this link: DRT.

2.2.2 Data Quality

There are several ways to measure the data quality such as bit error rate, chip error rate, symbol error rate, and frame error rate. The chip error rate and symbol error rate are measuring the quality of data along the transmission path. The frame error rate and the bit error rate are measuring the quality of data at the throughput.

2.2.3 Picture/Vision Quality

There are color acuity, depth perception, flicker perception, motion perception, noise perception, and visual acuity. The percentage of pixel (picture element) loss rate can be characterized in vertical resolution loss and horizontal resolution loss of a pixel.

2.2.4 Service Quality

Three items are required for service quality.

1. *Coverage.* The system should serve an area as large as possible. With radio coverage, however, because of irregular terrain configurations, it is usually not practical to cover 100 percent of the area for two reasons:

   a. The transmitted power would have to be very high to illuminate weak spots with sufficient reception, a significant added cost factor.

   b. The higher the transmitted power, the harder it becomes to control interference.

   Therefore, systems usually try to cover 90 percent of an area in flat terrain and 75 percent of an area in hilly terrain. The combined voice quality and coverage criteria in AMPS cellular systems[3] state that 75 percent of users rate the voice quality between good and excellent in 90 percent of the served area, which is generally flat terrain. The voice quality and coverage criteria would be adjusted as per decided various terrain conditions. In hilly terrain, 90 percent of users must rate voice quality good or excellent in 75 percent of the served area. A system operator can lower the percentage values stated above for a low-performance and low-cost system.

2. *Required grade of service.* For a normal start-up system, the grade of service is specified for a blocking probability of .02 for initiating calls at the busy hour. This is an average value. However, the blocking probability at each cell site will be different. At the busy hour, near freeways, automobile traffic is usually heavy, so the blocking probability at certain cell sites may be higher than 2 percent, especially when car accidents occur. To decrease the blocking probability requires a good system plan and a sufficient number of radio channels.

3. *Number of dropped calls.* During Q calls in an hour, if a call is dropped and $Q - 1$ calls are completed, then the call drop rate is $1/Q$. This drop rate must be kept low. A high drop rate could be caused by either coverage problems or handoff problems related to inadequate channel availability or weak reception. How to estimate the number of dropped calls will be described in Chapter 11.

2.2.5 Special Features

A system would like to provide as many special features as possible, such as call forwarding, call waiting, voice stored (VSR) box, automatic roaming, short message service (SMS), multimedia service (MMS), push-to-talk (PTT), or navigation services. However, sometimes the customers have to pay extra charges for these special services.

2.3 UNIQUENESS OF MOBILE RADIO ENVIRONMENT

2.3.1 Description of Mobile Radio Transmission Medium

2.3.1.1 The Propagation Attenuation. In general, the propagation path loss increases not only with frequency but also with distance. If the antenna height at the cell site is 30 to 100 m and at the mobile unit about 3 m above the ground, and the distance between the cell site and the mobile unit is usually 2 km or more, then the incident angles of both the direct wave and the reflected wave are very small, as Fig. 2.4 shows. The incident angle of the direct wave is θ_1, and the incident angle of the reflected wave is θ_2. θ_1 is also called the *elevation angle*. The propagation path loss would be 40 dB/dec,[4] where "dec" is an abbreviation of *decade*, i.e., a period of 10. This means that a 40-dB loss at a signal receiver will be observed by the mobile unit as it moves from 1 to 10 km. Therefore C is inversely proportional to R^4.

$$C \propto R^{-4} = \alpha R^{-4} \qquad (2.3\text{-}1)$$

where C = received carrier power
R = distance measured from the transmitter to the receiver
α = constant

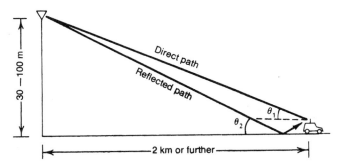

FIGURE 2.4 Mobile radio transmission model.

The difference in power reception at two different distances R_1 and R_2 will result in

$$\frac{C_2}{C_1} = \left(\frac{R_2}{R_1}\right)^{-4} \qquad (2.3\text{-}2a)$$

and the decibel expression of Eq. (2.3-2a) is

$$\Delta C \text{ (in dB)} = C_2 - C_1 \text{ (in dB)}$$

$$= 10 \log \frac{C_2}{C_1} = 40 \log \frac{R_1}{R_2} \qquad (2.3\text{-}2b)$$

When $R_2 = 2R_1$, $\Delta C = -12$ dB; when $R_2 = 10R_1$, $\Delta C = -40$ dB.

This 40 dB/dec is the general rule for the mobile radio environment and is easy to remember. It is also easy to compare to the free-space propagation rule of 20 dB/dec. The linear and decibel scale expressions are

$$C \propto R^{-2} \qquad \text{(free space)} \qquad (2.3\text{-}3a)$$

and

$$\Delta C = C_2 \text{ (in dB)} - C_1 \text{ (in dB)}$$

$$= 20 \log \frac{R_1}{R_2} \qquad \text{(free space)} \qquad (2.3\text{-}3b)$$

In a real mobile radio environment, the propagation path-loss slope varies as

$$C \propto R^{-\gamma} = \alpha R^{-\gamma} \qquad (2.3\text{-}4)$$

γ usually lies between 2 and 5 depending on the actual conditions.[5] Of course, γ cannot be lower than 2, which is the free-space condition. The decibel scale expression of Eq. (2.3-4) is

$$C = 10 \log \alpha - 10\gamma \log R \qquad \text{dB} \qquad (2.3\text{-}5)$$

2.3.1.2 Severe Fading. Because the antenna height of the mobile unit is lower than its typical surroundings, and the carrier frequency wavelength is much less than the sizes of the surrounding structures, multipath waves are generated. At the mobile unit, the sum of the multipath waves causes a signal-fading phenomenon. The signal fluctuates in a range

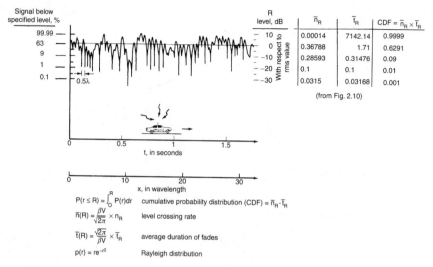

FIGURE 2.5 A typical fading signal received while the mobile unit is moving. (*Reprint after Lee, Ref. 4, p. 54.*)

of about 40 dB (10 dB above and 30 dB below the average signal). We can visualize the nulls of the fluctuation at the baseband at about every half wavelength in space, but all nulls do not occur at the same level, as Fig. 2.5 shows. If the mobile unit moves fast, the rate of fluctuation is fast. For instance, at 850 MHz, the wavelength is roughly 0.35 m (1 ft). If the speed of the mobile unit is 24 km/h (15 mi/h), or 6.7 m/s, the rate of fluctuation of the signal reception at a 10-dB level below the average power of a fading signal is 15 nulls per second (see Sec. 2.3.3).[6]

2.3.2 Model of Transmission Medium

A mobile radio signal $r(t)$, illustrated in Fig. 2.6, can be artificially characterized[5] by two components $m(t)$ and $r_0(t)$ based on natural physical phenomena.

$$r(t) = m(t)r_0(t) \tag{2.3-6}$$

The component $m(t)$ is called *local mean*, *long-term fading*, or *lognormal fading* and its variation is due to the terrain contour between the base station and the mobile unit. The factor r_0 is called *multipath fading*, *short-term fading*, or *Rayleigh fading* and its variation is due to the waves reflected from the surrounding buildings and other structures. The long-term fading $m(t)$ can be obtained from Eq. (2.3-7a).

$$m(t_1) = \frac{1}{2T} \int_{t_1-T}^{t_1+T} r(t)\, dt \tag{2.3-7a}$$

where $2T$ is the time interval for averaging $r(t)$. T can be determined based on the fading rate of $r(t)$, usually 40 to 80 fades.[5] Therefore, $m(t)$ is the envelope of $r(t)$, as shown in Fig.

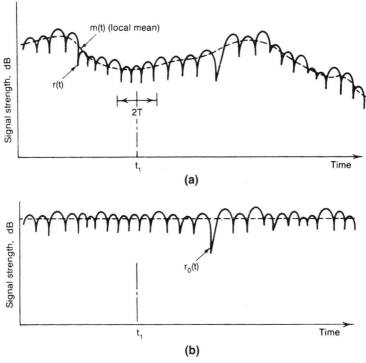

FIGURE 2.6 A mobile radio signal fading representation. (*a*) A mobile signal fading. (*b*) A short-term signal fading.

2.6*a*. Equation (2.3-7*a*) also can be expressed in spatial scale as

$$m(x_1) = \frac{1}{2L} \int_{x_1-L}^{x_1+L} r(x)\,dx \qquad (2.3\text{-}7b)$$

The length of 2*L* has been determined to be 20 to 40 wavelengths.[5] Using 36 or up to 50 samples in an interval of 40 wavelengths is an adequate averaging process for obtaining the local means.[4]

The factor *m(t)* or *m(x)* is also found to be a log-normal distribution based on its characteristics caused by the terrain contour. The short-term fading r_0 is obtained by

$$r_0 \text{ (in dB)} = r(t) - m(t) \qquad \text{dB} \qquad (2.3\text{-}8)$$

as shown in Fig. 2.6*b*. The factor $r_0(t)$ follows a Rayleigh distribution, assuming that only reflected waves from local surroundings are the ones received (a normal situation for the mobile radio environment). Therefore, the term *Rayleigh fading* is often used.

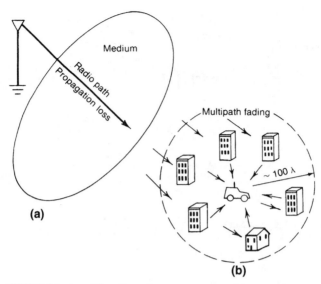

FIGURE 2.7 A mobile radio environment, two parts: (*a*) propagation loss;
(*b*) multipath fading.

2.3.3 Mobile Fading Characteristics

Rayleigh fading is also called multipath fading in the mobile radio environment. When
these multipath waves bounce back and forth due to the buildings and houses, they form
many standing-wave pairs in space, as shown in Fig. 2.7. Those standing-wave pairs are
summed together and become an irregular wave-fading structure. When a mobile unit
is standing still, its receiver only receives a signal strength at that spot, so a constant signal
is observed. When the mobile unit is moving, the fading structure of the wave in the space
is received. It is a multipath fading. The recorded fading becomes fast as the vehicle moves
faster.

2.3.3.1 The Radius of the Active Scatterer Region.   The mobile radio multipath fading
shown in Fig. 2.7 explains the fading mechanism. The radius of the active scatterer region
at 850 MHz can be obtained indirectly as shown in Ref. 7. The radius is roughly 100
wavelengths. The active scatterer region always moves with the mobile unit as its center.
It means that some houses were inactive scatterers and became active as the mobile unit
approached them; some houses were active scatterers and became inactive as the mobile
unit drove away from them.

2.3.3.2 Standing Waves Expressed in a Linear Scale and a Log Scale.   We first introduce
a sine wave in a log scale.

$$y = 10 \cos \beta x \qquad \text{dB} \qquad\qquad (2.3\text{-}9)$$

A log plot of the sine wave of Eq. (2.3-9) is shown in Fig. 2.8*a*. The linear expression of
Eq. (2.3-9) then is shown in Fig. 2.8*b*. The symmetrical waveform in a log plot becomes
an unsymmetrical waveform when plotted on a linear scale. It shows that the sine wave

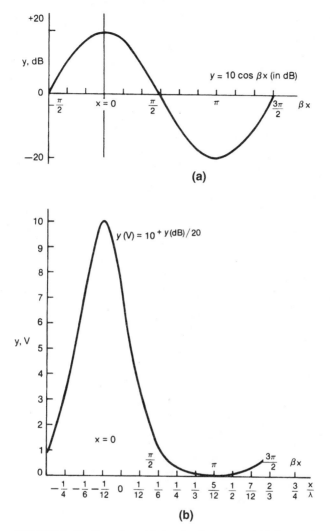

FIGURE 2.8   The linear plot and the log plot of a sine wave. (*a*) In linear scale; (*b*) in log scale.

waveform in a log scale becomes a completely different waveform when expressed on a linear scale and vice versa. Two sine waves, the incident wave traveling along the x-axis (traveling to the left) and the reflected wave traveling in the opposite direction, can be expressed as

$$e_0 = E_0 e^{j(\omega t - \beta x)} \tag{2.3-10}$$

and

$$e_1 = E_1 e^{j(\omega t + \beta x + 2\delta)} \tag{2.3-11}$$

where ω = angular frequency
     β = wave number (= $2\pi/\lambda$)
     2δ = time-phase lead of e_1 with respect to e_0 at $x = 0$

The two waves form a standing-wave pattern.

$$e = e_0 + e_1 = Re^{j(\omega t + \delta + \varphi)} \tag{2.3-12}$$

where φ is the phase angle of the two waves at $x \neq 0$, and the amplitude R becomes

$$R = \sqrt{(E_0 + E_1)^2 \cos^2(\beta x + \delta) + (E_0 - E_1)^2 \sin^2(\beta x + \delta)} \tag{2.3-13}$$

We are plotting two cases and assuming $\delta = 0$.

Case 1. $E_0 = 1$, $E_1 = 1$; that is, the reflection coefficient $= 1$,

$$\text{Standing wave ratio (SWR)} = \frac{E_0 + E_1}{E_0 - E_1} = \infty$$

and
$$R = 2 \cos \beta x \tag{2.3-14}$$

Case 2. $E_0 = 1$, $E_1 = 0.5$; that is, the reflection coefficient $= 0.5$, SWR $= 3$, and

$$R = \sqrt{(1.5)^2 \cos^2 \beta x + (0.5)^2 \sin^2 \beta x} \tag{2.3-15}$$

The linear expression of Eqs. (2.3-14) and (2.3-15) are shown in Fig. 2.9a. The log-scale expression of Eqs. (2.3-14) and (2.3-15) are shown in Fig. 2.9b. The waveform of Fig. 2.9b is the first sign of the fading signal, which resembles the real fading signal shown in Fig. 2.5.

2.3.3.3 First-Order and Second-Order Statistics of Fading.[5,6] Fading occurs on the signal reception when the mobile unit is moving. The first-order statistics, such as average power probability cumulative distribution function (CDF) and bit error rate, are independent of time. The second-order statistics, such as level crossing rate, average duration of fades, and word error rate, are time functions or velocity-related functions. The data signaling format is based on these characteristics. The description of the fading characteristic can be found in detail in two books, Refs. 4 and 5.

Some data can be found from Fig. 2.10a, the cumulative distribution function (CDF), and Fig. 2.10b, the level crossing rate. In Fig. 2.10a, the equation of CDF for a Rayleigh fading is used as follows:

$$P(r \leq R) = 1 - e^{-R^2/\overline{R^2}} \tag{2.3-16}$$

and
$$P(y \leq L) = 1 - e^{-L/\overline{L}} \tag{2.3-17}$$

where $\overline{R^2}$ and $\overline{L}$ are the mean square value and the average power, respectively. In Fig. 2.10a, about 9 percent of the total signal is below a level of -10 dB with respect to average power. In Fig. 2.10b, the level crossing rate (lcr) at a level R is

$$\overline{n}(R) = \frac{\beta v}{\sqrt{2\pi}} n_R \tag{2.3-18}$$

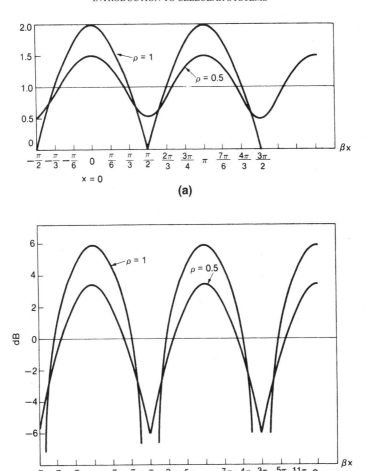

FIGURE 2.9 The linear plot and the log plot of a standing wave. (*a*) In linear scale; (*b*) in log scale.

where n_R is the normalized lcr which is independent of wavelength and the car speed. At a level of -10 dB, $n_0 = 0.3$ can be found from Fig. 2.10*b*. Assume that a signal of 850 MHz is received at a mobile unit with a velocity of 24 km/h (15 mi/h). Then

$$n_0 = \frac{\beta V}{\sqrt{2\pi}} = 50$$

and

$$\bar{n} = 50 \times 0.3 = 15$$

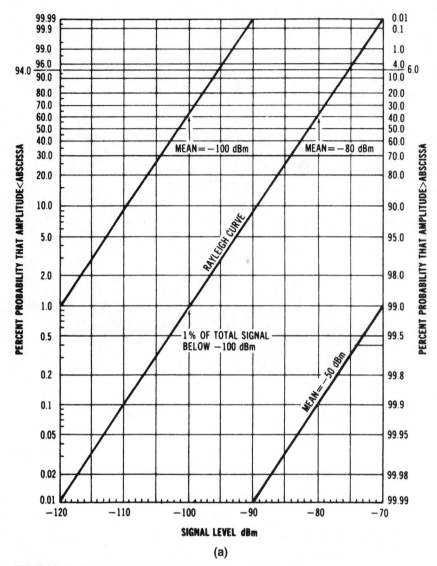

FIGURE 2.10 Fading characteristics. (*a*) CDF. (*After Lee, Ref. 8, p. 30.*)

Therefore, at a cellular frequency of 800 MHz and a vehicle velocity of 15 mi/h, the level crossing rate is 15 per second. It is easy to remember.

The average duration of fade is[6]

$$\bar{t} = \frac{\text{CDF}}{\bar{t}_0 \bar{t}_R} = \frac{\text{CDF}}{\bar{n}} \qquad (2.3\text{-}19)$$

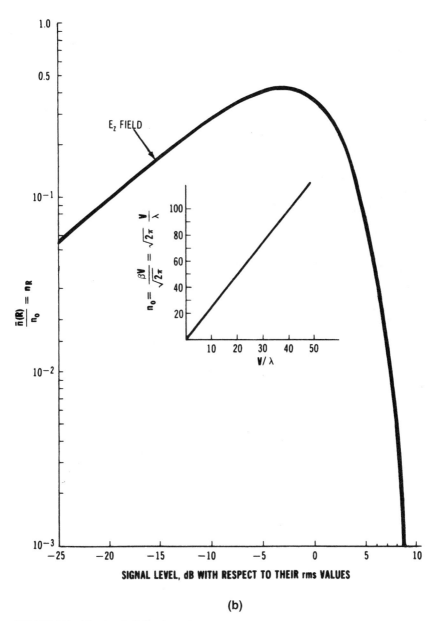

(b)

FIGURE 2.10 (*Continued*) (*b*) Level crossing rate.

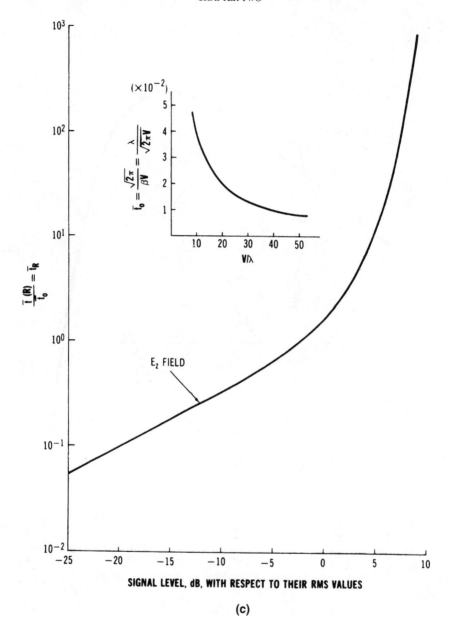

FIGURE 2.10   (*Continued*) (*c*) Average duration of fades.

Equation (2.3-19) is plotted in Fig. 2.10c, where t_0 and t_R are also shown. At -10 dB, the average duration of fades is

$$\overline{t_R} = \frac{\text{CDF}}{\overline{n}_R} = 0.0066\,\text{s} = 6.6\,\text{ms}$$

Now the average power level plays an important role in determining the statistics. Therefore, it should be specified by the system design. The second-order statistic of fading phenomenon is most useful for designing a signaling format for the cellular system. As soon as the signaling format is specified, we can calculate the bit error rate and the word error rate and find ways to reduce the error rates, which will be described in Sec. 15.2.

2.3.3.4 Delay Spread and Coherence Bandwidth

Delay spread. In the mobile radio environment, as a result of the multipath reflection phenomenon, the signal transmitted from a cell site and arriving at a mobile unit will be from different paths, and since each path has a different path length, the time of arrival for each path is different. For an impulse transmitted at the cell site, by the time this impulse is received at the mobile unit, it is no longer an impulse but rather a pulse with a spread width that we call the *delay spread*. The measured data indicate that the mean delay spreads are different in different kinds of environment.

Type of Environment	Delay Spread Δ, μs
Inside the building	<0.1
Open area	<0.2
Suburban area	0.5
Urban area	3

Coherence bandwidth. The coherence bandwidth is the defined bandwidth in which either the amplitudes or the phases of two received signals have a high degree of similarity. The delay spread is a natural phenomenon, and the coherence bandwidth is a defined creation related to the delay spread.

A coherence bandwidth for two fading amplitudes of two received signals is

$$B_c = \frac{1}{2\pi\,\Delta}$$

A coherence bandwidth for two random phases of two received signals is

$$B'_c = \frac{1}{4\pi\,\Delta}$$

2.3.4 Direct Wave Path, Line-of-Sight Path, and Obstructive Path

A *direct wave path* is a path clear from the terrain contour. The *line-of-sight path* is a path clear from buildings. In the mobile radio environment, we do not always have a line-of-sight condition.

When a line-of-sight condition occurs, the average received signal of the mobile unit at a 1-mi intercept is higher, although the 40 dB/dec path-loss slope remains the same. It

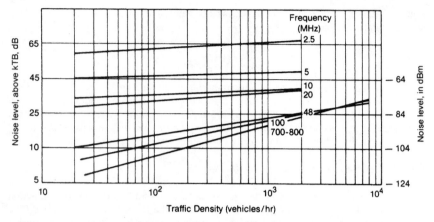

FIGURE 2.11 Average automotive-traffic-noise power for various traffic densities and frequencies. Detector noise bandwidth 30 kHz at room temperature (17°C). (*After Lee, Ref. 12.*)

will be described in Sec. 8.2. In this case, the short-term fading is observed to be a rician fading.[8] It results from a strong line-of-sight path and a ground-reflected wave combined, plus many weak building-reflected waves.

When an out-of-sight condition is reached, the 40-dB/dec path-loss slope still remains. However, all reflected waves, including ground reflected waves and building-reflected waves, become dominant. The short-term received signal at the mobile unit observes a Rayleigh fading. The Rayleigh fading is the most severe fading.

When the terrain contour blocks the direct wave path, we call it the *obstructive path*. In this situation, the shadow loss from the signal reception can be found by using the knife-edge diffraction curves shown in Sec. 8.7.2.

2.3.5 Noise Level in Cellular Frequency Band

The thermal noise kTB at a temperature T of 290 K (17°C) and a bandwidth B of 30 kHz is -129 dBm.[*] Assume that the received front-end noise is 9 dB, then the noise level is -120 dBm. Now there are two kinds of man-made noise, the ignition noise generated by the vehicles and the noise generated by 800-MHz emissions.

2.3.5.1 The Ignition Noise. In the past, 800 MHz was not widely used. Therefore, the man-made noise at 800 MHz is merely generated by the vehicle ignition noise.[10] The automotive noise[11] introduced at 800 MHz with a bandwidth of 30 kHz can be deduced from Ref. 12, as shown in Fig. 2.11.

2.3.5.2 The 800-MHz-Emission Noise. As a result of the cellular mobile systems operating in all the major cities in the United States and the spurious energy generated outside each channel bandwidth, the early noise data measurements[10] are no longer valid. The 800-MHz-emission noise can be measured at an idle channel (a forward voice channel) in the 869- to 894-MHz region while the mobile receiver is operating on a car battery in

---

[*]k is Boltzmann's constant, and $kT = -174$ dBm/Hz at $T = 290$ K.[9]

a no-traffic spot in a city. In this case, no automotive ignition noise is involved, and no cochannel operation is in the proximity of the idle-channel receiver. We found that in some areas the noise level is 2 to 3 dB higher than -120 dBm at the cell sites and 3 to 4 dB higher than -120 dBm at the mobile stations.

2.3.5.3   Emission Noise Above the 800 MHz.   Up to the operating frequency of 3 GHz, the emission noise level may remain the same level as that at the 800 MHz. Usually, the emission noise can be ignored because the interference level caused by the cochannels and adjacent channels is much higher than the emission noise level.

2.3.6   Amplifier Noise

A mobile radio signal received by a receiving antenna, either at the cell site or at the mobile unit, will be amplified by an amplifier. We would like to understand how the signal is affected by the amplifier noise. Assume that the amplifier has an available power gain g and the available noise power at the output is N_o. The input signal-to-noise (S/N) ratio is P_s/N_i, the output signal-to-noise ratio is P_o/N_o, and the internal amplifier noise is N_α. Then the output P_o/N_o becomes

$$\frac{P_o}{N_o} = \frac{g P_s}{g(N_i) + N_\alpha} = \frac{P_s}{N_i + (N_\alpha/g)} \tag{2.3-20}$$

The noise figure F is defined as

$$F = \frac{\text{maximum possible S/N ratio}}{\text{actual S/N ratio at output}} \tag{2.3-21}$$

where the maximum possible S/N ratio is measured when the load is an open circuit. Equation (2.3-21) can be used for obtaining the noise figure of the amplifier.

$$F = \frac{P_s/kTB}{P_o/N_o} = \frac{N_o}{(P_o/P_s)kTB} = \frac{N_o}{g(kTB)} \tag{2.3-22}$$

Also substituting Eq. (2.3-20) into Eq. (2.3-22) yields

$$F = \frac{P_s/kTB}{P_s/[N_i + (N_\alpha/g)]} = \frac{N_i + (N_\alpha/g)}{kTB} \tag{2.3-23}$$

The term kTB is the thermal noise as described in Sec. 2.3-5. The noise figure is a reference measurement between a minimum noise level due to thermal noise and the noise level generated by both the external and internal noise of an amplifier.

2.4   OPERATION OF CELLULAR SYSTEMS

2.4.1   Operation Procedures

This section briefly describes the operation of the cellular mobile system from a customer's perception without touching on the design parameters.[13,14] The operation can be divided into four parts and a handoff procedure.

Mobile unit initialization. When a user activates the receiver of the mobile unit, the receiver scans the set-up channels. It then selects the strongest and locks on for a certain time. Because each site is assigned a different set-up channel, locking onto the strongest set-up channel usually means selecting the nearest cell site. This self-location scheme is used in the idle stage and is user-independent. It has a great advantage because it eliminates the load on the transmission at the cell site for locating the mobile unit. The disadvantage of the self-location scheme is that no location information of idle mobile units appears at each cell site. Therefore, when the call initiates from the land line to a mobile unit, the paging process is longer. For a large percentage of calls originates at the mobile unit, the use of self-location schemes is justified. After a given period, the self-location procedure is repeated. When land-line originated calls occur, a feature called "registration" is used.

Mobile originated call. The user places the called number into an originating register in the mobile unit, and pushes the "send" button. A request for service is sent on a selected set-up channel obtained from a self-location scheme. The cell site receives it, and in directional cell sites (or sectors), selects the best directive antenna for the voice channel to use. At the same time, the cell site sends a request to the mobile telephone switching office (MTSO) via a high-speed data link. The MTSO selects an appropriate voice channel for the call, and the cell site acts on it through the best directive antenna to link the mobile unit. The MTSO also connects the wire-line party through the telephone company zone office.

Network originated call. A land-line party dials a mobile unit number. The telephone company zone office recognizes that the number is mobile and forwards the call to the MTSO. The MTSO sends a paging message to certain cell sites based on the mobile unit number and the search algorithm. Each cell site transmits the page on its own set-up channel. If the mobile unit is registered, the registered site pages the mobile. The mobile unit recognizes its own identification on a strong set-up channel, locks onto it, and responds to the cell site. The mobile unit also follows the instruction to tune to an assigned voice channel and initiate user alert.

Call termination. When the mobile user turns off the transmitter, a particular signal (signaling tone) transmits to the cell site, and both sides free the voice channel. The mobile unit resumes monitoring pages through the strongest set-up channel.

Handoff procedure. During the call, two parties are on a traffic channel. When the mobile unit moves out of the coverage area of a particular cell site, the reception becomes weak. The current cell site requests a handoff. The system switches the call to a new frequency channel in a new cell site without either interrupting the call or alerting the user. The call continues as long as the user is talking. The user does not notice the handoff occurrences. *Handoff* was first used by the AMPS system, then renamed *handover* by the European systems because of the different meanings in British English and American English. Description of handoff will appear in Chap. 11.

2.4.2 Maximum Number of Calls Per Hour Per Cell

To calculate the predicted number of calls per hour per cell Q in each cell, we have to know the size of the cell and the traffic conditions in the cell. The calls per hour per cell is based on how small the theoretical cell size can be. The control of the coverage of small cells is based on technological development.

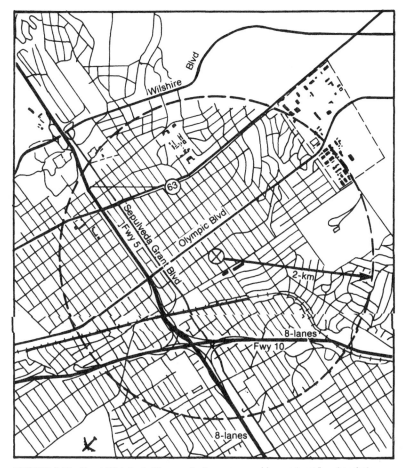

FIGURE 2.12 To establish the traffic capacity from a geographic map (west Los Angeles).

We assume that the cell can be reduced to a 2-km cell, which means a cell of 2-km radius. A 2-km cell in some areas may cover many highways, and in other areas a 2-km cell may only cover a few highways.

Let a busy traffic area of 12 km radius fit seven 2-km cells. The heaviest traffic cell may cover 4 freeways and 10 heavy traffic streets, as shown in Fig. 2.12. A total length of 64 km of 2 eight-lane freeways, 48 km of 2 six-lane freeways, and 588 km of 43 four-lane roads, including the 10 major roads, are obtained from Fig. 2.12. Assume that the average spacing between cars is 10 m during busy periods. We can determine that the total number of cars is about 70,000. If one-half the cars have car phones, and among them eight-tenths will make a call ($\eta_c = 0.8$) during the busy hour, there are 28,000 calls per hour, based on an average of one call per car if that car phone is used.

The maximum predicted number of calls per hour per a 2-km cell Q is derived from the above scenario. It may be an unrealistic case. However, it demonstrates how we can calculate Q for different scenarios and apply this method to finding the different Q in different geographic areas.

2.4.3 Maximum Number of Frequency Channels Per Cell

The maximum number of frequency channels per cell N is closely related to an average calling time in the system. The standard user's calling habits may change as a result of the charging rate of the system and the general income profile of the users. If an average calling time T is 1.76 min and the maximum calls per hour per cell Q_i is obtained from Sec. 2.4.2, then the offered load can be derived as

$$A = \frac{Q_i T}{60} \qquad \text{erlangs} \qquad (2.4\text{-}1)$$

Assume that the blocking probability is given (see Appendix A), then we can easily find the required number of radios in each cell.[15]

EXAMPLE 2.1 *Let the maximum calls per hour Q_i in one cell be 3000 and an average calling time T be 1.76 min. The blocking probability B is 2 percent. Then we may use Q from Eq. (2.4-1) to find the offered load A.*

$$A = \frac{3000 \times 1.76}{60} = 88$$

With the blocking probability $B = 2$ percent, the maximum number of channels can be found from Appendix A as $N = 100$.

EXAMPLE 2.2 *If we let $Q_i = 28,000$ calls per cell per hour, based on one scenaro shown in Sec. 2.4.2, $B = 2$ percent, and $T = 1.76$ min, how many radio channels are needed? The offered load A is obtained as*

$$A = \frac{28,000 \times 1.76}{60} = 821$$

Inserting the above known figures into the table of Appendix A, we find that $N = 820$ channels per cell.

EXAMPLE 2.3 *If there are 50 channels in a cell to handle all the calls and the average is 100 s per call, how many calls can be handled in this cell with a blocking probability of 2 percent? Because $N = 50$ and $B = 2$ percent, the offered load can be found from Appendix A as*

$$A = 40.3$$

The number of calls per hour in a cell is

$$Q_i = \frac{40.3 \times 3600}{100} = 1451 \text{ calls per hour}$$

EXAMPLE 2.4 *If the maximum number of calls per hour per cell is 1451 and there is a seven-cell reuse pattern* in the system ($K = 7$), and assuming that $B = 2$ percent and $T = 100$ s as in Example 2.3, then $N = 50$ as indicated. The total number of required channels for a $K = 7$ reuse system is*

$$N_t = 50 \times 7 = 350 \text{ radios}$$

---

*Its pattern is shown in Fig. 2.14 and described in Sec. 2.5.2.

If a large area is covered by 28 cells, $K_t = 28$; the total number of customers $M_t = \sum_{i=1}^{K_t} M_i$ in the system increases. Therefore, we may assume that the number of subscribers per cell M_i is somehow related to the percentage of car phones used in the busy hours (η_c) and the number of calls per hour per cell Q_i as

$$M_i = f(Q_i, \eta_c) \tag{2.4-2}$$

where the value Q_i is a function of the blocking probability B, the average calling time T, and the number of channels N.

$$Q_i = f(B, T, N) \tag{2.4-3}$$

If the $K = 7$ frequency reuse pattern is used, the total number of required channels in the system is $N_t = 7 \times N$. We must realize that it is the maximum number of calls per cell Q_i that determines the total required channels N_t, not the total number of subscribers M_t. In this case ($K_t = 28$ and $K = 7$), the total number of channels N_t has been used four times in the system.

2.5 CONCEPT OF FREQUENCY REUSE CHANNELS

A radio channel consists of a pair of frequencies, one for each direction of transmission that is used for full-duplex operation. A particular radio channel, say F_1, used in one geographic zone as named it a cell, say C_1, with a coverage radius R can be used in another cell with the same coverage radius at a distance D away.

Frequency reuse is the core concept of the cellular mobile radio system. In this frequency reuse system, users in different geographic locations (different cells) may simultaneously use the same frequency channel (see Fig. 2.13). The frequency reuse system can drastically increase the spectrum efficiency, but if the system is not properly designed, serious interference may occur. Interference due to the common use of the same channel is called *cochannel interference* and is our major concern in the concept of frequency reuse.

2.5.1 Frequency Reuse Schemes

The frequency reuse concept can be used in the time domain and the space domain. Frequency reuse in the time domain results in the occupation of the same frequency in different time slots. It is called *time-division multiplexing* (TDM). Frequency reuse in the space domain can be divided into two categories.

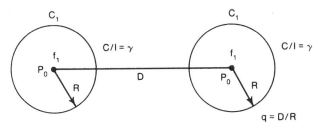

FIGURE **2.13** The ratio of D/R.

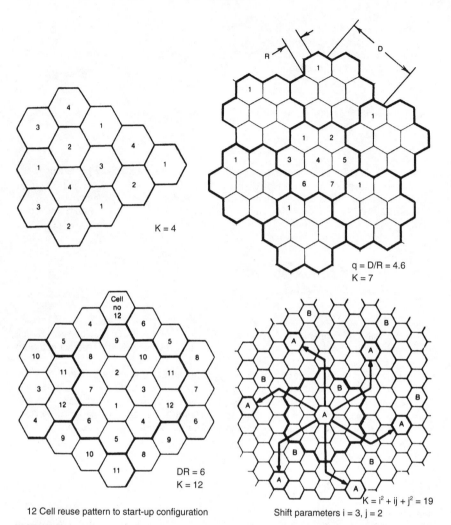

FIGURE 2.14   *N*-cell reuse pattern.

1. Same frequency assigned in two different geographic areas, such as AM or FM radio stations using the same frequency in different cities.

2. Same frequency repeatedly used in a same general area in one system[2]—the scheme is used in cellular systems. There are many cochannel cells in the system. The total frequency spectrum allocation is divided into K frequency reuse patterns, as illustrated in Fig. 2.14 for $K = 4$, 7, 12, and 19.

2.5.2   Frequency Reuse Distance

The minimum distance that allows the same frequency to be reused will depend on many factors, such as the number of cochannel cells in the vicinity of the center cell, the type of geographic terrain contour, the antenna height, and the transmitted power at each cell site.

The frequency reuse distance D can be determined[3,16,17] from

$$D = \sqrt{3K}\,R \tag{2.5-1}$$

Where K is the frequency reuse pattern shown in Fig. 2.13, then

$$D = \begin{cases} 3.46R & K = 4 \\ 4.6R & K = 7 \\ 6R & K = 12 \\ 7.55R & K = 19 \end{cases}$$

If all the cell sites transmit the same power, then K increases and the frequency reuse distance D increases. This increased D reduces the chance that cochannel interference may occur.

Theoretically, a large K is desired. However, the total number of allocated channels is fixed. When K is too large, the number of channels assigned to each of K cells becomes small. It is always true that if the total number of channels in K cells is divided as K increases, trunking inefficiency results.[18] The same principle applies to spectrum inefficiency: if the total number of channels are divided into two network systems serving in the same area, spectrum inefficiency increases.

Now the challenge is to obtain the smallest number K[17] that can still meet our system performance requirements. This involves estimating cochannel interference and selecting the minimum frequency reuse distance D to reduce cochannel interference. The smallest value of K is $K = 3$, obtained by setting $i = 1$, $j = 1$ in the equation $K = i^2 + ij + j^2$ (see Fig. 2.14).

2.5.3 Number of Customers in the System

When we design a system, the traffic conditions in the area during a busy hour are some of the parameters that will help determine both the sizes of different cells and the number of channels in them.

The maximum number of calls per hour per cell is driven by the traffic conditions at each particular cell. After the maximum number of frequency channels per cell has been implemented in each cell, then the maximum number of calls per hour can be taken care of in each cell. Now, take the maximum number of calls per hour in each cell Q_i and sum them over all cells. Assume that 60 percent of the car phones will be used during the busy hour, on average, one call per phone ($\eta_c = 0.6$) if that phone is used. The total allowed subscriber traffic M_t can then be obtained.

EXAMPLE 2.5 *During a busy hour, the number of calls per hour Q_i for each of 10 cells is 2000, 1500, 3000, 500, 1000, 1200, 1800, 2500, 2800, 900. Assume that 60 percent of the car phones will be used during this period ($\eta_c = 0.6$) and that one call is made per car phone. Summing over all Q_i gives the total Q_t*

$$Q_t = \sum_{i=1}^{10} Q_i = 17{,}200 \text{ calls per hour}$$

Because $\eta_c = 0.6$, the number of customers in the system is

$$M_t = \frac{17{,}200}{0.6} = 28{,}667$$

2.6 COCHANNEL INTERFERENCE
REDUCTION FACTOR

Reusing an identical frequency channel in different cells is limited by cochannel interference between cells, and the cochannel interference can become a major problem. Here we would like to find the minimum frequency reuse distance in order to reduce this cochannel interference.

Assume that the size of all cells is roughly the same. The cell size is determined by the coverage area of the signal strength in each cell. As long as the cell size is fixed, cochannel interference is independent of the transmitted power of each cell. It means that the received threshold level at the mobile unit is adjusted to the size of the cell. Actually, cochannel interference is a function of a parameter q defined as

$$q = \frac{D}{R} \tag{2.6-1}$$

The parameter q is the cochannel interference reduction factor. When the ratio q increases, cochannel interference decreases. Furthermore, the separation D in Eq. (2.6-1) is a function of K_I and C/I,

$$D = f(K_I, C/I) \tag{2.6-2}$$

where K_I is the number of cochannel interfering cells in the first tier and C/I is the received carrier-to-interference ratio at the desired mobile receiver.[3]

$$\frac{C}{I} = \frac{C}{\sum\limits_{k=1}^{K_I} I_k} \tag{2.6-3}$$

In a fully equipped hexagonal-shaped cellular system, there are always six cochannel interfering cells in the first tier, as shown in Fig. 2.15; that is, $K_I = 6$. The maximum number of K_I in the first tier can be shown as six (i.e., $2\pi D/D \approx 6$). Cochannel interference can be experienced both at the cell site and at mobile units in the center cell. If the interference is much greater, then the carrier-to-interference ratio C/I at the mobile units caused by the six interfering sites is (on the average) the same as the C/I received at the center cell site caused by interfering mobile units in the six cells. According to both the reciprocity theorem and the statistical summation of radio propagation, the two C/I values can be very close. Assume that the local noise is much less than the interference level and can be neglected. C/I then can be expressed, from Eq. (2.3-4), as

$$\frac{C}{I} = \frac{R^{-\gamma}}{\sum\limits_{k=1}^{K_I} D_k^{-\gamma}} \tag{2.6-4}$$

where γ is a propagation path-loss slope[5] determined by the actual terrain environment. In a mobile radio medium, γ usually is assumed to be 4 (see Sec. 2.3.1). K_I is the number of cochannel interfering cells and is equal to 6 in a fully developed system, as shown in Fig. 2.15. The six cochannel interfering cells in the second tier cause weaker interference than those in the first tier (see Example 2.6 at the end of Sec. 2.7.1).

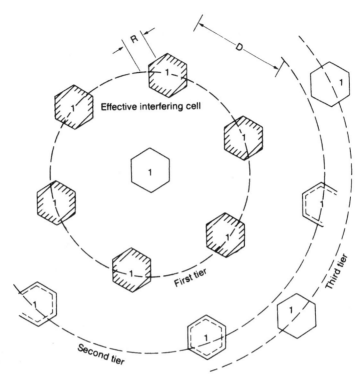

FIGURE 2.15   Six effective interfering cells of cell 1.

Therefore, the cochannel interference from the second tier of interfering cells is negligible. Substituting Eq. (2.6-1) into Eq. (2.6-4) yields

$$\frac{C}{I} = \frac{1}{\sum_{k=1}^{K_I}\left(\frac{D_k}{R}\right)^{-\gamma}} = \frac{1}{\sum_{k=1}^{K_I}(q_k)^{-\gamma}} \tag{2.6-5}$$

where q_k is the cochannel interference reduction factor with kth cochannel interfering cell

$$q_k = \frac{D_k}{R} \tag{2.6-6}$$

2.7 DESIRED C/I FROM A NORMAL CASE IN AN OMNIDIRECTIONAL ANTENNA SYSTEM

2.7.1 Analytic Solution

There are two cases to be considered: (1) the signal and cochannel interference received by the mobile unit and (2) the signal and cochannel interference received by the cell site.

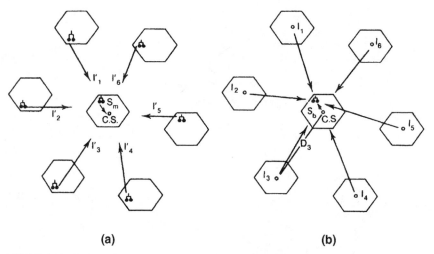

(a) **(b)**

FIGURE 2.16 Cochannel interference from six interferers, (*a*) Receiving at the cell site; (*b*) receiving at the mobile unit.

Both cases are shown in Fig. 2.16. N_m, and N_b are the local noises at the mobile unit and the cell site, respectively. Usually, N_m and N_b are small and can be neglected as compared with the interference level. The effect of the cochannel interference on spectrum efficiency systems will appear in Sec. 15.4. As long as the received carrier-to-interference ratios at both the mobile unit and the cell site are the same, the system is called a *balanced system*. In a balanced system, we can choose either one of the two cases to analyze the system requirement; the results from one case are the same for the others.

Assume that all D_k are the same for simplicity, as shown in Fig. 2.15; then $D = D_k$, and $q = q_k$, and

$$\frac{C}{I} = \frac{R^{-\gamma}}{6D^{-\gamma}} = \frac{q^\gamma}{6} \tag{2.7-1}$$

Thus

$$q^\gamma = 6\frac{C}{I} \tag{2.7-2}$$

and

$$q = \left(6\frac{C}{I}\right)^{1/\gamma} \tag{2.7-3}$$

In Eq. (2.7-3), the value of C/I is based on the required system performance and the specified value of γ is based on the terrain environment. With given values of C/I and γ, the cochannel interference reduction factor q can be determined. Normal cellular practice is to specify C/I to be 18 dB or higher based on subjective tests and the criterion described in Sec. 2.2. Because a C/I of 18 dB is measured by the acceptance of voice quality from present cellular mobile receivers, this acceptance implies that both mobile radio multipath fading and cochannel interference become ineffective at that level. The path-loss slope γ is equal to about 4 in a mobile radio environment.[19]

$$q = D/R = (6 \times 63.1)^{1/4} = 4.41 \tag{2.7-4}$$

The 90th percentile of the total covered area would be achieved by increasing the transmitted power at each cell; increasing the same amount of transmitted power in each cell does not affect the result of Eq. (2.7-4). This is because q is not a function of transmitted power. The computer simulation described in the next section finds the value of $q = 4.6$, which is very close to Eq. (2.7-4). The factor q can be related to the finite set of cells K in a hexagonal-shaped cellular system by

$$q = \overset{\Delta}{=} \sqrt{3K} \tag{2.7-5}$$

Substituting q from Eq. (2.7-4) into Eq. (2.7-5) yields

$$K = 7 \tag{2.7-6}$$

Equation (2.7-6) indicates that a seven-cell reuse pattern[*] is needed for a C/I of 18 dB. The seven-cell reuse pattern is shown in Fig. 2.14.

Based on $q = D/R$, the determination of D can be reached by choosing a radius R in Eq. (2.7-4). Usually, a value of q greater than that shown in Eq. (2.7-4) would be desirable. The greater the value of q, the lower the cochannel interference. In a real environment, Eq. (2.6-5) is always true, but Eq. (2.7-1) is not. Because Eq. (2.7-4) is derived from Eq. (2.7-1), the value q may not be large enough to maintain a carrier-to-interference ratio of 18 dB. This is particularly true in the worst case, as shown in Chap. 9.

EXAMPLE 2.6 *Compare interference from the first tier of 6 interferers with that from 12 interferers (first and second tiers) (see Fig. 2.15).*

From the first tier,

$$\frac{C}{I} = \frac{C}{\displaystyle\sum_{i=1}^{6} I_I} = \frac{R_1^{-4}}{6D_1^{-4}} = \frac{a_1^4}{6} \tag{E2.6-1}$$

From the first and second tiers,

$$\frac{C}{I} = \frac{C}{\displaystyle\sum_{i=1}^{6}(I_{1i} + I_{2i})} = \frac{1}{6(a_1^{-4} + a_2^{-4})} \tag{E2.6-2}$$

Because we have found $a_1 = 4.6$, then from the second tier, $a_2 = D_2/R_1 = 2D_1/R_1 = 2a_1 = 9.2$. Substituting a_1 and a_2 into Eqs. (E2.6-1) and (E2.6-2), respectively, yields

$$\left(\frac{C}{I}\right)_{1\text{st tier}} = 18.72 \text{ dB}$$

$$\left(\frac{C}{I}\right)_{1\text{st and 2nd tiers}} = 18.46 \text{ dB}$$

We realize that a negligible amount of interference is contributed by the six interferers from the second tier.

---

[*]In this seven-cell reuse pattern, the total allocated frequency band is divided into seven subsets. Each particular subset of frequency channels is assigned to one of seven cells.

2.7.2 Solution Obtained From Simulation

The required cochannel reduction factor q can be obtained from the simulation also. Let one main cell site and all six possible cochannel interferers be deployed in a pattern, as shown in Fig. 2.15. The distance D from the center cell to the cochannel interferers in the simulation is a variable. $D = 2R$ can be used initially and incremented every $0.5R$ as $D = 2R, 2.5R, 3R$. For every particular value of D, a set of simulation data is generated.

First, the location of each mobile unit in its own cell is randomly generated by a random generator. Then the distance D_k from each of the six interfering mobile units to the center cell site (assuming $K_I = 6$) is obtained. The desired mobile signal as well as six interference levels received at the center cell site would be randomly generated following the mobile radio propagation path-loss rule, which is 40 dB/dec, along with a log-normal standard deviation of 8 dB at its mean value.[20] Summing up all the data from six simulated interferences,

$$I = \sum_{k=1}^{K_I - 6} -I_k$$

and dividing it by the simulated main carrier, value C becomes C/I.

This C/I is for a particular D, the distance between the center cell site and the cochannel cell sites (cochannel interferers). Repeat this process, say 1000 times, for each particular value of D, based on the criterion stated in Sec. 2.2.4 (that 75 percent of the users say voice quality is "good" or "excellent" in 90 percent of the total covered area). Then from 75 percent of the users' opinion, $C/I = 18$ dB needs to be achieved[18] with a proper value of D. Assuming that mobile unit locations are chosen randomly and uniformly, then 90 percent of the area corresponds to 900 out of 1000 mobile unit locations.

To find a proper value for D, each mobile unit location associates with its received C/I. Some C/I values are high and some are low. This means that the lowest 100 values of C/I should be discarded. The main C/I value should be derived from the remaining 900 C/I values. This associates a particular C/I for a particular separation D. Repeating this process for different values of D, the corresponding mean C/I values are found. The C/I versus D curve can be plotted, depicting $C/I = 18$ dB as corresponding to $D = 4.6R$, as illustrated in the Bell Lab publication.[4] Then

$$q = \frac{D}{R} = 4.6 \tag{2.7-7}$$

Comparing the values of q obtained from an analytic solution shown in Eq. (2.7-4) and q obtained from a simulation solution shown in Eq. (2.7-7), the results are surprisingly close.

Although a simulation (statistical) approach deals with a real-world situation, it does not provide a clear physical picture. The two agreeable solutions illustrated in this section prove that the simple analytic method is implementable in a cellular system based on hexagonal cells.

2.8 HANDOFF MECHANISM

The handoff is the process mentioned in Sec. 2.4.1. It is a unique feature that allows cellular systems to operate as effectively as demonstrated in actual use. There are two kinds of handoffs, hard and soft. The hard handoff is "brake before make." The soft handoff is

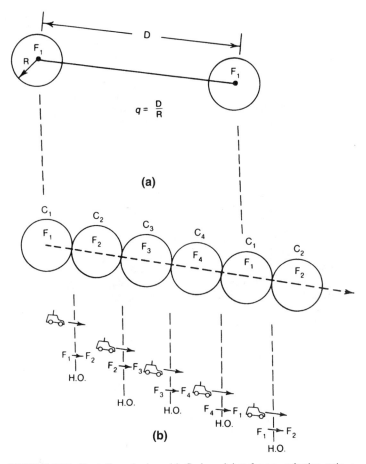

FIGURE 2.17 Handoff mechanism. (*a*) Cochannel interference reduction ratio q. (*b*) Fill-in frequencies.

"make before brake." To clearly describe the hard handoff concept, it is easy to use a one-dimensional illustration as shown in Fig. 2.17, although a real two-dimensional cellular configuration would cover an area with cells. The hard handoff concept as applied to a one-dimensional case will also apply to two-dimensional cases.

Two cochannel cells using the frequency F_1 separated by a distance D are shown in Fig. 2.17a. The radius R and the distance D are governed by the value of q. Now we have to fill in with other frequency channels such as F_2, F_3, and F_4 between two cochannel cells in order to provide a communication system in the whole area.

The fill-in frequencies F_2, F_3, and F_4 are also assigned to their corresponding cells C_2, C_3, and C_4 (see Fig. 2.17b) according to the same value of q.

Suppose a mobile unit is starting a call in cell C_1 and then moves to C_2. The call can be dropped and reinitiated in the frequency channel from F_1 to F_2 while the mobile unit moves from cell C_1 to cell C_2. This process of changing frequencies can be done automatically by the system without the user's intervention. This process of hard handoff is carried on in the cellular system, for FDMA and TDMA systems.

The soft handoff is used in CDMA systems. Because in CDMA, $K = 1$, the soft handoff is carried out when the mobile enters the neighboring cell. In the overlapped area between two cells, two traffic channels, one from each cell, serve one mobile call during the soft handoff.

The handoff processing scheme is an important task for any successful mobile system. How does one make any one of the necessary handoffs successful? How does one reduce all unnecessary handoffs in the system? How is the individual cell traffic capacity controlled by altering the handoff algorithm? All these questions will be answered in Chap. 11.

2.9 CELL SPLITTING

2.9.1 Why Splitting?

The motivation behind implementing a cellular mobile system is to improve the utilization of spectrum efficiency.[19] The frequency reuse scheme is one concept, and cell splitting is another concept. When traffic density starts to build up and the frequency channels F_i in each cell C_i cannot provide enough mobile calls, the original cell can be split into smaller cells. Usually the new radius is one-half the original radius (see Fig. 2.18). There are two ways of splitting. In Fig. 2.18a, the original cell site is not used, while in Fig. 2.18b, it is.

$$\text{New cell radius} = \frac{\text{old cell radius}}{2} \tag{2.9-1}$$

Then, based on Eq. (2.9-1), the following equation is true.

$$\text{New cell area} = \frac{\text{old cell area}}{4} \tag{2.9-2}$$

Let each new cell carry the same maximum traffic load of the old cell; then, in theory,

$$\frac{\text{New traffic load}}{\text{Unit area}} = 4 \times \frac{\text{traffic load}}{\text{unit area}}$$

2.9.2 How Splitting?

There are two kinds of cell-splitting techniques:

1. *Permanent splitting.* The installation of every new split cell has to be planned ahead of time; the number of channels, the transmitted power, the assigned frequencies, the choosing of the cell-site selection, and the traffic load consideration should all be considered. When ready, the actual service cut-over should be set at the lowest traffic point, usually at midnight on a weekend. Hopefully, only a few calls will be dropped because of this cut-over, assuming that the downtime of the system is within 2 h.

2. *Dynamic splitting.* This scheme is based on using the allocated spectrum efficiency in real time. The algorithm for dynamically splitting cell sites is a tedious job, as we cannot

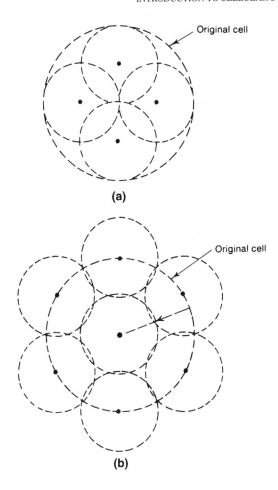

Original cell

(a)

Original cell

(b)   **FIGURE 2.18**   Cell splitting.

afford to have one single cell unused during cell splitting at heavy traffic hours. Section 12.6.2 will discuss this topic in depth.

2.10   CONSIDERATION OF THE COMPONENTS OF CELLULAR SYSTEMS

The elements of cellular mobile radio system design have been mentioned in the previous sections. Here we must also consider the components of cellular systems, such as mobile radios, antennas, cell-site, base-station controller, and MTSO. They would affect our system design if we do not choose the right one. The general view of the cellular system is shown in Fig. 2.19. Even though the EIA (Electronic Industries Association) and the FCC have specified standards for radio equipment at the cell sites and the mobile sites, we still need

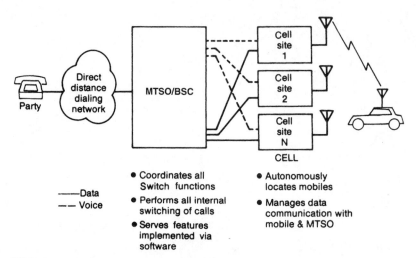

FIGURE 2.19 A general view of cellular telecommunications systems.

to be concerned about that equipment. The issues affecting choice of antennas, switching equipment, and data links are briefly described here.[21–23]

2.10.1 Antennas

Antenna pattern, antenna gain, antenna tilting, and antenna height[6] all affect the cellular system design. The antenna pattern can be omnidirectional, directional, or any shape in both the vertical and the horizon planes. Antenna gain compensates for the transmitted power. Different antenna patterns and antenna gains at the cell site and at the mobile units would affect the system performance and so must be considered in the system design.

The antenna patterns seen in cellular systems are different from the patterns seen in free space. If a mobile unit travels around a cell site in areas with many buildings, the omnidirectional antenna will not duplicate the omnipattern. In addition, if the front-to-back ratio of a directional antenna is found to be 20 dB in free space, it will be only 10 dB at the cell site. An explanation for these phenomena is given in Chapter 8.

Antenna tilting can reduce the interference to the neighboring cells and enhance the weak spots in the cell. Also, the height of the cell-site antenna can affect the area and shape of the coverage in the system. The effect of antenna height will be described in Chap. 8.

2.10.2 Switching Equipment

The capacity of switching equipment in cellular systems is not based on the number of switch ports but on the capacity of the processor associated with the switches. In a big cellular system, this processor should be large. Also, because cellular systems are unlike other systems, it is important to consider when the switching equipment would reach the maximum capacity.

The service life of the switching equipment is not determined by the life cycle of the equipment but by how long it takes to reach its full capacity. If the switching equipment is designed in modules, or as distributed switches, more modules can be added to increase the capacity of the equipment. For decentralized systems, digital switches may be more suitable. The future trend seems to be the utilization of system handoff. This means that switching equipment can link to other switching equipment so that a call can be carried from one system to another system without the call being dropped. We will discuss these issues in Chap. 13.

2.10.3 Data Links

The data links are shown in Fig. 2.19. Although they are not directly affected by the cellular system, they are important in the system. Each data link can carry multiple channel data (10 kbps data transmitted per channel) from the cell site to the MTSO. This fast-speed data transmission cannot be passed through a regular telephone line. Therefore, data bank devices are needed. They can be multiplexed, many-data channels passing through a wideband T-carrier wire line or going through a microwave radio link where the frequency is much higher than 850 MHz.

Leasing T1-carrier wire lines through telephone companies can be costly. Although the use of microwaves may be a long-term money saver, the availability of the microwave link has to be considered and is described in Chap. 13.

2.11 DIFFERENT CELLULAR SYSTEMS AND B3G-SYSTEMS

In 1984, the first analog cellular system, AMPS, was deployed in the United States. AMPS system will be described in Chapter 3. In 1992, the first digital cellular system, GSM (Special Mobile Group), was deployed in Germany. GSM is a European standard system. In the United States, an NA-TDMA system (IS-54 later IS-136) and a CDMA system (IS-95) have been developed. NA-TDMA was deployed in 1993, and CDMA is planned for deployment in 1995. A Japanese system, PDC (Personal Digital Cellular), was deployed in Osaka in June 1994. All the digital cellular systems and some noncellular digital systems will be described in Chap. 4. These systems are named 2G (second generation) systems. In Chapter 5, we will mention some B2G (Beyond 2G) systems. In chapter 6, we will mention 3G systems. In Chapter 7, B3G systems are mentioned.

REFERENCES

1. Bell Laboratories, "High-Capacity Mobile Telephone System Technical Report," December 1971, submitted to FCC.

2. F. H. Blecher, "Advanced Mobile Phone Service," *IEEE Transactions on Vehicular Technology*, Vol. VT-29, May 1980, pp. 238–244.

3. V. H. MacDonald, "The Cellular Concept," *Bell System Technical Journal*, Vol. 58, January 1979, pp. 15–42.

4. W. C. Y. Lee, *Mobile Communications Engineering*, McGraw-Hill Book Co., 1998, p. 121.

5. W. C. Y. Lee, *Mobile Communications Design Fundamentals*, John Wiley and Son, 1993, Chap. 2.

6. W. C. Y. Lee, "Statistical Analysis of the Level Crossings and Duration of Fades of the Signal from an Energy Density Mobile Radio Antenna", Bell System Technical Journal, Vol. 46, Feb. 1967, pp. 417–448.

7. W. C. Y. Lee, *Mobile Communications Engineering*, McGraw-Hill Book Co., 1998, p. 235.

8. W. C. Y. Lee, *Mobile Communications Design Fundamentals*, John Wiley & Son, 1993, pp. 26 and 30.

9. *ITT Reference Data for Radio Engineers*, Howard W. Sams & Co., 1993, 8th Ed., p. 34-6.

10. A. D. Spaulding and R. T. Disney, "Man-Made Radio Noise, Part I," U.S. Department of Commerce, Office of Technical Services Report 74-38, June 1974.

11. E. N. Skomal, *Man-Made Radio Noise*, Van Nostrand Reinhold Co., 1978, Chap. 2.

12. W. C. Y. Lee, *Mobile Communications Design Fundamentals*, John Wiley & Son, 1993, p. 232.

13. J. Oetting, "Cellular Mobile Radio—An Emerging Technology," *IEEE Communications Magazine*, Vol. 21, No. 8, November 1983, pp. 10–15.

14. "Advanced Mobile Phone Service," special issue, *Bell System Technical Journal*, Vol. 58. January 1979.

15. Siemens, "Telephone Traffic Theory and Table and Charts, Part 1," Telephone and Switching Division, Siemens, Munich, 1970.

16. W. C. Y. Lee, Lee's Essentials of Wireless Communications, McGraw-Hill Book Co., 2001, p. 8.

17. W. C. Y. Lee, *"Mobile Communications Design Fundamentals,"* John Wiley & Son, 1993, p. 141.

18. Bell Laboratories, "High-Capacity Mobile Telephone System Technical Report," December 1971, submitted to FCC.

19. W. C. Y. Lee, "Mobile Cellular System Conserves Frequency Resource," *Microwave Systems News & Communications Technology*, Vol. 15, No. 7, June 1985, pp. 139–150.

20. W. C. Y. Lee, *Mobile Communications Engineering*, McGraw-Hill Book Co., 1998, p. 164.

21. D. Bedson, G. F. McClure and S. R. McConaughey (eds.), *Land-Mobile Communications Engineering*, IEEE Press, 1984, Part III.

22. F. H. Blecher, "Advanced Mobile Phone Service," *IEEE Transactions on Vehicular Technology*, Vol. VT-29, May 1980, pp. 238–244.

23. S. W. Halpren, "Reuse Petitioning in Cellular Systems," *33rd IEEE Vehicular Technology Conference Record*, Toronto, May 1983.

CHAPTER 3

SPECIFICATIONS OF ANALOG SYSTEMS

The analog cellular system was a successful model in wireless communication and led to the digital cellular systems with several evolutions from FDMA to TDMA and to CDMA as of today. There are many clever techniques that have been implemented in the analog system. In the analog system, the signaling channels are only used for call establishing. After the call is connected, the traffic channel handles both voice and signaling by using the property of Manchester code. The use of SAT (Supervisory Audio Tone) for on-hook and off-hook as well as the identification of cells is also clever; of course, the invention of handoffs, used while at a weak-signal condition (at cell boundary), is another great contribution. Therefore, it is worthwhile to include discussion of the analog cellular system in this book.

In this chapter, we concentrate on U.S. analog cellular mobile specifications[1] as well as the elements and parameters of the analog system.[2-3] Also, we touch on the differences in other foreign analog cellular mobile systems.

3.1 DEFINITIONS OF TERMS AND FUNCTIONS

1. *Home mobile station* (*unit*). A mobile station that is subscribed in its cellular system.

2. *Land station.* A station other than a mobile station, which links to the mobile station.

3. *Control channel.* A channel used for the transmission of digital control information from a land station to a mobile station, or vice versa.

4. *Forward control channel* (FDCC). A control channel used from a land station to a mobile station.

5. *Reverse control channel* (RECC). A control channel used from a mobile station to a land station.

6. *Forward voice channel* (FVC). A voice channel used from a land station to a mobile unit.

7. *Reverse voice channel* (RVC). A voice channel used from a mobile station to a land station.

8. *Set-up channels.* A number of designated control channels.

9. *Access channel.* A control channel used by a mobile station to access a system and obtain service. The access channel always accesses from the mobile station to the cell site.

10. *Paging channel.* The act of seeking a mobile station when an incoming call from the land line has been placed to it.

11. *Digital color code* (DC). A digital signal transmitted by a forward control channel to detect capture of an interfering mobile station. There are four codes (See Sec. 3.2.8.)

12. *Flash request.* A message sent on a voice channel from a mobile station to a land station indicating a user's desire to invoke special processing, such as an emergency.

13. *Signaling tone.* A 10-kHz tone transmitted by the mobile station on a voice channel. It serves several functions.

14. *Handoff.* The act of transferring a mobile station from one voice channel to another voice channel. There are two kinds of handoffs:

a. Interhandoff, from one cell to another cell

b. Intrahandoff, within a cell

15. *Numeric information.* Used to describe the operation of the mobile station.

Numeric indicators

MIN	Mobile identification number
MIN1	24 bits that correspond to the seven-digit directory number assigned to the mobile station
MIN2	10 bits that correspond to the three-digit area code
BIS	Identifies whether a mobile station must check an idle-to-busy transition on a reverse control channel when accessing a system. In a forward control channel, busy-idle bit inserts in every 10-bit interval of a transmitted bit stream.
CCLIST	Scanned by a mobile station on a list of control channels
CMAX	Maximum number of control channels to be scanned by the mobile station (up to 21 channels)
MAXBUSY	Maximum number of busy occurrences allowed on a reversed control channel
MAXSZTR	Maximum number of seizure attempts allowed on a reversed control channel
NBUSY	Number of times a mobile station attempts to seize a reverse control channel and finds it busy
NSZTR	Number of times a mobile station attempts to seize a reverse control channel and fails
PL	Mobile station RF power level
SCC	A digital number that is stored and used to identify which SAT (see item 20 below) frequency a mobile station should be received on

16. *Paging.* The act of seeking a mobile station when an incoming call from the land station has been placed to it.

17. *Paging channel.* A forward control channel that is used to page mobile stations and send orders.

18. *Registration.* The procedure by which a mobile station identifies itself to a land station as being active.

19. *Roamer.* A mobile station that operates in a cellular system other than the one from which service is subscribed.

20. *Supervisory audio tone* (SAT). One of three tones in the 6-kHz region; there is one SAT frequency for each land station. In certain circumstances, there is one SAT frequency for each sector of each land station.

21. *System identification* (SID). A digital identification uniquely associated with a cellular system.

22. *Electronic serial number* (ESN). Each mobile station has an ESN assigned by the manufacturer.

23. *Group identification.* A subset of the most significant bits of SID that is used to identify a group of cellular systems.

24. *Channel spacing.* Thirty kilohertz per one-way channel. As an example, channel 1 is 825.030 MHz (mobile transmit) and 870.030 MHz (land transmit). Additional spectrum allocation of 10 MHz (5 MHz one way) for the cellular industry changes the channel numbering order.

3.2 SPECIFICATION OF MOBILE STATION (UNIT) IN THE UNITED STATES

3.2.1 Power

Let P_0 be the specified power and f_0 be the specified frequency channel. P and f are the operating power and frequency, respectively.

Power level (carrier-off condition) requires $P < -60$ dBm in 2 ms

Power level (carrier-on-condition) within 3 dB of specified power (P_0) within 2 ms

Power level (off-frequency condition), if $|f - f_e| > 1$ kHz, do not transmit; then $P < -60$ dBm

Power transmitted levels are maximum effective radiated power (ERP) with respect to a half-wave dipole

Mobile stations have three station class marks:[1]

Power Class	P, Power Level $= 0$	Tolerance
I	6 dBW (4.0 W)	(8 dBW $\leq P \leq 2$ dBW)
II	2 dBW (1.6 W)	(4 dBW $\leq P \leq -2$ dBW)
III	-2 dBW (0.6 W)	(0 dBW $\leq P \leq -6$ dBW)

Each mobile station power class I has eight full power levels (0 to 7), with power level 0 being the highest. Each level has a 4-dB drop. The total power control range for power class I (mobile) is 28 dB. The names CMAC and VMAC indicate the maximum control and maximum voice attenuation codes, respectively. For all three mobile station power classes, power level 7 is -22 dBW (or 8 dBm or 6.3 mW).

3.2.2 Modulation

1. *Compressor/expandor (compander).*[4] A 2:1 syllabic compander is used. Every 2-dB change in input level converts (compresses) to 1 dB at ouput (at the transmitted side). Then reverse the two numbers (expand) at the received side. It serves two purposes:

a. To confine the energy in the channel bandwidth

b. To generate a quieting effect during a speech pulse

2. *Preemphasis/deemphasis* (see Fig. 3.1).[4] The preemphasis network and its response are shown in Fig. 3.1. The improvement factor ρ_{FM} is[4]

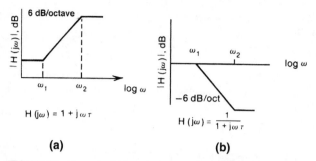

FIGURE 3.1 Preemphasis/deemphasis response. (*a*) Preemphasis response $\omega_1 = 1/\tau, \omega_2 = 2\pi f_2$. (*b*) Deemphasis response $\omega_1 = 1/\tau, \omega_2 = 2\pi f_2$.

$$\rho_{FM} = \frac{(f_2/f_1)^3}{3[f_2/f_1 - \tan^{-1}(f_2/f_1)]}$$

For $f_2/f_1 < 2$, ρ_{FM} approaches 1.
For wideband, $f_2 >> f_1$. Thus

$$\rho_{FM} = \frac{(f_2/f_1)^2}{3}$$

For $f_2 = 3$ kHz and $f_1 = 300$ Hz, the improvement factor ρ_{FM} is

$$\rho_{FM} = 10 \log \frac{100}{3} = 15.23 \text{ dB}$$

3. *Deviation limiter.* A mobile station must limit the instantaneous frequency deviation to ± 12 kHz. The deviation limiter of the frequency-to-voltage characteristic is shown in Fig. 3.2.

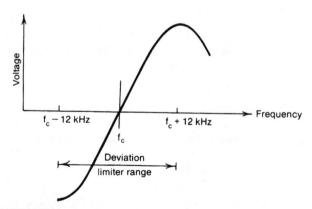

FIGURE 3.2 Deviation limiter characteristics.

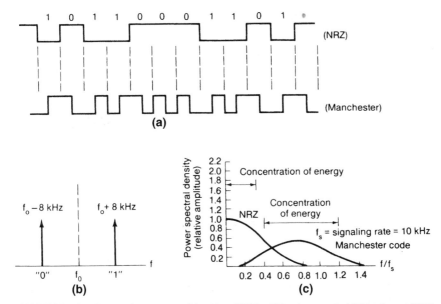

FIGURE 3.3 Waveforms and power spectral densities of NRZ and Manchester code. (*a*) Waveforms of NRZ and Manchester code. (*b*) Use of two frequency deviations to represent two levels. (*c*) Power spectral densities of NRZ and Manchester code.

4. *Wideband data signal.* A NRZ (non-return-to-zero) binary data stream is encoded to a Manchester (biphase) code, as shown in Fig. 3.3. It modulates to a ± 8-kHz binary FSK with a transmission rate of 10 kbps. The advantage of using a Manchester code in a voice channel is that the energy of this code is concentrated at the transmission rate of 10 kHz. Therefore, a burst of signals transmitted over the voice channel can be detected. The Manchester code is applied to both control channels and voice channels.

3.2.3 Limitation on Emission

It is very important that each mobile station have a limit on its emission. An RF signal emitted by any receiver has to be lese than some value, which in turn depends on different frequency bands. The values are shown in the box as follows.

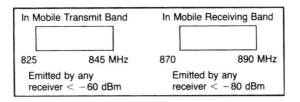

3.2.4 Security and Identification

1. *Mobile identification number* (MIN). A binary number of 34 bits ($2^{34} \approx 1.7 \times 10^{10}$) derived from a 10-digit directory telephone number.

2. *Electronic serial number* (ESN). A 32-bit binary number that uniquely identifies a mobile unit and must be set by the factory. Attempts to change the serial number circuit should render the mobile unit *inoperative*.

The manufacturer should not overlook this requirement, and each operating system has to check that this requirement is enforced from different manufactured units. This number will be used in the system for security purposes.

An amount of revenue can be lost to the system operation if the manufacturer fails to implement this requirement in the mobile unit and a false ESN can be used in place easily.

3. *First paging channel* (FIRSTCHP). An 11-bit system that identifies the channel number of the first paging channel when the mobile station is "home." It is stored in the mobile unit.

4. *Home system identification* (SID). Fifteen-bit system used to identify the home station. The least significant bit is 1 for a Block A system, otherwise 0 for a Block B system.

5. *Preferred system selection.* Provided as a means for selecting the preferred system as either system A or system B within a mobile station.

3.2.5 Supervision

3.2.5.1 SAT (Supervisory Audio Tone)[1,5]

1. *SAT function.* There are three SAT tones: 5970, 6000, and 6030 Hz. The tolerance of each tone is ±15 Hz. The features of the SAT tones are

    a. Each land station is assigned to one SAT among the three listed above.

    b. One SAT tone is added to each forward voice channel (FVC) by a land station. The mobile station detects, filters, and modulates on the reversed voice channel (RVC) with this same tone.

    c. SAT is suspended during transmission of wideband data (a burst of signaling of 10 kbps), information, or other control features on the reverse voice channel.

    d. It is not suspended when a signaling tone (10 kHz) is sent.

    e. The received audio transmission must be muted if the measured SAT and SCC do not agree with each other.

2. *SAT transmission.* The tone modulation index is 1/3. It is a narrowband FM. The deviation $\Delta F = \pm 2$ kHz is centered around each SAT tone.

3. *Fade timing status of SAT.* The transmitter is turned off if no valid SAT tone can be detected or the measured SAT does not agree with the SAT color code (SCC) of each cell site transmitted by the control signal, or if no SAT is received when the timer counts to 5 s. SCC is indicated in the set-up channel.

Signaling Tone. Signaling tones must be kept within 10 kHz ± 1 Hz and produce a nominal frequency deviation of ±8 kHz of the carrier frequency. It is used over the voice channel. It serves three functions.

1. Flush for special orders

2. Terminate the cells

3. Order confirmation

Malfunction Timer Set at 60 s. The transmission will cease when the timer exceeds 60 s. The timer never expires as long as the proper sequence of operations is taking place.

3.2.6 Call Processing

3.2.6.1 Initialization. When the user turns on the mobile station, the initialization work starts.

1. Mobile station must tune to the strongest dedicated control channel (usually one of 21 channels) within 3 s. Then, a system parameter message should be received.
2. If it cannot complete this task on the strongest dedicated control channel, it turns to the second strongest dedicated control channel and attempts to complete this task within the next 3-s interval.
3. Check whether it is in Enable or Disable status. Serving system status changed to Enable if the preferred system is System A. Serving system status changed to Disable if the preferred system is System B.

3.2.6.2 Paging Channel Selection

1. The mobile station must then tune to the strongest paging channel within 3 s. Usually paging channels are control channels.
2. Receive an overhead message train and update the following: Roam, system identification, local control status.

3.2.6.3 Idle Stage. A mobile station executes each of four tasks at least every 46.3 ms.

1. *Responds to overhead information.* Compare SID_s (stored) with SID_r (received). If $SID_s \neq SID_r$, return to initialization stage.
2. *Page match.* If the roam status is Disable, the mobile station must attempt to match for one-word message or two-word messages. If the roam status is Enable, the mobile station must attempt to match two words.
3. *Order.* After matching the MIN, respond to the order.
4. *Rescan access channels.* Because the vehicle is moving, information must be updated. Rescan at 2- to 5-min intervals, depending on different manufacturers.

3.2.6.4 Call Initiation. Origination indication (system access task).

1. *System access task.* When the system access task is started, an access timer is set for

Origination	max 12 s
Page response	max 6 s
An order response	max 6 s
Registration	max 6 s

2. *Scan access channels.* Choose one or, at most, two channels with the strongest signals. If the service request cannot be completed on the strongest signal, the mobile station can select the second strongest access channel (called the *alternate access channel*).
3. *Seize reverse control channel* (RECC).
   a. BIS = 1 status: The mobile station is ready for sending. The land station may ask the mobile station to check and wait for overhead message (WFOM) bit.

WFOM $= 1$ The mobile station waits to update overhead information (see item 5).

WFOM $= 0$ Delay a random time (0 to 92 ms) and send service request. It is an access attempt.

b. BIS $= 0$ status: This is the status of a "busy" condition. The mobile station increments NBUSY by 1 and then has to wait a random time interval of 0 to 200 ms to check the BIS status (0 to 1) again. When NBUSY exceeds MAXBUSY, the call is terminated.

4. *Access attempt parameters.* Maximum of 10 attempts. There is a random delay interval of 0 to 92 $\pm$ 1 ms for each attempt at checking the status of BIS. If BIS $= 1$, the mobile station just waits for the transmitting power to come up and sends out the service request message. The random time delay is used to avoid two or more mobile stations requesting services at the same time.

5. *Update overhead information.* Update overhead information should be completely received by the mobile station within 1.5 s after a call is initiated. Update overhead information is as follows. *The Overhead information (OHD)* will be sent by the land station and updated by the mobile station.

   a. Overhead control message (whether the system is overloaded or not).

   b. Access type parameter message sets the busy-idle status bits in the BIS field.

   c. Access attempt parameters message provides the following parameters.

   1. Maximum number of seizure tries allowed

   2. Maximum number of busy occurrences

   After the update overhead information has been completely received, the mobile station waits a random time interval of 0- to 750-ms and enters the seize reverse control channel task stated in item 3.

6. *Delay after failure.* The mobile station must examine the access timer every 1.5 s; if it does not expire, it reenters the access task after failure. The three failure conditions are as follows.

   a. Collision with other mobile station messages. If the collision occurs before the first 56 bits, the BIS changes from 1 to 0.

   b. The land station does not receive the signaling bits, the BIS remains 1 after the mobile station has sent 104 bits.

   c. The land station receives all the signaling bits but cannot interpret them and respond.

   When these conditions occur, the mobile station must wait a random time before making the next attempt. A random delay should be in the interval of 0 to 200 ms.

7. *Service request message.* A whole package of service request messages must be continuously sent to the land station. The format of each signaling word is shown in Fig. 3.4. There is a maximum length to the message consisting of five words: A, B, C, D, E. After a complete message is sent by the mobile station, an unmodulated carrier follows for 25 ms to indicate the end of the message.

8. *Await message response.* If there is no response after the request is sent for 5 s, the call is terminated, and a 120-impulse-per-minute fast tone is generated to the user. If decoded MIN bits match within 5 s, the mobile station must respond with the following messages.

   a. If access is an *origination* or *page response*.

   1. Initiate voice channel designation message. Update the parameters as set in the message.

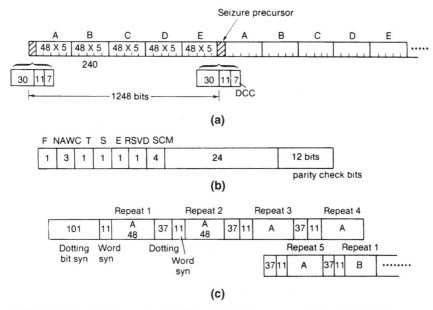

FIGURE 3.4   Signaling format of both RECC and RVC. (*a*) Reverse control channel (RECC) data stream. (*b*) A message word of RECC. (*c*) Signaling format of RVC.

2. For a directed-retry message, the mobile station must examine the signal strength on each of the retry channels and choose up to two channels with the strongest signals. The mobile station must then tune to the strongest retry access channel.

b. If the mobile station encounters the start of a new message before it receives the directed-retry message, the call has to be terminated.

3.2.7   Mobile Station Controls on the Voice Channel

3.2.7.1   Loss of Radio-Link Continuity.   While the mobile station is tuned to a voice channel, a fade timer must be started when no SAT tone is received. If the fade timer counts to 5 s, the mobile station must turn off.

3.2.7.2   Confirm Initial Voice Channel.   Within 100 ms of the receipt of the initial voice channel designation, the mobile station must determine that the channel number is within the set allocated to the home land station or from the other source.

3.2.7.3   Alerting

I. Waiting for order

    A. If an order cannot be received in 5 s, terminate the call.

    B. Order received. If order is received within 100 ms, the action to be taken for each order is

1. *Handoff*

  a. Turn off the home land station.

    1. A 10-kHz signal tone is on for 50 ms after the SAT tone.

    2. Turn off signaling tone.

    3. Turn off transmitter.

  b. Turn on the new site, adjust power level.

    1. Turn to new channel.

    2. Adjust to new SAT.

    3. Set SCC (signaling color code).

    4. Turn on new transmitter.

2. *Alert.* Turn on signaling tone, run 500 ms, and enter the Waiting for Answer task.

3. *Release*

  a. Send signaling tone for 1.8 s.

  b. Stop sending signaling tone.

  c. Turn off the transmitter.

4. *Audit.* Send order confirmation message to land station, remain in Waiting for Answer task, and reset the order timer for 5 s.

5. *Maintenance.* Turn on signaling tone, run for 500 ms, and enter the Waiting for Answer task.

6. *Change power*

  a. Adjust the transmitter to new ordered level.

  b. Send order confirmation to the land station.

  c. Local control. If the local control option is enabled in the mobile station, the local control order can be enabled if the group identification matches the SID_p in the mobile station's permanent security memory. A system operator can have a "local control" order for several markets and order under a group identification.

II. Waiting for answer. After requesting orders from the land station, the mobile station is in the Waiting for Answer status. An alert time must be set to 65 s. If no answer comes back in 65 s, the call is terminated. Events occur in the same order as listed in the Waiting for Order section above.

3.2.7.4 Conversation. A release-delay timer must be set to 500 ms during the conversation. The task can be used for the following conditions.

1. If the user terminates the call.

2. If the user requests a flush.

3. Within 100 ms of receipt of any orders, action will be taken by the mobile station for each order

3.2.8 Signaling Format

3.2.8.1 Signaling Rate. The signaling rate is 10 kbps $\pm$ 1 bps. It is slow enough to not cause the intersymbol interference. The Manchester code waveform is applied so that the energy of this signaling waveform is concentrated at 10 kHz, which can be distinguished from the energy concentrated around the carrier frequency for the baseband voice. (See Fig. 3.3c.)

3.2.8.2 Signaling Format. The reverse control channel (RECC) data stream is shown in Fig. 3.4a. The first word of 48 bits is called the *seizure precursor*, which consists of 30 synchronization bits, 11 frame bits, and 7 coded DCC (digital color code) bits.

Function	Coding
30 synchronization bits	10101010....
11 frame bits (word synchronization)	11100010010
7-bit coded DCC (00)	0000000
(01)	0011111
(10)	1100011
(11)	1111100

Each information word contains 48 bits. Each word block contains 240 bits, where each word is repeated five times.

The maximum data stream is one seizure precursor plus five word blocks: A, B, C, D, and E. The total number of bits is 1248 bits as shown in Fig. 3.4a.

In each information word, 36 bits are information bits and the other 12 bits are parity check bits, formed by encoding 36 bits into a (48, 36) BCH code that has a Hamming distance of 5 (described in Chap. 13). The format is shown in Fig. 3.4b for the first word. The interpretation of the data field is as follows.

F	First word indication field: 1, first word; 0, subsequent words
NAWC	Number of additional words coming
T	T field: 1, indicates an origination; 0, indicates page response
S	S field: 1, send serial number word; 0, otherwise
E	Extended address field: 1, extended address word sent; 0, not sent
SCM	Station class mark field (see Sec. 2.5.1)

3.2.8.3 Types of Messages. The types of messages to be transmitted over the reverse control channel (RECC) are:

• Page response message. When the mobile station receives a page from the land station, the mobile station responds back.

• Origination message. The mobile station originates the call.

• Order confirmation message. The mobile station responds to the order from the land station.

• Order message. The mobile station orders the tasks which should be performed by the land station and the mobile transmission switching office (MTSO).

3.2.8.4 Function of Each Word

Word A	An abbreviated address word. It is always sent to identify the mobile station.
Word B	An extended address word. It will be sent on request from the land station or in a roam situation. In addition, the local control field and the other field are shown in this word.
Word C	A serial number word. Every mobile unit has a unique serial number provided by the manufacturer. It is used to validate the eligible users.
Word D	The first word of the called address.
Word E	The second word of the called address.

3.2.8.5 Reverse Voice Channel (RVC).

The reverse voice channel (RVC) is also used by a wideband data stream sent from the mobile station to the land station. A 10 kbps $\pm$ 1 bps data stream is generated. A word is formed by encoding the 36 content bits into a (48, 36) BCH code, the same as the RECC.

1. *Signaling format.* The first 101 syn bits are used for increasing the possibility of successful syn. The signaling format of RVC is shown in Fig. 3.4c. There are two words: The first word repeats five times, and then the second word repeats five times.
2. *Types of messages.* There are two types of messages:
   a. Order confirmation message (one word) responds to the land station to confirm the order (e.g., handoff confirmation).
   b. Called-address message (two words) establishes a three-party call.

3.3 SPECIFICATION OF LAND STATION (UNITED STATES)

Most parts in the specification of the land station[1,5] are the same as the specification of the mobile station, such as the modulation of voice signals (Sec. 3.2.2), security and identification (Sec. 3.2.4), and supervision (Sec. 3.2.5). These sections will not be repeated in the specification of the land station.

3.3.1 Power

Maximum effective radiated power (ERP) and antenna height above the average terrain (HAAT) must be coordinated locally on an ongoing basis. Maximum power is 100 W at a HAAT of 500 ft. Normally, the transmitting 20 W at an antenna height of 100 ft above the local terrain is implemented.

3.3.2 Limit on Emission

The field strength limit at a distance of 100 ft or more from the receiver is 500 μV/m.

3.3.3 Call Processing

Call processing is the land station operation that controls the mobile station.

3.3.3.1   Overhead Functions for Mobile Station Initiation.   The overhead message train contains the first part of the system identification (SID1) and the number of paging channels (N).

3.3.3.2   On Control Channel

1. Overhead information is sent on the forward control channel and requires all mobile stations to either update or respond with new information during a system access.

Update the following information

- First part of the system identification (SID1)
- Serial number (S). IF S = 1, all mobile stations send their serial numbers during a system access; if S = 0, no need to send serial number.
- Registration (REGH, REGR). The land station is capable of registering the mobile stations.

REGH = 1	Enables registration for home mobile stations
REGH = 0	Otherwise
REGR = 1	Enables registration for roaming mobile stations
REGR = 0	Otherwise

- Extended address (E)

E = 1	Both MIN1 and MIN2 required
E = 0	Otherwise

- Discontinuous transmission (DTX)

DTX = 1	Let mobile stations use discontinuous transmission mode on the voice channel (reducing power consumption for portable units)
DTX = 0	Otherwise

- Number of paging channels (N)
- Read control-filler message (RCF) (see Sec. 3.3.4)

RCF = 1	ask the mobile unit to read control-filler message before accessing a system on a reverse control channel
RCF = 0	Otherwise

- Combined paging/access (CPA)

CPA = 1	Paging channel and access channel are the same
CPA = 0	Paging channel and access channel are not the same

- Number of access channel (CMAX)

Respond with the following information

- Local control. A system operation for home mobile stations and for the roaming mobile stations that are members.
- New access channels (NEWWACC). Send NEWACC information along the first access channel.
- Registration increment (REGINCR). Each time the mobile station increments a fixed value received on FOCC for its updated registration ID if it is equipped for autonomous registration.

- Registration ID (REGID). The last registration number received on FOCC and stored at the mobile station. Every time an increment occurs REGID (new) = REGID (old) + REGINCR, the mobile station identifies itself to a land station.
- Rescan. The rescan global action message must be sent to require all mobile stations to enter the initialization task.

2. The land station will use a control message (one word or two words) to page a mobile station through its home land station. The roaming mobile station must be paged with a two-word message.

3. Orders must be sent to mobile stations with a two-word control message. The orders can be audit and local control. By sending local orders with the order field set to local control and using system identifications (SID) that have identical group identifications, a home mobile station or a roaming mobile station which is a member of a group can be distinguished.

3.3.3.3 Land Station Support of System Access

1. *Overhead information.* The following information must be sent on a forward control channel to support system access that is used by mobile stations.

- *Digital color code* (DCC). The mobile station uses DCC to identify the land station.
- *Control mobile attenuation code* (CMAC). When a control-filler message is transmitted, the mobile station receiving the code has to adjust its transmitter power level before accessing a system on a reverse control channel.
- *Wait for overhead message* (WFOM). Set WFOM to 1 in the control-filler message; then the mobile station must wait for WFOM before accessing a system on a reverse control channel.
- *Overload control* (OLC). The mobile stations that are assigned to one or more of the 16 overload classes ($N = 1$ to 16) must not access the system for originations on the RECC.
- *Access-type parameters.* When the access-type parameters' global action message with the BIS field set to 0 is appended to a system parameter overhead message, the mobile stations do not check for an idle-to-busy status.
- *Access-attempt parameters* are the limit on the number of "busy" occurrences for mobile stations or the default values for the number of seizure attempts.

2. *Reverse control channel seizure by a mobile station.* When this equals 1, all mobile stations must check for an idle-to-busy status when accessing a system. A seizure precursor (48 bits including coded DCC) sent by a mobile station and received by the land station should match its encoded form of DCC.

   It must set the status of the busy-idle bits on the forward control channel between 0.8 and 2.9 ms of receipt of the last bit of 48 bits of the seizure precursor. The busy-idle bits must remain busy until

- 30 ms after the last word of message has been received
- ($24 N + 55$) ms otherwise, where N is the maximum number of words. It will not exceed 175 ms.

3. *Response to mobile station messages.* It is not required that the land station respond to the mobile station message. During periods of system overload or high usage, it may be desirable to permit mobile stations to "time-out" rather than sending release or other orders which use system capacity. The usual time-out period is 5 s. It means that after 5 s, if the mobile station does not receive any response from the land station, the mobile

station terminates the transmitted power. The following responses to mobile stations may be sent:

a. *Origination message.* Send one of the following orders.

1. Initial voice channel designation
2. Directed retry—direct to other cell site
3. Intercept—priority feature
4. Reorder—initiate again

b. *Page response message.* Send one of the following orders.

1. Initial voice channel designation
2. Directed retry
3. Release—turn off signaling tone and release the channel

c. *Order message.* Send one of the following orders.

1. Order confirmation
2. Release

d. *Order confirmation message.* "No message is sent."

3.3.3.4 Mobile Station Control on Voice Channel. The change of status of the supervisory audio tone (SAT) and signaling tone (ST) are used to signal the occurrence of certain events during the progress of a call, such as confirming orders, sending a release request, sending a flash request, and loss of radio-link continuity. In addition to the analog signaling (SAT and ST) to and from the mobile station, digital messages (in a burst mode with 10 kbps transmission rate) can be sent to and received from the mobile station. Response to the digital message is either a digital message or a status change of SAT and ST.

We use the notation "(SAT, ST) status" to describe the signaling condition.

SAT		ST		(SAT, ST)	
On	Off	On	Off	Status	Conditions
1			0	(1,0)	Mobile off-hook
1		1		(1,1)	Mobile on-hook
	0	1		(0,1)	Mobile in fade
	0		0	(0,0)	Mobile transmitter off

1. *Loss of radio-link continuity.* A designated SAT tone is continuously sent to the mobile station; the same SAT should be sent back on a reverse voice channel. If within 5 s the SAT has not been received, the land station would assume that the mobile station is lost and terminates the call.

2. *Initial voice channel confirmation*

   a. Confirmation will be received by the land station as a change in the SAT, ST status from (0,0) to (1,0).

   b. If the confirmation is not received, the land station must either resend the message or turn off the voice channel transmitter.

   c. If the mobile station was paged, the land station must enter the Wait for Order task or Conversation task.

3. *Alerting*

    a. *Waiting for Order task.* After being paged, the mobile station confirms the initial voice channel designation.

        1. *Handoff.* The mobile station confirms the order by a change in the (SAT, ST) status from (1,0) to (1,1) for 50 ms. The land station must remain in the Waiting for Order task.

        2. *Alert.* The mobile station confirms the order by changing (SAT, ST) status from (1,0) to (1,1). The land station must then enter the Waiting for Answer task.

        3. *Release.* The mobile station confirms the order by a change of (SAT, ST) status from (1,0) to (1,1) and holds the (1,1) status for 1.8 s. The land station must then turn off the transmitter.

        4. *Audit.* The mobile station confirms the order by a digital message. The land station remains in the Waiting for Order task.

        5. *Maintenance.* The mobile station confirms the order by a change in (SAT, ST) status from (1,0) to (1,1). The land station remains in the Waiting for Order mode.

        6. *Change power.* The mobile station confirms the order by a digital message.

        7. *Local control.* The confirmation and action depends on the message.

    b. *Waiting for Answer task.* When this task is entered, an alert timer must be set for 30 s. The following orders can be sent:

        1. *Handoff.* The mobile station confirms the order by a change of (SAT, ST) status from (1,1) to (1,0) for 500 ms followed by (1,0) to (1,1) held for 50 ms on the old channel. Then (1,1) status is sent on the new channel.

        2. *Alert.* If no confirmation is received, the land station must reset the alert timer to 30 s.

        3. *Stop alert.* The mobile station confirms the order by a change of (SAT, ST) status from (1,1) to (1,0).

        4. *Release.* The mobile station confirms the order by changing (SAT, ST) status from (1,1) to (1,0) for 500 ms followed by a change of (SAT, ST) from (1,0) to (1,1), which is then held for 1.8 s. The land station must turn off the transmitter.

        5. *Audit.* The mobile station confirms the order by a digital message.

        6. *Maintenance.* If no confirmation is received, the land station resets the alert timer to 30 s.

        7. *Change power.* The mobile station confirms the order by a digital message (see Sec. 3.2.1).

        8. *Local control.* The confirmation and action depends on the message.

4. *Conversation.* The mobile station signals an answer by a change in the (SAT, ST) status from (1,1) to (1,0). The land station enters the conversation task.

    a. *Handoff.* The mobile station confirms the order by a change in the (SAT, ST) from (1,0) to (1,1), which is then held for 50 ms. Then the land station must remain in the Conversation task.

    b. *Send called address.* The called mobile station confirms the order by a digital message with the called address information. This feature would save the established link if the called address were in error because of the transmission medium.

c. The functions *alert, release, audit, maintenance*, and *local control*. Same as in the Waiting for Order task.

d. *Change power*. The mobile station confirms the order by a digital message.

e. *Flash request*. The mobile station signals a flash by changing (SAT, ST) from (1,0) to (1,1) then holding (1,1) for 400 ms, then following with a transition to (1,0).

f. *Release request*. The mobile station signals a release by changing the (SAT, ST) status from (1,0) to (1,1), which is then held for 1.8 s. The land station must turn off the transmitter. This would be used for the mobile user who dials a called number and decides to terminate for any reason.

3.3.4 Signaling Formats

3.3.4.1 Forward Control Channel (FOCC). The FOCC is a continuous wideband 10 kbps $\pm$ 0.1 bps data stream sent from the land station to the mobile station. Each forward control channel consists of three discrete information streams (see Fig. 3.5):

Stream A (least significant bit of MIN = 0)

Stream B (least significant bit of MIN = 1)

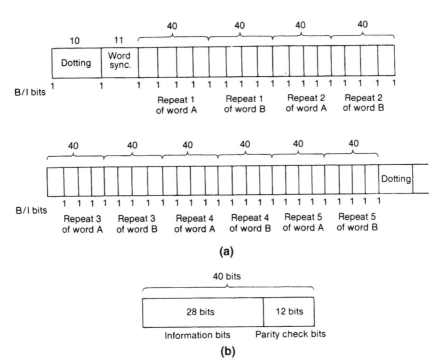

FIGURE 3.5 Forward control channel message stream (land-to-mobile). (*a*) Signaling format of FOCC. (*b*) A message word of FOCC.

Busy-idle stream (busy $= 0$, idle $= 1$); it is at a 1 kbps rate, i.e., one busy-idle bit every 10 data bits.

The 10-bit dotting sequence (1010101010) is for bit syn. The 10-bit length is assumed to be sufficient for bit syn because the mobile station is always monitoring the FOCC after initialization (see 3.2.6). The frame syn bits are the Barker sequence (11100010010). A word is formed by coding 28 control bits into a (40,28,5) BCH code. The total number of bits is 40, the number of information bits is 28, and the hamming distance is 5. The hamming distance d can be translated to the capability of error correction bits, t, as follows:

$$ t = \frac{d-1}{2} = 2 $$

Because this code will detect errors as well as correct them, it reduces to correct one bit in error and assure detection of two bits in error.

The code is a shortened version of the primitive (63,51,5) BCH code. It has 12 parity check bits. As long as the 12 parity check bits are retained, the shortened version can be any length. We use (40,28,5), for which a message of 28 bits is suitable (see Fig. 3.5b). The transmission rate is 10 kbps. The throughput is 1200 bps (see Fig. 3.5a).

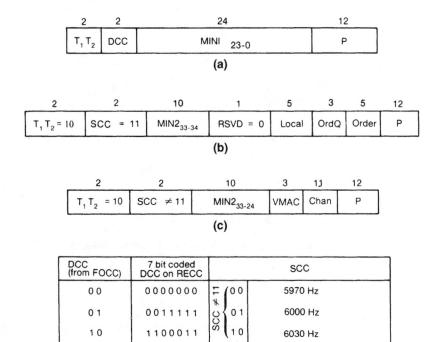

(a)

(b)

(c)

(d)

FIGURE 3.6 Mobile station control message. (*a*) Word 1—abbreviated address word (the busy-idle stream is not shown); (*b*) word 2—extended address word (SCC = 11); (*c*) word 2—extended address word (SCC ≠ 11); (*d*) DCC and SCC codes.

Types of messages

1. *Mobile station control message.* Consists of one, two, or four words.
   a. *Word 1.* Abbreviated address word (see Fig. 3.6a), $T_1 T_2$ = type field.

   $T_1 T_2 = 00$ Only word 1 is sent

   $T_1 T_2 = 01$ Multiple words are sent.

   DCC: digital color code field, 2 bits sent on FOCC. Then it is received by the mobile station and translated to a 7-bit coded DCC on RECC (see Fig. 3.6d).
   b. *Words 2 to 4.* Extended address word $T_1 T_2 = 10$, set in each additional word (see Fig. 3.6b and c). Let SCC = 11 or SCC $\neq$ 11 (see two bits indicated in Fig. 3.6d).

   1. *Word 2*
      a. By combining "order code" (ORDER) and "order qualification code" (ORDQ) in this word (see Fig. 3.6b), we can describe 11 functions.

Page (or origination)	Registration
Alert	Intercept
Release	Maintenance
Reorder	Send called address
Stop alert	Direct-retry status
Audit	

      b. Also changes the mobile station power levels in eight levels
   2. *Word 3.* First directed-retry word.
   3. *Word 4.* Second directed-retry word.

2. *Overhead message (OHD).* A 3-bit OHD field (see Fig. 3.7a) is used to identify the overhead message types. It locates just before the 12 parity check bits shown in Fig. 3.7b. The overhead types are grouped into the following functional classes.

Overhead message types

Code	Order
000	registration ID
001	control-filler
010	reserved
011	reserved
100	global action
101	reserved
110	word 1 of system parameter message
111	word 2 of system parameter message

(a)

2	2	20	1	3	12
$T_1 T_2$	DCC	REGID	END	OHD	P

(b)

FIGURE 3.7 Overhead message types and format.

BS	WS	Word	BS	WS	Word	BS	WS	Word	• • • • •
FVC									
101	11	40	37	11	40	37	11	40	(28, 12)
RVC									
100	11	48	37	11	48	37	11	48	(36, 12)

Repeat 11 times   for FVC   BS - Bit sync.
Repeat 5 times   for RVC   WS - Word sync.

FIGURE 3.8   Signaling format of FVC and RVC.

a. System parameter overhead message. The system parameter overhead message must be sent every 0.8 ± 0.3 s. It consists of two words: word 1 contains the first part of the system identification field, and word 2 contains the number of paging channels and number of access channels.

b. Global action overhead message. There are many global action overhead messages. Each of them consists of one word. The actions are registration increment, new access channel starting point, maximum busy occurrences, maximum seizure tries, and so forth.

c. Registration ID message. It consists of one word containing the registration ID field.

d. Control-filler message. It consists of one word and is sent whenever there is no other message to be sent on FOCC. It is used to specify a control mobile attenuation code (CMAC) which is used by mobile stations accessing the system, and a Wait for Overhead Message bit (WFOM) indicating whether mobile stations must read an overhead message train before accessing the system.

3. Data restriction

    a. The overhead message transmission rate is about once per second.

    b. Design the control-filler message to exclude the frame-sync (word sync) sequence.

    c. Restrict the use of certain control office codes.

3.3.4.2 Forward Voice Channel (FVC). During the call period, FVC is used for signaling. At the beginning, the 101-bit dotting sequence is used for bit sync then for all the repeat dotting sequences; each of them only contains 37 bits, as shown in Fig. 3.8. The word length is 40 bits and repeats 11 times. The reason for repeating 11 times is to be sure that the handoff message would reach the mobile station before the signal dropped below the unacceptable level at the mobile station. The FVC signaling is mainly used for handoff, and the signal level when the handoff occurs is usually very weak. Therefore, the purpose of the FVC is to be sure that the mobile station will get the message and not have a chance to send back a response on receipt because of a weak signal condition.

3.3.5   Additional Spectrum Radio (ASR) Issues

The FCC has allocated an additional 83 voice channels to each system (Band A and Band B). ASR will have 832 channels, half of them, 416 channels (333 channels plus 83 channels), are operated for each system. The 21 control channels still remain the same, but the total number of voice channels becomes 395. The new numbering scheme is shown below.

Numbering scheme						
(Base Tx) → 869	870	880	890	891.5	894 MHz (Base Tx)	
(Mobile Tx) → 824	825	835	845	846.5	849 MHz (Mobile Tx)	

(# of channels) →	(New) 33(A)	333(A)	333(B)	(New) 50(A)	(New) 83(B)	

(Ch. numbering) → 991	1 1023	333 334	666 667	716 717	799

ASR is identified by using the station class mark field as shown in Fig. 3.4*b*. The station class mark (SCM) consists of 4 bits and is specified as shown below.

Power Class	SCM	Transmission	SCM	Bandwidth	SCM
Class I (4 W)	XX00	Continuous	X0XX	20 MHz	0XXX
Class II (1.2 W)	XX01	Discontinuous	X1XX	25 MHz (ASR)	1XXX
Class III (0.6 W)	XX10				
Reserved	XX11				

The full spectrum frequency management charts for Block A and Block B are shown in Table 3.1.

3.4 DIFFERENT SPECIFICATIONS OF THE WORLD'S ANALOG CELLULAR SYSTEMS

In general, cellular systems can be classified by their operating frequencies: 450 MHz or 800 MHz. Also, they can be distinguished by the spacing between their channels (also called the *channel bandwidth*): 30, 25, or 20 kHz. Japanese NTT has deployed a 12.5-kHz channel spacing in their cellular system.

The large-capacity cellular telephones used in the world are listed in Table 3.2. There are five major systems, and their message protection schemes are different. The major differences are

1. The principle of majority decision (PMD)

2. The automatic repeat request (ARQ)

These schemes each have their merits. In a very severe fading environment, PMD is a good candidate. In a fairly light fading environment, ARQ is a good candidate. Table 3.3 lists the system of each country's use. There are 25 countries that have cellular systems.

Today there is no compatibility among the analog cellular systems serving European countries. In 1982, they agreed to set up a pan-European digital cellular standard, called GSM (special mobile group) specification, which was implemented in 1992 and is described in Chap. 4.

TABLE 3.1 Full Spectrum Frequency Management

Block A

1A	2A	3A	4A	5A	6A	7A	1B	2B	3B	4B	5B	6B	7B	1C	2C	3C	4C	5C	6C	7C
1	2	3	4	5	6	7	8	9	10	11	12	13	14	15	16	17	18	19	20	21
22	23	24	25	26	27	28	29	30	31	32	33	34	35	36	37	38	39	40	41	42
43	44	45	46	47	48	49	50	51	52	53	54	55	56	57	58	59	60	61	62	63
64	65	66	67	68	69	70	71	72	73	74	75	76	77	78	79	80	81	82	83	84
85	86	87	88	89	90												102	103	104	105
106	107	108	109	110	111												123	124	125	126
127	128	129	130	131	132												144	145	146	147
148	149	150	151	152	153												165	166	167	168
169	170	171	172	173	174												186	187	188	189
190	191	192	193	194	195												207	208	209	210
211	212	213	214	215	216												228	229	230	231
232	233	234	235	236	237												249	250	251	252
253	254	255	256	257	258												270	271	272	273
274	275	276	277	278	279												291	292	293	294
295	296	297	298	299	300												312	X	X	X
313*	314	315	316	317	318	319	320	321	322	323	324	325	326	327	328	329	330	331	332	333
667	668	669	670	671	672	673	674	675	676	677	678	679	680	681	682	683	684	685	686	687
688	689	690	691	692	693	694	695	696	697	698	699	700	701	702	703	704	705	706	707	708
709	710	711	712	713	714	715	716	X	991	992	993	994	995	996	997	998	999	1000	1001	1002
1003	1004	1005	1006	1007	1008	1009	1010	1011	1012	1013	1014	1015	1016	1017	1018	1019	1020	1021	1022	1023

Block B

1A	2A	3A	4A	5A	6A	7A	1B	2B	3B	4B	5B	6B	7B	1C	2C	3C	4C	5C	6C	7C
334	**335**	**336**	**337**	**338**	**339**	**340**	**341**	**342**	**343**	**344**	**345**	**346**	**347**	**348**	**349**	**350**	**351**	**352**	**353**	**354**
355	356	357	358	359	360	361														375
376	377	378	379	380	381	382														396
397	398	399	400	401	402	403														417
418	419	420	421	422	423	424														438
439	440	441	442	443	444	445														459
460	461	462	463	464	465	466														480
481	482	483	484	485	486	487														501
502	503	504	505	506	507	508														522
523	524	525	526	527	528	529														543
544	545	546	547	548	549	550														564
565	566	567	568	569	570	571														585
586	587	588	589	590	591	592	593	594	595	596	597	598	599	600	601	602	603	604	605	606
607	608	609	610	611	612	613	614	615	616	617	618	619	620	621	622	623	624	625	626	627
628	629	630	631	632	633	634	635	636	637	638	639	640	641	642	643	644	645	646	647	648
649	650	651	652	653	654	655	656	657	658	659	660	661	662	663	664	665	666	667	668	669
720	721	722	723	724	725	726	727	728	729	730	731	732	733	734	735	736	737	738	739	740
741	742	743	744	745	746	747	748	749	750	751	752	753	754	755	756	757	758	759	760	761
762	763	764	765	766	767	768	769	770	771	772	773	774	775	776	777	778	779	780	781	782
783	784	785	786	787	788	789	790	791	792	793	794	795	796	797	798	799				

*Boldface numbers indicate 21 control channels for Block A and Block B respectively.

81

TABLE 3.2 Large-Capacity Analog Cellular Telephones Used in the World

System	Japan	America North	England	Scandinavia	Germany
	NTT	AMPS	TACS	NMT	C450
Transmission frequency (MHz):					
Base station	870–885	869–894	917–960	463–467.5	461.3–465.74
Mobile station	925–940	824–849	572–905	453–457.5	451.3–455.74
Spacing between transmission and receiving frequencies (MHz)	65	45	45	10	10
Spacing between channels (kHz)	25,12.5	30	25	25	20
Number of channels	600	322 (Control channel 21×2)	1320 (Control channel 21×2)	180	222
Coverage radius (km)	5 (urban area) 10 (suburbs)	2–20	2–20	1.8–40	5–30
Audio signal: Type of modulation	FM	FM	FM	FM	FM
Frequency deviation (kHz)	±5	±12	±9.5	±5	±4
Control signal: Type of modulation	FSK	FSK	FSK	FSK	FSK
Frequency deviation (kHz)	±4.5	±8	±6.4	±3.5	±2.5
Data transmission rate (kb/s)	0.3	10	8	1.2	5.28
Message protection	Transmited signal is checked when it is sent back to the sender by the receiver.	Principle of majority decision is employed.	Principle of majority decision is employed.	Receiving steps are predetermined according to the content of the message.	Message is sent again when an error is detected.

Source: Report from International Radio Consultative Committee (CCIR).

TABLE 3.3 World's Analog Cellular Systems

NTT	AMPS	TACS	NMT	C450	NEC
Japan	U.S.	England	4 Nordic countries	Germany	Australia
	Canada	Hong Kong	Spain		Singapore
	South Korea	China	The Netherlands		Hong Kong
	Hong Kong		Belgium		Jordan
	Taiwan		Oman		Colombia
	Australia		Saudi Arabia		Mexico
	China		Tunisia		Kuwait
	Mexico		Malaysia		
	Brazil		Australia		
	Argentina		Ireland		
	Chile				

Source: Report from International Radio Consultative Committee (CCIR).

REFERENCES

1. FCC OST, "Cellular System Mobile Station—Land Station Compatibility Specification," *OST Bulletin*, No. 53, July 1983.
2. "Advanced Mobile Phone Service," special issue, *Bell System Technical Journal*, Vol. 58, January 1979.
3. "Code of Federal Regulations," FCC, part 22 1986, pp. 85–190.
4. P. F. Panter, *Modulation, Noise, and Spectral Analysis*, McGraw-Hill Book Co., 1965, p. 447.
5. EIA Interim Standard, "Cellular System Mobile Station-Land Station Compatibility Specification," IS-3-D EIA March, 1987.

CHAPTER 4
DIGITAL CELLULAR SYSTEMS (2G SYSTEMS)

Many digital cellular and cordless phone systems have been developed. The cellular systems are GSM, NA-TDMA, CDMA, PDC, and 1800-DCS, and the cordless phone systems are DECT and CT-2 schemes. Although analog cellular systems are limited to using frequency-division multiple-access (FDMA) schemes, digital cellular systems can use FDMA, time-division multiple-access (TDMA), and code-division multiple-access (CDMA). When a multiple-access scheme is chosen for a particular system, all the functions, protocols, and network are associated with that scheme. This chapter covers GSM, NA-TDMA, and CDMA in great detail and briefly describes other systems. At the begining of this chapter, a general description of digital systems is provided.

4.1 INTRODUCTION TO DIGITAL SYSTEMS

4.1.1 Advantages of Digital Systems

In an analog system, the signals applied to the transmission media are continuous functions of the message waveform. In the analog system, either the amplitude, the phase, or the frequency of a sinosoidal carrier can be continuously varied in accordance with the voice or the message.

In digital transmission systems, the transmitted signals are discrete in time, amplitude, phase, or frequency, or in a combination of any two of these parameters. To convert from analog form to digital form, the quantizing noise due to discrete levels should be controlled by assigning a sufficient number of digits for each sample, and a sufficient number of samples is needed to apply the Nyquist rate for sampling an analog waveform.

One advantage of converting message signals into digital form is the ruggedness of the digital signal. The impairments introduced in the medium in spite of noise and interference can always be corrected. This process, called *regeneration*, provides the primary advantages for digital transmission. However, a disadvantage of this ruggedness is increased bandwidth relative to that required for the original signal.

The increased bandwidth is used to overcome the impairment introduced into the medium. In addition to the cost advantage, power consumption is lower and digital equipment is generally lighter in weight and more compact. In mobile cellular systems, there are more advantages in applying digital technology.[1-3]

4.1.2 Digital Technologies

4.1.2.1 Digital Detection. There are three forms of digital detection: coherent detection, differentially coherent detection, and noncoherent detection. Coherent detection requires a reference waveform accurate in frequency and phase, and the use of a phase-coherent carrier tracking loop for each modulation technique. In a mobile radio environment, noncoherent detection is much easier to implement than coherent detection is. A form of detection that is intermediate in difficulty of implementation is called *differential PSK*. Differential PSK does not need absolute carrier phase information, and it circumvents the synchronization problems of coherent detection. The phase reference is obtained by the signal itself, which is delayed in time by an exact bit of spacing. This system maintains a phase reference between successive symbols and is insensitive to phase fluctuation in the transmission channel as long as these fluctuations are small during each duration of a symbol interval T. In differential binary-phase shift-keying (DBPSK) a symbol is a bit. The weak point of this scheme is that whenever there is an error in phase generated by the medium, two message error bits will result.

There are several aspects of digital detection.[4]

Carrier Recovery. Carrier recovery for the suppressed carrier signal $A(t) \sin(\omega_0 t)$ plus noise $n(t)$ can be obtained by two methods. A squaring or frequency-doubling loop can be used (see Fig. 4.1). The loop contains a phase-locked loop as shown in Fig. 4.2. The phase-locked loop maintains a constant phase ϕ_n of $\cos(2\pi f_0 t + \phi_n)$, which is the recovered carrier. Another carrier-recovery technique uses the Costas loop, which generates a coherent phase reference independent of the binary modulation by using both in-phase and quadrature channels. The Costas loop (Fig. 4.3) is often preferred over the squaring loop because its circuits are less sensitive to center-frequency shifts and are generally capable of wider bandwidth operation. In addition, the Costas loop results in circuit simplicity.

Carrier-Phase Tracking (Phase-Locked Loop). Carrier-tracking accuracy depends on several system parameters, including the phase noise in the carrier introduced by various oscillator short-term stabilities, carrier-frequency drifts, carrier-tracking-loop dynamics, transient response, the acquisition-performance requirement, and the signal-to-noise ratio S/N in the carrier-tracking loop. The phase-locked loop in the carrier-recovery tracking

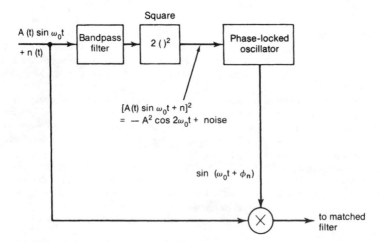

FIGURE 4.1 Block diagram of the square-law carrier-recovery technique.

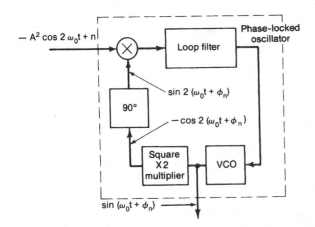

FIGURE 4.2 Phase-locked oscillator.

loop must have sufficient noise bandwidth to track the phase noise of the carrier. For a given carrier-phase–noise spectrum, one can compute the phase-locked-loop noise bandwidth B required to track the carrier. Clearly, too large a noise bandwidth can permit the occurrence of the thermal noise effect.

Phase-Equalization Circuits—For Cophase Combining

1. *Feedforward.* A circuit using two mixers to cancel random FM can be used (see Fig. 4.4(a)) as a phase-equalization circuit in each branch of an N-branch equal-gain diversity combiner.

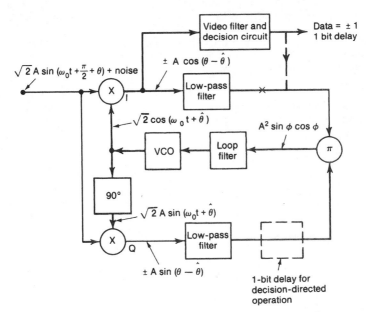

FIGURE 4.3 Costas loop OSK carrier-recovery circuit and bit detector; the phase error is defined as $\phi = \theta - \hat{\theta}$. The decision-directed configuration is shown in dashed lines.

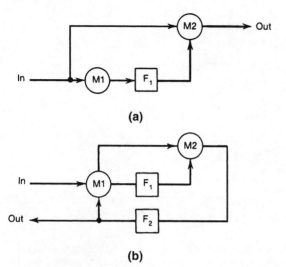

(a)

(b)

FIGURE 4.4 Cophase combining techniques. (*a*) Feed-forward cophase combining; (*b*) feedback cophase combining.

2. *Feedback.* A modified circuit from the feedforward circuit is shown in Fig. 4.4(*b*). This circuit is also used for each branch of an N-branch equal-gain diversity combiner. The feedback combiner is also called a Granlund combiner.

3. *The total combining circuit.* As shown in Fig. 4.5, either a feedback or a feedforward circuit can be used in the combiner to form a two-branch equal-gain combiner. The circuit connects to a coherent match-filter receiver for BPSK as shown in Fig. 4.6.

Bit Synchronization. Power-efficient digital receivers require the installation of a bit synchronizer. Bit synchronization commonly applies self-synchronization techniques, that is, it extracts clock time directly from a noisy bit stream. There are four classes of bit synchronizer.

1. *Nonlinear-filter synchronizer.* This open-loop synchronizer is commonly used in high-bit rate links that normally operate at high signal-to-noise ratios.

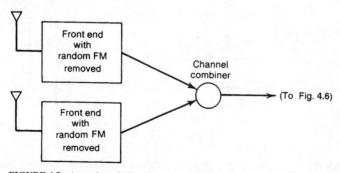

FIGURE 4.5 A two-branch diversity receiver.

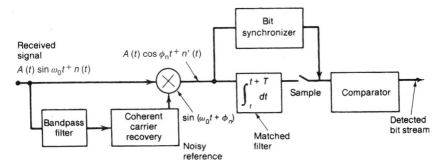

FIGURE 4.6 Coherent matched-filter receiver for BPSK.

2. *The data-transition tracking synchronizer.* This closed-loop synchronizer combines the operations of bit detection and bit synchronization. It can be employed at low signal-to-noise ratios and medium data rates.

3. *Early-late synchronizer.* This synchronizer uses early- and late-gate integral and dump channels, which have absolute values. It is simpler to implement than the data-transition tracking synchronizer and less sensitive to dc offsets.

4. *Optimum synchronizer.* This synchronizer provides an optimal means of searching for the correct synchronization time slot during acquisition. However, this approach generally is not practical.

4.1.2.2 Modulation for Digital Systems.   There are several aspects of digital modulation, and they are described below.

Requirements.   Basic digital modulation techniques are amplitude-shift keying (ASK), frequency-shift keying (FSK), phase-shift keying (PSK), and hybrid modulation techniques involving amplitude, frequency, and phase-shift keying.

In mobile cellular systems, the selection of a digital modulation for radio transmission involves satisfaction of the following requirements: (a) narrower bandwidths, (b) more efficient power utilization, and (c) elimination of intermodulation products.

a. *Narrower bandwidths.* For all the forms of modulation, it is desirable to have a constant envelope and, therefore, utilize relatively narrower bandwidths. In these cases, FSK and PSK are recommended. For example, multiphase-shift-keying (MPSK) for large values ($M > 4$) has greater bandwidth efficiency than does BPSK or QPSK but power use is less efficient.

b. *More efficient power utilization.* It is preferable to provide more channels for a given power level. Therefore, enhanced power utilization is essential. Besides, the FCC has limited the effective radiation power (100 W) to be radiated from each base-station antenna. This limitation governs the number of channels which can be served given the power allowed for each channel.

c. *Elimination of intermodulation products.* QPSK is commonly used with a transmission efficiency of about 1 to 2 bps/Hz. This value has been found to offer satisfactory trade-off between efficient frequency utilization and transmitter power economy. However, in mobile radio links, when nonlinear class C power amplifiers are used, any spurious radiation should be suppressed. For reducing the spurious signals, we are selecting a constant or low-fluctuation envelope property. There are two types of broadly classified modulations.

Modulation Schemes. There are several modulation schemes.

1. *Modified QPSK.* There are two kinds of QPSK besides a regular QPSK with restricted phase-transition rules.

   a. *QPSK.* The conventional QPSK shown in Fig. 4.7a has phase ambiguity. The ideal QPSK signal waveform

$$A \sin [\omega_0 t + \theta_m(t)] = \pm \frac{A}{\sqrt{2}} \sin \left(\omega_0 t + \frac{\pi}{4} \right) \pm \frac{A}{\sqrt{2}} \cos \left(\omega_0 t + \frac{\pi}{4} \right) \qquad (4.1\text{-}1)$$

where $\theta_m = (0, \pi/2, \pi, 3\pi/2)$ and the value of θ_m should match the sign of Eq. (4.1-1); that is, $\theta_m = 0$ for $(+, +)$, $\theta_m = \pi/2$ for $(+, -)$, $\theta_m = \pi$ for $(-, +)$, and $\theta_m = 3\pi/2$ for $(-, -)$.

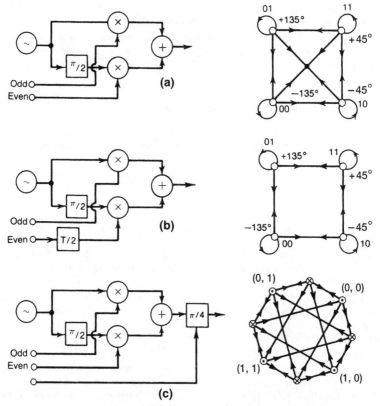

FIGURE 4.7 Modulator constitution and signal-space diagrams of (*a*) conventional QPSK, (*b*) offset QPSK, and (*c*) $\pi/4$ shift. (*After Hirade et al., Ref. 5, p. 14.*)

Bit Pair	Absolute Phase
0 0	0
0 1	$\pi/2$
1 1	π
1 0	$3\pi/2$

b. *Offset QPSK (OQPSK)*. This scheme is a QPSK, but the even-bit stream is delayed by a half-bit interval with respect to the odd 1 bit as shown in Fig. 4.7b.

c. $\pi/4$-*shift QPSK*. A phase increment of $\pi/4$ is added to each symbol shown in Fig. 4.7c.

Both OQPSK and $\pi/4$ shift QPSK have no π-phase transition; therefore, no phase ambiguity would occur as in QPSK. However, intrinsically they produce a certain amount of residual envelope fluctuation. Sometimes, a phase-locked loop (PLL) is inserted at the modulation output to remedy this problem.

2. *The differential encoding of QPSK (DQPSK)*. This is the same as in DBPSK, but the differential encoding of the bit pairs selects the phase change rather than the absolute phase. However, DQPSK has phase ambiguity just like QPSK.

Bit Pair	Phase Changes
0 0	0
0 1	$\pi/2$
1 1	π
1 0	$3\pi/2$

The QPSK carrier recovery would be slightly different than that of BPSK.[5]

3. *Modified FSK—continuous-phase frequency-shift-keying (CP-FSK) with low modulation index*[6]

a. Minimum-shift-keying (MSK)—also called *fast FSK* (FFSK)

b. Sinusoidal FSK (SFSK)

c. Tamed FSK (TFSK) or tamed frequency modulation (TFM)

d. Gaussian MSK (GMSK)

e. Gaussian TFM (GTFM)

Because all the schemes listed above are CP-FSK (and have a low modulation index, they intrinsically have constant envelope properties, unless severe bandpass filtering is introduced to the modulator output. In MSK the frequency shift precisely increases or decreases the phase by 90° in each T second. Thus, the signal waveform is

$$s(t) = \sin\left(\omega_0 t + 2\pi \int_0^t s_i d\tau + \frac{n\pi}{2}\right) \quad 0 < t < T$$

where

$$s_i = \begin{cases} s_1 = \dfrac{1}{4T} & \text{for a data bit 1} \\ s_2 = -\dfrac{1}{4T} & \text{for a data bit 0} \end{cases} \qquad (4.1\text{-}2)$$

or

$$s(t) = \sin\left(\omega_0 t + \frac{n\pi}{2} \pm \frac{\pi t}{2T}\right) \tag{4.1-3}$$

or

$$s(t) = \cos\left(\pm\frac{\pi t}{2T}\right)\sin\left(\omega_0 t + \frac{n\pi}{2}\right) + \sin\left(\pm\frac{\pi t}{2T}\right)\cos\left(\omega_0 t + \frac{n\pi}{2}\right)$$

Comparing Eq. (4.1-1) with Eq. (4.1-3), we find that the two equations are very similar. In fact, the phase-modulation waveforms of the I- and Q-channel modulations of OQPSK are modulated by sine and cosine waveforms, and thus the output will be identical to that of MSK. Note that it is necessary to modulate both the I and Q channels during each bit interval to retain the constant envelope of $s(t)$.

Because the phase is continuous from bit to bit, the spectral sidebands of MSK or OQPSK fall off more rapidly than in BPSK or QPSK (see Fig. 4.8). Although MSK demonstrates a superior property in terms of its out-of-band spurious spectrum suppression without any filtering, its out-of-band spurious spectrum suppression will not satisfy the severe requirements in the single carrier per channel (SCPC) communications. The sharp edges in MSK phase-transition trajectories (Fig. 4.9) can be smoothed by some premodulation baseband filtering. The SFSK shows a smoother phase transition than does the MSK but little improvement in the suppression of out-of-band spurious spectrum. The TFM is a modified MSK using the partial response encoding rule as the phase-transition rule. The smoothed phase trajectory of TFM is shown in Fig. 4.9. The outstanding suppressions for the out-of-band spectrum of TFM is shown in Fig. 4.8. However, this outstanding suppression of the out-of-band spurious spectrum can be achieved by using a suitable premodulation baseband filtering on MSK, such as a

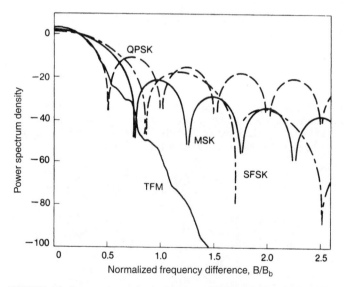

FIGURE 4.8   Power spectrum density functions of QPSK, MSK, SFSK, and TFM. (*After Hirade et al., Ref. 5, p. 15.*)

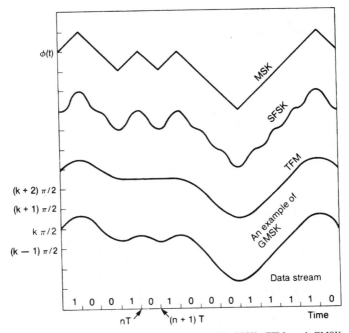

FIGURE 4.9 Phase-transition trajectories of MSK, SFSK, TFM, and GMSK. *(After Hirade et al., Ref. 5, p. 15.)*

baseband gaussian filtering, as shown in Fig. 4.10. The GMSK with $B_b T = 0.2$ has the same power spectrum density curves as does TFM, where B_b is the baseband bandwidth. Furthermore, GMSK is easier to implement than TFM.

The following parameters are defined and are in the figures that follow.

B_i Ideal bandpass

B_s Channel separation (bandwidth)

f_b Bit rate of voice coding $= 1/T$

$1/T$ Transmission bit rate (16 kbps)

$B_i T$ normalized bandwidth of the ideal bandpass filter

$b_b T$ normalized bandwidth of a Gaussian filter

Figure 4.11 shows the fractional power in percentage of GMSK signal exceeding the normalized bandwidth $B_i T$ with different values of $B_b T$ ($B_b T = \infty$ means no filter). This becomes conventional MSK. Figure 4.12 shows that the relative power radiated in the adjacent channel for $B_s T$ is equal to 1.5. Let $B_s = 30$ kHz, then the bit rate $f_b = (1/T) = 20$ kbps. For a normalized filter bandwidth $B_b T = 0.24$ or $B_b = 4.8$ kHz, and the relative power in the adjacent channel is -60 dB.

4. *QAM (Quadrature Amplitude Modulation)*[7,8]

QAM signaling can be viewed as a combination of amplitude shift keying (ASK) and phase shift keying (PSK). It can also be viewed as an amplitude shift keying in two dimensions. In an M-ary QAM signal, the signal in each state I is

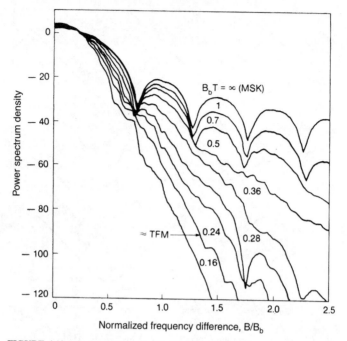

FIGURE 4.10 Power spectrum density functions of GMSK. (*After Hirade et al., Ref. 5, p. 15.*)

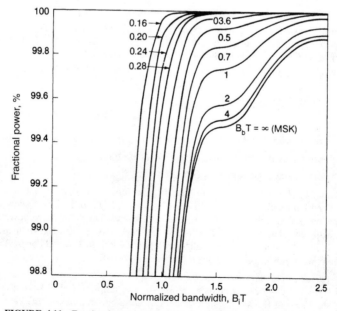

FIGURE 4.11 Fractional power of GMSK signal. (*After Hirade et al., Ref. 5, p. 15.*)

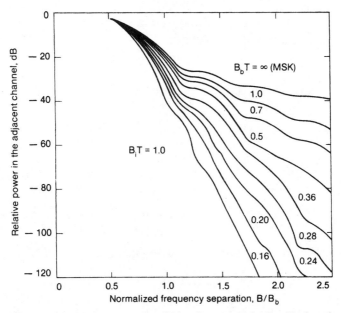

FIGURE 4.12 Relative power radiated in the adjacent channel. (*After Hirade et al., Ref. 5, p. 16.*)

$$s_i(t) = R_e\left[v_i(t)e^{j2\pi f_c t}\right]$$
$$= Aa_i \cos (2\pi f_c t) + Ab_i \sin (2\pi f_c t) \quad 0 < t < T \tag{4.1-4}$$

where A is a constant, $\sqrt{2}A$ representing the amplitude of the lowest state, and (a_i, b_i) is a pair of identifying states in the constellation of the ith state. The 16-QAM constellation diagram is shown in Fig. 4.13.

The probability of error for QAM can be determined from the probability of error for PAM. For the probability of error of a $\sqrt{M}$-ary PAM is expressed as

$$P_{\sqrt{M}} = 2\left(1 - \frac{1}{\sqrt{M}}\right) Q\left(\sqrt{\frac{3}{M-1} \frac{S_{av}}{N_0}}\right) \tag{4.1-5}$$

where S_{av}/N_0 is the average SNR per symbol of an M-QAM, and

$$S_{av} = 2\left(\frac{A^2 \sum_1^{\sqrt{M}} a_i^2}{\sqrt{M}}\right) \tag{4.1-6}$$

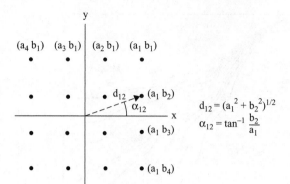

FIGURE 4.13 The 16-QAM constellation diagram.

The probability of a symbol error for an M-ary QAM is

$$P_M = 1 - (1 - P_{\sqrt{M}})^2 \qquad (4.1\text{-}7)$$

When $P_{\sqrt{M}}$ is a small value:

$$P_M = 2P_{\sqrt{M}} - P_{\sqrt{M}}^2 - 2P_{\sqrt{M}} \qquad (4.1\text{-}8)$$

Figure 4.14 shows the bit error rate for an M-QAM on nonfading and Rayleigh fading channels. Although M-QAM is a power-efficient modulation, the bit error probability increases as M increases. Besides, the envelope of M-QAM is not a constant. It means that the partial information is carried on the envelope and can be distorted while the envelope is distorted by the Gaussian noise or Rayleigh fading.

5. *OFDM Modem*[8,9]

Orthogonal frequency division multiplexing (OFDM) is a modulation technique where source symbols are transmitted in parallel by applying to a large number of orthogonal subcarriers. The OFDM signal $s(t)$ can be expressed

$$s(t) = R_e\left[v(t)e^{j2\pi f_c t}\right] \qquad (4.1\text{-}9)$$

The complex envelope $v(t)$ of an OFDM signal $s(t)$ can be expressed

$$v(t) = \sum_{k=0}^{K} v_k(t) = A \sum_{k=0}^{K} \sum_{n=0}^{N-1} x_{k,n}\phi_n(t - kT) \qquad (4.1\text{-}10)$$

where A is the carrier amplitude and k is the kth block of N serial source symbols.
The N orthogonal waveforms $[\phi_n(t)]$ in Eq. (4.1-10) are chosen as

$$\phi_n(t) = h_a(t)\exp\left\{\frac{j2\pi\left(n - \frac{N-1}{2}\right)t}{T}\right\} \qquad (4.1\text{-}11)$$

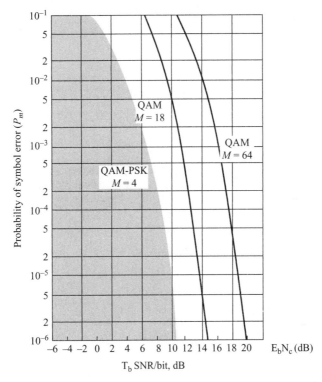

FIGURE 4.14 Probability of a symbol error for QAM and PSK in the 10^{-1} to 10^{-6} range. (*From Proakis, 1989.*) For $M = 4$, the performance of QPSK is the same as that of 4-QAM.

and $h_a(t)$ can be a rectangular amplitude shaping pulse, $h_a(t) = U_T(t)$. The source symbol block x_k at time $t = kT_s$ can be expressed as

$$x_k = (x_{k,0}, x_{k,1}, x_{k,2}, x_{k,3}, \cdots x_{k,N-1})$$

A block of N serial source symbols has a symbol duration T_s, where T_s can be less than the rms time delay spread Δ of the medium ($T_s < \Delta$). The block of N serial source can be converted to a block of N parallel modulated symbols, each in a duration of $T = NT_s$. Let the block length N be chosen so that $NT_s \gg \Delta$. Because the symbol rate ($1/T$) on each subcarrier is much less than the serial source rate

$$\left(\frac{1}{T} < \frac{1}{T_s} \right)$$

the effects of delay spread are greatly reduced, and we can even try to eliminate the equalizer. The source symbol block x_k in time domain is applied to N subcarrier and converted to X_k in frequency domain as shown in Fig. 4.15. The N transmitted signals are of equal energy and equal duration, and the signal subcarriers are separated by $1/T$ hertz, making the signals orthogonal among themselves. The medium dispersion will still

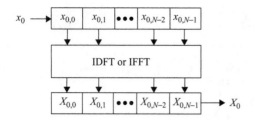

FIGURE 4.15 Block diagram of OFDM transmitter using IDFT or IFFT.

cause consecutive modulation symbol blocks to overlap, and creates a so-called residual intersymbol interference (ISI). It can be reduced by introducing the guard intervals between the blocks. The source symbol duration with guard interval is

$$T'_s = \frac{T_s}{1 + \dfrac{G}{N}} \qquad (4.1\text{-}12)$$

where G should be greater than the time delay spread Δ.

The attractive advantage of using OFDM is that the modulation can be expressed in a discrete frequency domain after going through the inverse fast Fourier transform (IFFT). Let the source symbol block at the first block, $k = 0$, the complex envelope

$$v_0(t) = A \sum_{n=0}^{N=1} x_{0,n} \exp\left\{\frac{j2\pi nt}{NT_s}\right\} \qquad 0 < t < T \qquad (4.1\text{-}13)$$

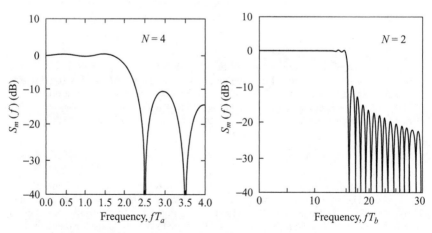

FIGURE 4.16 PSD of OFDM with $N = 4$ and $N = 32$.

The complex envelope $v_0(t)$ is sampled at $t = kT_s$ and forms a sequence through IFFT operation.

$$X_{0,k} = v_0(kT_s) = A \sum_{n=0}^{N-1} x_{0,n} \exp\left\{ \frac{j2\pi nk}{N} \right\} \qquad (4.1\text{-}14)$$

Then, $X_{0,k}$ passes a D/A converter and is subcarrier-modulated. OFDM is a means of providing power-efficient modulation for an OFDM signal expressed in Eq. (4.1-9), the power spectrum density (PSD) of its complex envelope is

$$S(f) = \frac{A^2}{T}\sigma_x^2 \sum_{n=0}^{N-1} \left| H\left[f - \frac{1}{T}\left(n - \frac{N-1}{2} \right) \right] \right|^2 \qquad (4.1\text{-}15)$$

where

$$\sigma_x^2 = \frac{1}{2}E[|x_{k,n}|^2]$$

and

$$H(f) = F^{-1}[h(t)]$$

The PSD of OFDM with $N = 4$ and $N = 32$ is shown in Fig. 4.16. For large N, the PSD becomes more flat at

$$f = \frac{1.6}{T_s} \left(\text{or } \frac{1.6N}{T} \right)$$

Therefore, as the block length N is large, the PSD of OFDM approaches that of single-carrier modulation. This is power-efficient modulation.

4.1.2.3 Demodulation for Digital Systems.

4.1.2.3 Demodulation for Digital Systems. When the signal is received, we would like to know the performance of the various demodulation schemes. Some demodulation schemes are better than others regardless of what the modulated signal is like. The orthogonal coherent detector proposed by de Buda[6] can be used for both MSK and TFM.

BER performance is always a good criterion for the comparison of different modulation schemes. Measured BER performance is shown in Fig. 4.17 with a normalized channel bandwidth $B_i T = 0.75$. The family of curves show the BERs for the different filter bandwidths. Also, TFSK (TFM) is plotted for comparison. GMSK with the filter bandwidth of $B_b T = 0.19$ is superior to TFSK. However, one disadvantage of narrowing the channel spectrum is increasing the BER, that is, degrading performance. Sometimes we have to consider whether it is worthwhile to use a gaussian filter.

4.1.3 ARQ Techniques

4.1.3.1 Different Techniques.[10,11] Automatic-repeat-request (ARQ) techniques include the coding and retransmission request strategy for delivering a message. Preceding the message is a header which contains the source and destination address and useful routing information. Every ARQ message must have a header. There are two principal ARQ techniques.

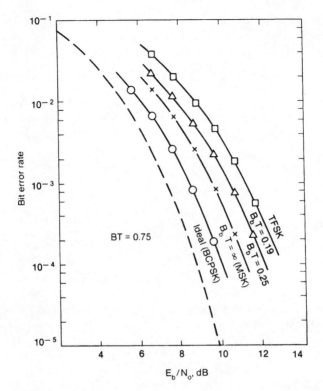

FIGURE 4.17   Measured BER performance. (*After Hirade et al., Ref. 5, p.17.*)

1. *Stop-and-wait ARQ.* The message originator stops at the end of each transmission to wait for a reply from the receiver (see Fig. 4.18*a*). Then the following steps can be taken.

   a. No forward error correction is used—ARQ(*a*).

   b. Both forward error correction and error detection coding are used—ARQ(*b*).

   c. Error-detection parity bits are sent, but not the forward error-correction parity bits, which assumes that the probability of an error-free message is great—ARQ(*c*).

2. *Selective retransmission.* When many words are transmitted at once, each word individually can apply error detection, not the message as a whole. Only those words containing detected errors are sent back. The scheme is called *selective retransmission*. Selective retransmission with ARQ(*b*) is shown in Fig. 4.18*b*. Selective retransmission with ARQ(*c*) is shown in Fig. 4.18*c*.

4.1.3.2   The Expected Number of Transmissions

Stop-and-Wait ARQ [Apply ARQ(a) *and ARQ*(b) *Only].*   Let P_{ew} be a word error rate (WER), and let a message consist of N words. Now the required number of transmissions depends on all N words being successfully transmitted. The expected number of transmissions is

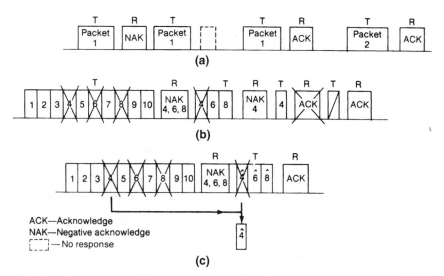

FIGURE 4.18 ARQ transactions (*a*) Stop-and wait ARQ; (*b*) selective retransmission with ARQ(*b*); (*c*) selective retransmission with ARQ(*c*).

$$E_N = \frac{1}{(1 - P_{ew})^N} \qquad (4.1\text{-}16)$$

assuming independence errors between words and that all words have the same P_{ew}. This assumption can be considered valid for cases where vehicle speed is high. Equation (4.1-16) indicates that the number of transmissions E_N increases more quickly with increasing the message length, that is, as N increases. Equation (4.1-16) is plotted in Fig. 4.19a.

Selective Retransmission (ST) with ARQ(b).　Assume that the number of transmissions of one word is independent of the number of transmissions of any other word. The expected number of transmissions required for sending an N-word message with fewer than i transmissions is

$$E_N = \sum_{i=1}^{\infty} \left[1 - \left(1 - P_{ew}^{i-1} \right)^N \right] \qquad (4.1\text{-}17)$$

Equation (4.1-17) is plotted in Fig. 14.19*b*. By comparing Fig. 4.19*a* with Fig. 4.19*b*, we see that stop-and-wait ARQ would require a greater number of transmissions to deliver a message than would selective retransmission with the same block error probability.

Selective Retransmission (SRT) with ARQ(c).　In this scheme, ARQ(*c*) defined in the stop-and-wait ARQ is applied to the selective retransmission scheme. Let the first-transmission probability be P_1 and a retransmission probability be P_2. The expected number of transmissions required for sending an N-word message with fewer than i transmissions is

$$E_N = 1 + \sum_{i=2}^{\infty} \left[1 - \left(1 - P_1 P_2^{i-2} \right)^N \right] \qquad (4.1\text{-}18)$$

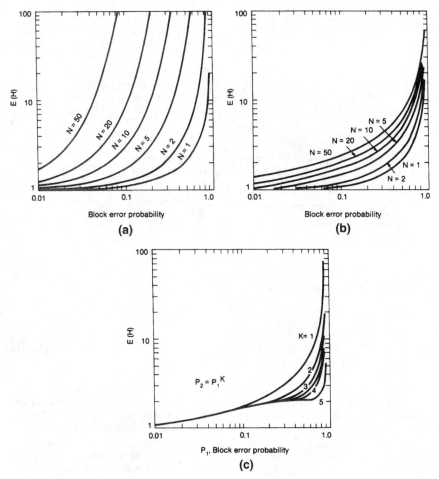

FIGURE 4.19 Expected number of transmissions for different kinds of ARQ. (*a*) $E(H)$, expected number of transmissions to deliver an N-block message for stop-and-wait ARQ. (*b*) $E(H)$, expected number of transmissions to deliver an N-block message for SRT ARQ(*b*). (*c*) $E(H)$, expected number of transmissions to deliver a 10-block message for SRT ARQ(*c*) for various retransmission-failure probabilities.

Because the forward error correction is added to retransmission, P_2 is smaller than P_1. Let P_2 be a positive integer power of P_1; that is, $P_2 = P_1^k$, where k represents the various powers of the feedforward error correction code. Equation (4.1-18) is plotted in Fig. 4.19*c* for $N = 10$. When $k = 1$, the curve shown in Fig. 4.19*c* is the same as $N = 10$ in Fig. 4.19*b*.

4.1.3.3 Transmission Efficiency **R**.

The transmission efficiency is the ratio of the number of information bits to the total number of transmission bits. Let a message consist of N words, where B is number of bits per word, and

$$B = H + L \tag{4.1-19}$$

where H is the header bits and L is the information bits. Then

Stop-and-wait ARQ technique

$$R = \frac{NL}{(H + NB)E_N} \qquad (4.1\text{-}20)$$

where E_N is as shown in Eq. (4.1-16).

Selective retransmission

$$R = \frac{NL}{HE_N + NBE_1} \qquad (4.1\text{-}21)$$

where E_N is as shown in Eq. (4.1-17) and

$$E_1 = \frac{1}{(1 - P_{\text{ew}})} \qquad (4.1\text{-}22)$$

Selective retransmission with ARQ(c)

$$R = \frac{NL}{HE_N + NBE_1} \qquad (4.1\text{-}23)$$

where E_N is as shown in Eq. (4.1-18), and E_1 is

$$E_1 = 1 + \sum_{i=2}^{\infty} \left[1 - \left(1 - P_1 P_2^{i-2}\right)\right] \qquad (4.1\text{-}24)$$

4.1.3.4 Undetected Error Rates.
In the previous sections, we saw that each transmission results in one of two outcomes, success or failure. This is called "hard detection." There is also a "soft detection." In soft detection three probabilities per transmission are denoted: P_c (success), P_d (detected error), and P_u (undetected error) per word. When each of these probabilities is identified for each transmission, then we can perform further calculations.

Stop-and-wait ARQ [Apply ARQ(a) and ARQ(b)]. We can find the undetected error probability per single-word message.

$$P_{\text{um}} = \frac{P_u}{P_c + P_u} \qquad (4.1\text{-}25)$$

where

$$P_c = 1 - P_{\text{ew}} \qquad (4.1\text{-}26)$$

and

$$P_u \le P_{\text{ew}} \, 2^{-m} \qquad (4.1\text{-}27)$$

where m is the number of error-detection parity bits. The undetected error probability per N-word message is

$$P_{\text{um}} = \frac{1 - (1 - P_{\text{ew}})^N}{1 + (1 - P_{\text{ew}})^N(2^m - 1)} \qquad (4.1\text{-}28)$$

Selective Retransmission. In this technique, we consider b parity bits per each word instead of m parity bits for the whole message. The probability of undetected error for a single-word message is

$$P_{um} = \frac{P_{ew}}{P_{ew}(1 - 2^b) + 2^b} \qquad (4.1\text{-}29)$$

The probability of undetected error for a N-word message is

$$P_{um} = 1 - \left[1 - \frac{P_{ew}}{P_{ew}(1 - 2^b) + 2^b} \right]^N \qquad (4.1\text{-}30)$$

The word error rate P_{ew} is a function of vehicle speed. Since the word error rate P_{ew} is derived from the bit error rate, each bit in error can be dependent on or independent of the adjacent bit error related to the vehicle speed. Therefore, the word error rate is not easy to obtain. Any oversimplified model may give incorrect answers. We can obtain the word error rate from two extreme cases, one assuming that the speed approaches infinity and the other assuming that the speed approaches zero as described in Section 15.2.2.

4.1.4 Digital Speech[12]

Since digital technologies have evolved, an important study focuses on efficient methods for digitally encoding speech. Speech quality implies a measure of fidelity, which is difficult to specify qualitatively because human perception is involved. The two criteria used are

What is being said (low fidelity accepted by military systems)

Who says it (high fidelity important to commercial systems)

For instance, a military system examiner who comments that someone's speech quality is excellent may be referring to intelligibility and low system noise. It is irrelevant who speaks on the other side (of the examiner) or that the examiner has never spoken to this person before.

4.1.4.1 Transmission Rates in Speech Coding. These rates are totally dependent on quality characterizations such as toll quality, commentary quality, communications quality, and synthetic quality. We may use the mean opinion score (MOS) referred in Sec. 2.2.1 to grade the voice quality.

1. *Toll quality* ($4 < MOS < 4.5$). An analog speech signal is of toll quality when its frequency range is 200 to 3200 Hz; its signal-to-noise ratio is greater than or equal to 30 dB; and its harmonic distortion is less than or equal to 2.3 percent. Digital speech has to have a quality comparable to that of the toll quality of an analog speech signal.

Toll-Quality Transmission

Coder	kbps
Log PCM	56
ADM	40
ADPCM	32
Sub-band	24
Pitch Predictive ADPCM	24
APC, ATC, ϕV, VEV	16

2. *Commentary quality (MOS > 4.5)*. In general, the signal at bit rates exceeding 64 kbps generates a commentary-quality speech signal which is better than toll quality, but the input bandwidths are significantly wider than in a noncellular telephone system (up to 7 kHz).

3. *Communications quality (3 < MMOS < 4)*. At rates below 16 kbps, the signal in the range of 7.2 to 9.6 kbps is a communications-quality speech signal. The signal is highly intelligible but has noticeable reductions in quality and speaker recognition.

Communications-Quality
Transmission

Coder	kbps
Log PCM	36
ADM	24
ADPCM	16
Sub-band	9.6
APC, ATC, ϕV, VEV	7.2

4. *Synthetic quality (2.5 < MOS < 3)*. At 4.8 kbps and below, the signal provides synthetic quality and speaker recognition is substantially degraded.

Synthetic-Quality Transmission

Coder	kbps
CV, LPC	2.4
Orthogonal	1.2
Formant	0.5

4.1.4.2   Classes of Coder.   There are two classes of coder: waveform coders and source coders.
Waveform Coders.   The speech waveform can be characterized by

1. Amplitude distribution (in time domain)

2. Autocorrelation function (in time domain)

3. Power spectral density (in frequency domain)

4. Spectral flatness measure (removing redundancy in speech waveform)

5. Fidelity criteria for waveforms

$$\text{Coding noise} = \frac{1}{T} \int_0^T (\text{coding error})^2 dt$$

where the coding error is equal to the amplitude difference (samples of a coded waveform minus the original input waveform).

The signal-to-noise ratio is expressed as

$$\frac{S}{N} = \left[\frac{(\text{input waveform})^2}{\text{coding noise}} \right]$$

There are two types of speech waveform coders.

1. *Time-domain coders.* Pulse code modulation (PCM), differential pulse code modulation (DPCM), and delta modulation (DM) are commonly used. Adaptive predictive coding (APC) in time-domain coding systems is limited to linear predictors with changing coefficients based on one of the following three types:

    a. Spectral fine structure—in more periods.

    b. Short-time spectral envelope—determined by the frequency response of the vocal tract and by the spectrum of the vocal-cord sound pulses.

    c. Combination of types *a* and *b*: In time-domain coders, speech is treated as a single full-band signal: in time-domain predictive coders, speech redundancy is removed prior to encoding by prediction and inverse filtering so that the information rate can be lower.

2. *Frequency-domain coders.* The speech signal can be divided into a number of separate frequency components, and each of these components can be encoded separately. The bands with little or no energy may not be encoded at all. There are two types of coding:

    a. *Subband coding (SBC).* Each subband can be encoded according to perceptual criteria that are specific to that band.

    b. *Adaptive transform coding (ATC).* An input signal is segmented and each segment is represented by a set of transform coefficients which are separately quantized and transmitted.

Source Coders—Vocoders. The synthetic quality of source vocoder speech is not appropriate for commercial telephone application. It is designed for very low bit-rate channels. Vocoders use a linear, quasi-stationary model of speech production.

Sound Source Characteristics: The sound can be generated by voiced sounds, fricatives, or stops. The source for voiced sounds is represented by a periodic pulse generator. The source for unvoiced sounds is represented by a random noise generator. They are mutually exclusive.

System Characterization: The acoustic resonances of the vocal tract modulate the spectra of the sources. Different speech sounds correspond uniquely to different spectral shapes. Vocoders depend on a parametric description of the vocal-tract transfer functions.

1. Channel vocoder/Frequency-Domain vocoder—speech signal evaluated at specific frequencies
2. Time-Domain vocoder—speech signal evaluated at specific times
3. LPC (linear prediction code) vocoder—linear prediction coefficients that describe the spectral envelope
4. Formant vocoder—specified frequency values of major spectral resonances
5. Autocorrelation vocoder—specified short-time autocorrelation function of the speech signal
6. Orthogonal function vocoder—specifies a set of orthonormal functions

First three basic source vocoders and their related vocoders are described as follows:

Frequency-Domain Vocoders. A single coder is called a *channel vocoder*. Instead of transmitting the telephone signal directly, only the spectrum of each speech signal is transmitted; 16 values along the frequency axis are needed. Each takes 20 ms and requires a bandwidth of $1/(2 \times 20 \text{ ms}) = 25$ Hz and the total frequency requirement is (16×25) or 400 Hz, which is one-tenth of the bandwidth of the speech signal itself.

Time-Domain Vocoders. Speech samples would have to be spaced $1/(2 \times 4000) = 0.125$ ms apart, which would require 30 samples to ensure a good quality. Then the frequency requirement is $30/(2 \times 0.125 \text{ ms})$ or 120 kHz. For digital transmission, the number of bits per correlation sample used by a time-domain vocoder should be about twice as high for spectral samples in frequency-domain vocoders. Therefore, time-domain vocoders are not desirable. Yet, one of the most successful innovations in speech analysis and synthesis is linear predictive coding (LPC), which is based on autocorrelation analysis.

LPC Vocoders.[13] LPC vocoders constitute an APC system in which the prediction residual has been replaced by pulse and noise sources. For the telephone band, the number of predictor coefficients is 8. For low-quality voice, the number can be as small as 4. The RELP (regular-pulse excited LPC) used by GSM, the VSELP (Vector-Sum Excited LPC) used by TDMA (IS-54) and the modified VSELP used by CDMA.

VSELP Vocoders. Each subframe is 5 ms (40 symbols) long. It consists of two parts, the first part is the generation of pulse excitation and the second part is the speech waveform synthesis. The detail of VSELP is described in Sec. 4.3.3.2.

AMR (Adaptive Multirate) Speech Vocoders. A family of LPC coders. It provides coding rates of 12.2 kbps, 10.2 kbps, 7.95 kbps, 7.40 kbps, 6.70 kbps, 5.90 kbps, 5.15 kbps, and 4.75 kbps. The 12.2 kbps rate is the same coding scheme as used in the GSM enhanced full-rate coding scheme. The 7.4 kbps rate is the same coding scheme as used in NA-TDMA networks. The AMR coder allows for the speech bit rate to change dynamically during a call. Each AMR speech frame is 20 ms in duration, and it is possible to change the speech-coding rate from one speech frame to the next. The AMR coder also supports voice activity detection (VAD) and discontinuous transmission (DTX), with comfort noise generation. The net effect is that little or nothing is sent over the air interface when nothing is being said.

Hybrid Waveform Coders-Vocoders. A hybrid arrangement of SBC, APC, and LPC is coming into vogue where a portion (lower-frequency band) of the transmission is accomplished by waveform techniques and a portion (upper-frequency band) by voice-excited vocoder techniques.

4.1.4.3 Complexity of Coders. A relative count of logic gates is used to judge the complexity of the coders as follows:

Relative Complexity		Coder
1	ADM:	Adaptive delta modulator
1	ADPCM:	Adaptive differential PCM
5	Sub-band:	Subband coder (with CCD filters)
5	P-P ADPCM:	Pitch-predictive ADPCM
50	APC:	Adaptive predictive coder
50	ATC:	Adaptive transform coder
50	ϕV:	Phase vocoder
50	VEV:	Voice-excited vocoder
100	LPC:	Linear-predictive coefficient (vocoder)
100	CV:	Channel vocoder
200	Orthogonal:	LPC vocoder with orthogonalized coefficients
500	Formant:	Formant vocoder
1000	Articulatory:	Vocal-tract synthesizer; synthesis from printed English text

Of these coders, LPC is attractive because of its performance and degree of complexity.

4.1.4.4   Digital Voice in the Mobile Cellular Environment.   Because voice communication is the key service in cellular mobile systems, when we think of the digital systems, we must think of a digital voice.

In present-day mobile cellular systems, transmission of a digital voice in a multipath fading environment is a challenging job. The major considerations in implementing digital voice in cellular mobile systems are discussed below, along with a tentatively recommended transmission rate for the cellular mobile system.

Digital Voice in the Mobile Radio Environment

1. The criterion for judging a good digital voice through a wire line is employed in three existing digital voice schemes.

   a. In a continuously variable step delta (CVSD)[14] modulation scheme, the present transmission rate is 16 kbps. This is not toll-quality voice transmission and is commonly used by the military.

   b. In a LPC scheme, the present transmission rate of 2.4 kbps provides a synthetic quality voice, but a rate of 4.8 kbps using vector quantization[15] may provide a communications-quality voice. A rate of 16 kbps can provide a toll-quality voice.[16]

   c. In a pulse code modulation (PCM) scheme, the present transmission rates of 32 kbps and 64 kbps are commonly used; 32 kbps is used by the military while 64 kbps is used commercially.

   Of the three schemes, LPC seems most attractive because of its low transmission rate. However, LPC is more vulnerable in terms of distortion to the mobile fading environment.

2. Digital voice has to be processed in real time, which imposes constraints on the digital processing time. This adversely affects LPC but not CVSD.

3. When sending a digital stream (voice) through a radio channel in a fading environment, in general, an LPC scheme needs more code protection than CVSD scheme does because LPC is not implemented in a continuous waveform in either the frequency domain or the time domain while CVSD is implemented in a continuous waveform in the time domain.

4. Because the mobile unit is moving, sometimes rapidly, sometimes slowly, insertion of extra synchronization bits is needed in the normal digital stream.

Considerations for a Digital Voice Transmission in Cellular Mobile System. The following factors are significant.

1. *Digital transmission rate*

    a. *Analog cellular signaling rate.* The present signaling format is designed on the assumption that the mobile unit moves at an average of 30 mi/h and that the transmission rate is 10 kbps. The 21 synchronization bits (10 synchronization bits and 11 frame bits) occur in front of ten code words of 48 bits each to ensure that the bits are not falling out of synchrony before the resynchronization takes place.

    b. *Consideration of LPC scheme.* If a rate of 4.8 kbps using LPC for a communications-quality voice is accepted its rate is almost half of the present transmission rate, and at this transmission rate a 48-bit word would be acceptable in a fading environment. The resynchronization scheme for a mobile receiver should take place in front of every code word of 48 bits [(21 synchronization bits) + (a code word of 48 bits) = 69 bits]. The number of synchronization bits is almost half the number of bits in a code word. Therefore, the transmission rate would be approximately $(4.8 \times 1.5) = 7.2$ kbps.

    c. *Redundancy of transmission.* The protection of synchronization in a mobile radio environment is not sufficient. If the digital stream were to occur in a signal fade, partial or whole code words would be lost. In order to prevent fading, redundancy of transmission is often used. We would take a minimum redundancy scheme; for example, we would transmit the same message bits three times and take a "2-out-of-3 majority vote" on each bit to minimize the fading impairment of the message bits. For LPC of 4.8 kbps, an RF transmission rate of $(4.8 \text{ kbps} \times 1.5) 3 = 21.6$ kbps is needed.[*] It is reasonable for a 30-kHz channel to carry a transmission rate of 21.6 kbps over a severe fading medium. When an RF transmission rate is given, the channel bandwidth can be narrower with a trade-off of transmitted powers. This point has been described in Sec. 15.4.8.

    d. *Modulation, diversity, coding, ARQ, and scrambling.* Diversity and modulation can help in reducing the RF transmission rate for the digital voice. However, ARQ schemes, fancy coding schemes, and complicated scrambling schemes cannot be implemented for voice transmission. This is because the digital voice must be processed in real time, and these three schemes usually require a fair amount of time for processing. These schemes can be used for data transmission.

2. *Word error rate.* In the multipath fading environment, the bit error rate P_e is not the only parameter for voice-quality measurement; the word error rate P_w is also important and varies with vehicle speed. However, information on the word error rate for transmission of digital voice over a mobile radio environment only appears in two extreme cases (see Sec. 15.2.3). Assume that we know the required P_e and P_w. We can convert P_e and P_w to a required carrier-to-noise ratio C/N. If a two-branch diversity scheme is applied after a 2-out-of-3 majority-vote redundancy scheme has been used, the bit error rate of 10^{-3} in a relatively slow fading case requires a C/N level of approximately 15 dB. With the C/N level, a word error rate of a 40-bit word is about 10^{-3} (see Fig. 15.3a). In general, if the word error rate is the same as or lower than the bit-error rate for a given C/N, the C/N level is acceptable. In our case, P_w and P_e are the same at $C/N = 15$; therefore, the $C/N = 15$ dB is justified.

---

[*] Applying diversity schemes can reduce this rate.

3. *Relationship between C/N and E_b/N_0.* The relationship between the carrier-to-noise ratio C/N, the energy-per-bit-to-noise-per-hertz ratio E_b/N_0, the transmission rate R, and the bandwidth B can be expressed as

$$\frac{C}{N} = \frac{E_b}{N_0} \frac{R}{B} \qquad (4.1\text{-}31)$$

When the number of levels C/N increases, the bandwidth decreases. Keeping E_b/N_0 constant, we see that when the bandwidth decreases, the required carrier-to-noise ratio C/N increases. Previously we calculated that $C/N = 15$ dB works for a two-level (binary) system. If the number of waveform levels increases, the C/N will be higher than 15 dB.

EXAMPLE 4.1 *Let $E_b/N_0 = 15$ dB for a two-level system and R_0 and B_0 be the transmission rate and transmission bandwidth, respectively, of the two-level system. Now if we reduce the bandwidth $B_1 = 0.5B_0$, then*

$$\left(\frac{C}{N}\right)_1 = (31.6)\frac{R_0}{0.5B_0} = 2\left(\frac{C}{N}\right)_0$$

$$= \left(\frac{C}{N}\right)_0 + 3\,\text{dB}$$

This means that the power increases by 3 dB. If the transmitted power was 50 W, now it is 100 W.

4.1.4.5 Evaluation of Digital Voice Quality.
In general, there are two methods for evaluating digital voice quality.

1. *Listener's opinion.* Use one 16-kbps voice coder and one 8-kbps voice coder in a specified digital system. Then find the two required carrier-to-interference ratios C/I based on the listener's opinion in a Rayleigh fading environment. Then compare the same voice quality with that from an analog FM system at $C/I \geq 18$ dB.
2. *Diagnostic rhyme test (DRT).* The voice quality of a digital format is often tested by DRT. Using the DRT score of 90 as a criterion, above 90 means acceptable for synthetic-quality voice and below 90 means unacceptable. Thus, the bit error should be less than 10^{-3} for an LPC of 2400 bps in a gaussian noise environment. Voice evaluation for an LPC of 4.8 kbps does not appear in the literature. The voice quality in CVSD based on the same DRT criterion requires a bit error rate of only 4 percent or less. The DRT is not designed for toll-quality voice test.

4.2 GLOBAL SYSTEM FOR MOBILE (GSM)

CEPT, a European group, began to develop the Global System for Mobile TDMA system in June 1982.[17-21] GSM has two objectives: pan-European roaming, which offers compatibility throughout the European continent, and interaction with the integrated service digital network (ISDN), which offers the capability to extend the single-subscriber-line system to a multiservice system with various services currently offered only through diverse telecommunications networks.

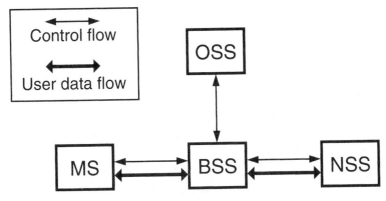

FIGURE 4.20   The external environment of the BSS.

System capacity was not an issue in the initial development of GSM, but due to the unexpected, rapid growth of cellular service, 35 revisions have been made to GSM since the first issued specification. The first commercial GSM system, called D2, was implemented in Germany in 1992.

4.2.1   GSM Architecture[19–20]

GSM consists of many subsystems, such as the mobile station (MS), the base station subsystem (BSS), the network and switching subsystem (NSS), and the operation subsystem (OSS) (see Fig. 4.20).

4.2.1.1   The Mobile Station.   The MS may be a stand-alone piece of equipment for certain services or support the connection of external terminals, such as the interface for a personal computer or fax. The MS includes mobile equipment (ME) and a subscriber identity module (SIM). ME does not need to be personally assigned to one subscriber. The SIM is a subscriber module which stores all the subscriber-related information. When a subscriber's SIM is inserted into the ME of an MS, that MS belongs to the subscriber, and the call is delivered to that MS. The ME is not associated with a called number—it is linked to the SIM. In this case, any ME can be used by a subscriber when the SIM is inserted in the ME.

4.2.1.2   Base Station Subsystem.   The BSS connects to the MS through a radio interface and also connects to the NSS. The BSS consists of a base transceiver station (BTS) located at the antenna site and a base station controller (BSC) that may control several BTSs. The BTS consists of radio transmission and reception equipment similar to the ME in an MS. A transcoder/rate adaption unit (TRAU) carries out encoding and speech decoding and rate adaptation for transmitting data. As a subpart of the BTS, the TRAU may be sited away from the BTS, usually at the MSC. In this case, the low transmission rate of speech code channels allows more compressed transmission between the BTS and the TRAU, which is sited at the MSC.

GSM uses the open system interconnection (OSI). There are three common interfaces based on OSI (Fig. 4.21): a common radio interface, called *air interface*, between the MS and BTS, an interface A between the MSC and BSC, and an A-bis interface between the BTS and BSC. With these common interfaces, the system operator can purchase the product of manufacturing company A to interface with the product of manufacturing company B. The difference between interface and protocol is that an interface represents the point of contact between two adjacent entities (equipment or systems) and a protocol provides information flows through the interface. For example, the GSM radio interface is the transit point for information flow pertaining to several protocols.

4.2.1.3 Network and Switching Subsystem. NSS (see Fig. 4.22) in GSM uses an intelligent network (IN). The IN's attributes will be described later. A signaling NSS includes the main switching functions of GSM. NSS manages the communication between GSM users and other telecommunications users. NSS management consists of:

Mobile service switching center (MSC). Coordinates call set-up to and from GSM users. An MSC controls several BSCs.

Interworking function (IWF). A gateway for MSC to interface with external networks for communication with users outside GSM, such as packet-switched public data network (PSPDN) or circuit-switched public data network (CSPDN). The role of the IWF depends on the type of user data and the network to which it interfaces.

Home location register (HLR). Consists of a stand-alone computer without switching capabilities, a database which contains subscriber information, and information related to the subscriber's current location, but not the actual location of the subscriber. A sub-division of HLR is the authentication center (AUC). The AUC manages the security data for subscriber authentication. Another sub-division of HLR is the equipment identity register (EIR) which stores the data of mobile equipment (ME) or ME-related data.

Visitor location register (VLR). Links to one or more MSCs, temporarily storing subscription data currently served by its corresponding MSC, and holding more detailed data than the HLR. For example, the VLR holds more current subscriber location information than the location information at the HLR.

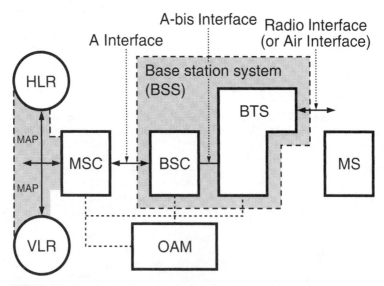

FIGURE 4.21 Functional architecture and principal interfaces.

Gateway MSC (GMSC). In order to set up a requested call, the call is initially routed to a gateway MSC, which finds the correct HLR by knowing the directory number of the GSM subscriber. The GMSC has an interface with the external network for gatewaying, and the network also operates the full Signaling System 7 (SS7) signaling between NSS machines.

Signaling transfer point (STP). Is an aspect of the NSS function as a stand-alone node or in the same equipment as the MSC. STP optimizes the cost of the signaling transport among MSC/VLR, GMSC, and HLR.

As mentioned earlier, NSS uses an intelligent network. It separates the central data base (HLR) from the switches (MSC) and uses STP to transport signaling among MSC and HLR.

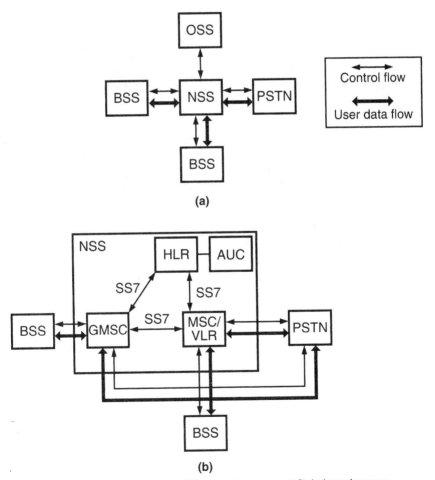

FIGURE 4.22   NSS and its environment. (*a*) The external environment; (*b*) the internal structure.

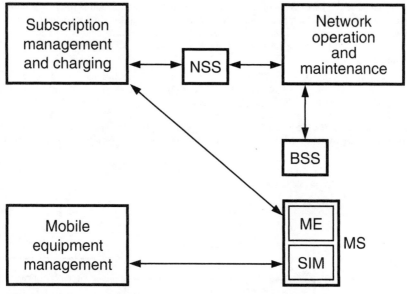

FIGURE 4.23 OSS organization.

4.2.1.4 Operation Subsystem. There are three areas of OSS, as shown in Fig. 4.23: (1) network operation and maintenance functions, (2) subscription management, including charging and billing, and (3) mobile equipment management. These tasks require interaction between some or all of the infrastructure equipment. OSS is implemented in any existing network.

4.2.2 Layer Modeling (OSI Model)

The Open System Interconnection (OSI) of GSM consists of five layers: transmission (TX), radio resource management (RR), mobility management (MM), communication management (CM), and operation, administration, and maintenance (OAM) (Fig. 4.24). The lower layers correspond to short-time-scale functions, the upper layers are long-time-scale functions.

The TX layer sets up a connection between MS and BTS. The RR layer refers to the protocol for management of the transmission over the radio interface and provides a stable link between the MS and BSC. The BSS performs most of the RR functions. The MM layer (1) manages the subscriber databases, including location data, and (2) manages authentication activities, SIM, HLR, and AUC. The NSS (mainly the MSC) is a significant element in the CM layer. The following functions are parts of the CM layer:

1. *Call control*. The CM layer sets up calls, maintains calls, and releases calls. The CM layer interacts among the MSC/VLR, GMSC, IWF, and HLR for managing circuit-oriented service, including speech and circuit data.

2. *Supplementary services management*. Allows users to have some control of their calls in the network, and has specific variations from the basic service.

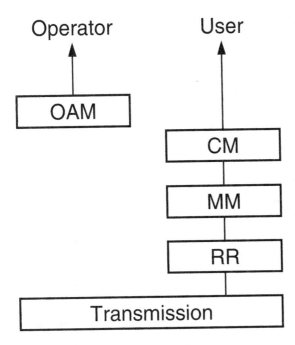

FIGURE 4.24 The functional planes of GSM.

3. *Short message service (SMS).* Related to the point-to-point SMS. A SMS service center (SMS-SC) may connect to several GSM networks. Short message transmission requires setting up a signaling connection between the mobile station and the MSC. The two functions of SMS are

a. Mobile-originating short message

b. Mobile-terminating short message

OSS is an integral part of the OAM layer. All the subsystems, such as BBS and NSS, contribute to the OAM operation and maintenance functions.

4.2.3 Transmission

4.2.3.1 Speech. A 4-kHz analog speech signal converts to a 64-kbps digital signal, then down-converts to 13 kbps before modulation. Using a rate of 13 kbps instead of 64 kbps allows the 13-kbps data rate transmission to occur over a narrowband channel. Because the radio spectrum is a precious and limited resource, using less bandwidth per channel provides more channels within a given radio spectrum.

Digital speech uses:

1. *Regular pulse excitation (RPE):* Generates the impulse noise to simulate the nature of speech.

2. *Linear prediction coding (LPC):* Generates speech waveform by using a filter with eight transmitted coefficients with a speech frame of 20 ms; 260 bits represent a 20-ms speech frame. There are two modes of voice transmission in GSM, continuous (normal mode) and discontinuous.

The discontinuous transmission (DTX) mode decreases effective radio transmission encoding of speech at 13 kbps from a bit rate around 500 bps without speech. In active speech the frame is 260 bits in each 20 ms, and in inactive speech, the frame is 260 bits in 480 ms (24 times longer than normal mode).

A voice activity device (VAD) detects the DTX mode. In the voice protocol, a silence detection (SID) frame precedes the start of DTX. The speech coder provides an additional bit of information indicating whether the speech frame needs to be sent, depending on the VAD algorithm.

A SID starts at every inactivity period and repeats at least twice per second, as long as inactivity lasts. During the inactive speech period determined by VAD, and during every inactive period, artificial noise is generated at the receiver, substituting for background noise.

4.2.3.2 Data Service. The highest data rate is 9600 bps and has two different modes. A forward error correction mechanism is provided in the transparent (T) mode. In the non-transparent (NT) mode, information is repeatedly sending when it is not acknowledged by the other end, and may be asked for an automatic repeat request (ARQ). Three different users' data rates are employed in the T connection: 2400 bps, 4800 bps, and 9600 bps. After insertion of the auxiliary information bits, the intermediate rates bits become 3.6 kbps, 6 kbps, and 12 kbps, corresponding to the user's 2.4 kbps, 4.8 kbps, and 9.6 kbps, respectively.

The basic GSM data rate is also 12 kbps (6 kbps on the half-rate channel) in an NT connection, but the available throughput varies with the quality of basic transmission and the transmission delay. Generally, the NT mode has less transmission error but also less throughput. The NT mode may be considered for a packet data flow application. The user data stream is sliced into blocks of 200 bits, and, with addition of the redundancy and auxiliary information, the user data stream becomes 240 bits per block. These blocks are used in NT while the ARQ scheme is applied.

An adaptation function called interworking function (IWF) at the network side, and terminal adapting function (TAF) at the terminal, is used to accommodate variable transmission rates (Fig. 4.25). The radio link protocol (RLP) is used for transporting signaling messages between the TAF and IWF.

Data can transmit over these planes, as shown in Fig. 4.25:

1. End-to-end transmission—direct transmission through hard wire.

2. TAF to IWF transmission through subscriber units.

3. GSM radio transmission through subscriber units; acts like a voice call in the air.

Although speech interconnection with the ISDN is not a problem, data transmission raises its own problems, as shown in Fig. 4.26. ISDN uses the capacity of a bidirectional 64 kbps/channel, but GSM must use the radio spectrum efficiently, through a bidirectional 13 kbps/channel. Interconnection of data services between GSM and ISDN is not possible without a rate-adapted (RA) box, as shown in Fig. 4.26.

4.2.3.3 Modulation. Gaussian minimum-shift keying (GMSK), where $BT = 0.3$ is the normalized bandwidth of a gaussian filter, is the modulation scheme of GSM, where B is the baseband bandwidth, and $1/T$ is the transmission rate. $B = 1/T \times 0.3 = 270\,\text{kbps} \times 0.3 = 81\,\text{kHz}$. Minimum means the *minimum tone separation*. GMSK uses a small spectrum

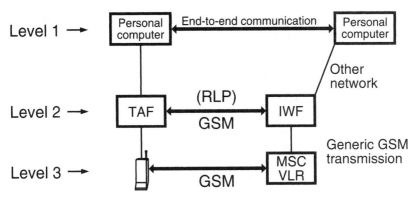

FIGURE 4.25   Data transmission planes.

bandwidth to send a GSM carrier channel. The modulation rate of a GSM carrier channel is 270 kbps.

4.2.4   GSM Channels and Channel Modes

4.2.4.1   Channel Structure.   The services offered to users have four radio transmission modes, three data modes, and a speech mode. The radio transmission modes use the physical channels.

4.2.4.2   Physical Channels.   There are three kinds of physical channels, also called traffic channels (TCHs):

1. *TCH/F (full rate).* Transmits a speech code of 13 kbps or three data-mode rates, 12, 6, and 3.6 kbps.

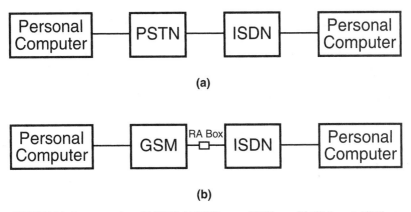

FIGURE 4.26   Interconnection with ISDN. (*a*) PSTN user to ISDN user; (*b*) GSM user to ISDN user.

2. *TCH/H (half rate).* Transmits a speech code of 7 kbps or two data modes, 6 and 3.6 kbps.

3. *TCH/8 (one-eighth rate).* Used for low-rate signaling channels, common channels, and data channels.

4.2.4.3 Logical Channels

Common channels. All the common channels are embedded in different traffic channels. They are grouped by the same cycle (51 × 8 BP), where BP stands for burst period (i.e., time slot), which is 577 μs.

Downlink common channels. There are five downlink unidirectional channels, shared or grouped by a TCH.

- Frequency correction channel (FCCH) repeats once every 51 × 8 BPs; used to identify a beacon frequency.

- Synchronization channel (SCH) follows each FCCH slot by 8 BPs.

- Broadcast control channel (BCCH) is broadcast regularly in each cell and received by all the mobile stations in the idle mode.

- Paging and access grant channel (PAGCH). Used for the incoming call received at the mobile station. The access grant channel is answered from the base station and allocates a channel during the access procedure of setting up a call.

- Call broadcast channel (CBCH). Each cell broadcasts a short message for 2 s from the network to the mobile station in idle mode. Half a downlink TCH/8 is used, and special CBCH design constraints exist because of the need for sending two channels (CBCH and BCCH) in parallel.

The mobile station (MS) finds the FCCH burst, then looks for an SCH burst on the same frequency to achieve synchronization. The MS then receives BCCH on several time slots and selects a proper cell, remaining for a period in the idle mode.

Uplink common channel. The random-access channel (RACH) is the only common uplink channel. RACH is the channel that the mobile station chooses to access the calls. There are two rates: RACH/F (full rate, one time slot every 8 BP), and RACH/H (half rate, using 23 time slots in the 51 × 8 BP cycle, where 8 BP cycle [i.e. a frame] is 4.615 ms).

Signaling channels. All the signaling channels have chosen one of the physical channels, and the logical channels names are based on their logical functions:

Slow associated control channel (SACCH). A slow-rate TCH used for signaling transport and used for nonurgent procedures, mainly handover decisions. It uses one-eighth rate. The TCH/F is always allocated with SACCH. This combined TCH and SACCH is denoted TACH/F. SACCH occupies 1 time slot (0.577 ms) in every 26 frames (4.615 ms × 26). The time organization of a TACH/F is shown in Fig. 4.27.

Fast associated control channel (FACCH). Indicates cell establishment, authenticates subscribers, or commands a handover.

Stand-alone dedicated control channel (SDCCH). Occasionally the connection between a mobile station and the network is used solely for passing signaling information and not for calls. This connection may be at the user's demand or for other management operations such as updating the unit's location. It operates at a very low rate and uses a TCH/8 channel.

Radio slots are allocated to users only when call penetration is needed. There are two modes, dedicated and idle. The mode used depends on the uplink and the downlink. In

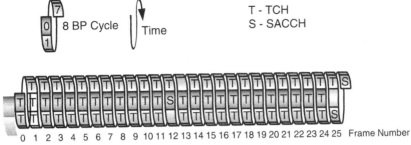

T - TCH
S - SACCH

0 1 2 3 4 5 6 7 8 9 10 11 12 13 14 15 16 17 18 19 20 21 22 23 24 25   Frame Number

FIGURE 4.27   Time organization of a TACH/F.

GSM terminology, the downlink is the signal transmitted from the base station to the mobile station, and the uplink is the signal transmitted in the opposite direction. (*Note*: The terrestrial communication terms *uplink* and *downlink* are not to be confused with the same terms used in satellite communications. In many instances the position of the mobile station can be higher than the base station antenna because of the terrain contour. Using the terms in the kind of situation may cause confusion, therefore it is more important for the reader to remember the *definitions* of these terms as used in terrestrial communications. This approach is analogous to using the term *handover* instead of *handoff* in discussions about European cellular telecommunications—as long as the definition itself is clear, the terms will be understood.)

Voice/data channels. Each time slot of a voice channel contains 260 bits per block. The entire block contains 316 bits. Each time slot of a data channel contains 120 or 240 bits per block.

Channel modes. Because of the precious value of the radio spectrum, individual users cannot have their own TCH at all times.

Dedicated mode. Uses TCH during call establishment and uses SACCH to perform location updating in the dedicated mode. TCH and SACCH are dedicated channels for both uplink and downlink channels.

Idle mode. During noncall activities, the five downlink channels are in the idle mode: FCCH; SCH; BCCH, which is broadcasting regularly; PAGCH and CBCH, which sends one message every 2 s. During idle mode, the mobile station listens to the common downlink channels, and also uses SDCCH (uplink channel) to register a mobile location associated with a particular base station to the network.

4.2.5   Multiple-Access Scheme

4.2.5.1   General Description.   GSM is a combination of FDMA and TDMA. The total number of channels in FDMA is 124, and each channel is 200 kHz. Both the 935–960 MHz uplink and 890–916 MHz downlink have been allocated 25 MHz, for a total of 50 MHz. Duplex separation is 45 MHz. If TDMA is used within a 200-kHz channel, 8 time slots are required to form a frame, frame duration is 4.615 ms, and the time slot duration burst period is 0.577 ms. There is a DCS-1800 system, which has the same architecture as the GSM, but it is upconverted to 1800 MHz. The downlink is 1805–1880 MHz (base TX) and the uplink is 1700–1785 MHz (mobile Tx).

4.2.5.2   Constant Time Delay Between Uplink and Downlink. The numbering of the uplink slots is derived from the downlink slots by a delay of 3 time slots. This allows the slots of one channel to bear the same time slot number in both directions. In this case, the mobile station will not transmit and receive simultaneously because the two time slots are physically separated. Propagation delay when the mobile station is far from the BTS is a major consideration. For example, the round trip propagation delay between an MS and BTS which are 35 km apart is 233 μs. As a result, the assigned time slot numbers of the uplink and downlink channels may not be the same (less than 3 time slots apart). The solution is to let BTS compute a time advance value. The key is to allow significant guard time by taking into account that BCCH is using only even time slots. This avoids the uncertainty of numbering the wrong time slot. Once a dedicated connection is established, the BTS continuously measures the time offset between its own burst schedule and the reception schedule of mobile station bursts on the bidirectional SACCH channel. The time compensation for the propagation delay (sending to the mobile station via SACCH) is 3 time slots minus the time advance.

4.2.5.3   Frequency Hopping. GSM has a slow frequency-hopping radio interface. The slow hopping is defined in bits per hop. Its regular rate is 217 hops/s, therefore, with a transmission rate of 270 kbps, the result is approximately 1200 bits/hop.

   If the PAGCH and the RACH were hopping channels, then hopping sequences could be broadcast on the BCCH. The common channel is forbidden from hopping and using the same frequency.

4.2.5.4   Different Types of Time Slots. Each cell provides a reference clock from which the time slots are defined. Each time slot is given a number (TN) which is known by the base station and the mobile station. The time slot numbering is cyclic. TN0 is a single set broadcast in any given call and repeated every 8 BPs for the confirmation of all common channels. The organization of TN0 (first of eight time slots) in sequence is as follows: FCCH (1), SCH (1), BCCH (4), PAGCH (4), FCCH (1), SCH (1), PAGCH (8), FCCH (1), SCH (1), PAGCH (8), FCCH (1), SCH (1), PAGCH (8), FCCH (1), SCH (1), PAGCH (8).

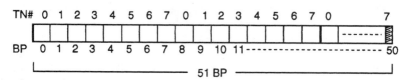

The symbol PAGCH (4) means that the PAGCH channel information appears in consecutive ones of every 8 BP cycle 4 times. Each of the remaining seven TNs (TN1 to TN7) is assigned to one TACH/F channel.

4.2.5.5   Bursts and Training Sequences. In TDMA, the signal transmits in bursts. The time interval of the burst brings the amplitude of a transmitted signal up from a starting value of 0 to its normal value. Then a packet of bits is transmitted by a modulated signal. Afterward, the amplitude decreases to zero. These bursts occur only at the mobile station transmission or at the base station if the adjacent burst is not transmitted.

   There are tail bits and training sequence bits within a burst. The tail bits are three 0 bits added at the beginning and at the end of each burst which provide the guard time.

   The training sequence is a sequence known by the receiver that trains an equalizer, a device that reduces intersymbol interference. The training sequence bits are inserted in the middle of a time slot sometimes called a *midamble,* for the same purpose as a preamble, so that the equalizer can minimize its maximum distance with any useful bit. There are eight different training sequences, with little correlation between any two sequences to distinguish the received signal from the interference signal.

There are several kinds of bursts:

1. The normal burst used in TCH:

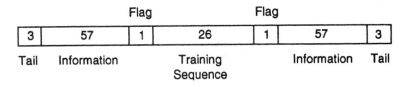

The 1-bit binary information indicating data or signaling is called the *stealing flag*.

2. The access burst used on the RACH in the uplink direction:

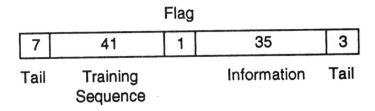

3. The F and S bursts. The F burst is used on the FCCH and has the simplest format. All of the 148 bits are zero, producing a pure sine wave. Five S bursts in each 51×8 BP cycle are used on the SCH. One S burst is shown below:

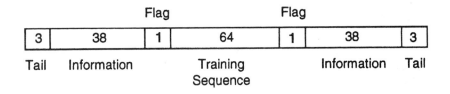

4.2.6   Channel Coding and Interleaving

4.2.6.1   Channel Coding.   Channel coding improves transmission quality when interference, multipath fading, and Doppler shift are encountered. As a result, the bit error rate and frame error rate or word error rate are reduced, but throughput is also reduced. Four kinds of channel codings are used in GSM:

1. Convolutional codes (L, k) are used to correct random errors: k is the input block bits, and L is the output block bits. Convolutional codes have three different rates in GSM:

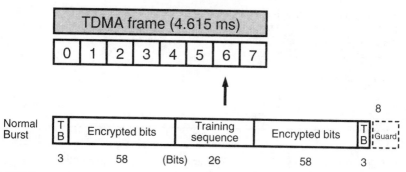

FIGURE 4.28 TDMA frame and normal burst.

(1) the one-half rate ($L/k = 2$), (2) the one-third rate ($L/K = 3$), and (3) the one-sixth rate ($L/k = 6$).

2. Fire codes (L, k) are used as a block code to detect and correct a single burst of errors, where k is the information bits and L is the coded bits.

3. Parity check codes (L, k) are used for error detection. L is the bits of a block, k is the information bits, $L - k$ is the parity check bits.

4. Concatenation codes use convolutional code as an inner code and fire code as an outer code. Both the inner code and the outer code reduce the probability of error and correct most of the channel code. The advantage of using concatenation code is a reduction of the implementation complexity as compared with a single coding operation.

GSM's speech code is sent at a rate of 13 kbps, which represents 260 bits in each 20-ms speech block. After channel coding, each block contains 456 bits and the transmission rate is 22.8 kbps, or 114 bits for time slots. Adding the overhead bits such as tail bits (6), training bits (26), flag bits (2), and guard time bits (8), the total bits of a traffic channel is 156 bits in one time slot of 0.577 ms, as shown in Fig. 4.28.

4.2.6.2 Interleaving.   Interleaving scrambles and/or spreads a sequence of bits prior to transmitting them. The sequence of bits is put back in order at the receiving end. Bursts of errors occur during transmission because of signal fading. After being received, these bursts of errors are then converted to random errors and put back in the correct sequence after decoding. Interleaving's major drawback is the corresponding delay at the receiving end.

Interleaving schemes are relatively simple in GSM. A code word of 456 bits could be spread into the following format:

1. Four full bursts—divide 456 bits into 4 parts, each one filling up a whole burst. This interleaving format takes 4.615 ms × 4 = 18.46 ms.

2. Eight half bursts—divide 456 bits into 8 parts, each one filling up half a burst. This interleaving format takes 4.615 ms × 8 = 36.92 ms. Four parts share with the previous and four parts with the new partial code word.

The interleaving and coding for different transmission modes are shown in Table 4.1. Interleaving is a powerful scheme which converts burst errors into random errors, and although it is very effective for data transmission, it is not effective for voice transmission. Voice transmission, operates in real time, and a long delay in response cannot be tolerated.

TABLE 4.1 Interleaving and Coding for the Different Transmission Modes

Channel and Transmission Mode	Input Rate (kbit/s)	Input Bock (in bits)	Coding	Ouput Block (in bits)	Interleaving
TCH/FS 1a 1b II	13	50 132 78	Parity (3 bits) convolutional 1/2 Convolutional 1/2 None	456	On 8 half-bursts
TCH/F9.6	12	240	Convolutional 1/2 punctured 1 bit out of 15	456	Complex, on 22 unequal burst portions
TCH/H4.8	6	240	Convolutional 1/2 punctured 1 bit out of 15	456	Complex, on 22 unequal burst portions
TCH/F4.8	6	120	Addition of 32 null bits Convolutional 1/3	456	Complex, on 22 unequal burst portions
TCH/F2.4	3.6	72	Convolutional 1/6	456	On 8 half bursts
TCH/H2.4	3.6	144	Convolutional 1/3	456	Complex, on 22 unequal burst portions
SCH		25	Parity (10 bits) Convolutional 1/2	78	On 1 S burst
RACH (+ Handover Access)		8	Parity (6 bits) Convolutional 1/2	36	On 1 access burst
Fast associated signalling on TCH/F and/H		184	Fire code 224/184, Convolutional 1/2	456	On 8 half bursts
TCH/8, SACCH; BCCH, PAGCH		184	Fire code 224/184, Convolutional 1/2	456	On 4 full bursts

Source: *Reprinted from Ref. 19 p. 246.*

Without interleaving and overhead bits, the transmit rate for a speech channel is 22.8 kbps, 114 bits per time slot, and 456 bits per four time slots.

4.2.7 Radio Resource (RR) Management

In a mobile network, radio channels must allocate for call setup, handover and release, on a call bias. This management is additional to the conventional fixed network call handling procedures. There are three management functions; location, handover, and roaming. The implementation of the RR functions require some kind of protocol between the mobile station and the network.

4.2.7.1 Link Protocol. We studied the means of transporting user information in previous sections. But in addition to the user's information, the signaling transfer information exchanges must be sent and understood by every piece of signaling transport equipment. Most information exchange functions are distributed to different kinds of equipment. There are three link protocols to provide information exchanges.

Radio link protocol (RLP), specified in GSM link access protocol over the radio link called LAPDm.

LAPD, the link access protocol (LAP) adapted from ISDN D channel.

Message transfer part (MTP), the protocols used for signaling transport on an SS7 network.

The radio link protocol's signaling message rate is 22.8 kbps. The signaling message rate on the other link protocol is 64 kbps.

4.2.7.2 Interfaces Associated with Link Protocols

Interface	Link Protocol
MS-BTS	LAPDm (GSM spec)
BTS-BSC	LAPD (adopted from ISDN)
BSC-MSC	MTP (SS7 protocol)
MSC/VLR/HLR—SS7 network	MTP (SS7 protocol)
MSC-MSC (call-related signaling)	TUP (telephone user part)
BSC-relay MSC (non-call-related signaling)	ISUP (ISDN user part)
	BSS MAP (MAP/B)
MSC-MSC (non-call-related signaling)	MAP (mobility application part)

Non-call-related signals correspond to protocols in the MSC that are different from those in other MSCs or other HLRs and are grouped together in the MAP. We can distinguish them by MAP/X, where X can be B, C, D, and so forth.

MAP/B   Protocol between BSC and relay MSC

MAP/C   Protocol between GMSC and an HLR

MAP/D   Protocol between another MSC/VLR and HLR

MAP/E   Protocol between MSCs

Figure 4.29 shows the relationships of MAP/X protocols.

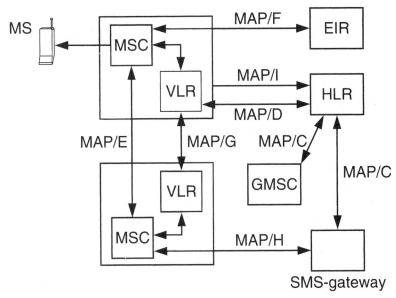

FIGURE 4.29   MAP/C to MAP/I protocols.

4.2.8 Mobility Management (MM)

The mobility of cellular system users requires mobility management for location updates, handovers, and roaming. A handover occurs when a voice channel changes as the mobile station enters another cell during a call. Roaming is the ability to initiate a call in one network system and deliver it to another network system by using MM and location update management.

4.2.8.1   Location Update Management.   The subscription is always associated with its home public land mobile network (PLMN). The roaming customer is associated with visited PLMNs. We may identify whether the call is from PLMN or visited PLMN from the location of the MS.

In the PLMN selection process, the MM normally looks for cells only in the home (serving) PLMN. If no service is available, the user can choose either the automatic mode (the network searches) or the manual mode (the user searches) to search for the desired PLMN. In the limited-service case, the MM continuously monitors only the 30 strongest carriers. Limited service usually takes care of coverage at the border areas of a foreign country.

4.2.8.2   Cell Selection.   Choosing the best cell from an MS depends on three factors: (1) the level of the signal received by the mobile station, (2) the maximum transmission power of the mobile station, and (3) two parameters p_1 and p_2 specified by the cell. This is called the C_1 criterion.

$$C_1 = A - \max(B, O)$$

$$A = \text{received level average} - p_1$$

$$B = p_2 - \text{maximum RF power of the MS}$$

$$p_1 = \text{a value between } -110 \text{ and } -48 \text{ dBm}$$

$$p_2 = \text{a value between } 13 \text{ and } 43 \text{ dBm}$$

Both values of p_1 and p_2 are broadcast from the cells.

$$\text{MS maximum power} = 29 \text{ to } 43 \text{ dBm}$$

The cell selection algorithm is as follows:

* A SIM must be inserted.
* The strongest C_1 is chosen by obtaining C_1 from candidate cells; the C_1 has to be higher than 0.
* All cells must not be barred from service.

4.2.8.3 Authentication. Authentication protects the network against unauthorized access.

First Phase. A PIN (personal identification number) code protects the SIM. The PIN is checked by the SIM locally, so the SIM is not sent out over the radio link.

Second Phase. The GSM network makes an inquiry by sending a random number (RAND). The 128-bit RAND is sent from the network to the MS, and mixes with the MS's secret parameter, K_i, in an A3 processing algorithm, which produces a 32-bit-long SRES (signed result) number. The SRES is then sent to the network from the MS for verification (see Fig. 4.30).

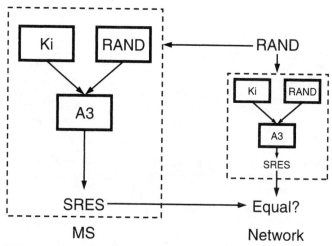

FIGURE 4.30 The authentication computation.

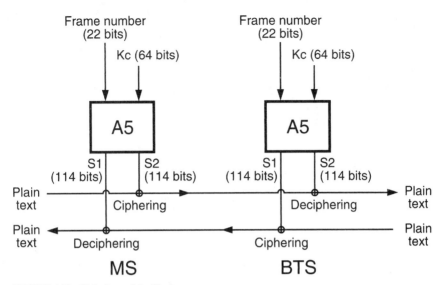

FIGURE 4.31   Ciphering and deciphering.

4.2.8.4 Encryption.   Encryption protects against unauthorized listening. The MS uses the RAND received from the network and mixes K_i through a different algorithm, called A5, and generates K_c (64 bits). The ciphering sequences are generated from the K_c (see Fig. 4.31). The frame number and K_c move to a ciphering algorithm, A5, and generate S_2 (114 bits), which plays an exclusive-or operation between the 114 bits of plain text and ciphering sequence S_2, as shown in Fig. 4.31.

4.2.8.5 User Identity Protection—Security Management.   SIM (MS side) and AUC (network side) are the repositories of the subscriber's key K_i. Key K_i never transmits over the air. Both sides perform A3 and A5 computations.

4.2.9 Communication Management

The CM layer provides telecommunications services such as speech, fax, and data to users via RR and MM layers, as shown in Fig. 4.32. The users include GSM calling party, GSM called party, and the users in both GSM calling and called parties. The management functions of CM are call control, service management, and short message service.

4.2.9.1 Call Control.   CC manages the most circuit-oriented services (speech, circuit data) through the MSC/VLR, GMSC, IWF, and HLR. CC functions set up calls (mobile-originating or base-originating), maintain calls, and release calls. To establish calls, the MS number has to be assigned. MS/ISDN is a mobile station ISDN number, part of the same numbering plan as ISDN numbers. Mobile station roaming number (MSRN) is the routing number, another number which can be a GSM subscriber or third party international mobile subscriber identity (IMSI) and provided by MS to access a foreign network. Figure 4.33 illustrates a domestic call through a GMSC. Figure 4.34 illustrates an international call.

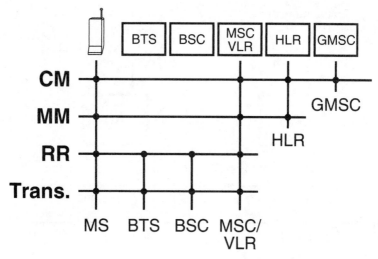

FIGURE 4.32   General protocol architecture of GSM.

4.2.9.2 Handover.   The GSM handover algorithm is not specified as a standard. It is a feature of mobile assistance handover (MAHO) and is carried out within the unit. The MS scans for another radio carrier under direction from a base station. It monitors those time slots which are not its own assigned time slots for receiving the signal. In this case, on the request of a base station, the signal strength of a specified radio carrier is measured in one time frame, and, on request, the measurements are forwarded to the base station to assist in the handover process. This is called MAHO. The MSC uses two sets of information to decide whether a handover should be initiated and which BTS is the candidate BTS for the handover. The two sets are (1) the signal strengths of the MS as received at the neighboring BTSs and (2) the signal strengths of neighboring BTSs received at the MS. The latter information is from MAHO.

4.2.9.3 Supplementary Services Management (SSM).   CC provides supplementary services such as call waiting, call forwarding, and automatic answering. SSM is a point-to-point

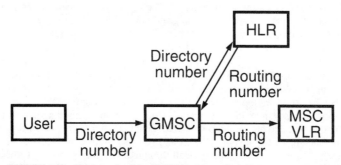

FIGURE 4.33   The key role of the GMSC for a domestic call.

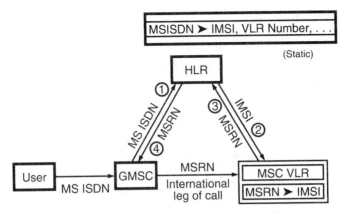

FIGURE 4.34 The provision of the MSRN for an international call.

management service. An SSM service center (SSM-SC) may connect to several GSM networks. SSM consists of two functions:

1. Mobile terminating short message
2. Mobile originating short message

4.2.9.4 Short Message Services. CC provides point-to-point short message services (SMS-PP). GSM is connected to the short message service center. The signaling transmission uses digital audio tones [digital tone multifrequency (DTMF)] to control voice mailbox, answering machine, conferencing, etc.

4.2.10 Network Management (NM)

An NM center oversees the following administration tasks:

1. Subscriber management—subscription administration
2. Billing and accounting
3. Maintenance
   a. Minimizing failures
   b. Monitoring operations and indicating by alarm improper operation situations
4. Subscriber administration tasks provide the selected approval code for ME (mobile equipment) within the international mobile equipment identity (IMEI) number. The code totals 15 digits and consists of type approval code (TAC) + final assembly code (FAC) + serial number which stores in EIR.
5. In the GSM telecommunication management network (TMN), all operation and maintenance machines compose a network which is linked to all traffic handling machines. The GSM Q3 is a network management protocol for operation systems functions and traffic handling machines. Two aspects of using GSM Q3 protocol are important. (a) Standardizing data communication protocols on the application level, such as file transfer. (b) Embodying the network modelling in GSM Q3 protocol.

4.2.11 Overview of GSM

4.2.11.1 Summary of Physical Layer Parameters

Transmission rate	260 kbps (over a 200 KHz carrier)
TDMA structure	8 time slots per radio carrier
Time slot	0.577 ms
No. of bits/Time slot	156
Frame interval	8 time slots = 4.615 ms
Radio carrier number	124 radio carriers (935–960 MHz downlink, 890–915 MHz uplink)
Modulation scheme	Gaussian minimum shift keying with $BT = 0.3$
Frequency hopping	Slow frequency hopping (217 hops/s)
Equalizer	Equalization up to 16-μs time dispersion

4.2.11.2 GSM's Strength. GSM is the first to apply the TDMA scheme developed for mobile radio systems. It has several distinguishing features:

1. Roaming in European countries
2. Connection to ISDN through RA box
3. Use of SIM cards
4. Control of transmission power
5. Frequency hopping
6. Discontinuous transmission
7. Mobile-assisted handover

4.3 NORTH AMERICAN TDMA

4.3.1 History

North American TDMA (NA-TDMA) is a digital cellular system[22–24] sometimes called American digital cellular (ADC) or digital AMPS (DAMPS), or North American digital cellular (NADC) or IS-54 system. This TDMA system was approved and design on it was started in 1987 by a group named TR45-3 after the industry debated between frequency-division multiple access and time-division multiple access. The reason those members voted for TDMA was due to the big influence of European GSM, which is the TDMA system. However, the requirements of designing a digital cellular system in Europe and in North America are different. In Europe, there is a virgin band (935–960 MHz downlink and 890–915 MHz uplink) for the digital cellular system. In North America, there is no new allocated band for the digital cellular system. The digital cellular system has to share the same allocated band with the analog system (AMPS, described in Chap. 3). Also, the digital and the analog systems have to be coexistent. In this circumstance, the low-risk approach is to use the same signal signature as the analog system (i.e., FDMA). Besides, because of the urgent need for large system capacity, the time for designing a new North American system had to be very short. The North American digital system was needed to be available in 1990, in only 3 years. To design a digital FDMA system would be a straightforward task. Since the analog system is a FDMA system, all the physical data gathered for the analog system in the past 20 years could be used for designing the FDMA digital system, and design time would be shortened. On the other hand, to design a TDMA digital system in the same band shared with an FDMA analog system, much more physical parameters would have to be developed and time would be needed to understand them. Without a good understanding of the limitation of coexistence between two different signal signatures, FDMA and TDMA, it would be very difficult to complete a digital system with good performance in a very short time. If GSM had taken 8 years to develop, NA-TDMA might also need as much time to be revised in order for it to be mature.

Because of the requirement of coexistence, a dual-mode mobile unit was decided on (i.e., the unit can work on both analog and digital systems). In a dual-mode mobile unit, the 21 call set-up channels for the analog system are available in the unit. Why not share the same call set-up channels (analog) for both the analog voice channels and digital voice channels? In this case, no additional spectrum is needed for the digital set-up channels.[25] The spectrum is saved for adding more digital voice. Furthermore, for the sake of speeding up the completion of North American digital systems, the call set-up channels of the digital system could be shared with the analog system to make the call processing the same between the two systems. Thus, the first phase of the NA-TDMA system could be completed earlier. IS-54 did not perform well. In 1994, an improved system design was made, and IS-54 was changed to IS-136.

4.3.2 NA-TDMA Architecture

The NA-TDMA architecture is similar to GSM architecture. The only difference is that in NA-TDMA, there is only one common interface, which is the radio interface as shown in Fig. 4.35. The NA-TDMA uses the intelligent network. All the components such as HLR, VLR, AUC, and EIR are the same as used in GSM (see Sec. 4.2). In developing the NA-TDMA system, there were two phases:

First phase: To commonly share the 21 set-up channels that are used for the analog system. The first-phase system is only for voice transmission. Both modes, AMPS and digital, are built in the same unit. The handoff procedure has to take care of the following four features:

1. AMPS cell to AMPS cell
2. TDMA cell to TDMA cell
3. AMPS cell to TDMA cell
4. TDMA cell to AMPS cell

Second phase: (1) generate new digital set-up channels (they were in the voice band) to access to TDMA voice channels so that a digital stand-alone unit can be provided and (2) specify a data-service signal protocol for transmitting data.

4.3.3 Transmission and Modulation

4.3.3.1 TDMA Structure (Digital Channels). In NA-TDMA, the set-up channels are analog channels shared with the AMPS system. One digital channel (a 30-kHz TDMA channel) contains 25 frames per second. Each frame is 40-ms long and has 6 time slots. Each time slot is 6.66-ms long. One frame contains 1944 bits (972 symbols), as shown in Fig. 4.36. Each slot contains 324 bits (162 symbols) and the duration between bits is 20.57 μs. Therefore, one radio channel is transmitted at 48.6 kbps but only 24,000 symbols per second over the radio path. Each frame consists of 6 time slots. The maximum effect on

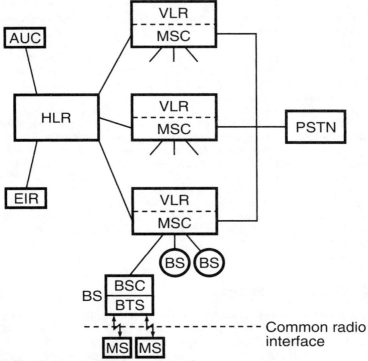

VLR: Visitor location registration
HLR: Home location registration
BS: Base station
AUC: Authentication center
EIR: Equipment identity register
BSC: Base station controller
BTS: Base transceiver station

FIGURE 4.35 NA-TDMA system architecture.

the signal for a forward time slot is one-half full symbol period and for a reverse time slot is 6 symbol periods (Fig. 4.36*b*).

Frame Length. There are two frame lengths, full rate and half rate. Each full-rate traffic channel shall use two equally spaced time slots of the frame. The overall length in each slot is shown in Fig. 4.36*b*.

Channel 1 uses time slots 1 and 4

Channel 2 uses time slots 2 and 5

Channel 3 uses time slots 3 and 6

Each half-rate traffic channel shall use one time slot of the frame:

Channel 1 uses time slot 1

Channel 2 uses time slot 2

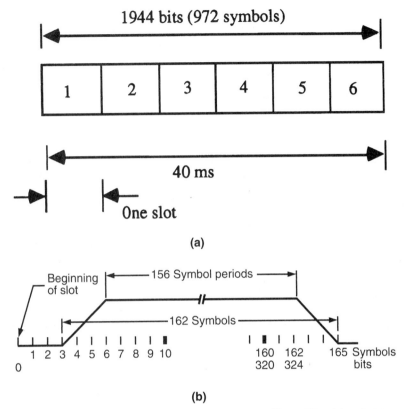

FIGURE 4.36   TDMA frame and slot: (*a*) TDMA frame structure, (*b*) overall length in each slot.

Channel 3 uses time slot 3
Channel 4 uses time slot 4
Channel 5 uses time slot 5
Channel 6 uses time slot 6

Frame Offset.   At the mobile station, the offset between the reverse and forward frame timing (without time advanced applied), is

$$\text{Forward frame} = \text{reverse frame} + (1 \text{ time slot} + 44 \text{ symbols})$$

$$= \text{reverse frame} + 206 \text{ symbols}$$

The time slot (TS) 1 of frame N (in forward link) occurs 206 symbol periods after TS 1 of frame N in the reverse link.

Modulation Timing

Modulation timing within a forward time slot. The first modulated symbol (the first symbol of the sync word) used by the mobile unit shall have maximum effect on the

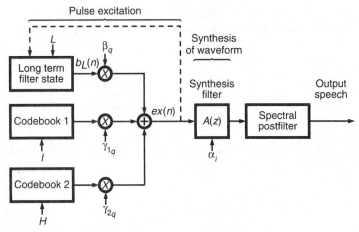

FIGURE 4.37   VSELP speech decoder.

signal (156 symbols) transmitted from the base antenna, one-half symbol (1 bit) period after beginning the time slot.

Modulation timing within a reverse time slot. The first modulated symbol has a maximum effect on the signal transmitted at the mobile unit 6 symbol periods after the beginning of the reverse time slot.

Power Level. In the AMPS system, there are eight power levels. In TDMA there are an additional three levels. Therefore, in total, TDMA has 11 power levels, as shown in Table 4.2. In the carrier-off condition, the output power of the transmitting antenna must fall to -60 dBm within 2 ms. In the carrier-on condition, the output power of the transmitting antenna must come to within 3 dB of the specified level.

TABLE 4.2   Mobile Station Nominal Power Level

Mobile Station Power Level (PL)	Mobile Attenuation Code (MAC)	Nominal Effective Radiated Power, dBW, for Mobile Station Power Class							
		I	II	III	IV	V	VI	VII	VIII
0	000	6	2	-2	-2	*	*	*	*
1	001	2	2	-2	-2	*	*	*	*
2	010	-2	-2	-2	-2	*	*	*	*
3	011	-6	-6	-6	-6	*	*	*	*
4	100	-10	-10	-10	-10	*	*	*	*
5	101	-14	-14	-14	-14	*	*	*	*
6	110	-18	-18	-18	-18	*	*	*	*
7	111	-22	-22	-22	-22	*	*	*	*
Dual-mode only									
8					-26 ± 3 dB	*	*	*	*
9					-30 ± 6 dB	*	*	*	*
10					-34 ± 9 dB	*	*	*	*

4.3.3.2   Speech Coding (Full Rate).   The NA-TDMA speech coding is a class of speech coding known as code excited linear predictive (CELP) coding. The code is called vector-sum excited linear predictive (VSELP) coding. It uses a codebook to vector-quantize the excitation (residual) signal such that the computation required for the codebook search process at the sender can be significantly reduced. The speech coder sampling rate is 7950 bps. Speech is broken into frames; each frame is 20-ms long and contains 160 symbols. Each frame is further divided into subframes 40 samples (5 ms) long. At the mobile station, the analog speech is converted to uniform pulse-code modulation (PCM) format. The speech coder is preceded by the following voice processing stages: (1) level adjustment, (2) bandpass filter, and (3) analog-to-digital conversion. The VSELP speech decoder is shown in Figure 4.37. The first part is the generation of pulse excitation and the second part is the speech waveform synthesis. Adding the two parts results in quality speech. All the values of parameters H, I, γ, β, L, $\alpha_1 \ldots \alpha_{10}$ for a 20-ms frame of speech are received with a low rate of transmission. Then those parameters are inserted into proper places in the speech decoder, and the speech is recovered at the receiving end.

The delays due to the air interface between the base station and the mobile station may exceed 100 ms, and echo control measures therefore necessary. In a half-rate speech coder, the speech frame of 20 msec may contain 80 symbols.

4.3.3.3   Modulation.   NA-TDMA uses a constant envelope modulation with $\pi/4$-shifted differential quadrature phase shift keying (DQPSK). The modulation scheme uses the phase constellation shown in Fig. 4.38. The rotation of $\pi/4$ occurs alternately at the odd state $\oplus$ and even state $\otimes$. The Gray code is used in the mapping. Every signal phase represents a di-bit symbol as shown in Fig. 4.38. Any two adjacent signal phases differ only in a single bit. The information is encoded differentially; symbols do not correspond to absolute phases, but to the phase difference between two adjacent symbols. A binary data stream

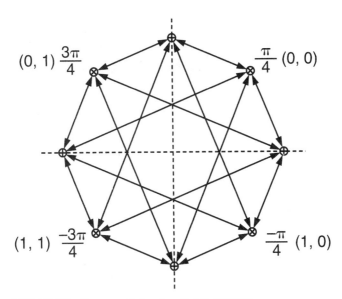

FIGURE 4.38   Phase constellation of a $\pi/4$-shifted DQPSK.

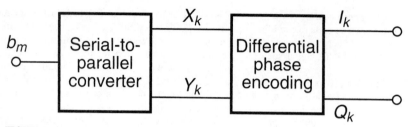

FIGURE 4.39　A binary data stream conversion.

b_m is separated into two streams: X_k is the even-numbered bit stream, and Y_k is the odd-numbered bit stream (Fig. 4.39). The streams $\{X_k\}$ and $\{Y_k\}$ are encoded onto $\{I_k\}$ and $\{Q_k\}$ by:

$$I_k = I_{k-1} \cos [\Delta\phi(X_k, Y_k)] - Q_{k-1} \sin [\Delta\phi(X_k, Y_k)] \tag{4.3-1}$$

$$Q_k = I_{k-1} \sin [\Delta\phi(X_k, Y_k)] + Q_{k-1} \cos [\Delta\phi(X_k, Y_k)] \tag{4.3-2}$$

where I_{k-1}, Q_{k-1} are the amplitudes at the previous pulse time. The phase change $\Delta\phi$ is determined by the following table:

X_k	Y_k	$\Delta\phi$ (Even State)	$\Delta\phi$ (Odd State)
1	1	$-3\pi/4$	π
0	1	$3\pi/4$	$\pi/2$
0	0	$\pi/4$	0
1	0	$-\pi/4$	$-\pi/2$

The signals I_k and Q_k at the output of the differential phase encoding device can take one of the four values $0, \pm 1, 1/\sqrt{2}$.

The Baseband Filters.　The baseband filter shall have (1) linear phase and (2) square-root-raised cosine frequency response as shown in Fig. 4.40 where T is the period that equals 41.1 μs. The QPSK modulation with two components I_k and Q_k is differentially encoded as shown in Fig. 4.39.

The Transmitted Signal.　The resultant transmitted signal $S(t)$ is given by:

$$S(t) = \sum_n g(t - nT) \cos\phi_n \cdot \cos w_c t + \sum_n g(t - nt) \sin\phi_n(t) \sin w_c t \tag{4.3-3}$$

where $g(t)$ is the pulse shaping with a time response of $H(f)$:

$$g(t) = \frac{1}{2\pi} \int_{-\infty}^{\infty} H(f) e^{jw_c t} dt \tag{4.3-4}$$

and w_c is the radian carrier frequency. ϕ_n is from the differential encoding

$$\phi_n = \phi_{n-1} + \Delta\phi_n \tag{4.3-5}$$

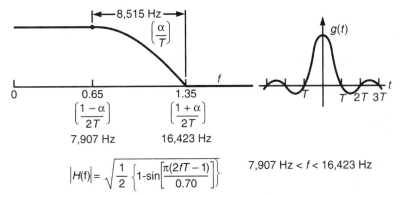

$$|H(f)| = \sqrt{\frac{1}{2}\left\{1\text{-sin}\left[\frac{\pi(2fT-1)}{0.70}\right]\right\}}$$

$$7{,}907 \text{ Hz} < f < 16{,}423 \text{ Hz}$$

FIGURE 4.40　Baseband filter characteristics.

4.3.4　Time Alignment and Limitation of Emission

4.3.4.1　Time Alignment.　It is necessary to control the TDMA time slot burst (advancing or retarding) transmission from the mobile unit, so that it arrives at the base station receiver in the proper time relationship with respect to other time slot burst transmissions. An error in time alignment causes errors in two signals in the overlap at the head or tail of a time slot.

System Access.　The mobile station receives an initial traffic channel designation (ITCD) message (order code 01110), which is contained in word 2 (extended address word), then moves to a traffic channel. The mobile station first synchronizes to the forward traffic channel. The time alignment is sent by a physical layer control message over a shortened burst transmission. The mobile station, while operating on a digital traffic channel, is transmitting over a slot interval 324 bits long at certain times. The mobile station continues to transmit a shortened burst at the standard offset reference position until a time alignment message is received from the base station. The mobile station adjusts its transmission time during the next available slot.

Time Alignment in Handoff Message.　A mobile handoff message contains estimated time alignment information. Analog-to-digital and digital-to-digital handoff messages contain a shortened burst indicator (SBI) field:

SBI = 00　A handoff to a small-diameter cell

SBI = 01　A handoff from sector to sector

SBI = 10　A handoff to a large-diameter cell.

The shortest burst format

3 symb.　　　　　　　　　　　　　　　　　　　　22 symb.

The shortened burst contains:

G1　3 symbol length guard time

R　3 symbol length ramp time

S   14 symbol length sync work

D   6 symbol length coded digital verification color code (CDVCC) (on reverse channel)

G2   22 symbol length guard time

The fields V, W, X, Y consist of

V = 4 zero bits (2 symbols)

W = 8 zero bits (4 symbols)

X = 12 zeros (6 symbols)

Y = 16 zeros (8 symbols)

In the shortened burst format, the symbol interval between any two sync words (total 6 sync words) is a unique interval. After detection of any two or more sync words, the timing alignment is determined at the base station.

4.3.4.2 Limitations on Emissions from Digital Transmission. The total emission power is shown in Fig. 4.41. This limitation is for the suppression of the energy within the cellular band. In addition, the transmitter emissions in each 30-kHz band anywhere in the mobile station receive band must not exceed −80 dBm at the transmit antenna connector.

4.3.5 Error Corrections

4.3.5.1 Speech Data Classes. Channel error correcting for the speech code employs three mechanisms:

1. A rate one-half convolutional code to protect the more vulnerable bits of the speech code.

2. Interleaving the transmitted data for each speech coder frame over two time slots to reduce the burst error due to Rayleigh fading.

3. Use of a cyclic redundancy check (CRC). After the error correction is applied at the receiver, these CRC bits are checked to see if most perceptually significant bits were received properly.

The 159-bit speech coder frame is separated into two classes:

Class 1   77 bits

Class 2   82 bits

Class 1 bits are the important bits to which the convolutional coding is applied. Among the 77 bits, there are 12 most perceptually significant bits in which a 7-bit CRC is used for error detection purposes. Class 2 bits are unimportant bits and are transmitted without any error protection.

4.3.5.2 Cyclic Redundancy Check. The 12 most perceptually significant bits of the 77 bits are coded in CRC. The generator polynomial is

$$g(X) = 1 + X + X^2 + X^4 + X^5 + X^7 \qquad (4.3\text{-}6)$$

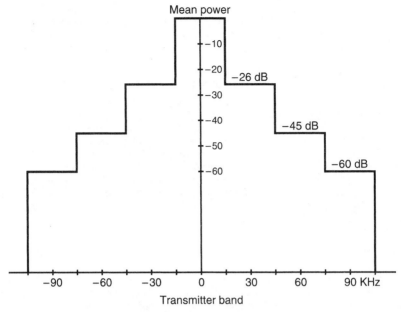

FIGURE 4.41 Suppression inside cellular band.

A 7-bit CRC is used for error detection if one or more of the 12 significant bits are in error. The 12 most significant bits form an input polynomial:

$$a(X) = \sum_{k=0}^{11} B_k X^k \qquad (4.3\text{-}7)$$

The polynomial $b(X)$ is the remainder of the division of $a(x)$ and $g(x)$ obtained from

$$\frac{a(X)X^7}{g(X)} = q(X) + \frac{b(X)}{g(X)} \qquad (4.3\text{-}8)$$

where $q(X)$ is the quotient of the division which is discarded.
The remainder $b(X)$ can be generated from Eq. (4.3-6) and Eq. (4.3-7)

$$b(X) = \sum_{k=1}^{7} C_k X^{k-1} \qquad (4.3\text{-}9)$$

The input 77 bits $B_1 \cdots B_{77}$ (including 12 significant bits) adding $C_1 \cdots C_7$ and 5 zero bits become 89 inportant bits.

0-3	4 - 80	81 - 82	84 - 88
4 bits CRC	77 bits	3 bits CRC	5 bits (five 0's) tail bits

A cyclic redundancy check is performed at the receiving end. After decoding of the class 1 bits, the received CRC $b'(x)$ bits are checked to determine if any errors have been detected. The process of checking the error in CRC uses the received 12 most perceptually significant bits $a'(x)$ in each frame divided by the generator polynomial in Eq. (4.3-6):

$$\frac{a'(X) \cdot X^7}{g(X)} = q'(X) + \frac{b''(X)}{g(X)} \qquad (4.3\text{-}10)$$

The received CRC $b'(x)$ are compared with the CRC bits $b''(x)$ generated by Eq. (4.3-10); if $b'(x) \neq b''(x)$, an error has occurred. The causes of error are (1) the data was corrupted by channel errors or (2) an FACCH message was transmitted in place of the speech data. As a result, the speech quality is degraded. A bad frame masking strategy is taking place. There are six states. The state 0 means no error is detected. When each successive speech frame is found to be in error, the state machine moves to the next higher state. Moving to a higher state means more repeats. If two successive frames occur with no detected errors, the state machine is returned to state 0.

4.3.6   Interleaving and Coding

4.3.6.1   Convolutional Encoding.   The 89 important bits are input to convolutional coder and 176 bits are at the output of the coder. Then adding 82 unimportant bits become 260 bits total for a 20 ms speech frame. Convolutional encoding uses a code rate of 1/2 and memory order 5. The five memory elements generate 32 states in this code. Since the code is 1/2 rate, two outputs alternately come out and are in a sequential order. CC0 is the convolutional code at one output and the other CC1 is the other output.

4.3.6.2   Interleaving and Deinterleaving.   The encoded speech after the convolutional code is interleaved over two time slots (Fig. 4.42). Each time slot contains two frames. The encoded speech is placed into a rectangular interleaving array columnwise. The two encoded speech frames are referred to as X and Y.

```
OX    26X  ···  234X
1Y    27Y       235Y
2X
3Y

24X   50X       258X
25Y   51Y       259Y
```

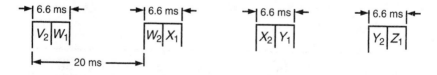

$X = X_1 + X_2$ encoded speech frame

FIGURE 4.42   Interleaving slots arrangement.

The speech code consists of 88 class 1 bits (after CRC coding) and 80 class 2 bits. The class 2 bits are intermixed with the convolutionally coded class 1 bits. The bits in the above array are then transmitted row-wise. The place of the coded class 1 bits and class 2 bits are in a certain mixed order.

Deinterleaving. At the receiving end, each time slot contains the interleaved data from two speech coder frames, X_1 and X_2, which are 20 ms apart. The received data are placed row-wise into a 26 × 10 deinterleaving array. Once the data from the two time slots are used to fill the deinterleaving array, all the data for frames X are available and can be decoded. After deinterleaving, one entire speech coder frame is available.

Delay Interval Requirement. The mobile station and the base station shall have a delay interval compensation of up to one symbol length.

4.3.7 SCM and SID

Station class mark (SCM) must be stored in a mobile station. It formerly used 4 bits for identifying the maximum powers of three different kinds of mobile stations. Now SCM uses 5 bits and can identify eight different power levels.

Power Class	Max. Power, dBm	Min. Power, dBm	Number of Power Levels	SCM	Transmission	SCM	Bandwidth	SCM
I	6	−22	0–7	0XX00	Continuous	XX0XX	20 MHz	X0XXX
II	2	−22	1–7	0XX01	Discontinuous	XX1XX	25 MHz	X1XXX
III	−2	−22	2–7	0XX10				
IV	−2	−34 ± 9 dB	2–10	0XX11				
V				1XX00				
VI				1XX01				
VII				1XX10				
VIII				1XX11				

Home system identification (SID) is a 15-bit system identification indicator

14	13 12	0
	2 bits	System number

00	USA
01	Other countries
10	Canada
11	Mexico

The first two bits indicate the country of origin:

00   United States
01   Other countries
10   Canada
11   Mexico

4.3.8   NA-TDMA Channels

In NA-TDMA, there are no common channels such as those used in GSM. The digital call set-up uses the 21 set-up channels which are shared with the analog system.

4.3.8.1   Supervision of the Digital Voice Channel.   The supervision channels in NADC are similar to those in GSM:

- *Fast associated control channel.* FACCH is a blank and burst channel equivalent to a signaling channel for the transmission of control and supervision messages between the base station and the mobile station. It consists of 260 bits. Mostly FACCH is used for handoff messages.
- *Slot associated control channel.* SACCH is a signaling channel including twelve code bits present in every time slot transmitted over the traffic channel whether these contain voice or FACCH information.

4.3.8.2   Mobile-Assisted Handoffs (MAHO).   The mobile station performs signal quality measurements on two types of channels:

1. Measures the RSSI (received signal strength indicator) and the BER (bit error rate) information of the current forward traffic channel during a call.
2. Measures the RSSI of any RF channel which is identified from the measurement order message from the base station.

MAHO consists of three messages:

1. Start measurement order
   - Measurement order message—sent from the base station to the mobile station.
   - Measurement order acknowledge message—sent from the mobile station to the base station.
2. Stop measurement order
   - Stop measurement order—sent from the base station to the mobile station.
   - Mobile acknowledge—sent from the mobile station to the base station.
3. Channel quality message (mobile to base only)

The mobile transmits the signal quality information over either the SACCH or FACCH. In the case of discontinuous transmission (DTX):

- Whenever the mobile is in the DTX high state, the mobile transmits channel quality information over the SACCH
- When the mobile is in the DTX low state, the mobile transmits the channel quality information over the FACCH

4.3.8.3   Handoff Action.   When a handoff order is received, the mobile station is at DTX high state and stays at that state. If the mobile station is at DTX low state it must enter the DTX high state and wait for 200 ms before taking the handoff action. Handoff to a digital traffic channel is described as follows:

1. Turn on signaling tone for 50 ms, turn off signaling tone, turn off transmitter which was operating on the old frequency.
2. Adjust power, tune to new channel, set stored DVCCs to the DVCC field of the received message.
3. Set the transmitter and receiver to digital mode, set the transmit and receive rate based on the message-type field.
4. Set time slot based on the message-type field.
5. Set the time alignment offset to the value based on the TA field.
6. Once the transmitter is synchronized, enter the conversation task of the digital traffic channel.

4.3.9   Discontinuous Transmission on a Digital Traffic Channel

In DTX, certain mobile stations can switch autonomously between two transmitter power-level states: DTX high and DTX low. In the DTX high state, the power level of transmitter at the mobile station is indicated by the most recent power-controlling order. In this state, the CDVCC (coded digital verification color code) is sent at all times. CDVCC is used to distinguish the current traffic channel from traffic co-channels. Decoding CDVCC (12, 8) becomes $DVCC_r$. $DVCC_r$ is received and checked with DVCCs for identification. There are 255 codes (2^8, but 0 is not used). In the DTX low state, the transmitter remains off and CDVCC is not sent except for the transmission of FACCH messages. All the SACCH messages will be sent as a FACCH message. After sending all the messages, the transmitter will return to the off state.

4.3.10   Authentication

A secret number PIN (personal identification number) is assigned to each subscriber. The mobile station, on receipt of a random challenge global action message, updates its internal stored RAND variable used as input to the authentication algorithm AUTH1. The mobile uses its PIN, its ESN and the MIN to compute a response to RAND in accordance with AUTH1. The mobile then responds to the page by transmitting its MIN, the output of AUTH1, RANDC (random confirmation), and COUNT (call history parameter). See also Sec. 4.4.5 for similarity.

4.3.11   Signaling Format

4.3.11.1   Signaling Format in Different Channels.   A reverse digital traffic channel (RDTC) is used to transport user information and signaling. A forward digital traffic channel (FDTC) has same format as the RDTC (reverse digital traffic channel). Two control channels are used: the FACCH is a blank and burst channel, the SACCH is a continuous channel, and interleaving is on the SACCH. The signaling formats of these two channels are shown in Fig. 4.43.

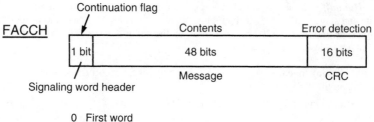

FACCH

0 First word
1 Subsequent word

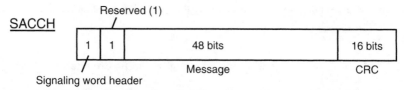

SACCH

FIGURE 4.43   Signaling formats of FACCH and SACCH.

Interleaving on the FACCH bits from 0 to 259 is

Row Number	FACCH Bits Interleaving									
0	215	256	223	258	230	219	257	227	259	189
1	0	25	50	75	231	89	114	139	164	190
2	1	26	51	76	232	90	115	140	165	191
⋮	⋮									
14	13	38	63	88	244	102	127	152	177	203
15	14	39	64	216	245	103	128	153	178	204
⋮	⋮									
25	24	49	74	229	255	113	138	163	118	214

The Y row (odd) of this frame combines alternately with the X row (even) of the previous frame to form a FACCH block. In SACCH code, the output of the convolutional coder is diagonally interleaved as the 12 coded bits are transmitted over 12 time slots.

4.3.11.2   Message Structure.   All messages contain:

1. An application message header
2. Mandatory fixed parameters
3. Mandatory variable parameters
4. Remaining length
5. Optional variable parameters

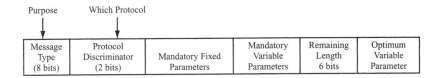

Message Type (8 bits)	Protocol Discriminator (2 bits)	Mandatory Fixed Parameters	Mandatory Variable Parameters	Remaining Length 6 bits	Optimum Variable Parameter

Purpose ↓   Which Protocol ↓

4.3.12   Word Format

The same word format is used for FACCH and SACCH shown in Section 4.3.11.

4.3.13   Enhanced NA-TDMA (IS-136)

The IS-136 is modified from IS-54 by creating digital control channels. Sometimes it is also called D-AMPS, as it was designed to operate alongside the AMPS system.

A. The Network Architecture
The architecture is similar to GSM as shown in Fig. 4.44.

B. Physical Layer (Layer 1)

  1. The transmission parameters

  - Operates in 800/1900 MHz band
  - Channel bandwidth 30 kHz
  - TDMA frame 40 ms in 6 time slots

  2. Channel data rates

  - 1st time slot: a half rate channel
  - 2nd and 5th time slots: a full rate channel
  - 2nd, 3rd, 5th, 6th time slots: a double rate channel

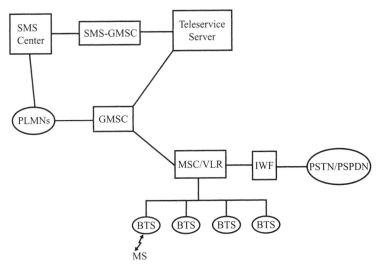

FIGURE 4.44   The IS-136 network architecture.

C. Data Link Layer (Layer 2)

This layer provides addressing, error detection, media access control (MAC), frame delimiting and flow control.

D. Network Layer (Layer 3)

This layer provides establishing, maintaining, and terminating connections.

E. Channel Types

1. Digital Control Channel (DCCH)

- Conveys setup information
- Provides signaling and message services
- Occupies a full rate digital channel (2 time slots)
- Divides into four logical channels

    a. SPACH (SMS Point-to-Point, Paging, Access Response Channel)

    b. BCCH (Broadcast Control Channel)

    c. SCF (Shared Channel Feedback)

    d. RACH (Random Access Control Channel)

2. Digital Traffic Channel (DTC)

- Two basic types: half-rate and full-rate channels
- Two ways of transferring control information

    in-band signaling

    out-of-band signaling using SACCH (slow associated control channel)

F. Data services: two types of services

1. Teleservices

- Small amount of data
- SMS through the DCCH
- Operator services

2. Analog circuit switched data services

- It can provide 9.6 kbps data rate

3. Digital circuit switched data services (through IWF)

- It can provide three data rates, 9.6, 19.2, and 28.8 kbps

4. Maximum rate

- It can use three channels to provide 28.8 kbps

G. GSM's enhancements are adopted in IS-136

4.4 CDMA

CDMA development[26-30] started in early 1989 after the NA-TDMA standard (IS-54) was established. A CDMA demonstration to test its feasibility for digital cellular systems was held in November 1989. The CDMA "Mobile Station-Base Station Compatibility Standard for Dual Mode Wideband Spread Spectrum Cellular System" was issued as IS-95 (PN-3118, Dec. 9, 1992). CDMA uses the idea of tolerating inteterference by spread-spectrum modulation. The power control scheme in a CDMA system is a requirement for digital cellular application. However, it was a challenging task and has been solved. Before describing the structure of the system, we list the key terms of CDMA systems.

4.4.1 Terms of CDMA Systems

Active set: The set of pilots associated with the CDMA channels containing forward traffic channels assigned to a particular mobile station (MS).

CDMA channel number: An 11-bit number corresponding to the center of the CDMA frequency assignment.

Code channel: A subchannel of a forward CDMA channel. A forward CDMA channel contains 64 code channels. Certain code channels are assigned to different logic channels.

Code channel zero: Pilot channel.

Code channels 1 through 7: Either paging channels or traffic channels.

Code channel 32: A sync channel or a traffic channel.

The remaining code channels are traffic channels.

Code symbol: The output of an error-correcting encoder.

Dim-and-burst: A frame in which the primary traffic is multiplexed with either secondary traffic or signal traffic. It is equivalent to the blank-and-burst function in AMPS.

Forward CDMA channel: Contains one or more code channels.

Frame: A basic timing interval in the system. For the access channel, paging channel, and traffic channel, a frame is 20-ms long. For the sync channel, a frame is 26.666-ms long.

Frame offset: A time skewing of traffic channel frames from system time in integer multiples of 1.25 ms. The maximum frame offset is 18.75 ms.

GPS (Global Position System): System used for providing location and time information to the CDMA system.

Handoff (HO): The act of transferring communication with a mobile station from one base station to another.

Hard HO: Occurs when (1) the MS is transferred between disjoint active sets, (2) the CDMA frequency assignment changes, (3) the frame offset changes, and (4) the MS is directed from a CDMA traffic channel to an analog voice channel but not vice versa.

Soft HO: HO from CDMA cell to CDMA cell at the same CDMA frequency.

Idle HO: Occurs when the paging channel is transferred from one base station (BS) to another.

Layering: A method of organization for communication protocols. A layer is defined in terms of its communication protocol to a peer layer.

Layer 1: Physical layer presents a frame by the multiplex sublayer and transforms it into an over-the-air waveform.

Layer 2: Provides for the correct transmission and reception of signaling messages.

Layer 3: Provides the control of the cellular telephone system. The signaling messages orginate and terminate at layer 3.

Long code: A PN (pseudonoise) sequence with period $2^{42}-1$ using a tapped n-bit shift register.

Modulation symbol: The output of the data modulator before spreading. There are 64 modulation symbols on the reverse traffic channel, 64-ary orthogonal modulation is used, and six code symbols are associated with one modulation symbol. On the forward traffic channel, each code symbol (data rate is 9600 bps) or each repeated code symbol (data rate is less than 9600 bps) is 1 modulation symbol.

$$\text{Reverse}: \overbrace{110101}^{53}\ \overbrace{101110}^{48} \longrightarrow \text{(Walsh function 53)}^{64\,\text{bits}}\ \text{(Walsh function 48)}^{64\,\text{bits}}$$

$$6 \text{ code symbols} \longrightarrow 1 \text{modulation symbol}$$

Forward: 1 code symbol $=$ 1 modulation symbol

Multiplex option: The ability of the multiplex sublayer and lower layers to be tailored to provide special capabilities. A multiplex option defines the frame format and the rate decision rules.

Multiplex sublayer: One of the conceptual layers of the system that multiplexes and demultiplexes primary traffic, secondary traffic, and signaling traffic.

Nonslotted mode: An operating mode of an MS in which the MS continuously monitors the paging channel.

Null traffic data: A frame of sixteen 1's followed by eight 0's sent at the 1200 bps rate. Null traffic channel data serve to maintain the connectivity between MS and BS when no service is active and no signaling message is being sent.

Paging channel: A code channel in a forward CDMA channel used for transmission of (1) control information and (2) pages from BS to MS. The paging channel slot has a 200-ms interval.

Power control bit: A bit sent in every 1.25 ms interval on the forward traffic channel to the MS that increases or decreases its transmit power.

Primary CDMA channel: A preassigned frequency used by the mobile station for initial acquisition.

Primary paging channel: The default code channel (code channel 1) assigned for paging.

Primary traffic: The main traffic stream between MS and BS on the traffic channel.

Reverse traffic channel: Used to transport user and signaling traffic from a single MS to one or more BSs.

Shared secret data (SSD): A 128-bit pattern stored in the MS.

SSD is a concatenation of two 64-bit subsets.

SSD-A is used to support the authentication.

SSD-B serves as one of the inputs to generate the encryption mask and private long code.

Secondary CDMA channel: A preassigned frequency (one of two) used by the mobile station for initial acquisition.

Secondary traffic: An additional traffic stream carried between the MS and the BS on the traffic channel.

Slotted mode: An operation mode of MS in which the MS monitors only selected slots on the paging channel.

Sync channel: Code channel 32 in the forward CDMA channel which transports the synchronization message to the MS.

Pilot channel: An unmodulated, direct-sequence (DS) signal transmitted continuously by each CDMA BS. The pilot channel allows a mobile station to acquire the timing of the forward CDMA channel, provides a phase reference for coherent demodulation, and provides a means for signal strength comparisons between base stations for determining when to hand off.

System time: The time reference used by the system. System time is synchronous to universal time coordination (UTC) time and uses the same time origin as GPS time. All BSs use the same system time. MSs use the same system time, offset by the propagation delay from the BS to the MS.

Time reference: A reference established by the MS that is synchronous with the earliest arriving multipath component that is used for demodulation. The time reference establishes transmit time and the location of zero in PN space.

Walsh chip: The shortest identifiable component of a 64-walsh function. On the forward CDMA channel, one chip equals 1/1.2288 MHz or 813.802 ns. On the reverse CDMA channel, one chip equals 4/1.2288 MHz or 3255 ns.

4.4.2 Output Power Limits and Control

4.4.2.1 Output Power. The mean output power of the mobile station shall be less than −50 dBm/1.23 MHz (−111 dBm/Hz) for all frequencies within ±615 kHz of the center frequency.

4.4.2.2 Gated Output Power. The MS shall transmit at nominal controlled levels during gated-on periods. A typical output power in a gated-on period is shown in Figure 4.45. The transmitter noise floor should be less than −60 dBm/1.23 MHz.

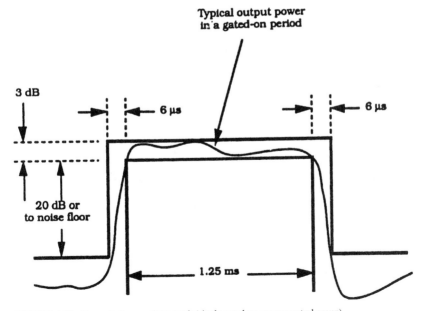

FIGURE 4.45   Transmission envelope mask (single gated-on power control group).

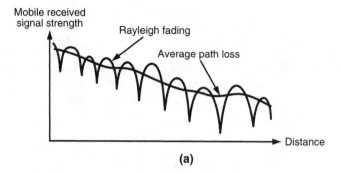

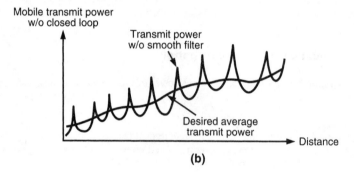

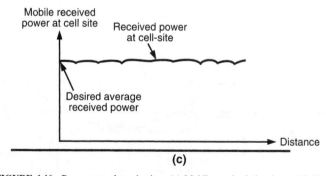

FIGURE 4.46 Power control mechanism. (*a*) Mobile received signal strength in log-normal shadowing and Rayleigh fading; (*b*) transmit power without closed-loop control and without nonlinear filtering; (*c*) mobile power received at cell site.

4.4.2.3 Controlled Output Power. Implementing CDMA power control is a must in the cellular CDMA system for the reverse link transmission in order to eliminate the near-far interference. If all the mobile transmitters within a cell site's area of coverage are so controlled, then the total signal power received at the cell site from all mobiles will be equal to the nominal received power times the number of mobiles.

4.4.2.4 CDMA Reverse-Link Open-Loop Power Control. The mobile station receives a signal suffering both the log-normal and Rayleigh fadings from the forward link, as shown in Fig. 4.46a. The average path loss is obtained as shown in the figure. If the transmitting and receiving ends are sharing the same frequency channel, then reversing the received signal strength as shown in Fig. 4.46b, indicated as the transmit power without smoothing filter, would eliminate the power variation at the cell site. Because CDMA uses duplexing channels, the Rayleigh fading on the forward channel and the reverse channel are not the same. Therefore, the desired average transmit power is sent back on the reverse channel.

At the cell site, the available information on instantaneous value versus the expected value of frame error rate (FER) of the received signal is examined to determine whether to command a particular mobile to increase or decrease its transmit power. This mechanism is called CDMA closed-loop power control. The mobile power received at a cell site after close-loop control is shown in Fig. 4.46c.

In transmission mode, the MS has two independent means for output power adjustment:

1. Open-loop output power

- The mobile station shall transmit the first probe on the access channel:

$$\overline{P_A} = \text{mean output power, dBm} = - \text{ mean input power, dBm}$$

$$- 73 + \text{NOMPWR, dB} + \text{INITPWR, dB}$$

where NOMPWR = the correction of received power at the base station and INITPWP = adjustment of the received power less than the required signal power. When INITPWR = 0, $\overline{P_A} = \pm 6$ dB.

- For initial transmission on the reverse channel,

$$\overline{P_I} = \text{mean output power, dBm} = \overline{P_A}$$

$$+ \text{ the sum of all access probe correction, dBm}$$

- For normal reverse traffic channel,

$$\overline{P_R} = \text{mean output power, dBm} = \overline{P_I}$$

$$+ \text{ the sum of all closed-loop power control correction, dB}$$

- For example, without any correction or adjustment,

$$\text{Mean output power} = - \text{ mean input power} - 73$$

$$= - (-90 \text{ dBm}) - 73$$

$$= + 17 \text{ dBm}$$

2. Closed-loop output power (involving both the mobile station and base station). The mobile station shall adjust its mean output power level in response to each valid power control bit received on the forward traffic channel. The change in mean output power per single power control bit shall be 1 dB nominal, within ±0.5 dB of the nominal change.

4.4.3 Modulation Characteristics

4.4.3.1 Reverse CDMA Channel Signals. The reverse CDMA channel is composed of access channels and reverse traffic channels. Since the MS does not establish a system time as at the BS, the reverse channel signal received at the BS cannot use coherent detection. Thus the modulation characteristics for the forward channel and reverse channel are different. The modulation of the reverse channel is 64-ary orthogonal modulation at a data rate of 9600, 4800, 2400, or 1200 bps, as shown in Fig. 4.47 at point A. The actual burst transmission rate is fixed at 28,800 code symbols per second. This results in a fixed Walsh chip rate of 307.2 thousand chips per second (kcps). Each Walsh chip is spread by four PN chips. The rate of the spreading PN sequence is fixed at 1.2288 million chips per second (Mcps). The reverse traffic channel modulation parameters and the access channel modulation parameters are listed in Tables 4.3 and 4.4, respectively.

Convolutional Encoding. At point B in Fig. 4.47, with a $K = 9$ (9 shift registers) and rate 1/3 convolutional encoder:

1. On the access channel, each code symbol has a fixed data rate of 4800 bps, and each symbol repeats one time consecutively.

2. On the reverse traffic channel, the full data rate is 9600 kbps. For the data rate of 4800 kbps, each symbol repeats one time consecutively. For the data rate of 2400 kbps, each symbol repeats three times consecutively. For the data rate of 1200 kbps, each symbol repeats seven times consecutively.

Interleaving. At point C in Fig. 4.47, the interleaving algorithm will form an array with 32 rows and 18 columns. At 9600 kbps, the interleaver forms a 32 × 18 matrix as in Table 4.5.

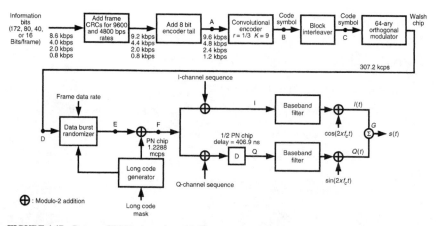

FIGURE 4.47 Reverse CDMA channel modulation process.

TABLE 4.3 Reverse Traffic Channel Modulation Parameters

Parameter	Date Rate, bps				Units
	9600	4800	2400	1200	
PN chip rate	1.2288	1.2288	1.2288	1.2288	Mcps
Code rate	1/3	1/3	1/3	1/3	bits/code symbol
Transmit duty cycle	100.0	50.0	25.0	12.5	%
Code symbol rate	28,800	28,800	28,800	28,800	sps
Modulation	6	6	6	6	code symbol/mod symbol
Modulation symbol rate	4800	4800	4800	4800	sps
Walsh chip rate	307.20	307.20	307.20	307.20	kcps
Mod. symbol duration	208.33	208.33	208.33	208.33	μs
PN chips/code symbol	42.67	42.67	42.67	42.67	PN chip/code symbol
PN chips/mod. symbol	256	256	256	256	PN chip/mod symbol
PN chips/Walsh chip	4	4	4	4	PN chips/Walsh chip

At 9600 bps, the transmission sequence is to send row by row in a sequence order up to row 32. At 4800 bps, the transmission sequence is to send by the unique order of rows as follows:

Row Number$\rightarrow$

1 3 2 4 5 7 6 8 9 11 10 12 13 15 14 16 17 19 18 20 21 23 22 24 25 27 26 28 29 31 30 32

Expressed in a formula, the transmission sequence is

$$J, J + 2, J + 1, J + 3$$

for $J = 1 + 4i$ and $i = 0, 1, 2, 3, \ldots, (32 / 4 - 1)$.
At 2400 bps, the transmission sequence is by a unique order of rows as follows:

$$J, J + 4, J + 1, J + 5, J + 2, J + 6, J + 3, J + 7$$

for $J = 1 + 8i$ and $i = 0, 1, 2 \ldots, (32 / 8 - 1)$.

TABLE 4.4 Access Channel Modulation Parameters

Parameter	Date Rate, bps	Units
	4800	
PN chip rate	1.2288	Mcps
Code rate	1/3	bits/code symbol
Code symbol repetition	2	symbols/code symbol
Transmit duty cycle	100.0	%
Code symbol rate	28,800	sps
Modulation	6	code sym/mod. symbol
Modulation symbol rate	4800	sps
Walsh chip rate	307.20	kcps
Mod. symbol duration	208.33	μs
PN chips/code symbol	42.67	PN chip/code symbol
PN chips/mod. symbol	256	PN chip/mod. symbol
PN chips/Walsh chip	4	PN chips/Walsh chip

TABLE 4.5 Interleaving Algorithm

Column Row	1	2	3	4	5	6	7	8	9	10	11	12	13	14	15	16	17	18
1	1	33	65	97	129	161	193	225	257	289	321	353	385	417	449	481	513	545
2	2																	
3	3																	
4	4																	
5	5																	
6	6																	
⋮	⋮																	
32	32	64	96	128	160	192	224	256	288	320	352	384	416	448	480	512	544	576

At 1200 bps, the transmission sequence is by a unique order of rows as follows:

$$J, J+8, J+1, J+9, J+2, J+10, J+3, J+11, J+4,$$

$$J+12, J+5, J+13, J+6, J+14, J+7, J+15$$

for $J = 1 + 16i$ and $i = 1, 2$.

For access channel code symbols, the interleaver rows follow this order:

$$J, J+16, J+8, J+24, J+4, J+20, J+12, J+28, J+2,$$

$$J+18, J+10, J+26, J+6, J+22, J+14, J+30$$

for $J = 1, 2$.

Orthogonal Modulation for Reverse Channel. As at point D in Fig. 4.47, the 64-ary Walsh codes consist of 64 codes each 64 bits long. They are orthogonal to each other as shown in Table 4.6. Every sixth symbol interpretating each Walsh code of 64 chips is sent out. For example,

Each 20-ms reverse traffic channel frame shall be divided into 16 equal-length (i.e., 1.25 ms) power control groups numbered from 0 to 15.

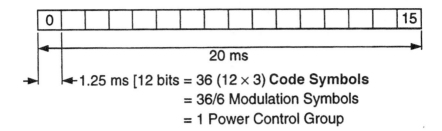

20 ms

1.25 ms [12 bits = 36 (12 × 3) Code Symbols
= 36/6 Modulation Symbols
= 1 Power Control Group

The reverse traffic channel and the access channel shall be direct-sequence spread by the long code prior to transmission. The long code shall be periodic with period $2^{42} - 1$ chips and shall satisfy the linear recursion specified by the polynomial

$$p(x) = x^{42} + x^{35} + x^{33} + x^{31} + x^{27} + x^{26} + x^{25} + x^{22} + x^{21}$$
$$+ x^{19} + x^{18} + x^{17} + x^{16} + x^{10} + x^{7} + x^{6} + x^{5} + x^{3} + x^{2} + x^{1} + 1$$

Each PN chip of the long code shall be generated by a 42-shift-register long-code generator.

Data Burst Randomizing.   At point E in Fig. 4.47, the data burst randomizer has generated a masking pattern of 0s and 1s that randomly masks out the redundant data generated by the code repetition. The mask pattern is determined by the data rate of the frame and by a block of 14 bits taken from the long code. These 14 bits shall be the last 14 bits of the long code used for spreading.

Direct Sequence Spreading.   At point F in Fig. 4.47, prior to transmission, the reverse traffic channel and the access channel are direct-sequence spread by the long code. This spreading operation involves modulo-2 addition of the data burst randomizer output stream and the long code. This long code shall be periodic with period $2^{42} - 1$ chips.

Quadrature Spreading.   The sequences used for the spread in quadrature are shown in Fig. 4.47 at point F. These sequences are periodic with period 2^{15} chips, and the spread polynomials of channel I and Q pilot PN sequences are

$$P_I(x) = x^{15} + x^{13} + x^{9} + x^{8} + x^{7} + x^{5} + 1$$
$$P_Q(x) = x^{15} + x^{12} + x^{11} + x^{10} + x^{6} + x^{5} + x^{4} + x^{3} + 1$$

which are of period $2^{15} - 1$. The pilot PN sequence repeats every 26.66 ms ($2^{15}/1228800$ s). There are exactly 75 repetitions in every 2 s. Reverse CDMA channel I and Q mapping for an offset QPSK modulation is shown in Fig. 4.48.

TABLE 4.6 64-Ary Orthogonal Symbol Set

```
          11 1111 1111 2222 2222 2233 3333 3333 4444 4444 4455 5555 5555 6666
   0123 4567 8901 2345 6789 0123 4567 8901 2345 6789 0123 4567 8901 2345 6789 0123

 0 0000 0000 0000 0000 0000 0000 0000 0000 0000 0000 0000 0000 0000 0000 0000 0000
 1 0101 0101 0101 0101 0101 0101 0101 0101 0101 0101 0101 0101 0101 0101 0101 0101
 2 0011 0011 0011 0011 0011 0011 0011 0011 0011 0011 0011 0011 0011 0011 0011 0011
 3 0110 0110 0110 0110 0110 0110 0110 0110 0110 0110 0110 0110 0110 0110 0110 0110

 4 0000 1111 0000 1111 0000 1111 0000 1111 0000 1111 0000 1111 0000 1111 0000 1111
 5 0101 1010 0101 1010 0101 1010 0101 1010 0101 1010 0101 1010 0101 1010 0101 1010
 6 0011 1100 0011 1100 0011 1100 0011 1100 0011 1100 0011 1100 0011 1100 0011 1100
 7 0110 1001 0110 1001 0110 1001 0110 1001 0110 1001 0110 1001 0110 1001 0110 1101

 8 0000 0000 1111 1111 0000 0000 1111 1111 0000 0000 1111 1111 0000 0000 1111 1111
 9 0101 0101 1010 1010 0101 0101 1010 1010 0101 0101 1010 1010 0101 0101 1010 1010
10 0011 0011 1100 1100 0011 0011 1100 1100 0011 0011 1100 1100 0011 0011 1100 1100
11 0110 0110 1001 1001 0110 0110 1001 1001 0110 0110 1101 1001 0110 0110 1001 1001

12 0000 1111 1111 0000 0000 1111 1111 0000 0000 1111 1111 0000 0000 1111 1111 0000
13 0101 1010 1010 0101 0101 1010 1010 0101 0101 1010 1010 0101 0101 1010 1010 0101
14 0011 1100 1100 0011 0011 1100 1100 0011 0011 1100 1100 0011 0011 1100 1100 0011
15 0110 1001 1001 0110 0110 1001 1001 0110 0110 1001 1001 0110 0110 1001 1001 0110

16 0000 0000 0000 0000 1111 1111 1111 1111 0000 0000 0000 0000 1111 1111 1111 1111
17 0101 0101 0101 0101 1010 1010 1010 1010 0101 0101 0101 0101 1010 1010 1010 1010
18 0011 0011 0011 0011 1100 1100 1100 1100 0011 0011 0011 0011 1100 1100 1100 1100
19 0110 0110 0110 0110 1001 1001 1001 1001 0110 0110 0110 0110 1001 1001 1001 1001

20 0000 1111 0000 1111 1111 0000 1111 0000 0000 1111 0000 1111 1111 0000 1111 0000
21 0101 1010 0101 1010 1010 0101 1010 0101 0101 1010 0101 1010 1010 0101 1010 0101
22 0011 1100 0011 1100 1100 0011 1100 0011 0011 1100 0011 1100 1100 0011 1100 0011
23 0110 1001 0110 1001 1001 0110 1001 0110 0110 1001 0110 1001 1001 0110 1001 0110

24 0000 0000 1111 1111 1111 1111 0000 0000 0000 0000 1111 1111 1111 1111 0000 0000
25 0101 0101 1010 1010 1010 1010 0101 0101 0101 0101 1010 1010 1010 1010 0101 0101
26 0011 0011 1100 1100 1100 1100 0011 0011 0011 0011 1100 1100 1100 1100 0011 0011
27 0110 0110 1001 1001 1001 1001 0110 0110 0110 0110 1001 1001 1001 1001 0110 0110

28 0000 1111 1111 0000 1111 0000 0000 1111 0000 1111 1111 0000 1111 0000 0000 1111
29 0101 1010 1010 0101 1010 0101 0101 1010 0101 1010 1010 0101 1010 0101 0101 1010
30 0011 1100 1100 0011 1100 0011 0011 1100 0011 1100 1100 0011 1100 0011 0011 1100
31 0110 1001 1001 0110 1001 0110 0110 1001 0110 1001 1001 0110 1001 0110 0110 1001

32 0000 0000 0000 0000 0000 0000 0000 0000 1111 1111 1111 1111 1111 1111 1111 1111
33 0101 0101 0101 0101 0101 0101 0101 0101 1010 1010 1010 1010 1010 1010 1010 1010
34·0011 0011 0011 0011 0011 0011 0011 0011 1100 1100 1100 1100 1100 1100 1100 1100
35 0110 0110 0110 0110 0110 0110 0110 0110 1001 1001 1001 1001 1001 1001 1001 1001

36 0000 1111 0000 1111 0000 1111 0000 1111 1111 0000 1111 0000 1111 0000 1111 0000
37 0101 1010 0101 1010 0101 1010 0101 1010 1010 0101 1010 0101 1010 0101 1010 0101
38 0011 1100 0011 1100 0011 1100 0011 1100 1100 0011 1100 0011 1100 0011 1100 0011
39 0110 1001 0110 1001 0110 1001 0110 1001 1001 0110 1001 0110 1001 0110 1001 0110

40 0000 0000 1111 1111 0000 0000 1111 1111 1111 1111 0000 0000 1111 1111 0000 0000
41 0101 0101 1010 1010 0101 0101 1010 1010 1010 1010 0101 0101 1010 1010 0101 0101
42 0011 0011 1100 1100 0011 0011 1100 1100 1100 1100 0011 0011 1100 1100 0011 0011
43 0110 0110 1001 1001 0110 0110 1001 1001 1001 1001 0110 0110 1001 1001 0110 0110
```

(Continued)

TABLE 4.6   64-Ary Orthogonal Symbol Set (*Continued*)

```
        11   1111 1111 2222 2222 2233 3333 3333 4444 4444 4455 5555 5555 6666
      0123   4567 8901 2345 6789 0123 4567 8901 2345 6789 0123 4567 8901 2345 6789 0123
```

```
44 0000 1111 1111 0000 0000 1111 1111 0000 1111 0000 0000 1111 1111 0000 0000 1111
45 0101 1010 1010 0101 0101 1010 1010 0101 1010 0101 0101 1010 1010 0101 0101 1010
46 0011 1100 1100 0011 0011 1100 1100 0011 1100 0011 0011 1100 1100 0011 0011 1100
47 0110 1001 1001 0110 0110 1001 1001 0110 1001 0110 0110 1001 1001 0110 0110 1001

48 0000 0000 0000 0000 1111 1111 1111 1111 1111 1111 1111 1111 0000 0000 0000 0000
49 0101 0101 0101 0101 1010 1010 1010 1010 1010 1010 1010 1010 0101 0101 0101 0101
50 0011 0011 0011 0011 1100 1100 1100 1100 1100 1100 1100 1100 0011 0011 0011 0011
51 0110 0110 0110 0110 1001 1001 1001 1001 1001 1001 1001 1001 0110 0110 0110 0110

52 0000 1111 0000 1111 1111 0000 1111 0000 1111 0000 1111 0000 0000 1111 0000 1111
53 0101 1010 0101 1010 1010 0101 1010 0101 1010 0101 1010 0101 0101 1010 0101 1010
54 0011 1100 0011 1100 1100 0011 1100 0011 1100 0011 1100 0011 0011 1100 0011 1100
55 0110 1001 0110 1001 1001 0110 1001 0110 1001 0110 1001 0110 0110 1001 0110 1001

56 0000 0000 1111 1111 1111 1111 0000 0000 1111 1111 0000 0000 0000 0000 1111 1111
57 0101 0101 1010 1010 1010 1010 0101 0101 1010 1010 0101 0101 0101 0101 1010 1010
58 0011 0011 1100 1100 1100 1100 0011 0011 1100 1100 0011 0011 0011 0011 1100 1100
59 0110 0110 1001 1001 1001 1001 0110 0110 1001 1001 0110 0110 0110 0110 1001 1001

60 0000 1111 1111 0000 1111 0000 0000 1111 1111 0000 0000 1111 0000 1111 1111 0000
61 0101 1010 1010 0101 1010 0101 0101 1010 1010 0101 0101 1010 0101 1010 1010 0101
62 0011 1100 1100 0011 1100 0011 0011 1100 1100 0011 0011 1100 0011 1100 1100 0011
63 0110 1001 1001 0110 1001 0110 0110 1001 1001 0110 0110 1001 0110 1001 1001 0110
```

Access Channel and Reverse Traffic Channel

1. Access channel

- Time alignment—an access channel frame shall begin only when system time is an integral multiple of 20 ms.

- Modulation rate—a fixed rate of 4800 bps.

- The reverse CDMA channel may contain up to 32 access channel numbers, 0 through 31, per supported paging channel (Fig. 4.49*a*). Each access channel is associated with a single paging channel on the corresponding forward CDMA channel (Fig. 4.49*b*). The forward CDMA channel structure will be described later.

- Frame structure:

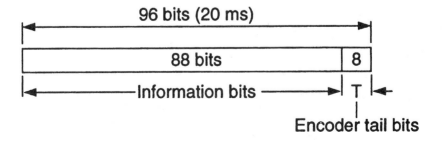

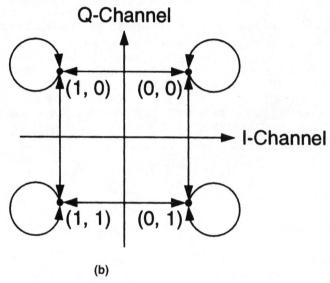

I	Q	Phase
0	0	$\pi/4$
1	0	$3\pi/4$
1	1	$-3\pi/4$
0	1	$-\pi/4$

(a)

(b)

FIGURE 4.48   Reverse CDMA channel quadrature spreading. (*a*) Reverse CDMA channel I and Q mapping; (*b*) offset QPSK constellation and phase transition.

2. Reverse traffic channel
  • A variable data rate of 9600, 4800, 2400, or 1200 bps
  • All frames have a duration of 20 ms

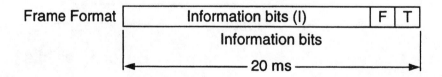

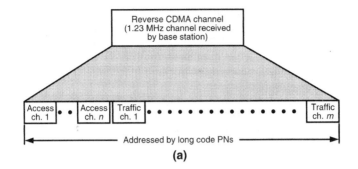

(a)

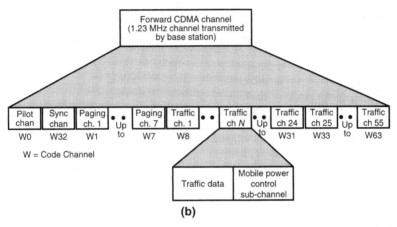

(b)

FIGURE 4.49 CDMA channel structure. (*a*) Example of logical reverse CDMA channels received at a base station; (*b*) example of a forward CDMA channel transmitted by a base station.

Information bits (I)	172 bits (for 9600 bps)
	80 bits (for 4800 bps)
	40 bits (for 2400 bps)
	16 bits (for 1200 bps)
Frame quality indicator (F)	12 bits (for 9600 bps)
(detect errors by CRC)	8 bits (for 4800 bps)
	0 bits (for 2400 bps)
	0 bits (for 1200 bps)
Tail bits (T)	8 bits for all data rates

where the generator polynomials for frame quality indicators (F) are

$$g(x) = x^{12} + x^{11} + x^{10} + x^9 + x^8 + x^4 + x + 1 \quad \text{(for 9600 bps)}$$

$$g(x) = x^8 + x^7 + x^4 + x^3 + x + 1 \quad \text{(for 4800 bps)}$$

Reverse traffic channel preamble. Used to aid the BS in performing initial acquisition of the reverse traffic channel. The preamble shall consist of frames of 192 zeros at the 9600-bps rate.

Null reverse traffic channel. Used when no service option is active. It is a keep-alive operation. The null traffic channel data shall consist of a frame of 16 ones followed by 8 zeros at the 1200-bps rate.

Information bits and time reference. The information bits (172 bits) can be used to provide for the transmission of primary traffic and signaling or secondary traffic. Signaling traffic may be transmitted via blank-and-burst with the primary traffic and signaling traffic sharing the frame. Five different information bit structures described in Fig. 4.50 are for the mobile station use.

The time reference will be established at the MS. The time of occurrence of the earliest arriving multipath component is used for demodulation. The time reference from the forward traffic channel is used for the transmit time of the reverse traffic channel. The time reference from the paging channel is used for the transmit time of the access.

4.4.3.2 Forward CDMA Channel Signals.   The forward CDMA channel consists of the following code channels: the pilot channel, the sync channel, paging channels (1 to 7), and forward traffic channels. They are code channels. Each is orthogonally spread by one of 64 Walsh function codes and is then spread by a quadrature pair of PN sequences at a fixed chip rate of 1.2288 Mcps. The example of a forward CDMA channel transmitted by a BS is shown in Fig. 4.51. Each traffic channel consists of traffic data and mobile power control subchannels.

4.4.3.3 Forward CDMA Channel Structure.   The structures of pilot channels, sync channel, paging channel, and forward traffic channel data are shown in Fig. 4.51. There are two parts, modulation and quadrature spreading. In the modulation part, the data rate is measured at the input.

Data rates at the input

1. The pilot channel sends all 0s at 19.2 kbps rate.

2. The sync channel operates at a fixed rate of 1200 bps.

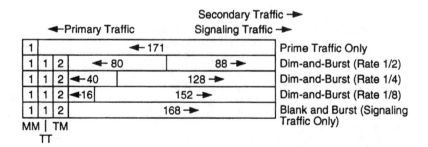

MM - mixed mode bit

TT - traffic type bit

TM - traffic mode bits

FIGURE 4.50   Information bits for primary traffic and secondary traffic.

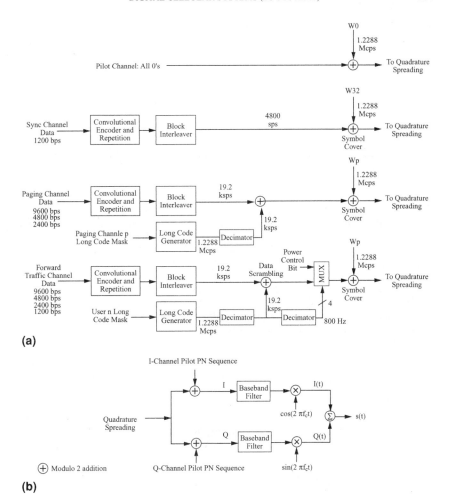

(a)

(b)

FIGURE 4.51   Forward CDMA channel structure. (*a*) Modulation; (*b*) quadrature spreading.

3. The paging channel supports the fixed data rate at 9600, 4800, or 2400 bps.

4. The forward traffic channel supports variable data rate operation at 9600, 4800, 2400, or 1200 bps.

Modulation. The modulation of the pilot channel has not used the error-correction prior to transmission. The channel takes each bit and spreads it into a 64-bit Walsh code. The data rate of 19.2 kbps becomes 1.2288 Mcps. The modulation parameters of sync channel, paging channel, and forward traffic channel are listed in Tables 4.7, 4.8, and 4.9, respectively. The sync channel, paging channel, and forward traffic channel are encoded prior to transmission. The rate of convolutional code is 1/2 with constraint length of 9 (9 shift registers).

Code symbol repetition. For paging and forward traffic channels, repetition depends on the data rate of each channel. A low data rate needs more repeats in order to make up the modulation symbol rate of 19.2 kbps.

TABLE 4.7 Sync Channel Modulation Parameters

Parameter	Data Rate, bps 1200	Units
PN chip rate	1.2288	Mcps
Code rate	1/2	bits/code symbol
Code repetition	2	mod. symbol/code symbol*
Modulation symbol rate	4800	sps
PN chips/modulation symbol	256	PN chips/mod. symbol
PN chips/bit	1024	PN chips/bit

*Each repetition of a code symbol is a modulation symbol.

For a sync channel, each encoded symbol is repeated two times and the modulation symbol rate is 4800 sps. The 4800-sps data are modulated with Walsh function code W32 which has been multiplied by 4. In other words, each symbol becomes $4 \times 64 = 256$ cps.

Block Interleaving. The purpose of using block interleaving is to try to avoid burst errors while sending the data through a multipath fading environment. The input of the sync channel interleaver is shown in Table 4.10 and the output is shown in Table 4.11, where the arrows in each column show the sequential order of the data flow. For the forward traffic channel and paging channel, the input of the interleaver is shown in Table 4.12 and the output of the interleaver is shown in Table 4.13.

Data scrambling. Data scrambling shall be accomplished by performing modulo-2 addition of the interleaver output symbol with the binary value of the long-code PN chip ($2^{42} - 1$); the long-code mask is for privacy. Also, the long-code data rate after passing through two decimators is reduced to 800 Hz, which is used for multiplexer (MUX) timing control. The circuit is shown in Fig. 4.52.

Power control subchannel. At the rate of one bit every 1.25 ms (i.e., 800 bps), a 0 bit indicator is sent to the MS to increase the mean output power level or a 1 bit is sent to decrease it. There are 16 possible starting positions. Each position corresponds to one of the first 16 modulation symbols. Figure 4.53 indicates the randomization of power control bit positions. The reverse traffic channel sends a bit with 6 Walsh symbols in 1.25 ms. The base station measures signal strength, converts the measured signal strength to a power control bit, and transmit with a 4-bit binary number (levels 0 to 15) by scrambling bits 23, 22, 21, and 20. In Fig. 4.53, the value of bits 23, 22, 21, and 20 is 1011 binary

TABLE 4.8 Paging Channel Modulation Parameters

Parameter	Data Rate, bps 9600	Data Rate, bps 4800	Data Rate, bps 2400	Units
PN chip rate	1.2288	1.2288	1.2288	Mcps
Code rate	1/2	1/2	1/2	bits/code symbol
Code repetition	1	2	4	mod. symbol/code symbol*
Modulation symbol rate	19,200	19,200	19,200	sps
PN chips/modulation symbol	64	64	64	PN chips/mod. symbol
PN chips/bit	128	256	512	PN chips/bit

*Each repetition of a code symbol is a modulation symbol.

TABLE 4.9 Forward Traffic Channel Modulation Parameters

Parameter	Data Rate, bps				Units
	9600	4800	2400	1200	
PN chip rate	1.2288	1.2288	1.2288	1.2288	Mcps
Code rate	1/2	1/2	1/2	1/2	bits/code symbol
Code repetition	1	2	4	8	mod symbol/code symbol*
Modulation symbol rate	19,200	19,200	19,200	19,200	sps
PN chips/modulation symbol	64	64	64	64	PN chips/mod. symbol
PN chips/bit	128	256	512	1024	PN chips/bit

*Each repetition of a code symbol is a modulation symbol.

TABLE 4.10 Sync Channel Interleaver Input (Array Write Operation)

1	9	17	25	33	41	49	57
1	9	17	25	33	41	49	57
2	10	18	26	34	42	50	58
2	10	18	26	34	42	50	58
3	11	19	27	35	43	51	59
3	11	19	27	35	43	51	59
4	12	20	28	36	44	52	60
4	12	20	28	36	44	52	60
5	13	21	29	37	45	53	61
5	13	21	29	37	45	53	61
6	14	22	30	38	46	54	62
6	14	22	30	38	46	54	62
7	15	23	31	39	47	55	63
7	15	23	31	39	47	55	63
8	16	24	32	40	48	56	64
8	16	24	32	40	48	56	64

TABLE 4.11 Sync Channel Interleaver Output (Array Read Operation)

1	3	2	4	1	3	2	4
33	35	34	36	33	35	34	36
17	19	18	20	17	19	18	20
49	51	50	52	49	51	50	52
9	11	10	12	9	11	10	12
41	43	42	44	41	43	42	44
25	27	26	28	25	27	26	28
57	59	58	60	57	59	58	60
5	7	6	8	5	7	6	8
37	39	38	40	37	39	38	40
21	23	22	24	21	23	22	24
53	55	54	56	53	55	54	56
13	15	14	16	13	15	14	16
45	47	46	48	45	47	46	48
29	31	30	32	29	31	30	32
61	63	62	64	61	63	62	64

TABLE 4.12   Forward Traffic and Paging Channel Interleaver Input (Array Write Operation at 9600 bps)

1	25	49	73	97	121	145	169	193	217	241	265	289	313	337	361
2	26	50	74	98	122	146	170	194	218	242	266	290	314	338	362
3	27	51	75	99	123	147	171	195	219	243	267	291	315	339	363
4	28	52	76	100	124	148	172	196	220	244	268	292	316	340	364
5	29	53	77	101	125	149	173	197	221	245	269	293	317	341	365
6	30	54	78	102	126	150	174	198	222	246	270	294	318	342	366
7	31	55	79	103	127	151	175	199	223	247	271	295	319	343	367
8	32	56	80	104	128	152	176	200	224	248	272	296	320	344	368
9	33	57	81	105	129	153	177	201	225	249	273	297	321	345	369
10	34	58	82	106	130	154	178	202	226	250	274	298	322	346	370
11	35	59	83	107	131	155	179	203	227	251	275	299	323	347	371
12	36	60	84	108	132	156	180	204	228	252	276	300	324	348	372
13	37	61	85	109	133	157	181	205	229	253	277	301	325	349	373
14	38	62	86	110	134	158	182	206	230	254	278	302	326	350	374
15	39	63	87	111	135	159	183	207	231	255	279	303	327	351	375
16	40	64	88	112	136	160	184	208	232	256	280	304	328	352	376
17	41	65	89	113	137	161	185	209	233	257	281	305	329	353	377
18	42	66	90	114	138	162	186	210	234	258	282	306	330	354	378
19	43	67	91	115	139	163	187	211	235	259	283	307	331	355	379
20	44	68	92	116	140	164	188	212	236	260	284	308	332	356	380
21	45	69	93	117	141	165	189	213	237	261	285	309	333	357	381
22	46	70	94	118	142	166	190	214	238	262	286	310	334	358	382
23	47	71	95	119	143	167	191	215	239	263	287	311	335	359	383
24	48	72	96	120	144	168	192	216	240	264	288	312	336	360	384

(11 decimal). The power control bit starting position is the eleventh position within 1.25 ms of the seventh slot.

Orthogonal spreading. In the forward channel, each code channel transmits one of 64 Walsh functions at a fixed chip rate of 1.2288 Mcps to provide orthogonal channelization among all code channels on a given forward CDMA channel.

PN Sequence Offset

Pilot channel. A pilot channel is transmitted all times on Walsh function W0 by the base station. Pilot PN sequence offset is used for identifying each base station. Time offset may be revised within a CDMA cellular system.

Sync channel. The sync channel is an encoded, interleaved, spread, and modulated spread signal. The sync channel uses the same pilot PN sequence offset as the pilot channel for a given base station.

Receiver at MS. The MS demodulation process shall perform complimentary operations to the BS modulation process. The MS shall provide a minimum of four processing elements. Three of them are capable of tracking and demodulating multipath components of the forward CDM channel. At least one element shall be a searcher element capable of scanning and estimating the signal strength at each pilot PN sequence offset. The signal strength of the pilot is used to select the desired BS during the idle or initialization stage.

TABLE 4.13 Forward Traffic and Paging Channel Interleaver Output (Array Read Operation at 9600 bps)

1	9	5	13	3	11	7	15	2	10	6	14	4	12	8	16
1	9	5	13	3	11	7	15	2	10	6	14	4	12	8	16
65	73	69	77	67	75	71	79	66	74	70	78	68	76	72	80
129	137	133	141	131	139	135	143	130	138	134	142	132	140	136	144
193	201	197	205	195	203	199	207	194	202	198	206	196	204	200	208
257	265	261	269	259	267	263	271	258	266	262	270	260	268	264	272
321	329	325	333	323	331	327	335	322	330	326	334	324	332	328	336
33	41	37	45	35	43	39	47	34	42	38	46	36	44	40	48
97	105	101	109	99	107	103	111	98	106	102	110	100	108	104	112
161	169	165	173	163	171	167	175	162	170	166	174	164	172	168	176
225	233	229	237	227	235	231	239	226	234	230	238	228	236	232	240
289	297	293	301	291	299	295	303	290	298	294	302	292	300	296	304
353	361	357	365	355	363	359	367	354	362	358	366	356	364	360	368
17	25	21	29	19	27	23	31	18	26	22	30	20	28	24	32
81	89	85	93	83	91	87	95	82	90	86	94	84	92	88	96
145	153	149	157	147	155	151	159	146	154	150	158	148	156	152	160
209	217	213	221	211	219	215	223	210	218	214	222	212	220	216	224
273	281	277	285	275	283	279	287	274	282	278	286	276	284	280	288
337	345	341	349	339	347	343	351	338	346	342	350	340	348	344	352
49	57	53	61	51	59	55	63	50	58	54	62	52	60	56	64
113	121	117	125	115	123	119	127	114	122	118	126	116	124	120	128
177	185	181	189	179	187	183	191	178	186	182	190	180	188	184	192
241	249	245	253	243	251	247	255	242	250	246	254	244	252	248	256
305	313	309	317	307	315	311	319	306	314	310	318	308	316	312	320
369	377	373	381	371	379	375	383	370	378	374	382	372	380	376	384

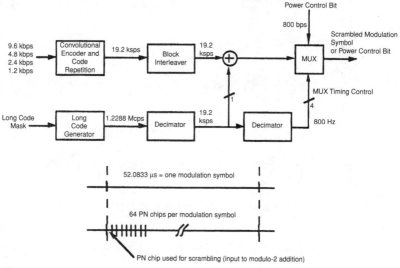

FIGURE 4.52 Data scrambler function and timing.

Also, the signal strength of the pilot is used for the MS to determine when the handoff shall be requested and which new BS is the candidate. The information on handoff will be sent to the BS via the reverse signaling traffic channel (see Table 4.14). The multiplex option is the same on both the forward traffic channel and the reverse traffic channel.

Forward Traffic Channel Frames. There are 14 categories for multiplex option 1. Among those categories, 12 are listed in Table 4.14 and are considered good frames. Categories 9 and 10 are bad frames:

Category 9: 9600-bps frame, primary traffic only, with bit errors.

Category 10: Insufficient frame quality.

4.4.4 Joint Detection (JD)

Joint detection receivers are used to equalize signals that have been distorted by intersymbol interference (ISI) due to multipath environment and multiple access interference (MAI) by the multiusers. It is mostly used for improving CDMA systems performance.

A. The joint detection techniques are

1. Matched filter: Maximizes the SNR at the required sampling instant at the output.
2. Whitening filter: When the correlated non-white Gaussian noise at the input of the filter, the output of the filter becomes white uncorrelated Gaussian noise samples.
3. Zero-forcing linear equalizer: Derived from the principles of Maximum Likelihood Sequence Estimation (MLSE).

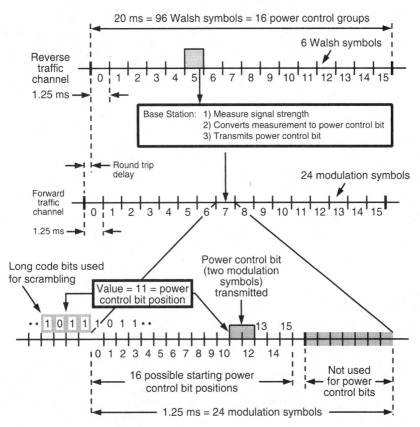

FIGURE 4.53 Randomization of power control bit positions.

4. Zero-forcing decision feedback equalizer: Introduces a nonlinearity into the system by feedback of previous estimates of data symbols in order to remove MAI.

B. Advantages of using joint detection

  1. JD combats MAI and ISI both at the same time.

  2. All the users' signals are detected simultaneously.

C. Requirement of using joint detection

  1. The burst synchronization and chip synchronization should be provided.

  2. Channel estimates are required by the joint detection.

4.4.5 Authentication, Encryption, and Privacy

Authentication refers to the process by which the base station confirms the identity of the mobile station (i.e., the identical sets of shared secret data). SSD is a 128-bit pattern in

TABLE 4.14   Reverse and Forward Traffic Channel Information Bits for Multiplex Option 1

| Transmit Rate (bits/s) | Format bits | | | Primary Traffic bits/ Frame | Signaling Traffic bits/ Frame | Secondary Traffic bits/ Frame | Categories of Received Traffic Channel Frame |
	Mixed Mode (MM)	Traffic Type (TT)	Traffic Mode (TM)				
9600	'0'	–	–	171	0	0	1
9600	'1'	'0'	'00'	80	88	0	2
9600	'1'	'0'	'01'	40	128	0	3
9600	'1'	'0'	'10'	16	152	0	4
9600	'1'	'0'	'11'	0	168	0	5
9600	'1'	'1'	'00'	80	0	88	11
9600	'1'	'1'	'01'	40	0	128	12
9600	'1'	'1'	'10'	16	0	152	13
9600	'1'	'1'	'11'	0	0	168	14
4800	–	–	–	80	0	0	6
2400	–	–	–	40	0	0	7
1200	–	–	–	16	0	0	8

the MS. SSD-A consists of 64 bits and SSD-B consists of 64 bits. SSD-A supports the authentication procedure initialized with mobile station specific information, random data, and the mobile station's A key (64 bits long). A key may be also called PIN. SSD-B supports CDMA voice privacy and message confidentiality.

The purposes for using authentication are (1) MS registration, (2) MS origination, and (3) MS termination. When the information element AUTH in the system parameters overhead message is set to 1 and the MS attempts to register, originate, or terminate, then the auth-signature procedure is executed, and AUTHR is obtained (see Fig. 4.54) and sent with RANDC (eight most significant bits of RAND confirmation) and COUNT to the base station for validation.

4.4.5.1   Authentication of MS Data Bursts

1. The BS sends an SSD update message on either the paging channel or the forward traffic channel. In the SSD update message, there is a RANDSSD field which is used for the computation of SSD at the home location register/authentication center (HLR/AUC). (The A key is stored at the MS and the HLR/AUC.) The MS shall then execute the SSD generation procedure by using RANDSSD, ESN, and A key to produce SSD-A-New and SSD-B-New.

2. The MS shall select a 32-bit random number RANDBS to BS in a base station challenge order via the access channel or reverse traffic channel.

3. Both BS and MS shall execute an auth-signature procedure by using SSD-A-New and RANDBS, and both obtain an 18-bit AUTHBS.

4. The BS sends the AUTHBS in the base station challenge order confirmation on the paging channel or the forward traffic channel.

5. The MS compares the two AUTHBS, one from its own MS and one from the BS. If the comparison is successful, it sets SSD-A and SSD-B to SSD-A-New and SSD-B-New, respectively. Also, the MS shall send an SSD update confirmation order to the BS indicating the successful comparison. If the comparison is not successful, it discards the

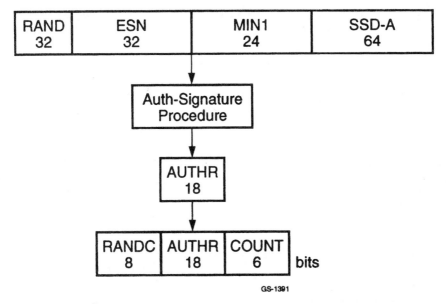

FIGURE 4.54   Authentication parameters for base station validation.

two new SSDs and sends an SSD update rejection order to the BS, indicating unsuccessful comparison.

On receipt of the SSD update confirmation order, the BS sets SSD-A and SSD-B to the values received from the HLR/AUC. The SSD update message flow is shown in Fig. 4.55.

4.4.5.2 Signaling Message Encryption.   In an effort to protect sensitive subscriber information (such as PIN), the availability of encryption algorithm information is governed under the U.S. International Traffic and Arms Regulation (ITAR) and export administration regulations. Messages shall not be encrypted if authentication is not performed. Signaling message encryption is controlled for each call individually.

4.4.5.3 Voice Privacy.   Voice privacy is provided in the CDMA system by means of the private long-code mask used for PN spreading. Voice privacy control is provided on the traffic channels only. All calls are initiated by using the public long-code mask for PN spreading. To initiate a transition to the private or public long-code mask, either the BS or the MS sends a long-code transition request order on the traffic channel.

4.4.6   Malfunction Detection

The BS detects the malfunction of an MS by asking the MS to respond to the lock order, lock until power-cycled order, and maintenance required order. This feature identifies the malfunctional MS and prevents the MS from contaminating the CDMA system by sending a signal to disconnect the MS transmit power.

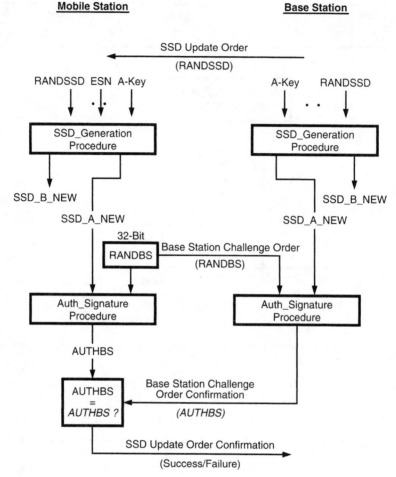

FIGURE 4.55 SSD update message flow.

4.4.7 Call Processing

MS call processing consists of the following states:

4.4.7.1 MS Initialization State

- The MS selects which system to use.
- It acquires the pilot channel of a CDMA system within 20 ms.
- It obtains system configuration and timing information for a CDMA system.
- It synchronizes its timing to that of a CDMA system.

4.4.7.2 MS Idle State

- The MS shall perform paging channel monitoring procedures. The paging channel is divided into 200-ms slots called *paging channel slots*. Paging and control messages for an MS operating in the nonslotted mode can be received in an array of the paging channel slots. Therefore, the nonslotted mode of operation requires the MS to monitor all slots. An MS operating in the slotted mode generally monitors the paging channel for one or two slots per slot cycle. The MS can control the length of the slot cycle.
- Unless otherwise specified in the requirements for processing a specific message, the MS shall transmit an acknowledgment in response to any message received that is addressed to the MS.
- The MS shall maintain all active registration timers.

The CDMA system supports nine different forms of registration. Five of them is in autonomous registration and four of them are in registrations under different requests.

Autonomous registrations:

1. *Power-up registration.* The mobile station registers when it powers on, switches from using the alternate serving system, or switches from using the analog system.
2. *Power-down registration.* The mobile station registers when it powers off if previously registered in the current serving system.
3. *Timer-based registration.* The mobile station registers when a timer expires.
4. *Distance-based registration.* The mobile station registers when the distance between the current base station and the base station in which it last registered exceeds a threshold.
5. *Zone-based registration.* The mobile station registers when it enters a new zone.

Registrations under different requests:

6. *Parameter-change registration.* The mobile station registers when certain of its stored parameters change.
7. *Ordered registration.* The mobile station registers when the base station requests it.
8. *Implicit registration.* When a mobile station successfully sends an origination message or page response message, the base station can infer the mobile station's location, causing an implicit registration.
9. *Traffic channel registration.* Whenever the base station has registration information for a mobile station that has been assigned to a traffic channel, the base station can notify the mobile station that it is registered.

4.4.7.3 System Access State.
The MS sends messages to the BS on the access channel and receives messages from the base station on the paging channel. The entire process of sending one message and receiving acknowledgment for that message is called an *access attempt*. Each transmission in the access attempt is called an *access probe*. The mobile station transmits the same message in each access probe in an access attempt. Each access probe consists of an access channel preamble and an access channel message capsule. There are two types of messages sent on the access channel: a response message and a request message. The access attempt ends after an acknowledgment is received.

4.4.7.4 MS Control on the Traffic Channel State.
The mobile station communicates with the BS using the forward and reverse traffic channels. There are five functions:

1. The MS verifies that it can receive the forward traffic channel and begins transmitting on the reverse traffic channel.
2. The MS waits for an order on an alert with information message.
3. The MS waits for the user to answer the call.
4. The MS's primary service option application exchanges primary traffic packets with the base station.
5. The MS disconnects the call.

4.4.8 Handoff Procedures

4.4.8.1 Types of Handoffs. The MS supports four handoff procedures:

1. *Soft handoff.* The MS commences communication with a new base station without interrupting communication with the old base station. Soft handoff means an identical frequency assignment between the old BS and new BS. Soft handoff provides different-site selection diversity to enhance the signal.
2. *CDMA-to-CDMA hard handoff.* The MS transmits between two base stations with different frequency assignments.
3. *CDMA-to-analog handoff.* The MS is directed from a forward traffic channel to an analog voice channel with a different frequency assignment.
4. *Softer handoff.* Handoffs between sectors within a cell.

4.4.8.2 Pilot Sets. The information obtained from the pilot channel is used for the handoff. A pilot is associated with the forward traffic channels in the same forward CDMA channel. A pilot channel is identified by a pilot sequence offset. Each pilot channel is assigned to a particular BS. The MS can obtain four sets of pilot channels:

1. *Active set.* The pilot associated with the forward traffic channels assigned to the MS.
2. *Candidate set.* The pilots that are not in the active set but are received by MS with sufficient strength.
3. *Neighbor set.* The pilots that are not in the active set or the candidate set and are likely candidates for handoff.
4. *Remaining set.* The set in the current system on the current CDMA frequency assignment, excluding the above three sets.

4.4.8.3 Pilot Requirement

1. The base station specified for each of the above pilots sets the search window in which the mobile station is to search for usable multipath components of the pilots in the set.
2. The MS assists the base station in the handoff process by measuring and reporting the strengths of received pilots.
3. A handoff drop timer shall be maintained for each pilot in the active set and candidate set. When the signal strength level is below TDROP (also called T-DROP), T-TDROP is set to zero (i.e., it expires within 100 ms). There are 15 T-TDROP values. The highest value of T-TDROP is 319 s. When the MS receives a signal strength level from the neighboring cell exceeding a given TADD (also called T_ADD) level in decibels, the soft handoff starts. When the MS receives a signal strength level from the home cell below TDROP,

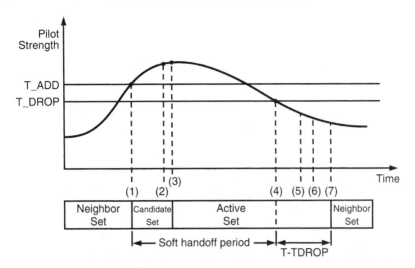

(1) Pilot strength exceeds T_ADD. Mobile station sends a *plot strength measurement message* and transfers pilot to the candidate set.

(2) Base station sends a *handoff direction message.*

(3) Mobile station transfers pilot to the active set and sends a *Handoff completion message.*

(4) Pilot strength drops below T_DROP. Mobile station starts the handoff drop timer.

(5) Handoff drop timer expires. Mobile station sends a *pilot strength measurement message.*

(6) Base station sends a *handoff direction message.*

(7) Mobile station moves pilot from the active set to the neighbor set and sends a *handoff completion message.*

FIGURE 4.56   Handoff threshold example.

the soft handoff ends. The handoff action would take place after the received level from the home cell is below the TDROP. If the time between TADD and TDROP is very short, the T-TDROP time has to be longer. Also, in certain circumstances, it is preferable to reduce the call drops and sacrifice voice quality.

4. The MS shall measure the arrival time for each pilot reported to the base station. The time of the earliest arriving usable multipath component of the pilot is used to measure relative to the MS's time reference in units of PN chips.

5. Soft handoff

   a. All forward traffic channels associated with pilots in the active set of the MS carry modulation symbols identically to those of the power control subchannel. When the active set contains more than one pilot, the MS should provide diversity combining of the associated forward traffic channels. The MS shall provide for differential propagation delays from zero to at least 150 μs.

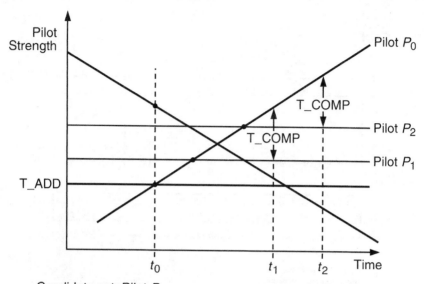

Candidate set: Pilot P_0

Active set: Pilots P_1, P_2

t_0 — *Pilot strength measurement message* sent, $P_0 >$ T_ADD

t_1 — *Pilot strength measurement message* sent, $P_0 > P_1 +$ T_COMP

t_2 — *Pilot strength measurement message* sent, $P_0 > P_2 +$ T_COMP

FIGURE 4.57 Pilot strength measurements triggered by a candidate pilot.

b. For reverse traffic channel power control during soft handoff, the handoff direction message identifies sets of forward traffic channels that carry identical closed-loop power control subchannels. A set consists of one or more forward traffic channel transmissions with identical power control information. The MS will obtain at most one power control bit from each set of identical closed-loop power control subchannels. If the power control bits obtained from all sets are equal to 0, the MS shall increase its power; if they are equal to 1, the MS shall decrease its power.

c. The typical message exchanges between the MS and the BS during handoff are shown in Fig. 4.56. There are seven messages during the soft handoffs. The first message that the MS sends is a pilot strength measurement message when the neighboring pilot strength exceeds TADD. The soft handoff starts. The seventh message is that the MS should move pilot from the active set to the neighboring set and send a handoff completion message. The soft handoff is then completed.

The pilot strength measurement triggered by a candidate pilot is shown in Fig. 4.57. During the soft handoff starts, the two pilots P_1 and P_2 are indicated in the active set. There is a P_0 in the candidate set that is stronger than a pilot in the active set only if the difference between their respective strengths is at least T-Comp (level in decibels) as shown in Fig. 4.57.

4.5 MISCELLANEOUS MOBILE SYSTEMS

In the previous sections, GSM, NA-TDMA, and CDMA were introduced. This section will briefly introduce other systems such as PDC, CT-2, DECT, CDPD, PCN, and PCS. iDEN and PHS will be described in Chapter 5.

4.5.1 TDD Systems

Time-division duplexing (TDD) systems are digital systems and use only one carrier to transmit and receive information. There are two kinds of TDD systems (see Fig. 4.58):

- TDD/FDMA—each carrier serves only one user.
- TDD/TDMA—each carrier can have many time slots and each slot can serve one user. Then N transmit time slots can serve N users.

A TDD system is used when only one chunk of spectrum is allocated. In cellular systems, there are two chunks of spectrum, separated by 20 MHz. In each cellular channel, the base transmit frequency and the mobile transmit frequency are 45 MHz apart. Therefore, the separation in frequency between transmitting and receiving is adequate to avoid interference. In TDD, there is no separation in frequency between transmitting and receiving but a separation in time interval.

The advantages of TDD are as follows:

1. When only one chunk of spectrum is available, TDD is the best use of spectrum.
2. Diversity can be applied at one end (terminal) to serve both ends, as the fading characteristics of one carrier are the same when received at both ends. At the base station, the information on selecting antennas for the space-diversity selective combining receiver can be used to switch to one of two transmitting antennas. Thus the mobile unit (or portable unit) can achieve the same diversity gain with a nondiversity receiver.

One of the concerns is that the TDD system has to be a synchronized system with a master clock. Otherwise, when one BS transmits and another BS receives, equivalent cochannel (co-time slot) interference occurs. Another concern is that the signal structures of TDD and of a frequency duplexing division (FDD) are different. Therefore, the two systems should not coexist in the same area because of their mutual interference.

In this section, several TDD systems will be briefly described.

4.5.1.1 Cordless Phone 2 (CT-2).[31] CT-2 was developed by GPT Ltd. in the United Kingdom and was the first TDD system for mobile radio communications. All the other TDD systems such as PHS and DECT adopted CT-2's structure. CT-2 is a portable payphone booth. Calls can be dialed out but not dialed in, and there is no handoff.

System Structure.   The structure is similar as PHS in Fig. 5.22.

- The CS is called the telepoint or phone zone
- Carrier frequency: 864.1 to 868.1 MHz
- Total spectrum: 4 MHz
- Channel access: FDMA/TDD
- Number of channels: 40

TDD/FDMA

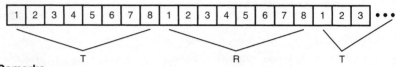

TDD/TDMA

■ Remarks

   • All cell sites have to be synchronized in order to eliminate the near-far
     interference from nieghboring sites
   • The guard time in TDD slot would be longer than in regular TDMA slots
   • The diversity scheme can be applied at one end to serve both ends
   • Do not increase spectrum efficiency from a traffic/capacity point of view

FIGURE 4.58   Time-division duplexing.

• Channel bandwidth: 100-kHz spacing
• Handset output power: 1 to 10 mW

   Characteristics

• Overall data rate: 72 kbps
• Data rate per speech channel: 32 kbps
• Speech coding: ADPCM
• Modulation: GMSK

4.5.1.2   Cordless Phone 3 (CT-3).   Originally called DCT900, CT-3 was developed by
Ericsson as an upgrade from the CT-2 version.

   System Structure

• Time slots: 64
• Two-way call system: call send and call delivery
• Slow-speed handoff
• Caller authentication
• Encryption
• Roaming

   Characteristics

• Handset effective radiated power (ERP): 80 mW
• Modulation: filtered minimum-shift keying (MSK)

- Spectrum range: 8 MHz
- Frequency: 800 to 1000 MHz
- Bandwidth: 1 MHz
- RF output power: 80 mW peak, 5 mW average
- Number of slots per frame: 8
- Overall data rate: 640 kbps
- Data rate per speech code: 32 kbps
- Speech coding: ADPCM

4.5.1.3   Digital European Cordless Telecommunication System (DECT).[32,33]   DECT is a European standard system. It is a CT-2–like system, and the applications are slightly different from the cellular system.

Applications

1. Use the public network to mobile communications within the home and the immediate vicinity.
2. Provide business communications locally. In this case, the PSTN has been replaced by the PBX. The base station has been renamed the radio fixed port (RFP), also called a *cluster controller*. The RFP can be treated as the microcell site.
3. Provide mobile public access. It is a PCS application. The system monitors the location of the active handsets and provides call delivery capability, like a cellular system.
4. Local loop. Using DECT to provide wireless local loops is a cost-effective alternative to running copper wires to residential premises.

System Structure

- Duplex method: TDD
- Access method: TDMA
- RF power of handset: 10 mW
- Channel bandwidth: 1.728 MHz/channel
- Number of carriers: 5 (a multiple-carrier system)
- Frequency: 1800 to 1900 MHz

Characteristics

- Frame: 10 ms
- Time slots: 12

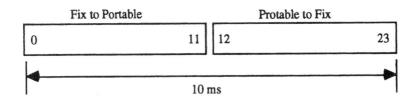

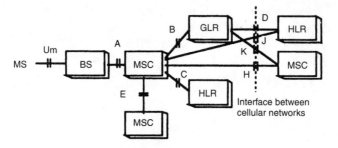

Um: Mobile user-network Interface
MS: Mobile Station
BS: Base Station
MSC: Mobile service Switching Center
HLR: Home Location Register
GLR: Gate Location Register

FIGURE 4.59   PDC network reference model.

- Bit rate—38.8 kb/slot
- Modulation—GFSK (Gausian FSK)
- Handoff—Yes

4.5.2   Other Full-Duplexed Systems

We have addressed the full-duplexed system such as GSM, NA-TDMA, and CDMA in the previous sections. In this section PDC, PCN, and PCS will be briefly described.

4.5.2.1   Personal Digital Cellular (PDC).[34,35]   PDC is a standard system in Japan. The system is a TDMA cellular system operating at 800 MHz and 1.5 GHz, which used to be called Japanese digital system (JDC). 1.5 GHz PDC was in service publicly in Osaka in 1994. The PDC network reference model is shown in Fig. 4.59. This system provides nine interfaces among the cellular network. Um is the air interface, which was standardized. Interfaces B, C, D, E, J, K, and H were defined by cellular carriers in Japan. Interface A is an option for operators.

Signaling Structure.   The signaling structure of PDC has three layers (Fig. 4.60). The third layer consists of three functional entities: call control, mobility management, and radio transmission management. In general, the structure of PDC is very similar to that of NA-TDMA.

System Structure

- Multiplex access: TDMA
- Number of time slots: 3

Characteristics

- 800 MHz
   810–826 MHz
   940–956 MHz

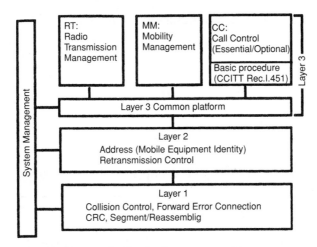

FIGURE 4.60   Subscriber line signaling structure model.

- 1500 MHz
    1429–1441 MHz
    1453–1465 MHz
    1477–1489 MHz
    1561–1513 MHz
- Modulation: $\pi/4$, DQPSK
- Speech coder: VSELP

4.5.2.2   Personal Communication Network (PCN).[36]   The PCN system was first initiated by Lord Young in 1988. The characteristics of PCN are as follows:

1. Operational frequency: 1.7 to 1.88 GHz (1710–1785 MHz and 1805–1880 MHz)
2. Uses 30 GHz or up for microwave backbone system
3. Covers both small cells and large cells (rural areas)
4. Coverage inside and outside buildings
5. Handover
6. Call delivery
7. Portable handset
8. Uses intelligent network

PCN uses the DCS-1800 system, which is similar to GSM, but upconverts the frequency to 1.7–1.88 GHz. Therefore, the network structure, the signaling structure, and the transmission characteristics are similar between PCN and GSM, but the operational frequencies are different.

• Wideband PCS — for cellular-like systems

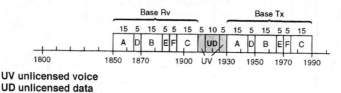

UV unlicensed voice
UD unlicensed data

• Narrowband PCS — for two-way paging systems

Five 50 kHz channels paired with 50 kHz channels

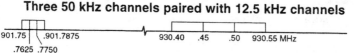

Three 50 kHz channels paired with 12.5 kHz channels

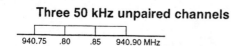

Three 50 kHz unpaired channels

940.75   .80   .85   940.90 MHz

FIGURE 4.61   FCC's PCS allocation.

4.5.2.3 Personal Communication Service.[37]   See Appendix C for (1) MTA in the United States, (2) broadband PCS designated in major trading areas (MTA), and (3) basic trading areas (BTA) in the United States.

Ever since cellular systems were deployed in 1983 in the United States, the rapidly growing wireless communication systems have faced limitations of spectrum utilization. However, the trend is toward personal communications and includes wireless communications for pedestrians and for in-building communications. In 1989, Lord Young of the United Kingdom was promoting a PCN system operating at 1.8 GHz. PCN uses a GSM version of cellular communication. The spectrum range is 1710–1785 MHz and 1805–1880 MHz.

In 1991, the FCC issued a Notice of Proposed Rule Making, Docket No. 90-134, considering allocating spectrum between 1.85 and 2.2 GHz. The FCC has now allocated 120 MHz of spectrum into seven bands as shown in Fig. 4.61 for wideband PCS and narrowband PCS allocated spectrum. The auction of PCS bands started in 1994.

There were many systems, such as GSM, NADC, CDMA, PCN, and DECT, as described in this chapter, that were being considered as candidates to be adapted as the future PCS system. How to improve the equalizer for the TDMA[28] and reduce the interference for CDMA were the major concerns. However, users want to carry one unit with which they can place a call to wherever they want and receive calls wherever they may be. Of course, the unit has to be small in size, light in weight, and provide long talking time. Three systems currently used in PCS are CDMA, NADC and GSM.

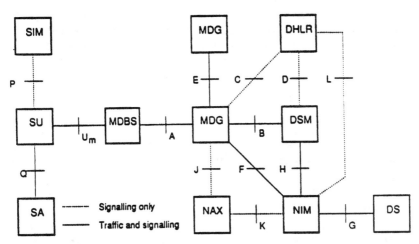

FIGURE 4.62   CDPD network reference model.

4.5.3 Noncellular Systems

There are two systems that can be mentioned in this section: CDPD, and satellite mobile systems. PHS and iDEN are described in Chapter 5.

4.5.3.1 Cellular Digital Packet Data (CDPD) System.[38]   CDPD is a packet switching system that uses idle voice channels from the cellular system band to carry out traffic. This system can be assigned a dedicated channel or it can hop to idle channels.

In the network reference model of CDPD in Fig. 4.62, acronyms are defined as follows:

SIM   Subscriber identity module
SU   Subscriber unit [also can be indicated as mobile-end station (M-ES)]
EIR   Equipment identity register
MDBS   Mobile data base station
MDG   Mobile data gateway
NIM   Network interface manager
DHLR   Data home location register
NAX   Network address translator
DSM   Data service manager [also can be indicated as mobile data information station (MD, IS)]
DS   Data service
NG   Network gateway

The network in Fig. 4.62 is self-explanatory. There are two communication interfaces, called *reference points*, identified with a letter (e.g., A or Um). On a given reference point there may be many physical devices to transport the signal such as routes, switches, multiplexers, demultiplexers, and modems.

System Operation.   The MDBS is collocated at the cellular cell site. DSM is a control center for CDPD. DSM operates independently from the MTSO of cellular systems. In the MDBS, a forward-link logical channel is always on to send the overhead message or send the data to the user. There are two set-ups:

1. *For a dedicated channel setup.* The MS, at the initialization stage, scans the assigned N CDPD channels to lock on a strong CDPD channel. The CDPD channel will be changed while the MS is moving from one cell to another cell.

2. *For a frequency-hopping channel setup.* There is a device called a *sniffer* installed in the MDBS. The sniffer monitors the cellular control channels on both the forward and reverse links and chooses an idle cellular channel for CDPD.

Transmission Structure

- Roaming support
- Security and authentication across the airlink
- Forward channel block: Reed-Solomon (63,47) data symbols
- Reverse channel block: 8-bit delay maximum plus dotting sequence (38 bits) plus reverse sync work (22 bits); Reed-Solomon (63,47) data symbols
- Frequency-agile with in-band control
- Channel hopping and dedicated channel
- Cell transfer controlled by M-ES (SU in Fig. 4.62).
- Power control
- AMPS-compatible
- Essentially transparent to AMPS
- Modulation: GMSK (same as GSM)
- Data rate: 19.2 kbps
- Link protocol: LAPD
- Point-to-point, broadcast, and multicast delivery

4.5.3.2   Mobile Satellite Communications.   In the future, mobile satellite communications will enhance terrestrial radio communication, either in rural areas or in global communication to become a broad sense PCS system. Mobile satellite communications is classified by three satellite altitude positions. One uses stationary satellites which are 22,000 mi above the earth. Another uses low-earth-orbit (LEO) satellites which are 400 to 800 mi above the earth. The third uses medium-earth-orbit satellites (MEO) anywhere between the stationary satellite altitude and LEO satellite altitude.

Stationary Satellites.   To cover the entire earth, only four stationary satellites are required. The required number of stationary satellites is low and the life span is 10 to 15 years. Thus the cost is low. Immarsat[39] is introduced to PCS. However, the time delay due to the long range can be 0.25 s (two ways) and does not include the other delays such as signal processing and network routing. Also, at high latitudes, the stationary satellite has a low elevation angle as seen from the earth. For instance, in Chicago, the elevation angle is 19°. Under this condition, the buildings and the hills block the direct path between the satellite and the mobile. This causes multipath fading and shadow loss. Also, the transmit power and size of antenna to send the signal up to the satellite from a mobile station is limited.

TABLE 4.15 Comparative Low-Earth-Orbiting Mobile Satellite Service Applications*

System Characteristics	Loral/QUALCOMM GLOBALSTAR	Motorola IRIDIUM	TRW ODYSSEY	Constellation ARIES (b)	Ellipsat ELLIPSO (c)
Number of satellites	46	66	12	48	24
Constellation altitude (NM)	750	421	5600	550	1767×230
Unique feature	Transponder	Onboard Processing	Transponder	Transponder	Transponder
Circuit capacity (U.S.)	6500	3835	4600	100	1210
Signal modulation	CDMA	TDMA	CDMA	FDMA/CDMA	CDMA
Gateways in U.S.	6	2	2	5	6
Gateway	C-band existing	New Ka-Band	New Ka-band	Unknown	Unknown
Coverage	Global	Global	Global	Global	Northern hemisphere

LEO Satellites.   Many LEO satellites are required to cover the earth. The Iridium[40] system (Motorola) needs 66 satellites, and Globalstar[41] needs 48 satellites. The average satellite life is 5 years. The cost of utilizing LEO mobile satellite systems is high. The satellite will circle the earth with a period between 1 to 2 h, depending on the satellite altitude. Handoffs between satellite antenna spot beams and between satellites may create difficulties for switching signals in space. However, there is no noticeable delay in talk time, and the mobile transmit power is not an issue. A comparison of LEO mobile satellite service applications among different systems is shown in Table 4.15.

MEO Satellites.   MEO satellites may share the advantages and disadvantages of both stationary satellites and LEO satellites. Odyssey Personal Communication Satellite System[42] developed by TRW belongs to MEO satellites.

REFERENCES

1. J. Swerup and J. Uddenfeldt, "Digital Cellular," *Personal Communications Technology*, May 1986, pp. 6–12.

2. M. Bohm, "Mobile Telephone for Everyone Through Digital Technology," *Telecommunications*, July 1985, pp. 68–72.

3. W. C. Y. Lee, "How to Evaluate Digital Cellular Systems," presented to the FCC, Washington, D.C., September 3, 1987.

4. J. J. Spilker, Jr., *Digital Communications by Satellite*, Prentice-Hall, 1977, Chap. 14.

5. K. Hirade and K. Murota, "A Study of Modulation for Digital Mobile Telephony," *29th IEEE Vehicular Technology Conference Record* (Arlington Heights, Illinois, March 27–30, 1979), pp. 13–19.

6. R. de Buda, "Coherent Demodulation of Frequency Shift Keying with Low Deviation Ratio," *IEEE Transactions on Communications*, Vol. COM-20, June 1972, pp. 466–470.

7. J. Prokis, *Digital Communications*, McGraw-Hill, 1989, pp. 278–285.

8. R. van Nee, R. Prasad, OFDM for Wireless Multimedia Communications, Artech House, 2000, Chapter 2.

9. W. C. Y. Lee, *Mobile Communications Engineering*, 2nd Edition, McGraw-Hill, 1998, p. 306.

10. R. A. Comroe and D. J. Costello, Jr., "ARQ Schemes for Data Transmission in Mobile Radio Systems," *IEEE Transactions on Vehicular Technology*, Vol. VT-33, August 1984, pp. 88–97.

11. P. J. Mobey, "Mobile Radio Data Transmission Coding for Error Control," *IEEE Transactions on Vehicular Technology*, Vol. VT-27, August 1978, pp. 99–109.

12. J. L. Flanagen, M. R. Schroeder, B. S. Atal, R. E. Crochiere, N. S. Jayant, and J. M. Tribolet, "Speech Coding," *IEEE Transactions on Communications*, Vol. COM-27, April 1979, pp. 710–737.

13. J. Makhoul, "Linear Prediction: A Tutorial Review," *Proceedings of the IEEE*, Vol. 63, April 1975, pp. 560–580.

14. J. M. Gilmer, "CVSD Intelligibility Testing." 1985 IEEE Milcom Conference, Boston, October 20–23, 1985, *Conference Record*, pp. 181–186.

15. J. Makhoul, S. Roucos, and H. Gish, "Vector Quantizations in Speech Coding," *Proceedings of the IEEE*, Vol. 33, November 1985, pp. 1551–1588.

16. T. C. Bartee, *Digital Communications*, Howard H. Sams & Co., 1986, Chap. 8.

17. *Conference Proceedings*, Digital Cellular Radio Conference, Hagen FRG, October 1988 (21 papers describe the GSM system).

18. Bernard J. T. Mallinder, "An Overview of the GSM System," *Conference Proceedings*, Digital Cellular Radio Conference, Hagen FRG, October 1988.

19. M. Mouly, M. B. Pautet, "The GSM System Mobile Communications," M. Mouly et M. B. Pautet, 49, vue Louis Bruneau, F-91120 Palaisea, France, 1992.

20. "European Digital Cellular Telecommunications System (Phase 2): General Description of a GSM Public Land Mobile Network," ETSI, 06921 Sophia Antipolis Cedex, France, October 1993, GSM 01-12.

21. *Conference Proceedings*, Third Nordic Seminar on Digital Land Mobile Radio Communication, September 12–15, 1988, Copenhagen (21 papers describe the GSM system).

22. Cellular System, IS-54 (incorporating EIA/TIA 553), "Dual-Mode Mobile Station-Base Station Compatibility Standard," Electronic Industries Association Engineering Department, PN-2215, December 1989 (NADCA-TDMA system).

23. Cellular System, IS-55, "Recommended Minimum Performance Standards for Mobile Stations," PN-2216, EIA, Engineering Department, December 1989 (NADC-TDMA system).

24. Cellular System, IS-56, "Recommended Minimum Performance Standards for Base Stations," PN-2217, EIA, Engineering Department, December 1989 (NATC-TDMA system).

25. W. C. Y. Lee, "Cellular Operators feel the squeeze," *Telephony*, Vol. 214, No. 2, May 30, 1988, pp. 22–23.

26. Cellular System, IS-95, "Dual-Mode Mobile Station-Base Station Wideband Spread Spectrum Compatibility Standard," PN 3118, EIA, Engineering Department, December 1992 (CDMA System).

27. Cellular System, IS-96, "Recommended Minimum Performance Standards for Mobile Stations Supporting Dual-Mode Wideband Spread Spectrum Cellular Base Stations," PN-3119, EIA, Engineering Department, December 1993 (CDMA system).

28. Cellular System, IS-97, "Recommended Minimum Performance Standards for Base Stations Supporting Dual-Mobile Wideband Spread Spectrum Cellular Mobile Stations," PN-3120, EIA, Engineering Department, December 1993 (CDMA system).

29. A. Salmasi and K. S. Gilhousen, "On the System Design Aspects of Code Division Multiple Access Applied to Digital Cellular and Personal Communications Networks," *IEEE VTC '91 Conference Record*, St. Louis, May 19–22, 1991, pp. 57–62.

30. S. C. Yang, CDMA RF System Engineering, Artech House, 1998.

31. Cordless Telephone 2/Common Air Interface (CT2/CAI), "Management of International Telecommunications, MIT 12-850-201, McGraw-Hill, Inc. DataPro Information Service Group, Delran, N.J., February 1994.

32. *Digital European Cordless Telecommunications*, Part I, "Overview," DE/RES 3001-1, Common Interface, Radio Equipment and Systems, ETS 300 175-1, ETSI, B.P. 152, F-06561 Valbonne Cedex, France, August 1991.

33. Sybo Dijkstra, Frank Owen, "The Case for DECT," *Mobile Communications International*, pp. 60–65, September–October–November 1993.

34. "PDC—Digital Cellular Telecommunications System, RCR STF-27A Version," January 1992, Research & Development Center for Radio System (RCR), Nippon Ericsson K.K.

35. H. Takamura, A. Nakajima, K. Yamamoto, "Network and Signaling Structure Based on Personal Digital Cellular Telecommunication System Concept," VTC '93, *Conference Record*, pp. 922–926.

36. A. R. Potter, "Implementation of PCNs using DCS/800," *IEEE Communications Magazine*, Vol. 30, December 1992, pp. 32–37.

37. FCC, "Spectrum Allocation for PCS," FCC 90-314, Sept. 23, 1993.

38. "CDPD—Cellular Digital Packet Data, Cell Plan II Specification," prepared by PCSI, San Diego, CA 92121, January 1992.

39. N. Hart, H. Haugli, P. Poskett, and K. Smith, "Immarsat's Personal Communications System," *Proc. Third International Mobile Satellite Conference*, Pasadena, pp. 303–304, June 16–18, 1993.

40. J. E. Hatlelid and L. Casey, "The Iridium System: Personal Communications Anytime, Anyplace," *Proc. Third International Mobile Satellite Conference*, Pasadena, pp. 285–290, June 16–18, 1993.

41. R. A. Wiedeman, "The Globalstar Mobile Satellite System for Worldwide Personal Communications," *Proc. Third International Mobile Satellite Conference*, Pasadena, pp. 291–296, June 16–18, 1993.

42. C. Spitzer, "Odyssey Personal Communications Satellite System," *Proc. Third International Mobile Satellite Conference*, Pasadena, pp. 291–296, June 16–18, 1993.

CHAPTER 5
B2G SYSTEMS

Those wireless systems developed after digital TDMA and CDMA systems are classified as B2G systems: these are GPRS, EDGE, HSCSD, iDEN, PHS, and RTT1X (IS-95B). Each of them is described in this chapter.

5.1 GPRS (GENERAL PACKET RADIO SERVICE)

5.1.1 GPRS Air Interface

GSM is not necessarily an efficient system for the support of data traffic. The GPRS is a solution[1,2] that provides more efficient packet-based data services at higher data rates. Besides, UMTS Release 99 reuses a great deal of GPRS functionality for WCDMA. In this section, we briefly describe the GPRS system, as the packed-switched system appearing in WCDMA will be shown in Chapter 6.

GPRS has the same basic air interface as GSM, a 200-kHz channel divided into eight time-slots. GPRS, however, defines four different channel coding schemes, CS-1 to CS-4 with different data rates. The most commonly used coding scheme for packet data transfer is coding scheme 2 (CS-2), which enables a given time slot to carry data at a transmission rate of 13.4 kbps. The data rate for usable data is approximately 20 to 30 percent less than the transmission rate.

The advantage of GPRS is the use of packet-switching technology. It enables multiple users to share air interface resources. Because this is a request-allocation procedure, the users feel their services to be "always on."

A given time slot is called Packet Data Channel (PDCH) when it is used to carry GPRS-related data traffic or control signaling. Although GPRS uses the same basic structure as GSM, it introduces a number of new logical channel types for Packet Common Control Channel (PCCCH) and for Packet Dedicated Control Channel (PDCCH).

The functions of those control channels are described as follows:

- Packet Common Control Channel (PCCCH)
  - Packet Random Access Channel (PRACH) is used by an MS to initiate a transfer of packet signaling or data in the uplink.
  - Packet Paging Channel (PPCH) is used by the network to page an MS prior to a downlink packet transfer.
  - Packet Access Grant Channel (PAGCH) is used by the network to assign resources to the MS prior to packet transfer in the downlink.
  - Packet Notification Channel (PNCH) is used for Point-to-Multipoint Multicast (PTM-M) notifications to a group of MSs.

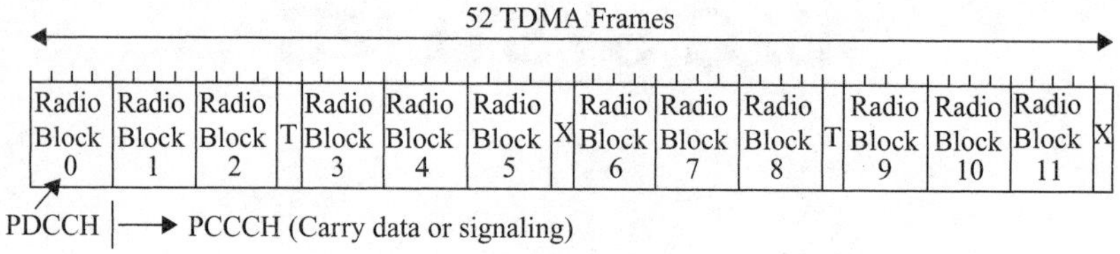

52 TDMA Frames

| Radio Block 0 | Radio Block 1 | Radio Block 2 | T | Radio Block 3 | Radio Block 4 | Radio Block 5 | X | Radio Block 6 | Radio Block 7 | Radio Block 8 | T | Radio Block 9 | Radio Block 10 | Radio Block 11 | X |

PDCCH |⟶ PCCCH (Carry data or signaling)

X = Idle Frame (2)
T = Frame Used for PTCCH (2)
Radio Block (RB) = 4 TDMA frames

FIGURE 5.1   GPRS air interface frame structure.

- Packet Dedicated Control Channel (PDCCH)
  - Packet Associated Control Channel (PACCH) is a bidirectional channel used to pass signaling and other information between the MS and the network during packet transfer.
  - Packet Timing Control Channel (PTCCH) is used for the control of the timing advance for MSs.
- Packet Data Traffic Channel (PDTCH) is used for the transfer of actual user data over the air interface in either uplink or downlink.

A general name for all GPRS channels is called the Packet Data Channel (PDCH), which uses a 52-multiframe structure as compared with a 26 multiframe structure for GSM. There are 12 radio blocks carrying user data and signaling. Each radio block is equivalent to four consecutive instances of a given slot. The GPRS air interface frame structure is shown in Fig. 5.1.

PBCCH uses Radio Block 0: broadcasts GPRS-specific system information.

PACCH uses Radio Block 1 to Radio Block 11 carrying signaling.

PDTCH uses Radio Block 1 to Radio Block 11 carrying data.

Comparison of the control and traffic channels between GSM and GPRS as follows:

Channels	GSM	GPRS
Common control channel	• CCH (one logical channel) RACH	• PCCCH (four logical channels) PRACH PPCH PAGCH PNCH
Broadcast channel	• BCCH	• PBCCH
Dedicated control channel	• DCCH	• PDCCH PACCH PTCCH
Dedicated traffic channels	• FACCH • DTCH	• FACCH • PDTCH

5.1.2 GPRS Network Architecture

GPRS's packet data network is overlaid on the GSM network. However, its packet data channels, packet data switching, and transport network are different from that of GSM. Figure 5.2 shows the GPRS network architecture. There are many new network elements.

PCU (Packet Control Unit) is responsible for a number of GPRS-related functions, such as access control, packet scheduling, and packet assembly and de-assembly.

SGSN (GPRS Support Node) is analogous to the MSC/VLR in the circuit-switched system. It connects to MSC/VLR, to short message service center (SMSC), HLR, and CGF (Charging Gateway Function).

GGSN (Gateway GPRS Support Node) is the point of interface with external packet data networks such as the internet.

The service area of a SGSN is divided into routing areas (RA). A MS may perform a RA update during an ongoing data session in a packet-switched cell known as a Packet

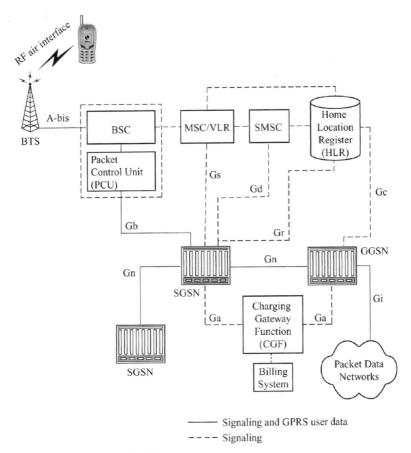

——— Signaling and GPRS user data

– – – – Signaling

FIGURE 5.2 GPRS network architecture.

Data Protocol (PDP) context. An update of location area only occurs after the call is finished in a circuit-switched call. Also, when the PDP context is established between SGSNs or between a new SGSN and GGSN, the old SGSN is removed from the path, whereas in a circuit-switched call, the old MSC remains as an anchor until the call is finished.

There are different interfaces between different network elements as shown in Fig. 5.2.

Gb (between PCU and SGSN) is a frame relay-based interface using BSS GPRS protocol (BSSGP).

Gr (between HLR and SGSN) is an SS7-based interface using MAP.

Gs (between MSC/VLR and SGSN) is an SS7-based interface using Signaling Connection Control Part (SCCP).

Gd (between SMSC and SGSN) is an SS7-based interface using MAP.

Gn (between GGSN and SGSN or between SGSN and SGSN) is an IP-based interface using the GPRS Tunneling Protocol (GTP).

Gc (between HLR and GGSN) is an SS7-based interface using MAP.

Ga (between SGSN and CGF, or between CGF and GGSN) is an SS7-based interface using MAP.

5.1.3 Transmission Plane and Signaling Plane

The logical interfaces are used between MS and SGSN

Transmission plane: for packet data transfer

Signaling plane: for signaling

A. The overall interface structure for the transmission plane is shown in Fig. 5.3. The MAC and RLC layers are appeared in GSM systems. The new Logic Link Control (LLC) provides a logical link and frame structure between the MS and SGSN. Any data between the MS and SGSN is sent in Logical Link Protocol Data Units (LL-PDUs). It supports the detection and recovery from lost or corrupted LL-PDUs, ciphering, and flow control. The information is encrypted across not only radio interface base GSM but also across the Abis interface and the Gb interface.

The SNDCP (Sub Network Dependent Convergence Protocol) resides between the LLC and the IP network to support multiple network protocols without having to change LLC layer. It also performs compression to increase the data throughput.

In GGSN, the IP layer repeats:

- One IP connection is for application layer.

- One IP connection is between GGSN and SGSN. The GTP-associated packet is in a wrapper for transmission at the GGSN. As the wrapper is removed, the packet is passed to the MS using SNDCP. The packet at MS passes to GGSN following the reverse procedure.

B. The overall interface structure for the signaling plane from MS to SGSN is shown in Fig. 5.4.

At the lower layer, the transmission plane and the signaling plane are the same. Above the LLC layer, the GMM/SM (GPRS Mobility Management and Session Management) protocol is used in the signaling plane instead of the SNDCP. GMM/SM is used for RA updating, authentication function, PDP context (session) establishment, modification, and deactivation.

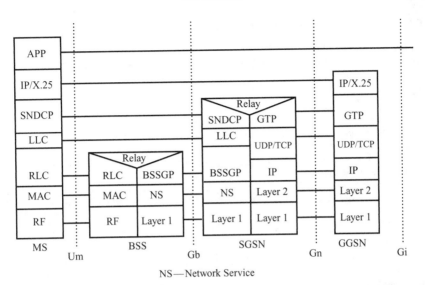

NS—Network Service

FIGURE 5.3   GPRS transmission plane.

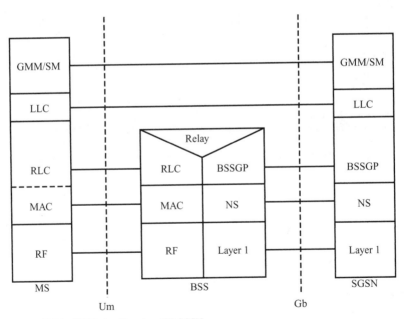

FIGURE 5.4   GPRS signaling plane MS-SGSN.

5.1.4 GPRS Traffic Performance

GPRS performs a GPRS Attach or Combined GPRS/GSM Attach when the MS may want to attach a single GPRS network (Class-C MS) or to simultaneously attach to both GSM and GPRS networks (Class-B MS), respectively.

A. GPRS Attach

A Class-C MS can be activated either when its power is on or when its browser is activated for packet traffic. A GPRS Attach is similar to the functionality of a location update in GSM. The process begins with a packet channel request from the MS. The network responds with a packet uplink assignment, which allocates a specific time slot or time slots to the MS. Upon receipt of the Attach request at BSS, the BSS uses the PACCH to acknowledge the receipt and forwards the Attach request to an SGSN. Based on the MM (Mobility Management) message in the request sent by the MS, the assigned resources will typically be sufficient for the MS to send user packet data.

B. Combined GPRS/GSM Attach

When a Class-B MS is powered up and needs to attach to both the GSM and GPRS services, the SGSN performs the procedures required of a GPRS and also interacts with the VLR to initiate a GSM Attach through a normal GSM location update.

C. Establishing a PDP Context

This transfer of GPRS packet data is through the establishment of a PDP context, that is, a data session. When an MS or the network initiates a PDP context, the MS moves from the standby state to the ready state. This request includes a number of important information elements, a requested network SAPI (Service Access Point Identifier), a requested LLC SAPI, a requested QoS, a requested PDP address, and a requested APN (Access Point Name) and sends to GGSN via SGSN. In responding to the SGSN's message, GGSN creates PDP Context Response, and then the SGSN sends Activate PDP Context Accept to the MS.

D. Routing Area Update

In GPRS, because of the nature of the sending packet, each PDU to or from the MS is sending the packet individually. No permanent resource is established between the SGSN and MS during a GPRS call. As the MS moves from one SGSN to another during an active PDP context, special functions need to be invoked so that packets are not lost during the transition.

First, the MS notices, from the PBCCH of the network, that it is in a new routing area. The MS, then, sends a routing area update to the new SGSN and sends an SGSN context Request message to the old SGSN. The GTP message is passed from the old SGSN to the new SGSN over the IP network. The new SGSN responds to the old one with the SGSN context Acknowledge, a GTP message. The new SGSN also sends an Update PDP Context Request to the GGSN to inform the GGSN of the new serving SGSN for the PDP context. The GGSN responds with the Update PDP Context Response message. Any subsequent PDUs from the GGSN to the MS are now sent via the new SGSN.

E. Networking Dimensioning for Traffic

1. Air Interface Dimensioning: To determine the required GPRS, an interface capacity is to estimate the amount of data traffic that a given call will be required to handle in a busy hour, because the voice transmission is in a real time, and the data transmission is not. Also, GPRS is overlaid on the GSM network. The voice and data transmission are sharing the same RF resource. The system operator has to adjust the distribution of traffic load between voice and data according to the total revenue received if the resource is limited. The capacity calculation is shown in Chapter 16. The RF capacity of a given GPRS based on the number of GPRS users in a cell can be calculated. The parameters of planning RF capacity of GPRS based on a single cell are listed as follows:

RF Carriers	Number of Carriers
TCH	Number of TCHs (based on the gross data rate)
Delay Time Allowed	Seconds or minutes
BER Required	b/s

2. Network Node Dimensioning
   The network elements that need to be dimensioned for GPRS traffic are BS, SGSN, and GGSN. The GPRS-specific dimensioning parameters are listed as follows:

Network Node	GPRS-Specific Dimensioning Factors
BSC	• Number of PDCHs
	• Number of Gb ports
SGSN	• Number of attached subscribers
	• Total throughput
	• Number of Gb ports
	• Number of cells
	• Number of routing areas
GGSN	• Number of simultaneous PDP contexts
	• Total throughput

5.2 EDGE (ENHANCED DATA RATES FOR GLOBAL EVALUATION)

5.2.1 Introduction

EDGE is a new time division multiplexing-based radio access technology to enhance packet radio service[2] that gives GSM and TDMA an evolutionary path toward 3G in 400, 800, 900, 1800, and 1900 MHz bands. Although EDGE reuses GSM carrier bandwidth and time-slot structures, it is not restricted to use in GSM cellular systems only. In fact, it can provide a generic air interface for higher data rates. It can be introduced smoothly into the existing systems without altering the cell planning. But as with GPRS, EDGE doesn't provide any additional voice capacity. The initial EDGE standard promised mobile data rates of 384 kbps. It allows data transmission speeds of 384 kbps to be achieved when all eight time slots are used. In fact, EDGE was formerly called GSM384, which means a maximum bit rate of 48 kbps per time slot. Even higher speeds may be available in good radio conditions. Actual rates will be lower with rates falling as one goes away from the cell site. GPRS is based on Gaussian minimum-shift keying (GMSK), which only yields a moderate increase in data bit rates per time slot. EDGE, on the other hand, is based on a new modulation scheme that allows a much higher bit rate across the air interface. This modulation technique is called eight-phase-shift keying (8 PSK). It automatically adapts to radio circumstances and thereby offers its highest rates in good propagation conditions close to the site of base stations. This shift in modulation from GMSK to 8 PSK is the central change with EDGE.

The idea behind EDGE is to eke out even higher data rates on the current 200-kHz GSM radio carrier while still working with current circuit (and packet) switches.

Only one EDGE transceiver unit will need to be added to each cell. With most vendors, it is envisioned that software upgrades to the BSCs and base stations can be carried out remotely. The new EDGE-capable transceiver can also handle standard GSM traffic and will automatically switch to EDGE mode when needed. EDGE capable terminals will also be needed—existing GSM terminals do not support the new modulation techniques and will need to be upgraded to use EDGE network functionality.

5.2.2 Network Architecture

The network architecture for EDGE is basically the same as that for GPRS: basically the same network elements, the same interfaces, the same protocols, and the same procedures. Some minor differences in the network are insignificant when compared to the enhancements to the air interface, which is where we shall focus.

5.2.2.1 Modulation. EDGE uses the same 200-kHz channels and 8 time-slot structure as used for GSM and GPRS. In EDGE, however, 8 PSK modulation is introduced in addition to the 0.3 Gaussian Minimum Shift Keying (GMSK), which is currently used in GSM.

The objective with EDGE is to offer higher bandwidth efficiency using the same 200-kHz channel. This higher bandwidth efficiency is achieved through 8 PSK. In general, PSK involves a phase change of the carrier signal according to the incoming bit stream. With 8 PSK, the incoming bit stream in groups of three bits (8 states) at a time can allow phase changes of $45°$, $90°$, $135°$, $180°$, $225°$, $270°$, or $315°$. The specific phase change of the signal represents the change from one set of three bits to the next. With EDGE, the symbol rate is still 270.833 ksymbols/second, as it is in GSM. Each symbol, however, is three bits, such that we have a bit rate of 812.5 kbps.

Of course, we do not get this great increase in bandwidth efficiency for free. In addition to any extra cost associated with producing devices that can support 8 PSK modulations, we must also contend with the fact that 8 PSK is more sensitive to noise than GMSK and makes it more difficult for a receiver to determine the exact phase change. Because of the fact that the states in 8 PSK are quite close together, the amount of noise tolerated for errors has to be relatively small—smaller than the amount of noise that GMSK can handle. The direct result of this is that if a BTS supports both GMSK and 8 PSK modulations and has the same output power for both, then the cell coverage is smaller for 8 PSK than for GMSK. To overcome this limitation, however, the specifications for EDGE are such that both the coding scheme and modulation scheme can be adjusted in response to RF conditions. Thus, as user moves toward the edge of a cell, the effect of lower signal to noise will mean that the network can reduce the user's throughput, by changing the coding scheme to include greater error detection. As a result, the user will receive a slower throughput.

5.2.2.2 Coding Schemes. With the advent of EDGE, we find a number of new channel coding schemes in addition to the coding schemes that exist for GSM voice and GPRS data. For packet data services in an EDGE network, we refer to *Enhanced GPRS* (EGPRS) and the new coding schemes for EGPRS are termed *Modulation and Coding Scheme-1 to Modulation and Coding Scheme-9* (MCS-1 to MCS-9). The reason why they are not just called coding schemes is the fact that for MCS-1 to MCS-4, GMSK modulation is used, whereas 8-PSK modulation is used for MCS-5 to MCS-9.

Table 5.1 shows the modulation scheme and data rate applicable to each MCS.

TABLE 5.1 Modulation and Coding Schemes for GPRS and EDGE

GPRS Coding Scheme	EDGE Coding Scheme	Modulation	RLC Blocks per Radio Block (20 ms)	Input Data Payload (bits)	Net Data Rate (kbps)	Remarks
CS1	MCS-1	GMSK	1	176	8.8	Error protection
CS2	MCS-2	GMSK	1	224	11.2	Error protection
CS3	MCS-3	GMSK	1	296	14.8	Error protection
CS4	MCS-4	GMSK	1	352	17.6	No error protection
	MCS-5	8-PSK	1	448	22.4	Error protection
	MCS-6	8-PSK	1	592	29.6	Error protection
	MCS-7	8-PSK	2	2×448	44.8	Error protection
	MCS-8	8-PSK	2	2×544	54.4	Error protection
	MCS-9	8-PSK	2	2×592	59.2	No error protection

MCS-4 using GMSK offers no error protection for the user data, nor does MCS-9 using 8 PSK. MCS-4 offers the same data rate as CS-4 in GPRS. The difference is due to the fact that in EGPRS, the RLC/MAC header is coded differently from the rest of the PDU and contains additional bits for error correction. The objective is to ensure that at least the header can be decoded. The same does not apply for CS-4.

5.2.2.3 Channel Types. The channel types applicable to EDGE are the same as those applicable to GPRS: we have a number of PDCHs that carry PCCCH, PBCCH, and PDTCHs. These channels are shared among GPRS and EDGE users. Thus, both GPRS users and EDGE users can be multiplexed on a given PDTCH. During those radio blocks when an EDGE user uses the PDTCH, the modulation may be either GMSK or 8 PSK, whereas it must be GMSK when used by a GPRS user.

Similar to the manner in which the network controls the coding scheme to be used by a GPRS user, the network also controls the MCS to be used by an EDGE user in both the uplink and downlink. This is done through the addition of new information elements in the Packet Uplink Assignment and Packet Downlink Assignment messages.

One important aspect of GPRS and EDGE users sharing the same PDTCH on the uplink is the use of the USF (uplink state flag). The USF is used with dynamic allocation, is sent on the downlink, and is used to indicate which MS has access to the next RLC/MAC block on the uplink. If a given PDTCH is being used for both GPRS and EDGE MSs, then it is important that both types of MS be able to decode the USF, so that they may appropriately schedule uplink transmissions.

Consequently, when a PDTCH is used for both GPRS and EDGE, GMSK modulation must be used for any radio block that assigns uplink resources to a GPRS MS. All other radio blocks may use 8 PSK modulation. Note that this forced use of GMSK for radio blocks destined for an 8 PSK MS only applies with dynamic allocation.

5.2.3 Network Control

The phase one of EDGE emphasizes enhanced circuit-switched data (ECSD) and enhanced GPRS (EGPRS).

The NA-TDMA terminals that support 30-kHz circuit-switched services scan for a 30-kHz control channel (DCCH) according to TIA/EIA 136 procedures. If an acceptable 200-kHz EGPRS carrier exists, a pointer to this system will be available on the DCCH. On finding this, the terminal will leave the 30-kHz system and start scanning of the 200-kHz system. When it finds it, it starts behaving as if it were a GSM/GPRS terminal. To answer a circuit-switched page, the mobile suspends packet data traffic and starts looking for a 30-kHz control channel. Mobile terminals that only support 200-kHz carriers immediately start looking for a 200-kHz packet data system.

EDGE is currently being developed in two modes: compact and classic. Compact employs a new 200-kHz control channel structure. Synchronized base stations are used to maintain a minimum spectrum deployment of 1 MHz in a $K = 3$ frequency reuse pattern. EDGE Classic on the other hand employs the traditional GSM 200-kHz control structure with a $K = 4$ frequency reuse pattern.

5.3 *HSCSD (HIGH SPEED CIRCUIT SWITCHED DATA)*

GSM Circuit Switched Data supports one user per channel per time slot. High Speed Circuit Switched Data (HSCSD)[4] gives a single user simultaneous access to multiple channels (up to four) at the same time. As such, there is a direct trade-off between greater speed and the associated cost from using more radio resources—it is expensive for end users to pay for multiple simultaneous calls.

Assuming a standard Circuit Switched Data transmission rate of 14.4 kilobits per second (kbps), using four time slots with HSCSD allows theoretical speeds of up to 57.6 kpbs. This is broadly equivalent to providing the same transmission rate as that available over one ISDN B-Channel. Some Mobile Switching Centers (MSCs) are limited to 64 kbps maximum throughput—this restriction is removed with GPRS.

In networks where HSCSD is deployed, GPRS may only be assigned third priority, after voice as number one priority and HSCSD as number two. In theory, HSCSD can be preempted by voice calls—such that HSCSD calls can be reduced to one channel if voice calls are seeking to occupy these channels. HSCSD does not disrupt voice service availability, but it does affect GPRS. Even given preemption, it is difficult to see how HSCSD can be deployed in busy networks and still confer an agreeable user experience (i.e., continuously high data rate). HSCSD is therefore more likely to be deployed in startup networks or those with plenty of spare capacity, as it is relatively inexpensive to deploy and can turn some spare channels into revenue streams. HSCSD is however easier to implement in mobile networks than GPRS, because some GSM vendor solutions require only a software upgrade of base stations and no new hardware. This is not the case with D-AMPS (IS-136) networks and some GSM vendor solutions.

There are a couple of reasons why HSCSD may be the preferred bearer for certain applications when compared to GPRS. The fact that associated packets can be sent in different directions to arrive at the same destination should in theory make the transmission more robust, as there are many different ways of achieving the end result. However, this nature of packet transmission means that packets are subjected to variable delay and some could be lost. While packet retransmission is incorporated into the GPRS standards, naturally this process does take time, and in the case of applications such as video transmission can cause poor quality images. HSCSD system can avoid this situation.

Another preferred application for HSCSD could be the fact that although GPRS is complementary for communicating with other packet-based networks such as the Internet, HSCSD could be the best way of communicating with other circuit-switched communications media such as the PSTN and ISDN.

In the case of transmitting a big volume of data, sending by HSCSD instead of by packet data can eliminate the overhead of the packets. The data throughput should be higher. This can be another preferred application.

5.4 iDEN (INTEGRATED DIGITAL ENHANCED NETWORK)

5.4.1 History

Prior to 1994, iDEN was called MIRS (Mobile Integrated Radio System). MIRS is a cellular-like system developed by Motorola to operate at the special mobile radio (SMR) band. MIRS used DSC switches. The performance of MIRS was not desirable. Then Motorola adopted GSM switches made by Nortel and changed the name to iDEN. Besides the conventional functions such as circuit-switched voice and data, many new functions are implemented in iDEN system, such as Push-to-Talk (PTT), Dispatch calls, and Packet Data Service. In this section, we describe the unique functions and services of iDEN and do not iterate those conventional wireless functions and services in iDEN.

5.4.2 Description of iDEN's Attributes[3]

The iDEN system provides both full and half-duplex operations:

- Half duplex: where one user is transmitting (talking) and other users are receiving (listening).
- Full duplex: where there is an open bidirectional link that allows full two-way communication.

This melding of communication operations allows much of the voice traffic to be run in half duplex mode while providing full duplex functionality when required.

The iDEN system is an integration of traditional PTT, half duplex, analog radio technology, and feature-rich, full duplex digital cellular communications.

The iDEN system can provide the following features:

- Opens communication to other subscriber corporations and all telephones.
- Increases the coverage area.
- Allows private and group calling.
- Optimizes RF resources.
- Improves quality with tighter frequencies and digital technology.

iDEN provides the following services:

- Messaging (Short Message Service).
- Private, Two-way and Group Call Cellular Telephony Service.
- Voice Mail.
- Data Networking (Intranet, Virtual Private Network [VPN], Internet).

iDEN provides the following adaptive designs:

- Network scaling.
- RF Channel usage in several spectrum bandwidths.
- Circuit-switched (dial-up) and Packet-data (IP) digital data network.
- Dispatch capability for Private, Local and Wide Area Group calling.
- Alphanumeric Messaging (Short Messaging Service).
- Compact portable Mobile Station.

In iDEN logical environment, most communications can be logically organized and grouped. When a sufficient number of users is reached, call patterns and communication relationships can be organized into a 4-tier functional model. The units of the model are

- Global: all the potential users of voice and data communications.

- Fleet: the broad logical group of users based on a common bond usually consisting of between 15 and 65,000 users (95,000 for Software Release 8.0).

- Talk Group: a subset of a fleet based on the interrelationship of users in the fleet (manages, sales, transportation, drivers, etc.).

- User: an individual or a compatible device that has access to the network.

5.4.3 iDEN's Unique Features

A. Circuit-switched (dial-up) and packet-data (IP) digital data network

1. **Circuit Switched Data Networking:** using traditional dial-up technologies, an iDEN MS can access and use remote computing services based on the access rights and permissions of a host server or an Internet service provider.

2. **Packet Data Networking:** packet data allows an MS to be logically linked to a host system of the Internet. Using packet data, the MS becomes a remote mobile node on the associated network.

B. Dispatch Calling
Dispatch calls follow the half duplex model of communication. Communication is one way at a time. This applies to most voice communication.

Dispatch calling splits a single 25-MHz carrier into 6 channels. This division increases the carrier load from one (analog cellular) to a maximum of 6 per carrier.

During a dispatch talk, one channel on the carrier is used. All those in the group listening during a group call at a single cell site use only one channel—reducing resources. For everyone in the conversation, only one channel at each hosting EBTS (Enhanced BTS) is used. A channel is used and allocated for the duration of the conversation (until everybody hangs up or times out). This consolidation reduces the network traffic and allows dynamic channel assignment to maximize the network resources.

5.4.4 iDEN Communications Network

The layout of an overall iDEN network is shown in Fig. 5.5. It is basically a TDMA system. Each major component shown has subsystems that perform more specific tasks. The different components in iDEN compared with those in the other systems are mobile station, EBTS, dispatch call processing, interconnect call processing, and OMC. The architecture of those elements is shown in Fig. 5.6.

A. MS (mobile station) is capable of:

- *Multiservice*
- *Dispatch calling*
- *Interconnect calling*
- *Roaming*
- *Message mail*
- *Data communications*
- *PTT*

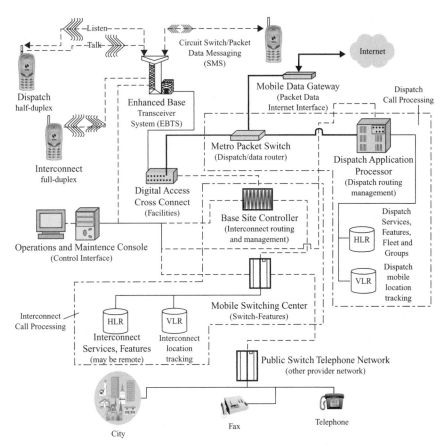

FIGURE 5.5 Simplified iDEN communications network.

B. EBTS (Enhanced BTS) consists of

- *Access Control Gateway (ACG):* Two units
    1. iDEN site controller (iSC) that integrates the access gateway, timing reference, and facilities termination functions. It discriminates between dispatch, interconnection, and packet data calls and routes the traffic accordingly.
    2. iDEN Monitor Unit (iMU) that integrates the Environment Alarm System (EAS) and the Base Monitor Radio (BMR).
- *Base Radio (BR):* One BR is used for each 25-kHz carrier; one EBTS supports 20 BRs as an omnisite and 24 BRs as a three-sector site. BRs and radio link traffic (voice and data) are controlled by ACG over a LAN.
- *Site Timing Reference:* Each EBTS uses GPS for site-to-site from synchronization.
- *Radio Link:* A 64-kbps digital base band signal subdivided into 6 time slots. Each time slot at the cell site is a radio link. Radio link functions are channel disconnect and reconnect, trolling, handover, and cell selection.

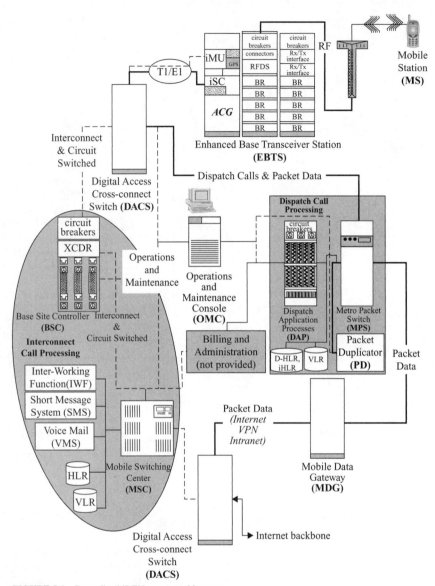

FIGURE 5.6 Generalized iDEN system architecture.

- *Switching Function:* For calls in the range of a single EBTS, the EBTS handles and controls handover in conjunction with the MS.
- *Network Management Agent:* Part of EBTS is the network management agent.

C. **Digital Access Connect Switch (DACS):** DACS is the attachment point of T1/E1 span lines and is required to connect the remote locations of iDEN system equipment to the mobile switching office (MSO).

D. **Metro Packet Switch (MPS):** MPS is a subsystem that connects the EBTS frame relay connections to the Dispatch Application Processor (DAP) and the Packet Duplicators (PD). MPS manipulates:

- The paths dispatch of voice packets during a dispatch call
- The data packet paths during a packet data networking

E. **Dispatch Application Processor (DAP):** DAP is mainly for dispatch and packet data control, maintaining the last dispatch location area for dispatch mobility. DAPs are usually deployed in groups. Each DAP consists of:

- Standard systems controller (SSC) cards, which provide the sever net communications routing for internal equipment.
- Input-out controller (IOC) cards, which provide for the connection of external equipment.
- Central processing unit (CPU), which provides the central processing engine and memory for the DAP.
- Router controller cards (RCC), which manage communication routing of control signaling, and operation and maintenance information between DAPs.
- Mass storage devices.

F. **Packet Duplicator:** The packet duplicators provide the functionality to allow broadcast, group, and multicast operation with dispatch calls.

G. **Mobile Data Gateway (MDG):** MDG is the interface to the Internet and WWW (Worldwide Web) for iDEN system during packet data operation.

H. **Base Site Controller (BSC):** BSC manages interconnect call processing between EBTS sites and other network devices such as their associated MSs. It functions are link concentration, radio-link conversion, data collection, and control information handling. The major BSC selves are divided by functions.

- *Base Site Controller–Control processor (BSC-CP):* Contains the memory and logic circuits to administer and monitor the routing of Interconnect Calls.
- *Base Site Controller–Transcoder (BSC-XCDR):* Converts the voice packets used on the radio link to the Pulse Code Modulation (PCM) used by local and interconnected Public Switch Telephone Networks (PSTNs).

I. **Mobile Switch Center (MSC):** MSC is a GSM-based Mobile Telephone Switch, which provides interconnect services. The MSC diagram is shown in Fig. 5.7. The same functions as GSM switch are provided.

J. **Operation and Maintenance Center (OMC):** Depending on the complexity and control requirements of iDEN system, the OMC exists in at least one form of three in every iDEN system:

- OMC-Radio (OMC-R): Required for radio system management.
- OMC-System (OMC-S): For possible switching system management.
- OMC-Network (OMC-N): For possible Network Operation Center (NOC).

Among the three forms, the OMC-R is needed in most of iDEN systems.

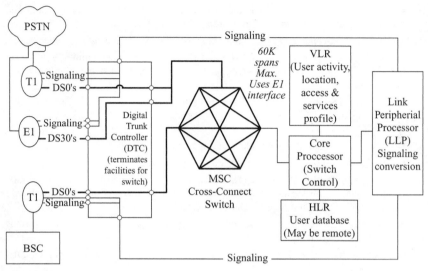

FIGURE 5.7   Mobile switching center components.

K. Administrative Data Center (ADC): ADC is for billing and administration, which is customer-supplied equipment.

5.4.5   Radio Link

A. Frequency Bands: The iDEN system uses 25-MHz frequency carrier pairs. One carrier is used for transmit, the other for receive. This is summarized on Table 5.2. Some bands cannot be combined. Software Release 8.0 also allows the use of more than one frequency range in a network. There are specific limitations to multiple range implementations as follows:

TABLE 5.2   iDEN Radio Frequency Spectral Bands

Frequency Spectral Bands	Channel Spacing	Carrier Pairs (MHz)	Link	Spacing	Offset
806–821	25 kHz	806–821	Uplink (from MS)	45 MHz	12 kHz
		851–866	Downlink (to MS)		
821–825*	25 kHz	821–825*	Uplink (from MS)	45 MHz	12 kHz
		866–870*	Downlink (to MS)		
896–901	25 kHz	896–901	Uplink (from MS)	39 MHz	12 kHz
		935–940	Downlink (to MS)		
1453–1465	25 kHz	1453–1465	Uplink (from MS)	48 MHz	12 kHz
		1501–1513	Downlink (to MS)		

*Requires Software Release 8.0.

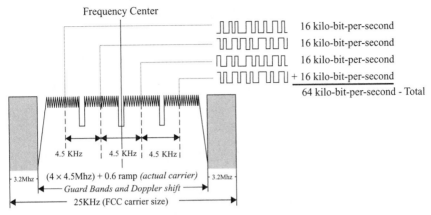

FIGURE 5.8 Logical RF channel sidebands.

- All radios (BRs) in a cell site (EBTS) must have the same frequency spectral band.
- All members of neighbor list must have the same frequency spectral band.

B. **RF Signal:** The iDEN RF signal consists of four independent side bands. The center frequencies of these side bands are 4.5-kHz apart from each other, and they're spaced symmetrically about a suppressed RF carrier frequency (Fig. 5.8). Each sideband is a logical 16-kbps data carrier. The resulting signal produces a 64 kilobit-per-second (64 kbps) gross-radio-channel-bit-rate. Data is transmitted on each of the four sidebands. Using four sidebands allows more data to be transmitted because it increases the data rate.

C. **Carrier Modulation:** The method used to modulate digital voice and data on the RF carrier is 16 Quadrature Amplitude Modulation (16-QAM). This implementation of the data transfer standard uses phase and amplitude modulation to create 16 offset points around the carrier waveform. Each point represents a bit pattern (Fig. 5.9). The

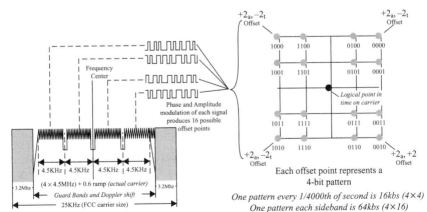

FIGURE 5.9 Quadrature Amplitude Modulation on 4 carrier sidebands.

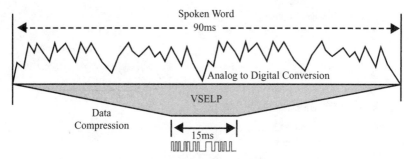

FIGURE 5.10   iDEN VSELP voice compression to 6:1 the radio link.

logical point in time on carrier is at the center. Each of 16 offset points represents a 4-bit pattern. One pattern of each of 4 side bands is 64 kbps (4 × 16).

D. Digital Voice Processing: The iDEN system converts analog voice into digital data for transmission across the radio link of the network. The iDEN system converts and compresses the analog voice into digital data that can be applied to the carrier using 16-QAM.

Voice sounds are converted to digital data by sampling the analog waveform and reducing it to a set of numbers. An algorithm that measures and predicts the waveform and converts it to a digital data stream interprets the analog voice. The 8-bit voice codec (vocoder) used is Vector Sum Excited Linear Predicting (VSELP).

By sampling the voice in small time-slices (milliseconds), summing the vectors (changes in amplitude slope), and predicting changes (gross sum of changes), the voice can be converted to digital with a response time to accurately reproduce speech. The data stream is then compressed before it is applied to the 4 carrier sidebands. This converts and compresses 90 ms of speech into 15 ms of digital data. The resultant data packets are applied to the radio link (Fig. 5.10).

E. TDMA Radio Carrier Access Method: Time Division Multiple Access (TDMA) allows more than one user or device to multiplex on (share) a given carrier. In the iDEN system, the radio carrier's digital data stream is divided by time (Fig. 5.11). Because the data stream runs much faster than is required during communication, other data

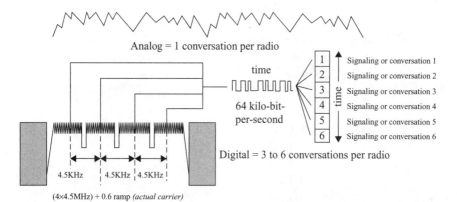

FIGURE 5.11   TDMA radio link time slots.

or conversations can be placed on a single radio carrier (may be interleaved) without degrading or interfering with each other. This increases the possible conversations per radio from one (analog cellular) to:

- 3 per radio (Interconnect)
- 4 per radio (2 Dispatch and 2 Interconnect)
- 6 per radio (Dispatch only)

The iDEN TDMA system divides the RF carrier into 6 discrete time slots of 15 ms in duration. Each of these time slots is a separate unit that contains overhead for transmitter turn-on, training and synchronization, propagation delay, or conversation. Auxiliary data embedded within each slot provides associated signaling. The sharing of the time slots (interleaving) increases the carriers' capacity.

Time slot 1 on a BR of each sector or cell is designated as a Primary Control Channel. These channels are used for call setup, MS contact, and MS location. Secondary Control Channels may be assigned if traffic volume is high enough to saturate the Primary Control Channels.

F. **Timeslot Allocation:** A typical iDEN option increases radio link time slots allocated to a single voice conversation for interconnect calls from 1 to 2 per frame as shown in Fig. 5.12. By doubling the time slots available, the voice-sampling rate can be increased. An increase of the voice sample rate results in improved audio quality. The voice bits are transmitted using two time slots of the 6 time-slot frames. This allows the use of the 8.0 kbps VSELP vocoder, which increases the voice-sampling rate to improve tone and richness. The iDEN system also uses forward error correction to reduce corrupted bits in the voice transmissions. This results in improved audio quality even in weak signal and interference areas. This 3:1 interleave is used in interconnect calls.

Doubling the number of time slots per call reduces the traffic-carrying capacity of the system. The time slot allocation methods provide flexibility for the operator to balance the requirements for superior audio quality against a reduction in capacity and support for other services. The breakdown on 3:1 interleave voice channels is

- Embedded signaling = 0.533333 kbps (24 bits per slot)
- FEC = 6.755555 kbps (304 bits per slot)

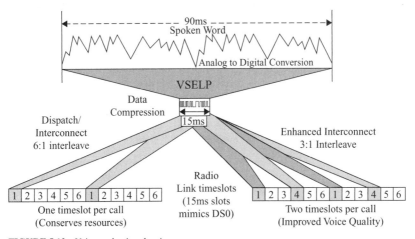

FIGURE 5.12 Voice packet interleaving.

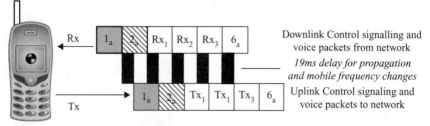

FIGURE 5.13   Time Division Duplex operation.

- Voice = 8 kbps (360 bits per slot)
- Total = 15.28888 kbps

Both 3:1 and 6:1 voice channels use the same transmission unit defined in the Layer 2 RF Interface protocol. The main difference is that 3:1 interleave slots are twice as often as 6:1 interleave slots. The method used will affect RF optimization and planning.

G. **TDD (Time Division Duplex): iDEN** also can support TDD system. To further optimize resources, the discrete time slots in conversation are divided and offset so transmit (Tx) and receive (Rx) control and voice information can share resources. Both the uplink to the network and the downlink to the mobile can share time slots during interconnect calls. Interconnect calls use two carriers. The Mobile Transmit and Receive frequencies are separate. With Time Division Duplex, the mobile dynamically shifts frequencies to send and receive voice, data, and signaling information.

   TDD further reduces the network's packet overhead and eliminates the need for RF duplexer on the MS. To reduce errors in propagation delay and allow the mobile to retune, the radio link's mobile receive packet is offset ahead of the mobile transmit packet (Fig. 5.13).

5.4.6   Dispatch Call Processing

A. **Dispatch only service:**   Because dispatch calls exist entirely within the iDEN system, the services, configuration, and administration of individual MSs on the system can be tightly controlled. If desired, a MS on the network may be excluded from using the PSTN networks. Conversely, a MS may be restricted from making dispatch calls. Both of these options are defined by service provisioning in the D-HLR and HLR.

   Figure 5.14 represents a simplified diagram of the iDEN system elements involved in Dispatch services. The MS sends, receives voice, and displays data. The EBTS converts the radio link to the land network link and discriminates between Dispatch, Packet Data, and Interconnect calls. The MPS routes dispatch call voice packets and packet data packets. The DAP determines service availability and location information. The APD (advanced packet duplicator) duplicates voice packet that needs to be sent to multiple MSs in group calling.

   The control and monitoring steps to complete a dispatch call are internal to the iDEN system. Aside from dialing, sending, and receiving, the steps to complete the call are user transparent. There are three major steps in a typical dispatch call.

- Establish radio link
- Route digital voice packets
- Duplicate packets for group calls

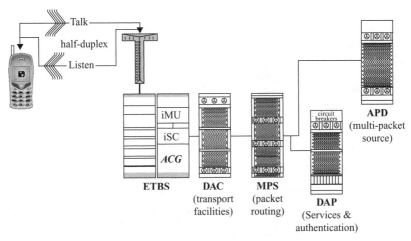

FIGURE 5.14   Simplified Dispatch diagram.

B. Dispatch call procedure: The simplified steps of a typical dispatch call are shown in Fig. 5.15.

1. A dispatch call is requested via PTT activation.

The call request packet is routed to the DAP.

The DAP recognizes the MSs group and finds the group members by dispatch location area (DLA).

2. The DAP sends location requests to the member's DLA to obtain current sector or cell.

3. The group member MSs respond with each current sector or cell location.

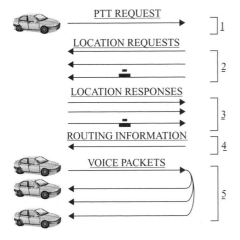

FIGURE 5.15   Typical Dispatch Call summary.

4. The DAP supplies each member's routing information to the MPS and PD.

5. Call voice packets are sent to the PD, where they are replicated and distributed to the MS sites.

C. Dispatch call types

1. Dispatch Private Call (DPC)

- A Private Call is similar to a one-to-one call. One user enters another user's designation (Fleet Member ID) and the call connection is one-way and exclusive. Other members of the fleet and group are not involved in the conversation.

- A private dispatch call was limited to another member of the same fleet in the same region.

- The caller enters the called MS's Fleet Member ID and presses the talk button on the MS to hail the iDEN system. The hail sends a request for service over the radio link control channel to the EBTS then to the DAP.

- During call setup, the DAP validates the MS (caller), the request, and the target (authentication). After validation, the DAP sends a location request to the called MS unit. If resources are not available to either the caller or called MS, the call is queued.

- If resources are available and the called party is available, a call reestablishment indicates to the originator that the called party has been located and is ready for the call.

- The called MS activates the audio. The caller's Fleet Member ID is sent to the called MS during the set-up process for display on the called user's MS or for returning another call. The called MS may display the caller's alias if it has the feature and is programmed to display the alias.

- The private call functionality is shown in Fig. 5.16. There are two phases:

  Phase 1: A Private Call (PC) is set up automatically. No other users hear the communication. When a PC is initiated, after the PC proceeding message, PC Page message is sent.

  Phase 2: Only the call returning a PC Page Response to the DAP is included in the PC. If no resources are available, the PC MS will be put into a queue. The DAP PC queue timer is adjustable. If no resources are available after the queue timer expires, the MS will receive an indication that the PC setup is being torn down.

2. Dispatch Group Calls (DGC)

Dispatch Group Calls allow MSs, which are members of predefined groups, to communicate in half-duplex (one person talking at a time and the others listening) among themselves. Only members of the group can participate in the conversation, and any

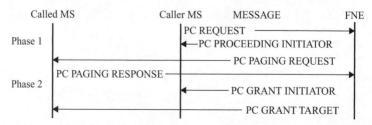

FIGURE 5.16 Private Call functionality.

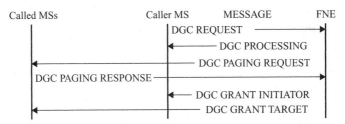

FIGURE 5.17 Dispatch Call setup.

authorized group member can either set up or participate in the call. The call can be set up without all group members being available and can involve members being served at different sites. Dispatch group call setup is shown in Fig. 5.17. Any group member can leave the group at any time. After one MS makes the request, the Fixed Network Equipment (FNE):

- Validates the Dispatch Group Call request.
- Determines the Dispatch Location Areas (DLAs) of the group's members.
- Page's member sends a Location Request in those DLAs.
- On Page response, assigns a channel at each site that needs to be added and have resources available.

There are three types of Dispatch Group Calls (DGC):

- Local Area Call: Communications between MS and the "Home" or "Local" service area.
- Selected Area Call: Communications between a caller and a group in a different service area.
- Wide Area Call: Communications between a caller and a group anywhere in the network.

If no servers are available at the caller's site, the call is queued. If a server is available at the caller's site but not at other sites, those sites are included into the call as servers become available. Pages will be sent out only in those Location Areas where active group members are registered (provisioned). Once an MS responds to the page, only those cells with active MSs will have voice channels assigned. After each transmission, the FNE maintains the call for the predefined hang time. If the hang time expires, the channels are disconnected and the call is torn down.

The types of Dispatch Group Calls that define the extent of the area of the call are Wide Area, Local Service Area, and Selected Service Area Dispatch Group Calls.

5.4.7 Packet Data Networking

Packet Data Networking is nonvoice communications that interface directly with Intranet, Virtual Private Network (VPN), Extranet, and Internet. Packet Data Networking allows the service provider to become a point-of-presence for mobile users on the Internet. This section will describe the fundamentals of Packet Data.

Packet Data Networking uses the iDEN system dispatch calling functions and infrastructure. An MS may travel freely throughout an iDEN system and teamed roaming partners.

If it is supported and provisioned, a user can originate or receive Packet Data. Interconnect facsimile and Dial-up services are not supported.

• The MS sends and receives data directly.
• The EBTS determines the cell as Packet Data and converts the radio link to data packets.
• The MPS routes data packets.
• The DAP determines services and location.
• The MDG routes the data to and from the Internet.
• The Billing Accumulator (BA) collects time and bit-transfer information for billing as desired by the service provider.

Packet Data Networking elements are shown in Fig. 5.18.

An MS may be a phone-type device, an emerging PDA, or Data Terminal Equipment (DTE) that is directly compatible with the iDEN system. Any MS, PDA, or RF computing device that provides digital data networking (Web browsing) and that is compatible with iDEN equipment may be used to create truly mobile computing. When a mobile is engaged in Packet Data, it exists as a mobile node on the Internet. The Mobile computing devices use Transmission Control Protocol/Internet Protocol (TCP/IP).

Intrasystem Mobility: Each MS is configured for packet data in its home DAP. The identification (IP address) and permissions for Packet Data are contained in the iHLR (iDEN HLR). The iHLR operates in the same manner as the D-HLR (Dispatch-HLR) except it identifies and verifies packet data services instead of dispatch calling services. The process of determining a handover and the handover procedures are similar to those in GSM. The required data reside in iHLR, iVLR and DAP for mobility management.

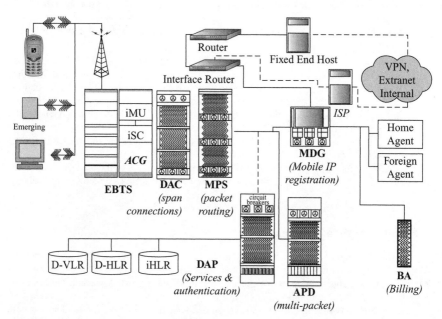

FIGURE 5.18   iDEN Packet Data networking elements.

Intersystem Mobility: For truly mobile computing, the iDEN system provides Packet Data remote system usage and roaming. Roaming uses the Home Agent and a Foreign Agent. Each of these is an MDG subsystem that serves an iDEN network. Each MDG contains a table of the addresses of all the roaming partner/remote MDGs (a virtual network).

5.5 *PHS (PERSONAL HANDY PHONE SYSTEM)*

PHS is a system that was developed in Japan and fit the need to replace the wireline telephones in many developing countries such as China. Therefore, this system became very popular after the 2G systems were deployed. In this section, we will describe the system's unique attributes.

5.5.1 Introduction

PHS is a wireless communication TDD system[4] that supports personal communication services (PCS). It uses small, low-complexity, lightweight terminals called personal stations (PSs). PHS can be used for public telepoint (a portable phone booth), wireless PBS, home cordless telephone, and walkie-talkie (PS-to-PS) communication.

PHS features wider coverage per cell; operation in a mobile outdoor environment; faster and distributed control of handoff; enhanced authentication, encryption, and privacy; and circuit and packet-oriented data services.

PHS is a micro-cellular mobile telephone system that works with 5E switch. It provides wireless local loop service in the 1895 to 1920 MHz band generally set aside for use by wireline service operators.

PHS creates a virtual local loop capacity on top of the existing facilities that connects the end user with the local switching center. By leveraging the existing outside plant, instead of just a single phone user per line, more than 20 subscribers per line can now be accommodated.

Because PHS uses micro-cellular dynamic channel allocation technology, which does not require the extensive traffic planning associated with cellular deployments, it can be deployed and in service quickly. Additionally, PHS can be rapidly incorporated into the existing 5E Switch as wireless local loop application to carry wireless voice and data traffic.

Deployments can start with minimum configurations. PHS offers a unique "need as you grow" strategy. The initial network investment is scaled to the actual number of subscribers supported within a geographic area. You only pay for what you need and you have network flexibility to accommodate growth.

5.5.2 PHS Network Structure and System Components

PHS Configuration: PHS includes the 5E PHS Service Center (PSC), Remote Access Interface Unit/Access Interface Unit (RAIU/AIU), Cell Stations, Cell Station Management System (CSMS), and Value Added Application Servers as shown in Fig. 5.19. The 5E PSC is the center of the call control for the network. The PSC with standard local/toll signaling interface, such as ISUP, is already part of the PSTN and can provide flexible network configurations for the operator. Based on the network coverage and traffic needs, the remote AIU provides up to 250-km radius of extended distance to provide ISDN access connection for

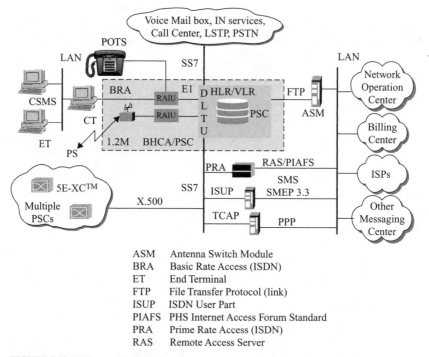

ASM   Antenna Switch Module
BRA   Basic Rate Access (ISDN)
ET   End Terminal
FTP   File Transfer Protocol (link)
ISUP   ISDN User Part
PIAFS PHS Internet Access Forum Standard
PRA   Prime Rate Access (ISDN)
RAS   Remote Access Server

FIGURE 5.19   PHS network structure.

various 3, 7, and 15 channel cell stations. The PSC includes the ASM high-speed TCP/IP interface to the billing center and network management center of an operator.

Handsets: With 32-kbps TDMA-TDD technology, its low transmission/reception power is 10 mW.

Cell Stations (CS): Three types of cell stations are available: Omni, Adaptive Array, and SDMA. PHS provides 500 mW for their 3, 7, 15 channel cell stations, and 20 mW for a 7 channel cell station.

Cell Station Management System: CSMS provides daily cell station remote data provisioning, traffic data collection and analysis, software updates, emergency operation, and maintenance. With the help of a digital map, CSMS can pinpoint the location of a troubled cell station. It can also help identify high-traffic needs and blind-spot areas for additional cell station installation to improve quality of service.

5.5.3   Value Added Service Platform

The PHS value added services is built on a unified platform with Application Programmable Interface (API), which provides great flexibility to add new applications and services. The PHS currently provides Short Message, Prepaid Phone, Location-based, Hi-Mode handset Web browsing service, and 32/64K data service. The unified PHS value added service platform can also provide standard TCP/IP interface for integrated services from the existing Internet Content Provider and/or customized services with third-party application providers. The Short Message Center can also provide a gateway function by interworking with CDMA/GSM short message centers.

- *Personal Mobility Communications:* PHS can be used as a primary or secondary line or as a family or business communications line. PHS provides citywide coverage. The same telephone number can be used to follow the customer everywhere within the service area.

- *Highspeed Wireless Data:* PHS offers wireless Internet connections with 32 or 64 kbps transmission rates. Customers can surf the Web, use text and numeric messaging, and send and receive e-mails with the fastest wireless data rate available today.

- *Wireline Replacement:* A customer can use PHS to replace their existing wireline, adding mobility without losing high-quality voice. Voice messaging, prepaid, short message service, and location-based system are attractive value added services.

- *Village Phone Service:* PHS can provide an economic solution for first-time customers formerly without telephone service. Customers have access to the same telecommunications services as those in larger geographic areas.

- *Portable Intercom Service (optional):* Small businesses and families can stay in contact with intercom or walkie-talkie style communications. The point-to-point handset feature allows quick and instant connections.

- *Pocket Demand:* PHS offers Centrex services for customers in campus-like environments such as universities, business complexes, hospitals, and private networks. Customers are now mobile and accessible at work. Pocket Demand can also offer a means of communication in critical disaster recovery situations.

5.5.4 PHS Physical Layer

5.5.4.1 Transmission Parameters

- Full duplex system
- Voice coder: 32-kbps adaptive differential pulse-code modulation (ADPCM).

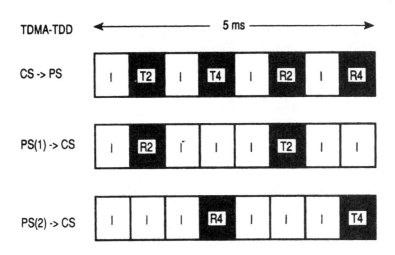

T: transmission R: reception, I: idle, Ti → Ri: Corresponding transmission/reception slot

FIGURE 5.20   Slot arrangement (corresponding to 32 kbps).

- Duplexing: TDD. The portable and base units transmit and receive on the same frequency but different time slots. The slot arrangement is shown in Fig. 5.20.
- Multiple access: TDMA-TDD, up to four multiplexed circuits.
- Modulation: $\pi/4$ DQPSK, roll-off rate $= 0.5$.
- Data rate: 192 ksps (or 384 kbps).
- Spectrum allocation: 1895 to 1918.1 MHz. This spectrum has been allocated for private and public use.
- Carrier frequency spacing: 300 kHz.
- Carrier frequency: 1895.15 MHz or 1895.15 + (N − 300 kHz) where N is an integer.

5.5.4.2 Function Channel Structure.   The control channel consists of the following logical channels:

1. *Broadcast control channel:* BCCH is a one-way downlink channel for broadcasting control information from CS to PS.
2. *Common control channel:* CCCH sends out the control information for call connection.
   a. *Paging channel:* PCH is a one-way downlink channel.
   b. *Signaling control channel:* SCCH is a bidirectional point-to-point channel.
3. *User packet channel:* UPCH is a bidirectional point-multipoint channel that sends control signal information and user packet data.
4. Associated control channel: ACCH is a bidirectional channel that is associated with the TCH. It carries out control information and user packet data. There is a SACCH and a FACCH.

The traffic channel is a point-to-point bidirectional channel and is used for transmitting user information.

5.5.4.3 Carrier Structure

Control carrier: A carrier in which only common usage slots can be assigned to study intermittent transmission in a cordless station (CS).

Communications carrier: A carrier in which the user can perform communication through the individual assigned slot. It also can allocate common usage slots for a communications carrier.

Carrier for direct communication between personal stations: A carrier providing direct communication without going through a CS. The connection control and conversation can be carried out on the same slot.

5.5.4.4 Structure and Interfaces of PHS System.   The structure of PHS is shown in Fig. 5.21a. The CS is connected to the telecommunications circuit equipment. The interfaces of PHS are shown in Fig 5.21b. There are three interface points:

Um is the interface point between personal station and cell station or between personal station and personal station. Conforms to the standard.

R is the interface point between I interface nonconforming terminal and mobile terminal equipment or terminal adapter. Outside scope of the standard.

S is the interface point between I interface conforming terminal or terminal adapter TA and mobile terminal equipment TE.

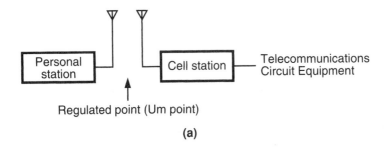

Regulated point (Um point)

(a)

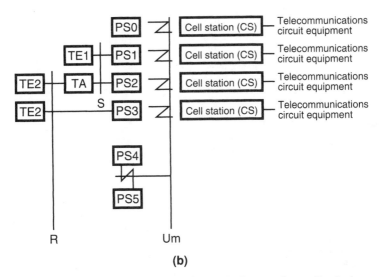

R   Um

(b)

FIGURE 5.21 System structure and interface of PHP. (*a*) Structure of personal handy phone system; (*b*) interface points.

The five different classes of PS in Fig. 5.21*b* are defined as follows:

PS0, PS4, PS5   Personal station, including integrated man/machine interface of terminals, and so forth.

PS1, PS2   Personal station with I interface.

PS3   Personal station without I interface.

Terminal equipment TE1 is with I interface, and TE2 is without I interface. TA is the interface conversion equipment for noninterface and I interface.

5.5.5 PHS Protocol

5.5.5.1 Protocol Model. In general, a communication protocol is made up of the call connection phase and the communications phase. In the Personal Handy Phone System protocol structure, it is divided into 3 protocol stages as shown below: A phase that establishes

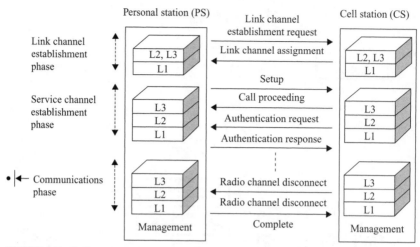

FIGURE 5.22 Basic structure of signals.

the radio interface handshake (link channel establishment phase), a phase that connects the call between the cell station (CS) that established the handshake and a personal station (PS) (service channel establishment phase), and a phase that performs communication and data transmission (communications phase).

In the link channel establishment phase, the special radio control channel structure is applied, and the service channel establishment phase and the communications phase use the hierarchical structure of layers 1 through 3 conforming to the OSI model. The basic signal structure is shown in Fig. 5.22. Here, the communications phase is defined as the term after the point when the services are provided from the CS side to PS. Here, services include in-band information.

5.5.5.2 Hierarchical Structure.

The call connection consists of the link channel establishment phase for establishing the link with the radio interface and the service channel establishment phase for establishing the radio link for telephone service such as voice transmission and nontelephone service such as ISDN.

1. *Link channel establishment phase:* Defined as the stage of using control channel functions to select a c-channel (hereafter referred to as link channel) with the quality and capacity required for each service's call connection and to select the protocol type required in the next phase of call connection. In the link channel establishment phase, layer 2 and layer 3 have a mixed structure as shown in Fig. 5.23.

2. *Service channel establishment phase:* Defined as the stage of using link channel functions obtained in the link channel establishment phase to select a channel (hereafter referred to as service channel) with the capacity required for providing service and to select the protocol type required in the communications phase. As shown in Fig. 5.24, layer 3 functions have a hierarchical structure that conforms to the OSI model that can be divided into RT (radio frequency transmission management), MM (mobility management), and CC (call control).

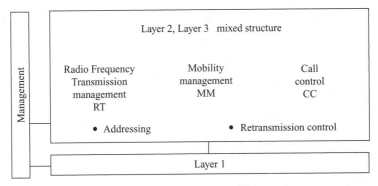

FIGURE 5.23 Hierarchical structure of link channel establishment phase.

3. *Communications phase:* The hierarchical structure of communication used via one radio channel (32 kbit/s speech, 3.1 kHz audio and 32 kbit/s unrestricted digital) shown in Fig. 5.25 and the hierarchical structure of communication used via two radio channel (64 kbit/s unrestricted digital) is shown in Fig. 5.25. As shown in Fig. 5.25, layer 3 functions have a hierarchical structure that conforms to the OSI model that can be divided into RT, MM, and CC. However, in the case of 64 kbit/s unrestricted digital information communication, the second TCH has only layer 1 function and RT function of layer 3.

5.5.6 PHS Basic Functions and Services

5.5.6.1 Basic Functions. The Personal Handy Phone System has the following functions:

1. It can be connected to the public telephone network.
2. It has a common radio interface.

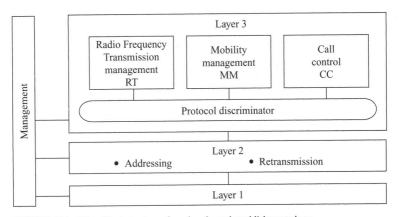

FIGURE 5.24 Hierachical structure of service channel establishment phase.

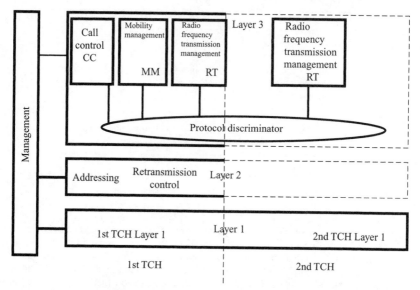

FIGURE 5.25 Hierarchical structure (communication using 1 radio channel or 2 radio channels).

3. The personal station, cell station, and relay station have a slot-unit interference detection function and can automatically allocate a less interfered channel.

4. If interference is received during communication, the personal station, cell station, and relay station can avoid interference in slot units. Interference avoidance is by channel switching, automatic reconnection, temporary stoppage of transmission, and so forth.

5. It has an identification code that identifies the cell station (system identification code [private] or operator identification code [public]) and an identification code that separately identifies the personal station (PS identification code). In the connection operation, these codes are sent mutually, which prevents erroneous connection and erroneous charging.

5.5.6.2 *Services*

A. Service features

Service attributes of the personal handy phone system:

Service Attribute	Service Item
Information transfer capability	Speech, 3.2-kHz audio, unrestricted digital
Transfer mode	Circuit mode
Information transfer rate	32k bit/s (only for unrestricted digital)
Communications format	Point-to-point

B. Service types

1. *Bearer services:* The bearer services used via communications channels are (a) 32-kbps speech; (b) 3.1-kHz audio, (c) 32-kbps digital data, (d) 64-kbps digital data.

2. *Teleservice:* Use via communication channels is not specified.

3. *Supplementary services (circuit mode):* Proper to PHS use as circuit mode services are

- DTMF signal transmission
- Hooking signal transmission
- Pause signal transmission
- Hold call
- Conference call
- Call waiting
- Call type notification
- PS remote control
- User-to-user signaling

5.6   IS-95B (RTT 1X)

IS-95B is an evolution of IS-95A. It can send packet data through IWF as shown in Fig. 5.26. Theoretically, it can provide data rates up to 115 kbps. However, in reality it can only achieve up to 64 kbps. The difference between IS-95A and IS-95B is the software upgraded in IS-95B. IS-95A can send the circuit data and IS-95B can send the packet data.

Whether IS-95B should be a 2G system or a 2.5G system has not been certified by the cellular industry. Also, IS-95B system specification[5] was quickly adopted and upgraded into cdma2000 1X. IX is an ITU-certified 3G standard. Therefore, IS-95B will be described in the section for the software upgrade.

In IS-95B, an active mobile always has a fundamental code channel at 9.6 kbps, and when high data rate is required, the base station assigns the mobile up to 7 supplementary code channels plus the fundamental code channel. Thus, the peak data rate is up to 76.8 kbps. Data rate is controlled at the base station and conveyed to the mobile though the supplementary channel assignment message.

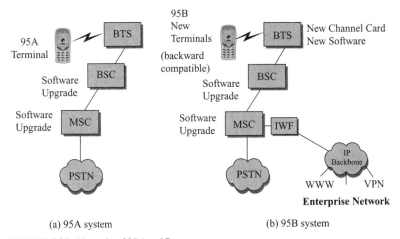

(a) 95A system   (b) 95B system

FIGURE 5.26   Networks of 95 A and B.

TABLE 5.3   Features of IS-95B

Features	Description	Impact
(A) IS-95B Prime features (done by software upgrade)		
1a. New Soft Handoff Algorithm	New Soft Handoff Algorithm, which uses new criteria (SOFT SLOPE, ADD/DROP INTERCEPT) to determine the need to add/drop a pilot	Capacity improvement, potential drop call rate increase in some rapidly changing pilots RF scenarios
2a. Access Entry Handoff	Allows IS-95B mobiles to transfer to another BTS's page channel after receiving the Page message before sending the Page Response	Improves termination success
3a. Access Handoff	Idle Handoff after probes transmitted while waiting for the BTS's response or prior to responding to the BTS	Improves access success
4a. Channel Assignment into Soft Handoff	Infrastructure activates multiple (up to 6) traffic channels after Origination or Page Response message to setup a call in Soft HO immediately, based on the list of pilots appended to Orig/Page Resp by the mobile	Improves access success, very small capacity hit.
5a. MAHHO	Mobiles will search other frequency and report signal strengths to the BTS prior to hard handoff	Improves hard handoff success rate, some voice quality degradation during visits to other frequency
6a. Enhanced Neighbor Search	Provides for variable search window size (per neighbor pilot) in the Extended Neighbor List Update and General Neighbor List messages	Improves handoff performance at the borders of cells with very dissimilar sizes
7a. True IMSI	CDMA International Mobile Station Identity	Compliance with international requirements
8a. Open Loop power estimate correction	Adjusts the initial open loop power estimate to take into account the interference	Improves access success
9a. Mobile Numeric Parameters	Values for T40, T50, T58, T70, T71, T72, T73, N1, N8, and N13 as per IS-95B	Improved call processing
(B) IS-95B Enhanced features (done by software upgrade)		
1b. Synchronized Message Capsule in Page slot	Ensures that 4 bits before the Synchronized Capsule Indicator (SCI) are padding bits (zeros), to allow for initialization of Viterbi decoder	Improves the standby time, minor reduction of Page Channel capacity possible
2b. NDSS	Allows the network to redirect a specific mobile to another preferred system	May improve call performance in multiband/multimode systems
3b. Access Probe Handoff	Idle Handoff inbetween access probes	Improves access success

TABLE 5.3 Features of IS-95B (*Continued*)

Features	Description	Impact
4b. Release Order on Access Channel	Mobiles can send a Release order in case of abandoned accesses due to power down or subscriber's command	Marginal improvement in Page channel and forward link capacity, more reliable Service Measurements
5b. Location Power-Up Function (PUF)	Intended to facilitate location determination via triangulation for emergency calls	Some capacity reduction on the reverse link
6b. Service Negotiation Enhancements	Intended to speed-up and simplify the service negotiation protocol by changes in Origination, Page Response, and Extended Handoff Direction messages	Possible faster call set-up
7b. Enhanced message encryption signaling	The signaling to support message encryption algorithms	Enhances the privacy
8b. System Reselection Enhancements	Mobile can perform system reselection based on the signal strengths criteria on the serving CDMA Channel in the idle mode	Can improve call performance in multifrequency or multiband/multimode systems
9b. Periodic PSMM	New order message to request periodic Pilot Strength Measurement reports on the serving frequency	Less voice degradation due to messaging on the forward link than with periodic PMRO messages
10b. Enhanced Roaming Indicator	Supported through ROAM_INDI field in Registration Accepted Order	New feature requirement
11b. PACA	Priority access channel assignment with queuing	New feature requirement
12b. CNAP	Support for Calling Name ID presentation, Calling, Called and Connected Party numbers and addresses. Redirecting number and addresses, etc.	New feature requirement

(C) IS-95B Optional features (done by software upgrade)

1c. Signaling Support for WLL applications	Support for Meter Pulse, Answer supervision, etc.	New feature requirement for some WLL applications
2c. High-Speed Data	Support for 64 kbps data rate (raw rates 76.8 and 115.2 kbps, depending on the Rate Set	Capacity reduction for voice calls

Figures 5.26*a* and 5.26*b* show the differences in the networks between IS-95A and IS-95B. In order to receive the packet data in the network of 95B shown in Fig. 5.26*b*, a new terminal is used. BTS will install a new channel card and new software; both BSC and MSC need a software upgrade. Then, the packet data can reach MSC and be on the way to IP backbone through IWF as shown in Fig. 5.26*b*.

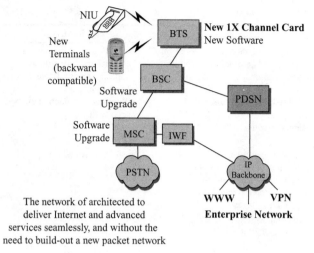

The network of architected to deliver Internet and advanced services seamlessly, and without the need to build-out a new packet network

FIGURE 5.27   Migration from IS-95B to CDMA 2000 1X.

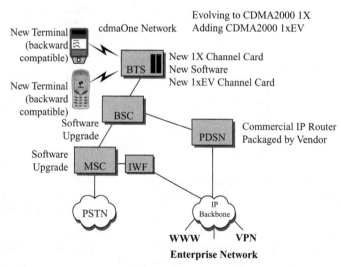

FIGURE 5.28   Migration from CDMA 2000 1X to 1xEV-DO.

The three classes of features in IS-95B have been provided by the software upgrade shown in Table 5.3: the prime features, the enhanced features, and the optimal features. Each feature has its description and impact; most of the features are migrated in cdma2000 1X.

Figure 5.27 shows the minimal requirement and incremental modifications to migrate from IS-95B to cdma2000 1X, as well as the easy network upgrade from cdma2000 1X to cdma2000 1XEV-DO as shown in Fig. 5.28.

REFERENCES

1. ETSI TC SMG, "Overall Description of the General Packet Radio Service (GPRS) Radio Interface Stage 2," GSM 03.64, January 1997.

2. T. Halonen, J. Romero, J. Melero, *GSM, GPRS and EDGE Performance*, John Wiley & Sons, 2002.

3. Motorola Network Solution Sector, "iDEN Technical Overview," Software Release 9.1, Motorola, Inc., 1999.

4. PHS – Personal Handy Phone Standard, Research Development Center for Radio System (RCR), "Personal Handy Phone Standard (PHS)," CRC STD-28, Dec. 20, 1993.

5. Kyoung Kim, *Handbook of CDMA System Design, Engineering and Optimization*, Prentice-Hall, PTR, 2000.

CHAPTER 6
3G SYSTEMS

ITU has called the future cellular networks 3G networks or IMT-2000; the previous term was Future Public Land Mobile Telephone System (FPLMTS). The performance for IMT-2000 air interference can be summarized as[1-3]:

- Wideband CDMA systems
- Spectrum bandwidth 5 MHz
- Full coverage and mobility for a data rate of 144 kbps to 384 kbps
- Limited coverage and mobility or no mobility for 2 Mbps
- High spectrum efficiency compared to 2G system
- High flexibility to introduce new and multimedia services

The 3G features:

- Provision of multirate services
- Packet data
- A user-dedicated pilot for a coherent uplink
- An additional DL pilot channel for beam forming
- Intercarrier handover
- Fast power control
- Multiuser detection

IMT-2000 has published a minimum performance requirement of a 3G wireless system, which is for both circuit-switched (CS) and packet-switched (PS) data:

- Data rate of 144 kbps in the vehicular environment
- Data rate of 384 kbps in the pedestrian environment
- Data rate of 2 Mbps in the fixed indoor and pico cell environment

The 3G systems concentrating on the three ITU-adopted systems using CDMA technology are WCDMA-UTRA (Europe), WCDMA-ARIB (Japan), and cdma2000 (North America).

3G consists of the three systems shown in Fig. 6.1, also called three modes because in the future, the three systems can have the features of hooks and extension to make intersystem connections among them.

Legend

FDD: Frequency Division Duplex
TDD: Time Division Duplex
CDM: Code Division Multiplexing
TDM: Time Division Multiplexing

IMT-2000

	FDD Direct Spread	FDD Multicarrier	TDD
Bandwidth	5 MHz	5 MHz/ 1.25 MHz	5 MHz/ 1.6 MHz
Chip Rate	3.84 Mcps	3.6864 Mcps/ 1.228 Mcps	3.84 Mcps/ 1.28 Mcps
Common Pilot	CDM	CDM	TDM
Dedicated Pilot	TDM	CDM	TDM
Synchronization	Asynchronous/ Synchronous	Synchronous as cdma2000	Synchronous
Core Network	GSM-MAP/ IP	ANSI-41/ IP	GSM-MAP/ IP

FIGURE 6.1　3G's three standard systems.

6.1 WCDMA-UMTS (UTRA-FDD) PHYSICAL LAYER

6.1.1 Description of Physical Layer

The radio access for UMTS is known as Universal Terrestrial Radio Access (UTRA).[4] Sometimes, WCDMA-UMTS is also called UTRA-FDD.

The physical layer structures WCDMA-UMTS naturally relate to radio interface when observing a single link between a terminal station and a base station. In the physical layer, we have to describe the transfer channels and physical channels, spreading and scrambling, modulation and power control.

WCDMA-UMTS's physical layer and higher layers have been extended from GSM systems, although the radio technology is basically adopted from cdmaOne. The difference in radio technology from cdma1X is the use of 5-MHz bandwidth channel instead of 1.25 MHz. With a 5-MHz bandwidth, the transmission medium reacts to the signal differently. The number of multipaths (also called fingers) is more; sometimes needing to collect 6–7 instead of 3 fingers in cdmaOne. Because of the large number of multipaths, the interference cancellation techniques become more complicated in the multiuser reception and the soft handover. The channelization codes used are known as Orthogonal Variable Spreading Factor (OVSF) codes in which Walsh codes belong. Also, the system is considering its interoperability among all 3G systems, the all-IP network, high-speed data, and multimedia applications.

The physical layer offers the transfer services of information to the other layers through the use of different types of channels. There are three types of channels: logical channels, transport channels, and physical channels. The different types of channels between different layers are shown in Fig. 6.2. Logical channels serve the information flow between the MAC layer and the RLC layer. Transport channels send the characteristics of the information over the radio channels. Physical channel defines the code and the frequency used by the radio link for the downlink as well as the relative phase, in-phase, or quantitative phase for the uplink.

In WCDMA-UMTS, the physical layer offer services to the MAC layer via transport channels. The data generated at higher layers is transferred by the logical channels and carried over the air with transport channels. Those transport channels are mapped in the physical layer to different physical channels.

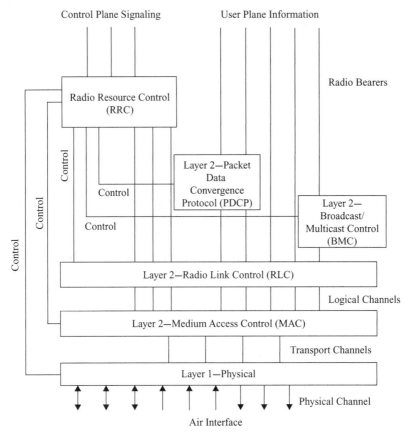

FIGURE 6.2 WCDMA air interface protocol structure.

6.1.2 Transport Channels[5]

The characteristics of information, which the transport channels are provided, are as follows:

- The control information for uplink or downlink
- The shared information for uplink or downlink
- Power control characteristics
- Managing the risk of collision
- Mobile station identification method
- Beam forming information (option)
- Data rate variation
- Broadcast coverage area (in a selected cell or entire cell)

Each transport channel carries the TFI (Transport Format Indicator) as shown in Fig. 6.3. At each time the expected data arrives at the specific transport channel from the higher layers.

TFCI: The physical layer combining the TFI information from different transport channels forms the TFCI (Transport Format Combination Indicator). The TFCI is transmitted in the physical control channel to inform the ME (Mobile Equipment) which transport channels are active in the current frame and provide TFI for the higher layers.

- Bank of Transport Channels {TC}
  Adding TFI to each TC becomes {TFI + TC}, where

$$\{TFI\} \rightarrow \text{Physical Control Channel (PCEH)}$$

$$\{TC\} \rightarrow \text{Coding and Multiplexing}$$

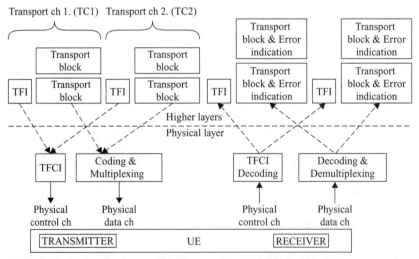

FIGURE 6.3 The interface between higher layers and the physical layer.

- BTFD (Blind Transport Format Detection) is in connection with the downlink dedicated channels.
- Transport channels can be divided into common channel and dedicated channel.
  A. Common channels: A resource shared among all or a group of users in a cell. There are six different common transport channels, four for downlink and two for uplink.

  For Downlink

  ○ Broadcast Channel (BCH): For mobile station to obtain system information, such as cell identities, spreading codes, access channel, and neighboring cell lists from the network.

  ○ Forward Access Channel (FACH): Carriers control information to MS in one cell.

  ○ Paging Channel (PCH): Send message to MS in the paging covered area.

  ○ Downlink Shared Channel (DSCH): A transport channel intended to carry dedicated user data and/or control information.

  For Uplink

  ○ Random Access Channel (RACH): Used for the cell originating from the mobile station after its synchronization.

  ○ Uplink Common Packet Channel (CPCH).

  Basic network needs BCH, RACH, FACH, and PCH as common transport channels and CPCH and DSCH as optional

  B. Dedicated channels (DCH): Identify by a specific code on a specific frequency and reserved for a single user. DCH channels are mapped into two physical channels.

  ○ DPDCH (Dedicated Physical Data Channel) carries higher layer information, such as user data. The bit rate can be varied from frame to frame.

  ○ DPCCH (Dedicated Physical Control Channel) carries physical layer control information. Bit rate is constant.

6.1.3 Physical Channels

Some physical channels carry only information relevant to physical layer procedure on the downlink channels such as:

- SCH (Synchronization Channel) ⎫ To be transmitted by every base
- CPICH (Common Pilot Channel) ⎭ station (not visible to higher layer)
- AICH (Acquisition Indication Channel)
- PICH (Paging Indication Channel)
- CSICH (CPCH Status Indication Channel) ⎫
- CD/CA-ICH (Collision Detection/Channel ⎬ If CPCH is used
  Assignment Indication Channel) ⎭

The different transport channels are mapped onto different physical channels. Some of the transport channels and physical channels are identical; we name them Group A.

Some physical channels were carriers for several transport channels, or a portion of a transport channel; we name them Group B.

The transport channels are mapped onto the physical channels as follows:

Transport Channels   **Physical Channels**

Group A
$\begin{cases} \text{BCH} \\ \text{RACH} \\ \text{DSCH} \\ \text{CPCH} \end{cases}$

$\longrightarrow$ PCCPCH (Primary Common Control Physical Channel)-(DL)
$\longrightarrow$ PRACH (Physical Random Access Channel)-(UL)
$\longrightarrow$ PDSCH (Physical Downlink Shared Channel)-(DL)
$\longrightarrow$ PCPCH (Physical Common Packet Channel)-(UL)

Group B
$\begin{cases} \text{FACH} \\ \quad \\ \text{PCH} \end{cases}$ $\longrightarrow$ SCCPCH (Secondary Common Control Physical Channel)-(DL)

$\text{DCH} \longrightarrow \begin{cases} \text{DPDCH (Dedicated Physical Data Channel): to carry data by one} \\ \text{or many DPDCH on each connection (UL)} \\ \quad \\ \text{DPCCH (Dedicated Physical Control Channel): to carry} \\ \text{control information by only one DPCCH on each connection (UL)} \end{cases}$

6.1.4   Transmission Characteristics[6,7]

A. Identical characteristics of both uplink and downlink.

- Spreading/channelization codes: OVSF codes
- Radio Frame structure   10 ms
- System Frame Number (SFN)   12 bits
- Chip Rate   3.84 Mcps
- Channel spacing   5 MHz
- Long code   38400 chips

B. Characteristics of uplink channels
The operations between spreading, scrambling, and modulation of WCDMA-UMTS Uplink is shown in Fig. 6.4. Spreading and scrambling form the CDMA signal. The relation between spreading and scrambling is shown in Fig. 6.5. The description of each function is depicted as follows:

- Pilot symbols: Used to demodulate coherently the message signals. The DPCH, CCPCH, and PRACH all carry pilot symbols.

- Spreading: Channelization code can identify the dedicated physical data channels (DPDCH) and dedicated physical control channels (DPCCH) from same and different terminals with its code length from 4 to 256 chips (1.0–66.7 Ms). The frames and slot structures of DPDCH and DPCCH for uplink are shown in Fig. 6.6.

- Scrambling: Uses Gold Code which has a pseudo random characteristics

    Code Length: Short code (256 chips for advanced multiuser detectors or interference cancellation received at the BS).

    Long Code: Long code (10 ms frame, 38400 chips with 3.84 Mcps is used to rake receiver at the base station).

    Short Code: Chosen from the extended S(2) code family (256 chips) is used when the BS uses advanced multiuser detection techniques.

    Code Numbers: Two scrambling code families contains millions of short codes. No code planning in cells is needed.

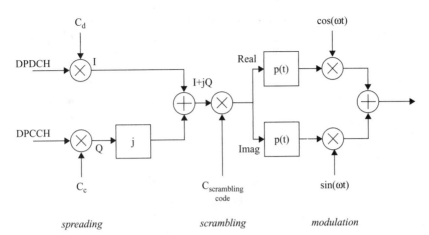

FIGURE 6.4 WCDMA-UMTS uplink spreading, scrambling, and modulation.

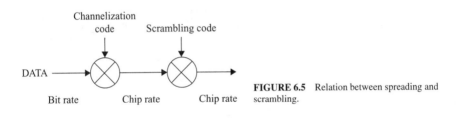

FIGURE 6.5 Relation between spreading and scrambling.

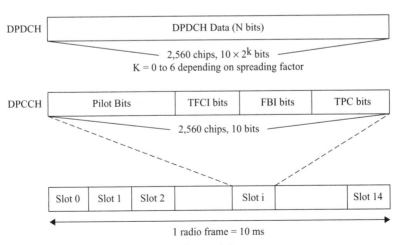

FIGURE 6.6 Uplink DPDCH and DPCCH frame and slot structure.

- Modulation: Combined I-Q/code multiplexing solution (called dual-channel QPSK) with complex scrambling.
- Power Control: Fast power control in uplink reduces the average required uplink transmission power.
- DTX: Insert in the user data channel (DPDCH) for power conservation.
- Channels: All dedicated channels and common channels are implemented with both spreading and scrambling. For link maintenance, two dedicated physical channels are not time multiplexed. Depending on higher layer requirements, a DPDCH or DPCCH can use either a short or a long code.

DPDCH ⎫	There are 16 different values of power levels for
DPCCH ⎭	making power difference between these two channels
PRACH	Physical random access channel
CPCH	Common packet channel

C. Characteristics of downlink channels

The relationship between spreading, scrambling, and modulation of WCDMA-UMTS downlink is shown in Fig. 6.7. In downlink, the DPDCH and DPCCH are shared in a DPCH as shown in Fig. 6.8. The DPCH serial bits in Fig. 6.7 are converted in parallel forms and mapped to the in-phase and quadrature branches. The description of each function is depicted as follows:

- Spreading – based on the OVSF codes and limited to 512 chips
- Scrambling – use Gold Codes over a timeframe of 10 ms (38400 chips)

   Code length 10 ms (38400 chips)

   Long code: 512 primary scrambling codes for identifying cells. Also secondary-scrambling codes can be used for beam steering operation.

   Short code: No short code is used for DL

- Channels

   SCH: Primary SCH contains a code of 256 chips

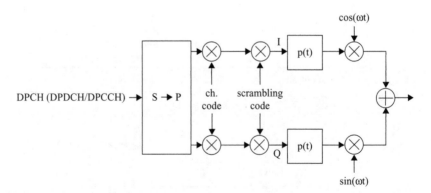

spreading   scrambling   modulation

FIGURE 6.7 WCDMA-UMTS downlink spreading, scrambling, and modulation.

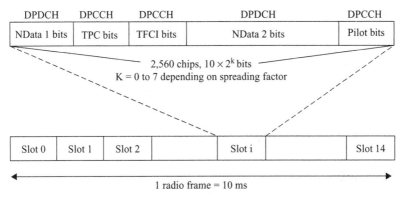

FIGURE 6.8 Downlink DPDCH and DPCCH frame and slot structure.

Secondary SCH: 16 sequences in use and generate a total of 64 different code words. It can be used to identify common channels that have continuous transmission.

Physical channels are listed in Sec. 6.1.3.

• Modulation: QPSK with time-multiplexed control and data stream.

6.1.5 User Data Transmission

The uplink DPCCH uses a slot structure with 15 slots in the 10-ms radio frame. The slot duration is 2560 chips or about 666 μs. The chip rate is 3.84 Mcps. For higher data rate, parallel code channels are used. For a spreading factor 4, it can have up to six parallel codes and raise the channel bit rate for data transmission up to 5740 kbps, which can accommodate 2 Mbps user data if the coding rate is one-half (see Table 6.1). The uplink dedicated channel structure is shown in Fig. 6.6. The number of 15 slots used for DPCCH is shown in the figure. User data transmission with the Random Access Channel (RACH) has a specific

TABLE 6.1 Uplink DPDCH Data Rates

DPDCH Spreading Factor	DPDCH Channel bit Rate (kbps)	Maximum User Data Rate with $\frac{1}{2}$-Rate Coding (Approx.)
256	15	7.5 kbps
128	30	15 kbps
64	60	30 kbps
32	120	60 kbps
16	240	120 kbps
8	480	240 kbps
4	960	480 kbps
4, with 6 parallel codes	5,760	2.3 Mbps

TABLE 6.2 Downlink Dedicated Channel Symbol and bit Rates

Spreading Factor	Channel Symbol Rate (kbps)	Channel bit Rate (kbps)	DPDCH Channel bit Rate Range (kbps)	Maximum User Data Rate with $\frac{1}{2}$-Rate Coding (Approx.)
512	7.5	15	3–6	1–3 kbps
256	15	30	12–24	6–12 kbps
128	30	60	42–51	20–24 kbps
64	60	120	90	45 kbps
32	120	240	210	105 kbps
16	240	480	432	215 kbps
8	480	960	912	456 kbps
4	960	1920	1872	936 kbps
4, with 3 parallel codes	2880	5760	5616	2.3 Mbps

future preamble that is sent prior to data transmission. These use a spreading factor (SF) of 256 and contain a signature sequence of 16 symbols, resulting in a total length of 4096 chips for the preamble. The message part can have SF varied from 256 down to 32 depending on the transmission need. Uplink common packet channel is for fast power control.

Downlink dedicated physical channel, (DPCH) symbol rates, and bit rates are the same as the uplink. However, the DPDCH channel bit rate is not fixed at downlink but in a range shown in Table 6.2. It applies time multiplexing for physical control information and user data transmission as shown in Fig. 6.8.

6.1.6 Physical Layer's Functions

a. Fast closed loop power control: One command per slot, command rate is 1500 Hz and basic step size is 1 dB.

    1. Operation with soft handover: The terminal reacts to multiple power control commands from several sources (several base stations) and makes decision whether to increase or decrease the power.

    2. Compressed mode: To converge power level more quickly.

b. Open loop power control: Only use prior to initiating the transmission on the RACH or CPCH. It is not very accurate.

c. Paging Procedures: In PCH for a paging group, there are paging indicators (PI) that appear periodically on paging indicator channel (PICH) when the paging messages for any of the terminals in that paging group.

d. RACH procedure

    First: Send 1 ms RACH preamble.

    Second: Received and decoded AICH to see whether the base station has received the preamble, if not, then retransmits with 1-dB power increase.

    Third: If yes, then transmit 10 ms or 20 ms message part of RACH.

e. CPCH sends a collision delectation (CD) preamble based on a signal structure. The base station acknowledges back on CD's indication channel.

f. Cell Search Procedure: There are three steps:

    1. The terminal searches the 256-chip primary synchronization code from the base station.

2. The terminal seeks the largest peak from the 64 possibilities for the secondary synchronization code word while the frame timing is known.

3. The terminal seeks the primary scrambling codes to find the cell to which it belongs.

g. Handover procedure: Because UTRA has two modes, FDD and TDD, the handover can be taken within the mode or to another mode.

1. Intra Mode Handover: Measured performance on CPICH within a system mode.

   i. Received Signal Code Power (RSCP) on one code after dispreading.

   ii. Received Signal Strength Indicator (RSSI), the total received power.

   iii. E_c/N_o is measured by using RSCP divided by RSSI, E_c/N_o level is used to determine if the handover should be taken or not.

   iv. Soft handover needs the relative timing information between the cells to allow coherent combining of signals in the Rake receiver from different cells.

2. Intermode handover: A dual mode FDD-TDD terminal operating in FDD and measuring the power level from the TDD cells available in the area. The TDD CCPCH bursts always send twice during the 10-ms TDD frame for the terminal to measure it.

h. Compressed mode measurement: It is also referred to as the slotted mode. The compressed mode means that the transmission and reception are halted for a short time, for a few milliseconds, in order to perform measurements on the other frequencies, or the fast power control purposes. In the compressed mode, there are three different ways to compress data rate.

1. Lowering the data rate.

2. Increasing the data rate by changing the spreading factor.

3. Reducing the symbol rate by puncturing.

The use of compressed mode has an impact on link performance and is largest at the cell edge, as the full power at the cell edge has no room to run fast power control any more.

6.2 WCDMA-ARIB PHYSICAL LAYER

ARIB's WCDMA,[8] is similar to UTRA; both use wideband CDMA. However ARIB has support for 1.25-Mhz bands, which UTRA does not support. ARIB has proposed two implementations for the system: a Frequency Division Duplex (FDD) implementation and a Time Division Duplex (TDD).

6.2.1 FDD Mode

6.2.1.1 Channels. There are three types of channels defined in WCDMA: logical, transport, and physical channels. The type of information they carry describes logical channels; transport channels are described by how the information is transmitted on the radio interface. Physical channels are defined differently for FDD and TDD. For FDD, a physical channel is defined by its carrier frequency, access code, and, in the uplink, by the relative phase of the signal (either the In-Phase or Quadrature component). Similarly, TDD defines a physical channel by its carrier frequency, access code, and relative phase for the uplink and also by the time slot in which it is transmitted.

A. Logical Channels

The following is a small list and description of the logical channels:

- **Control Channels**

  Logical Broadcast Control Channel (L-BBCH): Broadcasts control information from base station (BS) to mobile stations (MS).

  Logical Paging Channel (L-PCH): Transfers paging information from BS to MS.

  Logical Forward Access Channel (L-FACH): Carries control information from BS to MS when the network knows where the MS is located on the network.

  Logical Random Access Channel (L-RACH): Channel that carries control information from the MS to the BS (contention channel).

  Dedicated Control Channel (DCCH): Point-to-point bidirectional channel that transfers dedicated control information from a BS to a MS.

- **Traffic Channel (TCH)**

  Dedicated Traffic Channel (DTCH): Point-to-point bidirectional channel that carries user data.

  User Packet Traffic Channel (UPCH): Point-to-point bidirectional channel that carries user data in packets.

B. Transport Channels

Transport channels are defined by how they are transmitted over the radio interface. Each transport channel has a set of characteristics and transports logical channels. The following is a list of the transport channels and their important characteristics:

- **Common Channels**

  Broadcast Control Channel (BCCH)
  - Downlink only
  - Low fixed bit rate
  - Broadcasted in the entire coverage area of the cell

  Paging Channel (PCH)
  - Downlink only
  - Broadcasted in the entire coverage area of the cell
  - Possibility for sleep mode

  Forward Access Channel (FACH)
  - Downlink only
  - Possibility to use beam-forming

  Random Access Channel (DCH)
  - Uplink only
  - Risk of collision
  - Requirement for in-band MS identification

- **Dedicated Channels**

  Dedicated Channel (DCH)
  - Possibility to use beam forming
  - Possibility to change rate fast

C. Physical Channels

A physical channel in FDD is defined by its carrier frequency, access code, and, for the case of the uplink connection, the relative phase (In-Phase or Quadrature component). Physical channels are therefore used to carry the transport channel through the air interface. Here is the list and description of the physical channels defined in ARIB's proposal.

- **Perch Channel**

  The Perch channel is a unidirectional channel from the BS to the MS, which is used by MS for reception level measurements to select cells.

- **Common Physical Channel**

  Channel shared by multiple MS in the same sector. (A sector is a part of a cell.)

- **Dedicated Physical Channel**

  Dedicated point-to-point channel between MS and BS.

D. Mapping of Channels

Transports channels are mapped to the physical channels the following way:

- Perch: carries the BCCH

- Common Physical Channel: carries PCH, FACH, and RACH

- Dedicated Physical Channel: carries the DCH. Subdivided in the Dedicated Physical Data Channel (DPDCH) and the Dedicated Physical Control Channel (DPCCH).

6.2.1.2 Transmission Technologies and Parameters

A. Chip Rate

Different chip rates for the implementation of WCDMA are possible. Chip rates of 4.096 Mcps, 8.192 Mcps, and 16.384 Mcps are supported. A chip rate of 1.024 Mcps is used for environment where only a bandwidth of 1.25 MHz is available.

B. Modulation and Spreading

Two different modulation schemes are used: one for the uplink and another one for the downlink. The main difference between the two is the fact that the uplink case uses phase multiplexing (it uses the In-Phase and Quadrature component to transmit different messages), and downlink case uses two-phase components to transmit same message.

1. Uplink Modulations and Spreading

   Figure 6.9 shows the modulation and spreading block diagram for the uplink connection, again for the transmission of the DPCCH and DPDCH.

   The two channels are spread to the chip rate using two different OVSF codes, C_c and C_d. The complex built signal is then scrambled with a complex scrambling code, which is a 2^{10} chips segment (which lasts the time of a Superframe: 737.28 ms) of a Gold Sequence of length $2^{41} - 1$.

   Again, the difference between UTRA (Fig. 6.4) and ARIB (Fig. 6.9) for the uplink modulation and spreading scheme is very small. It consists of a difference of 180 degrees on the phase of the carrier of the Quadrature component.

2. Downlink Modulations and Spreading

   Figure 6.10 illustrates the modulation and spreading for the downlink connection for the transmission of the DPDCH and DPCCH channels. In the case of the downlink, the spreading is done using a real channelization code (access code), C_c on the diagram. This access code is chosen among a set of OVSF codes (Hadamard-Walsh codes, for example). Using OVSF codes allows the system to adjust the data rate to the required level while maintaining orthogonality between users.

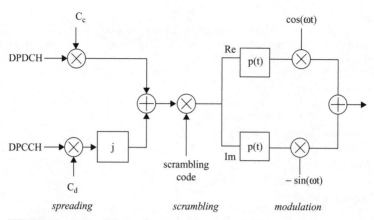

FIGURE 6.9 ARIB uplink spreading, scrambling, and modulation.

A complex scrambling code, which is cell-specific, does scrambling. The complex scrambling code is constructed with a segment of a Gold sequence of 10 ms or 40960 chips at 4.096 Mcps.

ARIB (Fig. 6.10) and UTRA (Fig. 6.7) modulation and spreading schemes for the downlink are very similar. However, UTRA uses both real scrambling and channelization codes. There is also a difference of 180 degrees on the phase of the carrier of the Quadrature component between the two proposed standards.

C. Pulse Waveform

As for UTRA, ARIB W-DMA uses a Root-Raised Cosine function with a roll-off factor of 0.22 in the frequency domain.

D. Detection

ARIB, like UTRA, transmits Pilot symbols on each channel to allow coherent detection. The way Pilot symbols are multiplexed with Data depends on the channel type.

E. Bandwidth Usage

ARIB supports ship rates of 1.024 Mcps, 4.096 Mcps, 8.192 Mcps, and 16.38 Mcps; the bandwidth used will be respectively 1.25 MHz, 5 MHz, 10 MHz, and 20 MHz.

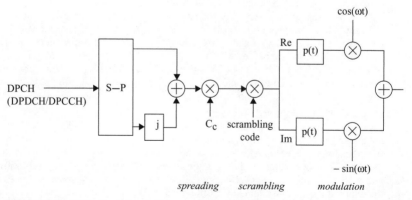

FIGURE 6.10 ARIB downlink spreading, scrambling, and modulation.

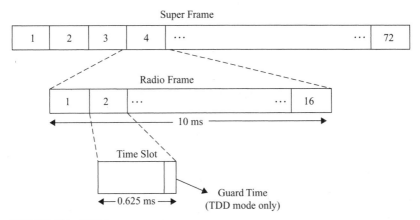

FIGURE 6.11   ARIB frame structure.

6.2.2   TDD Mode

A. Description
For the TDD mode of operation,[9-11] both the uplink and the downlink use the same frequency band. The two links cannot transmit at the same time and therefore are allocated time slots where they can broadcast the information. Each time slot ends with a guard period where no information transmission is allowed. This guard period is present to make sure that there is no loss of information due to propagation time delays.

The frame structure is pretty much the same as the one for FDD. A superframe contains 72 radio frames of 10 ms. Each radio frame contains 16 time slots of 0.625 ms each. Figure 6.11 illustrates the frame structure for ARIB's proposal:

The only difference with FDD in the frame structure is the guard period. The allocation units are time slots, and they can be allocated to either the uplink or the downlink. The first time slot of a frame is always reserved for downlink transmission of control information.

Each downlink time slot contains control information. Data is time-multiplexed with control information so that control is transmitted as often as possible.

The TDD mode also used CDMA so that many messages could be transmitted at the same time. ARIB's proposal suggests the use of multicode transmission to match the data rate required. That way, a user that requires more bandwidth would be allocated more access codes, hence more physical channels. For more flexibility, the codes are assigned independently for the uplink and downlink.

B. Channels
The transport channels and physical channels characteristics are the same for both FDD and TDD. Again, the only difference is that physical channel in TDD is defined by its frequency, access code, relative phase (quadrature or in-phase) for the uplink and also by its time slot.

6.2.3   Common Physical Layer Features for Both FDD and TDD Modes

- Modulation chip rate: $N \times 1.024$ Mcps, where $N = 1, 4, 8, 16$
- Pulse Shaping: Root-Raised Cosine (RRC) with roll-off factor 0.22

- Modulation:
  Uplink
    QPSK Data modulation
    QPSK Spreading modulation
  Downlink
    BPSK Data modulation
    QPSK Spreading modulation
- Channel spacing: 5 MHz for the basic chip rate of 3.84 Mcps.

6.3   WCDMA-TDD PHYSICAL LAYER

WCDMA TDD has two systems: UTRA-TDD (Europe) and TD-SCDMA (China).

Release 99 issued in December 1999 defined the UTRA-FDD and UTRA-TDD. These two standards were complementary. UTRA-FDD to be employed in Micro and Macro cells, and UTRA-TDD to cover micro cells, pico cells, and indoor.

The structure of channels of the two WCDMA-TDD systems are very similar, thus we just specify the structure of channels of UTRA-TDD. However, the modulation and spreading are different. Also, the parameters in a physical channel are different.

6.3.1   WCDMA-TDD Channel Structure

6.3.1.1   WCDMA-TDD[9–11] Specifies Two Types of Channels: Logical and Physical

A. Logical Channels

Two types of logical channels are defined: Traffic and Control. Traffic channels (TCH) are used to transfer user and/or signaling data. Signaling data consists of control information related to the process of a call. Control channels carry synchronization and information related to the radio transmission.

Control channels are grouped in two categories. Dedicated Control Channels (DCCH), which carry point-to-point connection oriented messages, and Common Control channels (CCCH), which carry point-to-multipoint or point-to-point connection or connection-less oriented messages. The CCCH is composed of the following channels, which are similar to the common transport channels for the FDD mode.

- BCCH (Broadcast Control Channel): Downlink point-to-multipoint control channels that broadcast network and cell specific information.
- PCH (Paging Channel): Downlink point-to-multipoint control channels that carry paging messages.
- FACH (Forward Access Channel): Downlink point-to-point or point-to-multipoint control channel designed to carry signaling messages.
- SCH (Synchronization Channel): Downlink point-to-multipoint channel used by the mobile to acquire frequency, chip, and slot synchronization.
- RACH (Random Access Channel): Uplink contention access channel that is used by mobiles to transmit control messages and requests.

B. Physical Channel

Its carrier frequency, access code, and time slot defines a physical channel in TDD mode.

In UTRA-TDD[9]

Time slots are units of time in UTRA-TDD, which have duration of 625 us each, or 2560 chips at 4.096 Mcps. They are part of a larger structure called frame, which lasts 10 ms or 16 time slots. Frames are also part of a larger structure of 24 frames (240 ms) named multiframe.

In TD-SCDMA[10,11]

A time frame of 5 ms that will provide seven time slots. Each time slot is 625 μs or 853 chips at 1.28 Mcps. The first time slot is used for control signaling. The rest of the six time slots are data slots in which three are used for downlink and three for uplink in a symmetric traffic services; or any number of six time slots can be used for downlink and the rest for the uplink in asymmetric services. The chip rate is 1.28 Mcps and the carrier bandwidth is 1.6 MHz, that is, about one-third bandwidth of standard WCDMA 5 MHz bandwidth.

6.3.2 Channel Mapping

Here is a short description of how the logical channels that we discussed are mapped to the physical channels:

- TCH: Traffic Channels
  Mapped into one or more set of slots and codes within a frame.

- BCCH: Broadcast Control Channel
  Transmitted in a predefined slot (slot#0) called Beacon within particular frames in the multiframe. In frames where the BCCH is not transmitted, the resource is allocated to other control channel: PCH, SCH, or FACH. Up to 8 base stations may transmit a BCCH signal in the same time slot. This allows a mobile to evaluate the power received from each of them for eventual handover.

- PCH: Paging Channel
  The PCH is usually mapped in the beacons slots or into a combination of time slots and codes to match the required rate. The location of the PCH is indicated in the BCCH.

- RACH: Random Access Channel
  Each transmission occupies only one burst (half a time slot). Each uplink slot is therefore subdivided in two. If required, more slots may be allocated to the RACH. The location of the RACH is indicated in the BCCH.

- FACH: Forward Access Channel
  Mapped into any combination of downlink resources (frequency, slot, and code). Its location is indicated in the BCCH. The FACH is sent every frame.

- SCH: Synchronization Channel
  The SCH permits time synchronization among mobiles and base stations. It allows a mobile to synchronize on frequency, chip, and slot to locate the position of the current frame within a multiframe. Each base station transmits one SCH every multiframe on the beacon slot. Special arrangements are made to make sure only one base station transmits its SCH in a frame.

6.3.3 Spreading (Channelization) Codes

TDD uses TDMA as well as Direct-Sequence CDMA (DS-CDMA). This allows a number of different possibilities for allocating resources. UTRA is considering two different options for code multiplexing.

The first option involves the use of access codes (CDMA). Each user in the time slot gets assigned a different spreading code, and up to 8 different codes can be allocated per time slot. The same mobile station may use more than one access code on the same time slot, depending on the data rate needed. Therefore, the spreading factor is fixed and this option is called Multicode transmission with fixed spreading.

The other option also uses access codes and is called Single code transmission with variable spreading. Each user in this transmission scheme gets one code but employs a different spreading factor depending on the required data rate. Generally, the spreading factor would be chosen such that an integer number of time slots are completely occupied and another one partially used with a different spreading factor. In that last time slot, a different mobile shares the bandwidth, by using different spreading codes with possibly different spreading factors.

6.3.4 Modulation and Spreading

The transmission mode is similar to the FDD mode:

In UTRA-TDD

- Chip rate 3.84 Mbps (fixed)
- Pulse shaping: root-raised cosine (RRC) with roll-off factor 0.22
- Modulation

    Uplink

        QPSK Data modulation

        QPSK Spreading modulation

    Downlink

        BPSK Data modulation

        QPSK spreading modulation

- Channel spacing: 5 MHz

The same structure for the modulation is used for TDD and FDD as shown in Fig. 6.4 for uplink and Fig. 6.7 for downlink.

In TD-SCDMA

- Chip rate 1.28 Mcps, that is, one-third of 3.84 Mcps (fixed).
- Pulse shaping and modulation are the same as UTRA-TDD.
- Channel spacing is 1.6 MHz, which is approximately one-third of 5 MHz.

6.3.5 Bandwidth Requirement and Capacity

In UTRA-TDD

The TDD mode of transmission needs a minimum bandwidth of 5 MHz (4.1 MHz using the 3-dB definition). This is achieved by using the time division property, so that both uplink and downlink can be transmitted at the same carrier frequency. Other 5-MHz frequency bands, not necessarily adjacent, can also be allocated to increase throughput.

The number of voice channels that can be accommodated for a single carrier is approximately 120, for a total bandwidth of 5 MHz. FDD was 250 voice channels for a total bandwidth of 10 MHz (5 MHz on the downlink and 5 MHz on the uplink).

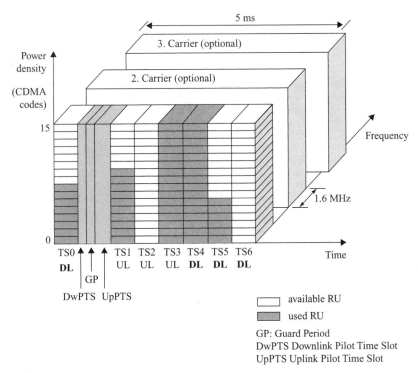

FIGURE 6.12   TD-SCDMA air interface principle.

In TD-SCDMA

Time Division Multiple Access (TDMA) in combination with Time Division Duplex (TDD) significantly improves the network performance by allowing radio resources to process network traffic in both directions, per uplink and downlink. TDMA uses a 5-ms frame for repetitive transmissions. This frame is subdivided into 7 time slots, which can be flexibly assigned to either several users or to a single user who may require multiple time slots.

The TD-SDMA air interface principle is shown in Fig 6.12 that combines four multiple access technologies: TDMA, CDMA, FDMA, and SDMA (space diversity multiple access) as shown in Fig. 6.13. It also uses smart antenna technology to reach a data rate of 2 Mbps, and its voice capacity is 3–5 times higher than GSM.

6.4   UMTS NETWORK ARCHITECTURE

6.4.1   Description

The protocol layers above the physical layer are data link layer (layer 2) and the network layer (layer 3). In layer 2 are two sublayers: Medium Access Control (MAC) protocol and Radio Link Control (RLC) protocol.

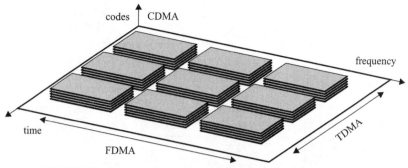

○ TD-SCDMA advanced radio interface takes advantage
  of all available Multiple Access techniques: TDMA, CDMA, FDMA, SDMA

○ TD-SCDMA provides an optimal and adaptive
  allocation of the radio resources

FIGURE 6.13   TD-SCDMA combines four multiple access techniques.

The physical layer offers services to the MAC layer via transport channels. In the physical layer, the design is to how and with what characters the data is transferred. The logical channels are characterized by what type of data is transmitted. MAC layer offers services to the RLC layer by means of logical channels. RLC layer offers service to higher layers. On the control plane, the RRC layer for signaling transport takes the RLC services. On the user plan, the RLC services are taken either by the service (specific protocol layers PDCP or BMC) or by other high-layer u-plane functions (e.g., speech coder) shown in the WCDMA radio interface protocol architecture in Fig. 6.14.

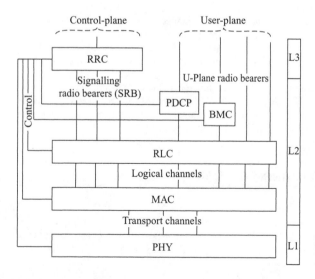

FIGURE 6.14   UTRA-FDD Radio Interface protocol architecture.

The two protocols:

1. The PDCP (Packet Data Convergence Protocol) is used for packet switches service, and its main function is the harder compression.
2. The BMC (Broadcast Multicast Control Protocol) is used to convey the radio interface messages originating from cell broadcast center.
The service offered by both protocols is called Radio Bearer.

The RRC layer offers services to higher layers through access points. The entire higher layer signaling such as mobility management, call control, session management, and so forth is placed into RRC messages for transmission over the radio interface. The control interfaces between the RRC and all the lower layer protocols are used to command the lower layers to perform certain types of measurements and to report measurement results and errors to the RRC. There are three types of channels transmitting information between layers; physical channels, transport channels, and logical channels. Those types of channels perform their unique operations.

6.4.2   MAC Layer[12,13]

6.4.2.1   Logical Channels. As mentioned earlier, the transport channels convey information passed from the MAC layer to the PHY layer. However, the information can originate higher in the protocol stack and is conveyed from RLC layer to the MAC layer through the logical channels. Therefore, the logical channels are mapped to transport channels, which in turn are mapped to physical channels.

The data transfer services of the MAC layer are provided on logical channels. There are different kinds of data transfer services offered by MAC. Logical channels can be classified into two groups: control channels and traffic channels. The MAC layer architecture is shown in Fig. 6.15. MAC-b handles the broadcast channel (BCH). MAC-c/sh handles the common channels and shared channels. MAC-d handles dedicated channels.

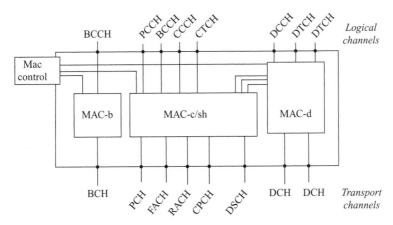

FIGURE 6.15   MAC layer architecture.

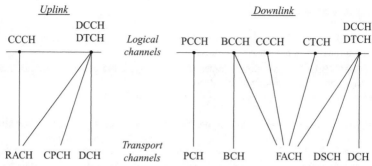

FIGURE 6.16 Mapping between logical channels and transport channels, uplink and downlink directions.

A. The control channels are

BCCH (Broadcast Control Channel [DL]): Transmits system information.

PCCH (Paging Control Channel [DL]): Pages an MS across one or more cells.

DCCH (Dedicated Control Channel [DL and UL]): A bidirectional point-to-point between an MS and the RNC for sending control information.

CCCH (Common Control Channel [DL and UL])

1. Used for the uplink by MS that wants to access the network but do not already have any connection with the network.

2. Used for the downlink to respond to such access attempts.

B. The traffic channels are

DTCH (Dedicated Traffic Channel [UL and DL]): A bidirectional point-to-point channel, dedicated to one MS, for the transfer of user information.

CTCH (Common Traffic Channel [DL]): A point-to-multipoint downlink channel for transfer of user information for all or a group of specified MS.

C. Mapping between logical channels and transport channels is shown in Fig. 6.16. On the uplink side, three logical channels are mapped to three transport channels. On the downlink side, five logical channels are mapped to five transport channels. The mapping is based on the operation of the MAC layer and shows the MAC functions when data is processed through the layer.

6.4.2.2 MAC Functions. MAC layer is a layer between PHY layer and RLC layer, therefore, the information conveys to PHY layer through transport channels and conveys to RLC layer through logical channels. The functions of MAC layer are

1. Handling the data flows in one MS and between MSs with priority and dynamic scheduling.

2. Identifying MSs in the MAC header on common transport channels.

3. Handling service multiplexing and de-multiplexing of higher layer PDUs for common transport channels and dedicated transport channels.

4. Monitoring traffic volume in RLC transmission buffer. Also provides traffic status to RRC.

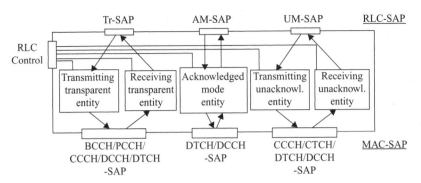

FIGURE 6.17 RLC layer architecture.

5. Switching between common and dedicated transport channels based on a switching decision from RRC.

6. Ciphering is performed if a radio bearer is using transparent RLC mode.

7. Use different access service classes (ASC) to provide different priorities of RACH usage.

6.4.3 RLC Layer[14]

A. RLC layer architecture
The RCL layer architecture is shown in Fig. 6.17. The three RLC entity types, transparent mode (Tr), acknowledged mode (AM), and unacknowledged mode (UM), are associated with its service access point (SAP). The transparent and unacknowledged modes of RLC are used as unidirectional; each one has transmitting and receiving entities. The acknowledged mode is bidirectional.

1. Transparent mode: No protocol overhead is added to higher layer area, thus the transmission can be of the streaming type in which higher layer data is not segmented.

2. Unacknowledged mode: No retransmission protocol is in use and data delivery is no guarantee of arrival. It is used for cell broadcast service and voice over IP (VoIP).

3. Acknowledged modes: An automatic repeat request (ARQ) scheme is used for error correction. The quality versus delay performance of RLC can be controlled by RRC. The acknowledged mode is the normal RLC mode for packet type services, such as Internet browsing and e-mail downloading.

B. RLC Functions
The RLC functions are most related to the quality of link connections.

1. Segmentation and reassembly of variable-length higher layer PDUs into or from smaller RLC payload units (PUs).

2. Concatenation and Padding: in case the contents of an RLC SDU do not fill an integral number of RLC PUs. When concatenation is not applicable, the remaining data is filled with padding bits.

3. Transfer of user data is controlled by QoS setting. The error correction by retransmission is in the acknowledged data transfer mode.

4. Delivery of higher layer PDUs in sequence by RLC using the acknowledged data transfer service and has duplication detection.

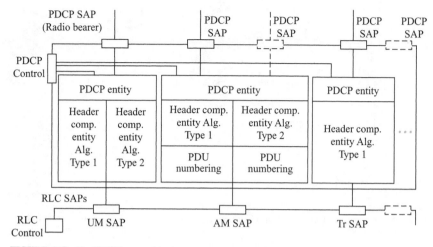

FIGURE 6.18   The PDCP layer architecture.

5. Detects and recovers from errors in the operation of the RLC protocol.

6. Using the same ciphering algorithm as MAC layer ciphering.

7. Suspensions and resumptions are local operations at RLC but commanded by RRC via the control interface.

6.4.4 PDCP Layer[15]

A. Architecture

The Packet Data Convergence Protocol (PDCP) exists only in the user plane and only for services from PS network. PDCP layer architecture is shown in Fig. 6.18. Every PDCP entity uses zero, one, or several header compression algorithm types with a set of configurable parameters. Several PDCP entities may use the same algorithm types. The RRC Radio Bearer established or reconfigured procedures indicated to the PDCP through the PDCP control SAP.

B. PDCP Function

1. Compression of redundant protocol control information at the transmitting entity and decompression at the receiving entity.

2. Transfers user data received from the NAS* and forwards it to the appropriate RLC entity and vice versa.

3. Support for loss-less serving RNS (SRNS) relocation. This is only applicable when PDCP is using acknowledged mode RLC with delivery in sequence.

6.4.5 BMC Layer[16]

A. Architecture

BMC (Broadcast/Multicast Control) protocol exists only in the user plane, originating from the broadcast domain along the radio interface. It is used for the SMS Cell

---

*Non-access stratum (NAS) carries signaling and user data message between UE and CN that are independent of the underlying access mechanism, e.g. access stratum (AS).

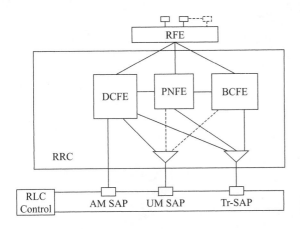

FIGURE 6.19 RRC layer architecture.

Broadcast Service (CBS). Each SMS CB message is targeted to a group of cells mapped by RNC.

B. BMC Functions

1. The BMC in RNC stores the cell broadcast messages received over CBC/RNC.

2. Traffic volume monitoring and scheduling of BMC message over the CBC/RNC interface.

3. Transmission of BMC message to MS and delivery of CB messages to the upper layer.

6.4.6 RRC Layer

A. Architecture

RRC layer handles the main part of control signaling between MS and RAN. RRC messages carry all parameters required to set up, modify, and release MAC layer and PHY layer protocol entities. The RRC layer architecture is shown in Fig. 6.19. There are four functional entities:

1. DCFE (Dedicated Control Functional Entity): Handles all functions and signaling specific to one MS. DCFE can utilize services from all SRB (see Fig. 6.14).

2. PNFE (Paging and Notification control Function Entity): Handles paging of idle mode in MS.

3. BCFE (Broadcast Control Function Entity): Handles the system information broadcasting.

4. RFE (Routing Function Entity): The routing of higher layer messages to different MM/CM entities on MS side or different core network domain on the RAN side.

B. RRC Functions[17]

1. Broadcast of system information, paging, and initial call selection and reselection in idle mode.

2. Establishment, maintenance, and release of an RRC connection between MS and RAN in connected mode.

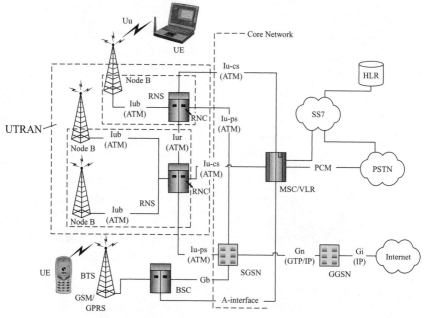

FIGURE 6.20   3GPP Release 1999 network architecture.

3. Control of Radio Bearers, transport channels, physical channels, and security functions.

4. Connection of mobility functions, MS positioning function, reception of MS measurement reporting, and support for DL open loop power control and outer loop power control in MS.

5. Cell broadcast service related functions.

6.4.7   Overview of 3GPP Release 99 Network[18]

6.4.7.1   General Description.   In 3GPP terminology, Mobile Equipment (ME) is the radio terminal used for radio communication. The User Equipment (UE) contains ME and the UMTS Subscriber Identity Module (USIM). USIM is a chip that contains some subscription-related information, plus security keys. UE is also called Mobile Station (MS). The network architecture for 3GPP Release 99 is shown in Fig. 6.20. The interface between the UE and the Node B is called Uu. Node B is named for BTS in 3GPP specification. The interface between Node B and RNC is called Iub. RNC is analogous to a BSC in GSM. Combining an RNC and many Node Bs is called Radio Network Subsystem (RNS).

An interface between the RNCs is called Iur. The primary purpose of this interface Iur is to support inter-RNC mobility and soft handover between Node Bs and different RNCs. An interface between RNC and the core network is called Iu. Iu interface has two different components. The interface between RNC and a single MSC/VLR is called Iu-CS. CS stands

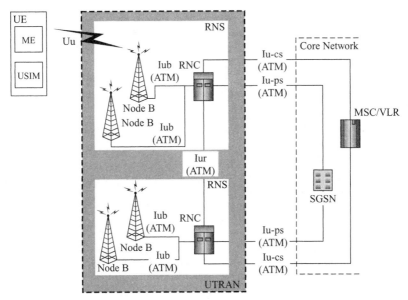

FIGURE 6.21 UTRAN architecture.

for Circuit Switched. The interface between RNC and SGSN (Serving GPRS Support Node) is called Iu-ps. PS stands for Packet switched. In Fig. 6.20, all the interfaces in the UTRAN of 3GPP Release 99 are based on Asynchronous Transfer Mode (ATM). ATM was chosen because it can support a valuable bit rate for packet-switched services and a constant bit rate for circuit-switched services. In Fig. 6.20 is the possibility for an existing core network such as GPRS to be upgraded to support UTRAN. A MSC could connect to both a GSM BSC and a UTRAN RNC.

The radio access network (RAN) of WCDMA is known as UTRAN (UMTS Terrestrial Radio Access Network). A UTRAN consists of several RNSs illustrated in the ultimate UTRAN architecture diagram shown in Fig. 6.21.

6.4.7.2 Role of the RNC

A. The RNC controlling one or several Node Bs through Iub interfaces is called Controlling RNC (CRNC) of the Node B. CRNC is responsible for the load and congestion control of its own cells, also for the allocation for new radio links to be established in those cells.

B. RNC as two logical roles with respect to the ME and UTRAN connections as shown in Fig. 6.22.

1. Serving RNC (SRNC): One UE connected to UTRAN through only one SRNC. Basic Radio Resource Management (RRM) operations are executed in SRNC, such as the handover decision, and outer loop power control.

2. Drift RNC (DRNC): Can be any RNC other than the SRNC. It controls cells used by the mobile. One UE may have zero, one, or more DRNCs.

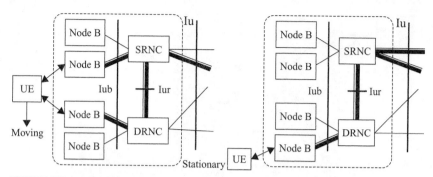

FIGURE 6.22 Logical role of the RNC for one UE UTRAN connection. The left-hand scenario shows one UE in inter-RNC soft handover (combining is performed in the SRNC). The right-hand scenario represents one UE using resources from one Node B only, controlled by the DRNC.

6.4.7.3 A Generic Model for UTRAN Interfaces.[19]

All the interfaces, such as Iu-CS, Iu-PS, Iur, and Iub interfaces, have two main components; the radio network layer and the transport network layer, as shown in Fig. 6.23. The radio network layer represents the application information (user data or control information) to be carried. The transport network layer represents the transport technology (ATM transport or others). The transport network layer could be different, but the radio network layer should be kept as no difference.

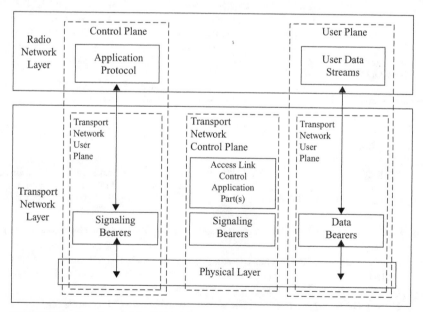

FIGURE 6.23 Generic model for UTRAN terrestrial interfaces.

As shown in Fig. 6.23, in the vertical domain, there are three planes: the control plane, the user plane, and the transport network user plane.

1. The control plane is used by control signaling, including the application protocol for establishing the bearers, which is transport user data, but the user data itself is carried on the user plane. The signaling bearers that carry the application signaling are analogous to the SS7 signaling links that are used between BSC and MSC in GSM.
2. The user plane is carrying the actual user data. The data packets are sent or received by the UE as part of a data session.
3. The transport network control plane contains functionality that is specific to the transport technology being used. It is not visible to the radio network layer. It involves the use of an Access Link Control Application Part (ALCAP). It is a generic term that describes a protocol or a set of protocols used to set up a transport bearer.

6.4.7.4 UMTS Packet Data Sessions. The packet data services used in Release 99 architecture as shown in Fig. 6.20 is largely the same mechanisms as used for GPRS data. The Gb interface of GPRS is replaced by the Iu-PS interface, which uses RAN Application Part (RANAP) as the application protocol. The IP over ATM is used between the SGSN and RNC. Thus an IP network is set up from GGSN to SGSN to RNC. The GTP-C (GPRS – Tunneling Protocol in Control plane) starts at GGSN and terminates at the SGSN shown in Fig. 6.24. It is because the application protocol between RNC and SGSN is RANAP rather than GTP. The GTP-U tunnel in the user plane can be relayed from the GGSN through the SGSN to the RNC.

From an interface perspective, UMTS provides greater flexibility than GPRS in terms of allocation of resources for packet data traffic. The UMTS can offer a greater range of data speeds and also provides a selection of different channel types of air interface for packet data. In the uplink, the RACH, CPCH, and DCH are available, and in the downlink, the DCH, FACH, and DSCH are available. RNC controls the choice of channels to be used depending

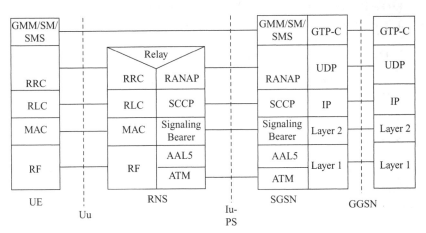

UMTS GPRS Control Plane UE to SGSN to GGSN

FIGURE 6.24 UMTS GPRS control plane protocol stacks.

on the characteristics of session required by the user, such as high-volume streaming versus low-volume bursting traffic.

6.5 EVOLUTION OF UMTS-3GPP RELEASE 4 AND BEYOND (RELEASE 5, 6, 7)

The distributed network architecture is migrated from the use of Frame Relay in GPRS and then followed by ATM in Release 99, followed by IP in Release 4.[20] The core network architecture for 3GPP Release 99 is not greatly different from the core network architecture of GPRS. In 3GPP Release 4 and beyond, we find significant enhancements to the core network.

6.5.1 Release 4 Core Network Architecture

A. Basically, MSC is broken into an MSC and a MGW (media gateway).

MSC server: (1) contains all of the mobility management and (2) call control logic.

MGS: (1) media path is via one or more MGWs and (2) establishes, manipulates, and releases media stream or voice streams under the control of the MS server.

B. For CS calls

1. Control signaling for CS calls is between RNC and the MSC server.

2. Media path for CS calls is between the RNC and the MGW.

3. MGN takes calls from the RNC and routes those calls toward their destinations over a packet backbone.

4. The packet backbone is IP-based for voice-over-IP (VoIP).

C. For improving PS domain

1. One backbone network is for both CS and PS traffic.

2. The control protocol between the MSC server (or GMSC server) and the MGW is ITUH.248 protocol.

3. The Release 4 Distributed Network Architecture will simultaneously support both UTRAN and GSM access networks. The Release 4 Distributed Network Architecture is shown in Fig. 6.25. It is modified from the architecture from Release 99 shown in Fig. 6.20.

6.5.2 VoIP Technology[21]

The Distributed Network Architecture of Release 4[20] is suitable to VoIP. In the IP-based backbone, IP corresponds to Layer 3 of OSI seven-layer protocol stack, as shown in Fig. 6.26. IP can simply pass a packet of data from one router to another though the network to its destination by taking IP address in the IP packet header. This simple operation provides no protection against a loss of packets, which might happen if congestion occurs during the operation. Furthermore, different packets can go on different routes through the network, thus the different delays from the different packets make the packets out of sequence when they arrive at the destination. In data network, the TCP (Transmission Control Protocol) is issued to ensure an error-free, in-sequence delivery of packets to the destination as

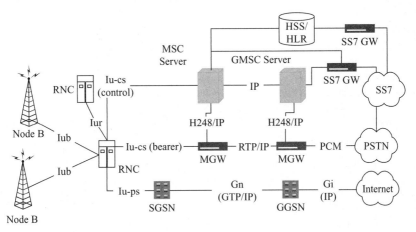

FIGURE 6.25   3GPP Release 4 distributed network architecture.

shown in Fig. 6.26. TCP is a layer higher than IP. When a session is set up between two applications, the application data is first passed to TCP where a TCP header is found. Then the data is passed to IP where an IP header is found. The data then is forwarded to the destination through the network.

A. TCP Layer

  1. TCP Header

  a. Source and destination port numbers: Identify the application data at each end.

  b. Sequence numbers and acknowledges numbers: Enable the detection of lost packets.

  c. Checksum: Enables the detection of corrupted packets.

  2. TCP uses this information to request retransmission of lost or corrupted packets and to deliver packets to the destination in the correct order.

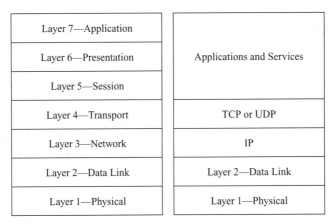

FIGURE 6.26   OSI and IP protocol stacks.

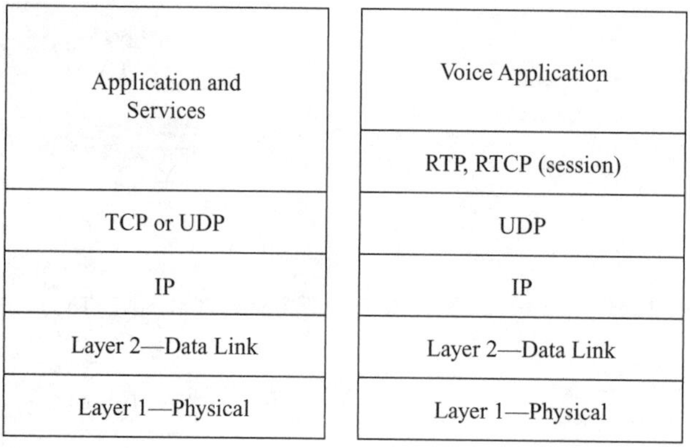

Application and Services	Voice Application
	RTP, RTCP (session)
TCP or UDP	UDP
IP	IP
Layer 2—Data Link	Layer 2—Data Link
Layer 1—Physical	Layer 1—Physical

FIGURE 6.27 IP and VoIP protocol layers.

3. TCP has to first establish a connection between two peer TCPs at each end.

4. This involves a sequence of messages between the TCPs prior to the transfer of user data.

5. For voice transmission, the UDP (User Datagram Protocol) is used instead of TCP. It is a simple protocol. It does not support recovery from loss of error and does not ensure an in-sequence delivery of packets. It is used for simple request response types of transactions, rather than the sequential transfer of multiple packets. An application of using UDP is the DNS (Domain Name Service), a classic one-shot request response protocol. It is strictly used for voice transmission. The reason for speech is excessive delay, and jitter is far more critical than occasional packet loss. A limited loss, less than 5 percent, can be tolerated without noticeable speech quality degradation.

B. Application Layer

1. To improve voice quality, the coding scheme can be used. The application of both source and destination need to know the coding scheme.

2. The Application needs timing information so that packets can reach the user in a synchronized manner and help resolve against delay in the network.

3. Application needs to know when packets are lost, so that a previous packet could be replayed to fill the gap when it is appropriate.

C. RTP, RTCP Layer in VoIP Protocol Layers

RTP (Real-Time Transport Protocol)[22] is created in the VoIP protocol layer shown in Fig. 6.27. It resides between UDP and Voice Application layers. This created layer can be treated as Session layer. RTP can be used to fulfill these needs mentioned in the Application layer. Whenever a packet of coded voice is sent, it is sent as the payload of an RTP packet.

1. RTP Header

   a. Voice coding scheme being sent.

   b. A sequence number of packets.

   c. A timestamp for the instant at which the voice packet was sampled.

   d. An identification for the source of the voice packet.

2. RTCP (RTP Control Protocol) is a companion protocol of RTP. It has functions as follows:

   a. It does not carry coded voice packets.

Audio/Video Application	Terminal/Application Control				
Audio/Video Codecs	RTCP	H.225.0 RAS Signaling	H.225.0 Call Signaling (Q.931)	H.245 Control Signaling	H.323
RTP					
UDP			TCP		
IP					
Layer 2—Data Link					
Layer 1—Physical					

FIGURE 6.28 H.323 protocol layers.

   b. It is a signaling protocol, including a number of messages to be exchanged between session users, regarding the quality of the session.

   c. The information of lost RTP packets, delay, and interarrival jitter.

   d. RTCP session is open when an RTP session is opened.

   e. When a UDP port number is assigned to an RTP session for transferring the voice packets, a separate port number is also assigned for RTCP session.

   f. RTP and RTCP simply provide information to the Applications at either end and let those Applications deal with loss, delay, or jitter with different protocols.

D. H.323 Protocols

In VoIP system, signaling protocols are invoked before or during a call for setting up a call, monitoring call progress, and terminating a call. The set of protocols is known as H.323, which title is Packet-based multimedia communications systems. H.323 protocol stack includes RTP, RTCP, H.225.0, and H.245, shown in Fig. 6.28. The last two protocols define the actual messages that are exchanged between H.323 end points. The end point can be a terminal, a gateway, a gatekeeper, or a MCU.

   1. H.225.0 is a two-part protocol:

     The first part of H.225.0 is a call signaling (Q.931): establishment and tear down of connections between H.323 end points.

     The second part of H.225.0 is a RAS signaling: RAS for Registration, Admission, and Status, which provides information for maintenance.

   2. H.245 is a control protocol used between two or more end points. The main purpose is to manage the media streams between H.323 session participants.

E. H.323 Call Establishment and Release

Let the two terminals establish a VoIP call between them and two different gatekeepers control the two terminals. There are six stages: request, setup, connecting, link connection, terminating, and disconnecting. The procedure of call establishment and release is shown in Fig. 6.29. The functions of those three signaling protocols, H.225.0 RAS signaling, H.225.0 call signaling, and H.245 control signaling, are indicated in the figure. Sometimes an H.323 fast connect procedure can be carried out by eliminating H.245 control signaling for opening/closing a logical channel and for end session.

   1. A logical channel contains mandatory parameters such as type of data (i.e., vocoder types) to be sent, an RTP session ID, an RTP payload type (i.e., a packet of coded voice), and an indication as to whether silence suppression is to be used.

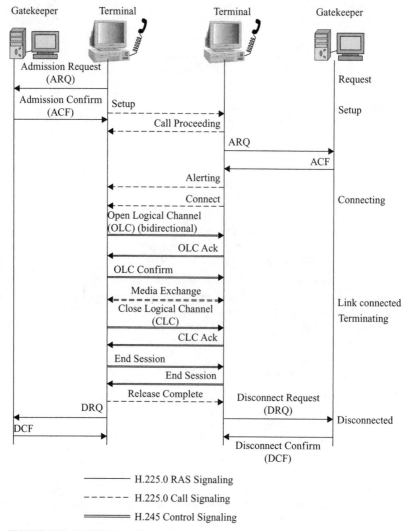

FIGURE 6.29   H.323 Call establishment and release.

2. End session: once all logical channels in a session are closed, then the session itself is terminated.

F. The SIP (Session Initiation Protocol)

SIP is a power alternative to H.323. It has a more flexible solution, simpler than H.323, easier to implement, and better suited to the support of intelligent user devices and the implementation of advanced features.

1. SIP Network Architecture

SIP is used to establish sessions between users. In SIP Network, there are two basic classes of network entities, clients, and servers. Thus SIP is a client-server protocol. SIP enables the use of proxies, which act as both clients and servers.

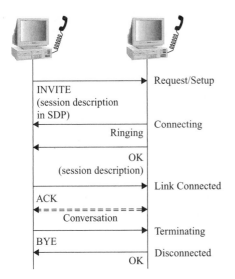

Request/Setup

Connecting

Link Connected

Terminating

Disconnected

FIGURE 6.30 SIP basic call establishment and release.

a. A client is an application program that sends SIP requests. It may be found within a user's device, a SIP phone.

b. Four different types of servers are served: proxy servers, redirect servers, user agent servers, and registers.

c. In SIP, the information in SIP message that is the type and coding of information to be shared by two users at two ends requires session descriptions. These session descriptions are coded according to the SDP (Session Description Protocol).

2. SIP Call Establishment and Release

SIP Call Establishment is very simple as shown in Figure 6.30. In SIP call, no gatekeepers are needed. The SDP carries all information used by SIP. The call begins with an INVITE, which indicates the address of the sender containing in URI (Uniform Resource Indicator). The call process shown in Fig. 6.30 explains the simple SIP call process.

6.5.3 3GPP Release 5 Core Architecture (HSDPA, IMS, PoC)

Release 4 is an enhancement to Release 99 core network. However, 3GPP Release 5[23] is a totally new core network architecture as shown in Fig. 6.31. Release 5 can realize larger capacities, better user experiences and network efficiency, and better enable new and integrated multimedia solutions. The UTRAN can be connected to two different logical core network domains; the PS main and the IP multimedia (IM) domain. The CS main is eliminated because of the omission of MSC server. When a terminal wants to use the services of the core network, it indicates which domain it wants to use. The IM domain is a new domain; it uses the services of the PS domain. The IM domain is based on the SIP. The IM architecture enables voice and data calls to be handled in a uniform manner from the UE to the destination. Moreover, the use of SIP means that a great deal of service control can be located in the UE rather than the network, to make it easier for the subscriber to customize services to meet personal need. All IM traffic is packed based and is transported using PS domain nodes such as the SGSN and GGSN. Three

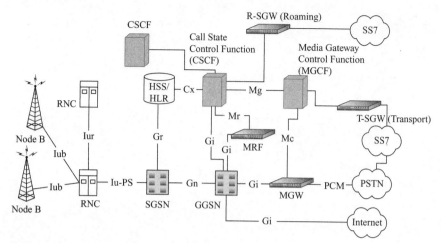

FIGURE 6.31 3GPP Release 5 IP multimedia network architecture. (SGW-Signaling gateway, MRF- multimedia resource function)

accomplishments, HSDPA, IMS and PoC, on the Release 5 features are described in the following:

A. HSDPA (High Speed Downlink Packet Access)[24]

HSDPA is a packet-based data service in downlink with data transmission rate up to 8–14 Mbps (and 20 Mbps for MIMO system in Release 6) over a 5 MHz bandwidth. The MIMO technology is described in Chapter 8. HSDPA implementations include Adaptive Modulation and Coding (AMC), Multiple-Input Multiple-Output (MIMO), Hybrid Automatic Request (HARQ), Fast Cell Site Selection (FCSS) search, and advanced receiver design. The features of HSDAP are as follows:

Feature	HSDPA
Downlink Frame Size	2 ms (3 slots)
Channel Feedback	Channel quality reported at 2 ms rate or or 500 Hz
Data user multiplexing	TDM/CDM
Adaptive Modulation and Coding	QPSK & 16-QAM Mandatory
Hybrid-ARQ	Chase or Incremental Redundancy (IR)
Spreading Factor	SF = 16 using UTRA OVSF Channelization Codes
Control Channel Approach	Dedicated Channel pointing to Shared Channel

HSDPA in Releases 5 and 6 will be capable of providing data rates of up to 10 Mbps as well as twofold base station capacity under ideal conditions. The techniques are employed to achieve the high data rates yet maintaining compatibility with currently available equipment. HSDPA is a new transport channel, the *downlink shared channel* (HS-DSCH) that is optimized for shared data. It also provides higher order modulation, short *transmission time interval* (TTI), fast link adaptation, fast scheduling, and fast HARQ.

B. IMS (IP Multimedia Subsystem) is based on IP core networking standards the enable 3G operators to simply and cost-effectively introduce multimedia services including VoIP, delivery of instant message, interactive mobile gaming, friend list/network presence detection, Push-to-Talk Over Cellular (PoC), and a variety of advanced multimedia services.

C. PoC (Push-to-Talk Over Cellular)

Push-to-Talk (PTT) is a feature that can instantly talk to a group of people in the network. PoC is the feature of PTT used in the cellular network. The OMA (Open Mobile Alliance) has a PoC.

The solution builds on the extensive 3GPP IMS (IP multimedia subsystem) architecture—leveraging IP protocols for signaling and voice transport. Using SIP (Session Initiation Protocol) as a general purpose signaling mechanism, subscriber handsets establish contact with a PoC server. SIP-enabled presence extensions produce buddy lists displayed on each talk group member's handset.

With the drive toward a consistent IMS environment between GSM and cdma2000, and extending even toward nonmobile networks such as WLAN, OMA PoC promises to extend universal group communication to collections of subscribers on disparate networks. Building on the IMS architecture with its generic application of SIP-based signaling and the IP-based RTP (Real-time Transport Protocol) sets the stage for other "Push To" services such as "Push to Video," which are needed for both consumer-friendly and business-oriented "see-what-I-see" services.

Future enhancements to 3GPP Release 5 will mainly be driven by the need for improved user experience powered by packet-based services combining real-time and non-real-time components available in both stationary and mobile environments.

6.5.4 3GPP Release 6 (MBMS, EUDCH)[25]

Release 6 is focused on improving capacity, quality of service, and service enabler and delivery for multimedia packet-based services. There are several new features:

A. One key feature targeted for 3GPP Release 6 is the Multimedia Broadcast Multicast Service (MBMS) feature, which identifies capabilities to address the same information to many users in one cell using the same radio resources. The MBMS is a unidirectional point-to-multipoint service in which data is transmitted from a single source entity to multiple recipients. Transmitting the same data to multiple recipients allows network resources to be shared. By this, the MBMS architecture enables the efficient usage of radio-network and core-network resources, with an emphasis on radio interface efficiency. MBMS is provided over a broadcast or multicast service area that can cover the whole network or be a small geographical area such as a shopping mall or sports stadium allowing for region specific content distribution. Examples of broadcast services are advertisements for upcoming or ongoing Multicast services or localized advertisements such as ads for attractions or shops within the broadcast area. An example of a service using the multicast mode could be near real-time distribution of video clips from national and regional sports events for which a subscription is required.

B. Another significant feature targeted for Release 6 is the Enhanced Uplink for Dedicated Channels (EUDCH) feature. As the importance of IP-based services increases, demand to improve the coverage and throughput as well as reduce the delay of the uplink also increases. Applications that could benefit from an enhanced uplink may include services like video clips, multimedia, e-mail, telematics, gaming, video streaming, and so forth. The EUDCH feature investigates enhancements that can be applied to UMTS in order to improve the performance on the uplink dedicated transport channels. To enhance uplink performance, features similar to those introduced for HSDPA in the downlink are being considered, including:

- Adaptive modulation and coding schemes.
- Hybrid ARQ protocols.
- Node B controlled scheduling.
- Physical layer or higher layer signaling mechanisms to support the enhancements.
- Shorter frame size (such as TTI) and improved QoS.

C. Other features include:

1. Generic User Profile (GUP) framework.
2. Advanced receiver performance specifications (e.g., diversity receive at the terminal).
3. Access network sharing.
4. Trace management.
5. Remote control of electrical antenna tilt.
6. IMS enhancements (e.g., to support messaging, conferencing, networking with CS and PS networks).
7. Enhancements to support WLAN integration.
8. QoS improvements.
9. New SIP capabilities.
10. Wideband AMR speech codec (i.e., to support wideband speech like music).
11. Mechanisms to standardize IP flow-based bearer level charging.
12. Aimed to better enable applications such as emergency services.
13. Enhanced Push-to-Talk over Cellular (PoC) such as presence, instant messaging.
14. PS streaming services and Voice and Video over IP.

Clearly, there are rich Release 6 feature contents planned that will significantly enhance spectral/network efficiency and greatly enhance the end user experience.

6.5.5 3GPP Release 7

For Release 7, the scope, content, and timeline have not been defined.

Increased spectral efficiency of the radio interface is of paramount importance in order to make the most out of the limited suitable spectrum and the operators' investment in site resources. Multiple-Input Multiple-Output (MIMO) antenna systems, motivated by an information theoretic consideration, promise a considerable increase in spectral efficiencies. Therefore, support for MIMO systems is one key element considered for evolution of the UMTS radio interface. A large effort is expected to go into the maintenance and enhancement of the considerable new capabilities that have been introduced in the previous two releases. For example, IMS will further be enhanced (e.g., by explicit support for wireline access allowing fixed-mobile convergence). In addition, the integration of alternative radio technologies such as WLAN will be considered (e.g., by allowing handover and closer integration with legacy voice services).

6.6 cdma2000 PHYSICAL LAYER

cdma2000[26–29] is an evaluation of cdmaOne, which extrapolates the air interface specification of IS-95 to meet the requirement for IMT-2000 as one among the third generation of cellular systems. cdma2000 supports backward compatibility with IS-95.

The physical layer is responsible for:

1. Transmitting and receiving bits over the physical medium, which is the air. The bits have to convert into waveforms by modulation.

2. Carrying out coding functions to perform error control functions at the bit and frame levels.

cdma2000 accepts both signal carrier and multiple carrier implementations. It also has proposed two kinds of multiplexing: FDD and TDD. The physical layer channels for both FDD and TDD are the same. However, FDD is first to implement. Physical channels are distinguished in two groups: dedicated and common channels.

6.6.1 Physical Channels

Physical channels are distinguished in two groups: dedicated and common channel.

A. Dedicated Physical Channel (DPHCH)

1. Forward Dedicated Physical Channel (F-DPHCH): There are four dedicated channels.

   - Fundamental channel (F-FCH): Provides for transportation of dedicated data.
   - Supplemental Channel (F-SCH): Allocated dynamically to supply a required data rate.
   - Dedicated Control Channel (F-DCCH): Used to transport mobile-specific control information.
   - Dedicated Auxiliary Pilot Channel (F-DAPICH): Used with antenna beam-forming and beam-steering to increase coverage or data rate of a desired user. This channel is optional.

2. Reversed Dedicated Physical Channel (R-DPHCH): There are three dedicated channels.

   - Fundamental Channel (R-FCH): Same function as F-FCH.
   - Supplemental Channel (R-SCH): Same function as F-SCH channel.
   - Dedicated Control Channel (R-DCCH)

B. Common Physical Channel (CPHCH)

1. Forward Common Physical Channel (F-CPHCH)

   - Pilot Channel (F-PICH): Carries the Pilot symbol and provides capabilities for channel estimation and coherent detection and soft handoff.
   - Common Auxiliary Pilot Channel (F-CAPICH): Provides a fine-tuning on coherent detection and soft handoff.
   - Sync Channel (F-SYNC): Provides the mobile station with system information and synchronization.
   - Common Assignment Channel (F-CACH): Support the reservation access mode on the R-EACH (Enhanced Access Channel). The message that assigns the R-CCCH is transmitted on the F-CACH.

- Paging Channel (F-PCH): It can enable paging functions, also provides a means for short burst data communications. Each mobile is assigned an 80-ms slot and decodes periodically to receive page messages. Two channels F-BCCH and F-CCCH can substitute it.

- Broadcast Control Channel (F-BCCH): Serves to broadcast system–specific and cell-specific overhead information.

- Common Control Channel (F-CCCH): It provides a means for paging functions and support different data rates for short burst data communications.

  The F-BCCH and F-CCCH do not have to operate at the same data rates and the same power level.

- Quick Paging Channel (F-QPCH): The idea of having F-QPCH is to decrease the time and mobile station needs to monitor the F-PCH or F-CCCH. The period at which the mobile station must decide F-PCH or F-CCCH as short as 1.28 ms.

- Common Power-Control Channel (F-CPCCH): Serves two purposes:

  a. To allow power control of the R-CCH and R-PICH works during the reservation access.

  b. To control the R-PICH when the mobile station is in the traffic state.

- Packet Data Control (F-PDCH): A shared packet data channel that supports high-speed operation traffic. Access to this channel is handled through MAC layer scheduling.

2. Reverse Common Physical Channel

- Access Channel (R-ACH): Used for mobile stations communications messages to the base station for backward compatibility reasons.

- Common Control Channel (R-CCCH): To transport control information.

- Enhanced Access Channel (R-EACH): An enhanced access product relative to that of the R-ACH.

- Dedicated Control Channel (R-DCCH): Same function as F-DCCH.

- Pilot Channel (R-PICH): Provides the signal for coherent detection.

- Channel Quality Indicator Channel (R-CQICH): A support channel for adoptive coding and modulation over the F-PDCH.

- Acknowledgment Channel (R-ACKCH): Check whether the CRC of the decoded packet has passed or failed.

C. Improvements in cdma2000 Physical Layer
The original intention of the IS-2000 family of standards is to evolve progressively to higher data rates using wider bandwidths (i.e., 3x ... 12x). However, the current trend seems to be one of the deploying high data rate solutions that use 1.25 MHz of bandwidth (e.g., 1xEV-DO). There are several advantages of using solutions like 1xEV-DO; one can select dedicated 1.25-MHz carriers to optimize for high rate data.

1xEV-DO and 1xEV-DV are described in Sec. 6.8.

Besides using 1xEv-DO to increase data rate, cdma2000 1x has also enhanced its IS-95 in two areas of improvements signaling and transmission, to enable data rates at or above 144 kbps:

1. In Signaling Area
In order to implement high-rate packet-switched data, cdma2000 needs to dynamically acquire and release air link resources. An efficient signaling is required to

perform quick acquisitions and releases of these resources. These new signaling mechanisms include:

- On the forward link, there are new overhead/signaling physical channels. They are quick paging channel (F-QPCH), forward common control channel (F-CCCH), broadcast control channel (F-BCCH), common power control channel (F-CPCCH), and common assignment channel (F-CACH).

- On the forward link, IS-2000 can also transmit shorter signaling messages. It can use shorter 5-ms frames (i.e., 1/8 rate) on the forward fundamental channel for this purpose.

- On the reverse link, there are new overhead/signaling physical channels. They are reverse dedicated control channel (R-DCCH), enhanced access channel (R-EACH), and reverse common control channel (R-CCH).

- On the reverse link, there are shorter signaling messages. IS-2000 can transmit shorter 5-ms frames on the enhanced access channel (R-EACH). This is done to reduce the probability of access collision.

2. In Transmission Area
A higher air link capacity is obviously needed to implement high-rate data, and various changes are made to improve air link capacity to beyond that of IS-95. These changes are also made to affect a more efficient use of air link resources. Some major changes are listed below:

- Forward supplemental channel (F-SCH) and reverse supplemental channel (R-SCH) are added to transport high-rate user data.

- Forward link now has fast closed-loop power control (compared with the slower power control in IS-95). Power control groups are transmitted on the reverse pilot channel to enable fast closed-loop power control of the forward link.

- In addition to power controlling the traffic channels, IS-2000 can also power control the signaling channel (i.e., forward dedicated control channel [F-DCCH]).

- Reverse link now has a reverse pilot channel (R-PICH) to support coherent modulation on the reverse link.

6.6.2 Radio Interface Parameters of cdma2000 FDD[29]

The radio interface parameters of cdma2000 are similar to IS-95.

A. **Channel Structure**
After the physical channel generates a frame, then the physical layer performs the same functions as does in IS-95.

- Adding the CRC bits for detecting frame errors
- Coding the FEC bits
- Interleaving for combating the long term fading

The final data stream as input $\{d_i\}$ goes through single carrier forward link radio access shown in Fig. 6.32.

B. **Chip Rates**: cdma2000 supports a range of chip rates; all can be expressed by: $N \times 1.2288$ Mcps, $N = 1, 3, 6, 9, 12$. When $N > 1$, there are two ways by which cdma2000 can spread the signal. The first one, Multicarrier, basically de-multiplexes the message signal into N information signals and spreads each of those on a different carrier, at a

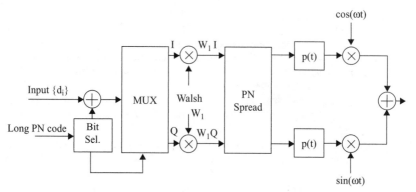

FIGURE 6.32 cdma2000 Single Carrier Forward link Modulation and Spreading.

chip rate of 1.2288 Mcps. The second one, Direct Spread, simply spreads the message signal directly with a chip rate of $N \times 1.2288$ Mcps. In the Multicarrier mode, each carrier has an IS-95 signal format. The two methods are illustrated next.

C. Modulation and Spreading

1. For Single Carrier

a. Forward Link

Figure 6.32 illustrates the modulation and spreading process for forward-link, single carrier of cdma2000. The input consists of a single channel that is already coded, punctured, and interleaved according to the cdma2000 specifications. Each channel has different possible configurations, but the modulation and spreading process is the same for all channels.

First, a long PN code scrambles the channel. The rate of the scrambling code depends on the code rate of the input. Only the PCH, DCCH, FCH, and SCH are scrambled.

Then the MUX maps the codes to polar form, transfers the serial data to parallel, and also provides the possibility of puncturing the data stream, to insert a bit of power control (indicated by the Bit Sel. Box). A Walsh code running at the chip rate (1.2288 Mcps) then multiplies the data. The same code is used for both the In-Phase and Quadrature component. Each channel gets a different Walsh code assigned and might be of different length (OVSF codes), to adjust the Spreading Factor to the data rate required.

Both Q data and I, after coded with Walsh code W_1, are then complex PN multiplied, also at the chip rate. This is accomplished by using the Complex Spreading shown in Fig. 6.33. PN_I and PN_Q are two different short PN sequences.

The diagram shown in Fig. 6.33 is to realize the following operation at the output of PN spread box:

$$(I + jQ) \cdot W_1 \cdot \left[(PN)_I + j(PN)_Q \right] = \left[W_1 \cdot I \cdot (PN)_I - W_1 \cdot Q \cdot (PN)_Q \right] +$$

$$j \left[W_1 \cdot I(PN)_Q + W_1 \cdot Q \cdot (PN)_I \right] \qquad (6.6\text{-}1)$$

The real part of Eq. (6.6-1) is the same as the upper part output of the PN spread box corresponding to the input of the in-phase branch of the QPSK modulator. The imaginary part of Eq. (6.6-1) is the same as the lower part output of the PN spread box corresponding to the input of the quadrature branch of the QPSK modulator.

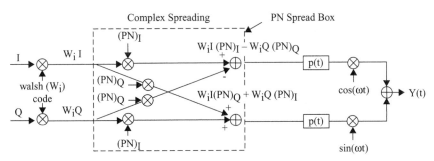

FIGURE 6.33 *PN* spread box.

Finally, the information is modulated, using p(t) as a waveform, which is the same as the one used in IS-95.

The same structure is used for Direct Spread, but the chip rate is modified to $N \times 1.2288$ Mcps.

cdma2000 uses XPSK, whereas IS-95 uses BPSK. QPSK transmits two independent symbol streams in two dimensions; QPSK thus can double the data rate of IS-95 using the same bandwidth.

b. Reverse Link

Figure 6.34 illustrates the reverse link modulation and spreading process. The channel illustrated here is the Reverse Dedicated Channel. It consists of a Reverse Pilot Channel, which is always present, a Reverse Fundamental Channel (R-FCH), one or more Reverse Supplemental Channel (R-SCH), and a Reverse Dedicated Control Channel (R-DCCH). The R-SCH, R-SCH, and R-DCCH may not always be used.

Each channel is spread with a Walsh codeword as indicated in Fig. 6.34. Channels that require higher data rates get a smaller codeword. The R-DCCH is spread with the sequence (00001111), the R-FCH with the sequence (0011), and the R-SCH is spread with (01) if there is only one supplemental channel present or (0101) if two are used. The second supplemental channel would then be spread with the sequence (0110). It is possible to have more supplemental channels by using a longer Walsh codeword.

The spread Pilot Channel and the R-DCCH are mapped to the In-Phase component. The spread R-FCH and R-SCH are mapped to the Quadrature component. Both components are then complex multiplied by the two PN sequences provided, PN_I and PN_Q, which are themselves multiplied by a long code. The complex multiplication process was illustrated in Fig. 6.33. The two short PN sequences have the same properties as their IS-95 equivalents and have a period of 2^{15} chips. The mobile station aligns the PN sequences in time with the synchronization channel so that the base station knows their state. The long code has a period of $2^{42} - 1$ chips.

The reverse link supports Direct Spread cdma for chip rates that are multiples of the basic 1.2288 Mcps. Chip rates of 3X correspond to 3.684 Mcps.

2. Multicarrier

a. Forward Link

Figure 6.35 illustrates the structure of forward link multicarrier cdma2000. It is very similar to the single carrier implementation. After scrambling, the user data is demultiplexed to feed the N IQ-Modulators ($N = 3, 6, 9$, or 12) so that each

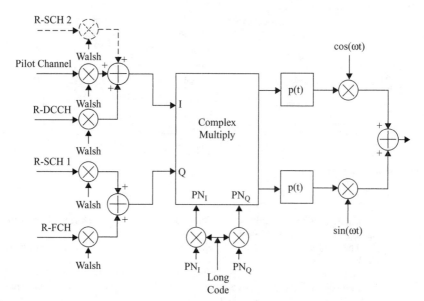

FIGURE 6.34 Reverse link Modulation and Spreading (Single Carrier).

frequency carries part of the data stream. The N carriers are Walsh code modulated to the chip rate of 1.2288 Mcps. The Walsh codes may be different for each.

As for the single carrier case, provision is made to puncture the data stream to add a bit for power control. The Bit Sel. box in Fig. 6.35 also indicates it.

The carriers are located on a different frequency with a spacing of 1.25 MHz between each.

b. Reverse Link
There is no Multicarrier implementation for the reverse link connection. Instead, the direct spread of 5 MHz is used as shown in Fig. 6.36.

3. Transmission Characteristics for Both Single Carrier and Multicarrier

- **Guard Regions**
cdma2000 allocates Guard regions of 625 kHz, on each side of the allocated bandwidth, to prevent interference with neighboring bands. So the figure for the total bandwidth must include these two Guard regions.

- **Pulse Waveform**
The pulse waveform for the transmission is the same as the one defined for IS-95.

- **Frame Structure**
cdma2000 supports two frame lengths, depending on the channel used: 5 ms and 20 ms. For voice data, frames of 20 ms are used to enhance the demodulation performance through longer interleaving span.

- **Transmission Characteristics**

    Modulation chip rate $= N \times 1.2288$ Mcps

    Pulse shaping $=$ same as IS-95

    Modulation

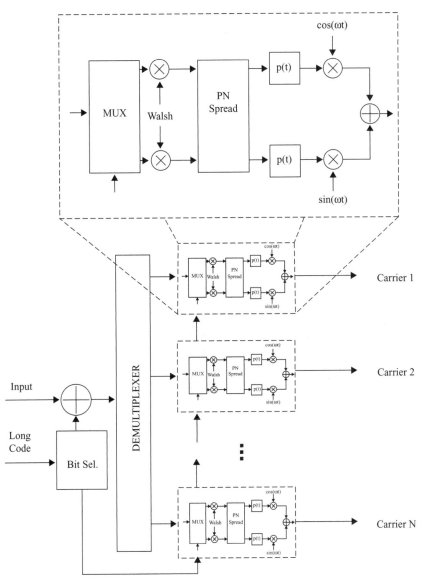

FIGURE 6.35   Multicarrier Forward link cdma2000 Modulation and Spreading.

Reverse Link
  BPSK Data modulation
  QPSK Spreading modulation
Forward Link
  QPSK Data modulation
  QPSK spreading modulation

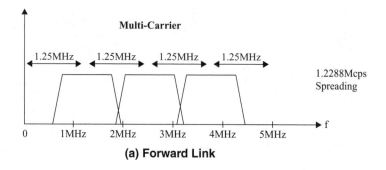

(a) Forward Link

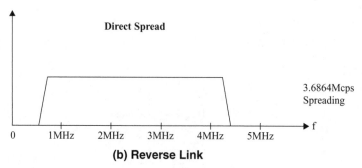

(b) Reverse Link

FIGURE 6.36   Channel bandwidths for FDD.

Detection: coherent for both reverse link and forward link

Channel Spacing: $(N + 1) \times 1.25$ MHz

- **Other Characteristics**
  cdma2000 plans to use multiple antennas to enhance the performance of the transmission link. Note that the multicarrier implementation is particularly well suited
  for diversity systems, as the signal to be transmitted is already de-multiplexed in
  multiple carriers. Provision is also made to use multiple antennas in the direct-
  spread implementation.

6.6.3   Transmission Characteristics for cdma2000 TDD

A. Description
TDD transmission mode[30–31] is available in areas where it is not possible to get a paired
frequency band. TDD uses the same modulation characteristics (chip rates, pulse wave
form, modulation type) and processing gain as FDD mode. In essence, TDD is just an
extension of FDD, where some functionality is added: Guard Time and Burst Generation.

B. Frame Structure of cdma2000 TDD
TDD also uses frame lengths of either 5 ms or 20 ms. Time slots last 1.25 ms each, so for
5 ms frames, there is a possibility of 4 time slots and for 20 ms frames, up to 16. We call
Burst Generation the process of placing the data in a suitable form for transmission in
short time slots. Every time slot finishes with a Guard Time of a minimum of 52.08 μs.
The Guard Time (GT) can be adjusted depending on the transmission scheme as shown
in Fig. 6.37.

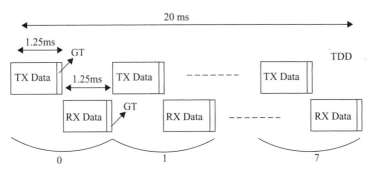

FIGURE 6.37   CDMA2000 TDD frame structure.

C. Physical Resources
In the TDD case, a physical resource is not only specified by the frequency and access code but also by its time slot.

D. An Outline of Transmission Characteristics
- Modulation chip rate: $N \times 1.2288$ Mcps
- Pulse Shaping: same as IS-95
- Modulation

    Reverse Link (RL)

    BPSK Data modulation

    QPSK Spreading modulation

    Forward Link (FL)

    QPSK Data modulation

    QPSK Spreading modulation
- Channel Spacing: $(N + 1) \times 1.25$ MHz

6.7 cdma2000 NETWORK

In cdma2000, four different protocol layers are specified:[29,32]

1. Physical (Layer 1) described in Sec. 6.6.
2. MAC sublayer (Layer 2) for controlling higher layers' access to the physical medium.
3. Link access control (LAC) sublayer (Layer 2) for responding to the reliability of signaling.
4. Upper layer (Layer 3) for an overall control of the cdma2000 system.

6.7.1 MAC Sublayer

A. Four Entities
In the MAC sublayer, there are four different entities: Radio Link Protocol (RLP), Signaling Radio Burst Protocol (SRBP), Common Channel Multiplex Sublayer, and Dedicated Channel Multiplex Sublayer as shown in Fig. 6.38.

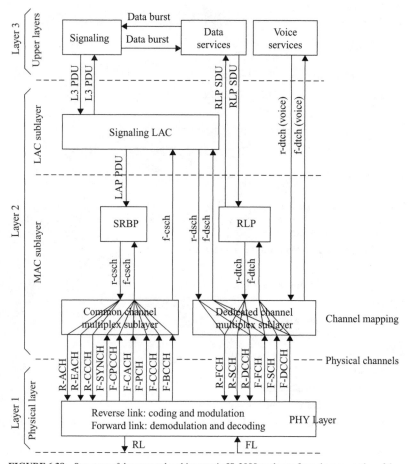

FIGURE 6.38   Structure of the protocol architecture in IS-2000 as shown from the perspective of the mobile.

- The radio link protocol (RLP) handles user packet data. RLP is performing in the Dedicated Channel Multiplex Sublayer.

- The Signaling Radio Burst Protocol (SRBP) handles common-channel signaling using radio burst techniques. The SRBP is performing in the Common Channel Multiplex Sublayer.

- The Common Channel Multiplex Sublayer performs the mapping between the logical common channels (i.e., those channels are shared among multiple users) and the physical common channels.

- Dedicated channel multiplex sublayer performs the mapping between the logical dedicated channels (i.e., those channels are dedicated to specific users) and the physical dedicated channels.

The primary function of the MAC sublayer is to multiplex logical channels onto different physical channels before sending and to de-multiplex physical channels into different logical channel after receiving. The two multiplex sublayers of the MAC as mentioned above handle these two functions.

The dedicated channels can be used for both signaling and user data; common channels are only used for signaling. The same arrangement of channels appears in WCDMA. However, the transport channels used in WCDMA for exchanging information between physical layer and logical channels replay MAC layer directly as a means to exchange information between Layer 1 and Layer 2.

B. Primitives
The messages sending and receiving between layers/sublayers are primitives, a form of these communication messages. Two widely used types of primitives are

- *Request primitives:* A service requester (MS) uses request primitives to request a service or a resource.

- *Indication primitives:* A service provider uses indication primitives to indicate an event requested by service requester has occurred.

C. Logical Channels
The multiplex sublayers, both common channels and dedicated channels, are responsible for the mapping between logical channels and physical channels. The mapping between logical channels and physical channels on the forward link are shown in Table 6.3(*A*) and on the reverse link shown in Table 6.3(*B*). The forward-dedicated traffic channel (F-DTCH) Logical Channel Data (common or dedicated) should be reliably delivered from end to end. In executing reliable delivery, the MAC sublayer assembles data received from higher layers and passes the assembled data to the physical layer for transmission. The MAC sublayer also receives data from the physical layer, disassembles the data, and passes the disassembled data to higher layers. The mapping connections between logical channels and physical channels are also shown in Table 6.3.

D. SDU (Service Data Unit)
On the transmit site, the MAC sublayer assembles data blocks received from a higher layer into an SDU and delivers the SDU to the physical layer for transmission. The MAC sublayer receives an SDU, disassembles the SDU into data blocks, and delivers them to higher layers.

Adding one or more data blocks with a header can assemble another SDU. All SDUs can be sent either by common channels or dedicated channels.

E. Multiplex Sublayer's Interaction
Multiplex sublayer can interact not only with physical layer (Layer 1) below, but can interact with four entities above it, RLP and Voice service on the dedicated channel side, LAC (Link Access protocol), and SRBP on the common channel side. LAC is described later.

6.7.2 RLP Layer

RLP controls the process of user packet data that travels on dedicated user channels. The RLP is a Layer 2 protocol that responds for the delivery and receipt of user packet data. An important function of Layer 2 entity is to control packet errors introduced by the physical layer. There are several techniques to control packet errors.

1. Positive acknowledgment (ACK): Acknowledgment of receiving successfully.

2. Negative acknowledgment (NAK): Acknowledgment of receiving unsuccessfully.

3. Retransmission: Retransmit when neither an acknowledgment nor a NAK is received.

TABLE 6.3 Mapping Between Logical Channels and Physical Channels

Logical Channels		Physical Channels	
Channel Designation	*Channel Name*	*Channel Designation*	*Channel Name*
(A) Forward link			
F-CSCH	Forward common signaling channel	F-SYNCH	Sync channel
		F-PCH	Paging channel
		F-CCCH	Forward common control channel
		F-BCCH	Broadcast control channel
		F-CPCCH	Common power control channel
		F-CACH	Common assignment channel
F-DSCH	Forward dedicated signaling channel	F-DCCH	Forward dedicated control channel
		F-FCH	Forward fundamental channel
F-DTCH	Forward dedicated traffic channel	F-DCCH	Forward dedicated control channel
		F-FCH	Forward fundamental channel
		F-SCH	Forward supplemental channel
(B) Reverse link			
R-CSCH	Reverse common signaling channel	R-ACH	Access channel
		R-EACH	Enhanced access channel
		R-CCCH	Reverse common control channel
R-DSCH	Reverse dedicated signaling channel	R-DCCH	Reverse dedicated control channel
		R-FCH	Reverse fundamental channel
R-DTCH	Reverse dedicated traffic channel	R-DCCH	Reverse dedicated control channel
		R-FCH	Reverse fundamental channel
		R-SCH	Reverse supplemental channel

Other data link control protocols in Layer 2 are

1. Logical Link Control (LLC): for operating over a LAN using IEEE 802 standards.
2. Link Access Protocol: balanced for connecting a device to a packet switched network using the X.25 standard.

Three Classes of Frames in RLP

1. Control frames: carrying control information that have the highest priority.
2. Retransmitted data frames: retransmit the old data frames.
3. New data frame: transmit with the lowest priority.

Three Service Types of RLP

RLP1: implements packet data service over IS-95A traffic channels, with a data rate of 9.6 or 14.4 kbps.

RLP2: implements packet data service over IS-95B traffic channels, which are fundamental and supplemental code channels.

RLP3: implements packet data service over cdma2000 traffic channels with a data rate up to 2 Mbps.

6.7.3 SRBP (Signaling Radio Burst Protocol) Layer

Functions of SRBP

A. The SRBP controls the process of signaling messages that travel on the common signaling channels in the physical layer. There are six forward common signaling channels: F-SYNCH, F-CPCCH, F-CCCH, F-PCH, F-CACH, and F-BCCH. There are three reverse common signaling channels: R-ACH, R-EACH, and R-CCCH. SRBP is the entity that generates and computes parameters, such as the power level of each successive access probe, the randomization delay of each access subattempt for the transmission, and reception of common signaling messages.

B. The SRBP also assembles SDUs for the physical layer to transmit on the physical channels and pass the received SDUs from the physical layer to the LAC sublayer, as shown in Fig. 6.38.

6.7.4 System Access Modes

The cdma2000 can operate its access in one of four different access modes; the four modes are

A. Basic Access Mode

- In R-ACH, the access procedure in this mode is the same as that used in IS-95. The mobile keeps transmitting access probes at increasing power levels (each at a 5-ms frame) until it gets a response back from the base station. Mobiles also transmit their attempts pseudorandom to gain access.

- In R-EACH, when the primary sector's E_c/I_o exceeds the mobile's access threshold, the mobile can access probes on the R-EACH. Each R-EACH probe carries an entire set of enhanced access data, which may require several 20 ms, 10 ms, or 5 ms frames to transport. The R-EACH probe consists of the preamble and enhanced access header.

B. Reservation Access Mode

- In R-EACH, a mobile transmits a short burst of 5 ms of a message on the R-EACH to attempt to reserve a space on the R-CCCH.

- In R-CCH, the mobile transmits the rest of access data on R-CCCH whose resources are scheduled by the base station and are free from collision.

- In F-CACH, after receiving the header of R-CCCH, the base station transmits an EACAM (Early Acknowledgment Channel Assignment Message) back to the mobile on F-CACH.

- In R-CCCH, after verifying that the received EACAM is intended for the mobile, it starts to transmit the enhanced access data on the allocated R-CCCH.

C. Power Controlled Access Mode

- In F-CPCCH, the base station uses the F-CPCCH to power control the R-EACH, provide a fast acknowledgment to the mobile, and to let the mobile know the specific F-CPCCH.

- In R-EACH, the mobile uses the power control bits received on F-CPCCH to adjust the power being transmitted on R-CCCH.

D. Designated Access Mode

- In F-CCCH, the mobile is in response on the R-CCCH to the requests received on the F-CCCH. The mobile does not initiate access or autonomously send access request.

- In F-CCCH, R-CCCH is power controlled in this mode by F-CPCCH at the base station.

- R-EACH is not used in designated access mode.

6.7.5 LAC Sublayers

The signaling LAC entity provides a data link protocol. The data link protocol ensures that signaling data generated by the upper layers are correctly delivered across the air link. It is, also, responsible for the delivery of user packet data across the air interface, as shown in Fig. 6.38. Both LAC and RLP are implementing data link protocols, but the difference is

- RLP provides a best effort transport of user packet data whose delivery is not assured.

- LAC provides a reliable delivery of signaling data, as the signaling data is very important to protect in any communication network to ensure a smooth operation.

In cdma2000, LAC is treated as an interface between MAC sublayer and Layer 3. To ensure reliable delivery of signaling data, the LAC entity depends on five sublayers to perform a variety of functions. These sublayers are shown in Fig. 6.39 and described as follows:

A. Authentication and Addressing Sublayers

This sublayer processes authentication-related fields such as addressing information (Mobile ESN and MIN). Authentication is applied only when a mobile is first trying to access the network using common signaling channels. Once the mobile has made access, it then uses dedicated traffic channels, and the authentication is no longer required.

B. ARQ Sublayer

The ARQ sublayer is the sublayer that is responsible for the reliable delivery of signaling data. In general, ARQ uses retransmission and positive and/or negative acknowledgment to provide reliable delivery.

The ARQ sublayer in LAC can deliver Layer 3 PDUs in two modes: (1) assured delivery and (2) unassured delivery. In assured delivery, the transmitting LA repeatedly sends signaling data at fixed intervals until it receives a positive acknowledgment from the receiving LAC.

In unassured delivery, the transmitting LAC sends signaling data, but the receiving LAC does not send any positive acknowledgment.

C. Utility Sublayer

The utility sublayer's functions are

- Assembling the radio environment report fields and attaching them to the PDU, if required. The utility sublayer at the mobile only performs this function.

- Padding the PDU to bring it to the required number of bits.

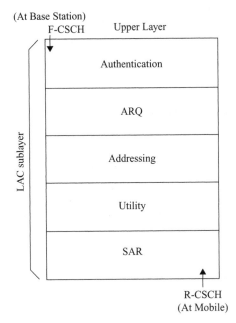

(At Base Station)
F-CSCH   Upper Layer

Authentication

ARQ

Addressing

Utility

SAR

LAC sublayer

R-CSCH
(At Mobile)   **FIGURE 6.39**   Structure of the LAC sublayer.

D. Segmentation and Reassembly (SAR) Sublayer

- On the transmit side, the segmentation and reassembly (SAR) sublayer segments the encapsulated PDUs into PDU fragments of sizes that can be transferred by the MAC sublayer. The SAR sublayer may also compute the CRC and append it to the PDU.

- On the receive side, the SAR sublayer reassembles the encapsulated PDU fragments received from the MAC sublayer into encapsulated PDUs. In addition, the SAR may check the CRC to verify valid receipts. The SAR sublayer then presents the encapsulated PDUs to the sublayers above in LAC for further processing.

6.7.6   Sublayer Processing

- *On the transmit side*, the LAC entity as a whole accepts Layer 3 PDUs from the upper layers, and the different sublayers perform their functions in sequence and attach their own control information to the data unit.

- *On the receive side*, the reverse process takes place:

  The sublayer processing done by the different sublayers in LAC for four scenarios: (1) common signaling on the forward link; (2) common signaling on the reverse link; (3) dedicated signaling on the forward link; and (4) dedicated signaling on the reverse link.

A. Common Signaling

1. Forward Link

Figure 6.39 shows the processing done by the different LAC sublayers at the base station when the base station transmits common signaling data to the mobile. In this case, all LAC sublayers are involved except the authentication sublayer. This is because the base station needs to authenticate the mobiles to prevent fraud.

The processing is also done by the LAC sublayers at the mobile when the mobile receives common signaling data from the base station. Here the reverse process takes place.

2. Reverse Link

When the mobile transmits on the reverse common signaling channel, there is a definite need for the base station to authenticate the mobile, as well as a need for that mobile to identify itself to the base station using addressing fields.

On the reverse link, the base station logically receives common signaling data on the R-CSCH.

B. Dedicated Signaling

1. Forward Link

The processing is done by the different LAC sublayers (at the base station) when the base station transmits dedicated signaling data to the mobile. In this case, only the ARQ, utility, and three SAR sublayers are involved; the addressing and authentication layers are not active.

2. Reverse Link

The LAC processing of dedicated signaling data on the reverse link is similar and symmetrical to those processing for dedicated signaling data on the forward link.

6.7.7 Communications Among Layers and Sublayers

In carrying out the communication, Layer 3, LAC, and MAC use primitives to pass data units and control information between Layer 3 and LAC and between LAC and MAC. The actual data unit transferred is used as one of the parameters of the primitive.

At the transmit side, when the LAC sublayer (or specifically the SAR sublayer) wants to send a PDU, the LAC sublayer invokes the SDU Ready primitive to request service from MAC layer. Four different primitives are used as shown in Fig. 6.40.

1. When Layer 3 has a PDU to send, it requests a service from the LAC sublayer by invoking the L2-Data primitive.

2. The LAC sublayer or the SAR sublayer wants to send a PDU from Layer 3, the LAC sublayer invokes the SDU Ready primitive to request service from the MAC layer.

3. If space is available for data transfer on the physical channels, MAC sends the Availability primitive to indicate the service requester that some event has occurred.

4. After receiving the Available primitive, LAC sends the MAC-Data primitive to MAC to request data transport service.

At the receive side, two different primitive are used (shown in Fig. 6.41) as interactive when receiving signal data.

1. MAC uses MAC-Data primitive to LAC.

2. After processing, LAC sends PDU to Layer 3 using the L2-Data primitive to indicate to Layer 3 that signaling data has been received.

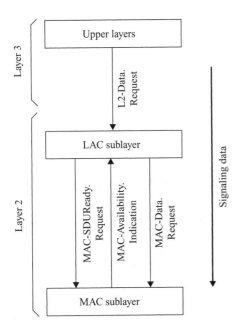

FIGURE 6.40 Interaction of primitives: transmit side.

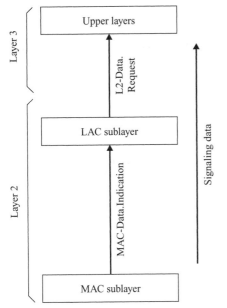

FIGURE 6.41 Interaction of primitives: receive side.

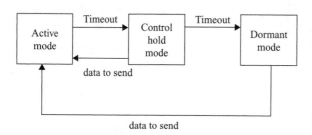

FIGURE 6.42 Three modes in packet data transmission.

6.7.8 Upper Layers

The signaling entity shown in Fig. 6.38 is the one that effectively controls the operation of the entire IS-2000 system by the following state transitions.

Four States: (1) mobile station initialization, (2) mobile station idle, (3) system access, and (4) mobile station control on the traffic channel. These states are similar to those in IS-95.

In packet data, transmissions are bursty in nature and use three modes while the mobile is in the traffic channel substate; active mode, control hold mode, and dormant mode. The active mode is active exchange of user packet data and dedicated signaling data between the MS and BTS. The control hold mode is actively maintaining MAC control and power control through the dedicated control channel. The dormant mode is used in MS idle state to keep information of the user's packet data service registration and PPP connection. The relationship of active, control hold, and dormant modes is shown in Fig. 6.42.

A mobile may be in one of several modes and transition between these modes. These modes are unique to IS-2000 and are implemented to accommodate bursty packet data transmissions and to conserve air link resources.

The signaling entity also controls and executes those functions that are necessary for the setup, maintenance, and tear-down of a call.

The signaling entity effectively controls and executes different functions that are required for call processing. These functions are registration, handoff, and power control. In performing these functions, the signaling entity originates and receives messages. In originating a message, the signaling entity (e.g., at the mobile) requests Layer 2 to deliver the message to its counterpart at the other side (e.g., at the base station). In receiving a message, the signaling entity takes delivery of the message from Layer 2 that was transmitted by the other side.

6.7.9 Power Control

In cdma2000, a host of new features to the function of power control is added. It improves its speed and accuracy related to the system capacity and quality. Power control in the reverse link is to minimize the variances of powers received from multiple transmitters at the base station and in the forward link is to minimize the variances of received powers in the same band, which allows more users to be on the system. The system can power control multiple physical channels on both forward link and reverse link. Also, the system can have a closed loop power control in both forward and reverse links at a rate of 800 times/second.

Different Types of Power Controls:

A. Closed Loop Power Control in the Forward Link

The closed loop power control on the forward link is to minimize the power received from multiple transmitters at the mobile. The mobile continuously monitors the forward link and measures the E_c/N_o and FER it receives.

1. Inner Loop

The MS requests the BS to power up and power down based on an E_b/N_o threshold in which the Power Control Bits (PCB) are determined that are multiplexed onto the R-PICH. PCBs are used to combat Rayleigh fading. PCBs are not error protected bits so that the BS can quickly recover them and adjust its transmit power accordingly. The power control decisions are made at the BS. It uses the inner loop implementation as shown in Fig. 6.43(a).

2. Outer Loop

Because the E_b/N_o and FER are constantly changing, the E_b/N_o threshold has to be dynamically adjusted to maintain an acceptable FER. This dynamic adjustment of the E_b/N_o threshold is implemented on the outer loop based on the E_b/N_o estimate and FER estimate to adjust E_b/N_o set point at the MS. The outer loop is monitoring the F-FCH. Use of this adjusted E_b/N_o set point to make the power control decisions. Those forward link power control functions are carried out by the mobile using both outer and inner loop implementation shown in Fig. 6.43(b).

B. Power Control in Reverse Link

The power control over the reverse link is used in each MS to make sure that the signal powers arrived at the BS for all the MS in the area are more or less the same. Thus the minimization of interference among the mobile signals in the reverse link can be obtained. The power control over the reverse link can be implemented by two ways: open loop and close loop.

1. Open Loop

In open loop power control, the mobile monitors its received power continuously and adjusts its transmit power accordingly. The open loop power control is done solely by the mobile and does not involve the base station at all. In cdma2000, the open loop power control on three types of reverse physical channels: R-EACH, R-CCH, and reverse traffic channels (R-DCCH, R-FCH, and R-SCH). For each of these channels, the open loop power control is performed in two separate parts: (1) the MS calculates the pilot channel transmit power of the R-PICH, which is almost active, and (2) the MS calculates the traffic channel transmit power of the reverse channels themselves.

2. Closed Loop

For the reverse link, the closed loop power control of cdma2000 is similar to that of IS-95. To power control the reverse link, the base station continuously monitors the reverse link and measures its link quality. If the link quality starts to get worse, then the base station will command the mobile, via the forward link, to power up. If the link quality becomes too good, then there is excess power on the reverse link. In this case, the base station will command the mobile to power down.

The inner loop of the closed loop power control on the reverse link can be implemented at both MS and BS. A predetermined E_b/N_o threshold is used by which power up and power down decisions are made. The function of the outer loop is only implemented at the MS and is to adjust the E_b/N_o threshold dynamically to maintain an acceptable FER.

At the BS Receiver: Estimate the E_b/N_o and FER based on the reversed physical channels, and then it can use inner loop only or inner plus outer loops to obtain the E_b/N_o set point. Then PCBs are calculated and multiplexed onto R-CPCCH, R-DCCH, and R-FCH before transmitting.

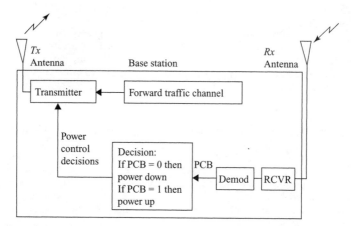

(a) Forward link power control functions carried out by the base station.

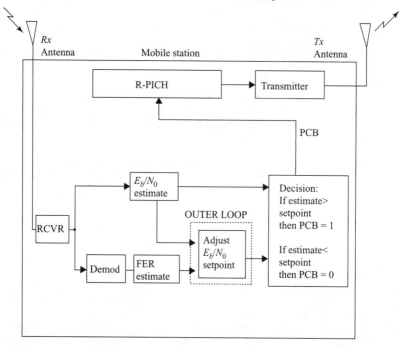

(b) Forward link power control functions carried out by the mobile.

FIGURE 6.43 Forward link power control functions.

At the BS Transmitter: A PCB is sent to command the mobile to power up or power down. PCBs are multiplexed onto the F-CPCCH, F-DCCH, or F-FCH depending on which reverse physical channel needs to be power controlled. PCBs are transmitted to the mobile at a maximum rate of 800 times per second.

At the MS Receiver: The MS receiver demodulates the receiving signal and detects the PCBs from F-CPCCH, F-DCCH, and F-FCH. It used their PCBs to make decision for R-EACH, R-CCCH, and Reverse Traffic Channels (R-FCH and R-SCH) at the MS.

At the MS Transmitter: The MS transmitter transmits the R-EACH, R-CCCH, and reverse traffic channels with their proper power after the closed loop correction from the decision maker based on PCBs. The MS does not use outer loop for power control in the reverse channels but uses outer loop for making better decisions on PCBs and sends on R-PICH to the base station for the forward link power control.

6.7.10 Network Architecture

The architecture of a wireless network that supports cdma2000 is described in this section. The cdma2000 wireless network is capable of providing circuit-switched voice service, circuit-switched data service, and packet-switched data service (shown in Fig. 6.44).

A. The Elements of the Network

Besides MS and BTS, the first six elements are the same as in cdmaOne for circuit-switched voice and data service; BSC, MSC, HLR, VLR, AC, and IWF. The IWF enables circuit-switched data service, and BSC carries out the mobility management. The additional two elements are for the purpose of providing packet-switched data service.

1. *Packet data serving node (PDSN):* The PDSN is the element that enables packet-switched data service.

The PDSN in packet switching is analogous to the MSC in circuit switching.

PDSN is essentially an Internet Protocol (IP) router that routes user data traffic to a public packet data network, such as the Internet.

The PDSN directs packet-switched traffic between the MS and a packet-switched network (e.g., Internet).

2. *Authentication, authorization, and accounting (AAA):* The AAA is a server that provides authentication, authorization, and accounting services for the PDSN, which in turn renders packet data network connectivity services to the mobile users.

Authentication is performed by the AAA and may simply require the user to provide an account number and the password. If this authentication is successful, then the MS is granted packet data service by the Authorization.

In addition, the AAA performs the function of accounting. For each MS, the AAA collects information on its usage of packet data service. The AAA then passes this information to a downstream billing application.

B. Two Supporting Functions

The cdma2000 network is capable of supporting simple IP and mobile IP functions:

1. Simple IP

An MS residing on its home PDSN has an IP address M, and the server on the Internet has an IP address S. Given these two addresses, IP packets can be simply exchanged between the MS and the different servers in the same PDSN.

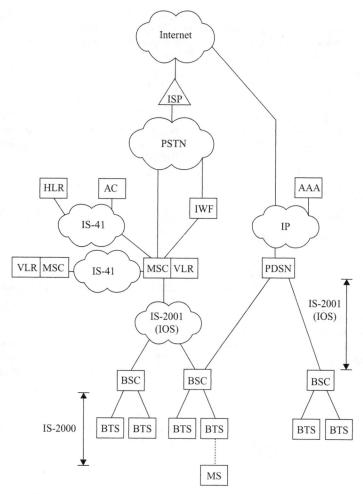

FIGURE 6.44 A typical 3G wireless network. The boldfaced parts are those that provide packet-switched data service.

2. Mobile IP

To support Mobile IP, two additional network elements are needed:

• Home Agent (HA): This is a router together with the foreign agent (FA), another router that provides mobile IP functionality. The HA is a router that resides on that MS' home IP network.

• Foreign Agent (FA): This is another router residing in another PDSN. When an MS visits a foreign IP network, the FA on the foreign network receives packets forwarded from the HA and delivers them to the MS.

6.8 cdma2000 EV-DO AND EV-DV

1xEV-DO stands for enhanced version of single carrier (1x) for data only. There are two versions: single mode and dual mode. Single mode version can only access the high-speed data rate (HDR) services on the EVDO radio channel at a rate of 2.4576 Mbps. The Dual mode version can access either the EVDO HDR channel or the IS-95 voice with medium-rate data traffic channels.

1xEV-DO takes advantage of the characteristics of data services.

a. The data rate requirements on the forward link are usually higher than those on the reverse link.

b. Data services can tolerate the latency.

c. Take the after burst period of data transmission to manage the control functions.

Also, it has an access terminal (AT) for data connectivity to the MS. The access network (AN) provides data connectivity between a packet-switched data network and AT, shown in Fig. 6.45. The AN consists of BSC and BTSs. In 1xEV-DO, the radio interfaces of forward link and reverse link are different.

6.8.1 Forward Link Physical Layer

A. Forward Link Channels
Three different channels are used on the forward link, pilot, forward traffic channel/control channel, and MAC channel.

1. Pilot Channels: Provides ATS with timing and phase reference
The pilot is multiplexed into the transmitted chip stream by the time division multiplexer.

2. Forward Traffic Channel/Control Channel
The physical layer constructs a forward traffic channel for transmitting physical layer packet and a control channel for transmitting MAC layer packet.

  a. Channel Structure: In a forward traffic channel, the physical layer packet can contain up to four MAC layer packets. Every MAC layer packet contains 1024 bits. In a control channel, one physical layer packet can only carry one MAC layer packet with 1024 bits long.

  b. Modulation: Transmitting a physical layer packet over a forward traffic channel, we can use different modulation schemes. It is based on the amount of data to be transmitted. It can use QPSK, 8 PSK and 16-QAM. In use of 16-QAM, 1xEV-DO can transmit at a rate of 2.45 Mbps over a RF bandwidth of 1.25 MHz. Table 6.4 shows the modulation schemes and data rates. The block diagram for both the forward traffic channel and control channel are shown in Fig. 6.46. A physical layer packet is sent over a series of functions encoding, scrambling, interleaving, modulation and repetition/puncture before de-multiplexing. It demux the output into 16 substreams and multiplying by 16 Walsh codes, to keep the power constant at each substream with a symbol rate at 76.8 ksps. Summing up 16 substreams of I or Q channels, the chip rate is 1.2288 Mcps at the summers of both I and Q channels to their respective TDMs. Both forward traffic channel and control channel share the same QPSK, 8 PSK, or 16-QAM modulator, but can be distinguished by different preambles.

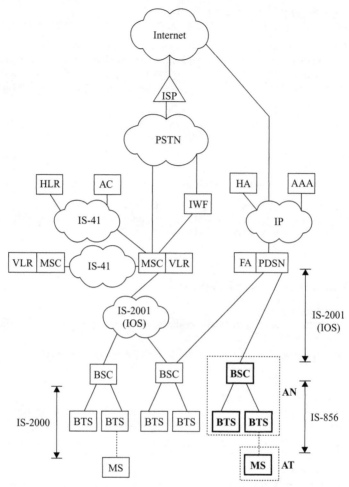

FIGURE 6.45 A typical wireless network using 1xEV-DO. The boldfaced parts are those that enable 1xEV-DO service.

TABLE 6.4 Forward Traffic Channel Modulation Schemes and Data Rates

Length of a Physical Layer Packet (bits)	Data Rates (kbps)	Code Rate	Modulation Scheme
1,024	38.4*, 76.8*, 153.6, 307.2,	1/5†	QPSK
2,048	307.2, 614.4, 1,228.8	1/3	QPSK
3,072	921.6, 1,843.2	1/3	8 PSK
4,096	1,228.8, 2,457.6	1/3	16-QAM

*Also used for control channel.

†For data rate of 614.4 kbps and physical layer packet length of 1,024, the code rate used is 1/3.

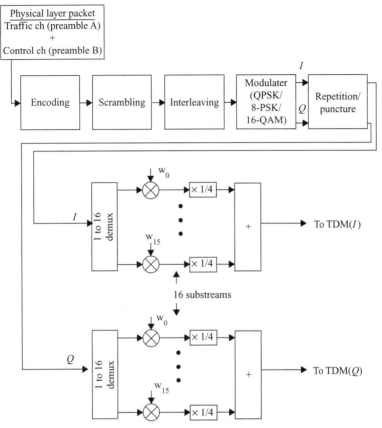

FIGURE 6.46   Block diagram: Forward traffic channel and control channel.

3. MAC Channel

It consists of RA Channel, RPC Channel, and DRC Lock Channel

a. RA (Reverse Activity) Channel

The AN uses the reverse activity channel to inform all ATs (in its coverage area) of the current traffic activity on the reverse link. ATs incorporate this information in making decisions to decrease their data rates because of high traffic load or to increase their data rates because of nominal traffic load on the reverse link. The reverse activity channel carries reverse activity bits. In time division multiplexing, reverse activity bits are onto the forward link, the physical layer transmits each reverse activity bit once every specified number of slots.

b. RPC (Reverse Power Control) Channel

The AN uses the reverse power control channel to power control ATs' reverse link transmission. Although there is no power control on the forward link, there is power control on the reverse link, and the reverse power control channel is used to send power control bits for that purpose.

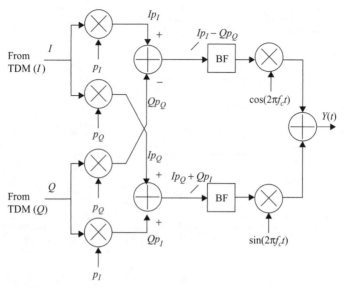

FIGURE 6.47   Modulation: Forward link.

c. DRClock (Data Rate Control Lock) Channel
The AN uses the DRClock channel to tell the AT if the AN is successfully receiving the DRC information sent by the AT.

B. Transmission Parameters

1. Time Division Multiplexing
On the forward link, the TDM chip stream generated by the time division multiplexer is organized into slots. Each slot lasts 1.67 ms and contains 2048 chips. This results in a final chip rate of 1.2288 Mcps (= 2048 chips / 1.67 ms). There are 16 slots in the time division multiplexed chip stream.

2. Modulation
The short PN Code spreads the output of TDM. The I and Q outputs of TDM are multiplied by a pair of the short PN, P_I and P_Q as shown in Fig. 6.47.

6.8.2   Forward Link MAC Layer

There is no power control in the forward link, and the forward link uses time division multiplexing (TDM) to multiplex different channels. Because in TDM different users may transmit at different times, there is no soft handoff on the forward link for EV-DO, and each AT is served by only one base station.

A message originates from higher layers that are transported across the physical layer, such as (1) user data messages, and (2) the signaling messages. For transmission and reception of these two types of messages on the forward link, two protocols are used: Forward Traffic Channel using MAC protocol and Control Channel using MAC protocol.

A. Forward Traffic Channel Using MAC Protocol for User Data Messages
The functions of the forward traffic channel using MAC protocol are not only to control the transmission and reception of packets on the forward traffic channel, but also to control their rate of transmission.

B. Control Channel Using MAC Protocol for Signaling Messages
It has the responsibility of managing the transmission and reception of signaling packets on the control channel.

6.8.3 Reverse Link Physical Layer

A. **Reverse Link Channels**

Two channels are used: Reverse Traffic Channel and Access Channel.

1. **Reverse Traffic Channel** (physical channel) is used to transport both user data messages and signaling messages. The messages are structured into physical layer packet. The reverse traffic channel's physical layer packet always contains just reverse traffic channel's MAC layer packet, consisting of five logical channels.

   a. *Data Channel:* transmitting physical layer packet.

   b. *Pilot Channel:* it functions as the cdma2000.

   c. *Reverse Rate Indicator (RRI) Channel:* report to AN what the data rate is currently being used by the data channel.

   d. *Data Rate Control (DRC) Channel:* AT uses the DRC channel on the reverse link to request different data rates on the forward link, also notify the AN of the AT's current home sector.

   e. *ACK Channel:* is used by AT to acknowledge the receipt of a forward traffic channel's physical layer packet.

2. **Access Channel**
   It is used by the AT to first contact the AN and respond to a message from the AN. An access channel's physical layer packet is transported using the access probe. Each access probe contains a preamble and a capsule. The preamble is transmitted on a pilot channel, and a capsule is transmitted on a data channel. Therefore, an access channel is using two physical channels: pilot channel and data channel. In an access probe period, the pilot channel is active during the transmission of capsule on the data channel.

B. **Modulation**

1. When the access channel is active, the chip stream of the pilot channel goes into I input, and the chip stream of the data channel goes into the Q input of a QPSK modulation.

2. When the reverse traffic channel is active, the summation of chip streams of the pilot channel, the RRI (reverse rate indicator) channel and the ACK channel become the I input, and the summation of chip streams of the data channel and the DRC channel becomes the Q input for a QPSK modulation shown in Fig. 6.48. The spreading codes are special PN codes, S_I and S_Q derived from long PN codes.

C. Reverse Power Control
   Both open loop and closed loop power controls are similar to those used in cdma2000. However, a characteristic of 1xEV-DO reverse power control is that when the reverse pilot channel power changes the power of other reverse channels, it also changes reference to the reverse pilot channel.

1. Open Loop Power Control
   When lowering the mean received power of the forward pilot channel, the open loop mean output power of the reverse pilot channel becomes higher. The open loop output power of the reverse pilot channel determines the power of three channels: Data Channel, DRC Channel, and ACK Channel.

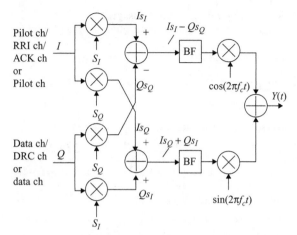

FIGURE   6.48 Modulation: Reverse link.

2. Closed Loop Power Control
   AT receives power control bits on the forward power control channel and changes the mean output power of the reverse pilot channel accordingly.

D. The Different Functions Between Forward Link and Reverse Link
   The reverse link is very similar to the reverse link of cdma2000. The different functions are

1. Use of power control schemes

2. Do not use TDM

3. Transmit data rate is less

4. Spreading codes are different

6.8.4 1xEV-DO Network

1xEV-DO[29] uses a seven-layer protocol architecture in supporting the connect-connectivity between AT and the packet-switched data network.

1xEV-DO is using new sets of protocols different from those of cdma2000. There is no connection logically between the BSC of cdma2000 and the AN of 1xEV-DO, although the two could be physically co-located. The seven layers are

1. **Application layer**

2. **Stream layer**

3. **Session layer**

4. **Connection layer**

5. **Security layer**

6. **MAC layer**

7. **Physical layer**

The MAC layer and physical layer were characterized in the previous sections. Here we briefly describe the other five layers.

A. **Application layer:** After the message is received from the upper layer (above application layer) to the RLP that is residing in application layer, the message itself becomes the payload. The RLP attaches a header to the payload to form a packet. The RLP passes the RLP packet to the stream layer.

B. **Stream layer:** The function of the stream layer is to multiplex streams of data (packets) coming from the application layer and attaches a header to form a stream layer packet. The stream protocol then passes the stream layer packet to the session layer.

C. **Session layer:** To manage this logical session between the AT and the AN, session management protocol is used. To maintain the logical address assigned to the AT, address management protocol is used. Also, to negotiate the configuration parameters of actual protocols, the session configuration protocol is used.

D. **Connection layer:** To manage the actual air link connection between the AN and AT. Because of connecting air link management, the protocols are formed for each of the functions such as air link management, route update, initialization, idle state, connected state, overhead message, and packet consolidation.

E. **Security layer:** To encrypt and authenticate packet. There are four protocols to handle four different functions, such as key exchange, encryption, authentication, and security.

6.8.5   1xEV-DV

The high-speed packet enhancement of cdma2000 Revision C and D is called 1xEV-DV system.[33-35] The objective of this enhancement was to improve the bandwidth efficiency of the cdma2000 system by creating a new set of high-speed packet data channels: the Forward Packet Data Channel (F-PDCH) and the Reverse Packet Data Channel (R-PDCH). This new set of high-speed packet data channels uses technologies such as fast packet scheduling, hybrid automatic repeat request, and adaptive modulation and coding.

• Fast Packet Scheduling: The purpose of performing fast packet scheduling for the F-PDCH and R-PDCH is to reduce the inherent delay in L3 message-based scheduling and channeling all the scheduling-associated control information to the physical or medium access control layer.

• Hybrid Automatic Repeat Request: One of the major enhancements in cdma2000 Revisions C and D is the inclusion of HARQ for the F-PDCH and R-PDCH. HARQ enhances the performance of a wireless system by making retransmissions in the physical layer that can be combined by either chase combining or incremental redundancy with previously received transmissions.

• Adaptive Modulation and Coding (AMC): For the F-PDCH, AMC is used to countermeasure against fading. The encoder packet size modulation and coding rate of each transmission are adapted as often as every 1.25 ms. For the R-PDCH, power control is used to counteract the effect of time-variant multipath fading.

EV-DV uses the flexible TDM-CDM multiplexing to send voice and data services on the same carrier. Because the nature of VoIP is a packet stream, the data and voice can share the same carrier. The bandwidth is first prioritized to voice traffic, and then the remaining bandwidth is shared between the data users. Because data traffic is typically running in bursts and does not necessarily have to be in a real-time delivery, there is plenty of bandwidth to go around. All of these fit into a single carrier of 1.25-MHz spectrum.

The EV-DV technology provides a 3.1-Mbps down channel and a 300-kbps up channel. EV-DV is backward compatible to IS-95A/B and CDMA1X. It can be used for a two-way video conference call at 15 frames per second and with full live images. The details of EV-DV technology can be found in References 34 and 35.

REFERENCES

1. E. Nikula, A. Toshala, E. Dahlman, L. Girad, A. Klein, "FRAMES Multiple Access for UMTS and IMT-2000, IEEE Personal Communications Magazine, April 1998, pp. 16–24.

2. ETSI Press Release, SMG Tdoc 40/98, "Agreement Reached on Radio Interface for Third Generation Mobile System, UMTS," Paris, France, January 1998.

3. ITU Press Release, ITU/99-22, "IMT-2000 Radio Interface Specifications Approved in ITU Meeting in Helsinki," Nov. 5, 1999.

4. 3GPP Technical Specification 25.401 UTRAN Overall Description.
3GPP Technical Specification 25.410 UTRAN Iu Interface: General Aspects and Principles.
3GPP Technical Specification 25.411 UTRAN Iu Interface: Layer 1.

5. 3GPP Technical Specification 25.211, Physical Channels and Mapping of Transport Channels on Physical Channels (FDD).

6. 3GPP Technical Specification 25.212, Multiplexing and Channel Coding (FDD).

7. 3GPP Technical Specification 25.213, Spreading and Modulation (FDD).

8. ARIB WCDMA, ARIB standard, RCR STD-40.

9. 3GPP "Physical Channels and Mapping of Transport Channels onto Physical Channels (TDD)," TSG Radio Access Network, 3GTS 25.221, V4.2.0, Sept. 2001.

10. W. L. Li, "TD-SCDMA and TD-SCDMA Forum," Workshop on Next Generation Networks: What, When and How?" Geneva, 9–10 July 2003.

11. S. Di-Giuseppe, M. Principato, R. Rodor, "TD-SCDMA: The Solution for TDD Bands," TD-SCDMA White Paper, Siemens, 2002.

12. 3G TS 25.301 Radio Interface Protocol Architecture.

13. 3G TS 25.321 MAC Protocol Specification.

14. 3G TS 25.322 RLC Protocol Specification.

15. 3G TS 25.323 PDCP Protocol Specification.

16. 3G TS 25.324 Broadcast/Multicast Control Protocol (BMC) Specification.

17. 3G TS 25.331 RRC Protocol Specification.

18. 3GPP TS 23.002 Network Architecture (Release 99).

19. 3GPP Technical Specification 25.420 UTRAN Iur Interface: General Aspects and Principles.
3GPP Technical Specification 25.421 UTAN Iur Interface: Layer 1.
3GPP Technical Specification 25.430 UTRAN Iub Interface: General Aspects and Principles.
3GPP Technical Specification 25.431 UTRAN Iub Interface: Layer 1.

20. 3GPP TS 21.102 Release 4 Specification.

21. D. Collins, *Carrier Grade Voice Over IP*, McGraw-Hill, 2001.

22. IETF RFC 1889, RTP: A Transport Protocol for Real-Time Applications.

23. 3GPP TS 21.103 Release 5 Specification.

24. 3GPP TS 25.855 High-Speed DownLink Packet Access (HSDPA); Overall UTRAN description.

25. 3GPP TS 21.104 Release 6 Specification and TS 21.105 Release 7 Specification.

26. V. K. Garg, *IS-95 CDMA and cdma2000*, Prentice-Hall PTR, 2000.

27. V. Vanghi, A. Damnjanovic, B. Vojcic, *The cdma2000 System for Mobile Communications*, Prentice-Hall PTR, 2004.

28. T. Ojanpera, R. Pasad, *Wideband CDMA for Third Generation Mobile Communications*, Artech House Publishers, Boston, 1998, Chapter 5 CDMA Air Interface Design, Chapter 1.

29. S. C. Yang, 3G CDMA 2000, Artech House, Inc., Boston, 2004.

30. B. Pelletier, H. Leib, "PCS Third Generation CDMA systems, Study of the Physical Layer," Wireless Communications Group at McGill University, August 2004.

31. H. Holma, Antti Toskala, *WCDMA for UMTS*, John Wiley & Sons, 2001.

32. C. Smith, D. Collins, *3G Wireless Works*, McGraw-Hill, 2002.

33. J. S. Lee, L. E. Miller, "CDMA System Engineering Handbook," Artech House, 1998.

34. 3GPP2 "cdma2000 Standard for Spread Spectrum Systems, Revision C," May 2002.

35. 3GPP2 "cdma2000 Standard for Spread Spectrum Systems, Revision D," Feb. 2004.

CHAPTER 7
B3G SYSTEMS

The maximum of 3G's data rate is only 2 Mbps, which is far less than the ADSL or cable modem data speed. Also, the requirement for 4G data rate has been set as indicated in Chap. 1, Sec. 1.1. The wireless loop area network (WLAN)[1] can offer a data speed much higher than 3G due to the different technologies. WLAN (including Wi-Fi and WiMAX) were later called the B3G (Beyond 3G) system by the industry. WiFi and WiMAX will be described in this chapter. The comparison of the data rate with different standards in WLAN is shown in Fig. 7.1.

7.1 IEEE-BASED WIRELESS STANDARD SYSTEMS

IEEE wireless standards use both licensed and unlicensed bands to provide wireless nomadic and mobility services as well as the ability to provide the last mile connection for customers as shown in Fig. 7.2.

Currently, IEEE 802.11 wireless-related working groups[2-3] and their respective frequency bands are indicated as (1) 802.11 Wireless Local Area Network (WLAN) operates at unlicensed band, 2.4 GHz (2.4 to 2.4825 GHz) and 5 GHz (5.15 to 5.35 and 5.47 to 5.825 GHz; (2) 802.15 Wireless Personal Area Network (WPAN) operates at unlicensed band, 2.4 GHZ; (3) 802.16 Broadband Wireless Access (BWA) operates at licensed and unlicensed bands, 10 to 66 GHz for LMDS and 2 to 11 GHz for MMDS; and (4) 802.16e extends 802.16 to operate below 6 GHz for mobility; initially focus three bands, on 2.5 GHz and 3.5 GHz licensed bands and 5.7 GHz U.S. unlicensed band. The comparison of IEEE-based wireless standards with 2G and 3G is shown in Fig. 7.2.

7.2 IEEE 802.11 SYSTEMS

802.11 WLAN[4] sometimes called Wi-Fi, is composed of a series of specifications (802.11, 802.11b, 802.11g, and 802.11a) as shown in Fig. 7.3. The goal is to provide wireless LAN services that are consistent with 802.3 Ethernet network. IEEE 802.11b specification operates in the 2.4-GHz band and has maximum data rate of 11 Mbps and a range about 100 meters. 802.11a supports up to 54 Mbps and operates at the 5-GHz unlicensed band, which is divided into four bands. Among them Dynamic Frequency Selection (DFS) and Transmit Power Control (TPC) are required in two of these bands. The 802.11 specifications hierarchy is shown in Fig. 7.4.

802.11g operates in 2.4-GHz band and can have backward compatibility with 802.11b. 802.11g uses Direct Sequence Spread Spectrum (DSSS) and transmits 1 and 2 Mbps using Barker codes and 5.5 and 11 Mbps using Complementary Code Keying (CCK)[5]. For higher

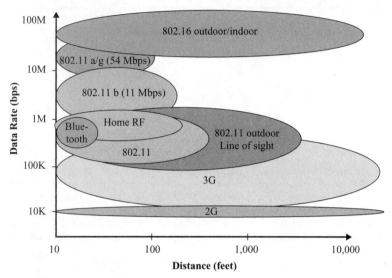

FIGURE 7.1 Wireless technology comparison.

data rate, transmission uses Orthogonal Frequency Division Multiplexing (OFDM) for 6, 9, 12, 18, 24, 36, 47, and 54 Mbps.

802.11n High Throughput is looking at data rate in excess of 100 Mbps.[6] The physical layer will most likely be OFDM. It includes advanced antenna techniques such as SIMO and MIMO.

The 802.11 standard supports four different physical layers for four different transmission technologies: Infrared (IR), Frequency Hopping Spread Spectrum (FHSS), Direct Sequence Spread Spectrum (DSSS), and OFDM. 802.11b uses Direct Sequence Spread Spectrum, 802.11a uses Orthogonal Frequency Division Multiplexing (OFDM), and 802.11g are a recent expansion of 802.11b uses OFDM.

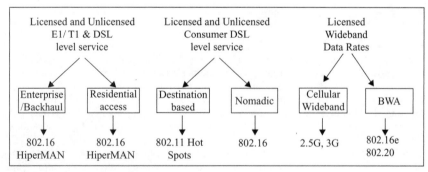

FIGURE 7.2 IEEE-based wireless standard versus cellular standards.

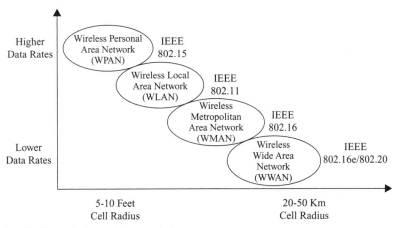

FIGURE 7.3 The IEEE wireless standards.

7.2.1 PPM, DSSS, and FHSS Transmission Technologies

The IEEE 802.11 standard places specifications on the parameters of the physical (PHY). In this section, the three transmission technologies, PPM (used in IR), DSSS, and FHSS, are briefly described. The technology of OFDM will be described in the following section. Their PHY layers, which actually handle the transmission of data between nodes, can use one of these three technologies. IEEE 802.11 makes provisions for data rates of either 1 Mbps or 2 Mbps and makes for operation in the 2.4–2.4835 GHz frequency band (in the case of spread-spectrum transmission), which is an unlicensed band for industrial, scientific, and medical (ISM) applications, and 300–428,000 GHz for IR transmission.

A. Infrared (IR): uses pulse position modulation (PPM). PPM systems usually employ short pulses of high peak power and low duty factor as an effective way of combating noise. PPM is usually operated synchronously. PPM therefore is generally considered to be more secure to eavesdropping, because IR transmissions require absolute line-of-sight links (no transmission is possible outside any simply connected space or

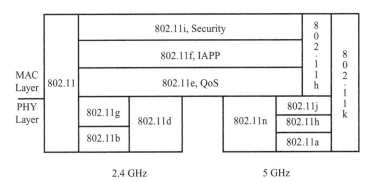

FIGURE 7.4 802.11 specifications hierarchy. (IAPP: interaccess point protocol)

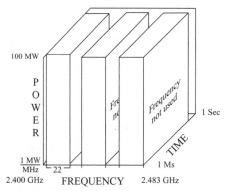

DSSS – Direct Sequence Spread Spectrum   **FIGURE 7.5**   The DSSS spread signal.

around corners), as opposed to radio-frequency transmissions, which can penetrate walls and be intercepted by third parties unknowingly. However, infrared transmissions can be adversely affected by sunlight, and the spread-spectrum protocol of 802.11 does provide some rudimentary security for typical data transfers.

B. Spread spectrum: designed to trade off bandwidth efficiency for reliability, integrity, and security. More bandwidth is consumed, producing a signal that is not easy to detect, provided the receiver knows the parameters of the spread-spectrum signal being broadcast. If a receiver is not tuned to the correct frequency, a spread-spectrum signal looks like background noise. The two types of spread-spectrum radios used for WLAN are DSSS and FHSS.

1. Direct Sequence Spread Spectrum (DSSS) means the narrowband signal is spread by directly multiplying it by a wideband pseudonoise (PN) code sequence or a smart code sequence known in advance to both transmitter and receiver as shown in Fig. 7.5. DSSS is used in CDMA systems as shown in Sec. 4.4 and Chap. 6. DSSS generates such a redundant code bit pattern for each data bit to be transmitted. This code bit is called a chip. The longer the chip pattern, the greater the probability that the original data can be recovered. Even if one or more bits in the chip pattern are damaged during transmission, the original data can be recovered without the need of retransmission. However, the data throughput is reduced as a trade-off. To an unintended receiver, DSSS appears as low-power wideband noise and is ignored by most narrowband receivers. DSSS is described in Chapter 4.

2. FHSS: uses a narrowband carrier that hops multiple carrier frequencies in a hopping pattern known to both the transmitter and receiver. By proper synchronization, FHSS has to maintain a single logical channel. To an unintended receiver, FHSS appears to be short-duration impulse noise. FHSS is usually used in military applications.

7.2.2   OFDM (Orthogonal Frequency Division Multiplexing) Technology[7–9]

A. Description
OFDM is a multicarrier transmission technique[10] to achieve high data rate in a multipath-fading environment that divides the available spectrum into many subcarriers (see Sec. 4.1.2.2). The subcarriers for each channel are made orthogonal (independent or unrelated) to one another, allowing them to be spaced very close together, without

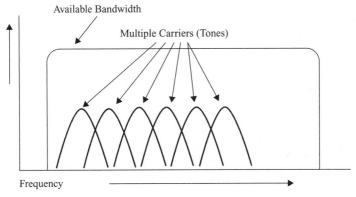

FIGURE 7.6 OFDM (Orthogonal Frequency Division Multiplexing).

individual carrier guard band overhead as in FDM as shown in Fig. 7.6. Orthogonality among subcarriers is achieved by dividing the carrier with an integer multiple that can make the process of the inverse of symbol duration of the parallel bit stream without causing interference among them. OFDM systems use bursts of data to minimize intersymbol interference (ISI) caused by time delay spread. Data is transmitted in bursts, and each burst consists of a cyclic prefix[11] followed by data symbols. The cyclic prefix is used to absorb transients from previous bursts caused by multipath signals and it should be greater than the delay spread of the multipath signals. By transmitting several symbols in parallel, the symbol rate is reduced, and the symbol duration is increased proportionately, which reduce the effects of ISI caused by the Rayleigh fading environment.

OFDM was selected to combat frequency selective fading and to randomize the burst errors caused by a wideband-fading channel. Selecting the best transmission rate is determined by a link adaptation scheme,[12] a process of selecting the best coding rate and modulation scheme based on channel conditions.

OFDM's key advantage is its efficiency to deal with multipath, as the ISI is removed by discarding guard interval resistant to narrowband interference. For a given delay spread, the implementation complexity is significantly lower than a single carrier system with an equalizer. In relatively slow time-varying channels, it is possible to significantly enhance the capacity by adapting the data rate per subcarrier according to the signal to noise ratio of that particular subcarrier. OFDM is robust against narrowband interference[13] because such interference affects only a small percentage of the subcarriers.

OFDM is more sensitive to frequency and phase noise[14] and it has a relatively large peak-to-average power ratio,[15] which tends to reduce the power efficiency of the RF amplifier.

B. Transmitter Structure

A typical OFDM transmitter is shown in Fig. 7.7a. After error correction coding and interleaver, the data stream moves to be symbols by QAM modulation. Then the symbol stream goes through serial-to-parallel process, and each symbol is assigned to each of the subcarriers. Each subcarrier is operating at a particular frequency with its assigned symbol. The symbols from all the subcarriers form a symbol frame in frequency domain. Each symbol frame in frequency domain will use an N-point IFFT (Inverse Fast Fourier

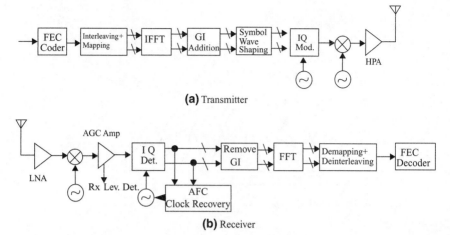

(a) Transmitter

(b) Receiver

FIGURE 7.7 Transmitter and receiver block diagram for the OFDM PHY.

Transformation) to convert each symbol frame into time frame. Then the time frames line up in series to form a digital data stream. Finally, the digital stream is converted into the analog waveform, the signal amplified and sent out through the antenna.

Different coding rate for convolutional coding are used based on required protection. More constellations of QAM modulation need higher coding protection. A combination of error detection, such as CRC and error correction such as convolutional coding in conjunction with interleaving, are used to provide better coding gain in the presence of frequency selective fading. Convolutional coding is usually punctured to provide higher bandwidth efficiency. Transmitter output has to meet strict criteria for out of band leakage. A spectrum mask is used to control the effect of bandwidth regrowth caused by amplifier clipping. Pulse shaping plays an important role in fighting the phase noise and frequency offset. It also provides a smoother transmit signal spectrum to combat the peak to average ratio issue[15] for OFDM.

Because of bandwidth limitation, only 48 subcarriers are used for data, the remaining 12 subcarriers are not used as shown in Fig. 7.8. The output of IDFT is converted to a serial sequence and a guard interval or CP (contention period) is added. The total duration of the OFDM symbol is the sum of the CP or guard duration plus the useful symbol duration. As long as the duration of the CP is longer than the channel impulse response, ISI is eliminated. Besides, 4 pilot subcarriers at frequency offset

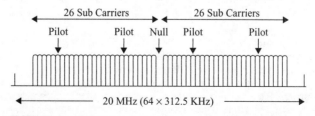

FIGURE 7.8 OFDM Subcarriers.

-21, -7, $+7$, and $+21$ are used at the receiver to estimate any residual phase error to improve coherent detection. Other offset subcarrier (from 49 to 52) is not used and each subcarrier frequency offset is 312.5 kHz.

C. Receiver Structure

A typical OFDM receiver is shown in Fig. 7.7*b*. The receiver must detect the frame, adjust AGC to proper level, utilize any diversity capability, and adjust for coarse frequency offset. Fast synchronization is critical. High phase noise and frequency offset of receiver oscillators interfere[16] with the synchronization process and require robust algorithm. Because received signal level can vary significantly due to shadowing and multipath, AGC needs to have a confirmation block after the correlator. It uses a repetitive pattern of preamble sequence to reduce false alarm probability. Once initial acquisition is accomplished, detection process starts to do channel estimation, cyclic prefix removal, frequency domain equalization,[17] and soft decoding. Initial channel estimation uses the preamble symbol.[18] After channel estimation and fine synchronization, guard intervals are removed. The receiver needs to make sure that the effect of pulse shaping is preserved and interference from adjacent blocks is minimized.

The AGC module is responsible for (1) setting the radio's coarse and fine gains to default values suitable for detecting packets that have a broad range of signal strengths; (2) determining whether a packet is present; (3) providing an initial estimate of when the packet started; (4) setting the radio's coarse gain to a suitable value for receiving the current packet; (5) refining the radio's gain by a fine AGC stage; (6) selecting the antenna with the best signal strength; (7) checking general properties of the received signal; and (8) providing abort signals if its behavior is inconsistent with that of a genuine packet.

D. Synchronization

Two frequency offsets are used to achieve synchronization: coarse and fine. Both are calculated using the short training symbols as soon as the start of packet (SOP) indicates activity in the medium.

Mobile node needs to sense the medium for specific time interval and ascertain whether the medium is available. The process is referred as Clear Channel Assessment (CCA). If the channel is unavailable, the transmission is suspended and random delay for reassessing the channel is assigned. The Mobile Node waits for an acknowledgment (ACK) frame. Normally, collisions are undetectable in a wireless environment because corruption of the data can be caused by either collision or fading. Thus, an ACK frame is necessary.

E. Carrier Multiplexing

Overlapping carriers are allowed because the subcarriers are orthogonal so that they are easily distinguished and able to separate from one another.

F. Orthogonality

The frequencies of the subcarriers are selected so that at each carrier frequency, all other subcarriers do not contribute any interference to the overall waveform.

G. Guard Time

Intersymbol Interference (ISI) occurs when the delay spread between different paths is large and causes a delayed copy of the transmitted bits to shift onto a previous arrived copy. Guard time is used to mitigate this problem.

H. Cyclic Prefix

The cyclic extension is used to overcome the intersymbol interference and intercarrier interference (ICI) issues while passing signal through a time-dispersive channel. A cyclic prefix is a copy of the last part of the OFDM symbol that is prepended to the transmitted symbol and removed at the receiver before the demodulation as shown in

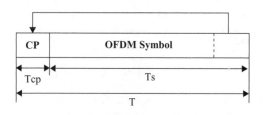

FIGURE 7.9 Cyclic Prefix from the OFDM Principle.

Fig. 7.9. The cyclic prefix[11] should be at least as long as the significant part of the impulse response experienced by the transmitted signal. It avoids ISI because it acts as a guard space between successive symbols and it converts the linear convolution with the channel impulse response into a cyclic convolution. A cyclic convolution is the time domain translates into a scalar multiplication in frequency domain, the subcarriers remain orthogonal and there is no ICI.

I. Convolution Coding

Convolution coding is not part of OFDM. However, OFDM signal is subject to narrowband interference or frequency specific narrow band fading, also known as deep fading. To keep a few faded subcarriers from controlling the bit error rate low, OFDM implementation often applies an error correction code across all the subcarriers. Implementations that use an error correction code in conjunction with OFDM are sometimes called coded OFDM (COFDM).

J. Windowing[19]

Transmission can be abrupt at symbol boundaries, causing a large number of high-frequency components (noise). It is common to add padding bits at the beginning and end of transmissions to allow transmitter to ramp up and ramp down from full power. Padding bits (training sequence) are frequently needed when error correction coding is used.

K. PLCP

The packet PPDU (PLCP Protocol Data Unit) structure is shown in Fig. 7.10. The function of PPDU will be described in Sec. 7.2.4.

L. AGC (Automatic Gain Control)

AGC is used for acquisition and initial timing acquisition. The other main purpose is for initial frequency offset estimation. Difference in phase between two successive

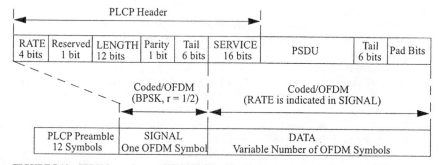

FIGURE 7.10   PPDU frame format (OFDM PLCP sublayer).

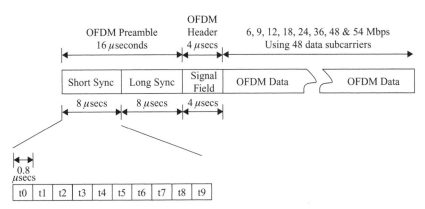

FIGURE 7.11   Short sync training symbols.

peaks gives offset that can resolve $+/-$ 612.5 kHz of offset. Sequence uses 12 out of 52 subcarriers while a 64-pt FFT creates a 3.2 μsec time domain sequence with a pattern that repeats four times (0.8 μsec periodicity). This sequence is repeated 2.5 times to create 10 symbol repetitions (8 μsec in length). Sequence is selected to have good autocorrelation properties.

Training sequence is used to have accurate estimates of the frequency offset at the receiver. To reduce the uncertainty in the channel estimation, short and long training sequences are provided. The short sync training is used to provide coarse and fine estimation of time and frequency errors. The short sync training symbols are shown in Fig. 7.11. The long training sequence is used to estimate the channel impulse response or channel state information (CSI). The long sync training symbols are shown in Fig. 7.12. With CSI, received signal can be demodulated and de-interleaved.

The AGC is also used to maintain a fixed signal power[20] to the A/D converter to prevent signal from saturating or clipping the output of the A/D converter.

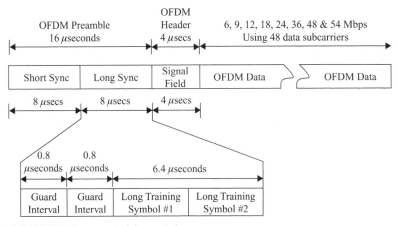

FIGURE 7.12   Long sync training symbols.

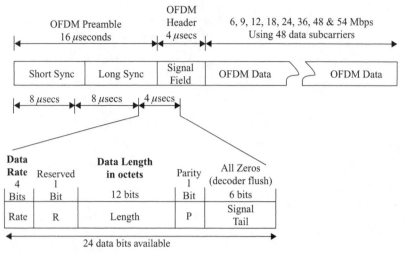

FIGURE 7.13   Signal field.

M. Signal Field

Signal field indicates data rate and packet length shown in Fig. 7.13. There are 24 data bits available in 4 μs.

N. OFDM Data Field

One OFDM symbol period is 4 μs (3.2 μsec data field + 0.8 μsec cyclic prefix). It is used to convey packet information on rate mode and amount of data being transmitted in octets. There are eight rate modes (6, 9, 12, 18, 24, 36, 48, 54 Mbps) as shown in Fig. 7.14. The lowest rate mode is used to maximize probability of reception. It is important that all base stations correctly decode in order to defer channel access.

Modulation μses 52 subcarriers: 48 subcarriers are modulated by coded data symbols, and 4 subcarriers are used as pilot/training symbols. Data is modulated by known BPSK PN sequence. The subcarrier spacing is 312.5 kHz with 80 samples at 20 MHz fundamental sample rates, which yields a 64-point FFT/IFFT.

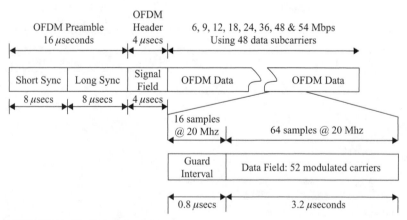

FIGURE 7.14   The OFDM data field.

O. Peak Power Cancellation Method[20]

An OFDM signal consists of a number of independently modulated subcarriers, which can be added up coherently sometimes, and results in a large peak-to-average power (PAP) ratio. To reduce the PAP ratio, several techniques have been used.

1. Reduce the peak amplitudes simply by nonlinearly distorting the signal at the peaks.

2. Use a particular forward-error correcting code set to exclude those OFDM symbols with a large PAR ratio.

3. Choose a scrambling sequence from a group sequence that gives the smallest PAP ratio.

7.2.3   Generic Physical Layer[21]

A. A General Description: IEEE 802.11 specifies three different physical layers for three different modulation schemes; Direct Sequence Spread Spectrum (DSSS), Frequency Hopping Spread Spectrum (FHSS), and Infrared (IR). The physical layer is subdivided into Physical Layer Convergence Protocol (PLCP) sublayer and Physical Medium Dependent (PMD) sublayer as shown in Fig 7.15. PLCP sublayer is PHY-specific, supports common PHYSAP (Service Access Point), performs clear channel assessment (CCA) signal, and reports the information to MAC layer. PMD sublayer is responsible for modulation and encoding.

The PHY Layer Management Entity (PLME) includes channel tuning and PHY Management Information Base (MIB). Station Management Entity (SME) interacts with both MAC management entity (MLME) and PHY layer management entity (PLME) as shown in Fig. 7.15 and will be described in Sec. 7.2.8.7.

B. OFDM PHY Layer.

   1. OFDM PLCP Sublayer

   a. PLCP (Physical Layer Convergence Protocol) format is including PLCP preamble, PLCP header, PSDU (PLCP SDU), tail bits, and pad bits. PLCP is shown in Fig. 7.15.

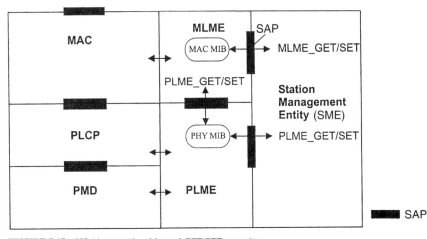

FIGURE 7.15   802.11 protocol entities and GET/SET operations.

TABLE 7.1 Major Parameters of the OFDM PHY

Information Data Rate	6, 9, 12, 18, 24, 36, 48, and 54 Mbit/s (6, 12 and 24 Mbit/s Are Mandatory)
Modulation	BPSK OFDM
	QPSK OFDM
	16-QAM OFDM
	64-QAM OFDM
Error correcting code	K = 7 (64 states) convolutional code
Coding rate	1/2, 2/3, 3/4
Number of subcarriers	52
OFDM symbol duration	4.0 μs
Guard interval	0.8 μs (T_{GI})
Occupied bandwidth	16.6 MHz

- Signal Field: *RATE* field and *LENGTH* field

  Rate Field: conveys information about the type of modulation and coding rate as used in the rest of the packet.

  Length Field: an unsigned 12-bit integer that indicates the number in PSDU that the MAC is currently requesting the PHY to transmit.

- Service Field: is needed to synchronize the descrambler in the receiver.
- PPDU Tail Bit Field: improves the error probability of the convolution decoder.
- PAD (Pad Bits): to accommodate the *TAIL* bits, and are computed from the length of the PDSU *(LENGTH)*

  b. PLCP Data shall be scrambled with a length 127 frame synchronous scrambler.

  c. DATA field shall be coded with a convolution encoder of coding rate, $R = \frac{1}{2}, \frac{2}{3}$, or $\frac{3}{4}$. Data shall be interleaved by a block interleaver with a blank size (compared to the number of bits in a single OFDM symbol).

  d. Subcarrier modulation mapping (for OFDM only): Using BPSK,QPSK,16-QAM, or 64-QAM modulations, depending on the RATE requested, shall modulate the OFDM subcarriers.

  e. Pilot subcarriers (for OFDM only): In each OFDM symbol, four subcarriers are dedicated to pilot signals in order to make the coherent detection robust against frequency offsets and phase noise.

  f. CCA (Clear Channel Assessment): PLCP shall provide the capability to perform CCA and report the result to the MAC.

2. Transmitter and Receiver for the OFDM PHY

   The general block diagram of the transmitter is shown in Fig. 7.7a and the receiver is shown in Fig. 7.7b. Both are using the OFDM technology. The major parameters of the OFDM PHY are shown in Table 7.1.

C. CSMA/CA Protocol

   The 802.11 standard specifies a carrier sense multiple access with collision avoidance (CSMA/CA) protocol. In this protocol, when a node receives a packet to be transmitted, it first listens to ensure no other node is transmitting. If the channel is clear, it then transmits the packet. Otherwise, it chooses a random "backoff factor" that determines the amount of time the node must wait until it is allowed to transmit its packet. During periods in which the channel is clear, the transmitting node decrements its backoff counter. When the channel is busy, it does not decrement its backoff counter. When the backoff counter reaches zero, the node transmits the packet. Because the probability that two nodes will choose the same backoff factor is small, collisions between packets are minimized. Collision detection, as is employed in Ethernet, cannot be used for the radio frequency transmissions of IEEE 802.11. The reason for this is that when a node is transmitting, it cannot hear any other node in the system that may be transmitting, as its own signal will drown out any others arriving at the node.

Similar to wired Ethernet networks, 802.11b WLANs employ CSMA (Carrier Sense, Multiple Access). But instead of using CD (Collision Detection), WLANs use CA (Collision Avoidance). This means that instead of each station trying to transmit as soon as the medium is free, WLAN devices will use a "Collision Avoidance" mechanism to prevent multiple stations sending at the same time.

7.2.4 Physical Layer for Specific Systems (802.11 b/a/g)

802.11 is composed of several alternative physical layers (802.11 b/a/g) (shown in Fig. 7.16), and the transmission and reception of 802.11 frames of different physical layers are specified in the section.

A. Physical Layer of 802.11b uses DSSS technology to support operation of up to 11 Mbps data rates in the 2.5-GHz band.

    1. PLCP (Physical Layer Convergence Protocol): Prepares 802.11 frames for transmission and directs the PMD (Physical Medium Dependent) to actually transmit signals, change radio channels, and receive signals.

Standard	802.11b	802.11a	802.11g	802.11n
Transmission Technique	DSSS	OFDM	OFDM	Probably OFDM
Channel Bandwidth	22 MHz	20 MHz	22 MHz	17-20 MHz
Data Rates	1 or 2 Mbps Barker codes, 5.5 or 11 Mbps Complementary Code Keying	6, 9.12, 18, 24, 36, 48 and 54 Mbps	1, 2, 5.5, 11 Mbps DSSS and 6, 9, 12, 18, 24, 36, 48, 54 Mbps OFDM	up to 100 Mbps
Channel Spacing	25 MHz	20 MHz	20 MHz	Not Determined
Frequency Band	2.4 GHz	5.8 GHz	2.4 GHz	5.8 GHz
Short Preamble	Optional	N/A	N/A	Not Determined

FIGURE 7.16 Comparison of all 802.11 standards.

2. PPDU (PLCP Protocol Data Unit): The actual frame that PLCP transmits, including the following fields:

   a. Sync Field: After detecting the sync, the receiver begins synchronizing (01010101....).

   b. Frame Delimiter Field: This field is always 1111001110100000 and defines the beginning of a frame.

   c. Signal Field

   • Rate Field: Identifies the data rate of the 802.11 frames, with its binary value equal to the data rate divided by 100 kbps. The PLCP field is always sent at the lowest rate, which is 1 Mbps. This ensures that the receiver is initially using the correct demodulation mechanism with different data rates.

   • Length Field: Represents the number of μseconds for transmitting the contents of the PPDU and for the receiver to use this information to determine the end of the frame.

   d. Service Field: Always sets to 00000000.

   e. Frame Check Sequence: Detects possible errors in the physical layer header containing 16-bit CRC.

3. Transmission Parameters

   DSSS Spreading: The available bandwidth is 30 MHz in 2.4 GHz. The spreading sequence is a binary code. For 1 Mbps and 2 Mbps operations, the spreading code is the 11-chip Barker sequence. The 802.11 transmitters combine the PPDU with a spreading sequence through the use of a binary adder.

   Both 5.5 Mbps and 11 Mbps rate operations use complementary code keying (CCK). The modulator simply refers to a table for the spreading sequence that corresponds to the pattern of data bits being sent. This is the most efficient processing of the data for achieving the higher data rates.

   DSSS Modulation:

   For 1 Mbps: PMD uses differential BPSK.

   For 2 Mbps, 5.5 Mbps, and 11 Mbps: PMD uses differential QPSK.

   Transmit Frequencies: There are fourteen channels, 5-MHz spacing each, from 2.412 to 2.484 GHz except Channel 14 has 12-MHz spacing.

   Power: 100 MW max for the United States.

B. Physical Layer of 802.11a.
   It uses OFDM technology to support operation of up to 54-Mbps data rates in the 5-GHz band.

   1. PLCP: Sends the 802.11 frames that are PPDU and includes the following fields.

   a. PLCP preamble field: Consists of 12 symbols (10 shorts and 2 long symbols) and enables the receiver to sync and acquire an incoming OFDM signal.

   b. Rate Field: Identifies the data rate of 802.11 frames. The lowest rate is 6 Mbps, then 9, 12, 18, 24, 36, 48 and 54 Mbps.

   c. Length Field: Same as 802.11b.

   d. Parity Field: Contains a single-bit for error code.

   e. Tail Field: Consists of six bits (all zeros) for receiver to process functions.

   f. Pad Bits Field: Contains a number of bits for modifying the frame size, which equals a specific multiple of bits coded in an OFDM symbol.

2. Transmission Parameter

a. OFDM Technology

Use of OFDM that divides a data signal across 48 separate subcarriers within a 20-MHz channel to provide transmissions of 6, 9, 12, 18, 24, 36, 48, or 54 Mbps. Data rates of 6, 12, and 24 Mbps are mandatory for all 802.11 products. OFDM is the basis for the HiperLAN Wireless LAN standards also. OFDM supports the global standard for HDSL too.

b. Modulation

For 6-Mbps operation, PMD uses BPSK for each subcarrier for higher data rates; PMD uses QAM with different levels for each subcarrier.

c. Transmit Frequencies

In the United States, the National Information Structure (U-NII) bands are used 5.15–5.25 GHz (lower) 5.25–5.35 GHz (middle), and 5.725–5.825 GHz (upper). Each band has four 20-MHz channels. The maximum transmit power for lower band is 40 MW, middle band is 200 MW, and upper band is 800 MW.

C. Physical Layer of 802.11g: operating at 2.4 GHz using two modes, CCK mode and OFDM mode.

1. Using CCK mode on DSSS radio

Under the direction of the PLCP, the PMD provides actual transmission and reception of PHY entities between two stations.

- CCK code word is modulated with the QPSK technology used in 2-Mbps wireless DSSS radios.

- At 2 Mbps per traffic channel, 2 bits per symbol are modulated with QPSK and spreaded to 11 Mcps needing 22-MHz.

2. OFDM Mode

It uses a combination of BPSK, QPSK, and L-QAM depending on the chosen data rates. The transmission parameters of 802.11g are similar to that of 802.11b.

3. Frame Format

An Extended Rate PHY (ERP) of AP (access point) supports three different preamble and header formats.

a. The long preamble and header: The PPDU provides interoperability with 802.11a when using the 1, 2, 5.5, and 11 Mbps data rates, and use the optional OFDM modulation at all OFDM rates.

b. The short preamble and header: Supports the rates 2, 5.5, and 11 Mbps.

c. The OFDM preamble and header

7.2.5 Available Bandwidth for Specific Systems (802.11b/a/g)

1. 802.11b/g

The available bandwidth for 802.11b and g is 83.5 MHz shown in Fig. 7.17. Both b and g supports 14 overlapping channels. For 802.11a, there is 300-MHz bandwidth available and up to 12 channels are available.

On 802.11b and g, the modulation scheme is a combination of high rate and low rate, as 11.g can operate at higher data rate and needs to provide backward compatibility with 802.11b. The 802.11a, however, does not have this restriction and can operate at single modulation scheme. The modulation scheme breakdown for 802.11 systems is shown in Fig. 7.18.

	802.11	802.11a	802.11b	802.11g
Standard	July 1997	Sept. 1999	Sept. 1999	August 2003
Bandwidth	83.5 MHz	300 MHz	83.5 MHz	83.5 MHz
Frequencies	2.400–2.4835 GHz	5.15–5.25 GHz 5.25–5.35 GHz 5.725–5.825 GHz	2.400–2.4835 GHz	2.400–2.4835 GHz
Non-Overlapping Channels	3	4 Indoor 4 Indoor/Outdoor 4 Outdoor	3	3
Data Rates	2, 1 Mbps	54, 48, 36, 24, 18, 12, 9, 6 Mbps	11, 5.5, 2, 1 Mbps	54, 36, 24, 22, 12, 11, 9, 6, 5.5, 2, 1 Mbps
Modulation	DQPSK, DBPSK	BPSK, QPSK, 16-QAM, 64-QAM	CCK, DQPSK, DBPSK	OFDM, CCK, DQPSK, DBPSK

FIGURE 7.17 Available bandwidth and channels for 802.11.

Rate (Mbps)	Encoding	802.11b		802.11g		802.11a	
		Mandatory	Optional	Mandatory	Optional	Mandatory	Optional
1	DBPSK	Barker-DSSS		Barker-DSSS			
2	DQPSK	Barker-DSSS		Barker-DSSS			
5.5	DBPSK	CCK-DSSS	PBCC	CCK-DSSS	PBCC		
6	BPSK			OFDM	CCK-OFDM	OFDM	
9	BPSK			OFDM, CCK-OFDM			OFDM
11	DQPSK	CCK-DSSS	PBCC	CCK-DSSS	PBCC		
12	QPSK			OFDM	CCK-OFDM	OFDM	
18	QPSK			OFDM, CCK-OFDM			OFDM
22	8PSK				PBCC		
24	16 QAM			OFDM	CCK-OFDM	OFDM	
33	8PSK				PBCC		
36	16 QAM			OFDM, CCK-OFDM			OFDM
48	64 QAM			OFDM, CCK-OFDM			OFDM
54	64 QAM			OFDM, CCK-OFDM			OFDM

FIGURE 7.18 Modulation scheme breakdown for 802.11a/b/g.

Channel ID	Frequency (MHz)	Americas (-A) CCK	Americas (-A) OFDM	EMEA (-E) CCK	EMEA (-E) OFDM	Israel (-I) CCK	Israel (-I) OFDM	Japan (-J) CCK	Japan (-J) OFDM
1	2412	X	X	X	X			X	X
2	2417	X	X	X	X			X	X
3	2422	X	X	X	X			X	X
4	2427	X	X	X	X			X	X
5	2432	X	X	X	X	X	X	X	X
6	2437	X	X	X	X	X	X	X	X
7	2442	X	X	X	X	X	X	X	X
8	2447	X	X	X	X	X	X	X	X
9	2452	X	X	X	X	X	X	X	X
10	2457	X	X	X	X	X	X	X	X
11	2462	X	X	X	X	X	X	X	X
12	2467			X	X	X	X	X	X
13	2472			X	X	X	X	X	X
14	2484							X	
Maximum Power (mW)		100	30	50	30	50	30	30	30

FIGURE 7.19 Worldwide 802.11b/g channel assignment and supported modulation. (EMEA: Europe, Middle East, Africa)

Adjacent channels have a separation of only 5 MHz, and most of the energy for each channel spans a 22-MHz band. The adjacent channels do interfere with each other.

In the United States, there are 11 different channels allocated for 11.b and g. Japan has up to 14 different channels, while EMEA has 13 channels that support both CCK and OFDM as shown in Fig. 7.19.

Figure 7.20 shows that this channel allocation only permits three nonoverlapping channels. For example, in the United States, these nonoverlapping channels are 1, 6, and 11. In Europe, because of the extra two channels (12 and 13), 1, 7, and 13 is a better allocation (due to wider separation) of no overlapping channels.

2. 802.11a Channels: Channels that can be used are defined for use by the 802.11a specification and depend on regulations for a given region. In the United States, 802.11a

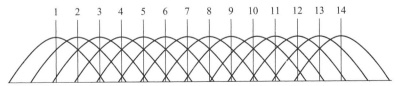

FIGURE 7.20 Channel allocation for the United States.

Regulatory Domain	Band (GHz)	Operating Channel Numbers	Center Frequencies (MHz)
United States	U-NII lower band (5.15-5.25)	36	5180
		40	5200
		44	5220
		48	5240
United States	U-NII middle band (5.25-5.35)	52	5260
		56	5280
		60	5300
		64	5320
United States	U-NII upper band (5.725-5.835)	149	5745
		153	5765
		157	5785
		161	5805

FIGURE 7.21   Valid operation channels for the United States in the 5-GHz band.

utilizes 12 channels, spread across 3 bands. Eight of the channels (lower band and middle band) are restricted to indoor use and 4 (52–64) can be used indoors or outdoors. Figure 7.21 shows the per band channel distribution of the United States.

A more complete list of channels that includes those supported in other regions of the world is shown in Figure 7.22.

Channel spacing for the U-NII lower and mid bands for indoor communications is shown in Figure 7.23a. The 8 indoor channels have 30-MHz guard bands at each end of the spectrum.

Channel spacing for U-NII Upper Band for Outdoor Communications is shown in Figure 7.23b. There are four carriers allocated in the 100-MHz band, each with spacing of 20 MHz.

There are differences on the maximum transmitted power allowed for each different band. The support for Dynamic Frequency Selection (DFS) and Transmit Power Control (TPC) are also different for different operating frequencies as shown in Fig. 7.24.

7.2.6   802.11a/b/g Throughput Comparisons

Throughput is obviously a big consideration when designing hotspots. A service provider provides aggressively to longing bandwidth services such as multimedia services. It is clear that the higher the data rate, the higher the throughput. Thus, 802.11g has higher throughput than 802.11b and 802.11a. There are other parts of the specification that affect the throughput. The most important one is the backwards compatibility between 802.11g and 802.11b. The 802.11g specifications require 802.11g APs to support communications with 802.11b client. As mentioned earlier, this support has come at the expense of throughput for both the 802.11b and 802.11g clients as well as the AP. Figure 7.25 shows the approximate throughputs that can be obtained with all the 802.11 technologies as well as throughputs obtained by an 802.11g AP while working in mix-mode using RTS/CTS and CTS-to-Self packet protection as mentioned in Sec. 7.2.8.2.

Channel	Frequency (MHz)	Americas	ETSI (Europe)	Japan
34	5170	-	-	x
36	5180	x	x	-
38	5190	-	-	x
40	5200	x	x	-
42	5210	-	-	x
44	5220	x	x	-
46	5230	-	-	x
48	5240	x	x	-
52	5260	x	x	-
56	5280	x	x	-
60	5300	x	x	-
64	5320	x	x	-
100	5500	-	x	-
104	5520	-	x	-
108	5540	-	x	-
112	5560	-	x	-
116	5580	-	x	-
120	5600	-	x	-
124	5620	-	x	-
128	5640	-	x	-
132	5660	-	x	-
136	5680	-	x	-
140	5700	-	x	-
149	5745	x	-	-
153	5765	x	-	-
157	5785	x	-	-
161	5805	x	-	-

FIGURE 7.22 The channel spacing for the U-NII lower and mid bands. These channels are used for indoor communications.

As shown in Fig. 7.25, the throughput for 802.11g actually drops in 11.b and g mixed environment compared with a pure 11.g environment.

7.2.7 802.11b and 802.11g Coexistence

802.11g standard supports much higher speeds than 802.11b. 802.11g supports multiple transmission rates all the way to 54 Mbps. 802.11g is a superset of 802.11b and is designed to maintain compatibility with 802.11b. 802.11g uses the same frequencies as 802.11b depending on regulatory domains. The AP transacts with 802.11b clients at their highest capable data rate given their configuration and position in the coverage cell, and does the same for 802.11g clients. This means that an 802.11b client can receive packets at the 11-Mbps data rate while an 802.11g client right next to the 802.11b client can receive packets at the 54-Mbps date rate. When 802.11b clients and 802.11g clients are in the same cell, the

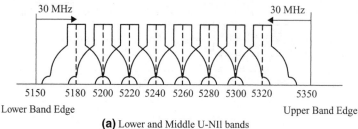

(a) Lower and Middle U-NII bands

Upper U-NII Bands: 4 Carriers in 100 MHz/ 20 MHz Spacing

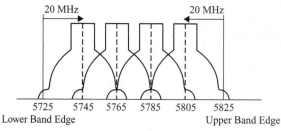

(b) Upper U-NII Bands

FIGURE 7.23   U-NII allocated band.

802.11g specification requires a protection mechanism that involves the use of the 802.11 RTS/CTS protocol shown in Fig. 7.26 and mentioned in Sec. 7.2.8.2.

It is this protection mechanism of 802.11g that slows the throughput of 11g clients when there are 802.11b in the coverage cell. The protection mechanism is not active when the cell has only 802.11g clients. With protection mechanism active, the AP still transmits to the clients at rates up to their capabilities. The protection mechanism slows 802.11g throughput but provides for the fewest collisions of packets.

RTS stands for "Request To Send" and CTS for "Clear To Send." This handshake was developed for stations to use at their own discretion when they detect the communications degrading or the medium being crowded. Rather than relying on the retransmission of undelivered packets, the stations (STAs) can clear the channel for transmission by sending an RTS message to the AP. If the AP determines it is OK for the station to transmit, it broadcasts out a CTS message to the requesting station. Both the RTS and CTS message contain information regarding how much time the client needs to deliver the packet in question. All clients that receive the CTS will then grant the channel to the requesting

Band	Maximum Power	DFS & TPC Required
5.15 to 5.25	50 mW	No
5.25 to 5.35	250 mW	Yes
5.47 to 5.725	250 mW	Yes
5.725 to 5.825	1 W	No

FIGURE 7.24   802.11a relations with DFS and TPC.

Technology	Data Rate (Mbps)	Approximate Throughput (Mbps)
802.11b	11	6
802.11g w 802.11b clients using RTS/CTS protection	54	8
802.11g w 802.11b clients using CTS-to-self protection	54	12
802.11g w no 802.11b clients	54	22
802.11a	54	26

FIGURE 7.25 Throughput comparisons of 802.11a, 802.11b, and 802.11g.

STA by making sure they don't transmit during the requested time period. 802.11b stations are able to understand RTS/CTS requests from 802.11g units because these messages are sent using modulation schemes shown in the 802.11b specification. Once an 802.11g STA has been granted the channel, it can switch back to OFDM if necessary. However, the interoperability handshake generates overhead, so that it can cut the 802.11g throughputs by over 50%. The detail description of RTS/CTS protocols is shown in the MAC layer section (Sec. 7.2.8.2).

7.2.8   MAC (Media Access Control) Layer[21]

The MAC layer is a set of protocols that is responsible for maintaining order in the use of a shared medium. MAC layer provides basic access mechanism, fragmentation, and encryption. MAC Layer Management Entity (MLME) shown in Fig. 7.15 handles synchronization, power management, roaming, and MAC MIB (management information base) handles multiplexing, queuing, scheduling, contention resolution, and so forth.

The 802.11 MAC layer is required to have a single MAC to support multiple PHYs. The MAC supports single and multiple channel PHYs and PHYs with different *Medium Sense* characteristics. It also allows overlap of multiple networks in the same area and same channel space through sharing the medium as well as reuse of the same medium. Because 802.11 uses the shared bandwidth, it needs to be *robust for interference* such as microwave and unlicensed spectrum users and cochannel interference. Mechanisms to deal with *Hidden Nodes* and provisions for *time-bounded services*, privacy, and access control are also needed.

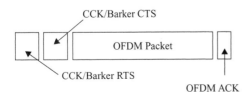

CCK/Barker CTS

OFDM Packet

CCK/Barker RTS

OFDM ACK

FIGURE 7.26 Illustration of using RTS/CTS formats.

The network needs to support a number of important features:

1. *High speed operation:* Normally operates at over 10 Mb/s and more than 50 Mb/s to support multimedia applications.

2. *Fair access:* Ensure all terminals are able to achieve similar throughput and delay characteristics.

3. *Time-bounded access:* include provision for both *ad hoc* and infrastructure-based networks.

4. *Flexible configurations:* include provision for both *ad hoc* and infrastructure-based networks.

5. *Security:* Militate against others taking advantage of the lack of physical security in a wireless network.

6. *Mobility support:* either provide mobility support or not make mobility support difficult at higher layers.

7. *Low power:* provide mechanisms that allow mobile terminals to minimize power consumption.

Wirelesses networking unique challenges include:

1. Hidden terminal problem: Two terminals transmitting to a third terminal may not be able to detect each other, making traditional carrier sense impossible.

2. Capture: Simultaneous Tx and Rx at a terminal is difficult, and making traditional collision detection impossible. One terminal in a network may continually over power another terminal, which could reduce access fairness.

3. Noise, interference and reflections: Data transmissions are corrupted much more often than in a wired network.

4. Limited spectrum: The network might operate with different spectrum or deal with simultaneous use of spectrum by other users.

5. Signal attenuation: Data transmissions have only limited range.

6. Signal open: Data transmissions are not secure.

The 802.11 standard has been designed to provide the required features and resolve the difficulties of working in a wireless environment as shown in Fig. 7.27.

Required feature	802.11 capability
High speed operation	PHY
Fair access	DCF, PCF
Time-bounded access	PCF
Flexible configuration	BSS, IBSS
Security	WEP
Mobility support	ESS
Low power	PS

Difficulty	802.11 capability
Hidden terminals	RTS/CTS
Capture	CSMA/CA, ACK
Noise and interference	PHY, ACK, fragmentation, multi-rate
Limited spectrum	licensing, PHY
Signal attenuation	PS mode
Signal open	WEP

FIGURE 7.27   802.11 capability on supporting required features and difficulty.

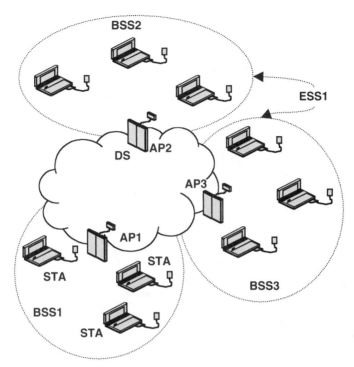

FIGURE 7.28   802.11 infrastructure model topology.

The 802.11 MAC supports both infrastructure and *ad hoc* network models. Infrastructure model includes: Stations (STA), which can be any wireless device; Access Point (AP), which connects BSS to DS and controls access by STAs; Basic Service Set (BSS), a region controlled by an AP and mobility is supported within a single BSS. Extended Service Set (ESS) is a set of BSSs forming a virtual BSS and mobility is supported between BSS's in an ESS. Distribution Service (DS) provides connection between BSSs as shown in Fig. 7.28.

Ad hoc model includes Stations (STA), which includes any wireless device that acts as distributed AP; Independent Basic Service Set (IBSS), with each BSS forming a self-contained network and no AP and no connection to the DS as shown in Fig. 7.29. The *Ad Hoc* network is described in Section 17.8.

The 802.11 MAC consists of basic access, data transmission, and management functions, as well as a variety of other features. The other various features are shown in Fig. 7.30.

7.2.8.1 DCF.   The model used for WLAN data transmission is called Distributed Coordination Function (DCF) access scheme. DCF carries the following events when end points try to transmit data.

1. Provides fair access in a noisy wireless environment with the option of prioritized access.

2. The scheme includes using a CSMA/CA-based protocol to ensure fair access while minimizing collisions. An STA may transmit a packet after sensing that the medium is idle for an Interframe Space (IFS) period.

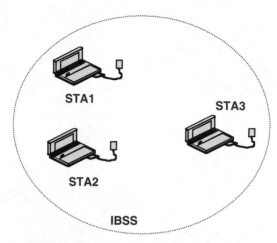

FIGURE 7.29 802.11 *Ad hoc* model topology.

3. Supporting prioritized access to allow higher priority to data and management traffic as required. Using different IFS periods for different classes of traffic may set different levels of priority. The 802.11 MAC defines the use of four IFS periods used by STAs as follows:

   a. SIFS (short IFS): Need time to maintain access at STAs. SIFS is the shortest interval and is used by Access Points to send acknowledgments and management traffic.

   b. PIFS (point-coordination-function IFS): Provides a collision-free period (CFP).

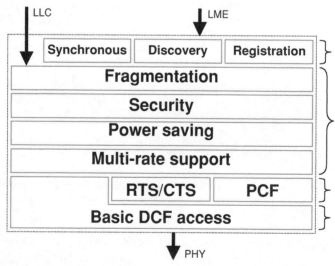

FIGURE 7.30 The 802.1 MAC Layer.

c. DIFS (distributed-coordination-functions IFS): Provides the contention period (CP). DIFS is the interval used by most other end points.

d. EIFS (extended IFS): When an incomplete or erroneous frame is received.

4. Specifies acknowledgments for all nonbroadcast and nonmulticast data packets and all nonbroadcast and nonmulticast management packets. The acknowledgment is sent with high priority by using SIFS and IFS period, and using acknowledgments for most packet sequences to ensure correct packet reception in a noisy environment.

After the IFS interval has expired, the end points begin their "Collision Avoidance" (CA) procedure. This procedure uses two values, called *aCWmin* and *aCWmax*. CW stands for "Contention Window." The CW determines what additional amount of time an end point should wait, after the IFS period, to attend to transmit a packet. This model determines the value of the CW used: Each end point has the values for aCWmin and aCWmax defined.

After IFS expires, the end point selects a value between 0 and aCWmax. The end point then waits the length of this value and determines if the medium is available to transmit. If the medium is available, then the end point transmits the packets. If the medium is unavailable, probably another device sent a packet; the end point then waits until the end of packet transmission from another device and the IFS period.

7.2.8.2 RTS/CTS Function. This function reduces the effect of hidden terminals, minimizes collisions, and provides a fast transmission check. A more detailed description of the RTS/CTS protection for 11g is shown in Fig. 7.31.

When RTS/CTS is in use, most stations will hear the RTS, and all stations will hear the CTS. In either case, each node receives information indicating the length of the subsequent OFDM packet and ACK transmission. Every station has an internal timer referred to as the network allocation vector (NAV). The NAV is set to have the same duration as the OFDM packet exchange. The NAV acts as in parallel with conventional carrier sensing and is referred to as a virtual carrier sense mechanism. The channel is not considered idle unless no active signal is detected and the NAV timer has expired. Once both criteria are met, stations can once again begin to contend for channel access. In this manner, 802.11b and 802.11g radios can operate in a mixed environment with an 802.11g AP. It should also be noted that every 802.11g client and AP must be capable of falling back and operating

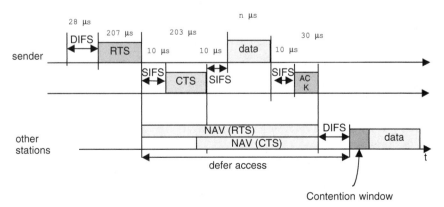

FIGURE 7.31 More detailed description of the 11.g RTS/CTS protection.

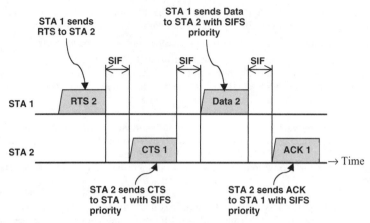

FIGURE 7.32   802.11 MAC: Illustration of RTC/CTS timing.

exactly like a legacy 802.11b device. Therefore, migration to 802.11g technologies can be smooth. As new 802.11g APs are brought online, legacy 802.11b APs can remain in service and will be fully interoperable with newer 802.11g clients.

To lessen the effect of the RTS/CTS protocol, a second method of reserving the channel was specified. This method is called CTS-to-Self and consists of the sending STA reserving the channel by bypassing the RTS and just sending a CTS message to itself. All stations that hear this message refrain from transmitting, thus clearing the channel. This method of channel reservation reduces the overhead, increasing the throughput. However, this method is vulnerable to the "Hidden-Node" problem. In the Hidden-Node case, two mobile stations can be too far apart to hear each other's messages, but not too far from the AP for association. When this situation occurs, one of the stations may not hear the CTS-to-Self message sent by the other, thus opening up the possibility for packet collisions. The situation gets worse the more stations that are connected to the same AP and far away from each other. Use of CTS-to-Self is a configuration option in some wireless cards. CTS-to-Self is not recommended in crowded wireless environments. Using CTS-to-Self messages may actually degrade the performance of a mixed-mode wireless network.

An STA uses the RTS/CTS access method to send a packet as follows: The STA 1 first sends an RTS using the basic access method, the receiving STA 2 sends a CTS with SIFS priority, the original STA 1 sends the data packet with SIFS priority, the receiving STA 2 sends the ACK with SIFS priority, and all packets in the exchange contain a field telling other STAs that the medium is reserved for the period until the end of the ACK (supporting virtual carrier sense) shown in Fig. 7.32. The RTS/CTS access method has a number of advantages: The short packets provide a fast transmission path check, the short packets minimize the length of any collision, and hidden terminals hear the medium reservation in the RTS and/or CTS.

7.2.8.3 *TSF (Timing Synchronization Function).*   Timing synchronization function (TSF) provides several functions:

1. Use Beacons for finding and staying with a BSS or IBSS (independent BSS). Under the TSF method, all stations maintain a local timer (accuracy $\pm 0.01\%$). Timing synchronization information is conveyed by periodic Beacon transmissions. BSS uses persistent common clock provided by AP in periodic Beacons. IBSS has no persistent common

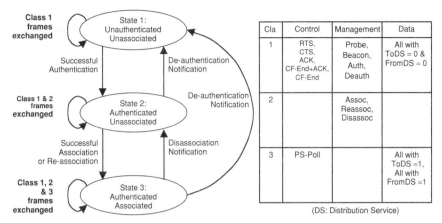

Cla	Control	Management	Data
1	RTS, CTS, ACK, CF-End+ACK, CF-End	Probe, Beacon, Auth, Deauth	All with ToDS = 0 & FromDS = 0
2		Assoc, Reassoc, Disassoc	
3	PS-Poll		All with ToDS =1, All with FromDS =1

(DS: Distribution Service)

FIGURE 7.33 802.11 MAC management functions: Beacon transmission methods (authentication and association).

clock and its synchronization uses distributed Beacons. The 802.11 MAC timing synchronization function enables low-power operation and PHY layer operation.

2. TSF is crucial for power management, as Beacons sent at well-known intervals and all station timers in IBSS and BSS are synchronized.

3. Hop timing for the 802.11 Frequency Hopping (FH) PHY uses TSF Timer for time Dwell Interval and all Stations are synchronized, so they hop at same time.

4. Beacon transmission also contains service set management. Information in the Beacon includes Service Set identity information (SSID), Capability information, Supported rates, PHY parameter set, Contention Free Period (CFP) parameters, IBSS parameters, and Traffic Information Matrix (TIM).

5. Scanning: The 802.11 MAC supports both passive and active network discovery. 802.11 MAC uses a common mechanism, called scanning, for all PHY layers, whether single or multichannel, for finding a network (IBSS or BSS). Scanning can be passive on each channel listening for Beacons on each channel or Active on each channel by sending a Probe Request and waiting for a Probe Response. Beacon or Probe Response contains information necessary to join the network.

6. Authentication: Beacon transmission contains authentication and association methods, which ensure secure and controlled access to a BSS (but not an IBSS) as shown in Fig. 7.33. In authentication area, the 802.11 MAC offers two authentication modes, the open authentication and the shared key authentication which uses the Wired Equivalent Privacy (WEP) algorithm as shown in Fig. 7.34.

7.2.8.4 PCF. The Point Coordination Function (PCF) access method provides centrally controlled access to the network. The PCF access method is used in an infrastructure-based network to provide AP controlled access to the wireless medium in a contention-free period (CFP). The central control of transmission allows the AP to provide time-bounded network access—the time-bounded protocol is not specified by 802.11. The contention-free period (CFP) is started with a beacon on a DTIM (Delivery TIM) boundary, is continued with regular beacons, and ends with a CF-End packet. The AP has control of the medium during

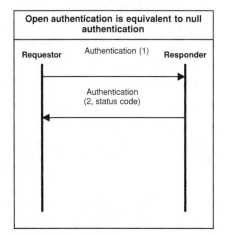 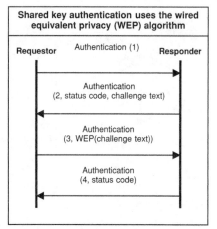

FIGURE 7.34   Authentication methods: Message flow for open and WEP authentications.

a CFP to transmit packets and to allow STAs to transmit packets after polling. The 802.11 MAC defines special rules to limit interference between APs operating CFPs in the same PHY channel.

CFP.   The CFP is started with a beacon on a DTIM boundary and is continued with regular beacons and ends with a CF-End packet. The AP establishes the CFP as follows: The AP starts the CFP by transmitting a beacon with PIFS priority. The beacon is sent when a normal DTIM beacon is due to be transmitted. The beacon contains information about the CFP, including its maximum allowed length to be set from which STAs will use to set their NAV timer. The AP continues the CFP as follows: (1) The AP starts the CFP by transmitting a beacon with SIFS priority; (2) The AP sends a beacon renewing the CFP whenever a beacon is due; (3) The beacon contains information about the CFP, including its remaining length, which STAs will use to reset their NAV timer; and (4) The AP ends the CFP by transmitting a CF-End packet as shown in Fig. 7.35.

Controlling Mechanism.   The AP has control of the medium during a CFP to transmit packets and to allow STAs to transmit packets after polling. STAs establish themselves as

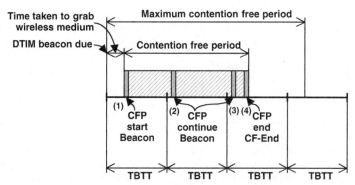

FIGURE 7.35   802.11 MAC: Example CFP Start/End timing diagram. (TBTT: target beacon transmission time)

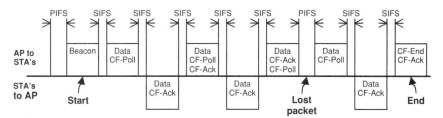

FIGURE 7.36 Data transmission: PCF.

CF-Poll during the association process. The rules for packet transmission during a CFP are as follows: (1) The AP may send data packets to any STA, which the STA acknowledges with an CF-Ack; (2) The AP may send a CF-Poll to Poll STA, which the STA acknowledges with a CF-Ack; (3) Reception of a CF-Poll gives the STA the right to send a single packet (or a null packet), which the AP acknowledges with an CF-Ack. Data Acks, CF-Polls, CF-Acks, and CF-Ends may be piggybacked as appropriate in the same transmission as shown in Fig. 7.36. All transmissions use a SIFS period, except when the AP does not receive an expected packet from an STA, in which case a PIFS period is used. During the CFP, the AP will poll a subset of STAs on its polling list according to a minimal set of rules.

During the CFP, the AP will poll a subset of STAs on its polling list according to a minimal set of rules. The AP must follow a minimal set of rules during the CFP to ensure interoperability. The rules are as follows: The AP shall send a CF-Poll to at least one STA on the polling list in a CFP. The AP will issue CF-Polls to a subset of STAs in ascending AID (association identifier) value. If all CF data frames have been delivered and all STAs on the polling list polled during a CFP, then the AP may poll any STA on the polling list and may send data or management frames to any STAs.

Interference Issues. The 802.11 MAC defines special rules to limit interference between APs operating CFPs in the same PHY channel. It is possible that two or more APs might operate in the same PHY channel. Although this will not cause any difficulty in DCF operation, it could cause interference in PCF operation. The 802.11 MAC defines the following rules to mitigate against this situation: The AP will use DIFS and a random back-off for the beacon to start the CFP if the beacon transmission is delayed due to a busy medium. The AP may optionally use the same delay to retransmit data and management frames during the CFP. The AP should check on regular occasions during the CFP that the medium is idle for DIFS plus a random period.

7.2.8.5 Power Saving (PS) Protocol. The 802.11 MAC supports a variety of power saving modes, which will promote longer battery life in mobile terminals. Mobile terminals rely on batteries for most of their power requirements. The 802.11 MAC promotes battery conservation in mobile terminals by defining operations during *active* and *power saving* modes for STAs. An STA in *power saving* mode turns off its transmitter and receiver circuitry for defined periods to save power. The 802.11 MAC defines a variation of the basic power saving protocol for BSS in the CP and CFP modes shown in Figs. 7.37 and 7.38, respectively, and IBSS in the CP mode shown in Fig. 7.39.

A. BSS in CP:

The 802.11 MAC defines a variation of the basic power saving protocol for a BSS in the CP. During power saving operations, the AP for a BSS in the CP maintains a list of associated STAs in PS mode.

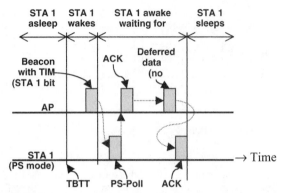

FIGURE 7.37 802.11 Illustration of power savings: STA is in a BSS in CP.

DTIM. For broadcast/multicast packets: it buffers all broadcast/multicast packets that do not have the *order* bit set (others are transmitted), transmits a Delivery Traffic Indication Matrix (DTIM) every few beacons, which contains an indication of whether the AP has buffered broadcast/multicast packets and transmits all broadcast/multicast packets immediately after the DTIM. If there are more multicast/broadcast packets to be transmitted before the next scheduled beacon, then a DTIM is also transmitted with the next beacon.

STA in Sleep Mode. For directed packets, AP buffers packets addressed to STAs in PS mode (other packets are handled normally) transmit a Traffic Indication Matrix (TIM) with every beacon, which contains an indication of the PS mode. It has at least one packet buffered responding to PS-Polls from an STA in PS mode by transmitting a single packet addressed to the STA from the buffer, and with the *more data* field if the AP has more packets buffered that are addressed to the STA. The response to the PS-Poll can be deferred by transmitting an ACK.

During power saving operations, an STA is in a BSS in the CP: For broadcast/multicast packets, it wakes up for every beacon containing a DTIM, unless the STA is willing to miss

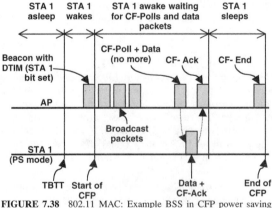

FIGURE 7.38 802.11 MAC: Example BSS in CFP power saving timing diagram.

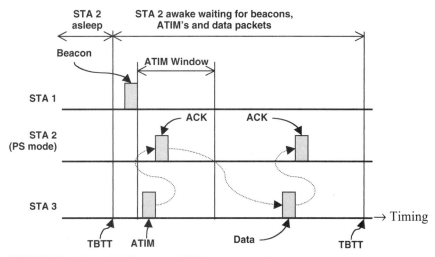

FIGURE 7.39 802.11 MAC: Illustration of IBSS power saving diagram.

broadcast/multicast packets. It remains awake if the DTIM indicates that the AP has broadcast/multicast packets buffered, until a received broadcast/multicast packet or a subsequent DTIM indicates there are no more broadcast/multicast packets buffered in the AP.

STA in Wake-up Mode. For directed packets: An STA wakes up to listen to selected beacons containing TIMs, transmits a PS-Poll to the AP when a TIM or DTIM indicates that the AP has a packet buffered that is addressed to the STA (using a CW of 0 to Cwmin when more than one bit set in TIM), remains awake after sending the PS-Poll until the STA either receives a packet in response to the PS-Poll or receives another beacon containing a DTIM or TIM indicating that the AP no longer has packets buffered that are addressed to the STA, and transmits another PS-Poll to the AP if the received packet (in response to a previous PS-Poll) indicates that the AP has more packets buffered that are addressed to the STA.

Also, every beacon contains an indication of the CF-Poll that the AP intends polling the STAs during the remainder of the CFP, transmits packets to the CF-Poll STAs in PS mode in order of ascending association ID, after any broadcast/multicast packets, with the *more data* bit set if the AP has more packets buffered for the CF-Poll STAs in PS mode.

B. BSS in CEP:

During power saving operations, an STA is in a BSS in the CFP: For broadcast/multicast packets, it wakes up for every beacon containing a DTIM during a CFP, unless the STA is willing to miss broadcast/multicast packets. It remains awake if the DTIM indicates the AP has broadcast/multicast packets buffered, until a received broadcast/multicast packet or a subsequent DTIM or TIM indicates there are no more broadcast/multicast packets buffered in the AP same as in the sleep mode.

STA in Awake Waiting Mode. For directed packets: It wakes up to listen to the beacon containing a DTIM at the start of the CFP, remains awake during the CFP until the STA receives a packet with the *more data* bit clear; or, with a DTIM or TIM indicating that the AP no longer has packets buffered that are addressed to the STA. The STA may send PS-Polls to the AP during the subsequent CP if the indicated buffered packets were not received during the CFP.

C. IBSS in CP:

The 802.11 MAC defines a variation of the basic power saving protocol for an IBSS in the CP. To send a packet to an STA in power saving mode in an IBSS: All STA's buffer packets addressed to the STA in PS mode, and the STAs packets in their PS buffer transmit an ATIM (Announcement TIM) packet in an ATIM window after each beacon to each STA (or broadcast/multicast destination) for which they have buffered packets. ATIM packets are transmitted using the basic DCF access method, with minor modifications. Any ATIMs that are not acknowledged are retransmitted. The packets corresponding to ATIMs not sent or acknowledged during an ATIM window are buffered until the next ATIM window. After the ATIM window, the STA first transmits any broadcast/multicast packets in the buffer. The STA then transmit the packets in the buffer corresponding to acknowledged ATIMs.

Summary. The 802.11 MAC defines a variation of the basic power saving protocol for an IBSS in the CP. All STAs in an IBSS that are in power saving mode: An STA wakes up for each beacon and for the subsequent ATIM window, acknowledges any received ATIM packets, remains awake until the end of the next ATIM window if an ATIM is received addressed to the STA (direct or broadcast/multicast), otherwise may sleep after the ATIM window finishes, may also remain awake to transmit packets to other STAs.

7.2.8.6 Fragmentation. The MAC may fragment and reassemble MSDUs (MAC service data unit) or MMPDUs (MAC management protocol data unit), and allow for fragment retransmission.

Fragment Method. A fragmentation method reduces the effect of transmission errors. Long unicast frames may be sent as burst of fragments that are individually acknowledged. Fragments and ACKs in the fragment burst are separated by a SIFS time. Fragments include an incrementing sequence control field and a "more fragments" indicator. The fragment burst finishes when the last fragment is transmitted or when an ACK is not received. Duration information in data fragments and ACK frames uses a NAV that lasts until the end of the fragment burst as shown in Fig. 7.40.

WEP. An optional "wired equivalent privacy" (WEP) mechanism protects authorized users of a WLAN from casual eavesdropping. WEP coverage is limited to wireless traffic. It is embedded in the 802.11 MAC entity and transmitted on wireless medium only; not sent to backbone. WEP implements an authentication service, to allow only authorized stations

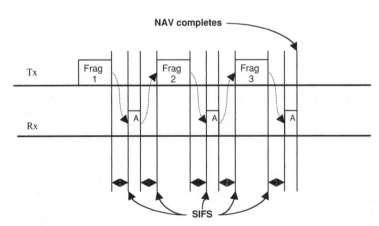

FIGURE 7.40   Illustration of fragmentation.

to use the WLAN, and a confidentiality service that encrypts data to inhibit third parties from reading it. WEP uses RC4 PRNG algorithm based on a 40-bit secret key (but no key distribution method standardized) and a 24-bit Initialization Vector (IV) that is sent with the data. It also includes an Integrity Check Value (ICV) to allow integrity check. WEP only encrypts the payload of Data frames. Encryption is done on per MMPDU basis.

Multirate Support. Multirate uses a set of rules relating to the selection of an appropriate rate. Control frames are transmitted at a basic rate from the BSSBasicRateSet as defined in the Beacon or at a mandatory PHY rate. All multicast or broadcast frames are transmitted at a basic rate. Data frames may be transmitted at any rate that is known to be supported by the receiving MAC or MACs in the case of piggybacked CF-ACKs. A responding STA shall transmit a CTS or ACK at the same rate as the immediately previous packet, if this is a mandatory PHY rate, or at the highest possible basic rate.

7.2.8.7 Layer Management

1. Overview of Management Model

   Both MAC and PHY layers conceptually include management entities, called MAC sublayer management and PHY layer management entities (MLME and PLME), shown in Fig. 7.15. These entities provide the layer management service interfaces through which layer management functions may be invoked.

   In order to provide correct MAC operation, a station management entity (SME) shall be present within each STA. The SME is a layer-independent entity that may be viewed as residing in a separate management plane or as residing "off to the side." Figure 7.15 depicts the relationship among entities.

   The various entities within this model interact in various ways via a service access point (SAP) across which are defined primitives. Other interactions are not defined explicitly within this standard, such as the interfaces between MAC and MLME and between PLCP and PLME, represented as double arrows shown in Fig. 7.15. The specific manner for these MAC and PHY management entities are integrated into the overall MAC.

   The management of six SAPs within this model shown in Fig. 7.15 are the following:

   • SAP between MAC and upper layer

   • SAP between MAC and PLCP

   • SAP between PLCP and PMD

   • SAP between SME and MLME

   • SAP between SME and PLME

   • SAP between MLME and PLME

   The latter two of the six SAPs support identical primitives and in fact may be viewed as a single SAP (called the PLME SAP) that may be used either directly by MLME or by SME. In this fashion, the model reflects what is anticipated to be a common implementation approach in which PLME functions are controlled by the MLME (on behalf of SME).

2. Generic Management Primitives

   The management information specific to each layer is represented as a management information base (MIB) for that layer. The MAC and PHY layer management entities are viewed as "containing" the MIB for that layer. The generic model of MIB-related management primitives exchanged across the management SAPs is to allow the SAP user-entity to either GET the value of a MIB attribute, or to SET the value of a MIB attribute as shown in Fig. 7.15. The invocation of a SET request primitive may require that the layer entity performs certain defined actions.

3. MLME SAP Interface

The services provided by the MLME to the SME are specified as follows:

- Establishing and maintaining the power management mode of a STA.
- Determining by scanning the characteristics of the available BSSs.
- Supporting authentication and de-authentication.
- To make a STA associated with an AP, reassociated with another AP or disassociated with an acting AP.
- Supporting the process of resetting the MAC.
- Supporting the process of creating a new BSS.

The SME uses the services provided by the MLME through the MLME SAP as shown in Fig. 7.15.

7.2.9 Wi-Fi

The Wi-Fi (Wireless Fidelity) Alliance[22] is a nonprofit international association formed in 1999 to certify interoperability of wireless Local Area Network products based on IEEE 802.11 specification. Currently, the Wi-Fi Alliance has more than 200 member companies from around the world, and more than 1500 products have received Wi-Fi℗ certification since certification began in March of 2000. The goal of the Wi-Fi Alliance's members is to enhance the user experience through product interoperability.

New wireless standards are constantly being introduced. This includes 802.11, 802.11b, 802.11a, 802.11g, 802.1X, WPA, WPA2, 802.11i, 802.11n, etc. The major standards bodies introducing these WLAN standards are the IEEE, the Wi-Fi Alliance (formerly WECA), and the IETF. Working in concert with the IEEE, the Wi-Fi Alliance is concerned with the practical implementation of IEEE WLAN standards, which was managed through an interoperability testing and certification process for vendor hardware solutions.

The current certification includes WMM (Wi-Fi Multi Media), WPA2 (Wi-Fi Protected Access 2), 11g, 11d, and 11a. The Wi-Fi Process flow is shown in Fig. 7.41.

Current Wi-Fi labs include:

1. Agilent Lab http://www.agilentcsg.timetrade.com in San Jose, CA; Melbourne, FL; Taipei, Taiwan; Tokyo, Japan; Edinburgh, UK.

2. ADT Lab http://www.adt.com.tw in Taoyuan, Taiwan.

3. CETECOM Lab http://www.cetecom.es/web/en/pag/0.htm in Malaga, Spain.

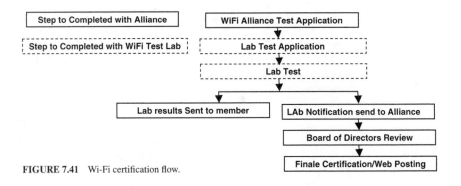

FIGURE 7.41 Wi-Fi certification flow.

4. NSTL Lab http://edata.nstl.com.tw/wifi_main.htm Labs located in Taipei, Taiwan, Blue Bell, Pennsylvania.

5. SGS Lab http://www.sgs.com/ in Taipei, Taiwan; Yokohama, Japan; Seoul, Korea.

6. TUV Lab http://www.us.tuv.com/product_testing/wifi/index.html in Cologne, Germany; Yokohama, Japan; Pleasanton, CA.

7.3 HOT SPOT

IEEE 802.11 has emerged as the worldwide standard for wireless LANs, and it has provided a ubiquitous experience for many users that need to have connectivity to Internet at different locations.

Wireless LAN (WLAN) saw its beginning in the enterprise in the late 1990s. Early adopter enterprises began deploying the technology in order to solve business problems, streamline processes, and enable the mobility of their workforce within the campus. The worldwide hot spot deployment actual and forecasts are shown in Fig. 7.42.

During the rapid growth of the Internet, numerous greenfield service providers envisioned another potential for WLAN—public access or public WLAN (PWLAN). These providers became known as wireless Internet service providers (WISPs). Their business model was to provide untethered Internet access at public locations by taking advantage of the unlicensed wireless spectrum of 802.11.

PWLAN gained momentum, especially among mobile operators that saw PWLAN as a complementary access technology to their existing mobile data networks. Demand for PWLAN services continue to grow as a result of increased adoption of WLAN technology within the enterprise and home networking markets, and as 802.11-enabled user devices become more common.

Functionally, a public hot spot[23] is a readily available wireless network connection where users with compatible wireless network devices such as PDAs, cell phones, notebook computers, or handheld games can connect to the Internet or private intranet, send and receive e-mail, and download files all without being encumbered by Ethernet cables as shown in Fig. 7.43 as an illustration. Many major cellular carriers offer public hot spots access.

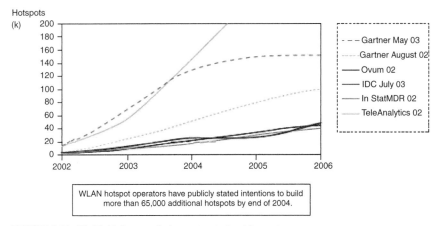

FIGURE 7.42 Worldwide hot spot deployment, actual and forecasts.

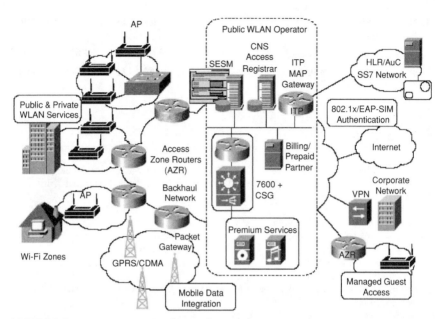

FIGURE 7.43   Hot spot network diagram using Cisco's equipments as an illustration.

Different ISP as well as service providers can support public hot spot. Customers can be connected to where they want to be. This provides users with flexibility and needed communications whenever and wherever they need as shown in Fig. 7.44.

EAP-SIM is a newly emerging EAP (Extensible Authentication Protocol) authentication protocol, designed for use with existing mobile telephone authentication systems and SIMs

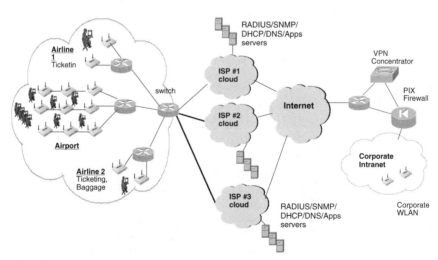

FIGURE 7.44   Airport model for multiple service providers.

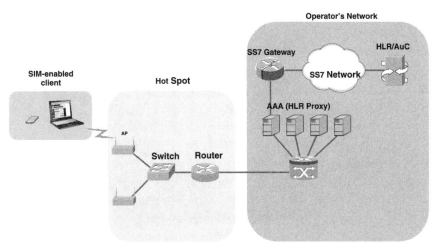

FIGURE 7.45 EAP-SIM, integration with WLAN and cellular.

(Subscriber Identity modules) for mobile phones. The EAP-SIM standard allows Wireless LAN users to authenticate access to a Wireless LAN network using a mobile phone SIM card as shown in Fig. 7.45.

Using Radiator EAP-SIM module operators and carriers are able to construct complete EAP-SIM wireless authentication and billing systems that interoperate with and utilize the existing worldwide GSM mobile phone authentication and billing systems, enabling a simple and seamless use and billing experience for roaming wireless LAN users.

7.4   802.16 AND ASSOCIATED STANDARDS

IEEE has established a hierarchy of complementary wireless standards.[24] These include IEEE 802.15 for the Personal Area Network (PAN), IEEE 802.11 for the Local Area Network (LAN), 802.16 for the Metropolitan Area Network, and the proposed IEEE 802.20 for the Wide Area Network (WAN). Each standard represents the optimized technology for a distinct market and usage model and is designed to complement the others. A good example is the proliferation of home and business wireless LANs and commercial hot spots based on the IEEE 802.11 standard. This proliferation of WLANs is driving the demand for broadband connectivity back to the Internet, which 802.16 can fulfill by providing the outdoor, long-range connection back to the service provider as shown in Fig. 7.46. For operators and service providers, systems built upon the 802.16 standard represent an easily deployable "third pipe" capable of delivering flexible and affordable last-mile broadband access for millions of subscribers in homes and businesses throughout the world.

The 802.16 standard, the "Air Interface for Fixed Broadband Wireless Access Systems," is also known as the IEEE WirelessMAN air interface.[25] This technology is designed from the ground up to provide wireless last-mile broadband access in the Metropolitan Area Network (MAN), delivering performance comparable to traditional cable, DSL, or T1 offerings.

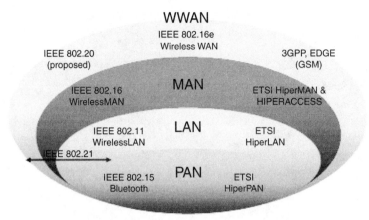

FIGURE 7.46   The IEEE 802.16 standard is one of a number of complementary wireless standards created by the IEEE to help ensure interoperability and reduce the risk of wireless technology deployment.

7.4.1   802.16a (a BWA System)

7.4.1.1   Physical Layer.   802.16a specifies a protocol[26] that supports low latency applications such as voice subscriber terminal (ST) and BTS. A single BTS will serve hundreds of ST. The standard is for Broadband Wireless Access (BWA) and is played by the World-wide Microwave Interoperability for Microwave Access (WiMAX) Forum (see Sec. 7.45). BWA is for both the physical layer environment (outdoor RF transmissions) and QoS needs, delivering high-speed Internet access to business, homes, and Wi-Fi hot spots.

- The 802.16 standard is addressed line-of-sight (LOS) environment at high-frequency bands operating in 10–66 GHz ranges.

- The 802.16a standard is designed for systems operating in bands between 2 GHz and 11 GHz for non-LOS (NLOS).

- To achieve 802.16a, three new PHY-layer specifications are

   A new single carrier PHY

   A 256 point FFT OFDM PHY

   A 2048 point FFT OFDM PHY

   Their major changes are for the lower frequency (2–11 GHz) and MAC-layer enhancements

- 802.16a supports both FDD and TDD transmissions

   The FDD and TDD frames are shown in Fig. 7.47, and a typical OFDM frame for FDD is shown in Fig. 7.48.

   The uplink and downlink duplexing in 802.16a is shown in Fig. 7.49.

- Time-Division Duplex (TDD)

   - DL & Ul time-share the same RF channel

   - Dynamic asymmatry

   - SS does not transmit/receive simultaneously (low cost)

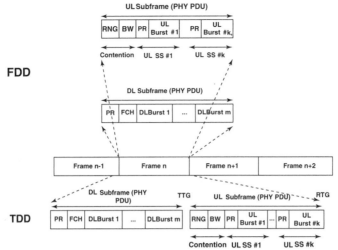

FCH: Frame Control Header   RNG: Contention Slot for Ranging Request   TTG: Tx/Rx Transmission Gap
PR: Preamble   BW: Contention Slot for BW Request   RTG: Rx/Tx Transmission Gap

FIGURE 7.47   FDD and TDD frames.

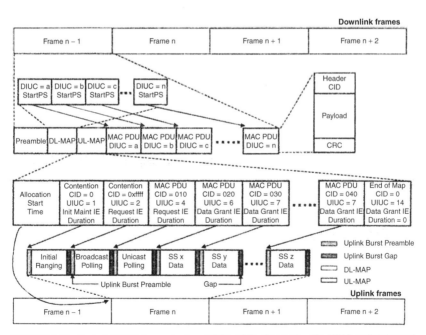

FIGURE 7.48   Typical OFDM frame structure (FDD). (CID: Connection ID, UIUC: uplink interval usage code, IE: information element)

Frequency

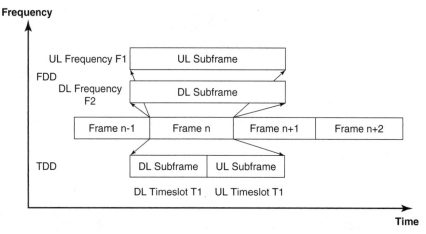

FIGURE 7.49   Uplink/downlink duplexing in 802.16a.

- Frequency-Division Duplex (FDD)
    - Downlink and Uplink on separate RF channels
    - Static asymmetry
    - Half-duplex SSs supported
    - SS does transmit/receive simuitaneously
- The OFDM signaling format is selected to support NLOS environment while maintaining a high level of spectral efficiency maximizing the use of available spectrum.
- The features of PHY layer: 802.16a delivers robust performance such as
    - Flexible channel widths (from 1.75 MHz to 20 MHz with many options in between).
    - Adaptive burst profiles.
    - Forward error correction with concatenated Reed-Solomon and convolutional encoding.
    - Optional AAS (Advanced Antenna Systems) to improve range/capacity.
    - DFS (dynamic frequency selection), minimizing interference
    - STC (space-time coding) to enhance performance in fading environments through spatial diversity.
    - Scalability, to increase the cell capacity:
        Automatic transmit power control
        Channel quality measurements for cell planning/deployment
        Reallocate spectrum through sectorization and cell splitting
        Support for multiple channel bandwidth
        TDD and FDD duplexing support

All the mentioned technologies are described in later chapters of this book.

Benefits of the PHY features:

Feature	Benefit
256-point FFT OFDM waveform	• Built-in support for addressing multipath in outdoor LOS and NLOS environments
Adaptive Modulation and variable error correction encoding per RF burst	• Ensures a robust RF link while maximizing the number of bits/second for each subscriber unit.
TDD and FDD duplexing support	• Address varying worldwide regulations where one or both may be allowed.
Flexible Channel sizes (e.g., 3.5 MHz, 5 MHz, 10 MHz, etc.)	• Provides the flexibility necessary to operate in many different frequency bands with varying channel requirements around the world.
Designed to support smart antenna systems	• Smart antennas are fast becoming more affordable, and as these costs come down their ability to suppress interference and increase system gain will become important to BWA deployments.

7.4.1.2 MAC Layer of 802.16a.[26]   MAC is used to access to the shared 802.16a medium, preventing simultaneous transmission from separate subscriber stations. 802.16a MAC consists of three sublayers.

1. Service Specific Convergence Sublayer (SSCS): It provides an interface to the upper layer entities through CS (Carrier Sense) of SAP (Service Access Point).

2. MAC CPS (Contention Period Sublayer): It provides the core MAC functions, including uplink scheduling, bandwidth request and grant, connection, ARQ, and ranging.

3. Privacy Sublayer (PS): It proves authentication and data encryption functions.

The two MAC architectures, one for base station and one for subscriber station, as shown in Figs. 7.50 and 7.51, respectively. The differences between these two are as follows:

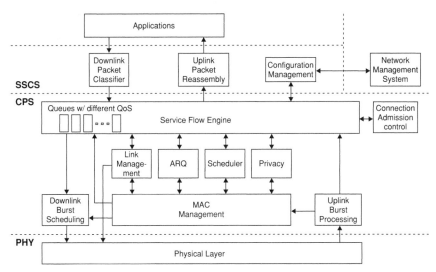

FIGURE 7.50   Base station MAC architecture.

at the base station, the network management system (NMS) controls the configuration management, also the connection administration control box controls service flow engine. At the subscriber station, the bandwidth request is implemented; also an autoconfiguration is placed as well.

Advanced topologies (mesh networks) and antenna technologies (beam forming, STC, antenna diversity) can be employed to improve coverage even further. The advanced antenna technologies are described in Chapters 8 and 16. The mesh network is described in Chapter 17.

802.16a MAC relies on a grant/request protocol for access to the medium, and it supports differentiated service levels. The protocol employs TDM data streams on the DL (downlink) and TDMA on the UL (uplink) with the hooks for a centralized schedule to support delay-sensitive services like voice and video.

By assuring collision-free data access to the channel, 16a MAC improves total system throughput and bandwidth efficiency.

Benefits of the MAC features:

Feature	Benefit
TDM/TDMA scheduled uplink/downlink frames	• Efficient bandwidth usage
Scalable from 1 to hundreds of subscribers	• Allows cost effective deployments by supporting enough subs to deliver a robust business case
Connection-oriented	• Per connection QoS
	• Faster packet routing and forwarding
QoS support Continuous Grant Real-Time Variable Bit Rate	• Low latency for delay sensitive services (TDM Voice, VoIP)
and Non-Real-Time Variable Bit Rate Best Effort	• Optimal transport for VBR traffic (e.g., video) Data prioritization
Automatic retransmission request (ARQ)	• Improves end-to-end performance by hiding RF layer induced errors from upper layer protocols
Support for adaptive modulation	• Enables highest data rates allowed by channel conditions, improving system capacity
Security and encryption (Triple DES)	• Protects user privacy
Automatic power control	• Enables cellular deployments by minimizing self-interference

7.4.1.3   Comparison of 802.11 and 802.16[27-28]

1. In the MAC layer of 802.11, CSMA/CA foundation of 802.11, basically a wireless Ethernet protocol, scaling is about the same, as with Ethernet. The MAC layer of 802.16 standard has been designed to scale from one up to 100s of users within one RF channel.

2. In 802.11 systems, the core design is either a basic CDMA approach or use OFDM with the same structure as DSL. The coverage is ten to a few hundreds of meters.

   802.16 (BWA)[28] standard is designed for both LOS and NLOS environments. The robust OFDM waveform supports high spectral efficiency over ranges from 2 to 40 kilometers with up to 70 Mbps in a single RF channel.

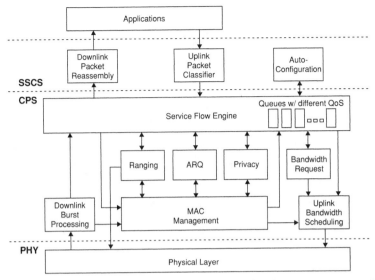

FIGURE 7.51 Subscriber station MAC architecture.

3. The 802.16 OFDM designed for BWA has in it the ability to encounter the multipath or reflections as shown in Fig. 7.52. 802.11 OFDM does not.

4. 802.11 MAC uses CSMA/CA approach and cannot deliver the QoS of a 802.16a MAC system.

7.4.2 802.16-2004

7.4.2.1 Physical Layer. 802.16-specified Fixed Broadband Wireless Access (FBWA) in the 10 to 66 GHz frequency range is shown in Fig. 7.53. The goal is to provide a wireless alternative to wireline broadband access, such as cable, DSL, and T1 and T3. 802.16a extended the frequency range to 2 to 11 GHz. 802.16c added profiles for 10 to 66 GHz equipment and defined a set of features and functions used for vendor conformance testing. 802.16-REVd-defined Air Interface for Fixed Broadband Access added 2–11 GHz profiles. 802.16-2004 (Local and Metropolitan Area Networks) is composed of 802.16 Fixed Broadband Wireless Access (10–66 GHz), 802.16a Fixed Broadband Wireless Access (2–11 GHz), and 802.16c Amendments (10–66 GHz). 802.16-2004 is sometimes known as 802.16d.

A wireless Metropolitan Area Network (WMAN) is a wireless network that covers an entire metropolitan area, such as a city and its suburbs. 802.16-2004 defines a "Fixed Wireless" MAN and 802.16e defines a "mobile" MAN as shown in Fig. 7.54, and the 802.16-2004 reference model is shown in Fig. 7.55.

802.16-2004 FBWA has point to multipoint (PMP), where traffic goes through base station (BS), and Mesh network, where communication can go directly between subscriber station (SS) options. It supports four different PHY on two distinct bands. The PHY can coexist operating in the 5-GHz unlicensed band.

One physical layer operates in the 10 to 66 GHz band and three physical layers operate in the 2 to 11 GHz band as shown in the 802.16-2004 reference model in Fig. 7.55. Both FDD and TDD modes are supported. In 10 to 66 GHz physical layer is a single carrier,

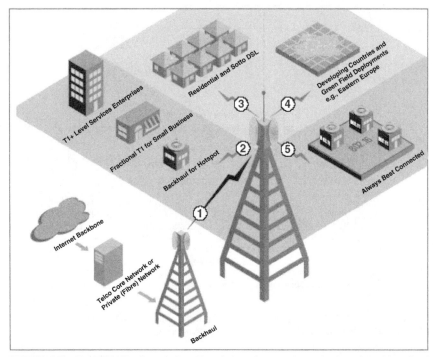

FIGURE 7.52   The IEEE 802.16 standard enables solutions that meet the needs of a variety of broadband access segments.

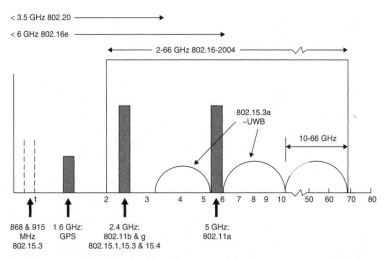

FIGURE 7.53   IEEE wireless standards operating frequencies.

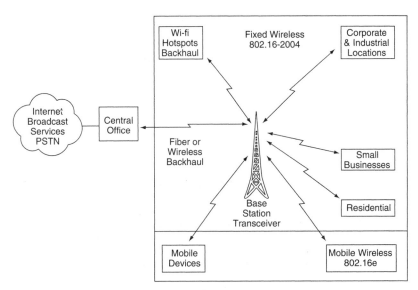

FIGURE 7.54 Broadband wireless access (BWA) fixed and mobile network.

which uses TDM/TDMA in the downlink and TDMA in the uplink. Channelization for the United States is 20 to 25 MHz and 28 MHz for Europe. The data rate range is from 32 to 134.4 Mbps through single carrier with QPSK, 16-QAM and 64-QAM as shown in Fig. 7.56.

802.16-2004 10–66 GHz supports both full duplex and half duplex devices. Subscriber stations operate in a full duplex mode and are multiplexed in TDM time slot. The half duplex devices are supported in TDMA format with preamble used for synchronization of each transmission.

Link Frame Structure (LFS) for FDD supports both full and half duplex. The Frame Control Header (FCH) is transmitted by the Base Station (BS) and it includes downlink and uplink MAPs. The DL-MAP defines the burst start times for TDM and TDMA transmissions to the mobile subscriber station (MSS). The UL-MAP provides mobile subscriber station (MSS) with scheduling information for the MSS transmission. The burst profile of FCH is

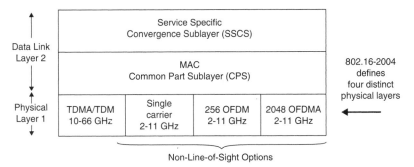

FIGURE 7.55 802.16-2004 reference model.

Channel Bandwidth MHz	Bit rates QPSK	Bit Rate 16 QAM	Bit rate 64-QAM
20	32 Mbps	64 Mbps	96 Mbps
25	40 Mbps	80 Mbps	120 Mbps
28	44.8 Mbps	89.6 Mbps	134.4 Mbps

FIGURE 7.56   802.16-2004 10 to 66 GHz single carrier supported data rate.

fixed and known by every subscriber station, and each subscriber station is associated with a specific burst.

The uplink uses TDMA, minislots of time are allocated to MSS for transmissions, and three types of bursts are supported: (1) Minislots for initial ranging access requests from new MSS, (2) minislots for request intervals such as requesting for bandwidth and responding to polls, (3) minislots for specific subscriber stations. The uplink MAP MAC message provides scheduling information on how the uplink is allocated.

There are three physical layer options for 802.16-2004: 2-11 GHz band (for single carrier TDM/TDMA), 256 OFDM and OFDMA. In the 2 to 11 GHz band, LOS is not a requirement, rain fade is not a problem, and frequency selective fading and delay spread due to multipath are issues. Power management and multiple antennas can be used to overcome the fluctuations in the radio environment. The single carrier TDM/TDMA physical layer of 802.16-2004 is similar to the TDM/TDMA solution for 11–66 GHz shown in Fig. 7.57. It uses TDM/TDMA in the downlink and TDMA in the uplink. It uses the same frame structure and supports both FDD and TDD.

The 256 OFDM Physical Layer supports variable channel bandwidths, and different channelization profiles are defined for interoperability (1.75 MHz, 3 MHz, 3.5 MHz, 5.5 MHz, 7 MHz, 10 and 20 MHz). It supports 256 subcarriers with 192 data carriers, 8 pilot carriers inserted at -88, -63, -38, -13 and $+13$, $+38$, $+63$, and $+88$ and 56 null carriers. The advantages of OFDM include high spectral efficiencies using the minimum subcarrier frequency separation, combined coding and interleaving to recover lost symbols due to fading or narrow band interference, removed intersymbol interference (ISI) caused by multipath delay spread, and use of smart antenna processing to exploit time, frequency, and spatial diversity. The smart antenna technologies are described in Sec. 8.15 and Sec. 16.5. The mesh network is described in Sec. 17.8.

The Orthogonal Frequency Division Multiple Access (OFDMA) is to have multiple users share subcarriers. It also supports variable channel bandwidth; channelization profiles include 1.25 MHz, 3.5 MHz, 7 MHz, 10 MHz, 14 MHz, 20 and 28 MHz. Subcarriers are

Coding rates:	Modulation:	Channelization profiles:
1/2	BPSK	3.5 MHz
2/3	QPSK	7 MHz
3/4	16-QAM	10 MHz
5/6	64-QAM	20 MHz
7/8	256-QAM	

FIGURE 7.57   802.16-2004 2 to 11 GHz TDMA/TDM physical layer characteristics.

divided into subchannels assigned to different subscriber stations. This means that multiple MSS can transmit at the same time.

802.16-2004 specifications include special considerations for operations in the license-exempt bands. High-Speed Unlicensed Metropolitan Area Network (HUMAN) defines operations in the 5-GHz unlicensed band (802.11a also operates in this band). In HUMAN, TDD operation is mandatory. Options include single carrier in a 10-MHz channel bandwidth, 256 OFDM in a 10-MHz channel, and OFDMA in a 10 or 20 MHz channel. Dynamic Frequency Selection (DFS) and Transmit Power Control (TPC) are two mandatory interference avoidance and sharing mechanisms.

7.4.2.2   MAC Layer.   802.16-2004 defines two Convergence Sublayers (CS), the Asynchronous Transfer Mode (ATM) CS to support ATM services and Packet CS to map packet-based protocols such as IEEE 802.3 Ethernet or IP. It supports Constant Bit Rate (CBR), Real-Time Variable Bit Rate (rt-VBR), Non-Real-Time Variable Bit Rate (nrt-VBR), and Best Effort (BE) QoS schemes.

802.16-2004 defines Fixed Broadband Wireless Access and supports four different PHY options. The MAC layer supports different levels of QoS including unsolicited Grant Service, Real-Time polling service, Non-Real-Time polling service, and Best Effort service. The convergence layer enables both ATM and IP services.

7.4.3   802.16e

7.4.3.1   Physical Layer for 802.16e.   A mobile PHY is designed to provide robust and efficient operation in harsh mobile environment, and at the same time coexistence with the fixed 802.16a. The PHY layer is based on OFDM/OFDMA, and is aligned with the 802.16a's OFDM mode.

1. The features of 802.16e[28]
   The common features with 802.16a are

- OFDM operation

- Constant FFT size of 256 for OFDM and 2048 for OFDMA

- A scalable physical layer for different channel bandwidths wih a maximum to 2048.

- 200 active subcarriers

- sampling ratios 8/7 or 7/6

   The differences with respect to the 802.16a PHY are

- UL OFDMA is a mandatory mode

- 40-50 UL (uplink) subcarriers

- Changes in the structure of UL burst

- Changes in preamble and pilot symbols to support mobility requirement.

- Use MIMO antenna array

   The comparison between 802.16 and 802.16e is shown in Fig. 7.58.

2. Coexistence of fixed and mobile users are shown in Fig. 7.58
   Both fixed and mobile users can cooperate and share the media.

- The super frame starts from a fixed preamble (DL frame prefix) and a burst carrying DL-MAP and UL-MAP messages for TDD.

- Fixed transmission leaves gaps for embedding of mobile transmissions into the super frame.

SECTION SUMMARY

	802.16-2004	802.16-2004	802.16e
Standard completion date	June 2004	June 2004	2005
Frequency Range	10-66 GHz	2-11 GHz	Below 6 GHz
Channelization	20, 25 and 28 MHz	Variable 1.5 to 20 MHz	Variable 1.5 to 20 MHz Uplink sub-channels
Licensed and Unlicensed	Yes	Yes	Licensed only
Cell Radius	1 to 3 miles	4 to 6 miles	4 to 6 miles
Line of sight	Yes	No	No
Data Rate	32 to 134.4 Mb/s in 28 MHz channel	1 to 70 Mb/s in 14 MHz channel	15 Mbps downlink 15 Mb/s uplink in 5 MHz channel
Access Technique	Single carrier	Single carrier 256-OFDM, 2K-OFDMA	OFDMA
Modulation	QPSK, 16QAM, 64QAM	QPSK, 16QAM, 64QAM	QPSK, 16QAM 64QAM
Mobility	None	None	12 to 60+ Mph

FIGURE 7.58   Comparing 802.16 and 802.16e.

- Mobile frame contains its own DL-MAP and UL-MAP that specify DL and UL allocations
- Partitioning of super frame period between fixed and mobile is flexible.
- For initial synchronization, either fixed DL frame prefix or fixed DL-MAP may point to the start of nearest mobile frame.

Figure 7.59 illustrates the structure of a TDD super-frame.

3. Uplink transmissions
   Two schemes are mutually exclusive:

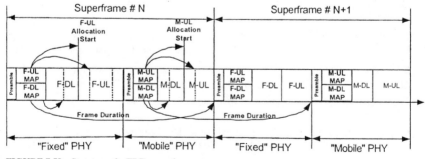

FIGURE 7.59   Structure of a TDD super frame.

- The cluster approach: The subcarriers are arranged in contiguous groups called clusters. This approach minimizes inter-subchannel interference and allows for robust channel estimation. A fast FH mechanism ensures frequency diversity is achieved.
- The scattered approach: The subcarriers are scattered across the band. This approach has no FH but maximizes the frequency diversity.

4. Downlink transmissions
OFDMA for DL is an optional mode

- A small number of DL subcarriers less than or equal to 8.
- The subscriber can process only one DL stream at a time, without significant buffering resources.

5. Additional PHY components

A. Interleaving and forward error correction (FEC): These schemes allow fine data granularity, which can be done by breaking the interleaving process into a two-step process.

- Interleaves over small groups of bits, to provide a small group of subcarriers.
- Interleaves between several groups of subcarriers.

B. Low PAPR (peak average power ratio) modes

- These modes may be optionally supported in the UL. The PAPR is reduced at the expense of data reduction. The PAPR mode is used depending on the selected sub-channelization scheme.

7.4.3.2 MAC Layer. The goal of 802.16e Mobile Wireless Metropolitan Area Network is to amend the PHY and MAC layers to support mobile operations below 6 GHz as shown in Fig. 7.60. PAPR mode is implemented. The goal is to define PHY and MAC enhancement to 802.16-2004 to support mobile operation below 6 GHz (support new regulatory allocations, particularly in the United States). The key feature is handover between Base Stations. There are several new services described as follows:

1. Scanning and Handover
The Mobile Subscriber Stations (MSS) periodically look for and monitor other base station, and the MSS may select to associate with neighbor BS to speed up potential

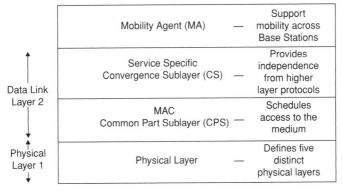

FIGURE 7.60   802.16e Mobile WMAN reference model.

future handoff. The MSS performs cell selection by synchronize with the new BS through listening for the preamble on the downlink channel. Once synchronized, it listens to the uplink MAP (UL-MAP) to determine when it can send the ranging Request Message.

a. BSs are required to transmit a broadcast message indicating all neighboring BS.

b. Follows the same handoff procedures as cellular systems.

2. EDCF

IEEE 802.16e defines the operation for EDCF (Extended DCF). EDCF is a model that allows end-devices that have delay-sensitive multimedia traffic to modify their aCWmin and ACWmax values to allow for statically greater (and more frequent) access to the medium.

When RTS/CTS is in use, most stations will hear the RTS, and all stations will hear the CTS. In either case, each node receives information indicating the length of the subsequent OFDM packet and ACK transmission.

3. Sleep Mode

a. The MSS makes a request to the BS to go into sleep mode.
The BS responds its readiness to go into sleep mode.

b. During a listening mode, the MSS stops decoding DL data and goes out of sleep mode.

c. MSS goes back to sleep mode if no message is received.

7.4.4   802.20

The goal of 802.20[24,29] is to define a standard to provide full mobility, broadband data at high speed, supporting mobility up to 150 Mph with data rate up to 6 Mbps. 802.20 operates in frequency bands below 3.5 GHz and supports 1.25 MHz and 5 MHz channel bandwidth (same as 3G cellular standards). Proposed data rate is 6 Mbps downlink and 3 Mbps uplink in a 5-MHz channel.

Two actions are specified as follows:

1. Targets for 1.25-MHz channel bandwidth: This is a reference bandwidth of 2×1.25 MHz for paired channels for FDD systems or a single 2.5-MHz channel for TDD systems. This is established to provide a common basis for measuring the bandwidth-dependent characteristics. Note that for larger bandwidths, the targets may scale proportionally with the bandwidth.

2. Various vehicular mobility classes: Recommendation ITU-R M.1034-1 establishes the following mobility classes or broad categories for the relative speed between a mobile and base station:

- Stationary (0 km/h)
- Pedestrian (up to 10 km/h)
- Typical vehicular (up to 100 km/h)
- High-speed vehicular (up to 500 km/h)
- Aeronautical (up to 1500 km/h)
- Satellite (up to 2700 km/h)

It also optimized the PHY and MAC layers for interworking with IETF IP based protocols such as mobile IP and adaptive antenna. Mobile IP allows mobile station moves between foreign agents (different subnet) while it registers with the new FA. The new FA informs the Home Agent (HA) of its IP address, and the HA then redirect the tunnel to the new FA.

Multiple Input Multiple Output (MIMO) antenna array, represents data sent and received on multiple antennas. It is the same technology used in 802.16e. It creates multiple signal paths within the same frequency, provides spatial multiplexing, and increases the capacity. MIMO can increase the range, data rate, as well as bit error rate. The advantages of using MIMO include spatial diversity gain to combat multipath fading and extended coverage. MxN diversity advantage with multiple antennas at transmitter and receiver: special efficiency gain is achieved through the opening of M parallel data pipe within the same RF channel, and interference suppression with the formation of up to N-1 nulls at receiver. The description of MIMO technology appears in Section 16.5.

The Physical Layer is undecided yet. There are several proposals. Flarion has proposed frequency hopping Orthogonal Frequency Division Multiple Access (FH-OFDMA), and Navini submitted a smart antenna Multicarrier Synchronous Code Division Multiple Access (MS-CDMA) proposal.

FH-OFDMA combines OFDMA and Frequency Hopping. OFDMA allows different mobile stations in the same cell to use different sets of tones for different subcarriers. Subcarrier can be allocated as small as one tone in a single OFDM symbol. Frequency Hopping enables mobile to hop to a different subcarrier every OFDM symbol period. This is referred to as fast tone hopping.

802.21 defines how devices can transition or "handoff" between different 802 interfaces, and includes both wired and wireless standards. 802.21 does not define handover between two APs within a given technology. For example, 802.11f defines handover between two 802.11 access points within an ESS, and 802.16e defines handover between two 802.16 base stations.

7.4.5   WiMAX Forum

WiMAX (Worldwide Interoperability for Microwave Access Forum)[30] was formed in April 2001, and the goal is to promote the adoption of IEEE 802.16 compliant equipment by operators of broadband wireless access systems. The organization is working to facilitate the deployment of broadband wireless networks based on the IEEE 802.16 standard by helping to ensure the compatibility and interoperability of broadband wireless access equipment. In this regard, the philosophy of WiMAX for the wireless MAN is comparable to that of the Wi-Fi Alliance in promoting the IEEE 802.11 standard for wireless LANs. In an effort to bring interoperability to Broadband Wireless Access, WiMAX is focusing its efforts on establishing a unique subset of baseline features grouped in what is referred to as "System Profiles" that all compliant equipment must satisfy. These profiles will establish a baseline protocol that allows equipment from multiple vendors to interoperate.

WiMAX has key benefits for operators. By choosing interoperable, standards-based equipment, the operator reduces the risk of deploying broadband wireless access systems. Economies of scale enabled by the standard help reduce monetary risk. Operators are not locked in to a single vendor because base stations will interoperate with subscriber stations from different manufacturers. Ultimately, operators will benefit from lower-cost and higher-performance equipment, as equipment manufacturers rapidly create product innovations based on a common, standards-based platform.

WiMAX's focus initially was on 802.16a 256 FFT Points of OFDM in the 2.5 and 3.5 GHz licensed bands. It is based on the vendor interests and completion of the ETSI HIPERMAN standard and desires to create a global interoperability standard. Completion of test suite and certification labs were done in summer 2004. The specifications of 802.16d was released in Dec. 2004. WiMAX is also focused on 802.16e. WiMAX specifies a version of 802.16e. The chip of WiMAX will be embedded in computer notebooks in 2006.

REFERENCES

1. Brian P. Crow, Indra Widjaja, Jeong Geon Kim and Prescott T. Sakai, "IEEE 802.11 Wireless Local Area Networks," *IEEE Communication Magazine*, Sept. 1997.

2. Daniel L. Lough, T. Keith Blankenship, Kevin J. Krizman, "A short Tutorial on Wireless LAN and 802.11," The Bradley Department of Electrical and Computer Engineering, Virginia Polytechnic Institute and State University, 1999.

3. IEEE 802.11, "Supplement to Standard for Telecommunications and Information Exchange Between Systems – LAN/MAN Specific Requirements – Part 11: Wireless MAC and PHY Specifications: High Speed Physical Layer in the 5-GHz Band," IEEE P802. 11a/D7.0, July 1999.

4. I. Howitt, "WLAN and WPAN Coexistence in UL Band," *IEEE Transactions on Vehicular Technology*, pp. 1114–1124, Vol. 50, No. 4, July 2001.

5. S. Halford, M. Webster, and J. Zyren, "CCK-OFDM Normative Text Summary," IEEE P802.11-01/436r1, July 2001.

6. R. van Nee, G. Awater, M. Morikura, H. Takanashi, M. Webster, and K. Halford, "New High Rate Wireless LAN Standards," *IEEE Communications Magazine*, December 1999.

7. Steve Halford and Karen Halford, "Implementing OFDM in Wireless Designs," Communications Design Conference, Palm Bay, FL, workshop 212, October 3, 2001.

8. Richard van Nee and Ramjee Prasad, "OFDM for Wireless Multimedia Communications," Artech House Publishers, 2000.

9. John Heiskala and John Terry, "OFDM Wireless LANs: A Technical and Practical Guide", SAMS, 2002.

10. Z. Wang and G. B. Giannakis, "Wireless Multicarrier Communications," *IEEE Signal Processing Magazine*, pp. 29–48, Vol. 17, No. 3, May 2000.

11. X. G. Xia, "Precoded and Vector OFDM Robust to Channel Spectral Nulls and with Reduced Cyclic Prefix Length in Single Transmit Antenna Systems," *IEEE Transactions on Communications*, pp. 1363–1374, Vol. 49, No. 8, August 2001.

12. P. Moose, "Matched Filters and OFDM link budgets," IEEE P802.11-01/390, May 2001.

13. Y. Zhao and S.G. Haggman, "Intercarrier Interference Self-Cancellation Scheme for OFDM Mobile Communications System's," *IEEE Transactions on Communications*, vol. 49, No. 7, pp. 1185–1191, July 2001.

14. T. Pollet, M. Van Bladel, M. Moeneclaey, "BER Sensitivity of OFDM Systems to Carrier Frequency Offset and Wiener Phase Noise," *IEEE Transaction on Communications*, vol. 43, No. 2, pp. 191–193, February 1995.

15. R. van Nee, "OFDM Codes for Peak-to-Average Power Reduction and Error Correction," IEEE Global Telecommunications Conference, London, pp. 740–744, November 1996.

16. P. Moose, "A Technique for Orthogonal Frequency Division Multiplexing Frequency Offset Correction," *IEEE Transactions on Communications*, pp. 2908–2914, Vol. 42, No. 10, October 1994.

17. N. Al-Dhahir and J. M. Cioffi, "Optimum Finite-Length Equalization for Multicarrier Transceivers," *IEEE Transactions on Communications*, Vol. 44, No. 1, pp. 56–64, January 1998.

18. J. H. Manton and Y. Hua, "Robust Frequency-Domain Precoders," *IEEE Communications Letters*, pp. 40–42, Vol. 5, No. 2, February 2000.

19. S. H. Multer-Weinfurtner, "Optimum Nyquist Windowing in OFDM Receivers," Vol. 49, No. 3, pp. 417–420, March 2001.

20. J. A. Davis and J. Jedwab, "Peak-to-Mean Power Control and Error Correction for OFDM Transmission Using Golay Sequences and Reed-Muller Codes," *Electronics Letters*, Vol. 33, 1997.

21. ANSI/IEEE Std 802.11 Part II: Wireless LAN Medium Access Control (MAC) and Physical Layer (PHY) Specifications. LAN MAN standards committee of IEEE Computer Society, 1999 Ed.

22. WiFi Alliance, www.wi-fi.org

23. Daniel Minoll, Hotspot Networks, WiFi for Public Access Locations, McGraw-Hill, 2002.

24. Telecommunications Research Associates, "Understanding the 802 Wireless Standards; 802.11, 802.15, 802.16 and 802.20," 2004, www.tra.com.

25. IEEE 802.16-2001, "IEEE Standard for Local and Metropolitan Area Networks – Part 16: Air Interface for Fixed Broadband Wireless Access Systems," April 8, 2002.

26. IEEE P802.16a/D3-2001: "Draft Amendment to IEEE Standard for Local and Metropolitan Area Networks – Part 16: Air Interface for Fixed Wireless Access Systems – Medium Access Control Modifications and Additional Physical Layers Specifications for 2–11 GHz," Mar. 25, 2002.

27. IEEE Standard 802.16: "A Technical Overview of the Wireless MAN^{TM} Air Interface for Broadband Wireless Access," IEEE org. group documentations 02/C802.16-02 05, http://grouper.ieee.org/groups/802/16/docs/02/C802.16-02.05.pdf.

28. Carl Eklund, Roger B. Marks, Kenneth L. Stanwood and Stanley Wang, "IEEE Standard 802.16: A Technical Overview," *IEEE Communication Magazine*, June 2002.

29. Ron Olexa, "Implementing 802.11, 802.16 and 802.20 Wireless Networks Planning, Troubleshooting and Operations," Newnes, 2005.

30. Intel White Paper, "IEEE 802.16 and WiMAX Broadband Wireless Access for Everyone," http://grouper.ieee.org/groups/802/16.

CHAPTER 8
CELL COVERAGE AND ANTENNAS

PART I: CELL COVERAGE

8.1 GENERAL INTRODUCTION

Cell coverage can be based on signal coverage or on traffic coverage. Signal coverage can be predicted by coverage prediction models and is usually applied to a start-up system. The task is to cover the whole area with a minimum number of cell sites. Because 100 percent cell coverage of an area is not possible, the cell sites must be engineered so that the holes are located in the no-traffic locations. The prediction model is a point-to-point model that is discussed in this chapter. We have to examine the service area as occurring in one of the following environments:

> *Human-made structures*
> In a building area
> In an open area
> In a suburban area
> In an urban area

> *Natural terrains*
> Over flat terrain
> Over hilly terrain
> Over water
> Through foliage areas

The results generated from the prediction model will differ depending on which service area is used.

There are many field-strength prediction models in the literature.[1-28] They all provide more or less an area-to-area prediction. As long as 68 percent of the predicted values from a model are within 6 to 8 dB (one standard deviation) of their corresponding measured value, the model is considered a good one. However, we cannot use area-to-area prediction models for cellular system design because of the large uncertainty of the prediction.

The model being introduced here is the point-to-point prediction model, which would provide a standard deviation from the predicted value of less than 3 dB. An explanation of this model appears in Refs. 23 and 24. Many tools can be developed based upon this model, such as cell-site choosing, interference reduction, and traffic handling.

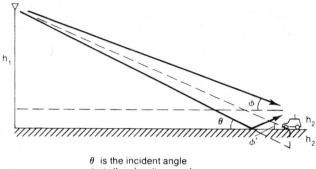

θ is the incident angle
φ is the elevation angle

FIGURE 8.1 A coordinate sketch in a flat terrain.

8.1.1 Ground Incident Angle and Ground Elevation Angle

The ground incident angle and the ground elevation angle over a communication link are described as follows. The ground incident angle θ is the angle of wave arrival incidently pointing to the ground as shown in Fig. 8.1. The ground elevation angle ϕ is the angle of wave arrival at the mobile unit as shown in Fig. 8.1.

EXAMPLE 8.1 *In a mobile radio environment, the average cell-site antenna height is about 50 m, the mobile antenna height is about 3 m, and the communication path length is 5 km. The incident angle is (see Fig. 8.1)*

$$\theta = \tan^{-1} \frac{50 \text{ m} + 3 \text{ m}}{5 \text{ km}} = 0.61°$$

The elevation angle at the antenna of the mobile unit is

$$\phi = \tan^{-1} \frac{50 \text{ m} - 3 \text{ m}}{5 \text{ km}} = 0.54°$$

The elevation angle at the location of the mobile unit is

$$\phi' = tan^{-1} \frac{50 \text{ m}}{5 \text{ km}} = 0.57°$$

8.1.2 Ground Reflection Angle and Reflection Point

Based on Snell's law, the reflection angle and incident angle are the same. Because in graphical display we usually exaggerate the hilly slope and the incident angle by enlarging the vertical scale, as shown in Fig. 8.2, then as long as the actual hilly slope is less than 10°, the reflection point on a hilly slope can be obtained by following the same method as if the reflection point were on flat ground. Be sure that the two antennas (base and mobile) have been placed vertically, not perpendicular to the sloped ground. The reason is that the actual slope of the hill is usually very small and the vertical stands for two antennas are correct. The scale drawing in Fig. 8.2 is somewhat misleading; however, it provides a clear view of the situation.

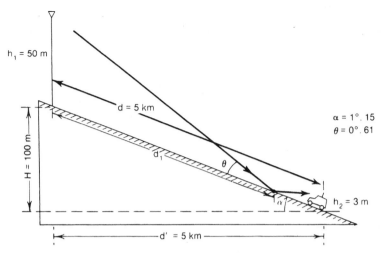

FIGURE 8.2 A coordinate sketch in a hilly terrain.

EXAMPLE 8.2 *Let $h_1 = 50$ m, $h_2 = 3$ m, $d = 5$ km, and $H = 100$ m as shown in Fig. 8.2.*

(a) Using the approximate method ($d = d' = 5$ km), the slope angle α of the hill is

$$\alpha = \tan^{-1} \frac{100 \text{ m}}{5 \text{ km}} = 1.14576°$$

the incident angle is

$$\theta = \tan^{-1} \frac{50 \text{ m} + 3 \text{ m}}{5 \text{ km}} = 0.61$$

and the reflection point location from the cell-site antenna

$$d_1 = 50/\tan\theta = 4.717 \text{ km}.$$

(b) Using the accurate method, the slope angle α of the hill is

$$\alpha = \tan^{-1} \frac{100 \text{ m}}{\sqrt{(5 \text{ km})^2 - (100 \text{ m})^2}} = \tan^{-1} \frac{100}{4999} = 1.14599°$$

The incident angle θ and the reflection point location d_1 are the same as above.

8.2 OBTAINING THE MOBILE POINT-TO-POINT MODEL (LEE MODEL)

This mobile point-to-point model is obtained in three steps: (1) generate a standard condition, (2) obtain an area-to-area prediction model, (3) obtain a mobile point-to-point model using the area-to-area model as a base. The philosophy of developing this model is to try to separate

TABLE 8.1 Generating a Standard Condition

Standard Condition	Correction Factors*
At the Base Station	
Transmitted power $P_t = 10$ W (40 dBm)	$\alpha_1 = 10 \log \frac{P'_t}{10}$
Antenna height $h_1 = 100$ ft (30 m)	$\alpha_2 = 20 \log \frac{h'_1}{h_1}$
Antenna gain $G_t = 6$ dB/dipole	$\alpha_3 = G'_t - 6$
At the Mobile Unit	
Antenna height, $h_2 = 10$ ft (3 m)	$\alpha_4 = 10 \log \frac{h'_2}{h_2}$
Antenna gain, $G_m = 0$ dB/dipole	$\alpha_5 = G'_m$

*All the parameters with primes are the new conditions.

two effects, one caused by the natural terrain contour and the other by the human-made structures, in the received signal strength.

8.2.1 A Standard Condition

To generate a standard condition and provide correction factors, we have used the standard conditions shown on the left side and the correction factors on the right side[10] of Table 8.1. The advantage of using these standard values is to obtain directly a predicted value in decibels above 1 mW expressed in dBM.

8.2.2 Obtain Area-to-Area Prediction Curves for Human-Made Structures[29]

The area-to-area prediction curves are different in different areas. In area-to-area prediction, all the areas are considered flat even though the data may be obtained from nonflat areas. The reason is that area-to-area prediction is an average process. The standard deviation of the average value indicates the degree of terrain roughness.

8.2.2.1 Effect of the Human-Made Structures. Because the terrain configuration of each city is different, and the human-made structure of each city is also unique, we have to find a way to separate these two. The way to factor out the effect due to the terrain configuration from the man-made structures is to work out a way to obtain the path loss curve for the area as if the area were flat, even if it is not. The path loss curve obtained on virtually flat ground indicates the effects of the signal loss due to solely human-made structures. This means that the different path loss curves obtained in each city show the different human-made structure in that city. To do this, we may have to measure signal strengths at those high spots and also at the low spots surrounding the cell sites, as shown in Fig. 8.3a. Then the average path loss slope (Fig. 8.3b), which is a combination of measurements from high spots and low spots along different radio paths in a general area, represents the signal received as if it is from a flat area affected only by a different local human-made structured environment. We are using 1-mi intercepts (or, alternatively, 1-km intercepts) as a starting point for obtaining the path loss curves.

Therefore, the differences in area-to-area prediction curves are due to the different man-made structures. We should realize that measurements made in urban areas are different from those made in suburban and open areas. The area-to-area prediction curve is obtained from the mean value of the measured data and used for future predictions in that area.

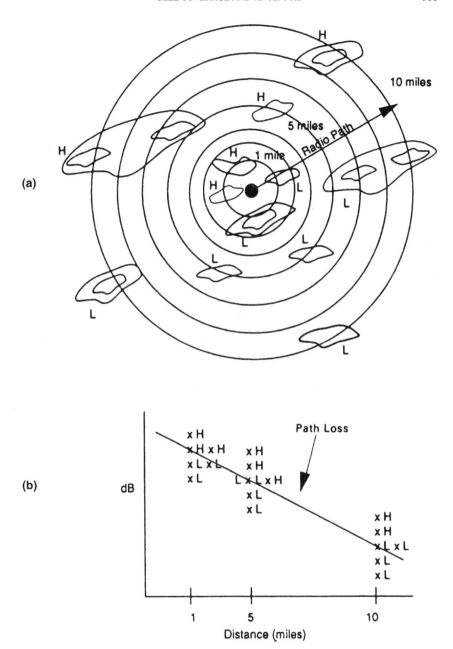

FIGURE 8.3 Propagation path loss curves for human-made structures. (*a*) For selecting measurement areas (*b*) path loss phenomenon.

Any area-to-area prediction model[1-28] can be used as a first step toward achieving the point-to-point prediction model.

One area-to-area prediction model which is introduced here[10] can be represented by two parameters: (1) the 1-mi (or 1-km) intercept point and (2) the path-loss slope. The 1-mi intercept point is the power received at a distance of 1 mi from the transmitter. There are two general approaches to finding the values of the two parameters experimentally.

1. Compare an area of interest with an area of similar human-made structures which presents a curve such as that shown in Fig. 8.3c. The suburban area curve is a commonly used curve. Because all suburban areas in the United States look alike, we can use this curve

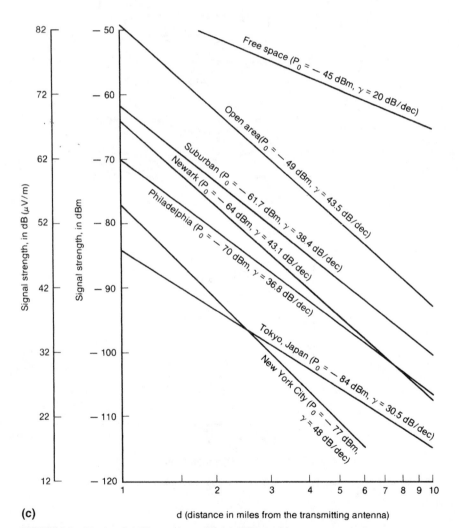

(c)   d (distance in miles from the transmitting antenna)

FIGURE 8.3 (*Continued*) (*c*) Propagation path loss in different cities.

for all suburban areas. If the area is not suburban but is similar to the city of Newark, then the curve for Newark should be used.

2. If the human-made structures of a city are different from the cities listed in Fig. 8.8c, a simple measurement should be carried out. Set up a transmitting antenna at the center of a general area. As long as the building height is comparable to the others in the area, the antenna location is not critical. Take six or seven measured data points around the 1-mi intercept and around the 10-mi boundary based on the high and low spots. Then compute the average of the 1 mi data points and of the 10 mi data points. By connecting the two values, the path-loss slope can be obtained. If the area is very hilly, then the data points measured at a given distance from the base station in different locations can be far apart. In this case, we may take more measured data points to obtain the average path-loss slope.

   If the terrain of the hilly area is generally sloped, then we have to convert the data points that were measured on the sloped terrain to a fictitiously flat terrain in that area. The conversion is based on the effective antenna-height gain as[23]

$$\Delta G = \text{effective antenna-height gain} = 20 \log \frac{h_e}{h_1} \qquad (8.2\text{-}1)$$

where h_1 is the actual height and h_e is the effective antenna height at either the 1- or 10-mi locations. The method for obtaining h_e is shown in the following section.

3. An explanation of the path-loss phenomenon is as follows. The plotted curves shown in Fig. 8.3c have different 1-mi intercepts and different slopes. The explanation can be seen in Fig. 8.3d. When the base station antenna is located in the city, then the 1-mi intercept could be very low and the slope is flattened out, as shown by Tokey's curve. When the base station is located outside the city, the intercept could be much higher and the slope is deeper, as shown by the Newark curve. When the structures are uniformly distributed, depending on the density (average separation between buildings) s shown in Fig. 8.3d, the 1-mi intercept could be high or low, but the slope may also keep at 40 dB/dec.

8.2.3   The Phase Difference between a Direct Path and a Ground-Reflected Path

Based on a direct path and a ground-reflected path (see Fig. 8.4), where a direct path is a line-of-sight (LOS) path with its received power

$$P_{\text{Los}} = P_0 \left(\frac{1}{4\pi d/\lambda} \right)^2 \qquad (8.2\text{-}2)$$

and a ground-reflected path with its reflection coefficient and phase changed after reflection, the sum of the two wave paths can be expressed as:

$$P_r = P_0 \left(\frac{1}{4\pi d/\lambda} \right)^2 \left| 1 + a_v e^{j\Delta\phi} \right|^2 \qquad (8.2\text{-}3a)$$

where $a_v = $ the reflection coefficient

   $\Delta\phi = $ the phase difference between a direct path and a reflected path

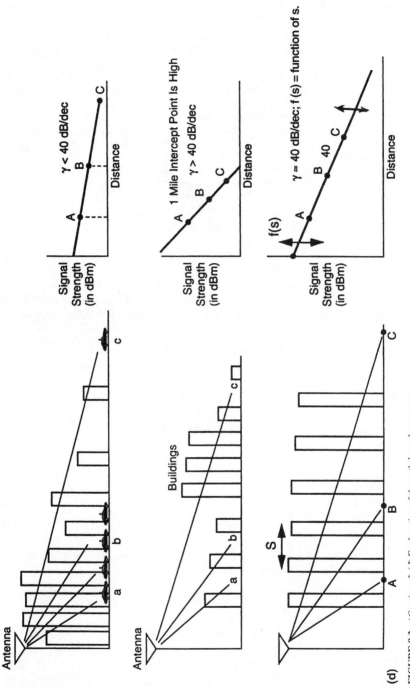

FIGURE 8.3 (*Continued*) (*d*) Explanation of the path-loss phenomenon.

356

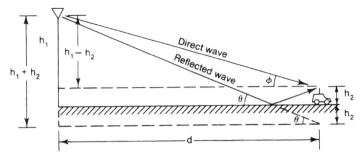

FIGURE 8.4 A simple model.

$$P_0 = \text{the transmitted power}$$

$$d = \text{the distance}$$

$$\lambda = \text{the wavelength}$$

Equation (8.2-2) indicates a two-wave model, which is used to understand the path-loss phenomenon in a mobile radio environment. It is not the model for analyzing the multipath fading phenomenon. In a mobile environment $a_e = -1$ because of the small incident angle of the ground wave caused by a relatively low cell-site antenna height.

Thus[29]

$$P_r = P_0 \left(\frac{1}{4\pi d/\lambda} \right)^2 \left| 1 - \cos \Delta\phi - j \sin \Delta\phi \right|^2$$

$$= P_0 \frac{2}{(4\pi d/\lambda)^2}(1 - \cos \Delta\phi) = P_0 \frac{4}{(4\pi d/\lambda)^2} \sin^2 \frac{\Delta\phi}{2} \qquad (8.2\text{-}3b)$$

where

$$\Delta\phi = \beta \Delta d \qquad (8.2\text{-}4)$$

and Δd is the difference, $\Delta d = d_1 - d_2$ from Fig. 8.4.

$$d_1 = \sqrt{(h_1 + h_2)^2 + d^2} \qquad (8.2\text{-}5)$$

and

$$d_2 = \sqrt{(h_1 - h_2)^2 + d^2} \qquad (8.2\text{-}6)$$

Because Δd is much smaller than either d_1 or d_2,

$$\Delta\phi = \beta \Delta d \approx \frac{2\pi}{\lambda} \frac{2h_1 h_2}{d} \qquad (8.2\text{-}7)$$

Then the received power of Eq. (8.2-3) becomes

$$P_r = P_0 \frac{\lambda^2}{(4\pi)^2 d^2} \sin^2 \frac{4\pi h_1 h_2}{\lambda d} \tag{8.2-8}$$

If $\Delta\phi$ is less than 0.6 rad, then $\sin(\Delta\phi/2) \approx \Delta\phi/2$, $\cos(\Delta\phi/2) \approx 1$ and Eq. (8.2-8) simplifies to

$$P_r = P_0 \frac{4}{16\pi^2 (d/\lambda)^2} \left(\frac{2\pi h_1 h_2}{\lambda d}\right)^2 = P_0 \left(\frac{h_1 h_2}{d^2}\right)^2 \tag{8.2-9}$$

From Eq. (8.2-9), we can deduce two relationships as follows:

$$\Delta P = 40 \log \frac{d_1}{d_2} \quad \text{(a 40 dB/dec path loss)} \tag{8.2-10a}$$

$$\Delta G = 20 \log \frac{h_1'}{h_1} \quad \text{(an antenna height gain of 6 dB/oct)} \tag{8.2-10b}$$

where ΔP is the power difference in decibels between two different path lengths and ΔG is the gain (or loss) in decibels obtained from two different antenna heights at the cell site. From these measurements, the gain from a mobile antenna height is only 3 dB/oct, which is different from the 6 dB/oct for h_1' shown in Eq. (8.2-10b). Then

$$\Delta G' = 10 \log \frac{h_2'}{h_2} \quad \text{(an antenna-height gain of 3 dB/oct)} \tag{8.2-10c}$$

EXAMPLE 8.3 *The distance $d = 8$ km. The antenna height at the cell site is 30 m, and at the mobile unit it is 3 m. Then the phase difference at 850 MHz is ($\beta \cdot \Delta d$), or 0.4 rad, which is less than 0.6 rad. Therefore, Eq. (8.2-9) can be applied.*

8.2.4 Why There Is a Constant Standard Deviation Along a Path-Loss Curve

When plotting signal strengths at any given radio-path distance, the deviation from predicted values is approximately 8 dB.[10,12] This standard deviation of 8 dB is roughly true in many different areas. The explanation is as follows. When a line-of-sight path exists, both the direct wave path and reflected wave path are created and are strong (see Fig. 8.2). When an out-of-sight path exists, both the direct wave path and the reflected wave path are weak. In either case, according to the theoretical model, the 40-dB/dec path-loss slope applies. The difference between these two conditions is the 1-mi intercept (or 1-km intercept) point. It can be seen that in the open area, the 1-mi intercept is high. In the urban area, the 1-mi intercept is low. The standard deviation obtained from the measured data remains the same along the different path-loss curves regardless of environment.

Support for the above argument can also be found from the observation that the standard deviation obtained from the measured data along the predicted path-loss curve is approximately 8 dB. The explanation is that at a distance from the cell site, some mobile unit radio paths are line-of-sight, some are partial line-of-sight, and some are out-of-sight.

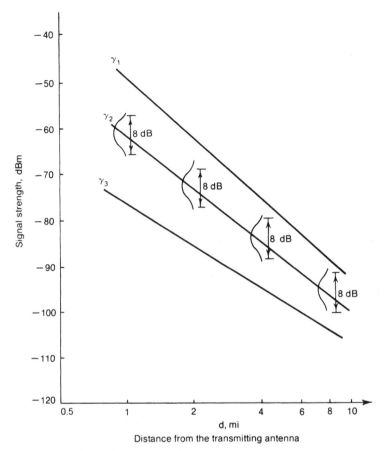

FIGURE 8.5   An 8-dB local mean spread.

Thus, the received signals are strong, normal, and weak, respectively. At any distance, the above situations prevail. If the standard deviation is 8 dB at one radio-path distance, the same 8 dB will be found at any distance. Therefore a standard deviation of 8 dB is always found along the radio path as shown in Fig. 8.5. The standard deviation of 8 dB from the measured data near the cell site is due mainly to the close-in buildings around the cell site. The same standard deviation from the measured data at a distant location is due to the great variation along different radio paths.

8.2.5   The Straight-Line Path-Loss Slope with Confidence

As we described earlier, the path-loss curves are obtained from many different runs at many different areas. As long as the distances of the radio path from the cell site to the mobile unit are the same in different runs, the signal strength data measured at that distance would be used to calculate the mean value for the path loss at that distance. In the experimental data, the path-loss deviation is 8 dB across the distance from 1.6 to 15 km (1 to 10 mi) where the general terrain contours are not generally flat. Figure 8.5 depicts this. The path-loss curve is γ. The received power can be expressed as

$$P_r = P_0 - \gamma \log \frac{r}{r_0} \tag{8.2-11}$$

The slope γ is different in different areas, but it is always a straight line in a log scale. If $\gamma = 20$ is a free-space path loss, $\gamma = 40$ is a mobile path loss.

8.2.5.1 Confidence Level.[30] A confidence level can only be applied to the path-loss curve when the standard deviation σ is known. In American suburban areas, the standard deviation $\sigma = 8$ dB. The values at any given distance over the radio path are concentrated close to the mean and have a bell-shaped (normal) distribution. The probability that 50 percent of the measured data are equal to or below a given level is[29]

$$P(x \geq C) = \int_C^\infty \frac{1}{\sqrt{2\pi}\,\sigma} e^{-(x-A)^2/2\sigma^2} dx = 50\% \tag{8.2-12}$$

where A is the mean level obtained along the path-loss slope, which is shown in Eq. (8.2-11) as

$$A = P_0 - \gamma \log \frac{r_1}{r_0}$$

Thus, level A corresponds to the distance r_1. If level A increases, the confidence level decreases, as shown in Eq. (8.2-12).

$$P(x \geq C) = P\left(\frac{x - A}{\sigma} \geq B\right) \tag{8.2-13}$$

Let $C = B\sigma + A$. The different confidence levels are shown in Table 8.2. We can see how to use confidence levels from the following example.

EXAMPLE 8.4 *From the path-loss curve, we read the expected signal level as -100 dBm at 16 km (10 mi). If the standard deviation $\sigma = 8$ dB, what level would the signal equal or exceed for a 20 percent confidence level?*

TABLE 8.2 The Different Confidence Levels

$P(x \leq C)$, %	$C = B\sigma + A$
80	$-0.85\sigma + A$
70	$-0.55\sigma + A$
60	$-0.25\sigma + A$
50	A
40	$0.25\sigma + A$
30	$0.55\sigma + A$
20	$0.85\sigma + A$
16	$1\sigma + A$
10	$1.3\sigma + A$
2.28	$2\sigma + A$

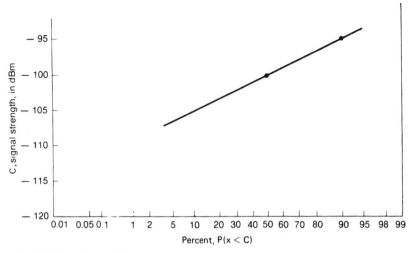

FIGURE 8.6   A log-normal curve.

$$P\left(\frac{x - A}{\sigma} \geq B\right) = 20\% \qquad x \geq B\sigma + A \qquad \text{(E8.4-1)}$$

or from Table 8.2 we obtain

$$x \geq 0.85 \times 8 + (-100) = -93.2\,\text{dBm}$$

The log normal curve with a standard deviation of 8 dB is shown in Fig. 8.6.

8.2.6   Determination of Confidence Interval

The confidence interval is often confused with confidence level. This usually happens when dealing with a particular run in a particular terrain contour. The signal strength of a run is shown in Fig. 2.6. The local mean is the envelope of the received signal, which also follows a log-normal distribution as shown in Fig. 8.6. The standard deviation of the local mean curve is a reflection of how much variation there is in terrain contour. If we know the standard deviation, then we can estimate how often the local mean (average power of the signal) falls within given limits (confidence interval).

The confidence intervals are defined as

$$P(m - \sigma \leq x \leq m + \sigma) = \int_{m-\sigma}^{m+\sigma} P(x)\,dz$$

$$= \int_{m-\sigma}^{m+\sigma} \frac{1}{\sqrt{2\pi}\,\sigma} e^{-(x-m)^2/2\sigma^2}\,dx$$

$$= \int_{-1}^{+1} \frac{1}{\sqrt{2\pi}} e^{-y^2}\,dy = 68\% \qquad \text{(8.2-14)}$$

or

$$P(m - 2\sigma \le x \le m + 2\sigma) = \int_{m-2\sigma}^{m+2\sigma} \frac{1}{\sqrt{2\pi}\,\sigma} e^{-(x-m)^2/2\sigma^2} dx = 95.45\% \qquad (8.2\text{-}15)$$

where m is the mean of all the data and σ is the standard deviation of all the data.

Equation (8.2-14) indicates that 68 percent of predicted data will fall in the range between $-\sigma$ and $+\sigma$ around this mean value. In other words, we are 68 percent confident that a predicted data point will fall between $m - \sigma$ and $m + \sigma$.

The standard deviation from Fig. 8.6 can be found from Table 8.2 as

$$\sigma = \frac{C - A}{B} \quad \left[\text{for a given percentage, } P(x \ge C)\right] \qquad (8.2\text{-}16)$$

EXAMPLE 8.5 *Find the standard deviation of a local mean curve as shown in Fig. 8.6. The confidence level for -95 dBm is found to be 10 percent, and the mean is -110 dBm. Then $C = -95$ dBm, $A = -110$ dBm, $B = 1.3$ (from Table 8.2), and*

$$\sigma = \frac{-95 - (-110)}{1.3} = 11.54 \text{ dB}$$

EXAMPLE 8.6 *If we do not have Fig. 8.6 in hand but we know the average power and its standard deviation, we can determine the percentage of signal above any level.*

Assuming that the average power is -90 dBm and the standard deviation is 9 dB, what would the signal level be if the confidence level is 30 percent?

The level would be (from Table 8.2)

$$0.55 \times 9 + (-90) = -85.05 \text{ dBm}$$

The confidence level and the confidence interval of a signal strength can be calculated from the predicted data applied to a mobile point-to-point model in an area of interest. However, the confidence level and the confidence interval of a signal strength cannot be found from a simple path-loss slope. In other words, it cannot be obtained from an area-to-area model unless the standard deviation of the model from which the curves were generated is known.

$F(50,70)$ is a common notation to indicate that a signal strength is predicted under a confidence level of 50 percent for time to 70 percent for coverage. A detailed description can be found in Ref. 29.

8.2.7 A General Formula for Mobile Radio Propagation

Here we are only interested in a general propagation path-loss formula in a general mobile radio environment, which could be a suburban area. The 1-mi intercept level in a suburban area is -61.7 dBm under the standard conditions listed in Table 8.1. Combining these data with the equation shown in Eq. (8.2-10b) from the theoretical prediction model, and Eqs. (8.2-10c) and (8.2-11) from the measured data, the received power P_r at the suburban area can be expressed as

$$P_r = (P_t - 40) - 61.7 - 38.4 \log \frac{r_1}{1 \text{ mi}} + 20 \log \frac{h_1}{100 \text{ ft}}$$

$$+ 10 \log \frac{h_2}{10 \text{ ft}} + (G_t - 6) + G_m \qquad (8.2\text{-}17)$$

Equation (8.2-17) can be simplified as

$$P_r = P_t - 157.7 - 38.4 \log r_1 + 20 \log h_1 + 10 \log h_2 + G_t + G_m \qquad (8.2\text{-}18)$$

where P_t is in decibels above 1 mW, r_1 is in miles, h_1 and h_2 are in feet, and G_t and G_m are in decibels. Equation (8.2-18) is used for suburban areas. We may like to change Eq. (8.2-18) to a general formula by using P_r at 10 mi as a reference which is -100 dBm, as shown in Fig. 8.3c. Also the 40 dB/oct slope used is generous. Then Eq. (8.2-18) changes to

$$P_r = P_t - 156 - 40 \log r_1 + 20 \log h_1 + 10 \log h_2 + G_t + G_m \qquad (8.2\text{-}19)$$

where the units of P_t, r_1, h_1, h_2, G_t, and G_m are stated below Eq. (8.2-18). Equation (8.2-19) can be used as a general formula in a mobile radio environment.

The most general formula is expressed as follows

$$P_r = P_t - K - \gamma \log r_1 + 20 \log h_1 + 10 \log h_2 + G_t + G_m \qquad (8.2\text{-}20)$$

where $P_r = P_t - K$ at $r_1 = 1$ mile, $h_1 = h_2 = 1'$, and $G_t = G_m = 0$. The value of K and γ will be different and need to be measured in different human-made environment.

8.2.8 Comments on the Propagation Models

There are many models published in the literatures.[31,32] Because of the different human-made environments with various terrain contours along the propagation path, a simple formula cannot predict the signal strength very accurately. Nevertheless, there is an uncertainty followed by the Gaussian distribution along the predicted value (mean value with a standard deviation of $\sigma = 8$ dB). Nowadays, in small cells or microcells, the 8-dB standard deviation uncertainty for prediction is too large. Then the point-to-point prediction along a particular path can be applied as stated in Sec. 8.7.

8.3 PROPAGATION OVER WATER OR FLAT OPEN AREA

Propagation over water or flat open area is becoming a big concern because it is very easy to interfere with other cells if we do not make the correct arrangements. Interference resulting from propagation over the water can be controlled if we know the cause.

In general, the permittivities ϵ_r of seawater and fresh water are the same, but the conductivities of seawater and fresh water are different. We may calculate the dielectric constants ϵ_c, where $\epsilon_c = \epsilon_r - j60\sigma\lambda$. The wavelength at 850 MHz is 0.35 m. Then ϵ_c (seawater) $= 80 - j84$ and ϵ_c (fresh water) $= 80 - j0.021$.

However, based upon the reflection coefficients formula[33,34] with a small incident angle, both the reflection coefficients for horizontal polarized waves and vertically polarized waves approach 1. Because the 180° phase change occurs at the ground reflection point, the reflection coefficient is -1. Now we can establish a scenario, as shown in Fig. 8.7. Because the two antennas, one at the cell site and the other at the mobile unit, are well above sea level, two reflection points are generated. The one reflected from the ground is close to the mobile unit; the other reflected from the water is away from the mobile unit. We recall that the only reflected wave we considered in the land mobile propagation is the one reflection point which is always very close to the mobile unit. We are now using the formula to find the field

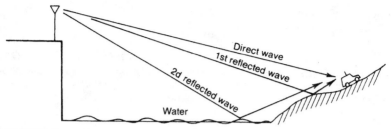

FIGURE 8.7 A model for propagation over water.

strength under the circumstances of a fixed point-to-point transmission and a land-mobile transmission over a water or flat open land condition.

8.3.1 Between Fixed Stations

The point-to-point transmission between the fixed stations over the water or flat open land can be estimated as follows. The received power P_r can be expressed as (see Fig. 8.8)

$$P_r = P_t \left(\frac{1}{4\pi d/\lambda} \right)^2 \left| 1 + a_v e^{-j\phi_v} \exp(j\Delta\phi) \right|^2 \qquad (8.3\text{-}1)$$

where $\quad P_t =$ the transmitted power

$d =$ distance between two stations

$\lambda =$ wavelength

$a_v, \phi_v =$ amplitude and phase of a complex reflection coefficient, respectively

$\Delta\phi$ is the phase difference caused by the path difference Δd between the direct wave and the reflected wave, or

$$\Delta\phi = \beta \Delta d = \frac{2\pi}{\lambda} \Delta d \qquad (8.3\text{-}2)$$

The first part of Eq. (8.3-1) is the free-space loss formula which shows the 20 dB/dec slope; that is, a 20-dB loss will be seen when propagating from 1 to 10 km.

$$P_0 = \frac{P_t}{(4\pi d/\lambda)^2} \qquad (8.3\text{-}3)$$

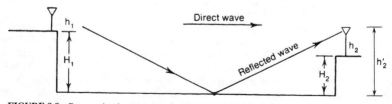

FIGURE 8.8 Propagation between two fixed stations over water or flat open land.

The $a_v e^{-j\phi_v}$ are the complex reflection coefficients and can be found from the formula[33]

$$a_v e^{-j\phi_v} = \frac{\epsilon_c \sin\theta_1 - (\epsilon_c - \cos^2\theta_1)^{1/2}}{\epsilon_c \sin\theta_1 + (\epsilon_c - \cos^2\theta_1)^{1/2}} \tag{8.3-4}$$

When the vertical incidence is small, θ is very small and

$$a_v \approx -1 \quad \text{and} \quad \phi_v = 0 \tag{8.3-5}$$

can be found from Eq. (8.3-4), ϵ_c is a dielectric constant that is different for different media. However, when $a_v e^{-j\phi_v}$ is independent of ϵ_c, the reflection coefficient remains -1 regardless of whether the wave is propagated over water, dry land, wet land, ice, and so forth. The wave propagating between fixed stations is illustrated in Fig. 8.8. Equation (8.3-1) then becomes

$$P_r = \frac{P_t}{(4\pi d/\lambda)^2} \left| 1 - \cos\Delta\phi - j\sin\Delta\phi \right|^2$$

$$= P_0(2 - 2\cos\Delta\phi) \tag{8.3-6}$$

as $\Delta\phi$ is a function of Δd and Δd can be obtained from the following calculation. The effective antenna height at antenna 1 is the height above the sea level.

$$h_1' = h_1 + H_1$$

The effective antenna height at antenna 2 is the height above the sea level.

$$h_2' = h_2 + H_2$$

as shown in Fig. 8.8, where h_1 and h_2 are actual heights and H_1 and H_2 are the heights of hills. In general, both antennas at fixed stations are high, so the reflection point of the wave will be found toward the middle of the radio path. The path difference Δd can be obtained from Fig. 8.8 as

$$\Delta d = \sqrt{(h_1' + h_2')^2 + d^2} - \sqrt{(h_1' - h_2')^2 + d^2} \tag{8.3-7}$$

Because $d \gg h_1'$ and h_2', then

$$\Delta d \approx d\left[1 + \frac{(h_1' + h_2')^2}{2d^2} - 1 - \frac{(h_1' - h_2')^2}{2d^2}\right] = \frac{2h_1'h_2'}{d} \tag{8.3-8}$$

Then, Eq. (8.3-2) becomes

$$\Delta\phi = \frac{2\pi}{\lambda}\frac{2h_1'h_2'}{d} = \frac{4\pi h_1'h_2'}{\lambda d} \tag{8.3-9}$$

Examining Eq. (8.3-6), we can set up five conditions:

1. $P_r < P_0$. The received power is less than the power received in free space; that is,

$$2 - 2\cos\Delta\phi < 1 \quad \text{or} \quad \Delta\phi < \frac{\pi}{3} \tag{8.3-10}$$

2. $P_r = 0$; that is,

$$2 - 2\cos\Delta\phi = 0 \quad \text{or} \quad \Delta\phi = \frac{\pi}{2}$$

3. $P_r = P_0$; that is,

$$2 - 2\cos \Delta\phi = 1 \quad \text{or} \quad \Delta\phi = \pm 60° = \pm\frac{\pi}{3} \tag{8.3-11}$$

4. $P_r > P_0$; that is,

$$2 - 2\cos \Delta\phi > 1 \quad \text{or} \quad \frac{\pi}{3} < \Delta\phi < \frac{5\pi}{3} \tag{8.3-12}$$

5. $P_r = 4P_0$; that is,

$$2 - 2\cos \Delta\phi = \max \quad \text{or} \quad \Delta\phi = \pi \tag{8.3-13}$$

The value of $\Delta\phi$ can be found from Eq. (8.3-9). Now we can examine the situations resulting from Eq. (8.3-9) in the following examples.

EXAMPLE 8.7 *Let a distance between two fixed stations be 30 km. The effective antenna height at one and h_1 is 150 m above sea level. Find the h_2 at the other end so that the received power always meets the condition $P_r < P_0$ at 850-MHz transmission ($\lambda = 0.35\,m$).*

Solution

$$\frac{4\pi h_1' h_2'}{\lambda d} \le \frac{\pi}{3} \tag{E8.7-1}$$

or

$$h_1' \le \frac{d\lambda}{12h_1'} = \frac{30,000 \times 0.35}{12 \times 150} = 6\ \text{m} \tag{E8.7-2}$$

EXAMPLE 8.8 *Using the same parameters given in Example 8.7, find the range of h_2 which would keep $P_r > P_0$, and find the maximum received power P_r for $P_r = 4P_0$.*
Solution

a. $\quad \dfrac{\pi}{3} \le \dfrac{4\pi h_1' h_2'}{\lambda d} \le \dfrac{5\pi}{3} \quad$ the range of h_2 for $P_r > P_0$ $\tag{E8.8-1}$

Substituting the values given in Example 8.7, we obtain

$$6\ \text{m} < h_2 < 30\ \text{m} \quad 42\ \text{m} < h_2 < 66\ \text{m} \tag{E8.8-2}$$

b. $\Delta\phi = \pi$ *for the maximum received power.*

$$h_2 = 18\ \text{m} \qquad h_2 = 54\ \text{m} \qquad h_2 = 6\ \text{m}\ [3(2n - 1)] \tag{E8.8-3}$$

where n is any integer.

8.3.2 Land-to-Mobile Transmission Over Water

The propagation model would be different for land-to-mobile transmission over water. As depicted in Fig. 8.7, there are always two equal-strength reflected waves, one from the water and one from the proximity of the mobile unit, in addition to the direct wave. The reflected wave, whose reflected point is on the water is counted because there are no surrounding objects near this point. Therefore the reflected energy is strong. The other reflected wave that has a reflection point proximal to the mobile unit also carries strong reflected energy to it.

Therefore, the reflected power of the two reflected waves can reach the mobile unit without noticeable attenuation. The total received power at the mobile unit would be obtained by summing three components.[34]

$$P_r = \frac{P_t}{(4\pi d/\lambda)^2} \left| 1 - e^{j\Delta\phi_1} - e^{j\Delta\phi_2} \right|^2 \qquad (8.3\text{-}14)$$

where $\Delta\phi_1$ and $\Delta\phi_2$ are the path-length difference between the direct wave and two reflected waves, respectively. Because $\Delta\phi_1$ and $\Delta\phi_2$ are very small usually for the land-to-mobile path, then

$$P_r = \frac{P_t}{(4\pi d/\lambda)^2} \left| 1 - \cos\Delta\phi_1 - \cos\Delta\phi_2 - j(\sin\Delta\phi_1 + \sin\Delta\phi_2) \right|^2 \qquad (8.3\text{-}15)$$

Follow the same approximation for the land-to-mobile propagation over water.

$$\cos\Delta\phi_1 \approx \cos\Delta\phi_2 \approx 1 \quad \sin\Delta\phi_1 \approx \Delta\phi_1 \quad \sin\Delta\phi_2 \approx \Delta\phi_2$$

Then

$$P_r = \frac{P_t}{(4\pi d/\lambda)^2} \left| -1 - j(\Delta\phi_2 + \Delta\phi_2) \right|^2$$

$$= \frac{P_t}{(4\pi d/\lambda)^2} \left[1 + (\Delta\phi_1 + \Delta\phi_2)^2 \right] \qquad (8.3\text{-}16)$$

In most practical cases, $\Delta\phi_1 + \Delta\phi_2 < 1$; then $(\Delta\phi_1 + \Delta\phi_2)^2 \ll 1$ and Eq. (8.3-16) reduces to

$$P_r = \frac{P_t}{(4\pi d/\lambda)^2} \qquad (8.3\text{-}17)$$

Equation (8.3-17) is the same as that expressing the power received from the free-space condition. Therefore, we may conclude that the path loss for land-to-mobile propagation over land, 40 dB/dec, is different for land-to-mobile propagation over water. In the case of propagation over water, the free-space path loss, 20 dB/dec, is applied.

8.4 FOLIAGE LOSS

Foliage loss is a very complicated topic that has many parameters and variations. The sizes of leaves, branches, and trunks, the density and distribution of leaves, branches, and trunks, and the height of the trees relative to the antenna heights will all be considered. An illustration of this problem is shown in Fig. 8.9. There are three levels: trunks, branches, and leaves. In each level, there is a distribution of sizes of trunks, branches, and leaves and also of the density and spacing between adjacent trunks, branches, and leaves. The texture and thickness of the leaves also count. This unique problem can become very complicated and is beyond the scope of this book. For a system design, the estimate of the signal reception due to foliage loss does not need any degree of accuracy.

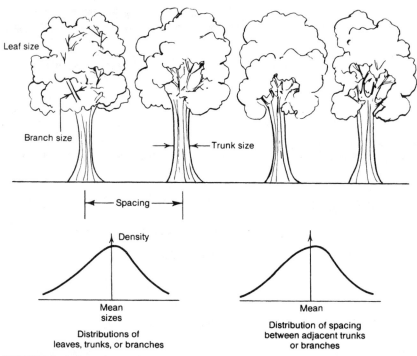

FIGURE 8.9   A characteristic of foliage environment.

Furthermore, some trees, such as maple or oak, lose their leaves in winter, while others, such as pine, never do. For example, in Atlanta, Georgia, there are oak, maple, and pine trees. In summer the foliage is very heavy, but in winter the leaves of the oak and maple trees fall and the pine leaves stay. In addition, when the length of pine needles reaches approximately 6 in., which is the half wavelength at 800 MHz, a great deal of energy can be absorbed by the pine trees. In these situations, it is very hard to predict the actual foliage loss.

However, a rough estimate should be sufficient for the purpose of system design. In tropic zones, the sizes of tree leaves are so large and thick that the signal can hardly penetrate. In this case, the signal will propagate from the top of the tree and deflect to the mobile receiver. We will include this calculation also.

Sometime the foliage loss can be treated as a wire-line loss, in decibels per foot or decibels per meter, when the foliage is uniformly heavy and the path lengths are short. When the path length is long and the foliage is nonuniform, then decibels per octaves or decibels per decade is used. Detailed discussion of foliage loss can be found in Refs. 35 to 39. In general, foliage loss occurs with respect to the frequency to the fourth power ($\sim f^{-4}$). Also, at 800 MHz the foliage loss along the radio path is 40 dB/dec, which is 20 dB more than the free-space loss, with the same amount of additional loss for mobile communications. Therefore, if the situation involves both foliage loss and mobile communications, the total loss would be 60 dB/dec (= 20 dB/dec of free-space loss + additional 20 dB due to foliage loss + additional 20 dB due to mobile communication). This situation would be the case

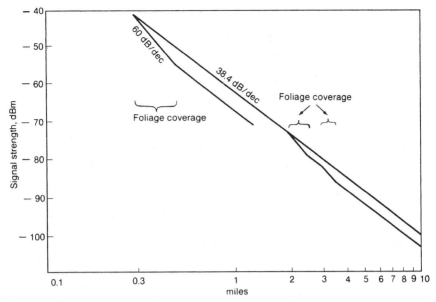

FIGURE 8.10   Foliage loss calculation in suburban areas.

if the foliage would line up along the radio path. A foliage loss in a suburban area of 58.4 dB/dec is shown in Fig. 8.10.

EXAMPLE 8.9   *In a suburban area two places are covered with trees: 2 to 2.5 mi away from the cell site and 3 to 3.5 mi away from the cell site. The additional loss due to foliage is 3 dB, according to Fig. 8.10.*

EXAMPLE 8.10   *In a suburban area, one place is 0.3 to 0.5 mi (a distance of 1056 ft) from the cell site with additional trees. The additional path loss is 5 dB due to the foliage, according to Fig. 8.10.*

As demonstrated from the above two examples, close-in foliage at the transmitter site always heavily attenuates signal reception. Therefore, the cell site should be placed away from trees. If the heavy foliage is close in at the mobile unit, the additional foliage loss must be calculated using the diffraction loss formula given in Sec. 8.7.2.

8.5   PROPAGATION IN NEAR-IN DISTANCE

8.5.1   Why Use a 1-mi Intercept?

1. Within a 1-mi radius, the antenna beamwidth, especially of a high-gain omnidirectional antenna, is narrow in the vertical plane. Thus the signal reception at a mobile unit less than 1 mi away will be reduced because of the large elevation angle which causes the mobile

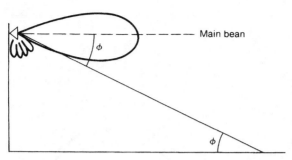

FIGURE 8.11   Elevation angle of the shadow of the antenna pattern.

unit to be in the shadow region (outside the main beam). The larger the elevation angle, the weaker the reception level due to the antenna's vertical pattern, as shown in Fig. 8.11.

2. There are fewer roads within the 1-mi radius around the cell site. The data are insufficient to create a statistical curve. Also the road orientation, in-line and perpendicular, close to the cell site can cause a big difference in signal reception levels (10–20 dB) on those roads.

3. The near-by surroundings of the cell site can bias the reception level either up or down when the mobile unit is within the 1-mi radius. When the mobile unit is 1-mi away from the cell site, the effect due to the near-by surroundings of the cell site becomes negligible.

4. For land-to-mobile propagation, the antenna height at the cell site strongly affects the mobile reception in the field; therefore, mobile reception 1 mi away has to refer to a given base-station antenna height.

8.5.2   Curves for Near-in Propagation

We usually worry about propagation at the far distance for coverage purposes. Now we also should investigate the near-in distance propagation. We may use the suburban area as an example. At the 1-mi intercept, the received level is −61.7 dBm based on the reference set of parameters; that is, the antenna height is 30 m (100 ft). If we increase the antenna height to 60 m (200 ft), a 6-dB gain is obtained. From 60 to 120 m (20 to 400-ft), another 6 dB is obtained. At the 120-m (400-ft) antenna height, the mobile received signal is the same as that received at the free space.

The antenna pattern is not isotropic in the vertical plane. A typical 6-dB omnidirectional antenna vertical beamwidth is shown in Fig. 8.12. The reduction in signal reception can be found in the figure and is listed in the table below.

At $d = 100$ m (328 ft) [mobile antenna height = 3 m (10 ft)], the incident angles and elevation angles are 11.77° and 10.72°, respectively.

Antenna Height h_1, m (ft)	Incident Angle θ, Degrees	Elevation Angle ϕ, Degrees	Attentuation α, dB
90 (300)	30.4	29.6	21
60 (200)	21.61	20.75	16
30 (100)	11.77	10.72	6

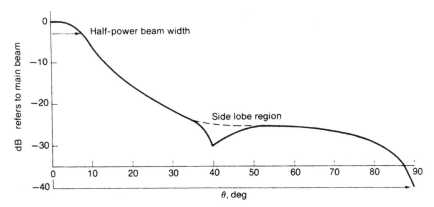

FIGURE 8.12   A typical 6-dB omnidirectional antenna beamwidth.

Because the incident angle becomes larger, the 40-dB/dec slope is no longer valid. If the antenna beam is aimed at the mobile unit, we will observe 24 dB/dec for an antenna height of 100 ft, 22 dB/dec for an antenna height of 200 ft, and 20 dB/dec for an antenna height of 400 ft or higher. The slope of 20 dB/dec is the free-space loss as shown in Fig. 8.13. The power of 11 dBm received at 0.001 mi is obtained from the free-space formula with an ERP of 46 dBm at the cell site as the standard condition (Table 8.1).

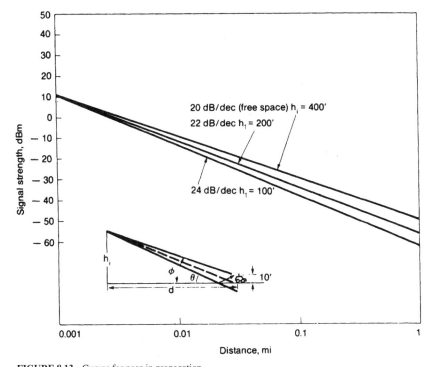

FIGURE 8.13   Curves for near-in propagation.

8.5.3 Calculation of Near-Field Propagation

The range d_F of near field can be obtained by letting $\Delta\phi$ in Eq. (8.2-7) be π.

$$\Delta\phi = \frac{4\pi h_1 h_2}{\lambda d_F} = \pi \qquad (8.5\text{-}1)$$

and then

$$d_F = \frac{4 h_1 h_2}{\lambda} \qquad (8.5\text{-}2)$$

The signal received within the nearfield ($d < d_F$) uses the free space loss formula (Eq. (8.3-17)), and the signal received outside the nearfield ($d > d_F$) can use the mobile radio path loss formula [Eq. (8.2-18)], for the best approximation.

8.6 LONG-DISTANCE PROPAGATION

The advantage of a high cell site is that it covers the signal in a large area, especially in a noise-limited system where usually different frequencies are repeatedly used in different areas. However, we have to be aware of the long-distance propagation phenomenon. A noise-limited system gradually becomes an interference-limited system as the traffic increases.[40–41] The interference is due to not only the existence of many cochannels and adjacent channels in the system, but the long-distance propagation also affects the interference.

8.6.1 Within an Area of 50-mi Radius

For a high site, the low-atmospheric phenomenon would cause the ground wave path to propagate in a non-straight-line fashion. The phenomenon is usually more pronounced over seawater because the atmospheric situation over the ocean can be varied based on the different altitudes. The wave path can bend either upward or downward. Then we may have the experience that at one spot the signal may be strong at one time but weak at another.

8.6.2 At a Distance of 320 km (200 mi)

Tropospheric wave propagation prevails at 800 MHz for long-distance propagation; sometimes the signal can reach 320 km (200 mi) away.

The wave is received 320 km away because of an abrupt change in the effective dielectric constant of the troposphere (10 km above the surface of the earth). The dielectric constant changes with temperature, which decreases with height at a rate of about 6.5°C/km and reaches −50°C at the upper boundary of the troposphere. In tropospheric propagation, the wave may be divided by refraction and reflection.

Tropospheric refraction.[40] This refraction is a gradual bending of the rays due to the changing effective dielectric constant of the atmosphere through which the wave is passing.

Tropospheric reflection. This reflection will occur where there are abrupt changes in the dielectric constant of the atmosphere. The distance of propagation is much greater than the line-of-sight propagation.

Moistness. Actually water content has much more effect than temperature on the dialec-tric constant of the atmosphere and on the manner in which the radio waves are affected. The water vapor pressure decreases as the height increases.

If the refraction index decreases with height over a portion of the range of height, the rays will be curved downward, and a condition known as *trapping,* or *duct propagation,* can occur. There are surface ducts and elevated ducts. Elevated ducts are due to large air masses and are common in southern California. They can be found at elevations of 300 to 1500 m (1000 to 5000 ft) and may vary in thickness from a few feet to a thousand feet. Surface ducts appear over the sea and are about 1.5 m (5 ft) thick. Over land areas, surface ducts are produced by the cooling air of the earth.

Tropospheric wave propagation does cause interference and can only be reduced by umbrella antenna beam patterns, a directional antenna pattern, or a low-power low-antenna-mast approach.

8.7 OBTAIN PATH LOSS FROM A POINT-TO-POINT PREDICTION MODEL: A GENERAL APPROACH

8.7.1 In Nonobstructive Condition[24,41−43]

In this condition, the direct path from the cell site to the mobile unit is not obstructed by the terrain contour. Here, two general terms should be distinguished. The *nonobstructive direct path* is a path unobstructed by the terrain contour. The *line-of-sight path* is a path that is unobstructed by the terrain contour and by man-made structures. In the former case, the cell-site antenna cannot be seen by the mobile user whereas in the latter case, it can be. Therefore, the signal reception is very strong in the line-of-sight case, which is not the case we are worrying about.

In the mobile environment, we do not often have line-of-sight conditions. Therefore, we use direct-path conditions, which are unobstructed by the terrain contour. Under these conditions, the antenna-height gain will be calculated for every location in which the mobile unit travels, as illustrated in Fig. 8.14. The method for finding the antenna-height gain is as follows.

8.7.1.1 Finding the Antenna-Height Gain[43]

1. Find the specular reflection point. Take two values from two conditions stated as follows.

   a. Connect the image antenna of the cell-site antenna to the mobile antenna; the intercept point at the ground level is considered as a potential reflection point.

   b. Connect the image antenna of the mobile antenna to the cell-site antenna; the intercept point at the ground level is also considered as a potential reflection point.

   Between two potential reflection points we choose the point which is close to the mobile unit to be the real one because more energy would be reflected to the mobile unit at that point.

2. Extend the reflected ground plane. The reflected ground plane which the reflection point is on can be generated by drawing a tangent line to the point where the ground curvature is, then extending the reflected ground plane to the location of the cell-site antenna.

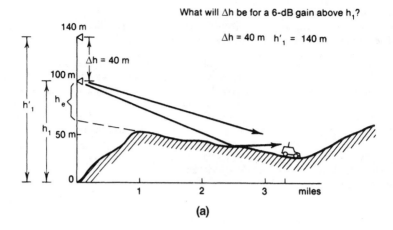

(a)

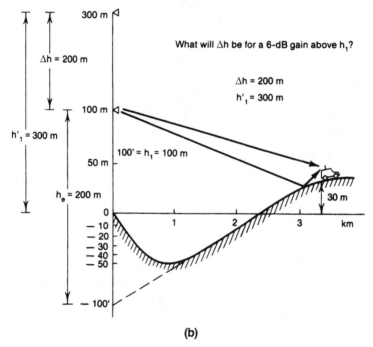

(b)

FIGURE 8.14   Calculation of effective antenna height: (*a*) case 1; (*b*) case 2.

3. Measure the effective antenna height. The effective antenna height is measured from the point where the reflected ground plan and the cell-site antenna location meet. Between these two cases shown in Fig. 8.14, h_e equals 40 m in Fig. 8.14*a* and 200 m in Fig. 8.14*b*. The actual antenna height h_1 is 100 m.

4. Calculate the antenna-height gain ΔG. The formula of ΔG is expressed as [see Eq. (8.2-10*b*)]

$$G = 20 \log \frac{h_e}{h_1} \qquad (8.7\text{-}1)$$

Then the ΔG from Fig. 8.14a is

$$\Delta G = 20 \log \frac{40}{100} = -8 \text{ dB} \qquad (\text{a negative gain in Fig. } 8.14a)$$

The ΔG from Fig. 8.14b is

$$\Delta G = 20 \log \frac{200}{100} = 6 \text{ dB} \qquad (\text{a positive gain in Fig. } 8.14b)$$

We have to realize that the antenna-height gain ΔG changes as the mobile unit moves along the road. In other words, the effective antenna height at the cell site changes as the mobile unit moves to a new location, although the actual antenna remains unchanged.

8.7.1.2 Another Physical Explanation of Effective Antenna Height. Another physical explanation of effective antenna height is shown in Fig. 8.15. In Fig. 8.15a, we have to ask which height is the actual antenna height h_1, or is the actual antenna height very important in this situation? As long as the value of H is much larger than h_2 and the length l of the

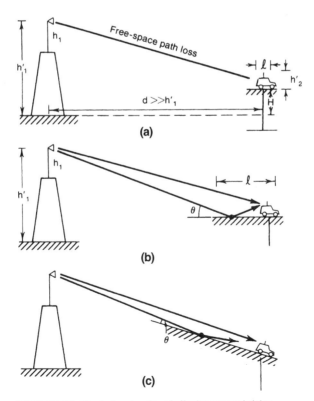

FIGURE 8.15 Physical explanation of effective antenna heights.

floor is roughly equal to the length of the vehicle, there is only one direct wave, and the free-space path loss is applied to the situation which provides a strong reception.

In Fig. 8.15b, the situation remains the same, except the length l is longer to allow a reflection point to be generated on the floor. Now two waves are created, one direct wave and one reflected wave. The stronger the reflected wave is, the larger the path loss is. The stronger reflected wave occurs at a very small incident angle θ. This means that a small incident angle corresponds to a large reflection coefficient because of the nature of the reflection mechanism, and the wave reflected from the ground is a 180° phase shift. Therefore, no matter what, the amount of reflected energy always becomes negative. The addition of a strong reflected wave to a direct wave tends to weaken the direct wave.

In Fig. 8.15c, as the incident angle θ approaches zero, the signal reception becomes very weak. The shadow-loss condition starts when both the direct wave and the reflected wave have been blocked. When the direction of the vehicle-site floor is reversed (i.e., going counter-clockwise), the incident angle θ increases and the reflection coefficient decreases. The energy reflected from the floor becomes less, and so the direct wave would reduce the small amount of energy resulting from the negative contribution from the reflected wave. The larger the incident angle of the reflected wave, the weaker the reflected wave, and the signal reception becomes the free-space condition.

When the incident angle of a wave is very small, two conditions shown in Fig. 8.16 can be considered.

1. Sparse human-made structures or trees along the propagation path. When there are few human-made structures along the propagation path, the received power is always higher

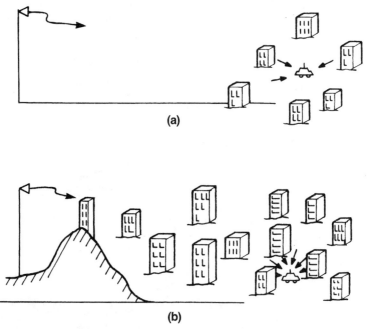

FIGURE 8.16 Man-made environment. (a) Sparse man-made structures. (b) Dense man-made structures.

than when there are many. This is why the power level received in an open area is higher than that received in a suburban area and higher still than that received in an urban area.

2. Dense human-made structures along the propagation path. There are two conditions.

a. A line-of-sight wave exists between the base station and the mobile unit. When the waves reflected by the surrounding buildings are relatively weak, less fading (rician fading)[41] is observed.

b. The mobile unit is surrounded by the scatters. If the direct reception is blocked by the surrounding buildings, Rayleigh fading is observed.

In the above two conditions the average received powers are not the same. However, if the reflected waves from surrounding buildings are very strong, the average received power from the two different conditions can be very close. It can be seen as an analog to conservation of energy. The total signal received at the mobile unit (or at the cell site) either from a single wave or from many reflected waves tentatively remains a constant. In both conditions, the propagation path loss is 40 dB/dec because both conditions are in a mobile radio environment unless the reflected wave is weak.

8.7.1.3   Comments on the Contribution of Antenna-Height Gain.   If we do not take into account the changes in antenna-height gain due to the terrain contour between the cell site and the mobile unit the path-loss slope will have a standard deviation of 8 dB. If we do take the antenna-height gain into account, values generally have a standard deviation within 2 to 3 dB.

The effects of terrain roughness are illustrated in Fig. 8.17a as changing different effective antenna heights, h_e and h'_e at different positions of the mobile unit. Then the effective antenna gain ΔG can be obtained from Eq. (8.7-1) as

$$\Delta G = 20 \log \frac{h_e}{h'_e}$$

Assume that the mobile unit is traveling in a suburban area, say northern New Jersey. The path-loss slope of this suburban area is shown in Fig. 8.3 and then plotted in Fig. 8.17b. Thus the antenna-height gains or losses are added or subtracted from the slope at their corresponding points. Now we can visualize the difference between an area-to-area prediction (use a path-loss slope) and a point-to-point prediction (after the antenna-height gain correction). The point-to-point prediction is based on the actual terrain contour along a particular radio path (in this case, the radio path and the mobile path are the same for simplicity), but the area-to-area prediction is not. This is why the area-to-area prediction has a standard deviation of 8 dB but the point-to-point prediction only has a standard deviation of less than 2 to 3 dB (see Sec. 8.8.2).

8.7.2   In Obstructive Condition

In this condition, the direct path from the cell site to the mobile unit is obstructed by the terrain contour. We would like to treat this condition as follows.

1. *Apply area-to-area prediction.* First, just apply the same steps in the area-to-area prediction as if the obstructive condition did not exist. If the area is in Philadelphia, the Philadelphia path-loss slope applies. All the correction factors would apply to finding the area-to-area prediction for a particular situation.

2. *Obtain the diffraction loss.* The diffraction loss can be found from a single knife-edge or double knife-edge case, as shown in Fig. 8.18.

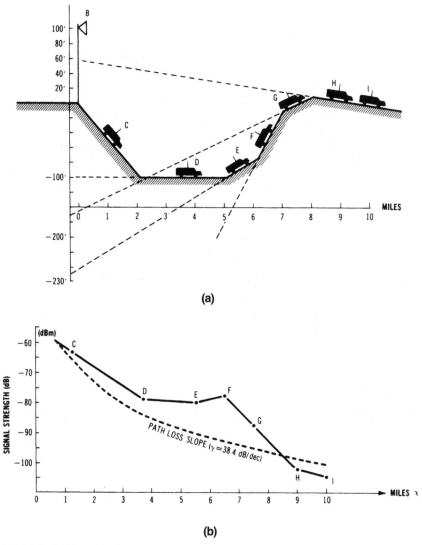

FIGURE 8.17 Illustration of the terrain effect on the effective antenna gain at each position. (*a*) Hilly terrain contour. (*b*) Point-to-point prediction. (*After Lee, Ref. 41, p. 88.*)

a. Find the four parameters for a single knife-edge case. The four parameters, the distances r_1 and r_2 from the knife-edge to the cell site and to the mobile unit, the height of the knife-edge h_p, and the operating wavelength λ, are used to find a new parameter v.

$$v = -h_p \sqrt{\frac{2}{\lambda}\left(\frac{1}{r_1} + \frac{1}{r_2}\right)} \qquad (8.7\text{-}2)$$

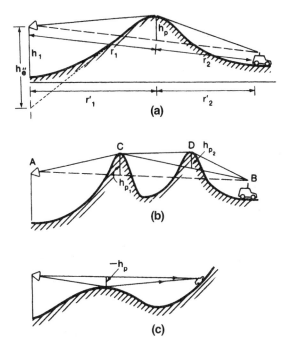

FIGURE 8.18 Diffraction loss due to obstructive conditions. (*a*) Single knife-edge; (*b*) double knife-edges; (*c*) nonclear path.

h_p is a positive number as shown in Fig. 8.18*a*, and h_p is a negative number as shown in Fig. 8.18*c*. As soon as the value of v is obtained, the diffraction loss L can be found from the curves shown in Fig. 8.19. The approximate formula below can be used with different values of v to represent the curve and be programmed into a computer.

$$1 \le v \quad L = 0\,\text{dB}$$

$$0 \le v < 1 \quad L = 20\log\,(0.5 + 0.62\,v)$$

$$-1 \le v < 0 \quad L = 20\log\,(0.5e^{0.95v})$$

$$-2.4 \le v < -1 \quad L = 20\log\,\left(0.4 - \sqrt{0.1184 - (0.1\,v + 0.38)^2}\right)$$

$$v < -2.4 \quad L = 20\log\,\left(-\frac{0.225}{v}\right) \tag{8.7-3}$$

When $h_p = 0$, the direct path is tangential to the knife-edge, and $v = 0$, as derived from Eq. (8.7-2). With $v = 0$, the diffraction loss $L = 6$ dB can be obtained from Fig. 8.19.

b. A double knife-edge case. Two knife edges can be formed by the two triangles *ACB* and *CDB* shown in Fig. 8.18*b*. Each one can be used to calculate v as v_1 and v_2. The

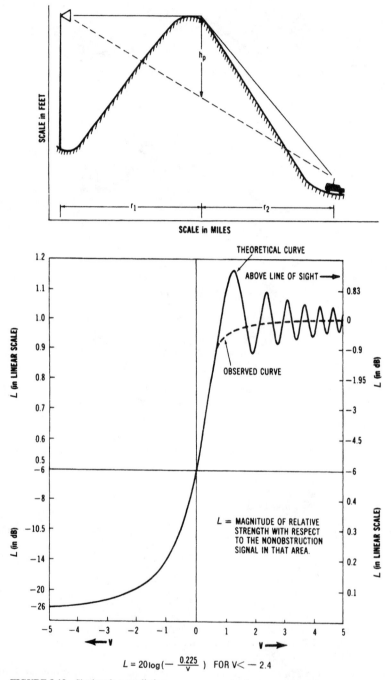

FIGURE 8.19   Shadow-loss prediction.

corresponding L_1 and L_2 can be found from Fig. 8.19. The total diffraction loss of this double knife-edge model is the sum of the two diffraction losses.

$$L_t = L_1 + L_2$$

8.7.3 Cautions in Obtaining Defraction Loss

We always draw the scales of the y and x axes differently. The same intervals represent 10 m or 10 ft in the y-axis but 1 km or 1 mi in the x-axis. In this way we can depict the elevation change more clearly. Then we have to be aware of the measurement of r_1 and r_2 shown in Fig. 8.18a. The simple way of measuring r_1 and r_2 is based on the horizontal scale as shown in the figure, where $r_1 = r_1'$ and $r_2 = r_2'$. It can be shown that the errors for $r_1 = r_1'$ and $r_2 = r_2'$ are insignificant if the scales used on both the x and y axes are the same.

When the heavy foliage is close in at the mobile unit, the loss due to foliage can be obtained from the diffraction loss. The average foliage configuration resembles the terrain configuration. Therefore the height of knife edge over the foliage configuration can be found. Then the diffraction loss due to the foliage is obtained.

8.8 FORM OF A POINT-TO-POINT MODEL

Lee[44] developed this point-to-point model in 1977, and its software implementation at AT&T Bell Lab, called ACE (Area Coverage Estimation), an in-house prediction tool called ADMS (Area Deployment of Mobile Systems), was used for deploying seven Baby Bell first-generation cellular systems in their markets in the early 1980s. Later, the portable version of ACE (PACE) could be sold as a product. Then, the model was modified by PacTel and AirTouch and called Pheonex[45] and used in AirTouch only markets, domestic (USA) and international (Europe, Korea and Japan), with successful results. The model had been taught in George Washington University as a short course from 1982 to 1998.[46] This model is a methodology, not a formula. The man-made environments are different in different areas, and to predict the signal strength on every local street is needed in the first build-up cellular system for coverage purposes. This model can provide quality coverage with minimum equipment. However, this model needs a terrain database and a computer program. Therefore, it is not easy to use as a formula for a quick prediction to be referred in academic papers. Nevertheless, the prediction results can provide an amazing match with the actual measured data as AirTouch constantly made evaluation internally with other market models.

8.8.1 General Formula of Lee Model[47−48]

Lee's point-to-point model has been described. The formula of the Lee model can be stated simply in three cases:

1. *Direct-wave case.* The effective antenna height is a major factor which varies with the location of the mobile unit while it travels.
2. *Shadow case.* No effective antenna height exists. The loss is totally due to the knife-edge diffraction loss.
3. *Over-the-water condition.* The free space path-loss is applied.

We form the model as follows:

$$
P_r = \begin{cases}
\begin{aligned}
&\text{Nonobstructive path} \\[4pt]
&= P_{r_0} - \gamma \log \underbrace{\frac{r}{r_0}}_{\text{By human-made structure}} + \underbrace{20 \log \frac{h'_e}{h_1} + \alpha}_{\text{By terrain contour}}
\end{aligned} \\[16pt]
\begin{aligned}
&\text{Obstructive path} \\[4pt]
&= P_{r_0} - \gamma \log \frac{r}{r_0} + 20 \log \frac{h''_e}{h_1} + L + \alpha \ (\text{where } h''_e \text{ is shown in Fig. 4.18}a) \\[6pt]
&= P_{r_0} - \gamma \log \underbrace{\frac{r}{r_0}}_{\text{By human-made structure}} + \underbrace{L + \alpha \ (\text{when } h''_e \approx h_1)}_{\text{By terrain contour}}
\end{aligned} \\[12pt]
\text{Land-to-mobile over water} = \text{a free-space formula}
\end{cases}
$$

(8.8-1)

(see Sec. 8.2 and Sec. 8.3)

Remarks

1. The P_r cannot be higher than that from the free-space path loss.
2. The road's orientation, when it is within 2 mi from the cell site, will affect the received power at the mobile unit. The received power at the mobile unit traveling along an in-line road can be 10 dB higher than that along a perpendicular road.
3. α is the corrected factor (gain or loss) obtained from the condition (see Sec. 8.2.1).
4. The foliage loss (Sec. 8.4) would be added depending on each individual situation. Avoid choosing a cell site in the forest. Be sure that the antenna height at the cell site is higher than the top of the trees.
5. Within one mile (or one kilometer) in a man-made environment, the received signal is affected by the buildings and street orientations. The macrocell prediction formula (Eq. 8.8-1) can not be applied in such area. A microcell prediction model by Lee is introduced and described in Ref. 48.

8.8.2   The Merit of the Point-to-Point Model

The area-to-area model usually only provides an accuracy of prediction with a standard deviation of 8 dB, which means that 68 percent of the actual path-loss data are within the ± 8 dB of the predicted value. The uncertainty range is too large. The point-to-point model reduces the uncertainty range by including the detailed terrain contour information in the path-loss predictions.

The differences between the predicted values and the measured ones for the point-to-point model were determined in many areas. In the following discussion, we compare the differences shown in the Whippany, N.J., area and the Camden-Philadelphia area. First, we plot the points with predicted values at the x-axis and the measured values at the y-axis, shown in Fig. 8.20. The 45° line is the line of prediction without error. The dots are data from the Whippany area, and the crosses are data from the Camden-Philadelphia area. Most of them, except the one at 9 dB, are close to the line of prediction without error. The mean value of all the data is right on the line of prediction without error. The standard deviation of the predicted value of 0.8 dB from the measured one.

In other areas, the differences were slightly larger. However, the standard deviation of the predicted value never exceeds the measured one by more than 3 dB. The standard deviation range is much reduced as compared with the maximum of 8 dB from area-to-area models.

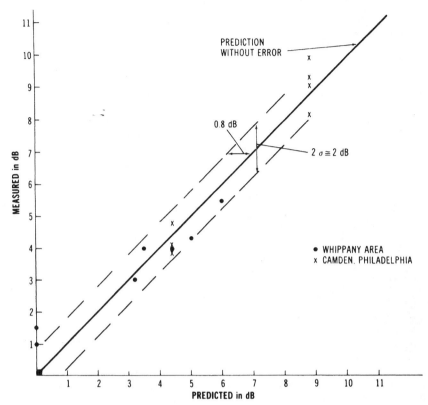

FIGURE 8.20 Indication of errors in point-to-point predictions under nonobstructive conditions. (*After Lee, Ref. 43.*)

The point-to-point model is very useful for designing a mobile cellular system with a radius for each cell of 10 mi or less. Because the data follow the log-normal distribution, 68 percent of predicted values obtained from a point-to-point prediction model are within 2 to 3 dB.

This point-to-point prediction can be used to provide overall coverage of all cell sites and to avoid cochannel interference. Moreover, the occurrence of handoff in the cellular system can be predicted more accurately.

The point-to-point prediction model is a basic tool that is used to generate a signal coverage map, an interference area map, a handoff occurrence map, or an optimum system design configuration, to name a few applications.

8.9 COMPUTER GENERATION OF A POINT-TO-POINT PREDICTION

The point-to-point prediction described in Sec. 8.8 can easily be used in a computer program. Here we describe the automated prediction in steps.[44]

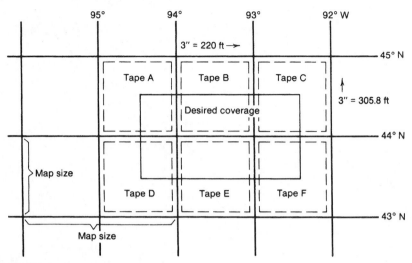

FIGURE 8.21 A coverage by six tapes.

8.9.1 Terrain Elevation Data

We may use either a 250,000:1 scale map, called a *quarter-million scale map*, or a 7.5-minute scale map issued by the U.S. Geological Survey. Both maps have the terrain elevation contours. Also, terrain elevation data tapes can be purchased from the DMA (Defense Map Agency). The quarter-million scale map tapes over the whole United States, but the 7.5-minute scale maps are only available for certain areas. Let us discuss the use of these two different scale maps.

1. Use a quarter-million scale map. Each elevation contour increment is 100 ft, which does not provide the fine detail needed for a mobile radio propagation in a hilly area. The quarter-million scale elevation data tapes made by DMA come from the quarter-million scale maps. The elevation data for two adjacent terrain contours is determined by extrapolation. Although the tape gives elevations for every 208 ft (0.01 in on the map), these elevations are not accurate because they are from the quarter-million scale map. However, in most areas, as long as the terrain contour does not change rapidly, the DMA tape can be used as a raw data base. DMA provides two kinds of tapes: a 3-second arc tape and a 0.01-in tape. The former has an elevation for every 3-second interval (about 61 to 91.5 m, or 200 to 300 ft, depending on the geographic locations) on the map. The latter has an elevation at intervals of 0.01 in (63.5 m, or 208 ft). Because the arc-second tape provides sample intervals of 3 seconds, a length of $1°$ has 1200 points. The advantage of using the arc-second tape is the continuity of sample points from one tape to another. However, for the arc-second tape the sample points are not equally far apart on the ground but are in the planar tape. Therefore, if the desired coverage is within one tape's geographic area, the planar tape is used. If the desired area is spread over more than one tape (see Fig. 8.21), the arc-second is used. The structures to a 250,000:1 scale digital elevation format is shown in Fig. 8.22.

2. Use a 7.5-minute map. A 7.5-minute map roughly covers 10×13 km^2, or 6×8 mi^2. The increment of elevation between two contours is 3 or 6 m (10 or 20 ft). The fine resolution

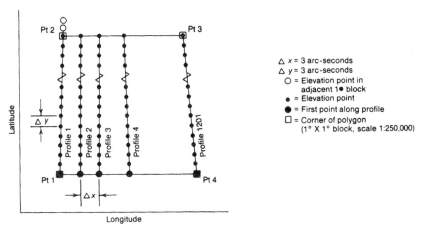

FIGURE 8.22   Structure of a 250,000:1 scale digital elevation format.

of elevation data proves to be useful for propagation prediction. There are three ways to deal with the 7.5-minute map.

a. Divide a 7.5-minute scale map into either a 30 × 45 grid map, where each grid is 300 × 300 m (1000 × 1000 ft), or into a 15 × 22.5 grid map, where each grid is 600 × 600 m (2000 × 2000 ft). An eyeball estimate of the elevation value in each grid is quite adequate.

b. Use DMA tapes in the area if the 7.5-minute tape is available. The 7.5-minute tape can have 150 3-second points. Therefore, a quarter-million scale tape can be replaced by 8 × 8 = 64 7.5 minute maps. The 7.5-minute tapes are used in those areas of the quarter-million map tapes when the terrain contour changes rapidly.

c. The elevation contour line of a 7.5-minute map with the same elevation contour can be digitized in different sample points on the map and stored in a database or on a tape. Then any two points along the terrain elevation contour can be plotted based on the actual contour lines. This is the most accurate method; however, sometimes the accuracy obtained from item *a* is sufficient for predicting the path loss.

8.9.2 Elevation Map

We prefer to use the arc-second tape since the continuity of sample points from tape to tape simplifies the calculation. In the area of N40° latitude, the average elevation of a 2000 × 2000 ft (roughly) grid can be found by taking 7 samples in latitude (a length of 2141 ft) and 10 samples in longitude (a length of 2200 ft).

$$\text{Average elevation} = \frac{\displaystyle\sum_{1}^{70} \text{sample elevations}}{70} \text{(in one grid)}$$

Figure 8.23 shows an elevation map whose grids are approximately 2200 × 2200 ft in area. The average elevation of each grid is given along with a (Y, X) tag.

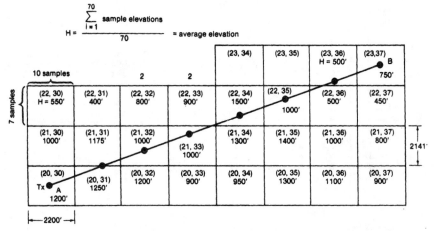

FIGURE 8.23 Elevation map.

8.9.3 Elevation Contour

Assuming that a transmitter is in a grid (20, 30) and the receiver is in a grid (23, 37), then an elevation contour can be plotted with an increment of 2200 ft for every elevation point in its corresponding grid, as shown in Fig. 8.24.

Assume that the antenna height is 100 m (300 ft) at the transmitter and 3 m (10 ft) at the receiver. We can plot a line between two ends and see that shadow-loss condition exists. An example the path loss calculation for this particular path is as follows.

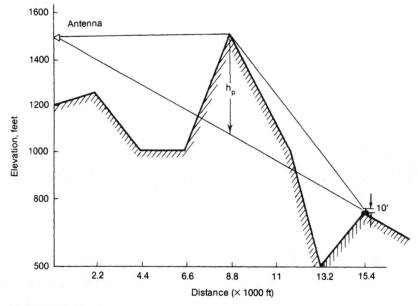

FIGURE 8.24 Elevation contour.

TABLE 8.3   Work Sheet for Example 8.11

Classification of area: suburban
Distance: 15,400 ft = 2.92 mi
From the curve: (see Fig. 8.3)
   P_r − 79.5 dBm

New data:	*Corrections:*
Transmitter power = 5 W	−3 dB
Antenna gain = −2 dB per dipole	−4 dB
Antenna height = 300 ft, $20 \log \dfrac{900}{100} = $	$\dfrac{+9.5 \text{ dB}}{+2.5 \text{ dB}}$

For flat-terrain case:
   New path loss $P_r' = -79.5 \text{ dBm} + 2.5 \text{ dB} = -77 \text{ dBm}$
For shadow-region case:
   $r_1 = 8800 \text{ ft} \quad r_2 = 6600 \text{ ft} \quad h_r = 450 \text{ ft} \quad f = 850 \text{ MHz}$
   $v = -9.63$
   $L = 32.6 \qquad \left[L = 20 \log \left(-\frac{0.225}{v} \right) \right]$
New path loss $P_x' = -77 \text{ dB} - 33 \text{ dB} = -110 \text{ dBm}$

EXAMPLE 8.11   *If the transmitter power is 5 W, the base station antenna gain is 2 dB above dipole, and its height is 300 ft, calculate the path loss from the path shown in Fig. 8.24. The results are given in Table 8.3.*

8.10   CELL-SITE ANTENNA HEIGHTS AND SIGNAL COVERAGE CELLS

8.10.1   Effects of Cell-Site Antenna Heights

There are several points that need to be clarified concerning cell-site antenna-height effects.

8.10.1.1   Antenna Height Unchanged.   If the power of the cell-site transmitter changes, the whole signal-strength map (obtained from Sec. 8.9) can be linearly updated according to the change in power.

   If the transmitted power increases by 3 dB, just add 3 dB to each grid in the signal-strength map. The relative differences in power among the grids remain the same.

8.10.1.2   Antenna Height Changed.   If the antenna height changes ($\pm \Delta h$), then the whole signal-strength map obtained from the old antenna height cannot be updated with a simple antenna gain formula as

$$\Delta g = 20 \log \frac{h_1'}{h_1} \tag{8.10-1}$$

where h_1 is the old actual antenna height and h_1' is the new actual antenna height. However, we can still use the same terrain contour data along the radio paths (from the cell-site antenna to each grid) to figure out the difference in gain resulting from the different effective antenna heights in each grid.

$$\Delta g' = 20 \log \frac{h_e'}{h_e} = 20 \log \frac{h_e \pm \Delta h}{h_e} \tag{8.10-2}$$

where h_e is the old effective antenna height and h'_e is the new effective antenna height. The additional gain (increase or decrease) will be added to the signal-strength grid based on the old antenna height.

EXAMPLE 8.12 *If the old cell-site antenna height is 30 m (100 ft) and the new one h'_1, is 45 m, the mobile unit 8 km (5 mi) away sees the old cell-site effective antenna height (h_e) being 60 m. The new cell-site effective antenna height h'_e seen from the same mobile spot can be derived.*

$$h'_e = h_e + (h'_1 - h_1) = h_e + (h'_e - h_e) = h_e + \Delta h = 60 + (45 - 30) = 75 \text{ m}$$

Since the difference between two actual antenna heights is the same as the difference between the two corresponding effective antenna heights seen from each grid, the additional gain (or loss) based on the new change of actual antenna height is

$$\Delta g' = 20 \log \frac{h'_e}{h_e} = 20 \log \left(1 + \frac{h'_1 - h_1}{h_e} \right) \tag{E8.12-1}$$

8.10.1.3 Location of the Antenna Changed. If the location of the antenna changes, the point-to-point program has to start all over again. The old point-to-point terrain contour data are no longer useful. The old effective antenna height seen from a distance will be different when the location of the antenna changes, and there is no relation between the old effective antenna height and the new effective antenna height. Therefore, every time the antenna location changes, the new point-to-point prediction calculation starts again.

8.10.1.4 Visualization of the Effective Antenna Height. The effective antenna height changes when the location of the mobile unit changes. Therefore, we can visualize the effective antenna height as always changing up or down while the mobile unit is moving. This kind of picture should be kept in mind. In addition, the following facts would be helpful.

Case 1: The mobile unit is driven up a positive slope (up to a high spot). The effective antenna height increases if the mobile unit is driving away from the cell-site antenna, and it decreases if the mobile unit is approaching the cell-site antenna. (See Fig. 8.25a.)

Case 2: The mobile unit is driven down a hill. The effective antenna height decreases if the mobile unit is driving away from the cell-site antenna, and it increases if the mobile unit is approaching the cell-site antenna. (See Fig. 8.25a.)

8.10.2 Visualization of Signal Coverage Cells

A physical cell is usually visualized as a signal-reception region around the cell site. Within the region, there are weak spots called *holes*. This is always true when a cell covers a relative flat terrain. However, a cell can contain a hilly area. Then the coverage patterns of the cell will look like those shown in Fig. 8.25b. Here the two cell sites are separated by a river. Because of the shadow loss due to the river bank, cell site A cannot cover area A', but cell site B can. The same situation applies to cell site B in area B'. Now every time the vehicle enters area A', a handoff is requested as if it were in cell B.

Therefore, in most cases, the holes in one cell are covered by the other sites. As long as the processing capacity at the MTSO can handle excessive handoff, this overlapped arrangement for filling the holes is a good approach in a noninterference condition.

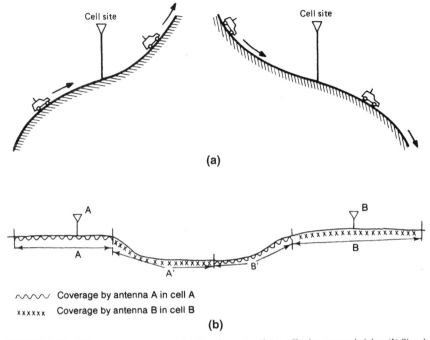

FIGURE 8.25 Different coverage concept. (*a*) Signal coverage due to effective antenna heights. (*b*) Signal coverage served by two cell sites.

8.10.3 Cell Breathing

In CDMA systems, the coverage of the cell expands and shrinks depending on the number of users in the cell. This is known as cell breathing.

Cell breathing occurs because the users of CDMA systems transmit at the same time. Each user is identified by its unique code.

The interference is averaged among the other users, so as users are added to the cell, the coverage shrinks, and as users leave the cell, the coverage expands. A user downloading data can significantly reduce the coverage, forcing voice users to "soft" handoff to another cell. The description of soft handoff is stated in Sec. 11.13. Such an increase in handoff rates would require that more cells be added to ensure coverage and eliminate any dead spots.

8.11 PROPAGATION PREDICTION IN AND THROUGH BUILDINGS

In the past, so many in-building propagation prediction models[49,50] appeared in the literature, mostly using ray-tracing techniques. Because we cannot visualize the ray paths bouncing back and forth inside the buildings, the ray paths created from the building layout

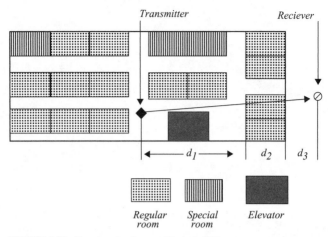

FIGURE 8.26   Top view: receiver outside the building.

are based on guessing. Therefore, the predicted results are up or down around the actual received signal. It is a statistical approach. We will simplify the statistical approach by using a group of known propagation slopes based on different areas inside the building, such as elevators, regular rooms, special rooms, open space, and so forth. Assume that the transmitter is installed in the hallway of the building, and the receiver can be located in three situations as shown in Fig. 8.26.[51]

A. Receiver is in an open space, the path loss is

$$L_{Los} = 20 \log \frac{4\pi d_1}{\lambda} + \gamma_{los} \qquad (8.11\text{-}1)$$

The distance d_1 is from the transmitter to the mobile station in the free space shown in Fig. 8.26. γ_{los} is the loss due to the two-ray model as shown in Fig. 8.4.

B. Receiver is in a room, the path loss is

$$L_{room} = L_{Los} + \gamma_1 \log \left(1 + \frac{d_2}{d_1}\right) \qquad (8.11\text{-}2)$$

where d_2 is the distance measured from the wall of the room where the signal penetrates into. γ_1 is the attenuation slope dependent on the structural material of the wall. γ_1 can be different from a regular room or from a special room such as utility room or elevator. From the measured data, the room attenuation slopes are mostly around 40 dB/dec for the regular rooms.

C. Receiver outside the building

$$L_{outside} = \gamma_{wall} + 20 \log \left(1 + \frac{d_3}{d_1 + d_2}\right) \qquad (8.11\text{-}3)$$

γ_{wall} is obtained from the measured data, typically between 15 and 20 dB. The general formula of a received power

$$P_r = P_t + G_t + G_r - L_{los} - L_{room} - L_{outside}$$

from situation A⟶

from situations A & B⟶

from situations A & B & C⟶ (8.11-4)

The model has been verified by using AirTouch and Qualcomm's building with a good agreement between predicted values and measured data.

8.12 MOBILE-TO-MOBILE PROPAGATION

8.12.1 The Transfer Function of the Propagation Channel

In mobile-to-mobile land communication,[52] both the transmitter and the receiver are in motion. The propagation path in this case is usually obstructed by buildings and obstacles between the transmitter and receiver. The propagation channel acts like a filter with a time-varying transfer function $H(f, t)$, which can be found in this section.

The two mobile units M_1 and M_2 with velocities V_1 and V_2, respectively, are shown in Fig. 8.27. Assume that the transmitted signal from M_1 is

$$s(t) = u(t)e^{jwt} \qquad (8.12\text{-}1)$$

The receiver signal at the mobile unit M_2 from an ith path is

$$s_i = r_i u(t - \tau_i)e^{j[(\omega_0 + \omega_{1i} + \omega_{2i})(t - \tau_i) + \phi_i]} \qquad (8.12\text{-}2)$$

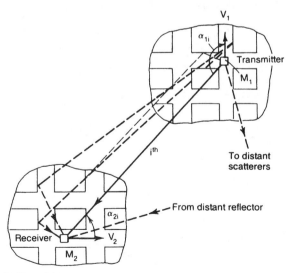

FIGURE 8.27 Vehicle-to-vehicle transmission.

where $u(t)$ = signal

                         ω_0 = RF carrier

                         r_i = Rayleigh-distributed random variable

                         ϕ_i = uniformly distributed random phase

                         τ_i = time delay on ith path

and

         ω_{1i} = Doppler shift of transmitting mobile unit on ith path

$$= \frac{2\pi}{\lambda} V_1 \cos \alpha_{1i} \tag{8.12-3}$$

         ω_{2i} = Doppler shift of receiving mobile unit on ith path

$$= \frac{2\pi}{\lambda} V_2 \cos \alpha_{2i} \tag{8.12-4}$$

where α_{1i} and α_{2i} are random angles shown in Fig. 8.27. Now assume that the received signal is the summation of n paths uniformly distributed around the azimuth.

$$s_r = \sum_{i=1}^{n} s_i(t) = \sum_{i=1}^{n} r_i u(t - \tau_i) \times \exp\{j[(\omega_0 + \omega_{1i} + \omega_{2i})(t - \tau_i) + \phi_i]\}$$

$$= \sum_{i=1}^{n} Q(\alpha_{i,t}) u(t - \tau_i) e^{j\omega_0(t - \tau_i)} \tag{8.12-5}$$

where

$$Q(\alpha_i, t) = r_i \exp\{j[(\omega_{1i} + \omega_{2i})t + \phi_i']\} \tag{8.12-6}$$

$$\phi_i' = \phi - (\omega_{1i} + \omega_{2i})\tau_i \tag{8.12-7}$$

Equation (8.12-5) can be represented as a statistical model of the channel, as shown in Fig. 8.28.
Let $u(t) = e^{j\omega t}$, then Eq. (8.12-5) becomes

$$s_r(t) = \left[\sum_{i=1}^{n} Q(\alpha_i, t) e^{-j(\omega_0 + \omega)\tau_i} \right] e^{j(\omega_0 + \omega)t} = H(f, t) e^{j(\omega_0 + \omega)t} \tag{8.12-8}$$

Therefore

$$H(f, t) = \sum_{i=1}^{n} Q(\alpha_i, t) e^{-j(\omega_0 + \omega)\tau_i} \tag{8.12-9}$$

where the signal frequency is $\omega = 2\pi f$. Equation (8.12-9) is expressed in Fig. 8.29(a).

Let $f = 0$; that is, only a sinusoidal carrier frequency is transmitted. The amplitude of the received signal envelope from Eq. (8.12-8) is

$$r = |H(0, t)| \tag{8.12-10}$$

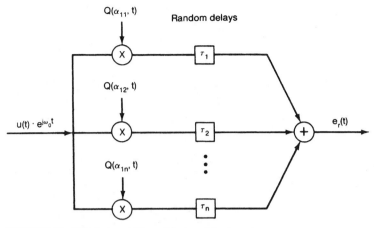

FIGURE 8.28   Statistical model for mobile-to-mobile channel.

where r is also a Rayleigh-distributed random variable with its average power of $2\sigma^2$ shown in the probability density function as

$$P(r) = \frac{r}{\sigma^2} e^{-r^2/2\sigma^2} \tag{8.12-11}$$

8.12.2   Spatial Time Correlation

Let $r_{x_1}(t_1)$ be the received signal envelope at position x_1 at time t_1. Then

$$r_{x_1}(t_1) = \sum_{i=1}^{n} r_i \exp j\left[(\omega_{1i} + \omega_{2i}) + \phi_i + \frac{2\pi}{\lambda} x_1 \cos \alpha_{1i} \right] \tag{8.12-12}$$

The same equation will apply to $r_{x_2}(t_2)$, at position x_2 at time t_2.
   The spatial time-correlation function of the envelope is given by

$$R(x_1, x_2, t_1, t_2) = \tfrac{1}{2} \langle r_{x_1}(t_1) r_{x_2}^*(t_2) \rangle \tag{8.12-13}$$

assuming that the random process r is stationary and "$*$" denotes complex conjugate. Then Eq. (8.12-13) can be rewritten as

$$R(\Delta x, \tau) = \sigma^2 J_0(\beta V_1 \tau) J_0(\beta V_2 \tau + \beta \Delta x) \tag{8.12-14}$$

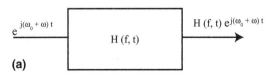

(a)

FIGURE 8.29 (*a*)   A propagation channel model.

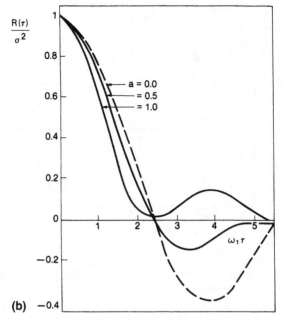

FIGURE 8.29 (*Continued*) (*b*) Normalized time-correlation function of the complex envelope for different values of $a = V_2/V_1$ versus $\omega_1 \Delta t$ where $\omega_1 = \beta V_1$. (*After Akki, Ref. 52.*)

where $\qquad\qquad \beta = 2\pi\lambda$

$\qquad\qquad J_0(\cdot) = $ zero-order Bessel function

$\qquad\qquad \tau = t_1 - t_2$

$\qquad\qquad \Delta x = x_1 - x_2$

The normalized time-correlation function is

$$\frac{R(\tau)}{\sigma^2} = J_0(\beta V_1 \tau) J_0(\beta V_2 \tau) \qquad\qquad (8.12\text{-}15)$$

Equation (8.12-15) is plotted in Fig. 8.29(*b*). The spatial correlation function $R(\Delta x)$ is

$$\frac{R(\Delta x)}{\sigma^2} = J_0(\beta \Delta x) \qquad\qquad (8.12\text{-}16)$$

Equation (8.12-16) is the same as for the base-to-mobile channel.

8.12.3 Power Spectrum of the Complex Envelope

The power spectrum $S(f)$ is a Fourier transform of $R(\tau)$ from Eq. (8.12-15).

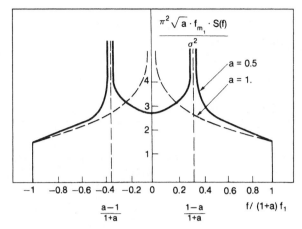

FIGURE 8.30 Power spectrum of the complex envelope for the case of $a = 0.5$ and $a = 1$ (where $a = V_2/V_1 = f_2/f_1$). (*After Akki, Ref. 52.*)

$$S(f) = \int_{-\infty}^{\infty} R(\tau)e^{-j2\pi f \tau} d(\tau) \qquad (8.12\text{-}17)$$

Substituting Eq. (8.12-15) into (8.12-17) yields

$$S(f) = \frac{\sigma^2}{\pi^2 f_1 \sqrt{a}} K \left\{ \frac{1+a}{2\sqrt{a}} \sqrt{1 - \left[\frac{f}{(1+a)f_1} \right]^2} \right\} \qquad (8.12\text{-}18)$$

where

$$a = f_2/f_1$$

$$f_1 = V_1/\lambda$$

$K(\cdot)$ = complete elliptic integral of the first kind.

Equation (8.12-18) is plotted in Fig. 8.30.
 If $V_2 = 0$ and $a = 0$, Eq. (8.12-18) can be reduced to

$$S(f) = \frac{\sigma^2}{\pi \sqrt{f_1^2 - f^2}} \qquad (8.12\text{-}19)$$

which is the equation for a base-to-mobile channel.

PART II: ANTENNAS

8.13 ANTENNAS AT CELL SITE

8.13.1 For Coverage Use: Omnidirectional Antennas

8.13.1.1 High-Gain Antennas. There are standard 6-dB and 9-dB gain omnidirectional antennas. The antenna patterns for 6-dB gain and 9-dB gain are shown in Fig. 8.31.

8.13.1.2 Start-Up System Configuration. In a start-up system, an omnicell, in which all the transmitting antennas are omnidirectional, is used. Each transmitting antenna can transmit signals from N radio transmitters simultaneously using a N-channel combiner or a broadband linear amplifier. Each cell normally can have three transmitting antennas which

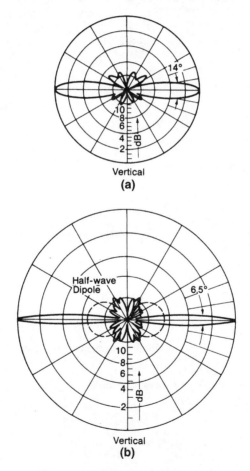

Vertical
(a)

Vertical
(b)

FIGURE 8.31 High-gain omnidirectional antennas (*reprinted from Kathrein Mobile Communications Catalog*). Gain with reference to dipole: (*a*) 6 dB; (*b*) 9 dB.

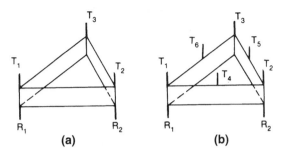

FIGURE 8.32   Cell-site antennas for omnicells: (*a*) for 3N channels; (*b*) for 6N channels.

serve 3N voice radio transmitters* simultaneously. Each sending signal is amplified by its own channel amplifier in each radio transmitter, or N channels (radio signals) pass through a broadband linear amplifier and transmit signals by means of a transmitting antenna (see Fig. 8.32*a*).

Two receiving antennas commonly can receive all 3N voice radio signals simultaneously. Then in each channel, two identical signals received by two receiving antennas pass through a diversity receiver of that channel. The receiving antenna configuration on the antenna mast is shown in Fig. 8.32. The separation of antennas for a diversity receiver is discussed in Sec. 8.14. For serving 6N voice radio transmitters from six transmitting antennas is shown in Fig. 8.32(*b*).

8.13.1.3 Abnormal Antenna Configuration.   Usually, the call traffic in each cell increases as the number of customers increases. Some cells require a greater number of radios to handle the increasing traffic. An omnicell site can be equipped with up to 90 voice radios for AMPS systems. In such cases six transmitting antennas should be used as shown in Fig. 8.32*b*. In the meantime, the number of receiving antennas is still two. In order to reduce the number of transmitting antennas, a hybrid ring combiner that can combine two 16-channel signals is found.[53] This means that only three transmitting antennas are needed to transmit 90 radio signals. However, the ring combiner has a limitation of handling power up to 600 W with a loss of 3 dB.

8.13.2   For Interference Reduction Use: Directional Antennas

When the frequency reuse scheme must be used in AMPS, cochannel interference will occur. The cochannel interference reduction factor $q = D/R = 4.6$ is based on the assumption that the terrain is flat. Because actual terrain is seldom flat, we must either increase q or use directional antennas.

8.13.2.1 Directional Antennas.   A 120°-corner reflector or 120°-plane reflector can be used in a 120°-sector cell. A 60°-corner reflector can be used in a 60°-sector cell. A typical pattern for a directional antenna of 120° beamwidth is shown in Fig. 8.33.

---

*The combiner of AMPS is designed for combining 16 voice channels. However, the AMPS cellular system divides its 312 voice channels into 21 sets; each set consists of only about 15 voice channels. Therefore the dummy loads have to be put on some empty ports of a 16-channel combiner.

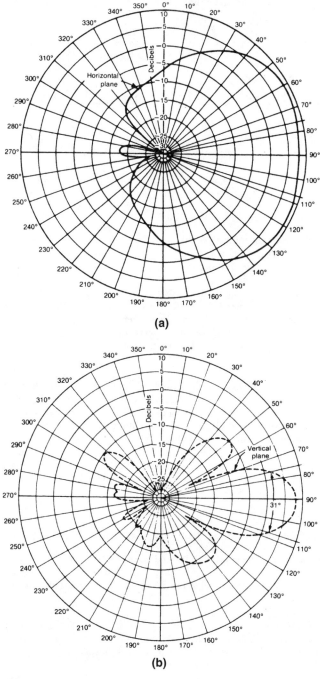

FIGURE 8.33 A typical 8-dB directional antenna pattern. (*Reprinted from Bell System Technical Journal, Vol. 58, January 1979, pp. 224–225.*) (*a*) Azimuthal pattern of 8-dB directional antenna. (*b*) Vertical pattern of 8-dB directional antenna.

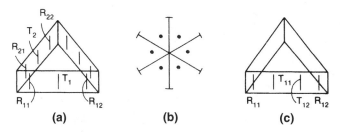

FIGURE 8.34 Directional antenna arrangement: (*a*) 120° sector (45 radios);
(*b*) 60° sector; (*c*) 120° sector (90 radios).

8.13.2.2   Normal Antenna (Mature System) Configuration

1. $K = 7$ cell pattern (120° sectors). In a $K = 7$ cell pattern for frequency reuse, if 333
channels are used, each cell would have about 45 radios. Each 120° sector would have
one transmitting antenna and two receiving antennas and would serve 16 radios. The two
receiving antennas are used for diversity (see Fig. 8.34*a*).

2. $K = 4$ cell pattern (60° sectors). We do not use $K = 4$ in an omnicell system because the
cochannel reuse distance is not adequate. Therefore, in a $K = 4$ cell pattern, 60° sectors
are used.[54] There are 24 sectors. In this $K = 4$ cell-pattern system, two approaches are
used.

   a. Transmitting-receiving 60° sectors. Each sector has a transmitting antenna carrying
   its own set of frequency radios and hands off frequencies to other neighboring sectors
   or other cells. This is a full $K = 4$ cell-pattern system. If 333 channels are used, with
   13 radios per sector, there will be one transmitting antenna and one receiving antenna
   in each sector. At the receiving end, two of six receiving antennas are selected for an
   angle diversity for each radio channel (see Fig. 8.34*b*).

   b. Receiving 60° sectors. Only 60°-sector receiving antennas are used to locate mobile
   units and handoff to a proper neighboring cell with a high degree of accuracy. All the
   transmitting antennas are omnidirectional within each cell. At the receiving end, the
   angle diversity for each radio channel is also used in this case.

8.13.2.3   Abnormal Antenna Configuration.

If the call traffic is gradually increasing,
there is an economic advantage in using the existing cell systems rather than the new
splitting cell system (splitting into smaller cells). In the former, each site is capable of
adding more radios. In a $K = 7$ cell pattern with 120° sectors, two transmitting antennas at each sector are used (Fig. 8.34*c*). Each antenna serves 16 radios if a 16-channel
combiner is used. One observation from Fig. 8.34*c* should be mentioned here. The two
transmitting antennas in each sector are placed relatively closer to the receiving antennas
than in the single transmitting antenna case. This may cause some degree of desensitization
in the receivers. The technology cited in Ref. 53 can combine 32 channels in a combiner;
therefore, only one transmitting antenna is needed in each sector. However, this one transmitting antenna must be capable of withstanding a high degree of transmitted power. If
each channel transmits 100 W, the total power that the antenna terminal could withstand is
3.2 kW.

The 32-channel combiner has a power limitation which would be specified by different
manufacturers. Two receiving antennas in each 120° sector remain the same for space
diversity use.

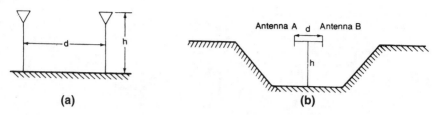

FIGURE 8.35 Diversity antenna spacing at the cell site: (*a*) $\eta = h/d$; (*b*) proper arrangement with two antennas.

8.13.3 Location Antennas

In each cell site a location receiver connects to the respective location antenna. This antenna can be either omnidirectional or shared-directional. The location receiver in AMPS can tune a channel to one of 333 channels either upon demand or periodically. This operation is discussed in Chaps. 11 and 12.

8.13.4 Setup-Channel Antennas

The setup-channel antenna usually shared with the voice-channel antenna is used to page a called mobile unit or to access a call from a mobile unit. It transmits only data. The setup-channel antenna can be an omnidirectional antenna or consist of several directional antennas at one cell site. In general, in both omnicell and sector-cell systems, one omnidirectional antenna is used for transmitting signals (data and voice) and another for receiving signals in each cell site. Setup-channel operational procedures are discussed in Chap. 12.

8.13.5 Space-Diversity Antennas Used at Cell Site

Two-branch space-diversity antennas are used at the cell site to receive the same signal with different fading envelopes, one at each antenna. The degree of correlation between two fading envelopes is determined by the degree of separation between two receiving antennas. When the two fading envelopes are combined, the degree of fading is reduced; this improvement is discussed in Ref. 55. Here the antenna setup is shown in Fig. 8.35*a*. Equation (8.13-1) is presented as an example for the designer to use.

$$\eta = \frac{h}{D} = 11 \qquad (8.13\text{-}1)$$

where h is the antenna height and D is the antenna separation. From Eq. (8.13-1), the separation $d \geq 8\lambda$ is needed for an antenna height of 100 ft (30 m) and the separation $d \geq 14\lambda$ is needed for an antenna height of 150 ft (50 m). In any omnicell system, the two space-diversity antennas should be aligned with the terrain, which should have a U shape[56] as shown in Fig. 8.35*b*.

Space-diversity antennas can separate only horizontally, not vertically; thus, there is no advantage in using a vertical separation in the design.[56] The use of space-diversity antennas at the base station is discussed in detail in Ref. 56.

8.13.6 Umbrella-Pattern Antennas

In certain situations, umbrella-pattern antennas should be used for the cell-site antennas.

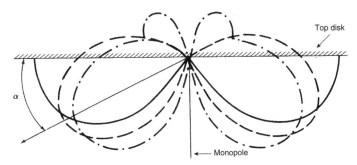

FIGURE 8.36 Vertical-plane patterns of quarter-wavelength stub antenna on infinite ground plane (solid) and on finite ground planes several wavelengths in diameter (dashed line) and about one wavelength in diameter (dotted line). (*After Kraus, Ref. 14.*)

8.13.6.1 Normal Umbrella-Pattern Antenna.[57] For controlling the energy in a confined area, the umbrella-pattern antenna can be developed by using a monopole with a top disk (top-loading) as shown in Fig. 8.36. The size of the disk determines the tilting angle of the pattern. The smaller the disk, the larger the tilting angle of the umbrella pattern.

8.13.6.2 Broadband Umbrella-Pattern Antenna.[58] The parameters of a *discone antenna* (a bioconical antenna in which one of the cones is extended to 180° to form a disk) are shown in Fig. 8.37*a*. The diameter of the disk, the length of the cone, and the opening of the cone can be adjusted to create an umbrella-pattern antenna as described in Ref. 58.

8.13.6.3 High-Gain Broadband Umbrella-Pattern Antenna. A high-gain antenna can be constructed by vertically stacking a number of umbrella-pattern antennas as shown in Fig. 8.37*b*.

$$E_0 = \frac{\sin[(Nd/2\lambda)\cos\phi]}{\sin[(d/2\lambda)\cos\phi]} \cdot \text{(individual umbrella pattern)}$$

where ϕ = direction of wave travel
  N = number of elements
  d = spacing between two adjacent elements

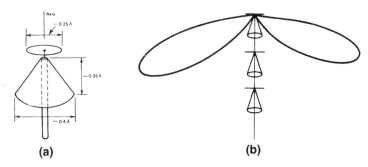

(a)   **(b)**

FIGURE 8.37 Discone antennas. (*a*) Single antenna. (*b*) An array of antennas.

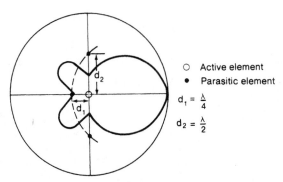

FIGURE 8.38 Application of parasitic elements. (*After Jasik, Ref. 59.*)

8.13.7 Interference Reduction Antenna[59]

A design for an antenna configuration that reduces interference in two critical directions (areas) is shown in Fig. 8.38. The parasitic (insulation) element is about 1.05 times longer than the active element. The separation d and the various values of parasitic element reactance X_{22} were shown by Brown for this application.[60]

8.14 UNIQUE SITUATIONS OF CELL-SITE ANTENNAS

8.14.1 Antenna Pattern in Free Space and in Mobile Environments

The antenna pattern we normally use is the one measured from an antenna range (open, nonurban area) or an antenna darkroom. However, when the antenna is placed in a suburban or urban environment and the mobile antenna is lower than the heights of the surroundings, the cell-site antenna pattern as a mobile unit received in a circle equi-distant around the cell site is quite different from the free-space antenna pattern. Consider the following facts in the mobile radio environment.

1. The strongest reception still coincides with the strongest signal strength of the directional antenna.[60]

2. The pattern is distorted in an urban or suburban environment.

3. For a 120° directional antenna, the backlobe (or front-to-back ratio) is about 10 dB less than the frontlobe, regardless of whether a weak sidelobe pattern or no sidelobe pattern is designed in a free-space condition. This condition exists because the strong signal radiates in front, bouncing back from the surroundings so that the energy can be received from the back of the antenna. The energy-reflection mechanism is illustrated in Fig. 8.39.

4. A design specification of the front-to-back ratio of a directional antenna (from the manufacturer's catalog) is different from the actual front-to-back ratio in the mobile radio environment. Therefore the environment and the antenna beamwidth determine how the antenna will be used in a mobile radio environment. For example, if a 60° directional antenna is used in a mobile radio environment, the actual front-to-back ratio can vary

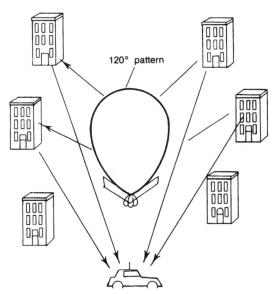

FIGURE 8.39 Front-to-back ratio of a directional antenna in a mobile radio environment.

depending on the given environment. If the close-in man-made structures in front of the antenna are highly reflectable to the signal, then the front-to-back ratio of a low-master directional antenna can be as low as 6 dB in some circumstances. In this case, the directional antenna beamwidth pattern has no correlation between it measured in the free space and it measured in the mobile radio environment. If all the buildings are far away from the directional antenna, then the front-to-back ratio measured in the field will be close to the specified antenna pattern, usually 20 dB.

8.14.2 Minimum Separation of Cell-Site Receiving Antennas

Separation between two transmitting antennas should be minimized to avoid the intermodulation discussed in Chap. 10. The minimum separation between a transmitting antenna and a receiving antenna necessary to avoid receiver desensitization is also described in Chap. 10. Here we are describing a minimum separation between two receiving antennas to reduce the antenna pattern ripple effects.

The two receiving antennas are used for a space-diversity receiver. Because of the near-field disturbance due to the close spacing, ripples will form in the antenna patterns (Fig. 8.40). The difference in power reception between two antennas at different angles of arrival is shown in Fig. 8.40. If the antennas are located closer; the difference in power between two antennas at a given pointing angle increases. Although the power difference is confined to a small sector, it affects a large section of the street as shown in Fig. 8.40. If the power difference is excessive, use of a space diversity will have no effect reducing fading. At 850 MHz, the separation of eight wavelengths between two receiving antennas creates a power difference of ± 2 dB, which is tolerable for the advantageous use of a diversity scheme.[61]

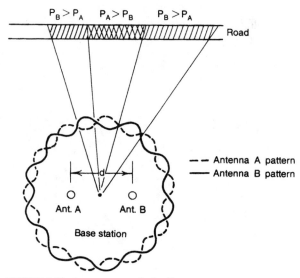

FIGURE 8.40   Antenna pattern ripple effect.

8.14.3 Regular Check of the Cell-Site Antennas

Air-pressurized cable is often used in cell-site antennas to prevent moisture from entering the cable and causing excessive attenuation. One method of checking the cell-site antennas is to measure the power delivered to the antenna terminal; however, few systems have this capability. The other method is to measure the VSWR at the bottom of the tower. In this case the loss of reflected power due to the cable under normal conditions should be considered. For a high tower, the VSWR reading may not be accurate.

If each cable connector has 1-dB loss due to energy leakage and two midsection 1-dB loss connectors are used in the transmitted system as shown in Fig. 8.41, the reflected power P_b indicated in the VSWR would be 4 dB less than the real reflected power.

8.14.4 Choosing an Antenna Site

In antenna site selection we have relied on the point-to-point prediction method (discussed in Chap. 8), which is applicable primarily for coverage patterns under conditions of light call traffic in the system. Reduction of interference is an important factor in antenna site selection.

When a site is chosen on the map, there is a 50 percent chance that the site location cannot be acquired. A written rule states that[62] an antenna location can be found within a quarter of the size of cell $R/4$. If the site is an 8-mi cell, the antenna can be located within a 2-mi radius. This hypothesis is based on the simulation result that the change in site within a 2-mi radius would not affect the coverage pattern at a distance 8 mi away. If the site is a 2-mi cell, the antenna can be located within a 0.5-mi radius.

The quarter-radius rule can be applied only on relatively flat terrain, not in a hilly area. To determine whether this rule can be applied in a general area, one can use the point-to-point prediction method to plot the coverage at different site locations and compare the differences. Usually when the point-to-point prediction method (tool) can be used to design a system, the quarter-radius rule becomes useless.

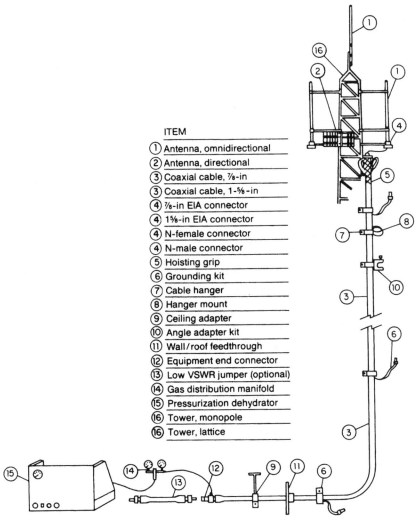

ITEM	
①	Antenna, omnidirectional
②	Antenna, directional
③	Coaxial cable, ⅞-in
③	Coaxial cable, 1-⅝-in
④	⅞-in EIA connector
④	1⅝-in EIA connector
④	N-female connector
④	N-male connector
⑤	Hoisting grip
⑥	Grounding kit
⑦	Cable hanger
⑧	Hanger mount
⑨	Ceiling adapter
⑩	Angle adapter kit
⑪	Wall / roof feedthrough
⑫	Equipment end connector
⑬	Low VSWR jumper (optional)
⑭	Gas distribution manifold
⑮	Pressurization dehydrator
⑯	Tower, monopole
⑯	Tower, lattice

FIGURE 8.41   Antenna system at cell site.

8.15   SMART ANTENNAS

8.15.1   Introduction[63-67]

A broad definition of smart antennas is used; namely, base station antennas with a pattern that is not fixed but adapts to the current radio conditions. The principal reason for introducing smart antennas is to increase capacity. Capacity can be defined as the total bit rate per unit bandwidth per unit area, or bit/s/Hz/m². Because the available frequency band is limited, the capacity is given by bit/s/Hz/cell, called cell density, which is a function of frequency reuse distance. From the cell density, and the user's demand in voice or data, we can calculate the number of users that can be served simultaneously by each cell site (i.e., base station). Techniques for increasing capacity in cellular system aim at interference reduction.

1. Coding schemes
2. Power control
3. Microcell
4. Frequency hopping
5. Repeaters
6. Diversity schemes (space, polarization, time)
7. Frequency management
8. Super conductive receiver (LNA)
9. Modulation schemes
10. Multiple access schemes
11. Smart antennas

One of the interference reduction schemes is "smart antenna," which is to change the base station antenna patterns to adapt to the current radio conditions. Smart antennas lead to a much more efficient use of the power and spectrum, increasing the useful received power as well as reducing interference; as a result, the carrier-to-noise ratio increases.

Besides the three multiple access schemes, FDMA, TDMA, and CDMA, the smart antennas add a new scheme to increase the number of users. It may call SDMA (space division multiple access). In the same cell, two users can use the same physical communication channel.

- Advantages of smart antennas
  1. Increase the number of users (capacity).
  2. Increased range.
  3. Increased a higher level of security.
- Elements of smart antennas
  1. Radiating elements (transmit elements), or an array of elements.
  2. A combining/dividing network.
  3. A control unit (a DSP)—the brain of the smart antennas.
  4. A sensor box (receiving elements or search beam) feeds the receiving information to the control unit as mobility management.
- Levels of intelligence received from the sensor box
  1. Switched (selected) beam: Switch beams between two fixed directive antennas based on the desired users.
  2. Beam tracking: Continuous tracking of the user.
  3. Adaptive mulling: The radiation pattern can not only track the desired user but also null out the interferers. This is the way to maximize the signal-to-interference ratio (SIR).
- Physical size of smart antenna: Because the element spacing for an array is a half wavelength (0.5λ), then an 8-element array will be about 1.2 meters at 900 MHz and 60 cm at 2 GHz. Therefore, the higher the frequency, the smaller the size of the smart antennas.

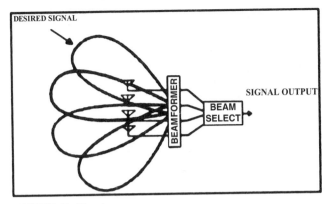

FIGURE 8.42   Phased array.

8.15.2   Types of Smart Antennas

There are two types, a phased array and an adaptive array.

A. Phased array: Consists of either a number of fixed beams with one beam tuned on toward the desired signal, or a single beam formed by a phase adjustment only steered toward the desired signal as shown in Fig. 8.42. The beam former can generate N fixed antenna patterns by changing the phases of N elements. The beam selector selects the beam according to the desired signal.

B. Adaptive antenna array: An array of multiple antenna elements, with the received signals weighted and combined to maximize the desired signal to interference plus noise power ratio (S/(I+N)). This essentially puts a main beam in the direction of the desired signal and nulls in the direction of the interference as shown in Fig. 8.43.

8.15.3   Applications

A. A smart antenna uses a phased or adaptive array that adjusts to the radio environment. For using the phased array, the beam is steered or different beams are selected as the desired user moves. For using the adaptive array, the beam pattern changes as the desired user and the interference move. The use of switching beam or adaptive beam for tracking is shown in Fig. 8.44.

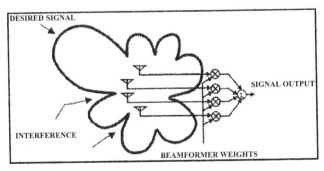

FIGURE 8.43   Adaptive array.

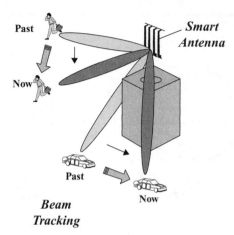

FIGURE 8.44 Smart antenna technology—Beam Tracking.

B. The interference reduction effectiveness on top of the basic beam steering can be found by

1. Basic beam steering: Refers to the class of algorithm that attempts to direct a beam toward the wanted mobile but makes no attempt to null cochannel interference signals.

2. Frequency hopping: Reduce the interference in an average sense among all the hopping channels.

3. Spatial filtering for interference reduction (SFIR): In this scheme, nulls are formed in the direction of interference sources in uplink and downlink. This improves the carrier to interference (C/I) ratio and allows the frequency reuse pattern to be tightened, thus increasing capacity.

4. The smart antenna also can achieve SDMA (spatial division multiple access): This involves the use of adaptive nulling to allow two or more mobiles in the same cell to share the same frequency and time slot. One beam is formed for each mobile with nulls in the direction of the other mobiles as shown in Fig. 8.45. The elements of SDMA are shown in Fig. 8.46. It is a space-time interference cancellation.

   SDMA requires better nulling performance than SFIR because the high dynamic range of uplink signals within a cell that means the C/I of the wanted signal can be far below 0 dB. In the SFIR case, the C/I is usually positive. However, SDMA has the advantage that it can be implemented in isolation in single cells (e.g., traffic hot spots), whereas SFIR must be implemented across whole clusters of cells. Of course SDMA also requires the establishment of new procedures to manage the air interface resources within each cell. For example, this may involve intracell handovers.

   SDMA is not appropriate in CDMA systems, as it implies reuse of spreading codes, which is undesirable for the SDMA application. However, the spreading codes can serve the purpose as SDMA does.

8.15.4 Multiple Antenna Communications

Digital communications using MIMO (multiple input, multiple output) has emerged as one of the most promising research areas in wireless communications, giving a chance to resolve

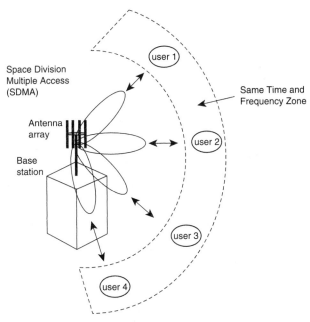

FIGURE 8.45 Smart antenna technology—SDMA.

some of the bottlenecks of traffic capacity in high-speed broadband wireless Internet access networks (3G and beyond).

MIMO refers to a link for which the transmitting end as well as the receiving end is equipped with multiple antenna elements, as illustrated in Fig. 8.47. The idea behind MIMO is that the signals on the transmit antennas on one end and that of the receive

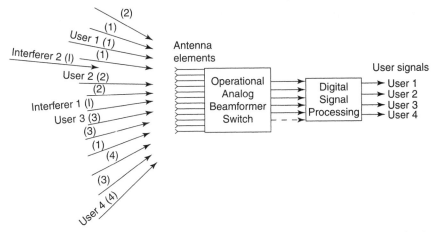

FIGURE 8.46 Smart antenna system. (All signals indicated by (1) are user 1's multipath signals; The signals indicated by (I) are interferens).

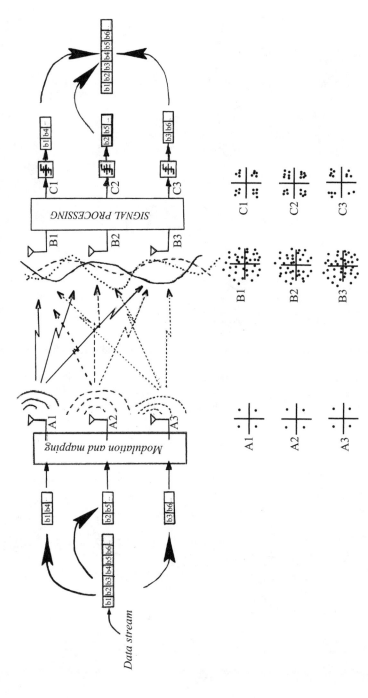

FIGURE 8.47 MIMO system.

antennas on the other end are "combined" in such a way that the quality (Bit Error Rate) or the data rate (Bit/Sec) of the communication will be improved.

MIMO systems use space-time processing techniques in that the time dimension (natural dimension of transmission signals) is joined with the spatial dimension brought by "smart antennas," a popular technology for improving wireless transmission. However, the underlying mathematical nature of MIMO environments can give performance that goes well beyond that of conventional smart antennas. In particular, MIMO systems have the ability to turn multipath propagation, usually a pitfall of wireless transmission, into an advantage for increasing the user's data rate.

In Fig. 8.47, the data stream to be transmitted is distributed among different subchannels, then goes through modulation and mapping, and is transmitted by corresponding antennas. Upon receipt, each receiving antenna receives three signals from the transmit antennas, then the entire received signal goes through signal processing to receive the desired signal.

The promise of MIMO techniques and the mechanisms to achieve it are on the horizon. Practical design of MIMO solutions involve both transmission algorithms and channel modeling to measure their performance as well as the radio network level considerations and to evaluate the overall benefits of MIMO setups. A detailed description of MIMO technology is given in Section 16.5.

8.16 MOBILE ANTENNAS

The requirement of a mobile (motor-vehicle–mounted) antenna is an omnidirectional antenna that can be located as high as possible from the point of reception. However, the physical limitation of antenna height on the vehicle restricts this requirement. Generally, the antenna should at least clear the top of the vehicle. Patterns for two types of mobile antenna are shown in Fig. 8.48.

8.16.1 Roof-Mounted Antenna

The antenna pattern of a roof-mounted antenna is more or less uniformly distributed around the mobile unit when measured at an antenna range in free space as shown in Fig. 8.49. The 3-dB high-gain antenna shows a 3-dB gain over the quarter-wave antenna. However, the gain of the antenna used at the mobile unit must be limited to 3 dB because the cell-site antenna is rarely as high as the broadcasting antenna and out-of-sight conditions often prevail. The mobile antenna with a gain of more than 3 dB can receive only a limited portion of the total multipath signal in the elevation as measured under the out-of-sight condition.[68] This point is discussed in detail in Sec. 8.16.3.

8.16.2 Glass-Mounted Antennas[53,69]

There are many kinds of glass-mounted antennas. Energy is coupled through the glass; therefore, there is no need to drill a hole. However, some energy is dissipated on passage through the glass. The antenna gain range is 1 to 3 dB depending on the operating frequency.

The position of the glass-mounted antenna is always lower than that of the roof-mounted antenna; generally there is a 3-dB difference between these two types of antenna. Also, glass-mounted antennas cannot be installed on the shaded glass found in some motor vehicles because this type of glass has a high metal content.

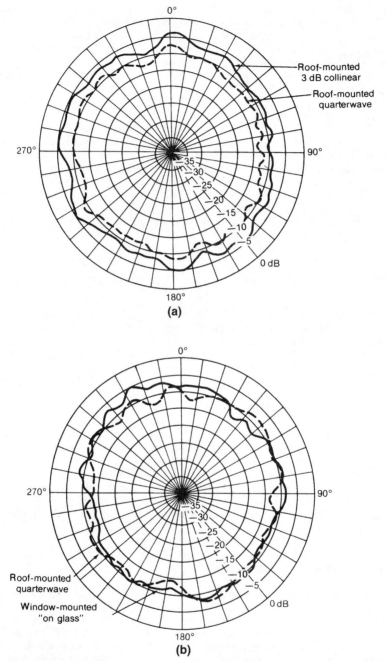

FIGURE 8.48 Mobile antenna patterns. (*From Antenna Specialist Co., Ref. 49.*) (*a*) Roof-mounted 3-dB-gain collinear antenna versus roof-mounted quarter-wave antenna. (*b*) Window-mounted "on-glass" gain antenna versus roof-mounted quarter-wave antenna.

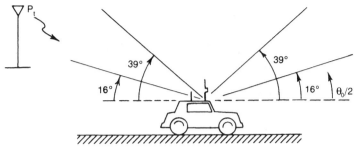

FIGURE 8.49   Vertical angle of signal arrival.

8.16.3   Mobile High-Gain Antennas

A high-gain antenna used on a mobile unit has been studied.[68] This type of high-gain antenna should be distinguished from the directional antenna. In the directional antenna, the antenna beam pattern is suppressed horizontally; in the high-gain antenna, the pattern is suppressed vertically. To apply either a directional antenna or a high-gain antenna for reception in a radio environment, we must know the origin of the signal. If we point the directional antenna opposite to the transmitter site, we would in theory receive nothing.

In a mobile radio environment, the scattered signals arrive at the mobile unit from every direction with equal probability. That is why an omnidirectional antenna must be used. The scattered signals also arrive from different elevation angles. Lee and Brandt[68] used two types of antenna, one $\lambda/4$ whip antenna with an elevation coverage of $39°$ and one 4-dB-gain antenna (4-dB gain with respect to the gain of a dipole) with an elevation coverage of $16°$, and measured the angle of signal arrival in the suburban Keyport-Matawan area of New Jersey. There are two types of test: a line-of-sight condition and an out-of-sight condition. In Lee and Brandt's study, the transmitter was located at an elevation of approximately 100 m (300 ft) above sea level. The measured areas were about 12 m (40 ft) above sea level and the path length about 3 mi. The received signal from the 4-dB-gain antenna was 4 dB stronger than that from the whip antenna under line-of-sight conditions. This is what we would expect. However, the received signal from the 4-dB-gain antenna was only about 2 dB stronger than that from the whip antenna under out-of-sight conditions. This is surprising.

The reason for the latter observation is that the scattered signals arriving under out-of-sight conditions are spread over a wide elevation angle. A large portion of the signals outside the elevation angle of $16°$ cannot be received by the high-gain antenna. We may calculate the portion being received by the high-gain antenna from the measured beamwidth. For instance, suppose that a 4:1 gain (6 dBi) is expected from the high-gain antenna, but only 2.5:1 is received. Therefore, 63 percent of the signal* is received by the 4-dB-gain antenna (i.e., 6 dBi) and 37 percent is felt in the region between 16 and $39°$. Consider the data in the following table.

	Gain, dBi	Linear ratio	$\theta_0/2$, degrees
Whip antenna (2 dB above isotropic)	2	1.58:1	39
High-gain antenna	6	4:1	16
Low-gain antenna	4	2.5:1	24

---

* For a Rayleigh fading signal, 63 percent will be below its power level.

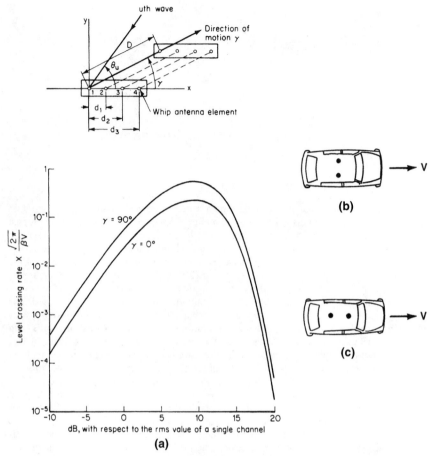

FIGURE 8.50 Horizontally spaced antennas. (*a*) Maximum difference in lcr of a four-branch equal-gain signal between $\alpha = 0$ and $\alpha = 90°$ with antenna spacing of 0.15λ (*b*) Not recommended. (*c*) Recommended.

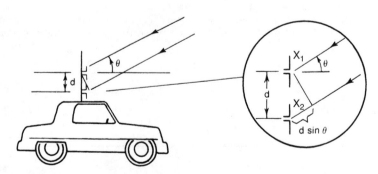

FIGURE 8.51 Vertical separation between two mobile antennas.

Therefore, a 2- to 3-dB-gain antenna (4 to 5 dBi) should be adequate for general use. An antenna gain higher than 2 to 3 dB does not serve the purpose of enhancing reception level. Moreover, measurements reveal that the elevation angle for scattered signals received in urban areas is greater than that in suburban areas.

8.16.4 Horizontally Oriented Space-Diversity Antennas

A two-branch space-diversity receiver mounted on a motor vehicle has the advantage of reducing fading and thus can operate at a lower reception level. The advantage of using a space-diversity receiver to reduce interference is discussed in Chap. 10. The discussion here concerns a space-diversity scheme in which two vehicle-mounted antennas separated horizontally by 0.5λ wavelength[69] (15 cm or 6 in) can achieve the advantage of diversity.

We must consider the following factor. The two antennas can be mounted either in line with or perpendicular to the motion of the vehicle. Theoretical analyses and measured data indicate that the inline arrangement of the two antennas produces fewer level crossings, that is, less fading, than the perpendicular arrangement does. The level crossing rates of two signals received from different horizontally oriented space-diversity antennas are shown in Fig. 8.50.

8.16.5 Vertically Oriented Space-Diversity Antennas[70]

The vertical separation between two space-diversity antennas can be determined from the correlation between their received signals. The positions of two antennas X_1 and X_2 are shown in Fig. 8.51. The theoretical derivation of correlation is[71]

$$\rho\left(\frac{d}{\lambda}, \theta\right) = \frac{\sin[(\pi d/\lambda)\sin\theta]}{(\pi d/\lambda)\sin\theta} \tag{8.15-1}$$

Equation (8.15-1) is plotted in Fig. 8.52. A set of measured data was obtained by using two antennas vertically separated by 1.5λ wavelengths. The mean values of three groups of measured data are also shown in Fig. 8.52. In one group, in New York City, low correlation coefficients were observed. In two other groups, both in New Jersey, the average correlation coefficient for perpendicular streets was 0.35 and for radial streets, 0.225. The following table summarizes the correlation coefficients in different areas and different street orientations.

	Correlation Coefficient	
Area	Average	Standard Deviation
New York City	0.1	0.06
Suburban New Jersey		
Radial streets	0.226	0.127
Perpendicular streets	0.35	0.182

From Fig. 8.52 we can also see that the signal arrives at an elevation angle of $29°$ in the suburban radial streets and $33°$ in the suburban perpendicular streets. In New York City the angle of arrival approaches $40°$.

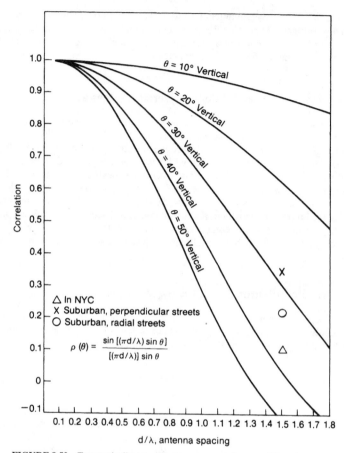

FIGURE 8.52   Two vertically spaced antennas mounted on a mobile unit.

8.17   HANDSETS, ANTENNAS, AND BATTERIES

The key elements of making long and quality calls are antennas and batteries. We describe handset antennas first, followed by the handset batteries.

8.17.1   Handset Considerations

Handset antenna design is an art that is greatly dependent on the characteristics of the mounting platform. The variation in shape and construction of handset devices dictates unique behavior in every new terminal. In addition, designing antennas and matching networks optimize performance for a given platform.

Another aspect of effective handset antenna design is the antenna's sensitivity to the surrounding environment. A handset must function in a variety of situations, whether in a chest pocket, on a table, or of course close to the head. Great attention to detail and experience is required during the design process to maintain optimal performance in all defined user scenarios.

8.17.2 RF Antenna Characterization

When characterizing an antenna for usage on a handset, it is important to consider three main characteristics:

1. The antenna fits to transceiver impedance match.
2. The antenna radiation is usually quantified by Mean Effective Gain or Efficiency.
3. The antenna interacts with other objects. A handset in use is most often close to an object, so distortion should be tolerated with its operation.
4. A terminal must comply with safety standards regarding electromagnetic power absorption in the human body, based on Specific Absorption Rate (SAR).

8.17.3 Different Types of Handsets and PCMCIA Antennas

A. Electrical Dipoles[72]
Half-wavelength dipole antennas are very popular within the antenna community. A dipole at this length is purely resistive and has an antenna resistance of 73 ohms. At 900 MHz, a half-wavelength is 0.15 m and at 1.8 GHz, 0.075 m. Half-wavelength antennas are seldom used at frequencies below 1 GHz for handheld terminals due to their large sizes. However, quarter-wavelength dipole antennas form a first half of the half-wavelength antenna. The handset's PCB provides the other half.

When a dipole is shorter than a half-wavelength, it becomes increasingly capacitive with decreasing antenna resistance. The radiation efficiency reduces. However, many improvements can be achieved based on the analysis of Ref. 72. In addition, thickening the rod of a dipole can also broaden the bandwidth of the antenna.

B. Small Loops[73]
The radiation behavior of a small loop is comparable to a small electrical dipole in free space. An electrical dipole operated within close proximity to a user exhibits decreased performance. However, when the loop is in operation close to a user, it makes constructive use of the user's body. The impedance of small loops is reactive with a small resistive part. Although the radiation efficiency reduces, antennas are widely used in pagers.

C. Helical Antennas[73]
Helical antennas appear electrically to be a number of short dipoles with small loops positioned in-between. The ingenious effect is that the capacitive behavior of a short dipole is balanced by the inductive behavior of a small loop. This number of short dipoles will dominate the radiated fields.

Sometimes two or four helices are intertwined. These antennas are called bifilar and quadrifilar antennas and are popular within space/satellite applications.

Helical antennas cannot be used as broadband antennas.

D. Meander Line Antennas (MLA)[74-76]
Rashed and Tai[74] proposed the meander line antenna for antenna size reduction such that the antennas were made from continuously folded wire intended to reduce the resonant length. The meander line antennas tend to resonante at frequencies much

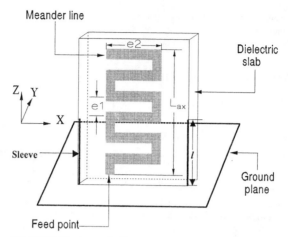

FIGURE 8.53 A meander line antenna on a small ground plane.

lower than a single element antenna of equal length. These antennas comprise one or more metallic traces that meanders back and forth in the antenna as shown in Fig. 8.53.

To begin the meander line antenna design, the changes in impedance and resonant frequency are observed by increasing the number of segments of the meaner line trace gradually until the design goal is achieved. When the meander line is printed on a small substrate sitting on a small ground plane as shown in Fig. 8.53, the input impedance reduces dramatically. Dual sleeves have been successfully used to tune the wire meander line antenna to 50Ω and widen the bandwidth. Therefore, dual sleeves are printed on both edges of the dielectric substrate. The length of the sleeves is adjusted for optimal matching. They are closely related to helical antennas in that the inductive behavior of the meander is balancing the capacitive properties characteristic of a short dipole. However, the trace is not making loops. Instead, it should be interpreted as small sections of transmission lines with short dipoles positioned in-between. In addition, in this case the radiated field is dominated by the electrical dipoles.

Compared to helical antennas, meander antennas offer a greater possibility to design antennas with multiband performance.

E. Planar Internal Antennas[76,77]

Due to the drive toward fitting antennas inside the handsets, planar antennas have grown increasingly popular. A classical planar antenna is the patch antenna, which is a rectangular metallic film mounted above a ground plane. Two popular methods to reduce size are as follows.

1. To use dielectrics with a high dielectricity constant. This adds weight and reduces the antenna bandwidth.

2. To incorporate grounding by adding inductance to the capacitive planar antenna shifts antenna resonace to a lower frequency.

Planar Inverted F Antennas (PIFA): the design of this group of antennas normally includes some kind of slot, thus adding electrical length to the antenna. The Inverted F is distinguished by the loop formed by the Ground enclosed box and the short right angle elements of the letter F as shown in Fig. 8.54a. L_F is the horizontal length from

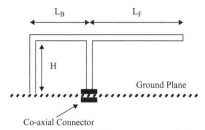

(a) Plane Inverted F antenna

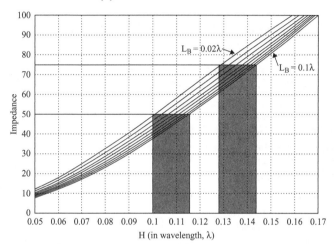

(b) Impedance(Ω) vs Height(λ) at resonance

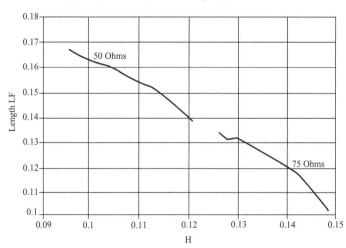

(c) Length (L$_F$) vs Height at resonance

FIGURE 8.54 Planar inverted F antenna and its designing chart.

the feed point to the open end of the antenna. L_B is the horizontal length from the feed point to the closed end of the antenna. H is the height between the ground plane and the horizontal element. The design of inverted F antenna is shown in Fig. 8.54*b* and 8.54*c*. In Fig. 8.54*c*, we obtain the height H from a given L_B and an impedance value (50 Ω or 75 Ω). Then with the height H and the given impedance, the length L_F can be found.

When designing antennas at frequencies above 1.7 GHz, parasitic elements are popular. The parasitic elements consist of a grounded strip that runs parallel to the antenna. The effect of these parasitic elements is upper band widening.

8.17.4 Battery Fundamentals

A. Basic Definitions

- Capacity: A cell is rate at 1000 mAh (milli-Amp-hours), then 1000 mA of current for 1 hour or 500 mA of current for 2 hours.

- "C" rate: Charging and discharging are expressed as a function of the "C" rate. If a 1200 mAh cell is charged at a 1C rate, then the charging current applied is 1200 mA. If it is charged at a 0.2C rate, then the charging current applied is 240 mA.

- Energy density of a cell is a measure of how much energy can be stored in a cell per unit volume or unit weight.

  Volumetric energy density in terms of watt-hours/liter (wh/l).

  Gravimetric energy density in terms of watt-hour/kilogram (wh/kg).

B. Thin Batteries for Handsets
The lithium-based battery, Li-Ion or Li-Polymer cells are intended to be single cell applications.

- Advantages

  Available in extremely thin form factors.

  Higher energy density than nickel-based cells (Ni-Cd, Ni-MH).

  No memory effect.

  Envelope material (aluminium-laminated film) allows complex form factors.

  Low self-discharge rate (<10% per month).

  No toxic substances.

- Disadvantages

  Fewer standard cell sizes.

  Less rugged envelope.

  Requires protection circuitry.

  More difficult to assemble into multicell configurations due to thin foil contacts.

  Currents to 2C.

C. Fuel Cells for Handsets in the Future
Full cell technology is considered an efficient and clean hydrogen-based energy source. It could replace the lithium-based battery. The user can instantly refill power for the fuel cell. In addition, the fuel cell gives longer talk and standby time. The challenges today are miniaturization and safety.

REFERENCES

1. Y. Okumura et al., "Field Strength and Its Variability in VHF and UHF Land-Mobile Radio Service," *Review of the Electrical Communication Laboratories* Vol. 16, Nos. 9 and 10, 1958, pp. 825–873.

2. M. Hata, "Empirical Formula for Propagation Loss in Land Mobile Radio Services," *IEEE Transactions on Vehicular Technology*, Vol. VT-29, No. 3, 1980, pp. 317–325.

3. A. Akeyama, T. Nagatsu, and Y. Ebine, "Mobile Radio Propagation Characteristics and Radio Zone Design Method in Local Cities," *Review of the Electrical Communication Laboratories* Vol. 30, No. 2, 1982, pp. 308–317.

4. A. G. Longley and P. L. Rice, "Prediction of Tropospheric Radio Transmission Loss Over Irregular Terrain, A Computer Method-1968," ESSA Technical Report ERL 79-ITS 67, NTIS acc. no. 676874, 1968.

5. A. G. Longley, "Radio Propagation in Urban Areas," OT Report 78-144, NTIS, 1978.

6. J. J. Egli, "Radio Propagation Above 40 MC Over Irregular Terrain," *Proceedings of the IRE*, Vol. 45, 1957, pp. 1383–1391.

7. K. Allsebrook and J. D. Parsons, "Mobile Radio Propagation in British Cities at Frequencies in the VHF and UHF Bands," *IEEE Transactions on Vehicular Technology*, Vol. VT-26, No. 4, 1977, pp. 313–323.

8. K. Bullington, "Radio Propagation for Vehicular Communications," *IEEE Transactions on Vehicular Technology*, Vol. VT-26, No. 4, 1977, pp. 295–308.

9. W. J. Kessler and M. J. Wiggins, "A Simplified Method for Calculating UHF Base-to-Mobile Statistical Coverage Contours over Irregular Terrain," *27th IEEE Vehicular Technology Conference*, 1977, pp. 227–236.

10. W. C. Y. Lee, *Mobile Communications Engineering*, McGraw-Hill Book Co., 1998, p. 125.

11. "Bell System Practices Public Land Mobile and UHF Maritime Systems Estimates of Expected Coverage," *Radio Systems General*, July 1963.

12. K. K. Kelly II, "Flat Suburban Area Propagation of 820 MHz," *IEEE Transactions on Vehicular Technology*, Vol. VT-27 November 1978, pp. 198–204.

13. G. D. Ott and A. Plitkins, "Urban Path-Loss Characteristics at 820 MHz," *IEEE Transactions on Vehicular Technology*, Vol. VT-27, November 1978, pp. 189–197.

14. W. R. Young, "Mobile Radio Transmission-Compared at 150 to 3700 MC," *Bell System Technical Journal*, Vol. 31, November 1952, pp. 1068–1085.

15. Robert T. Forrest, "Land Mobile Radio, Propagation Measurements for System Design," *IEEE Transactions on Vehicular Technology*, Vol. VT-24, November 1975, pp. 46–53.

16. G. Hagn, "Radio System Performance Model for Predicting Communications Operational Ranges in Irregular Terrain," *29th IEEE Vehicular Technology Conference Record*, 1970, pp. 322–330.

17. Robert Jensen, "900 MHz Mobile Radio Propagation in the Copenhagen Area," *IEEE Transactions on Vehicular Technology*, Vol. VT-26, November 1977.

18. G. L. Turin, "Simulation of Urban Location Systems," *Proceedings of the 21st IEEE Vehicular Technology Conference*, 1970.

19. D. L. Nielson, "Microwave Propagation Measurements for Mobile Digital Radio Applications," *IEEE Transactions on Vehicular Technology*, Vol. VT-27, August 1978, pp. 117–132.

20. V. Graziano, "Propagation Correlations at 900 MHz," *IEEE Transactions on Vehicular Technology*, Vol. VT-27, November 1978, pp. 182–188.

21. D. O. Reudink, "Properties of Mobile Radio Propagation Above 400 MHz," *IEEE Transactions on Vehicular Technology*, Vol. VT-23, November 1974, pp. 143–160.

22. M. F. Ibrahim and J. D. Parson, "Urban Mobile Propagation at 900 MHz," *IEEE Electrical Letters*, Vol. 18, No. 3, 1982, pp. 113–115.

23. W. C. Y. Lee, *Mobile Communications Engineering*, McGraw-Hill Book Co., 1998, Chap. 4.

24. W. C. Y. Lee, *Mobile Communications Design Fundamentals*, John Wiley & Sons, 1993, pp. 72–94.

25. N. H. Shepherd, "Radio Wave Loss Deviation and Shadow Loss at 900 MHz," *IEEE Transactions on Vehicular Technology*, Vol. VT-26, November 1977, pp. 309–313.

26. B. Bodson, G. F. McClure, and S. R. McConoughey, *Land-Mobile Communications Engineering*, IEEE Press, 1984.

27. H. F. Schmid, "A Prediction Model for Multipath Propagation of Pulse Signals at VHF and UHF over Irregular Terrain," *IEEE Transactions on Antennas and Propagation*, Vol. AP-16, March 1970, pp. 253–258.

28. H. Susuki, "A Statistical Model for Urban Radio Propagation," *IEEE Transactions on Communications*, Vol. Com-25, July 1977.

29. W. C. Y. Lee, *Mobile Communications Engineering*, McGraw-Hill Book Co., 1998, pp. 163–166.

30. J. S. Bendat and A. G. Piersol, *Random Data, Analysis and Measurement Procedures*, Wiley/Interscience, 1971.

31. IEEE VTS Committee on Radio Propagation "Lee's Model," *IEEE Transactions on Vehicular Technology*, Feb. 1988, pp. 68–70.

32. A. Neskovic, N. Neskovic, and G. Paunovic, "Modern Approaches in Modeling of Mobile Radio Systems Propagation Environment," IEEE Communications Survey and Tutorials, The Electronic Magazine of Original Peer-Reviewed Survey Article, 2000.

33. E. C. Jordan, *Electromagnetic Waves and Radiation Systems*, Prentice-Hall, 1950, p. 141.

34. W. C. Y. Lee, *Mobile Communications Engineering*, McGraw-Hill Book Co., 1998, p. 106.

35. S. Swarup and R. K. Tewari, "Propagation Characteristics of VHF/UHF Signals in Tropical Moist Deciduous Forest," *Journal of the Institution of Electronics and Telecommunication Engineers*, Vol. 21, No. 3, 1975, pp. 123–125.

36. S. Swarup and R. K. Tewari, "Depolarisation of Radio Waves in a Jungle Environment," *IEEE Transactions on Antennas and Propagation*, Vol. AP-27, No. 1, January 1979, pp. 113–116.

37. W. R. Vincent and G. H. Hagn, "Comments on the Performance of VHF Vehicular Radio Sets in Tropical Forests," *IEEE Transactions on Vehicular Technology*, Vol. VT-18, No. 2, August 1969, pp. 61–65.

38. T. Tamir, "On Radio-Wave Propagation in Forest Environments," *IEEE Transactions on Antenna and Propagation*, Vol. AF-15, November 1967, pp. 806–817.

39. T. Tamir, "On Radio-Wave Propagation Along Mixed Paths in Forest Environments," *IEEE Transactions on Antennas and Propagation*, Vol. AP-25, July 1971, pp. 471–477.

40. E. C. Jordan (ed.), *Reference Data for Engineers*, 7th ed., Howard W. Sams & Co., 1985, Chap. 33.

41. W. C. Y. Lee, *Mobile Communications Design Fundamentals*, John Wiley & Sons, 1993, pp. 30–31.

42. W. C. Y. Lee, "A New Propagation Path-Loss Prediction Model for Military Mobile Access," 1985 IEEE Military Communications Conference, Boston, Conference Record, Vol. 2, pp. 19–21.

43. W. C. Y. Lee, "Studies of Base Station Antenna Height Effect on Mobile Radio," *IEEE Transactions on Vehicular Technology*, Vol. VT-29, May 1980, pp. 252–260.

44. W. C. Y. Lee, "The New model of predicting point-to-point signal strength over a given terrain coutour," Bell Lab. internal memorandum, July 5, 1978.

45. W. C. Y. Lee, "Mobile Communications Design Fundamentals," John Wiley & Sons, 1993, pp. 88–94.

46. George Washington University, Continuing Engineering Education Program, course 1086, "Mobile Cellular Telecommunications Systems." A lecture note prepared by W. C. Y. Lee.

47. W. C. Y. Lee, "A New Propagation Path Loss Prediction model for military mobile Access," *IEEE Milcom*, 85:2, Boston, MA (Oct. 1985) 19.2.1–19.2.10.

48. W. C. Y. Lee, "Lee's Model" IEEE VTS 42nd Conference Proceedings, Denver, CO, May 10–13, 1992, pp. 343–348.

49. W. Honcharonko, H. L. Bertoni, I. Dialing, J. Qian, H. D. Yee, "Mechanisms governing UHF propagation on single floor in modern office buildings," *IEEE Trans. Veh. Technol.*, pp. 77–32, May 1992.

50. T. S. Rappaport, "Indoor radio communication for factories of the future," *IEEE Commun. Mag.*, pp. 15–24, May 1989.

51. D. J. Y. Lee and W. C. Y. Lee, "Propagation Prediction in and Through Buildings," *IEEE Transactions on Vehicular Technology*, Vol. 49, No. 5, Sept. 2000, pp. 1529–1533.

52. A. S. Akki, F. Haber, "A Statistical Model of Mobile-to-Mobile Land Communications Channels," *IEEE Transactions on Vehicular Technology*, Vol. VT-85, February 1986, p. 2.

53. Antenna Specialist Co. catalog product branches, Antenna Specialist Co., Cleveland, Ohio.

54. American Radio Telephone Service (ARTS) development license application to the Federal Communications Commission, Feb. 14, 1977. In the application, a proposed system from Motorola was described.

55. W. C. Y. Lee, "Mobile Radio Signal Correlation versus Antenna Height and Space," *IEEE Transactions on Vehicular Technology*, Vol. VT-25, August 1977, pp. 290–292.

56. W. C. Y. Lee, *Mobile Communications Design Fundamentals*, John Wiley & Sons, 1993, p. 210.

57. J. D. Kraus, *Antennas*, McGraw-Hill Book Co., 1950, p. 421.

58. A. G. Kandoian, "Three New Antenna Types and Their Applications," *Proceedings of the IRE*, Vol. 34, February 1946, pp. 70W–75W.

59. H. Jasik (ed.), *Antenna Engineering Handbook*, McGraw-Hill Book Co., 1961, pp. 5–7.

60. G. H. Brown, "Directional Antennas," *Proceedings of the IRE*, Vol. 25, January 1937, pp. 75–145.

61. W. C. Y. Lee, *Mobile Communications Engineering*, McGraw-Hill Book Co., 1998, p. 185.

62. V. H. MacDonald, "The Cellular Concept," *Bell System Technical Journal*, Vol. 58, January 1979, p. 27.

63. T. K. Sarkar, M. C. Wicks, M. Salazar-Palma, R. J. Bonneau, *Smart Antenna*, Wiley-IEEE Press, 2003.

64. J. C. Liberti and T. S. Rappaport, *Smart Antennas for Wireless Communications: IS-95 and Third-Generation CDMA Applications*, Prentice Hall, 1999.

65. J. H. Winters and M. J. Gans, "The Range Increase of Adaptive Versus Phased Arrays in Mobile Radio Systems," 28th Asilomar Conference on Signals, Systems and Computers, Pacific Grove, CA, USA, Oct. 31 Nov. 2, 1994, pp. 10915.

66. H. Steyskal, "Aspects of Digital Beamforming and Adaptive Arrays," Proc. COST259/260 Joint Workshop Spatial Channel Models and Adptive Antennas, Vienna, Austria, Apr. 20–21, 1999.

67. P. H. Lehne, M. Pettersen, "An Overview of Smart Antenna Technology for Mobile Communications Systems," Telenor Research and Development, IEEE Communications Surveys, 1999.

68. W. C. Y. Lee and R. H. Brandt, "The Elevation Angle of Mobile Radio Signal Arrival," *IEEE Transactions on Communications*, Vol. Com-21, November 1973, pp. 1194–1197.

69. W. C. Y. Lee, *Mobile Communications Design Fundamentals*, John Wiley & Sons, 1993, p. 233.

70. J. S. Bitler, "Correlation Measurements of Signals Received on Vertically Spaced Antennas," Microwave Radio Symposium, Boulder, Colorado, 1972.

71. M. J. Gans, private communications.

72. H. Nakano, H. Tagami, A. Yoshizawe, J. Yanauchi, "Shortening ratios of modified dipoles," *IEEE Trans. Antennas and Propagation*, Vol. 32, pp. 385–387, April 1948.

73. J. D. Kraus, *Antenna*, McGraw-Hill, 1950, Chapters 6, 7.

74. J. Rashed, C. T. Tai, "A new class of resonant antennas," *IEEE Trans. Antennas and Propagation*, Vol. 39, pp. 1428–1430, Sept. 1991.

75. E. Tsutomu, S. Yonehiko, S. Shinichi, K. Takashi, "Resonant Frequency and Radiation Efficiency of Meander Line Antennas," *Electronics and Communications in Japan*, Part 2, Vol. 83. No. 1, 2000.

76. M. Ali, et al, "Analysis of Integrated inverted-F antenna for Bluetooth Applications," Digest of 2000 IEEE-APS Conference on Antennas and Propagation for wireless communications, Waltham, MA November 6–8, pp. 21–24.

77. L. F. V. Neves Leal, "Design Curves for an Inverted F Antenna," 4th Year Design Report, School of Electrical and Information Engineering, University of Witwatersrand, August 2003.

CHAPTER 9

COCHANNEL AND CODE-CHANNEL INTERFERENCE REDUCTIONS

The cochannel interference is usually involved with FDMA, TDMA, and OFDMA systems. The interference occurred because the frequency reuse scheme is applied to those systems in which the channels operate at the same frequency but repeatedly in separate locations. If the specified separation is large, the cochannel interference is reduced, but the number of the cochannel in a given area is also reduced. As a result, the capacity is reduced. Therefore, we have to find an optimal separation from which the reduction level of cochannel interference is acceptable and the capacity reaches to a maximum.

In a single-carrier CDMA system, every cell uses the same CDMA frequency carrier, and within the carrier, using different spreading codes creates the number of traffic channels. Therefore, there is no cochannel interference in CDMA but code channel interference among the traffic channels. For reducing the code channel interference, the power control is a very critical element. We will address it in this chapter.

9.1 COCHANNEL INTERFERENCE

The frequency-reuse method is useful for increasing the efficiency of spectrum usage but results in cochannel interference because the same frequency channel is used repeatedly in different cochannel cells. Application of the cochannel interference reduction factor $q = D/R = 4.6$ for a seven-cell reuse pattern ($K = 7$) is described in Sec.2.7.[1]

The cochannel interference reduction factor $q = 4.6$ is based on the system required $C/I = 18$ dB of the AMPS system. From $q = 4.6$ we can obtain $K = 7$. Nevertheless, the system required C/I is different from a different system. For those systems with lower required C/I levels, the q values are less.

In this chapter, we try to use the AMPS system as an example to illustrate the ways of reducing cochannel interference. For other FDMA, TDMA, and OFDMA systems, the same methodology is applied.

In most mobile radio environments, use of a seven-cell reuse pattern is not sufficient to avoid cochannel interference for AMPS systems. Increasing $K > 7$ would reduce the number of cochannels per cell, and that would also reduce spectrum efficiency. Therefore, it might be advisable to retain the same number of radios as the seven-cell system but to sector the cell radially, as if slicing a pie. This technique would reduce cochannel interference and use channel sharing and channel borrowing schemes to increase spectrum efficiency.

9.2 EXPLORING COCHANNEL INTERFERENCE AREAS IN A SYSTEM

Problems in mobile telephone coverage (service), particularly holes (weak signal strength measured in dBm) that result in call drops during the customer's conversation, have been partially solved by applying the propagation (wave motion) studies discussed in Chap. 8 for the case where no cochannel interference exists.

When customer demand increases, the channels, which are limited in number, have to be repeatedly reused in different areas, which provides many cochannel cells, thus increases the system's capacity. But cochannel interference may be the result. In this situation, the received voice quality is affected by both the grade of coverage and the amount of cochannel interference. For detection of serious channel interference areas in a cellular system, two tests are suggested.

9.2.1 Test 1: Find the Cochannel Interference Area From a Mobile Receiver

Cochannel interference that occurs in one channel will occur equally in all the other channels in a given area. We can then measure cochannel interference by selecting any one channel (as one channel represents all the channels) and transmitting on that channel at all cochannel sites at night while the mobile receiver is traveling in one of the cochannel cells.

While performing this test, we watch for any change detected by a field-strength recorder in the mobile unit and compare the data with the condition of no cochannel sites being transmitted. This test must be repeated as the mobile unit travels in every cochannel cell. To facilitate this test, we can install a channel scanning receiver in one car.

One channel (f_1) records the signal level (no-cochannel condition), another channel (f_2) records the interference level (six-cochannel condition is the maximum), while the third channel receives f_2, which is not transmitting in the air. Therefore, the noise level is recorded only in f_3 (see Fig. 9.1).

We can obtain, in decibels, the carrier-to-interference ratio C/I by subtracting the result obtained from f_3 from the result obtained from f_1 (carrier minus interference $C - I$) and the carrier-to-noise ratio C/N by subtracting the result obtained from f_3 from the result obtained from f_2 (carrier minus noise $C - N$). Four conditions should be used to compare the results.

1. If the carrier-to-interference ratio C/I is greater than 18 dB throughout most of the cell, the system is properly designed for capacity.
2. If C/I is less than 18 dB and C/N is greater than 18 dB in some areas, there is cochannel interference.
3. If both C/N and C/I are less than 18 dB and $C/N = C/I$ in a given area, there is a coverage problem.
4. If both C/N and C/I are less than 18 dB and $C/N > C/I$ in a given area, there is a coverage problem *and* cochannel interference.

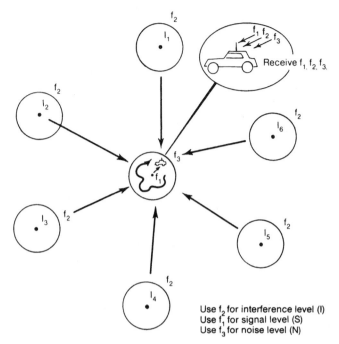

FIGURE 9.1   Test 1: cochannel interference at the mobile unit.

9.2.2   Test 2: Find the Cochannel Interference Area Which Affects a Cell Site

The reciprocity theorem can be applied for the coverage problem but not for cochannel interference. Therefore, we cannot assume that the first test result will apply to the second test condition. We must perform the second test as well.

Because it is difficult to use seven cars simultaneously, with each car traveling in each cochannel cell for this test, an alternative approach may be to record the signal strength at every cochannel cell site while a mobile unit is traveling either in its own cell or in one of the cochannel cells shown in Fig. 9.2.

First we find the areas in an interfering cell in which the top 10 percent level of the signal transmitted from the mobile unit in those areas is received at the desired site (Jth cell in Fig. 9.1). This top 10 percent level can be distributed in different areas in a cell. The average value of the top 10 percent level signal strength is used as the interference level from that particular interfering cell. The mobile unit also travels in different interfering cells. Up to six interference levels are obtained from a mobile unit running in six interfering cells. We then calculate the average of the bottom 10 percent level of the signal strength which is transmitted from a mobile unit in the desired cell (Jth cell) and received at the desired cell site as a carrier reception level.

Then we can reestablish the carrier-to-interference ratio received at a desired cell, say, the Jth cell site as follows.

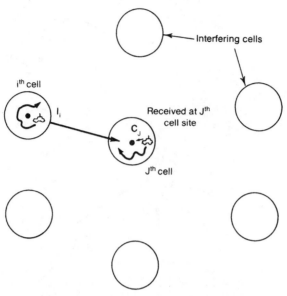

FIGURE 9.2   Test 2: cochannel interference at the cell site.

$$\frac{C_J}{I} = \frac{C_J}{\displaystyle\sum_{\substack{i=1 \\ i \neq J}}^{6} I_i}$$

The number of cochannel cells in the system can be less than six. We must be aware that all C_J and I_i were read in decibels. Therefore, a translation from decibels to linear is needed before summing all the interfering sources. The test can be carried out repeatedly for any given cell. We then compare

$$\frac{C_J}{I} \quad \text{and} \quad \frac{C_J}{N_J}$$

and determine the cochannel interference condition, which will be the same as that in test 1. N_J is the noise level in the Jth cell assuming no interference exists.

9.3   REAL-TIME COCHANNEL INTERFERENCE MEASUREMENT AT MOBILE RADIO TRANSCEIVERS

When the carriers are angularly modulated by the voice signal and the RF frequency difference between them is much higher than the fading frequency, measurement of the signal carrier-to-interference ratio C/I reveals that the signal is

$$e_1 = S(t) \sin(\omega t + \phi_1) \qquad (9.3\text{-}1)$$

and the interference is

$$e_2 = I(t) \sin(\omega t + \phi_2) \qquad (9.3\text{-}2)$$

The received signal is

$$e(t) = e_1(t) + e_2(t) = R \sin(\omega t + \psi) \qquad (9.3\text{-}3)$$

where

$$R = \sqrt{[S(t)\cos\phi_1 + I(t)\cos\phi_2]^2 + [S(t)\sin\phi_1 + I(t)\sin\phi_2]^2} \qquad (9.3\text{-}4)$$

and

$$\psi = \tan^{-1} \frac{S(t)\sin\phi_1 + I(t)\,\sin\phi_2}{S(t)\cos\phi_1 + I(t)\cos\phi_2} \qquad (9.3\text{-}5)$$

The envelope R can be simplified in Eq. (9.3-4), and R^2 becomes

$$R^2 = [S^2(t) + I^2(t) + 2S(t)I(t)\cos(\phi_1 - \phi_2)] \qquad (9.3\text{-}6)$$

Following Kozono and Sakamoto's[2] analysis of Eq. (9.3-6), the term $S^2(t) + I^2(t)$ fluctuates close to the fading frequency V/λ and the term $2S(t)I(t)\cos(\phi_1 - \phi_2)$ fluctuates to a frequency close to $d/dt(\phi_1 - \phi_2)$, which is much higher than the fading frequency. Then the two parts of the squared envelope can be separated as

$$X = S^2(t) + I^2(t) \qquad (9.3\text{-}7)$$

$$Y = 2S(t)I(t)\cos(\phi_1 - \phi_2) \qquad (9.3\text{-}8)$$

Assume that the random variables $S(t)$, $I(t)$, ϕ_1, and ϕ_2 are independent; then the average processes on X and Y are

$$\overline{X} = \overline{S^2(t)} + \overline{I^2(t)} \qquad (9.3\text{-}9)$$

$$\overline{Y^2} = 4\overline{S^2(t)I^2(t)}(\tfrac{1}{2}) = 2\overline{S^2(t)I^2(t)} \qquad (9.3\text{-}10)$$

The signal-to-interference ratio Γ becomes

$$\Gamma = \frac{\overline{S^2(t)}}{\overline{I^2(t)}} = k + \sqrt{k^2 - 1} \qquad (9.3\text{-}11)$$

where

$$k = \frac{\overline{X^2}}{\overline{Y^2}} - 1 \qquad (9.3\text{-}12)$$

Because X and Y can be separated in Eq. (9.3-6), the preceding computation of Γ in Eq. (9.3-11) could have been accomplished by means of an envelope detector, analog-to-digital converter, and a microcomputer. The sampling delay time Δt should be small enough to satisfy

$$S(t) \approx S(t + \Delta t), \qquad I(t) \approx I(t + \Delta t) \qquad (9.3\text{-}13)$$

and

$$\mathrm{E}\left[\cos[\phi_1(t) - \phi_2(t)] \cos[\phi_1(t + \Delta t) - \phi_2(t + \Delta t)]\right] \approx 0 \qquad (9.3\text{-}14)$$

Determining the delay time Δt to meet the requirement of Eq. (9.3-13) for this calculation is difficult and is a drawback to this measurement technique. Therefore, real-time cochannel interference measurement is difficult to achieve in practice.

9.4 DESIGN OF AN OMNIDIRECTIONAL ANTENNA SYSTEM IN THE WORST CASE

In Sec. 2.7, we proved that the value of $q = 4.6$ is valid for a normal interference case in a $K = 7$ cell pattern.[3] In this section, we would like to prove that a $K = 7$ cell pattern does not provide a sufficient frequency-reuse distance separation even when an ideal condition of flat terrain is assumed. The worst case is at the location where the mobile unit would receive the weakest signal from its own cell site but strong interferences from all interfering cell sites.

In the worst case the mobile unit is at the cell boundary R, as shown in Fig. 9.3. The distances from all six cochannel interfering sites are also shown in the figure: two distances of $D - R$, two distances of D, and two distances of $D + R$.

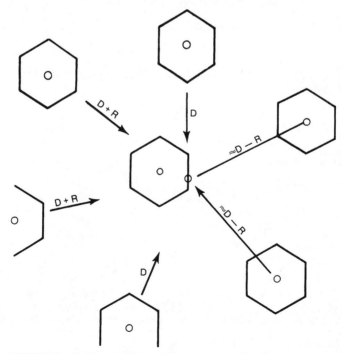

FIGURE 9.3 Cochannel interference (a worst case).

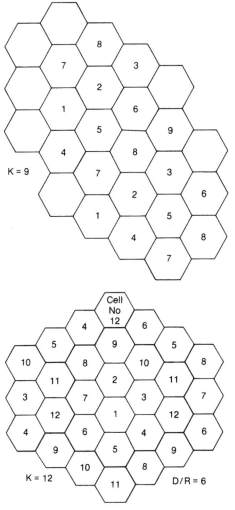

FIGURE 9.4 Interference with frequency-reuse patterns $K = 9$ and $K = 12$.

Following the mobile radio propagation rule of 40 dB/dec shown in Sec. 2.3, we obtain

$$C \propto R^{-4} \qquad I \propto D^{-4}$$

Then the carrier-to-interference ratio is

$$\frac{C}{I} = \frac{R^{-4}}{2(D - R)^{-4} + 2(D)^{-4} + 2(D + R)^{-4}}$$

$$= \frac{1}{2(q - 1)^{-4} + 2(q)^{-4} + 2(q + 1)^{-4}} \qquad (9.4\text{-}1a)$$

where $q = 4.6$ is derived from the normal case shown in Eq. (2.7-7). Substituting $q = 4.6$ into Eq. (9.4-1a), we obtain $C/I = 54$ or 17 dB, which is lower than 18 dB. To be conservative, we may use the shortest distance $D - R$ for all six interferers as a worst case; then Eq. (9.4-1a) is replaced by

$$\frac{C}{I} = \frac{R^{-4}}{6(D-R)^{-4}} = \frac{1}{6(q-1)^{-4}} = 28 = 14.47 \text{ dB} \qquad (9.4\text{-}1b)$$

In reality, because of the imperfect site locations and the rolling nature of the terrain configuration, the C/I received is always worse than 17 dB and could be 14 dB and lower. Such an instance can easily occur in a heavy traffic situation; therefore, the system must be designed around the C/I of the worst case. In that case, a cochannel interference reduction factor of $q = 4.6$ is insufficient.

Therefore, in an omnidirectional-cell system, $K = 9$ or $K = 12$ would be a correct choice. Then the values of q are

$$q = \begin{cases} \dfrac{D}{R} = \sqrt{3K} \\ 5.2 & K = 9 \\ 6 & K = 12 \end{cases} \qquad (9.4\text{-}2)$$

Substituting these values in Eq. (9.4-1), we obtain

$$\frac{C}{I} = 84.5 \,(=) \, 19.25 \text{ dB} \qquad K = 9 \qquad (9.4\text{-}3)$$

$$\frac{C}{I} = 179.33 \,(=) \, 22.54 \text{ dB} \qquad K = 12 \qquad (9.4\text{-}4)$$

The $K = 9$ and $K = 12$ cell patterns, shown in Fig. 9.4, are used when the traffic is light. Each cell covers an adequate area with adequate numbers of channels to handle the traffic.

9.5 DESIGN OF A DIRECTIONAL ANTENNA SYSTEM

When the call traffic begins to increase, we need to use the frequency spectrum efficiently and avoid increasing the number of cells K in a seven-cell frequency-reuse pattern. When K increases, the number of frequency channels assigned in a cell must become smaller (assuming a total allocated channel divided by K) and the efficiency of applying the frequency-reuse scheme decreases.

Instead of increasing the number K in a set of cells, let us keep $K = 7$ and introduce a directional-antenna arrangement. The cochannel interference can be reduced by using directional antennas. This means that each cell is divided into three or six sectors and uses three or six directional antennas at a base station. Each sector is assigned a set of frequencies (channels). The interference between two cochannel cells decreases as shown Fig. 9.5.

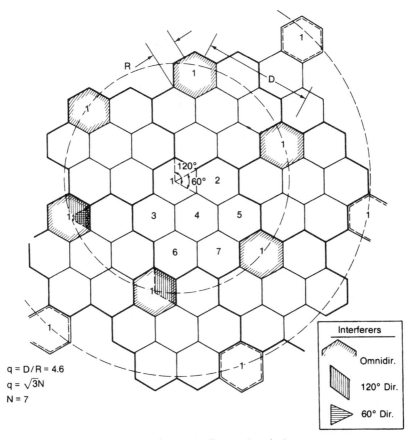

q = D/R = 4.6
q = $\sqrt{3N}$
N = 7

FIGURE 9.5 Interfering cells shown in a seven-cell system (two-tiers).

9.5.1 Directional Antennas In $K = 7$ Cell Patterns

9.5.1.1 Three-Sector Case. The three-sector case is shown in Fig. 9.5. To illustrate the worst-case situation, two cochannel cells are shown in Fig. 9.6a. The mobile unit at position E will experience greater interference in the lower shaded cell sector than in the upper shaded cell-sector site. This is because the mobile receiver receives the weakest signal from its own cell but fairly strong interference from the interfering cell. In a three-sector case, the interference is effective in only one direction because the front-to-back ratio of a cell-site directional antenna is at least 10 dB or more in a mobile radio environment. The worst-case cochannel interference in the directional-antenna sectors in which interference occurs may be calculated. Because of the use of directional antennas, the number of principal interferers is reduced from six to two (Fig. 9.5). The worst case of C/I occurs when the mobile unit is at position E, at which point the distance between the mobile unit and the two interfering antennas is roughly $D + (R/2)$; however, C/I can be calculated more precisely as follows.*

---

*The difference in results between using a closed form and an approximate calculation is small.

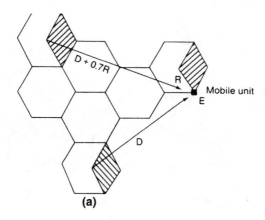

(a)

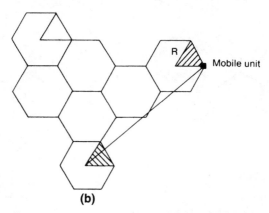

(b)

FIGURE 9.6 Determination of carrier-to-interference ratio C/I in a directional antenna system. (a) Worst case in a 120° directional antenna system ($N = 7$); (b) worst case in a 60° directional antenna system ($N = 7$).

The value of C/I can be obtained by the following expression (assuming that the worst case is at position E at which the distances from two interferers are $D + 0.7$ and D).

$$\frac{C}{I}(\text{worst case}) = \frac{R^{-4}}{(D + 0.7R)^{-4} + D^{-4}}$$

$$= \frac{1}{(q + 0.7)^{-4} + q^{-4}} \tag{9.5-1}$$

Let $q = 4.6$; then Eq. (9.5-1) becomes

$$\frac{C}{I}(\text{worst case}) = 285 \,(=) 24.5 \text{ dB} \tag{9.5-2}$$

The C/I received by a mobile unit from the 120° directional antenna sector system expressed in Eq. (9.5-2) greatly exceeds 18 dB in a worst case. Equation (9.5-2) shows that using directional antenna sectors can improve the signal-to-interference ratio, that is, reduce the cochannel interference. However, in reality, the C/I could be 6 dB weaker than in Eq. (9.5-2) in a heavy traffic area as a result of irregular terrain contour and imperfect site locations. The remaining 18.5 dB is still adequate.

9.5.1.2 Six-Sector Case. We may also divide a cell into six sectors by using six 60°-beam directional antennas as shown in Fig. 9.6*b*. In this case, only one instance of interference can occur in each sector as shown in Fig. 9.5. Therefore, the carrier-to-interference ratio in this case is

$$\frac{C}{I} = \frac{R^{-4}}{(D+0.7R)^{-4}} = (q+0.7)^4 \qquad (9.5\text{-}3)$$

For $q = 4.6$, Eq. (9.5-3) becomes

$$\frac{C}{I} = 794 \, (=) \, 29 \text{ dB} \qquad (9.5\text{-}4)$$

which shows a further reduction of cochannel interference. If we use the same argument as we did for Eq. (9.5-2) and subtract 6 dB from the result of Eq. (9.5-4), the remaining 23 dB is still more than adequate. When heavy traffic occurs, the 60°-sector configuration can be used to reduce cochannel interference. However, fewer channels are generally allowed in a 60° sector and the trunking efficiency decreases. In certain cases, more available channels could be assigned in a 60° sector.

9.5.2 Directional Antenna in $K = 4$ Cell Pattern

9.5.2.1 Three-Sector Case. To obtain the carrier-to-interference ratio, we use the same procedure as in the $K = 7$ cell-pattern system. The 120° directional antennas used in the sectors reduced the interferers to two as in $K = 7$ systems, as shown in Fig. 9.7. We can apply Eq. (9.5-1) here. For $K = 4$, the value of $q = \sqrt{3K} = 3.46$; therefore, Eq. (9.5-1) becomes

$$\frac{C}{I} \text{ (worst case)} = \frac{1}{(q+0.7)^{-4}+q^{-4}} = 97 = 20 \text{ dB} \qquad (9.5\text{-}5)$$

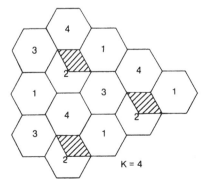

K = 4

FIGURE 9.7 Interference with frequency-reuse pattern $K = 4$.

If, using the same reasoning used with Eq. (9.5-4), 6 dB is subtracted from the result of Eq. (9.5-5), the remaining 14 dB is unacceptable.

9.5.2.2 Six-Sector Case. There is only one interferer at a distance of $D + R$ shown in Fig. 9.7. With $q = 3.46$, we can obtain

$$\frac{C}{I} \text{ (worst case)} = \frac{R^{-4}}{(D + R)^{-4}} = \frac{1}{(q + 1)^{-4}} = 355 = 26 \, \text{dB} \qquad (9.5\text{-}6)$$

If 6 dB is subtracted from the result of Eq. (9.5-6), the remaining 21 dB is adequate. Under heavy traffic conditions, there is still a great deal of concern over using a $K = 4$ cell pattern in a 60° sector. An explanation of this point is given in the next section.

9.5.3 Comparing $K = 7$ and $K = 4$ systems

A $K = 7$ cell-pattern system is a logical way to begin an omnicell system. The cochannel reuse distance is more or less adequate, according to the designed criterion. When the traffic increases, a three-sector system should be implemented, that is, with three 120° directional antennas in place. In certain hot spots, 60° sectors can be used locally to increase the channel utilization.

If a given area is covered by both $K = 7$ and $K = 4$ cell patterns and both patterns have a six-sector configuration, then the $K = 7$ system has a total of 42 sectors, but the $K = 4$ system has a total of only 26 sectors and, of course, the system of $K = 7$ and six sectors has less cochannel interference.

One advantage of 60° sectors with $K = 4$ is that they require fewer cell sites than 120° sectors with $K = 7$. Two disadvantages of 60° sectors are that (1) they require more antennas to be mounted on the antenna mast and (2) they often require more frequent handoffs because of the increased chance that the mobile units will travel across the six sectors of the cell. Furthermore, assigning the proper frequency channel to the mobile unit in each sector is more difficult unless the antenna height at the cell site is increased so that the mobile unit can be located more precisely. In reality the terrain is not flat, and coverage is never uniformly distributed; in addition, the directional antenna front-to-back power ratio in the field is very difficult to predict (see Sec. 8.4.2). In small cells, interference could become uncontrollable; thus the use of a $K = 4$ pattern with 60° sectors in small cells needs to be considered only for special implementations such as portable cellular systems (Sec. 15.6) or narrowbeam applications (Sec. 12.8). For small cells, a better alternative scheme is to use a $K = 7$ pattern with 120° sectors plus the underlay-overlay configuration described in Sec. 13.6.1.

9.6 LOWERING THE ANTENNA HEIGHT

Lowering the antenna height does not always reduce the cochannel interference. In some circumstances, such as on fairly flat ground or in a valley situation, lowering the antenna height will be very effective for reducing the cochannel and adjacent-channel interference. However, there are three cases where lowering the antenna height may or may not effectively help reduce the interference.

9.6.1 On a High Hill or a High Spot

The effective antenna height, rather than the actual height, is always considered in the system design. Therefore, the effective antenna height varies according to the location of the mobile unit, as described in Chap. 8. When the antenna site is on a hill, as shown in Fig. 9.8a, the effective antenna height is $h_1 + H$.

If we reduce the actual antenna height to $0.5h_1$, the effective antenna height becomes $0.5h_1 + H$. The reduction in gain resulting from the height reduction is

$$
\begin{aligned}
G = \text{ gain reduction} &= 20 \log_{10} \frac{0.5h_1 + H}{h_1 + H} \\
&= 20 \log_{10} \left(1 - \frac{0.5h_1}{h_1 + H} \right)
\end{aligned}
\tag{9.6-1}
$$

If $h_1 \ll H$, then Eq. (9.6-1) becomes

$$
G = 20 \log_{10} 1 = 0 \text{ dB}
$$

This simply proves that lowering antenna height on the hill does not reduce the received power at either the cell site or the mobile unit.

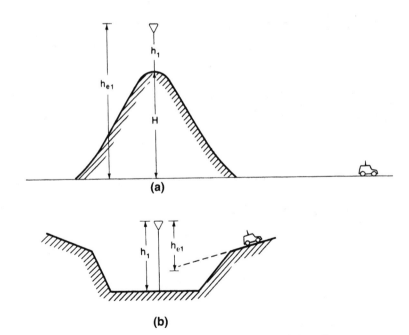

FIGURE 9.8 Lowering the antenna height (*a*) on a high hill and (*b*) in a valley.

9.6.2 In a Valley

The effective antenna height as seen from the mobile unit shown in Fig. 9.8b is h_{e1}, which is less than the actual antenna height h_1. If $h_{e1} = \frac{2}{3}h_1$ and the new antenna height is lowered to $\frac{1}{2}h_1$, then the new effective antenna height, determined from Chap. 8, is

$$h_{e1} = \frac{1}{2}h_1 - (h_1 - \frac{2}{3}h_1) = \frac{1}{6}h_1$$

Then the antenna gain is reduced by

$$G = 20 \ \log\frac{\frac{1}{6}h_1}{\frac{2}{3}h_1} = -12 \ \mathrm{dB}$$

This simply proves that the lowered antenna height in a valley is very effective in reducing the radiated power in a distant high elevation area. However, in the area adjacent to the cell-site antenna, the effective antenna height is the same as the actual antenna height. The power reduction caused by decreasing antenna height by half is only

$$20 \ \log\frac{\frac{1}{2}h_1}{h_1} = -6 \ \mathrm{dB}$$

9.6.3 In a Forested Area

In a forested area, the antenna should clear the tops of any trees in the vicinity, especially when they are very close to the antenna. In this case, decreasing the height of the antenna would not be the proper procedure for reducing cochannel interference because excessive attenuation of the desired signal would occur in the vicinity of the antenna and in its cell boundary if the antenna were below the treetop level. This phenomenon is described in Sec. 8.4.

9.7 REDUCTION OF COCHANNEL INTERFERENCE BY MEANS OF A NOTCH IN THE TILTED ANTENNA PATTERN

9.7.1 Introduction

Reduction of cochannel interference in a cellular mobile system is always a challenging problem. A number of methods can be considered, such as (1) increasing the separation between two cochannel cells, (2) using directional antennas at the base station, or (3) lowering the antenna heights at the base station. Method 1 is not advisable because as the number of frequency-reuse cells increases, the system efficiency, which is directly proportional to the number of channels per cell, decreases. Method 3 is not recommended because such an arrangement also weakens the reception level at the mobile unit. However, method 2 is a good approach, especially when the number of frequency-reuse cells is fixed. The use of directional antennas in each cell can serve two purposes: (1) further reduction of cochannel interference if the interference cannot be eliminated by a fixed separation of cochannel cells and (2) increasing the channel capacity when the traffic increases. In this chapter we try to further reduce the cochannel interference by intelligently setting up the directional antenna.

9.7.2   Theoretical Analysis

Under normal circumstances radiation from a cochannel serving site can easily interfere with another cochannel cell as shown in Fig. 9.9. Installation of a $120°$ directional antenna can reduce the interference in the system by eliminating the radiation to the rest of its $240°$ sector. However, cochannel interference can exist even when a directional antenna is used, as the serving site can interfere with the cochannel cell that is directly ahead. Let us assume that a seven-cell cellular system ($K = 7$) is used. The cochannel interference reduction factor q becomes

$$q = \sqrt{3N} = 4.6 \qquad (9.7\text{-}1)$$

and the cochannel cell separation D can be found if the cell radius is known.

$$D = qR = 4.6R \qquad (9.7\text{-}2)$$

With a separation of $4.6R$, the area of interference at the interference-receiving cell is illuminated by the central $19°$ sector of the entire ($120°$) transmitting antenna pattern at the serving cell (see Fig. 9.9). If three identical directional antennas are implemented in every cell, with each antenna covering a $120°$ sector, then every sector receives interference in the central $19°$ sector of the entire $120°$ angle at the interfering cell. Therefore, attempts should be made to reduce the signal strength of the interference in this $19°$ sector.

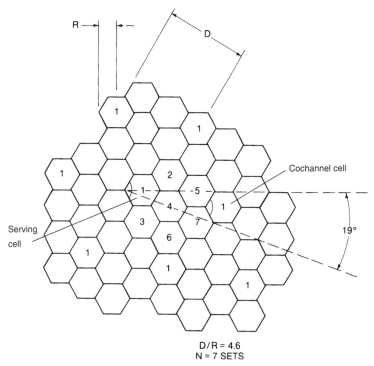

D/R = 4.6
N = 7 SETS

FIGURE 9.9   A seven-cell cellular configuration.

To tilt down the antenna pattern can reduce the signal strength in general. There are two ways to tilt down the antenna patterns; electronically and mechanically. The electronic downtilting is to change the phases among the elements of a colinear array antenna. The mechanical downtilting is to downtilt the antenna physically.

To achieve a significant gain of C/I in the interference-receiving cell (cochannel cell), we should consider using a notch in the center of the antenna pattern at the interfering cell (serving cell). An antenna pattern with a notch in the center can be obtained in a number of ways. One relatively simple way is to tilt the high-gain directional antenna mechanical downward such that the signal strength in a 19° sector angle can be reduced.[4] A discussion of this method follows.

9.7.3 The Effect of Mechanically Downtilting Antenna on the Coverage Pattern

Because the shape of the antenna pattern at the base station relates directly to the reception level of signal strength at the mobile unit, the following antenna pattern effect must be analyzed.[4]

When a high-gain directional antenna (the pattern in the horizontal x-y plane is shown in Fig. 9.10 and in the vertical x-z plane, in Fig. 9.11) is physically (mechanically) tilted at an angle θ in the x-y plane shown in Fig. 9.11, how does the pattern in the x-y plane change? The antenna pattern obtained in the x-y plane after tilting the antenna is shown in Fig. 9.11. When the center beam is tilted downward by an angle θ, the off-center beam is tilted downward by only an angle ψ as shown in Fig. 9.12. The pattern in the x-y plane can

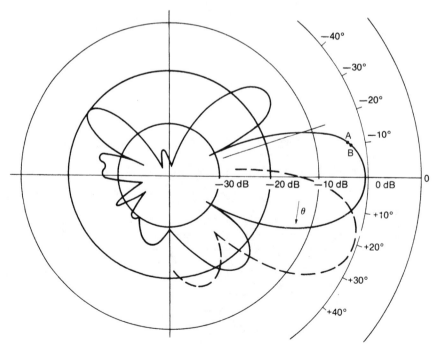

FIGURE 9.10   Vertical antenna pattern of a 120° directional antenna.

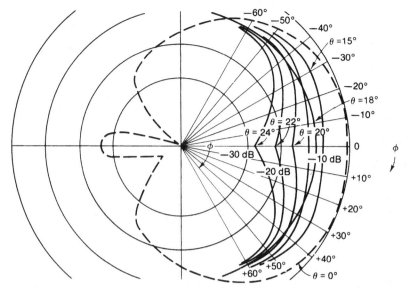

FIGURE 9.11   Notch appearing in tilted antenna pattern. (*Reprinted after Lee, Ref. 4.*)

be plotted by varying the angle ϕ. From the diagram in Fig. 9.12, we can obtain a derivation which provides the relationship among the angles ψ, θ, and ϕ as

$$\sin\frac{\theta}{2} = \frac{d}{l} \tag{9.7-3}$$

$$\frac{\overline{DB}}{\sin\phi} = \frac{l}{\sin(135° - \phi)} \tag{9.7-4}$$

$$\overline{CD} = l\frac{\sin 45°}{\sin(135° - \phi)} \tag{9.7-5}$$

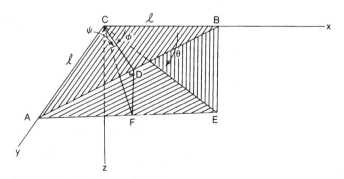

FIGURE 9.12   Coordinate of the tilting antenna pattern.

$$\frac{\overline{AD}}{\overline{DF}} = \frac{\overline{AB}}{2d} = \frac{\sqrt{2}l}{2d} \tag{9.7-6}$$

$$\overline{AD} = \overline{AB} - \overline{DB} \tag{9.7-7}$$

$$\cos \psi = \frac{2\overline{CD} - \overline{DF}}{2\overline{CD}} = 1 - \frac{\overline{DF}}{2\overline{CD}} \tag{9.7-8}$$

Substituting Eqs. (9.7-3) to (9.7-7) into Eq. (9.7-8), we obtain

$$\cos \psi = 1 - \cos^2\phi\,(1 - \cos\theta) \tag{9.7-9}$$

or

$$\psi = \cos^{-1}[1 - \cos^2\phi\,(1 - \cos\theta)] \tag{9.7-10}$$

If the physically tilted angle is $\theta = 18°$, then the off-center beam ψ is tilted downward.

$$\phi = \begin{cases} 0° \\ 45° \\ 90° \end{cases} \qquad \psi = \begin{cases} 18° = \theta \\ 12.7° \\ 0° \end{cases}$$

This list tells us that the physically tilted angle ϕ and the angle ψ are not linearly related, and that when $\phi = 90°$, then $\psi = 0°$. When the angle θ increases beyond 18°, the notch effect of the pattern in the x-y plane becomes evident, as indicated in Fig. 9.11.

9.7.4 Suggested Method for Reducing Interference

Suppose that we would like to take advantage of this notch effect. From Fig. 9.13, we notice that the interfering site could cause interference at those cells within a 19° sector in front of the cell.

In an ideal situation such as that shown in Fig. 9.13, the antenna pattern of the serving cell must be rotated clockwise by 10° such that the notch can be aimed properly

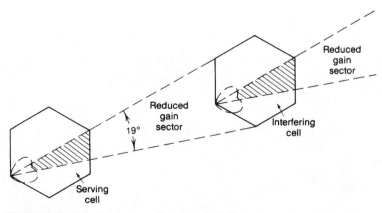

FIGURE 9.13 Reduced-gain sector of two cochannel cells.

at the interfering cell. The antenna tilting angle θ may be between 22° to 24° in order to increase the carrier-to-interference ratio C/I by an additional 7 to 8 dB in the interfering cell as shown in Fig. 9.11. Now we can reduce cochannel interference by an additional 7 to 8 dB because of the notch in the mechanically tilted-antenna pattern. Although signal coverage is rather weak in a small shaded area in the serving cell, as shown in Fig. 9.13, the use of sufficient transmitting power should correct this situation.

9.7.5 Cautions in Tilting Antennas

When a base-station antenna is tilted down mechanically or electronically by 10°, the strength of the received signal in the horizontal direction, as point A shown in Fig. 9.10, is decreased by 4 dB. But the strength of the received signal 1° below the horizontal (at point B) is decreased by 3.5 dB—only 0.5 dB stronger than in the 0° case. This is a very important observation. For example, the elevation angle at the boundary of a 2-mi serving cell with a 100-ft antenna mast is about 0.5°. This means that the serving cell and the interfering cell are separated by only 0.5° at most. Then by tilting the antenna down by 10°, the interference by the interfering cell is reduced by an additional 0.25 dB. This is an insignificant improvement, yet the total power received is 4 dB less than in the no-tilt case. If the tilt is increased to 20°, the received power drops by 16 dB and the reduction in interference due to tilting the antenna is only 1 dB at the interfering cell (see Fig. 9.10). The justification for implementing the tilting antenna is that the new carrier-to-interference ratio $(\alpha C/\beta I)$ after tilting is significantly higher than C/I before tilting, where α and β are those constants which can be expressed if the following expression holds.

$$\frac{\alpha C}{\beta I}\text{(linear scale)} \Rightarrow \frac{C}{I} + (\alpha - \beta)\text{(dB scale)}$$

In the above example, at a 10° tilt, $\alpha = 3.75$ dB (at point B pointing to the cell boundary) and $\beta = 4$ dB at point A pointing to the cochannel cell and the improved new carrier-to-interference ratio is $(C/I) + 0.25$ dB, which is an insignificant improvement. Therefore, the antenna vertical pattern and the antenna height play a major role in justifying antenna tilting. Some calculations are shown in Sec. 9.8.2. Sometimes, tilting the antenna upward may increase signal coverage if interference is not a problem.

9.8 UMBRELLA-PATTERN EFFECT

The umbrella pattern can be achieved by use of a staggered discone antenna as discussed in Sec. 8.13.6. The umbrella pattern can be applied to reduce cochannel interference just as the downward tilted directional antenna pattern is. The umbrella pattern can be used for an omnidirectional pattern, but not for a directional antenna pattern. The tilted directional antenna pattern can create a notch after tilting 20° or more in front of the beam, but the umbrella pattern cannot.

Of most concern for future cellular systems is the long-distance interference due to tropospheric propagation as mentioned in Sec. 8.6. In the future, one system may experience long-distance interference resulting from other systems located approximately 320 km (200 mi) away. Cochannel interference, especially cross talk, could be a severe problem. Therefore, the umbrella pattern might be recommended for every cell site where interference prevails.

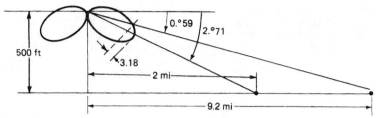

FIGURE 9.14 Coverage with the tilted-beam pattern.

9.8.1 Elevation Angle of Long-Distance Propagation

The elevation of the tropospheric layer[5] is 16 km (10 mi) and the propagation distance is about 320 km (200 mi); thus, the angle of the wave propagating through the tropospheric layers is roughly

$$\theta = \tan^{-1} \frac{10\,\mathrm{mi}}{100\,\mathrm{mi}} = 5.7°$$

It indicates that no strong power should be transmitted upward by 5° or more in order to avoid long-distance propagation.

9.8.2 Benefit of the Umbrella Pattern

The umbrella pattern, in which energy is confined to the immediate area of the antenna, is effective in reducing both cochannel and long-distance interference. Also, in hilly terrain areas there are many holes (weak signal spots). With a normal antenna pattern, we cannot raise the antenna high enough to cover these holes and decrease cochannel interference at the same time. However, the advantage of the umbrella pattern is that we can increase the antenna height and still decrease cochannel interference.

The frequency-reuse distance can be shortened by use of the umbrella pattern. To demonstrate this fact, we first calculate the two angles, one from the cell-site antenna to the cell boundary and the other from the cell-site antenna to the cochannel cell (the two angles are shown in Fig. 9.14).

Antenna Height, ft	Desired Maximum Beam Angle at Boundary of a 2-mi Cell, Degrees	Angle Toward Cochannel Cell at a Distance of $4.6R$ (9.2 mi), Degrees
100	0.54	0.12
300	1.63	0.35
500	2.71	0.59

Suppose that we are using an umbrella-pattern antenna with 11-dB gain,* and that the half-power beamwidth is above 5°. A tower of 500 ft is also used to cover a 2-mi cell.

---

* Normally, antenna gain is measured with respect to a dipole.

Then an approximate 3-dB difference due to the antenna pattern shown in Fig. 9.14 is obtained between the area at the maximum beam angle and the area at the angle reaching the cochannel cell.

$$\frac{R^{-4}}{6D^{-4}} = 18 \text{ dB} - 3 \text{ dB} = 15 \text{ dB}$$

$$q^4 = 6 \times 31.6 = 189.74$$

$$q = 3.7$$

where beam strengths in two regions are different by 3 dB. This demonstrates that the required frequency-reuse distance can be reduced. In other words, more protection against cochannel interference is possible with the use of an umbrella pattern than with an omnidirectional beam pattern.

9.9 USE OF PARASITIC ELEMENTS

Interference at the cell site can sometimes be reduced by using parasitic elements, creating a desired pattern in a certain direction. In such instances, the currents appearing in several parasitic antennas are caused by radiation from a nearby drive antenna. A driven antenna and a single parasite can be combined in several ways.

1. *Normal spacing.*[6] We may first generate two separate patterns as shown in Fig. 9.15a and 9.15b. A single parasite spaced approximately one-quarter wavelength from the driven element is shown in Fig. 9.15a. Because the current flowing in the parasite is much weaker than that in the driven antenna, the front-to-back ratio is usually high. The two parasites spaced one-half wavelength from the driven element are shown in Fig. 9.15b. A combination of Fig. 9.15a and 9.15b forming a pattern very similar to that of a parabola dish is shown in Fig. 9.15c. This is an effective arrangement for cell-site directional antennas with a non-wind-resistant structure: a four-element structure that has only one active element.

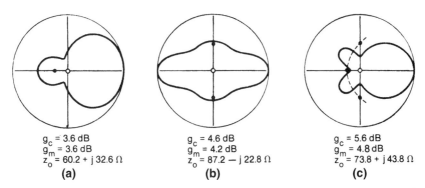

$g_c = 3.6 \text{ dB}$
$g_m = 3.6 \text{ dB}$
$z_o = 60.2 + j\, 32.6\ \Omega$
(a)

$g_c = 4.6 \text{ dB}$
$g_m = 4.2 \text{ dB}$
$z_o = 87.2 - j\, 22.8\ \Omega$
(b)

$g_c = 5.6 \text{ dB}$
$g_m = 4.8 \text{ dB}$
$z_o = 73.8 + j\, 43.8\ \Omega$
(c)

FIGURE 9.15 Parasitic elements with effective interference reduction. (*a*) One-quarter wavelength spacing; (*b*) one-half wavelength spacing; (*c*) combination of *a* and *b*. (*Reprint after Jasik, Ref. 6.*)

2. *Relatively close spacing.*[7] In relatively close spacing, two elements are placed as close as 0.04λ. Three cases can be described here.

   a. *The lengths of two elements are identical.* Two elements, one active and one parasitic, are separated by only 0.04λ. At this close spacing, the current flowing in the parasite is very strong. The two elements form a null along the y axis in the horizontal plane and along the z axis in the vertical plane. There is a directive gain of 3 dB relative to a single element. The horizontal pattern and the vertical pattern of the closely spaced arrangement are shown in Fig. 9.16a.

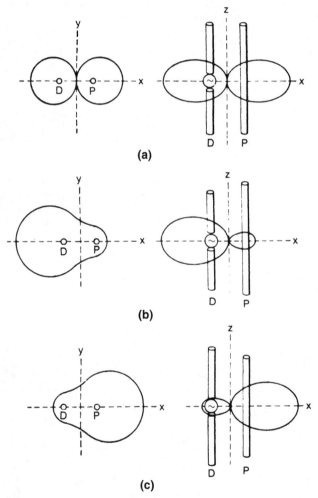

(a)

(b)

(c)

FIGURE 9.16   A close-in parasitic element with effective interference reduction (D = length of dipole; P = length of parasite). (a) $D = P$; (b) $D < P$; (c) $D > P$. (*Reprint after Jasik, Ref. 6.*)

b. *The length of the parasite is 5 percent longer than that of the active one.* In this case, the parasite acts as a reflector. The patterns are shown in Fig. 9.16*b* in both the horizontal and vertical planes. A directive gain of 6 dB is obtained.

c. *The length of the parasite is shorter than that of the active one.* In this case, the parasite acts as a director. The patterns are shown in Fig. 9.16*c* in the vertical and horizontal planes. A gain of 8 dB is obtained.

The pattern shown in Fig. 9.16*a* can be used for eliminating the interference to or from a given direction as shown by the null in the *y* axis. Two elements can be set up such that the *y* axis is aligned with the direction of interference.

Besides, we should emphasize that a directive antenna can be structured by a single parasite with a single active element (Fig.9.16*b* and 9.16*c*). Therefore, a corner reflector or a ground reflector is not needed.

9.10 POWER CONTROL

9.10.1 Who Controls the Power Level

The power level can be controlled only by the mobile switching office (MSO),[*] not by the mobile units, and there can be only limited power control by the cell sites as a result of system limitations.

The reasons are as follows. The mobile transmitted power level assignment must be controlled by the MSO or the cell site, not the mobile unit. Or, alternatively, the mobile unit can lower the power level but cannot arbitrarily increase it. This is because the MSO is capable of monitoring the performance of the whole system and can increase or decrease the transmitted power level of those mobile units to render optimum performance. The MSO will not optimize performance for any particular mobile unit unless a special arrangement is made.

9.10.2 Function of the MSO[*]

The MSO controls the transmitted power levels at both the cell sites and the mobile units. The advantages of having the MSO control the power levels are described in this section.

1. Control of the mobile transmitted power level. When the mobile unit is approaching the cell site, the mobile unit power level should be reduced for the following reasons.

a. Reducing the chance of generating intermodulation products from a saturated receiving amplifier. This point is discussed in Chap. 10.

b. Lowering the power level is equivalent to reducing the chance of interfering with other cochannel cell sites.

c. Reducing the near-end–far-end interference ratio (see Sec. 10.3.1).

Reducing the power level if possible is always the best strategy.

2. Control of the cell-site transmitted power level. When the signal received from the mobile unit at the cell site is very strong, the MSO should reduce the transmitted power level of that particular radio at the cell site and, at the same time, lower the transmitted power level at the mobile unit. The advantages are as follows.

---

[*]MSO is a general term used in this book to represent either a MTSO in AMPS or BSC in digital systems as mentioned in Chapter 2.

a. For a particular radio channel, the cell size decreases significantly, the cochannel reuse distance increases, and the cochannel interference reduces further. In other words, cell size and cochannel interference are inversely proportional to cochannel reuse distance.

b. The adjacent channel interference in the system is also reduced.

However, in most analog cellular systems, it is not possible to reduce only one or a few channel power levels at the cell site because of the design limitation of the combiner. The channel isolation in the combiner is 18 dB. If the transmitted power level of one channel is lower, the channels having high transmitted power levels will interfere with this low-power channel. (The channel combiner is described in Chap.10.) The manufacturer should design an unequal-power combiner for the system operator so that the power level of each channel can be controlled at the cell site. In digital systems, power control appears at each individual channel.

3. The power transmitted from a small cell is always reduced, and so is that from a mobile unit. The MSO can facilitate adjustment of the transmitted power of the mobile units as soon as they enter the cell boundary.

The power control used for reducing near-far interference especially in CDMA systems is described in Sec. 4.4.2.

9.10.3 Reduction of Code Channel Interference[8-11]

In CDMA systems, there can be only one CDMA carrier assigned in all cells that consists of up to 64 coded channels. Those coded channels are distinguished by using 64 Walsh codes. However, the correlation between two Walsh codes is zero only when two coded signals arrived at the same time, e.g., $\tau = 0$, but not zero when $\tau \neq 0$. Thus the Walsh codes are not perfect codes. Use of these Walsh codes in CDMA systems needs power control at the basestation to equalize the different signal strength received from different mobile units in the field. It is the scheme to eliminate the near-far problem so that the individual signals have the same signal strength, and can be detected separately, although the low correlation between any two Walsh codes exists. The property of perfect codes can be shown as follows.

A. Using a perfect spreading code. Assume a perfect spreading code $x(t_1)$ holding its orthogonality property as follows:

1. The autocorrelation of $x(t)$ is

$$< x_1(t) \cdot x_1(t + \tau) > \ = 1 \text{ when } \tau = 0 \qquad (9.10\text{-}1)$$

$$= 0 \text{ when } \tau \neq 0$$

2. The cross-correlation of two perfect spreading codes $x_1(t)$ and $x_2(t)$

$$< x_1(t) \cdot x_2(t + \tau) > \ = 0 \text{ when } \tau = 0 \qquad (9.10\text{-}2)$$

$$= 0 \text{ when } \tau \neq 0$$

Due to the property of Eq. (9.10-2), $x_1(t)$ will be received regardless if the power of $x_2(t)$ is higher than $x_1(t)$. Then there is no need for the power control scheme.

B. Nevertheless, the CDMA spreading codes are Walsh codes. The properties of Walsh codes hold the orthogonality among the Walsh codes when $\tau = 0$. The orthogonality property of Walsh codes is as follows:

1. The autocorrelation of a Walsh code χ_1

$$< x_1(t_1) - x_1(t_1 + \tau) > \; = \; 1 \text{ when } \tau = 0 \qquad (9.10\text{-}3)$$
$$\neq 0 \text{ when } \tau \neq 0$$

2. The cross-correlation of two Walsh codes χ_1 and χ_2

$$< x_1(t_1) - x_2(t_1 + \tau) > \; = \; 0 \text{ when } \tau = 0 \qquad (9.10\text{-}4)$$
$$= \varepsilon \text{ when } \tau \neq 0$$

From the above two equations, we found the Walsh codes only hold a perfect orthogonal property for multiple access transmission when $\tau = 0$. When $\tau \neq 0$, the cross-correlation of two codes is not zero as shown in Eq. (9.10-4). It means the desired code signal will be interfered by another code signal received with a time delay τ due to the multipath. In this case, the power control is needed to make all the code channels have the same power levels while receiving at the base station. The desired signal power (autocorrelation at $\tau = 0$) is then higher than the ε, which is the interference. The power control scheme is further shown in Chapters 4 and 6 for CDMA systems.

The power level to be controlled is usually based on the remote MS probably at the cell boundary. Because the mobiles are moving, the method of implementing the power control is shown in Sec. 4.4.2.

The code-channel interference can be reduced by using the Walsh code channels with power control, but can be eliminated by using a perfect spreading code without power control.

The perfect spreading code has some limitations and will be introduced in Section 18.2.

To choose a set of smart codes[8-11] that have a property close to the perfect code property used in CDMA systems may eliminate the use of power control. Further research is carrying on.

9.11 DIVERSITY RECEIVER

The diversity scheme applied at the receiving end of the antenna is an effective technique for reducing interference because any measures taken at the receiving end to improve signal performance will not cause additional interference.

The diversity scheme is one of these approaches. We may use a selective combiner to combine two correlated signals as shown in Fig. 9.17. The performance of other kinds of combiners can be at most 2 dB better than that of selective combiners. However, the selective combining technique is the easiest scheme to use.[12]

Figure 9.17 shows a family of curves representing this selective combination. Each curve has an associated correlation coefficient ρ; when using the diversity scheme, the optimum result is obtained when $\rho = 0$.

We have found that at the cell site the correlation coefficient $\rho \leq 0.7$ should be used[13] for a two-branch space diversity; with this coefficient the separation of two antennas at the cell site meets the requirement of $h/d = 11$, where h is the antenna height and d is the antenna separation (see Sec. 8.13.5).

At the mobile unit, we can use $\rho = 0$, which implies that the two roof-mounted antennas of the mobile unit are 0.5λ or more apart. This is verified by the measured data shown in Fig. 9.18.[14]

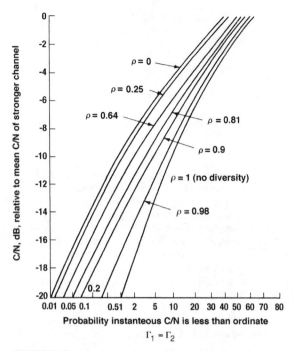

FIGURE 9.17 Selective combining of two correlated signals.

Now we may estimate the advantage of using diversity. First, let us assume a threshold level of 10 dB below the average power level. Then we compare the percent of signal below the threshold level both with and without a diversity scheme.

1. *At the mobile unit.* The comparison is between curves $\rho = 0$ and the $\rho = 1$. The signal below the threshold level is 10 percent for no diversity and 1 percent for diversity. If the signal without diversity were 1 percent below the threshold, the power would be increased by 10 dB (see Fig. 9.17). In other words, if the diversity scheme is used, the power can be reduced by 10 dB for the same performance as in the nondiversity scheme without reducing power. With 10 dB less power transmitted at the cell site, cochannel interference can be drastically reduced.

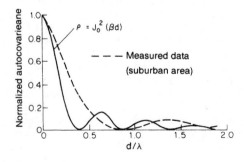

FIGURE 9.18 Autocorrelation coefficient versus spacing for uniform angular distribution (applied to diversity receiver). (*Reprint after Lee, Ref. 10.*)

2. *At the cell site.* The comparison is between curves of $\rho = 0.7$ and $\rho = 1$. We use curve $\rho = 0.64$ for a close approximation as shown in Fig. 9.17. The difference is 10 percent of the signal is below threshold level when a nondiversity scheme is used versus 2 percent signal below threshold level when a diversity scheme is used. If the nondiversity signal were 2 percent below the threshold, the power would have to increase by 7 dB (see Fig. 9.17). Therefore, the mobile transmitter (for a cell-site diversity receiver) could undergo a 7-dB reduction in power and attain the same performance as a nondiversity receiver at the cell site. Thus, interference from the mobile transmitters to the cell-site receivers can be drastically reduced.

9.12 DESIGNING A SYSTEM TO SERVE A PREDEFINED AREA THAT EXPERIENCES COCHANNEL INTERFERENCE

A system for a service area wthout cochannel interference can be designed by using the propagation prediction model described in Chap. 8. When cochannel interference does exist, the service in the area will deteriorate depending on the location of the interference (or interferers). First, let us assume that the ground is flat; then two theoretical equations for designing a system in a given service area can be derived for two different interference cases. Then the same approach can be used to design the systems for a service area where the ground is not flat.

9.12.1 Flat Ground

9.12.1.1 One-Interferer Case. An interferer (cochannel site) is a distance d away from the serving cell site, and the mobile unit is traveling along the boundary of the serving-cell coverage. When the interferer is inactive, the coverage boundary is at a distance R from the serving site. When the interferer becomes active, the distance from the serving site to the effective coverage boundary is r, which can be less than R if the interference is either strong or close to the serving site or both. If we use polar coordinates, the serving site is located at $(0, 0)$ with a transmitted power P_0, and the interferer is located at (d, θ_1) with a transmitted power P_1.

The mobile unit is located at $(r, 0)$, where r can be equal to or less than R. Assume the carrier-to-interference ratio requirement is C/I, then

$$\frac{C}{I} \leq \frac{P_0 r^{-4}}{P_1 \left[\sqrt{r^2 + d^2 - 2rd\cos(\theta - \theta_1)} \right]^{-4}} \qquad r \leq R \qquad (9.12\text{-}1)$$

Let $\theta_1 = 0$ without loss of generality, as shown in Fig. 9.19 as "interferer," and $P_0 = P_1$, then

$$\frac{C}{I} \leq \left(1 + \frac{d^2}{r^2} - \frac{2d}{r}\cos\theta \right)^2 \qquad (9.12\text{-}2)$$

When $r = R$, there is no interference. Then Eq. (9.12-2) becomes

$$\frac{C}{I} \leq \left(1 + \frac{d^2}{R^2} - \frac{2d}{R}\cos\theta \right)^2 \qquad (9.12\text{-}3)$$

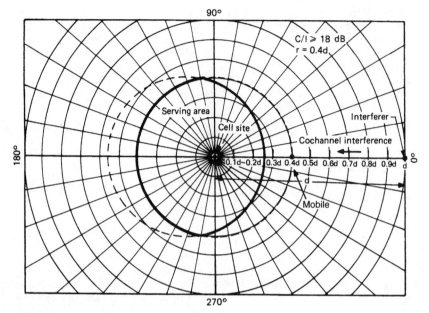

FIGURE 9.19 Serving area under cochannel interference.

Let $\theta = 0$, the strongest interference condition and $C/I = 18$ dB; then Eq. (9.12-3) becomes

$$63 \leq \left(1 - \frac{d}{R}\right)^4$$

or

$$d \geq 3.82R \tag{9.12-4}$$

When $r < d/3.82$, the serving area starts to decrease. Equation (9.12-2) can be converted to rectangular coordinates.

$$\frac{C}{I} \leq \left(1 + \frac{d^2}{x^2 + y^2} - \frac{2dx}{x^2 + y^2}\right)^2$$

or

$$\left(x + \frac{d}{\sqrt{C/I} - 1}\right)^2 + y^2 = d^2 \left(\frac{1}{\sqrt{C/I} - 1} + \frac{1}{(\sqrt{C/I} - 1)^2}\right) \tag{9.12-5}$$

where $x^2 + y^2 \leq R^2$, the serving area has its center at $(-d/\sqrt{C/I} - 1, 0)$, and the radius is $d(C/I)^{1/4}/(\sqrt{C/I} - 1)$. An illustration of Eq. (9.12-5) is shown in Fig. 9.19 as the boundary area.

9.12.1.2 Multiple-Interference Case. For K_I interferers, Eq. (9.12-1) can be modified as

$$\frac{C}{I} = \frac{P_0 r^{-4}}{\sum_{i=1}^{K_I} P_i \left[\sqrt{r^2 + d^2 - 2rd \, \cos(\theta - \theta_1)} \right]^{-4}}$$

$$K_I \leq 6, r \leq R \quad (9.12\text{-}6)$$

9.12.2 Nonflat Ground

The same approach is applied to the propagation model described in Chap. 8 in a real environment for predicting the serving areas.

REFERENCES

1. W. C. Y. Lee, "Elements of Cellular Mobile Radio Systems," *IEEE Transactions on Vehicular Technology*, Vol. 35, May 1986, pp. 48–56.

2. S. Kozono and M, Sakamoto, "Channel Interference Measurement in Mobile Radio Systems," *Proceedings of the 35th IEEE Vehicular Technology Conference*, Boulder, Colorado, May 21–23, 1985, pp. 60–66.

3. W. C. Y. Lee, *Mobile Communications Design Fundamentals*, John Wiley & Sons, 1993, Chap. 4.

4. W. C. Y. Lee, "Cellular Mobile Radiotelephone System Using Tilted Antenna Radiation Pattern," U.S. Patent 4,249,181, February 3, 1981.

5. K. Bullington, "Radio Propagation Fundamentals," *Bell System Technical Journal*, Vol. 36, 1957, pp. 593–626.

6. H. Jasik (Ed.) *Antenna Engineering Handbook*, McGraw-Hill Book Co., 1961, pp. 5–7.

7. A. B. Bailey, *TV and Other Receiving Antenna*, John Francis, Inc., New York, 1950.

8. H. Wei, L.-L. Yang, L. Hanzo, "Interference-Free Broadband Single – and Multicarrier DS-CDMA," *IEEE Communications Magazine*, Feb. 2005, Vol. 43, p. 68–73.

9. P. Z. Fan, et al, "A Class of Binary Sequences with Zero Correlation Zone," *IEEE Elect. Lett.*, 1999, Vol. 35, No. 10, pp. 777–779.

10. H. Chen, J. Yeh, N. Suehiro, "A Multicarrier CDMA Architecture Based on Orthogonal Complementary Codes for New Generations of Wideband Wireless Communications," *IEEE Communications Magazine*, Oct. 20001, Vol. 30, pp. 126–135.

11. W. C. Y. Lee, "CS-OFDMA: A New Wireless CDD Physical Layer Scheme," *IEEE Communication Magazine*, Feb. 2005, Vol. 43, pp. 74–79.

12. D. G. Brennan, "Linear Diversity Combining Techniques," *Proceedings of the IRE*, Vol. 47, June 1959, pp. 1075–1102.

13. W. C. Y. Lee, "Mobile Radio Signal Correlation Versus Antenna Height and Spacing," *IEEE Transactions on Vehicular Technology*, Vol. 25, August 1977, pp. 290–292.

14. W. C. Y. Lee, *Mobile Communications Design Fundamentals*, John Wiley & Sons, 1993, p. 228.

CHAPTER 10
TYPES OF NON-COCHANNEL INTERFERENCE

10.1 SUBJECTIVE TEST VERSUS OBJECTIVE TEST

Voice quality often cannot be measured by objective testing using parameters such as the carrier-to-noise ratio C/N, the carrier-to-interference ratio C/I, the baseband signal-to-noise S/N, and the signal to noise and distortion ratio (SINAD). In a mobile radio environment, multipath fading plus variable vehicular speed are the major factors causing deterioration of voice quality.

Only the following methods can help to correct this imbalance.

1. Let the received carrier level be high to increase the signal level.

2. Let the receiver sensitivity be high to lower the noise level.

3. Maintain a low distortion level in the receiver to increase SINAD.

4. Use a diversity receiver to reduce the fading.

5. Use a good system design in a mobile radio environment and a good adjacent-channel rejection to reduce the interference.

However, when a transceiver is deployed in a mobile radio environment, a subjective test is still the only way to test this receiver, using different types of analog modulation, such as single-sideband, double-sideband, amplitude, and frequency modulation (SSB, DSB, AM, FM), also different types of digital modulation, such as ASK, FSK, MSK, QPSK, QAM, etc.

10.1.1 The Subjective Test

A subjective test can be set up according to the criterion that 75 percent of the customers perceive the voice quality at a given C/N as being "good" or "excellent," the top two levels among the five circuit-merit (CM) grades.[1] The simulator of this test must be adjusted for different mobile speeds. The customers can hear different S/N levels at the baseband on the basis of the carrier-to-noise ratio C/N being changed at the RF transmitter. One typical set of curves from the customers' perception at a mobile speed at 25 km/h (or 16 mi/h) and one at 56 km/h (or 35 mi/h) are shown[2] in Fig. 10.1. Average all the test records for different vehicle speeds and determine a C/N that can satisfy the criterion we have established.

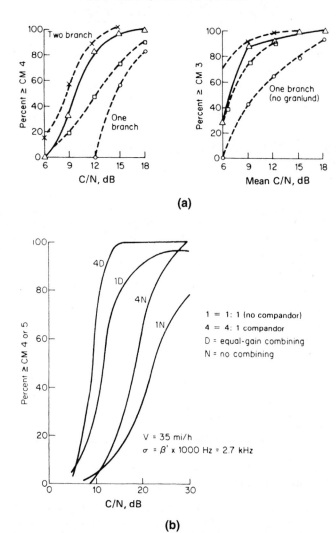

FIGURE 10.1 Results from subjective tests. (*Reprinted from W. C. Y. Lee, Mobile Communications Engineering, McGraw-Hill Book Co., 1997, pp. 505–507.*) (*a*) System-versus-performance comparison based on circuit merit CM4 vs. CM3. (*b*) System-versus-performance comparisons based on circuit merit CM4 and CM5.

10.1.2 The Objective Test

There are many objective tests at the baseband for both voice and data. The characterization of voice quality is very difficult, as mentioned previously, but evaluation of data transmission is easy. There are two major terms: bit-error rates and word error rates. The bit-error rate (BER) is the first-order statistic (independent of time or vehicle speed), and the word-error rate (WER) is the second-order statistic, which is affected by the vehicle speed. These rates are discussed in Chap. 12.

10.1.3 Measurement of SINAD

SINAD has been used as a measurement of communication signal quality at the baseband or in the cellular mobile receiver to measure the effective FM receiver sensitivity.[3] Some telephone industries use a "notched noise" measurement, in which a 1000-Hz tone is sent down the telephone line. The line noise is added onto the tone when it is received. By notching out the tone frequency, we can determine the remaining noise. This is a type of SINAD measurement.

1. The SINAD of the baseband output signal is defined as the ratio of the total output power to the power of the noise plus distortion only.

$$\text{SINAD} = \frac{\text{total output power}}{\text{nonsignal portion}}$$

$$= \frac{\text{signal} + \text{noise} + \text{distortion}}{\text{noise} + \text{distortion}} \tag{10.1-1}$$

The output power can be obtained by measuring the output from a voltmeter and then squaring the voltage, or directly from a power meter. In cellular radio equipment, an input of -116 dBm is equivalent to a SINAD of 12 dB.

2. A high signal level can be measured by

$$\text{SINAD} = \frac{\text{signal} + \text{noise}}{\text{noise}} \approx \frac{\text{signal}}{\text{noise}}$$

The SINAD shown in Fig. 10.2a can be obtained by measuring the signal at the upper position and measuring the noise reading received at the lower position, assuming that the distortion is insignificant.

3. Receiver sensitivity can be measured by modulating with a 1-kHz tone at 3-kHz peak modulation deviation as shown in Fig. 10.2b. The signal-generated attenuator should be adjusted until the SINAD meter shows 12 dB. Then the microvolt output is read from the attenuator dial, which reveals the "12 dB" of SINAD "sensitivity" of the receiver. This means that the signal input must be of a certain level for the signal at the output to be 12 dB higher than noise plus distortion. If the receiver noise is higher, the minimum input signal level should also be higher in order to maintain the 12-dB SINAD.

4. Noise voltage can be measured from a c-message weighting filter on any kind of telephone circuit. The frequency response of this c-message weighting filter is based on the human voice. The noise measured at the output of the filter is the noise withholding in the speech frequency spectrum. Therefore telephone line performance is measured by the amount of noise voltage through the c-message-weight filter.

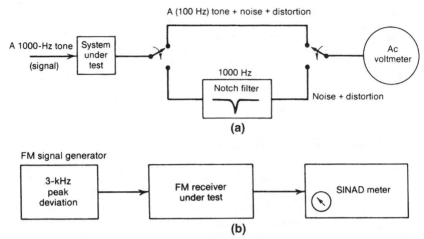

FIGURE 10.2 (*a*) A SINAD meter. (*b*) Measuring receiver sensitivity.

5. The SINAD meter also can be used as a distortion meter if the noise is very low in comparison to the distortion. The SINAD meter can be used to check the maximum distortion figures of the receiver. The input signal level is increased until no thermal noise can be heard; the receiver volume meter reads the audio power, and the SINAD meter reads the distortion.

10.2   ADJACENT-CHANNEL INTERFERENCE

The scheme discussed in Chap. 9 for reduction of cochannel interference can be used to reduce adjacent-channel interference. However, the reverse argument is not valid here. In addition, adjacent-channel interference can be eliminated on the basis of the channel assignment, the filter characteristics, and the reduction of near-end–far-end (ratio) interference. "Adjacent-channel interference" is a broad term. It includes next-channel (the channel next to the operating channel) interference and neighboring-channel (more than one channel away from the operating channel) interference. Adjacent-channel interference can be reduced by the frequency assignment.

10.2.1   Next-Channel Interference

Next-channel interference in an AMPS system affecting a particular mobile unit cannot be caused by transmitters in the common cell site but must originate at several other cell sites. This is because any channel combiner at the cell site must combine the selected channels, normally 21 channels (630 kHz) away, or at least 8 or 10 channels away from the desired one. Therefore, next-channel interference will arrive at the mobile unit from other cell sites if the system is not designed properly. Also, a mobile unit initiating a call on a control channel in a cell may cause interference with the next control channel at another cell site. The methods for reducing this next-channel interference use the receiving end. The channel filter characteristics[4] are a 6 dB/oct slope in the voice band and a 24 dB/oct falloff outside the voice-band region (see Fig. 10.3). If the next-channel signal is stronger than 24 dB, it

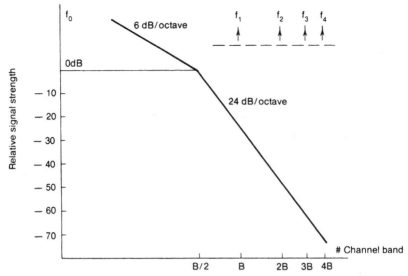

FIGURE 10.3   Characteristics of channel-band filter.

will interfere with the desired signal. The filter with a sharp falloff slope can help to reduce all the adjacent-channel interference, including the next-channel interference. The same consideration is applied to digital systems.

10.2.2   Neighboring-Channel Interference

The channels that are several channels away from the next channel will cause interference with the desired signal. Usually, a fixed set of serving channels is assigned to each cell site. If all the channels are simultaneously transmitted at one cell-site antenna, a sufficient amount of band isolation between channels is required for a multichannel combiner (see Sec. 10.7.1) to reduce intermodulation products. This requirement is no different from other nonmobile radio systems. Assume that band separation requirements can be resolved, for example, by using multiple antennas instead of one antenna at the cell site. There will be no intermodulation products. A truly linear broadband amplifier can realize this idea. However, it is a new evolving technology.

Another type of adjacent-channel interference is unique to the mobile radio system. In the mobile radio system, most mobile units are in motion simultaneously. Their relative positions change from time to time. In principle, the optimum channel assignments that avoid adjacent-channel interference must also change from time to time. One unique station that causes adjacent-channel interference in mobile radio systems is described in the next section.

10.2.3   Transmitting and Receiving Channels Interference

In FDMA and TDMA systems, the transmitting channels and receiving channels have to be separated by a guard band mostly 20 MHz. It is because the transmitting channels are so strong that they can mask the weak signals received from the receiving channels. The duplexer can only provide 30 dB to 40 dB isolation. The band isolation is the other means to reduce the interference.

iDEN Mobile Tx	Cellular Base Rec	iDEN Base Tx	Cellular Mobile Rec

M	A	B	A	B	M	A	B	A	B

800   810   820 830   840   850 860 870   880   890   900

		Mobile Tx	Base Tx
A	Cellular band A	824-835, 845-846.5 MHz	869-880, 890-891.5 MHz
B	Cellular band B	835-845, 846.5-849 MHz	880-890, 891.5-894 MHz
	iDEN	806-821 MHz	851-866 MHz

FIGURE 10.4   Cellular and iDEN spectrum in 800 MHz.

10.2.4 Interference from Adjacent Systems

The frequency bands allocated between AMPS and iDEN in 800-MHz systems are shown in Fig. 10.4. In 1993, iDEN transmitted in the band 851–866 MHz, using several broadband amplifiers to cover this band. The IM (2A-B) generated from the nonlinear amplifiers interfered with the cellular base received signals. Then, the broadband amplifiers were removed.

10.3   NEAR-END–FAR-END INTERFERENCE

10.3.1   In One Cell

Because motor vehicles in a given cell are usually moving, some mobile units are close to the cell site and some are not. The close-in mobile unit has a strong signal that causes adjacent-channel interference (see Fig. 10.5a). In this situation, near-end–far-end interference can occur only at the reception point in the cell site.

If a separation of $5B$ (five channel bandwidths) is needed for two adjacent channels in a cell in order to avoid the near-end–far-end interference, it is then implied that a minimum separation of $5B$ is required between each adjacent channel used with one cell.

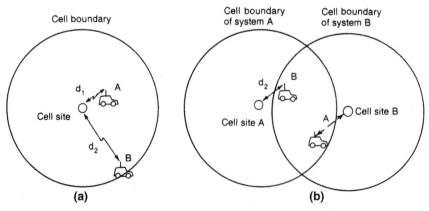

(a)   **(b)**

FIGURE 10.5   Near-end–far-end (ratio) interference. (*a*) In one cell; (*b*) in two-system cells.

Because the total frequency channels are distributed in a set of N cells, each cell only has $1/N$ of the total frequency channels. We denote $\{F_1\}$, $\{F_2\}$, $\{F_3\}$, $\{F_4\}$ for the sets of frequency channels assigned in their corresponding cells C_1, C_2, C_3, C_4.

The issue here is how can we construct a good frequency management chart to assign the N sets of frequency channels properly and thus avoid the problems indicated above. The following section addresses how cellular system engineers solve this problem in two different systems.

10.3.2 In Cells of Two Systems

Adjacent-channel interference can occur between two systems in a duopoly-market system. In this situation, adjacent-channel interference can occur at both the cell site and the mobile unit.

For instance, mobile unit A can be located at the boundary of its own home cell A in system A but very close to cell B of system B as shown in Fig 10.5b. The other situation would occur if mobile unit B were at the boundary of cell B of system B but very close to cell A of system A. Following the definition of near-end–far-end interference given in Sec. 10.3.1, the solid arrow indicates that interference may occur at cell site A and the dotted arrow indicates that interference may occur at mobile unit A. Of course, the same interference will be introduced at cell site B and mobile unit B.

Thus, the frequency channels of both cells of the two systems must be coordinated in the neighborhood of the two-system frequency bands. This phenomenon causes a great concern as indicated in the additional frequency-spectrum allocation charts in Fig. 10.6 as an example.

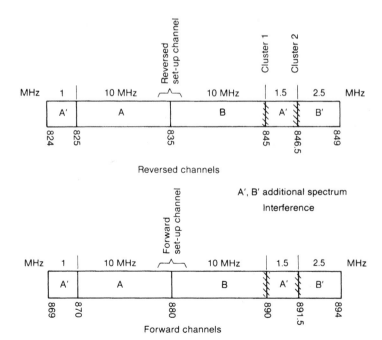

FIGURE 10.6 Spectrum allocation with new additional spectrum.

The two causes of near-end–far-end interference of concern here are

1. *Interference caused on the set-up channels.* Two systems try to avoid using the neighborhood of the set-up channels as shown in Fig. 10.6.
2. *Interference caused on the voice channels.* There are two clusters of frequency sets as shown in Fig. 10.6 that may cause adjacent-channel interference and should be avoided. The cluster can consist of 4 to 5 channels on each side of each system, that is, 8 to 10 channels in each cluster. The channel separation can be based on two assumptions.

   a. *Received interference at the mobile unit.* The mobile unit is located away from its own cell site but only 0.25 mi away from the cell site of another system.

   b. *Received interference at the cell site.* The cell site is located 10 mi away from its own mobile unit but only 0.25 mi from the mobile unit of another system.

These assumptions are discussed in the next section. If the two system operators do not agree to coordinate their use of frequency channels and some of the cell sites of system B are at the coverage boundaries of the cells of system A, then the two groups of frequencies shown in Fig. 10.6 must not be used if interference has to be avoided. Of course, if the two systems do coordinate their use of frequency channels, adjacent channels in the two clusters can be used with no interference.

These observations regarding adjacent-channel interference lead the author to conclude that the existence of two systems having all colocation cell sites in a city is desirable since near-end–far-end ratio interference might be easy to control or might not occur if frequency channel use is coordinated.

10.4   EFFECT ON NEAR-END MOBILE UNITS

10.4.1   Avoidance of Near-End–Far-End Interference

The near-end mobile units are the mobile units that are located very close to the cell site. These mobile units transmit with the same power as the mobile units that are far away from the cell site. The situation described below is illustrated in Fig. 10.7. The distance d_0 between a calling mobile transmitter and a base-station receiver is much larger than the distance d_I between a mobile transmitter causing interference and the same base-station receiver. Therefore, the transmitter of the mobile unit causing interference is close enough

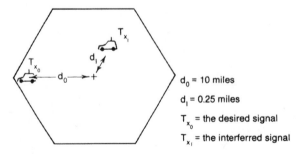

FIGURE 10.7   Near-end–far-end ratio interference.

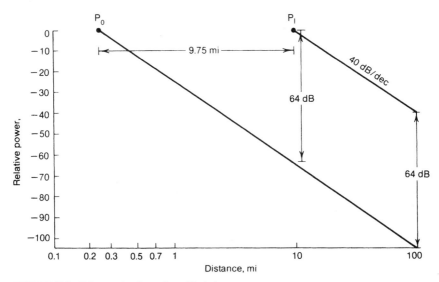

FIGURE 10.8 Using spacing for cochannel isolation.

to override the desired base-station signal.[5] This interference, which is based on the distance ratio, can be expressed as

$$\frac{C}{I} = \left(\frac{d_0}{d_I}\right)^{-\gamma} \tag{10.4-1}$$

where γ is the path-loss slope. The ratio d_I/d_0 is the near-end–far-end ratio. From Eq. (10.4-1) the effect of the near-end–far-end ratio on the carrier–adjacent-channel interference ratio is dependent on the relative positions of the moving mobile units.

For example, if the calling mobile unit is 10 mi away from the base-station receiver and the mobile unit causing the interference is 0.25 mi away from the base-station receiver, then the carrier-to-interference ratio for interference received at the base-station receiver with $\gamma = 4$ is

$$\frac{C}{I} = \left(\frac{d_0}{d_I}\right)^{-4} = (40)^{-4} = -64\,\text{dB} \tag{10.4-2}$$

This means that the interference is stronger than the desired signal by 64 dB (see Fig. 10.8).

This kind of interference can be reduced only by frequency separation with narrow filter characteristics. Assume that a filter of channel B has a 24 dB/oct slope[4]; then a 24-dB loss begins at the edge of the channel $B/2$. The increase from $B/2$ to B results in 24-dB loss, the increase from B to $2B$ results in another 24-dB loss, and so forth.

In order to achieve a loss of 64 dB, we may have to double the frequency band more than two times as

$$\frac{64}{L} = \frac{64}{24} = 2.67$$

where L is the filter characteristic. The frequency band separation for 64-dB isolation is

$$2^{-(C/I)/L}\left(\frac{B}{2}\right) = 2^{2.67}\left(\frac{B}{2}\right) = 3.18B \qquad (10.4\text{-}3)$$

Therefore, a minimum separation of four channels is needed to satisfy the isolation criterion of 64 dB. The general formula for the required channel separation is based on the filter characteristic L, which is expressed as follows.[5]

$$\text{Frequency band separation} = 2^{G-1}B \qquad (10.4\text{-}4)$$

where

$$G = \frac{\gamma \log_{10}\left(\frac{d_0}{d_I}\right)}{L} \qquad (10.4\text{-}5)$$

10.4.2 Nonlinear Amplification

When the near-end mobile unit is close to the cell site, its transmitted power is too strong and saturates the IF log amplifier if the received signal at the cell site exceeds −55 dBm. A typical log IF amplifier characteristic is shown in Fig. 10.9. Assume that the mobile unit transmitted power is 36 dBm and the antenna gain is 2 dBi. The power plus the gain is 38 dBm. The receiver power is −55 dBm at the cell cite.

The propagation loss $L = 38$ dBm − (−55 dBm) = 93 dB. We may calculate the free-space path loss, which is the maximum distance within which the saturation of the IF amplifier will occur. The calculation of free-space loss versus distance at 850 MHz is as follows.

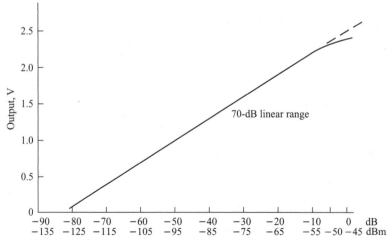

FIGURE 10.9   A typical intermediate-frequency log amplifier.

$$-55\,\text{dBm} = 10\log \frac{P}{(4\pi)^2(d/\lambda)^2}$$

$$= 38\,\text{dBm} - 20\log 4\pi - 20\log\left(\frac{d}{\lambda}\right)$$

$$20\log_{10}\left(\frac{d}{\lambda}\right) = 55 + 38 - 22 = 71 \qquad\qquad (10.4\text{-}6)$$

$$\frac{d}{\lambda} = 10^{71/20} = 3548$$

$$d = 3548\lambda = 4115\,\text{ft}$$

$$= 1241\,\text{m} = 1.24\,\text{km}$$

This means that when the mobile unit is within 1.24 km of the cell-site boundary, it is possible to saturate the IF amplifier, and it is likely that intermodulation will be generated because of the nonlinear portion of the characteristics. If the intermodulation (IM) product matches the frequency channel of another mobile unit far away from the cell site where reception is weak, then the IM can interfere with the other frequency received at the cell site.

Therefore, the near-end mobile unit can cause interference at the cell site with the far-end mobile unit by generating IM at the cell-site amplifier and by leaking into the signal of the far-end mobile unit received at the cell site.

10.5 CROSS TALK—A UNIQUE CHARACTERISTIC OF VOICE CHANNELS

When the cellular radio system was designed, the system was intended to function like a telephone wire line. A wire pair serves both directions of traffic at the line transmission. In a mobile cellular system there is a pair of frequencies, occupying a bandwidth of 60 kHz, which we simply call a "channel." A frequency of 30 kHz serves a received path, and the other 30 kHz accommodates a transmitted path.

Because of paired-frequency (as a wire pair) coupling through the two-wire–four-wire hybrid circuitry at the telephone central office, it is possible to hear voices in both frequencies (in the frequency pair) simultaneously while scanning on only one frequency in the air. Therefore, just as with a wire telephone line, the full conversation can be heard on a single frequency (either one of the two). This phenomenon does not annoy cellular mobile users; when they talk they also listen to themselves through the phone receiver. They are not even aware that they are listening to their own voices.

This unnoticeable cross-talk phenomenon in frequency pairs has no major impact on both wire telephone line and cellular mobile performance. But when real cross talk occurs it has a larger impact on the cellular mobile system than on the telephone line, because the amount of cross talk could potentially be doubled since cross talk occurring on one frequency will be heard on the other (paired) frequency. Cross talk occurring on the reverse voice channel (RVC) can be heard on the forward voice channel (FVC), and cross talk occurring on the forward voice channel can be heard on the reverse channel. Therefore, the cross-talk effect is twofold. A number of situations are conducive to cross talk.

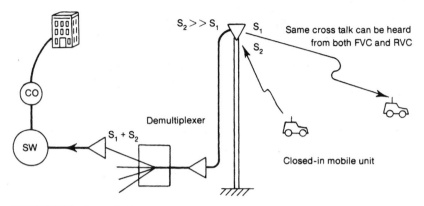

FIGURE 10.10   Cross-talk phenomenon.

Near-end mobile unit. Cross talk can occur when one mobile unit (unit A) is very close to the cell site and the other (unit B) is far from the cell site. Both units are calling to their land-line parties as shown in Fig. 10.10. The near-end mobile unit has a strong signal such that the demultiplexer cannot have an isolation (separation) of more than 30 dB. Then the strong signal can generate strong cross talk while the received signal from mobile unit B is 30 dB weaker than signal A.

Near-end mobile units can belong to one system or to another (foreign) system. If the foreign system units are operating in the new allocated spectrum channels, cross talk can occur. When the mobile unit is close to the cell site and the cell site is capable of reducing the power of the mobile unit, the near-end mobile interference can be reduced.

If the operating frequencies of both home system units and foreign system units are in the new allocated spectrum channels and the isolation of the multicoupler (demultiplexer) could be only 30 dB, cross talk would occur in the two interfering clusters of channels (Fig. 10.10) and could not be controlled by the system operator.

Close-in mobile units. When a mobile unit is very close to the cell site and if the reception at the cell site is greater than -55 dBm, the channel preamplifier at the cell site can become saturated and produce IM as a result of the nonlinear portion of the amplification. These IM products are the spurious (unwanted frequency) signal that leaks into the desired signal and produces cross talk. Also, as mentioned previously, the same cross talk can be heard from both the forward and reverse voice channels.

Cochannel cross talk. The cochannel interference reduction ratio q should be as large as possible to compensate for the cost of site construction and the limitation of available channels at each cellular site. There are other ways to increase q, as mentioned in Chap. 9. An adequate system design will help to reduce the cochannel cross talk.

The channel combiner. The signal isolation among the forward voice channels in a channel combiner is 17 dB.[4] The loss resulting from inserting the signal into the combiner is about 3 dB. The requirement of IM product suppression is about 55 dB. If one outlet is not matched well, the signal isolation is less than 17 dB. Therefore, for each channel an isolator is installed to provide an additional 30-dB of isolation with a 0.5-dB insertion loss. This isolator prevents any signal from leaking back to the power amplifier (see Sec. 10.7.1). Spurious signals can be cross-coupled to this weak channel while transmitting. This kind of cross-coupled interference can be eliminated by routinely checking impedance matching at the combiner.

Telephone-line cross talk. Sometimes cross talk can result from cable imbalance or switching error at the central office and be conveyed to the customer through the telephone line. Minimizing this type of cross talk should be given the same priority as reducing the number of call drops, discussed later (Sec. 11.10 and Sec. 13.1).

10.6 EFFECTS ON COVERAGE AND INTERFERENCE BY APPLYING POWER DECREASE, ANTENNA HEIGHT DECREASE, AND BEAM TILTING

Communications engineers sometimes encounter situations where coverage must be reduced to compensate for interference. There are several ways of doing this. Reorienting the directional-antenna patterns, changing the antenna beamwidth, or synthesizing the antenna pattern were discussed in Chap. 9. There are two additional methods, decreasing the power and decreasing the antenna height. Both methods are effective, and engineers often have difficulty choosing between them. Which one is better? The answer is dependent on the situation.

10.6.1 Choosing a Proper Cell Site

Given a fixed transmitted power and a cell-site antenna height, the coverage contours of a cell site for different signal reception levels can be obtained from either the measurement or from the prediction model described in Chap. 8. A typical contour is shown in Fig. 10.11. Because of the irregular terrain contours, contours between different reception levels are not equally spaced.

When a cell site is selected, we must determine whether an ultra-high-frequency (UHF) TV station is nearby (see Sec. 10.9) and whether any future nearby ongoing construction would affect signal coverage from the cell site later. We must check the local noise level and be sure that no spurious signals fall in the cellular frequency band.

Finally, if we are using an existing multiantenna tower, we must ensure that the grounding and shielding are adequate. Otherwise the interference level could become very high and weaken cell-site operation. Sometimes a special isolator may be provided if an AM broadcasting antenna is colocated on the same tower.

10.6.2 Power Decrease

As long as the setup of the antenna configuration at the cell site remains the same, and if the cell-site transmitted power is decreased by 3 dB, then the reception at the mobile unit is also decreased by 3 dB. This is a one-on-one (i.e., linear) correspondence and thus is easy to control.

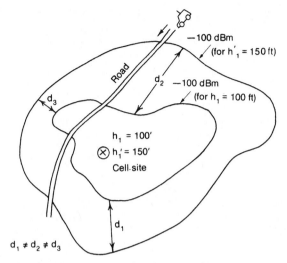

FIGURE 10.11   Signal-strength contour shape changing as the antenna height changes.

10.6.3   Antenna Height Decrease

When antenna height is decreased, the reception power is also decreased. However, the formula [see Eq. (8.10-2)]

$$\text{Antenna height gain (or loss)} = 20 \log \frac{h'_{e_1}}{h_{e_1}}$$

is based on the difference between the old and new effective antenna heights and not on the actual antenna heights. Therefore, the effective antenna height is the same as the actual antenna height only when the mobile unit is traveling on flat ground. It is easy to decrease antenna height to control coverage in a flat-terrain area. For decreasing antenna height in a hilly area, the signal-strength contour shown in Fig. 10.12a is different from the situation of power decrease shown in Fig. 10.12b. Therefore, a decrease in antenna height would affect the coverage; thus, antenna height becomes very difficult to control in an overall plan. Some area within the cell may have a high attenuation while another may not.

10.6.4   Antenna Patterns

The design of different antenna patterns is discussed and illustrated in Chap. 8. Here, we would like to emphasize that the design of the antenna pattern should be based on the terrain contour, the population and building density, and other conditions within a given area. Of course, this is often difficult to do. For instance, implementation of antenna tilting or use of an umbrella pattern might be necessary in certain areas in order to reduce interference.

Sidelobe control (i.e., control of secondary lobe formation in an antenna radiation pattern) is also very critical in the implementation of a directional antenna. Coverage can be controlled by means of the following methods.

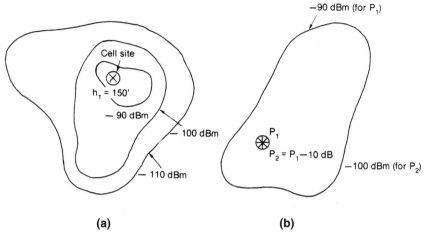

(a)   **(b)**

FIGURE 10.12   The signal-strength effect as measured by different parameters. (*a*) Different signal-strength contours. (*b*) Signal-strength changes with power changes.

10.6.4.1 Using Multiple Antennas.   In a multiple directional antenna pattern, the antennas can have different power outputs and each antenna can form a desired pattern. Two configurations can be mentioned.

1. All the antennas are facing outward (see Fig. 10.13*a*). The resultant pattern is always difficult to control because ripples and deep nulls frequently form.

2. With skewed directional antennas[6] (see Fig. 10.13*b*), the resultant pattern becomes smoother. Therefore, this configuration is more attractive.

10.6.4.2 Using a Synthesis of Power Pattern.   The use of steepest descent techniques for searching the antenna parameters by giving an actual pattern and a desired pattern is introduced here. The signal strength contour obtained from Chap. 8 will be used. The difference between the two patterns, actual and desired, or error ϵ_i, using the ith antenna element can be expressed as

$$\epsilon_i(\phi, d, I_i, \alpha_i, \gamma) = \sum_{j=1}^{M} W_j (P_j - Q_j)^2 \tag{10.6-1}$$

The parameters ϕ, d, and γ are shown in Fig. 10.13*c*, where I_i and α_i are the amplitude and phase of ith element, respectively. P_j is the desired field strength at the jth direction, and Q_j is the given (measured) field strength at the jth direction. All cells may be divided into M small angles, and the jth direction is one of these angles. In Eq. (10.6-1), W_j is a weighting function. When a nonuniform pattern is to be synthesized $W_j \neq 1$. The steepest descent technique can be applied to find the five parameters associated with pattern P_j which will yield the minimum ϵ_i in Eq. (10.6-1).

If we are using L elements, then P_j in Eq. (10.6-1) is the desired radiation field strength at the jth direction.

$$P_j = \sum_{i=1}^{L} P_i(\phi_j - \gamma_i) I_i \times \exp\left\{ -j\left[\frac{2\pi d_i}{\lambda} \cos(\phi_j - \phi_i) - \alpha_i \right] \right\} \tag{10.6-2}$$

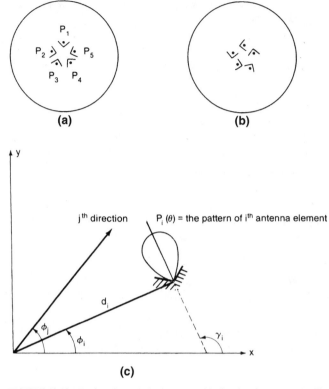

FIGURE 10.13 Engineering a desired pattern with directional antennas. (*a*) Five directional antennas facing outward; (*b*) a skewed configuration of five directional antennas; (*c*) the coordinate.

where $P_i(\phi)$ is the individual pattern of ith element. The magnitude and phase of the ith-element excitation are I_i and α_i, respectively. The remaining variables of Eq. (10.6-2) as shown in Fig. 10.13*c*. Since ϵ is a function of five parameters are indicated in Eq. (10.6-1), we start with an initial guess for the parameters ($\phi_0, d_0, I_0, \alpha_0, \gamma_0$), and then apply the iterative equation

$$\beta_{n+1} = \beta_n - k_{\beta_i} \nabla_{\beta_i} \epsilon_n \qquad (10.6\text{-}3)$$

where β = one of five parameters

$\nabla_{\beta_i} \epsilon_n$ = component of $\nabla \epsilon$ corresponding to the variable β evaluated at a given point, say, $\beta_n = \phi_n(\beta_n, d_n, I_n, \alpha_n, \gamma_n)$

k_{β_i} = gain constant for the parameter β_i

The value k_{β_i} cannot be small; otherwise the convergent process would be very slow. The iterative process is repeated until $n = N$ is reached, that is, $\nabla_{\beta_i} \epsilon_N = 0$. Then from Eq. (10.6-3), $\beta_{n+1} = \beta_n = \beta_i$ for any one of five parameters for the ith antenna element.

The same procedures apply for all elements, and all calculations can be performed by computer.

Caution. Because the terrain is not flat, the signal strengths in all directions are not uniformly attenuated at equal distances; thus, we must first obtain an antenna pattern (not desired) corresponding to a cell boundary in the actual field from a set of predetermined parameters (assume that the current distributions of all antenna elements are the same) and then convert the undesired pattern through the use of an iteration process to a desirable pattern that can be used in the field. The propagation model described in Chap. 8 will serve this purpose. Thus, we can apply this iterative process to practical problems.

10.6.5　Transmitting and Receiving Antennas at the Cell Site

At the base station, the transmitted power of 100 W (+50 dBm) plus an antenna gain of 9 dBi is assumed at one transmitting antenna. The receiving antenna, located at the same site, also has a gain of 9 dBi and receives a mobile signal of -100 dBm. The difference in signal strength is

$$(50 + 9 + 9)\ \text{dBm} - (-100\ \text{dBm}) = +168\ \text{dB}$$

If the space separation between a transmitting antenna and a receiving antenna is 15 m (50 ft) horizontally, the signal isolation between two antennas obtained from the free-space formula is 56 dB.

The 45-MHz bandpass filter followed by the receiving antenna has at least a 55-dB rejection for signals arriving from the 870- to 890-MHz transmission band. However, the two numbers added together is 111 dB, which is still not sufficient (57 dB short). That is why the transmitting antenna and receiving antenna are not mounted in the same horizontal plane, but rather on the same vertical pole, if they are omnidirectional. This restriction can be moderated for directional antennas because of the directive patterns.[7]

10.6.6　A 39-dBμ and a 32-dBμ Boundary

The Federal Communications Commission (FCC) has used a specified received signal strength[8] for the coverage boundary, which is 39 dBμ (dB in μV/m) for AMPS. This value converts to a received power of -93 dBm for dipole or monopole matching on a 50-Ω load at 850 MHz (see Secs. 15.3.3). The value of 39 dBμ (i.e., -93 dBm) should be tested to determine if it is too high for use at the cell boundary in the cellular system.

We can calculate an acceptable level as follows. As we know, the accepted carrier-to-noise ratio for good quality (agreed on by most system operators) is 18 dB for AMPS system. The thermal noise level kTB with a bandwidth of 30 kHz and a temperature of 17°C is -129 dBm.

The receiver front-end noise N_f of an average-quality receiver is 9 dB. The noise figure NF usually would add the front-end noise N_f of the receiver and the noise N_{cm} introduced from the cellular mobile environment.

$$\text{NF} = \sqrt{N_f^2 + N_{cm}^2}\quad \text{dB}$$

N_{cm} can either increase or decrease, depending on the system design. The earlier data indicate that N_{cm} can be neglected for 900-MHz curves.[9,10] If we now introduce a safety factor and let $N_{cm} = 6$ dB then

$$\text{NF} = \sqrt{(9)^2 + (6)^2} = 11\ \text{dB}$$

The total noise level is $N = kTB + \text{NF} = -118$ dBm. Because the required C/N is 18 dB, the lowest acceptable signal level is -100 dBm (-32 dBμ), which is 7 dB lower than -93 dBm (39 dBμ). In reality, the cell boundary or the handoff is based on the voice quality, that is, $C/N = 18$ dB or a level of -100 dBm; therefore, the FCC cell boundary of 39 dBμ or -98 dBm is 7 dB higher than the level provided by the system. Thus a cell boundary of 32 dBμ or -100 dBm proved to be sufficient for cellular coverage.

The two main advantages of using a 32-dBμ level (see Fig. 10.14) are that (1) fewer cell sites would be needed to cover a growth area and (2) less interference would be effected at the boundaries. A 32-dB boundary for cells in either boundary of a metropolitan statistical area (MSA) or a rural service area (RSA) is a proper operation, as opposed to a 39-dBμ boundary which is an artificial value.

In September 1991, the FCC was modifying rules pertaining to measurement of coverage. The idea was based on the reason which the author mentioned in the previous edition of

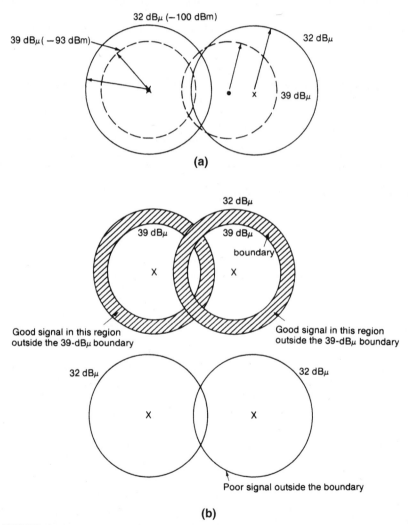

FIGURE 10.14   (*a*) Using a 32-dB boundary needs fewer cells to cover the area. (*b*) A signal outside its boundary generates noise.

this book. The FCC proposes the following formula to define a cellular geographic service area (CGSA):

$$d = 1.05 \times H^{0.34} \times P^{0.17} \quad \text{(FCC)} \tag{10.6-4}$$

where d is the distance from the cell site antenna to the reliable service area boundary in miles, H is the antenna height above average terrain in feet, and P is the effective radiated power (ERP) in watts. This formula approximates this distance to the 32-dBμ contour predicted by Carey.

The prediction based on the Lee model also can be derived from Eq. (8.2-18) as follows

$$d = 0.348 \times H^{0.52} \times P^{0.26} \quad \text{(Lee)} \tag{10.6-5}$$

10.7 EFFECTS OF CELL-SITE COMPONENTS

10.7.1 Channel Combiner

10.7.1.1 A Fixed-Tuned Channel Combiner at the Transmitting Side. A channel combiner is installed at each cell site. Then all the transmitted channels can be combined with minimum insertion loss and maximum signal isolation between channels. Of course, we can eliminate the channel combiner by letting each channel feed to its own antenna. Then a 16-channel site will have 16 antennas for operation. It is an economical and a physical constraint. In GSM, a multicarrier combiner is used.

A conventional AMPS combiner has a 16-channel combined capacity based on the frequency subset of 16 channels, and it causes each channel to lose 3 dB from inserting the signal through the combiner. The signal isolation is 17 dB because each channel is 630 kHz or 21 channels apart from neighboring channels (Fig. 10.15*a*). The intermodulation at the multiplexer is controlled by ferrite isolators, which provide a 30-dB reverse

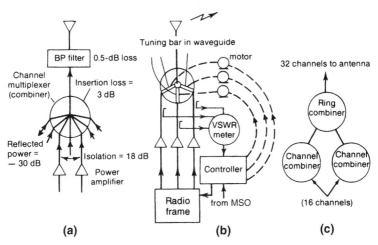

FIGURE 10.15   Different kinds of channel combiners. (*a*) Fixed-tuned combiner; (*b*) tunable combiner; (*c*) ring combiner.

loss. The intermodulation (IM) products are at least 55 dB down from the desired signals. Therefore, the IM will not affect channels within the transmitted band design from this.

Each cable fed into a combiner must be properly shielded. Because it is a nonlinear device, undesired signal leakage into another channel would occur before the combiner can produce the IM products, which would in turn, produce cross-coupled interference. Therefore, proper shielding and impedance match are very important. Fixed-tuned combiners are tuned to match the impedances of a set of fixed frequencies which are assigned to a combiner.

10.7.1.2 A Frequency-Agile Combiner.[11] This combiner is capable of returning to any frequency by remote control in real time. The remote control device is a microprocessor. The combiner is a waveguide-resonator combiner with a tuning bar in each input waveguide as shown in Fig. 10.15*b*. The bar is mechanically rotated by a motor, and the voltage standing-wave ratio (VSWR) can be measured when the motor starts to turn. The controller receives an optimum reading after a full turn and is stopped at that position by the controller. The controller also has a self-adjusting potential. This combiner can be used when a dynamic frequency assignment is applied. In many cases, it is preferable to redistribute the frequency channels to avoid prominent interference in certain areas. To use this kind of combiner, cell-site transceivers should also be able to change their operating frequencies, which are controlled by the MSO, accordingly. This kind of combiner can also be designed to be tuned electronically.

10.7.1.3 A Ring Combiner.[12] A ring combiner is used to combine two groups of channels into a single output. The insertion loss is 3 dB, and the signal isolation between channels is 35 to 40 dB. The function of a ring combiner is to combine two 16-channel combiners into one 32-channel output. Therefore, all 32 channels can be used by a single transmitting antenna. If a cell site has two antennas, up to 64 radio channels can be installed in it.

If all the channel-transmitted powers are low, it is possible to combine more than 32 channels by using two or three ring combiners before feeding them into one transmitting antenna. The total allowed transmitted power is a limiting factor. Some ring combiners have a 600-W power limitation. The use of ring combiners reduces adjacent channel separation. If two 16-channel regular combiners are combined with a ring combiner, the adjacent-channel separation at the ring combiner output can be 315 kHz, even though the adjacent-channel separation of each regular combiner is 630 kHz. It is simply a frequency offset of 315 kHz between two regular combiners.

10.7.2 Demultiplexer at the Receiving End

A demultiplexer is commonly used to receive 16 channels from one antenna. The demultiplexer is a filter bank as shown in Fig. 10.16. Then, each receiving antenna output passes through a 25-dB-gain amplifier to a demultiplexer. The demultiplexer output has a 12-dB loss from the split of 16 channels.

$$\text{Split loss} = 10 \log 16 = 12 \text{ dB}$$

and the IM product at the output of the demultiplexer should be 65 dB down.[4] The two space-diversity antennas each connect to an umbrella filter (block A or B band filter for AMPS) and have a 55-dB rejection from the other system band. If the undesired mobile unit is close to the cell site, then the preamplifier becomes saturated and generates IM at

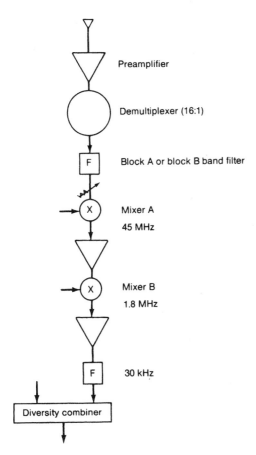

Preamplifier

Demultiplexer (16:1)

Block A or block B band filter

Mixer A
45 MHz

Mixer B
1.8 MHz

30 kHz

Diversity combiner

FIGURE 10.16   A typical cell-site channel receiver.

the output of the amplifier; these IM products (frequencies) could be felt in one of the weak incoming signals. This situation can lead to cross talk (see Sec. 10.4) which can be heard from both ends of the link because of a unique characteristic of cellular channels (see Sec. 10.5).

10.7.3   SAT Tone of AMPS System

10.7.3.1   General Description.   The major function of a supervisory audio tone (SAT) is to ensure that a SAT tone is sent out at the cell site, is received by the mobile unit on a forward voice channel, is converted on a corresponding reverse voice channel, and is then sent back to the cell site within 5 s. If the time out is more than 5 s, the cell site will terminate the call.

Every cell site has been assigned to one of three SAT tones. The assignment of three SAT tones in a system is shown in Fig. 10.17. The cells have the same SAT tones, and the same channels are separated by $\sqrt{3}D$, which is farther than the cochannel

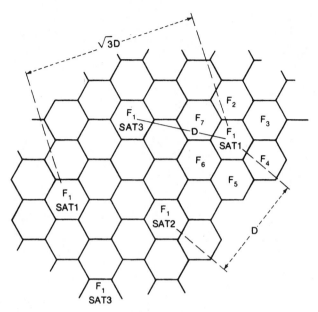

FIGURE 10.17   SAT spatial allocation.

distance D. Therefore, a receiver located at either the cell site or at the mobile unit and receiving the same frequency with different SAT tones will terminate the call.

10.7.3.2   Characteristics of SAT.   There are three SAT tones, 5970 H, 6000 H, and 6030 Hz, spaced 30-Hz apart. They are narrowband frequency-modulated (FM) with a deviation of $f_\Delta = 2$ kHz. The modulation index is $\beta = \frac{1}{3}$. Let the SAT tone signal be

$$x(t) = A_m \cos \omega_m t \qquad (10.7\text{-}1)$$

and the modulated carrier is

$$x_c(t) = A_c \cos(\omega_c t + \beta \sin \omega_m t) \qquad (10.7\text{-}2)$$

where $\beta = (A_m f_\Delta / f_m)$. Let the amplitude modulation $A_m = 1$; thus, since β is small, Eq. (10.7-2) becomes

$$x_c(t) \approx A_c \cos(\omega_c t) + \frac{A_c \beta}{2}$$

$$\times \cos\left[2\pi(f_c + f_m)t\left[- \frac{A_c \beta}{2}\cos\right]2\pi(f_c - f_m)t\right]$$

$$= R(t)\cos[\omega_c t + \phi(t)] \qquad (10.7\text{-}3)$$

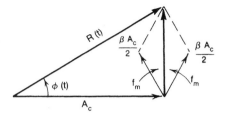

FIGURE 10.18   Narrowband FM for SAT.

where[13]

$$R(t) \approx \sqrt{A_c^2 + \left(2\frac{\beta}{2} A_c \sin \omega_m t \right)^2}$$

$$\approx A_c \left[1 + \frac{\beta^2}{4} - \frac{\beta^2}{4} \cos 2\omega_m t \right] \qquad (10.7\text{-}4)$$

$$\phi(t) \approx \arctan \left[\frac{2(\beta/2)A_c \sin \omega_m t}{A_c} \right] \approx \beta \sin \omega_m t \qquad (10.7\text{-}5)$$

The FM phasor diagram for $\beta \ll 1$ is shown in Fig. 10.18. Equation (10.7-4) represents an FM condition in which the amplitude of the carrier always remains constant. This means that the amplitude has no information content. This is a very common consideration in the mobile radio environment because of the severe fading that distorts the constant amplitude.

The SAT generator cannot deviate by more than ± 15 Hz while receiving the signal. The SAT detector uses this criterion to continuously accept or reject a returned SAT. It has been observed that two SATS with two different audio tone amplitudes can arrive at one cell. If the desired SAT tone is weaker than the undesired one by a certain ratio, then the SAT tone will deviate by ± 15 Hz. These conditions are discussed in Sec. 15.1.2. The filter bandwidth of the SAT tone detector relates to call-drop timing, which should be based on the unacceptable voice quality level. In theory, this level is different in different environment. Usually the smaller the filter bandwidth, the lower the call-drop rates. But the voice quality may be very poor before dropping the calls.

In IS-136 system, there are 2^8 digital color codes (DCC) using 8 bits to serve the purpose of SAT in AMPS. Because of the large number of DCC, the problem of using SAT does not exist in digital systems.

10.8 INTERFERENCE BETWEEN SYSTEMS

10.8.1 In One City

Let us assume that there are two systems operating in one city or one MSA. If a mobile unit of system A is closer to a cell site of system B while a call is being initiated through system A, adjacent channel interference or IM can be produced if the transmitted frequency

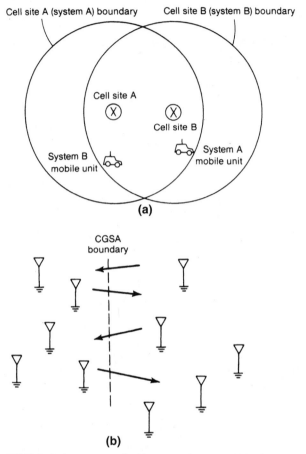

FIGURE 10.19   Intersystem interference. (*a*) System A cell sites in system B cell coverage; (*b*) interference between two cellular geographic service area (CGSA) systems.

of mobile unit A is close to the covered band of the received preamplifier at cell site B (see Fig. 10.19*a*). These IM products will then leak into the receiving channel of system B and cross talk will occur. This cross talk can be heard not only at the land-line side but also at the mobile unit because of the unique characteristics described in Sec. 10.5.

This cross-talk situation can be reduced by any of the following measures.

1. All cell sites in the two systems can be located together (*colocated*).

2. Adjacent channels (four or five channels) at each cluster (see Fig. 10.6) of the new allocated voice channels between two of the AMPS systems should not be used.

3. To prevent a strong mobile signal from saturating the preamplifier at the cell site, a foreign-system signal should be −55 dBm down from the cell-site reception point. Otherwise IM products can be produced and mixed with the desired system by passage through the system (band) block filter (see Fig. 10.16).

For instance, IM may occur in either of the following cases.

$$(2 \times 838 - 832)\,\text{MHz} = 844\,\text{MHz}\,(\text{system B at the cell site})$$

Either signal (838 or 832 MHz) is strong; the IM will leak into the 844-MHz channel.

$$(2 \times 834 - 836)\,\text{MHz} = 832\,\text{MHz}\,(\text{system A at the cell site})$$

Either signal (834 or 836 MHz) is strong; the IM will leak into the 832-MHz channel.

10.8.2 In Adjacent Cities

Two systems operating at the same frequency band and in two adjacent cities or areas may interfere with each other if they do not coordinate their frequency channel use. Most cases of interference are due to cell sites at high altitudes (see Fig. 10.19b). In any start-up system, a high-altitude cell site is always attractive to the designer. Such a system can cover a larger area, and, in turn, fewer cell sites are needed. However, if the neighboring city also uses the same system block, then the result is strong interference, which can be avoided by the following methods.

1. The operating frequencies should be coordinated between two cities. The frequencies used in one city should not be used in the adjacent city. This arrangement is useful only for two low-capacity systems.
2. If both systems are high capacity, then decreasing the antenna heights will result in reduction of the interference not only within each system but also between the two systems.
3. Directional antennas may be used. For example, if one system is high capacity and the other is low capacity, the low-capacity system can use directional antennas but still retain the high tower. In this situation frequency coordination between the two systems has to be worked out at the common boundary because all the allocated frequencies must be used by the high-capacity system in its service area but only some frequencies are used by the low-capacity system.

10.9 UHF TV INTERFERENCE

Two types of interference can occur between UHF television and 850-MHz cellular mobile phones.

10.9.1 Interference to UHF TV Receivers from Cellular Mobile Transmitters

Because of the wide frequency separation between cellular phone systems and the media broadcast services (TV and radio) and the significantly high power levels used by the UHF TV broadcast transmitters, the likelihood of interference from cellular phone transmissions affecting broadcasting is very small.[14,15] There is a slight probability that when the cell-site transmission is 90 MHz above that of a TV channel, it can interfere with the image-response frequency of typical home TV receivers. Interference between TV and cellular mobile channels is illustrated in Fig. 10.20.

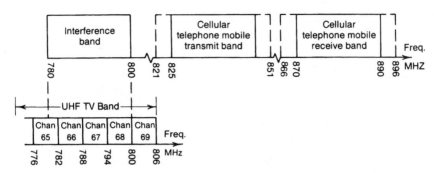

FIGURE 10.20 Cellular telephone frequency plan.

Some UHF TV channels overlap cellular mobile channels. There two types of service can interfere with each other only under following conditions.

1. *Band region with overlapping frequencies.* Two services have been authorized to operate within the same frequency band region.

2. *Image interference region.* This is explained as follows. The TV receiver or the cellular receiver (mobile unit or cell site) can receive two transmitted signals, for instance, one from a TV channel and one from a cellular system, and produce a third-order intermodulation product that falls within the TV or the mobile receive band.

Let

$$f_{Tm} = \text{mobile transmit frequency}$$

$$= f_{Rc} = \text{cell-site receive frequency} = f_{Tc} - 45 \text{ MHz}$$

$$f_{Rm} = \text{mobile receive frequency}$$

$$= f_{Tm} + 45 \text{ MHz} = f_{Tc} = \text{cell-site transmit frequency}$$

$$f_{T,\text{TV}} = \text{TV transmit frequency}$$

$$f_{R,\text{TV}} = \text{TV receive frequency}$$

Third-order intermodulation gives the following results in two cases of interfering UHF TV receivers.

Case 1. Let

$$2f_{Tm} - f_{T,\text{TV}} = f_{Rm} \qquad (10.9\text{-}1)$$

$$f_{Tm} = f_{Rm} - 45 \qquad (10.9\text{-}2)$$

then

$$f_{Tm} = f_{T,TV} + 45 \qquad (10.9\text{-}3)$$

Because the mobile transmit frequency f_{Tm} lies in the 825- to 845-MHz band, and the TV transmit frequency $f_{T,TV}$ lies in the 780- to 800-MHz band, f_{Tm} will interfere with the TV receiver as seen from Eq. (10.9-3). This interference region is called the *image interference region*.

Case 2. Let

$$2f_{Rc} - f_{T,TV} = f_{Tc} \tag{10.9-4}$$

then

$$2f_{Rc} = f_{Tc} - 45 \tag{10.9-5}$$

and

$$2f_{Tc} = f_{T,TV} + 90 \tag{10.9-6}$$

Because the cell-site transmit frequency f_{Tc} lies in the 870- to 890-MHz band, and $f_{T,TV}$ lies in the 780- to 800-MHz band, f_{Tc} will interfere with the TV receiver, as shown in Eq. (10.9-6). This interference region is called the image interference region.

In these two cases, an image-interference rejection range of 40 to 50 dB isolation across the UHF TV band is required to prevent this interference. The results from the two cases are as follows.

Case 1: When the mobile transmitter is located near a TV receiver (Eq. 10.9-3). The minimum grade B television service contour of an accepted TV receiver level is -63 dBm with a receiver antenna gain of 6 dB referring to dipole gain. Roughly, this kind of TV station has a coverage of a 56-km (35-mi) radius. Since the cellular telephone mobile unit has an effective radiated power (ERP) of about 37 dBm, the difference in signal levels between the TV receiver and the mobile transmitter can exceed 100 dB ($= 63 + 37$). The TV antenna height at each residence normally is about $h_2 = 10$ m. The mobile antenna height is about $h_1 = 2$ m. Assume that the cross-modulation loss between two frequency bands is 80 dB and the polarization coupling loss between the bands is 10 dB. Using the formula derived in Eq. (8.2-19), we obtain

$$-63 = 37 - 156 - 40 \log \frac{d_1}{d_0} + 10 \log h_1$$

$$+ 20 \log h_2 + 6 - (80 + 10) \, \text{dB} \tag{10.9-7}$$

Substitution of $h_1 = 2$ m (6 ft) and $h_2 = 10$ m (30 ft) into Eq. (10.9-7) yields

$$140 = -40 \log d_1 + 7.78 + 29.54$$

We can solve d_1 as

$$d_1 = 10^{-2.57} = 0.00239 \, \text{mi} = 14 \, \text{ft}$$

We find that the required non-interference distance from a transmitting cellular mobile unit to a TV receiver is only 14 ft. Besides, a mobile unit is always moving while the TV receivers usually are off; thus, the chance of mobile unit interference occurring within 14 ft of the receiver while TV receivers are operative is very slim. In addition, the chances are that the mobile unit would remain in the area of interference for only 5 to 10 s.

Case 2: When the cell site transmitter is located near a TV receiver (Eq. 10.9-6). Usually, cell-site antennas are located on high towers, and the vertical antenna pattern usually produces a null under the antenna tower. Therefore, even though Eq. (10.9-6) indicates the possibility of cell-site interference, the TV receivers near the cell site will not be in the area of the main antenna beam and, clearly, the horizontally polarized TV wave will not be distorted by the cellular vertically polarized waves when it reaches the TV receiving antenna on the roof of the house. Because of these differences between antenna beam pattern and wave polarization, no strong interference can be seen in this case. We find that the required distance could be less than 200 m (700 ft). We should also consider the following key points.

1. The polarization coupling loss from vertical (cellular) to horizontal (TV) waves can be 10 dB, according to Lee and Yeh's data.[16]

2. The percentage of active mobile units in that area is small.

3. In the UHF TV fringe area, cable TV (CATV) usually provides the service.

4. Only four TV channels (Channels 65 to 68) can experience interference. The chance of one TV set tuning to one of these four "interference channels" and the active mobile unit happening to be in that area at the same time is slim.

5. Even if transmission from the mobile unit does interfere with TV reception, the interference time is very short (<15 s). Therefore, no interference should be encountered.

10.9.2 Interference of Cellular Mobile Receivers by UHF TV Transmitters

This type of image interference can occur in the following four cases. Here, the image-interference region will be the same as that described in Sec. 10.9.1 but in the reversed direction.

Case 1. Let

$$2f_{Tm} - f_{T,TV} = f_{Rm} \tag{10.9-8}$$

Then

$$2f_{Tm} = 2(f_{Rm} - 45) \tag{10.9-9}$$

and

$$F_{T,TV} = 2f_{Tm} - f_{Rm} = f_{Rm} - 90 \text{ MHz} \tag{10.9-10}$$

Because the mobile unit receiver frequency f_{Rm} lies in the 870- to 890-MHz band, $f_{T,TV}$, which lies in the 780- to 800-MHz band, will interfere with the mobile unit receiver, as shown in Eq. (10.9-10).

Case 2. Let

$$2f_{Rc} - f_{T,TV} = f_{Tc} \tag{10.9-11}$$

Then

$$f_{Rc} = f_{Tc} - 45 \tag{10.9-12}$$

and

$$f_{Rc} = 2f_{Rc} - f_{T,TV} - 45 = f_{T,TV} + 45 \tag{10.9-13}$$

Because the cell-site receiver frequency f_{Rc} lies in the 825- to 845-MHz band, $f_{T,TV}$, which lies in the 780- to 800-MHz band, will interfere with the cell-site receiver as shown in Eq. (10.9-13). There are two additional, but less important, cases.

Case 3. When a mobile receiver approaches a TV transmitter, it is easy to find that transmission from the TV station will not interfere with the reception at the mobile receiver by following the same analysis shown in Sec. 10.9.1, case 2.

Case 4. When the cell-site receiver is only 1 mi or less away from the TV station, interference may result. However, when the cell site is very close to the TV station, the interference decreases as a result of the two vertical narrow beams pointing at different elevation levels. For this reason, it is advisable to mount a cell-site antenna in the same vicinity as the TV station antenna if the problems of shielding and grounding can be controlled.

10.10 LONG-DISTANCE INTERFERENCE

10.10.1 Overwater Path

The phenomenon is mentioned in several reports.[17,18]

1. A 41-mi overwater path operating at 1.5 GHz in Massachusetts Bay.[17]

   a. Low ducts (<50 ft thick); steady signal well above normal level is received.

   b. High ducts (≥100 ft thick); a high signal level generally on the average is received but with deep fading.

2. A 275-mi overwater path operating at 812 and 857 MHz between Charleston, South Carolina, and Daytona Beach, Florida.

   a. Charleston: Antenna height 500 ft above average terrain antenna pattern, omnidirectional ERP 220 W; receiving sensitivity less than 0.5 μV $= -113$ dBm (1 μV $= -107$ dBm) with a 50-Ω terminal.

   b. Daytona Beach: Antenna height 920 ft above average terrain antenna pattern, omnidirectional ERP 440 W; receiving sensitivity 0.7 μV $= -110$ dBm.

Federal Express engineers have discovered the following phenomenon through study of their system.[18] The mobile units in Charleston within 1 to 2 mi of shoreline are capable of clear communication with a repeater station in Daytona Beach. The same situation applies when the mobile unit is in Daytona Beach. These clear path communications occur regardless of weather, time of day, or season. This is a tropospherical propagation, and we should eliminate it in cellular systems to avoid interference among systems in North America. One way of doing this is by use of umbrella antenna patterns.

10.10.2 Overland Path

Tropospheric scattering over a land path is not as persistent as that over water and can be varied from time to time. Usually, tropospheric propagation is more pronounced in the morning. The distance can be about 200 mi. Federal Express engineers have observed this long-distance propagation throughout their nationwide system.

REFERENCES

1. V. H. MacDonald, "The Cellular Concept," *Bell System Technical Journal*, Vol. 58, January 1979, pp. 15–42.

2. S. W. Halpern, "Techniques for Estimating Subjective Opinion in High-Capacity Mobile Radio," *Microwave Mobile Symposium*, Boulder, Colorado, 1976.

3. F. E. Terman and J. M. Pettit, *Electronic Measurements*, McGraw-Hill Book Co., 1952.

4. N. Ehrlich, R. E. Fisher, and T. K. Wingard, "Cell-Site Hardware," *Bell System Technical Journal*, Vol. 58, January 1979, pp. 153–199.

5. W. C. Y. Lee, "Elements of Cellular Mobile Radio Systems," *IEEE Transactions on Vehicular Technology*, Vol. VT-35, May 1986, pp. 48–56.

6. J. Pecini and M. H. Idselis, "Radiation Pattern Synthesis for Broadcast Antennas," *IEEE Transactions on Broadcasting*," Vol. BC-18, September 1972, pp. 53–62.

7. W. C. Y. Lee, *Mobile Communications Design Fundamentals*, 2nd Edition, John Wiley & Sons, p. 210.

8. FCC Application for Cellular Operation License Requirement.

9. A. D. Spaulding and R. T. Disney, "Man-Made Radio Noise, Part I: Estimate for Business, Residential and Rural Areas," U.S. Department of Commerce, Office of Technical Services Report 74-38, June 1974.

10. E. N. Skomal, *Man-Made Radio Noise*, Van Nostrand Reinhold, 1978, Chap. 2.

11. Antenna Specialist Co., Cleveland, Ohio, A Frequency-Agile Combiner.

12. Antenna Specialist Co., Cleveland, Ohio, A Ring Combiner.

13. P. F. Panter, *Modulation, Noise, and Spectral Analysis*, McGraw-Hill Book Co., 1965, p. 248.

14. S. N. Ahmed and P. C. Constantinon, "A Mobile Interference Model into UHF Television Receivers," *IEEE Transactions on Vehicular Technology*, Vol. VT-32, May 1983, pp. 206–208.

15. R. E. Fisher, "UHF Television Interference Associated with Cellular Mobile Telephone Systems," *IEEE Transactions on Vehicular Technology*, Vol. VT-33, August 1984, pp. 244–249.

16. W. C. Y. Lee and Y. S. Yeh, "Polarization Diversity System for Mobile Radio," *IEEE Transactions on Communications*, Vol. COM-20, October 1972, pp. 912–923.

17. S. S. Attwood (Ed.), *Radio Wave Propagation Experiments*, Vol. 2, Columbia University Press, 1946, Part I, pp. 3–47 (Chaps. 1 and 2).

18. G. W. Moor and S. Walton, Federal Express Inc., private communication.

CHAPTER 11
HANDOFFS AND DROPPED CALLS

11.1 VALUE OF IMPLEMENTING HANDOFFS

11.1.1 Why Handoffs[1-5]

In an analog system, once a call is established, the set-up channel is not used again during the call period. Therefore, handoff is always implemented on the voice channel. In the digital systems, the handoff is carried out through paging or common control channel. The value of implementing handoffs is dependent on the size of the cell. For example, if the radius of the cell is 32 km (20 mi), the area is 3217 km² (1256 mi²). After a call is initiated in this area, there is little chance that it will be dropped before the call is terminated as a result of a weak signal at the coverage boundary. Then why bother to implement the handoff feature? Even for a 16-km radius, cell handoff may not be needed. If a call is dropped in a fringe area, the customer simply redials and reconnects the call. Today the size of cells becomes smaller in order to increase capacity. Also people talk longer. The handoffs are very essential.

Handoff is needed in two situations where the cell site receives weak signals from the mobile unit: (1) at the cell boundary, say, -100 dBm, which is the level for requesting a handoff in a noise-limited environment; and (2) when the mobile unit is reaching the signal-strength holes (gaps) within the cell site as shown in Fig. 11.1.

11.1.2 Types of Handoff

In digital systems there are different types of handoff, but in an analog system, there is only one type of handoff, which is the hard handoff.

A. Natures of handoff

1. Hard handoff: This is a break-before-make process and handoff between two frequencies. All FDMA, TDMA, and OFDMA digital systems, and analog systems, can perform hard handoffs.

2. Soft handoff: This is a make-before-break process. Because CDMA has to perform the handoff between two code channels, not two frequencies, it is difficult to perform the hard handoffs. Because of the soft handoffs, the process needs to secure two code channels during the handoff process. Therefore, the capacity is reduced in the soft handoff region, but the drop call is reduced also due to the diverse nature of switching two code channels.

3. Softer handoff: Handoff occurring between sectors only at the serving cell. It is a make-before-break type using combined diversity of two code channels.

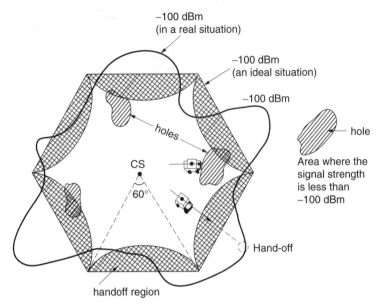

FIGURE 11.1   Occurrence of handoff.

B. Purposes of handoff

1. Intracell handoff: can be a sector-to-sector handoff.
2. Intercell handoff: a handoff from an old cell to a new cell.
3. Inter BSC/MSC handoff: using compressed mode, referred to as the slotted mode. In this mode, the transmission and reception are halted for a short time, of the order a few milliseconds, in order to perform measurements on the other frequencies from other systems.
4. Intersystem handoff: handoff between two same type systems.
5. Intercarrier handoffs: handoff occurs between two carriers.
6. Intermode handoff: the handoff occurs from one of the modes TDMA, CDMA, GSM, and GPRS to another mode.

C. Algorithms of handoff

1. MCHO (Mobile Control Handoff): It is the responsibility of MS to choose the best BS.
2. NCHO (Network Control Handoff): It is the responsibility of network to choose the best BS.
3. NCHO/MAHO (Network Control Handoff/Mobile Assists Handoff): It is the responsibility of network to choose the best BS, but with the information supplied by the mobile's assist.

11.1.3   Two Decision-Making Parameters of Handoff

There are two decision-making parameters of handoff: (1) that based on signal strength and (2) that based on carrier-to-interference ratio. The handoff criteria are different for these two types. In type 1, the signal-strength threshold level for handoff is -100 dBm in noise-limited systems and -95 dBm in interference-limited systems. In type 2, the value of C/I at the cell boundary for handoff should be at a level, 18 dB for AMPS in order to have toll quality voice. Sometimes, a low value of C/I may be used for capacity reasons.

Type 1 is easy to implement. The location receiver at each cell site measures all the signal strengths of all receivers at the cell site. However, the received signal strength (RSS) itself includes interference.

$$RSS = C + I \qquad (11.1\text{-}1)$$

where C is the carrier signal power and I is the interference. Suppose that we set up a threshold level for RSS; then, because of the I, which is sometimes very strong, the RSS level is higher and far above the handoff threshold level. In this situation handoff should theoretically take place but does not. Another situation is when I is very low but RSS is also low. In this situation, the voice quality usually is good even though the RSS level is low, but since RSS is low, unnecessary handoff takes place. Therefore, it is an easy but not very accurate method of determining handoffs. Some analog systems use SAT information together with the received signal level to determine handoffs (Sec. 15.1.2). Some CDMA systems use pilot channel information.

Type 2: Handoffs can be controlled by using the carrier-to-interference ratio C/I, which can be obtained as described in Sec. 9.3.

$$\frac{C + I}{I} \approx \frac{C}{I} \qquad (11.1\text{-}2)$$

In Eq. (11.1-2), we can set a level based on C/I, so C drops as a function of distance but I is dependent on the location. If the handoff is dependent on C/I, and if the C/I drops, it does so in response to increase in (1) propagation distance or (2) interference. In both cases, handoff should take place. In today's cellular systems, it is hard to measure C/I during a call because of analog modulation. Sometimes we measure the level I before the call is connected, and the level $C + I$ during the call. Thus $(C + I)/I$ can be obtained. Another method of measuring C/I is described in Sec. 9.3.

11.1.4 Determining the Probability of Requirement for Hard Handoffs[6]

To find the probability of requiring a hard handoff, we can carry out the following simulation. Suppose that a mobile unit randomly initiates a call in a 16-km (10-mi) cell. The vehicle speed is also randomly chosen between 8 and 96 km/h (5 to 60 mi/h). The direction is randomly chosen to be between 0 and $360°$; then the chance of reaching the boundary is dependent on the call holding time.

Figure 11.2 depicts the probability curve for requiring handoff. Table 11.1 summarizes the results. If the call holding time is 1.76 min, the only chance of reaching the boundary is 11 percent, or the chance that a handoff will occur for the call is 11 percent. If the call holding time is 3 min, the chance of reaching the boundary is 18 percent. Now we may debate whether a handoff is needed or not. In rural areas, handoffs may not be necessary. However, commercial mobile units must meet certain requirements, and handoffs may be necessary at different times. Military mobile systems may opt not to use the handoff feature and may apply the savings in cost to implement other security measures.

11.1.5 Number of Hard Handoffs Per Call

The smaller the cell size, the greater the number and the value of implementing handoffs. The number of handoffs per call is relative to cell size. From the simulation, we may find

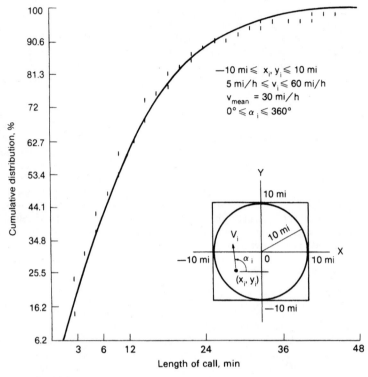

FIGURE 11.2 The probability of requiring handoff.

0.2 handoff per call in a 16- to 24-km cell

1–2 handoffs per call in a 3.2- to 8-km cell

3–4 handoffs per call in a 1.6- to 3.2-km cell

11.1.6 Area of Soft Handoffs in a Cell

In a 60° sector of a cell, as shown in Fig. 11.1 the handoff occurs at the cell boundary. In theory, the shade region indicates the handoff region, which is 20 percent of the sector. However, in a real situation, the soft handoff area can be much bigger, especially when the soft handoff algorithm is not effectively performed.

TABLE 11.1. Probability of Having a Handoff in a 10-mi Coverage Area

Handoff Probability, %	Call Length, min
11.3	1.76
18	3
42.6	6
59.3	9

11.2   *INITIATION OF A HARD HANDOFF*

At the cell site, signal strength is always monitored from a reverse voice channel. When the signal strength reaches the level of a handoff (higher than the threshold level for the minimum required voice quality), then the cell site sends a request to the mobile switching (MSO)* for a handoff on the call. An intelligent decision can also be made at the cell site as to whether the handoff should have taken place earlier or later. If an unnecessary handoff is requested, then the decision was made too early. If a failure handoff occurs, then a decision was made too late.

The following approaches are used to make handoffs successful and to eliminate all unnecessary handoffs. Suppose that −100 dBm is a threshold level at the cell boundary at which a handoff would be taken. Given this scenario, we must set up a level higher than −100 dBm—say, −100 dBm + Δ dB—and when the received signal reaches this level, a handoff request is initiated. If the value of Δ is fixed and large, then the time it takes to lower −100 dBm + Δ to −100 dBm is longer. During this time, many situations, such as the mobile unit turning back toward the cell site or stopping, can occur as a result of the direction and the speed of the moving vehicles. Then the signals will never drop below −100 dBm. Thus, many unnecessary handoffs may occur simply because we have taken the action too early. If Δ is small, then there is not enough time for the call to hand off at the cell site and many calls can be lost while they are handed off. Therefore, Δ should be varied according to the path-loss slope of the received signal strength (Sec. 8.2) and the level-crossing rate (LCR) of the signal strength (Sec. 2.3.3) as shown in Fig. 11.3.

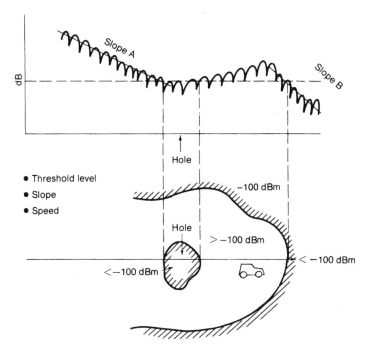

FIGURE 11.3   Parameters for handling a handoff.

---

*MSO is a general term which stands for either MTSO in AMPS, or BSC sometimes MSC in digital systems.

Let the value of Δ be 10 dB in the example given in the preceding paragraph. This would mean a level of -90 dBm as the threshold level for requesting a handoff. Then we can calculate the velocity V of the mobile unit based on the predicted LCR[7] at a -10-dB level with respect to the root-mean-square (rms) level, which is at -90 dBm; thus

$$V = \left\{ \begin{array}{ll} \dfrac{n\lambda}{\sqrt{2\pi}\,(0.27)} & \text{ft/s} \\[2mm] n\lambda & \text{mi/h} \end{array} \right\} \quad \text{at} -10\text{-dB level} \qquad (11.2\text{-}1)$$

where n is the LCR (crossings per second) counting positive slopes and λ is the wavelength in feet. Equation (11.2-1) can be simplified as

$$V(\text{mi/h}) \approx n(\text{crossings/s}) \text{ at 850 MHz and a } -10\text{-dB level} \qquad (11.2\text{-}2)$$

Here, two pieces of information, the velocity of vehicle V and the pathloss slope γ, can be used to determine the value of Δ dynamically so that the number of unnecessary handoffs can be reduced and the required handoffs can be completed successfully.

There are two circumstances where handoffs are necessary but cannot be made: (1) when the mobile unit is located at a signal-strength hole within a cell but not at the boundary (see Fig. 11.3) and (2) when the mobile unit approaches a cell boundary but no channels in the new cell are available.

In case 1, the call must be kept in the old frequency channel until it is dropped as the result of an unacceptable signal level. In case 2, the new cell must reassign one of its frequency channels within a reasonably short period or the call will be dropped.

The MSO usually controls the frequency assignment in each cell and can rearrange channel assignments or split cells when they are necessary. Cell splitting is described in Sec. 12.6.

11.3 DELAYING A HANDOFF

11.3.1 Two-Handoff-Level Algorithm

In many cases, a two-handoff-level algorithm is used. The purpose of creating two request handoff levels is to provide more opportunity for a successful handoff. A handoff could be delayed if no available cell could take the call.

A plot of signal strength with two request handoff levels and a threshold level is shown in Fig. 11.4. The plot of average signal strength is recorded on the channel received

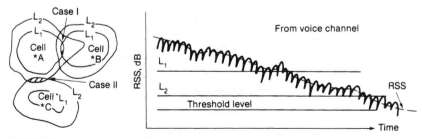

FIGURE 11.4   A two-level handoff scheme.

signal-strength indicator (RSSI), which is installed at each channel receiver at the cell site. When the signal strength drops below the first handoff level, a handoff request is initiated. If for some reason the mobile unit is in a hole (a weak spot in a cell) or a neighboring cell is busy, the handoff will be requested periodically every 5 s. At the first handoff level, the handoff takes place if the new signal is stronger (see case I in Fig. 11.4). However, when the second handoff level is reached, the call will be handed off with no condition (see case II in Fig. 11.4).

The MSO always handles the handoff call first and the originating calls second. If no neighboring calls are available after the second handoff level is reached, the call continues until the signal strength drops below the threshold level; then the call is dropped. In AMPS systems if the supervisory audio tone (SAT) is not sent back to the cell site by the mobile unit within 5 s, the cell site turns off the transmitter.

11.3.2 Advantage of Delayed Handoffs

Consider the following example. The mobile units are moving randomly and the terrain contour is uneven. The received signal strength at the mobile unit fluctuates up and down. If the mobile unit is in a hole for less than 5 s (a driven distance of 140 m for 5 s, assuming a vehicle speed of 100 km/h), the delay (in handoff) can even circumvent the need for a handoff.

If the neighboring cells are busy, delayed handoff may take place. In principle, when call traffic is heavy, the switching processor is loaded, and thus a lower number of handoffs would help the processor handle call processing more adequately. Of course, it is very likely that after the second handoff level is reached, the call may be dropped with great probability.

The other advantage of having a two-handoff-level algorithm is that it makes the handoff occur at the proper location and eliminates possible interference in the system. Figure 11.4, case I, shows the area where the first-level handoff occurs between cell A and cell B. If we only use the second-level handoff boundary of cell A, the area of handoff is too close to cell B. Figure 11.4, case II, also shows where the second-level handoff occurs between cell A and cell C. This is because the first-level handoff cannot be implemented.

11.4 FORCED HANDOFFS

A *forced handoff* is defined as a handoff that would normally occur but is prevented from happening, or a handoff that should not occur but is forced to happen.

11.4.1 Controlling a Handoff

The cell site can assign a low handoff threshold in a cell to keep a mobile unit in a cell longer or assign a high handoff threshold level to request a handoff earlier. The MSO also can control a handoff by making either a handoff earlier or later, after receiving a handoff request from a cell site.

11.4.2 Creating a Handoff

In this case, the cell site does not request a handoff but the MSO finds that some cells are too congested while others are not. Then, the MSO can request call sites to create early handoffs for those congested cells. In other words, a cell site has to follow the MSO's order and increase the handoff threshold to push the mobile units at the new boundary and to hand off earlier.

11.5 QUEUING OF HANDOFFS

Queuing of handoffs is more effective than two-threshold-level handoffs. The MSO will queue the requests of handoff calls instead of rejecting them if the new cell sites are busy. A queuing scheme becomes effective only when the requests for handoffs arrive at the MSO in batches or bundles. If handoff requests arrive at the MSO uniformly, then the queuing scheme is not needed. Before showing the equations, let us define the parameters as follows.

$1/\mu$ average calling time in seconds, including *new calls* and *handoff calls* in each cell

λ_1 arrival rate (λ_1 calls per second) for originating calls

λ_2 arrival rate (λ_2 handoff calls per second) for handoff calls

M_1 size of queue for originating calls

M_2 size of queue for handoff calls

N number of voice channels

a $(\lambda_1 + \lambda_2)/\mu$

b_1 λ_1/μ

b_2 λ_2/μ

The following analysis can be used to see the improvement. We are analyzing three cases.[8]

1. *No queuing on either the originating calls or the handoff calls.* The blocking for either an originating call or a handoff call is

$$B_o = \frac{a^N}{N!} P(0) \tag{11.5-1}$$

where

$$P(0) = \left(\sum_{n=0}^{N} \frac{a^N}{n!} \right)^{-1} \tag{11.5-2}$$

2. *Queuing the originating calls but not the handoff calls.* The blocking probability for originating calls is

$$B_{oq} = \left(\frac{b_1}{N} \right)^{M_1} P_q(0) \tag{11.5-3}$$

where

$$P_q(0) = \left[N! \sum_{n=0}^{N-1} \frac{a^{n-N}}{n!} + \frac{1 - (b_1/N)^{M_1+1}}{1 - (b_1/N)} \right]^{-1} \tag{11.5-4}$$

The blocking probability for handoff calls is

$$B_{oh} = \frac{1 - (b_1/N)^{M_1+1}}{1 - (b_1/N)} P_q(0) \qquad (11.5\text{-}5)$$

3. *Queuing the handoff calls but not the originating calls.* The blocking probability for handoff calls is

$$B_{hq} = \left(\frac{b_2}{N}\right)^{M_2} P_q(0) \qquad (11.5\text{-}6)$$

where $P_q(0)$ is as shown in Eq. (11.5-4). The blocking probability for originating calls is

$$B_{ho} = \frac{1 - (b_2/N)^{M_2+1}}{1 - (b_2/N)} P_q(0) \qquad (11.5\text{-}7)$$

EXAMPLE 11.1 *The following parameters are given. The number of channels at the cell site $N = 70$. The call holding time is 101 s $= 0.028$ h. The number of originating calls attempted per hour is expressed as $\lambda_1 = 2270$. The number of handoff calls attempted per hour is expressed as $\lambda_2 = 80$. Then*

$$A = \frac{\lambda_1 + \lambda_2}{\mu} = (2270 + 80)\,0.028 = 65.80$$

$$b_1 = \frac{\lambda_1}{\mu} = 2270 \times 0.028 = 63.60$$

$$b_2 = \frac{\lambda_2}{\mu} = 2.24$$

Given these parameters, Eqs. (11.5-1), (11.5-3), (11.5-5), (11.5-6), and (11.5-7) have been plotted in Figs. 11.5, 11.6, 11.7, and 11.8 respectively.

We have seen (Figs. 11.5 and 11.6) with queuing of originating calls only, the probability of blocking is reduced. However, queuing of originating calls results in increased blocking probability on handoff calls, and this is a drawback. With queuing of handoff calls only, blocking probability is reduced from 5.9 to 0.1 percent by using one queue space (see Fig. 11.7). Therefore it is very worthwhile to implement a simple queue (one space) for handoff calls. Adding queues in handoff calls does not affect the blocking probability of originating calls in this particular example (see Fig. 11.8). However, we should always be aware that queuing for the handoff is more important than queuing for those initiating calls on assigned voice channels because call drops upset customers more than call blockings.

11.6 POWER-DIFFERENCE HANDOFFS

A better algorithm is based on the power difference (Δ) of a mobile signal received by two cell sites, home and handoff. Δ can be positive or negative. The handoff occurs depending on a preset value of Δ.

$\Delta =$ the mobile signal measured at the candidate handoff site

$-$ the mobile signal measured at the home site $\qquad (11.6\text{-}1)$

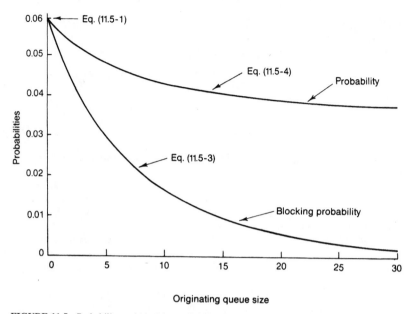

FIGURE 11.5   Probability and blocking probability graph showing blocking probability for originating calls queuing for originating calls ($N = 70$).

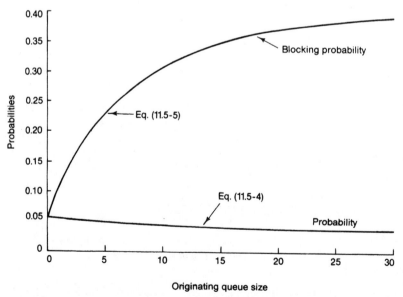

FIGURE 11.6   Probability and blocking probability graph showing blocking probability for handoff calls (queuing for originating calls) ($N = 70$).

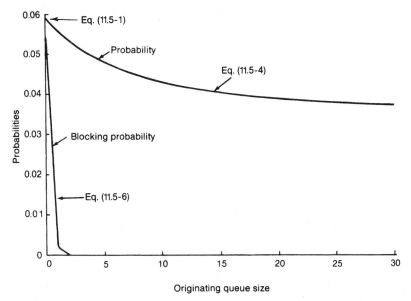

FIGURE 11.7   Probability and blocking probability graph showing blocking probability for handoff calls (queuing for handoff calls) ($N = 70$).

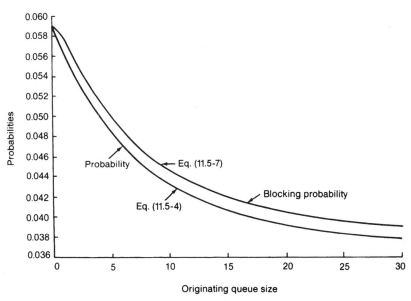

FIGURE 11.8   Probability and blocking probability graph showing blocking probability for originating calls (queuing for handoff calls) ($N = 70$).

For example, the following cases can occur.

$$\Delta > 3 \, dB \quad \text{request a handoff}$$

$$1 \, dB < \Delta < 3 \, dB \quad \text{prepare a handoff}$$

$$-3 \, dB < \Delta < 0 \, dB \quad \text{monitoring the signal strength}$$

$$\Delta < -3 \, dB \quad \text{no handoff}$$

Those numbers can be changed to fit the switch processor capacity. This algorithm is not based on the received signal strength level, but on a relative (power difference) measurement. Therefore, when this algorithm is used, all the call handoffs for different vehicles can occur at the same general location in spite of different mobile antenna gains or heights.

11.7 MOBILE ASSISTED HANDOFF (MAHO) AND SOFT HANDOFF

In a normal handoff procedure, the request for a handoff is based on the signal strength (or the SAT range of AMPS) of a mobile signal received at the cell site from the reverse link. In the digital cellular system, the mobile receiver is capable of monitoring the signal strength of the setup channels of the neighboring cells while serving a call. For instance, in a TDMA system, one time slot is used for serving a call, the rest of the time slots can be used to monitor the signal strengths of setup channels. When the signal strength of its voice channel is weak, the mobile unit can request a handoff and indicate to the switching office which neighboring cell can be a candidate for handoff. Now the switching office has two pieces of information: the signal strengths of both forward and reverse setup channels of a neighboring cell or two different neighboring cells. The switching office (MSO) therefore, has more intelligent information to choose the proper neighboring cell to handoff to.

The soft handoff is applied to one kind of digital cellular system named CDMA. In CDMA systems, all cells can use the same radio carrier. Therefore, the frequency reuse factor K approaches one. Because the operating radio carriers of all cells are the same, no need to change from one frequency to another frequency but change from one code to another code. Thus, there is no hard handoff. We call this kind of handoff a soft handoff. If sometimes there are more than one CDMA radio carrier operating in a cell, and if the soft handoff from one cell to another is not possible for some reason, the intracell hard handoff may take place first, then go to the inter-cell soft handoff.

11.8 CELL-SITE HANDOFF ONLY

This scheme can be used in a noncellular system. The mobile unit has been assigned a frequency and talks to its home cell site while it travels. When the mobile unit leaves its home cell and enters a new cell, its frequency does not change; rather, the new cell must tune into the frequency of the mobile unit (see Fig. 11.9). In this case only the cell sites need the frequency information of the mobile unit. Then the aspects of mobile unit control can be greatly simplified, and there will be no need to provide handoff capability at the mobile unit. The cost will also be lower.

This scheme can be recommended only in areas of very low traffic. When the traffic is dense, frequency coordination is necessary for the cellular system. Then if a mobile unit does not change frequency on travel from cell to cell, other mobile units then must change frequency to avoid interference.

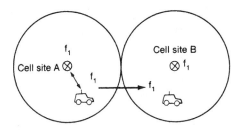

FIGURE 11.9   Cell-site handoff-only scheme.

Therefore, if a system handles only low volumes of traffic, that is, if the channels assigned to one cell will not reuse frequency in other cells, then it is possible to implement the cell-site handoff feature as it is applied in military systems.

11.9   INTERSYSTEM HANDOFF

Occasionally, a call may be initiated in one cellular system (controlled by one MSO)* and enter another system (controlled by another MSO) before terminating. In some instances, *intersystem handoff* can take place; this means that a call handoff can be transferred from one system to a second system so that the call be continued while the mobile unit enters the second system.

The software in the MSO must be modified to apply this situation. Consider the simple diagram shown in Fig. 11.10. The car travels on a highway and the driver originates a call

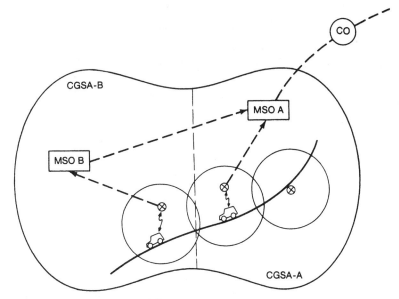

FIGURE 11.10   Intersystem handoffs.

_____

* In this section, MSO stands for MTSO in AMPS or MSC in digital systems.

in system A. Then the car leaves cell site A of system A and enters cell site B of system B. Cell sites A and B are controlled by two different MSOs. When the mobile unit signal becomes weak in cell site A, MSO A searches for a candidate cell site in its system and cannot find one. Then MSO A sends the handoff request to MSO B through a dedicated line between MSO A and MSO B, and MSO B makes a complete handoff during the call conversation. This is just a one-point connection case. There are many ways of implementing intersystem handoffs, depending on the actual circumstances. For instance, if two MSOs are manufactured by different companies, then compatibility must be determined before implementation of intersystem handoff can be considered. A detailed discussion of this topic appears in Sec. 13.4.

11.10 INTRODUCTION TO DROPPED CALL RATE

11.10.1 The Definition of Dropped Call Rate

The definition of a dropped call is after the call is established but before it is properly terminated. The definition of "the call is established" means that the call is setup completely by the setup channel. If there is a possibility of a call drop due to no available voice channels, this is counted as a blocked call not a dropped call.

If there is a possibility that a call will drop due to the poor signal of the assigned voice channel, this is considered a dropped call. This case can happen when the mobile or portable units are at a standstill and the radio carrier is changed from a strong setup channel to a weak voice channel due to the selective frequency fading phenomenon.

The perception of dropped call rate by the subscribers can be higher due to:

1. The subscriber unit not functioning properly (needs repair).
2. The user operating the portable unit in a vehicle (misused).
3. The user not knowing how to get the best reception from a portable unit (needs education).

11.10.2 Consideration of Dropped Calls

In principle, dropped call rate can be set very low if we do not need to maintain the voice quality. The dropped call rate and the specified voice quality level are inversely proportional. In designing a commercial system, the specified voice quality level is given relating to how much C/I (or C/N) the speech coder can tolerate. By maintaining a certain voice quality level, the dropped call rate can be calculated by taking the following factors into consideration:

1. Provide signal coverage based on the percentage (say 90 percent) that all the received signal will be above a given signal level.
2. Maintain the specified co-channel and adjacent channel interference levels in each cell during a busy hour (i.e., the worst interference case).
3. Because the performance of the call dropped rate is calculated as possible call dropping in every stage from the radio link to the PSTN connection, the response time of the handoff in the network will be a factor when the cell becomes small, the response time for a handoff request has to be shorter in order to reduce the call dropped rate.

4. The signaling of the handoff and the MAHO algorithm will also impact the call dropped rate.

5. The relationship among the voice quality, system capacity and call dropped rate can be expressed through a common parameter C/I.

11.10.3 Relationship Among Capacity, Voice Quality, Dropped Call Rate

Radio Capacity m is expressed as follows:

$$m = \frac{B_T/B_c}{\sqrt{\frac{2}{3}(C/I)_S}} \tag{11.10-1}$$

where B_T/B_c is the total number of voice channels. B_T/B_c is a given number, and $(C/I)_S$ is a required C/I for designing a system. The above equation is obtained based on six co-channel interferers which occur in busy traffic (i.e., a worst case). In an interference limited system, the adjacent channel interference has only a secondary effect. The derivation of Eq. (11.10-1) will be expressed in Chap. 15. Eq. (11.10-1) can be changed to the following form:

$$(C/I)_S = \frac{3}{2}\left(\frac{B_T/B_c}{m}\right)^2 = \frac{3}{2}\left(\frac{B_T}{B_c}\right)^2 \cdot \frac{1}{m^2} \tag{11.10-2}$$

Because the $(C/I)_S$ is a required C/I for designing a system, the voice quality is based on the $(C/I)_S$. When the specified $(C/I)_S$ is reduced, the radio capacity is increased. When the measured (C/I) is less than the specified $(C/I)_S$, both poor voice quality and dropped calls can occur.

11.10.4 Coverage of 90 Percent Equal-Strength Contour

The coverage in cellular cells always uses the coverage of 90 percent equal-strength contour. The prediction tool (Lee Model) described in Chap. 8 is used to predict the equal-strength contour at level C with 50 percent time and 50 percent area in a cell. For example, let $C = -102$ dBm, which is 18 dB above the ambient noise -120 dBm. If $C = -102$ dBm is 50 percent equal-strength contour, then increase the level to $C + 10$ dB contour which can be calculated from the following equation:

$$P(x' < A) = \int_{-x}^{A} \frac{1}{\sqrt{2\pi}\sigma} \exp\left[\frac{(y' - \overline{m})^2}{2\sigma^2}\right] dy'$$

$$= P\left(x < \frac{A - \overline{m}}{\sigma}\right) \tag{11.10-3}$$

Equation (11.10-3) is the cumulative distribution function where A is the desired signal level and $\overline{m}$ is the mean level. σ is long-term fading due to terrain contour. If $A = C + 10 = -92$ dB and $\sigma = 8$ dB:

$$P(x' < -92) = P\left(x < \frac{-92 - (-102)}{8}\right) = P\left(x < \frac{10}{8}\right) = 0.9082 \tag{11.10-4}$$

Equation (11.10-4) can also be interpreted as being at a -92 dBm contour, the signal above the level of -92 dBm is 90.8 percent. Of course, the level of -92 dBm is determined to be 18 dB above -120 dBm which is the ambient noise level. The $(C/N)_S$ of 18 dB is the required level for getting a voice quality.

11.11 FORMULA OF DROPPED CALL RATE

The dropped call rate can be calculated either using general formula or by a commonly used formula.

11.11.1 General Formula of Dropped Call Rate

The general formula of dropped call rate P in a whole system can be expressed as:

$$P = 1 - \left[\sum_{n=0}^{N} \alpha_n X^n \right] = \sum_{n=0}^{N} \alpha_n \cdot P_n \qquad (11.11\text{-}1)$$

where

$$P_n = 1 - X^n \qquad (11.11\text{-}2)$$

P_n is the probability of a dropped call when the call has gone through n handoffs and

$$X = (1 - \delta)(1 - \mu)(1 - \theta\tau)(1 - \beta)^2 \qquad (11.11\text{-}3)$$

δ = Probability that the signal is below the specified receive threshold (in a noise-limited system).

μ = Probability that the signal is below the specified cochannel interference level (in an interference-limited system).

τ = Probability that no traffic channel is available upon handoff attempt when moving into a new cell.

θ = Probability that the call will return to the original cell.

β = Probability of blocking circuits between BSC and MSC during handoff.

α_n = The weighted value for those calls having n handoffs, and $\sum_{n=0}^{N} \alpha_n = 1$

N = N is the highest number of handoffs for those calls.

Equation (11.11-3) needs to be explained clearly as follows:

1. z_1 and z_2 are two events, z_1 is the case of no traffic channel in the cell, z_2 is the case of no-safe return to original cell. Assuming that z_1 and z_2 are independent events, then

$$P(z_2|z_1) \cdot P(z_1) = P(z_2) \cdot P(z_1) = \theta \cdot \tau$$

2. $(1 - \beta)$ is the probability of a call successfully connecting from the old BSC to the MSC. Also, $(1 - \beta)$ is the probability of a call successfully connecting from the MSC to the new BSC. Then the total probability of having a successful call connection is

$$\begin{array}{ll} \text{BSC (old)} \rightarrow \text{MSC} & (1 - \beta) \\ \text{MSC} \rightarrow \text{BSC (new)} & (1 - \beta) \end{array} \Bigg\} \rightarrow (1 - \beta)^2$$

3. The call dropped rate P expressed in Eq. (11.11-1) can be specified in two cases:

  1. In a noise limited system (startup system): there is no frequency reuse, the call dropped rate P_A is based on the signal coverage. It can also be calculated under busy hour conditions.

     In a noise-limited environment (for worst case)

     $$\delta = \delta_1$$

     $$\mu = \mu_1$$

     $$\left.\begin{array}{l} \tau = \tau_1 \\ \theta = \theta_1 \\ \beta = \beta_1 \end{array}\right\} \text{ the conditions for the noise limited case}$$

  2. In an interference-limited system (mature system): frequency reuse is applied, and the dropped rate P_B is based on the interference level. It can be calculated under busy hour conditions.

     In an interference-limited environment (for worst case)

     $$\delta = \delta_2$$

     $$\mu = \mu_1$$

     $$\left.\begin{array}{l} \tau = \tau_2 \\ \theta = \theta_2 \\ \beta = \beta_2 \end{array}\right\} \text{ the conditions for the interference limited case}$$

Equation (11.11-1) has to make a distinguished difference between P_A and P_B. The cases of P_A and P_B do not occur at the same time. When capacity is based on frequency reuse, the interference level is high, the size of the cells is small, and coverage is not an issue. The call dropped rate totally depends on interference.

11.11.2 Commonly Used Formula of Dropped Call Rate

In a commonly used formula of dropped call rate, the values of τ, θ, and β are assumed to be very small and can be neglected. Then Eq. (11.11-3) becomes:

$$X = (1 - \delta)(1 - \mu) \tag{11.11-4}$$

Furthermore, in a noise-limited case, $\mu \to 0$, Eq. (11.11-1) becomes:

$$P_A = \sum_{n=0}^{N} \alpha_n P_n = \sum \alpha_n [1 - (1 - \delta)^n] \tag{11.11-5}$$

and in an interference-limited system, $\delta \to 0$, Eq. (11.11-1) becomes:

$$P_B = \sum_{n=0}^{N} \alpha_n P_n = \sum \alpha_n [1 - (1 - \mu)^n] \tag{11.11-6}$$

11.11.3 Handoff Distribution of Calls, α_n

The α_n is the weight value for those calls having n handoffs. Then the handoff distribution of all α_n's is needed for calculating Eq. (11.11-1), or Eq. (11.11-5), or Eq. (11.11-6). The relationship of all α_n's is:

$$\sum_{n=0}^{N} \alpha_n = 1$$

The handoff distribution of calls α_n can be assumed as follows:
The α_n in macrocells is used for calculating the dropped call rate P_A:

Kinds of Units	n Handoffs Per Call	Percent of Units	α_n
Handset units	$n = 0$	100%	$\alpha_0 = 1$
Mobile units	$n = 0$	20%	$\alpha_0 = 0.2$
	$n = 1$	60%	$\alpha_1 = 0.6$
	$n = 2$	20%	$\alpha_2 = 0.2$

The α_n in microcells is used for calculating the dropped call rate P_B:

Kinds of Units	n Handoffs Per Call	Percent of Units	α_n
Handset units	$n = 0$	80%	$\alpha_0 = 0.8$
Mobile units	$n = 1$	20%	$\alpha_1 = 0.2$
	$n = 0$	20%	$\alpha_0 = 0.2$
	$n = 1$	60%	$\alpha_1 = 0.6$
	$n = 2$	20%	$\alpha_2 = 0.2$

The values of α_n are used for calculating the dropped call rate. For instance, calculating the general formula of dropped call rate (Eq. (11.11-1)) in macrocells (noise-limited system) for mobile units.

$$P_A = 1 - [0.2X^0 + 0.6X^1 + 0.2X^2]$$

$$= 0.2P_0 + 0.6P_1 + 0.2P_2 \tag{11.11-7}$$

where X is expressed in Eq. (11.11-3). In Eq. (11.11-3), the values of τ, θ, and β are usually small. Therefore, the value of X is heavily dependent on δ and μ.

11.12 FINDING THE VALUES OF δ AND μ USED FOR DROPPED CALL RATE

The values of δ and μ can be derived for a single cell case and in the case of a handoff. The single cell case solution is used for estimating the blocked calls. The reason behind this is that the probability of δ and μ in a single case is used for the blocked call rate of setting up calls. Assuming that after a call is set up, the call will not be dropped in a cell until the mobile unit travels into the handoff region.

11.12.1 Formula for δ and μ

We first find the value of δ in a single cell by integrating Eq. (11.10-3) over a whole cell to find the area Q in which the measured x will be greater than $[A(r) - \overline{m}]/\sigma$. The mean value $\overline{m}$ is a specified receive level. A is the signal level which is a function of $A(r)$ that exceeds $\overline{m}$ at the distance r which is less or equal to the cell radius R.

$$Q = \int_0^R P\left(x > \frac{A(r) - \overline{m}}{\sigma}\right) \cdot 2\pi r dr \qquad (11.12\text{-}1)$$

The probability δ that the signal is below a specified receive threshold $\overline{m}$ in a noise-limited environment system is

$$\delta = \frac{\pi R^2 - Q}{\pi R^2}$$

$$= 1 - \frac{1}{\pi R^2} \int_0^R \left[1 - P\left(x < \frac{A(r) - \overline{m}}{\sigma}\right)\right] \cdot 2\pi r dr \qquad (11.12\text{-}2)$$

The probability μ that the signal is below the specified signal level C over the interference level I in an interference-limited system can also be expressed as:

$$\mu = \frac{\pi R^2 - Q}{\pi R^2}$$

$$= 1 - \frac{1}{\pi R^2} \int_0^R \left[1 - P\left(x < \frac{A(r) - C}{\sigma}\right)\right] \cdot 2\pi r \cdot dr \qquad (11.12\text{-}3)$$

we may use the numerical calculation to solve Eq. (11.12-2) and Eq. (11.12-3) for dropped calls due to handoffs.

11.12.2 Calculation of δ and μ in a Single Cell

δ is calculated numerically in a noise-limited case. The cell can be divided into five rings ($i = 1,5$) as shown in Fig. 11.11. Eq. (11.12-2), then can be expressed as:

$$\delta = 1 - \frac{\displaystyle\sum_{i=1}^5 P_i\left(x > \frac{A_i(r_i) - \overline{m}}{\sigma}\right) \cdot a_i}{\pi R^2} \qquad (11.12\text{-}4)$$

where

$$1 - p_i\left(x < \frac{A_i(r_i) - \overline{m}}{\sigma}\right) = P_i\left(x > \frac{A_i(r_i) - \overline{m}}{\sigma}\right)$$

p_i is the probability of having a successful call and P_i is the probability of a dropped call.

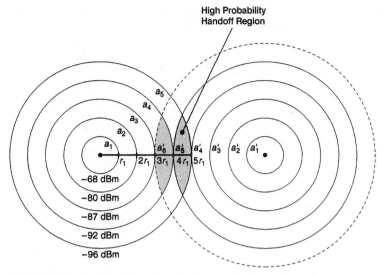

FIGURE 11.11   The diagram for calculating the dropped calls due to handoffs.

$$a_i = \pi[2i - 1]r_1^2 \qquad (i^{\text{th}} \text{ ring area})$$

$$\sum_{i=1}^{5} a_i = \pi R^2 \tag{11.12-5}$$

in a single cell. $A_5(r_5 = R)$ is the desired signal level at the cell radius $R = 5r_1$. Let

$$P_i\left(x > \frac{A_i(r_i) - \overline{m}}{\sigma}\right) = P_i$$

for simplicity. Eq. (11.12-4) can also be expressed as:

$$\delta = \frac{\sum_{i=1}^{5}(1 - P_i) \cdot a_i}{\pi R^2} \tag{11.12-6}$$

Equation (11.12-6) is also the equation for obtaining the value of μ in the interference case.

11.12.3 δ_h and μ_h Are Improved due to the Natural Two-Site Diversity in the Handoff Region

Due to natural situations providing equivalent two-site diversity in the handoff region, in region a_5, the probability of dropping a call P_5' is reduced by $1 - (1 - p_5)^2$ as compared with P_5. In region a_4, the probability of dropping a call P_4' is $1 - (1 - p_4)(1 - p_6)$ as compared with P_4. P_4' is the probability of a dropped call due to the fact that the handoff takes place in a_4 by the new cell coverage. Therefore, δ_h and μ_h are expressed as:

$$
\left.\begin{array}{c} \delta_h \\ \mu_h \end{array}\right\} = \frac{(1 - p_5)^2 a_5 + (1 - p_4)(1 - p_6)a_4 + (1 - p_3)a_3 + (1 - p_2)a_2 + (1 - p_1)a_1}{\pi R^2}
$$

(11.12-7)

Be aware that p_i is the probability of having a successful call and P_i is the probability of a dropped call.

EXAMPLE 11.1   *Given $\sigma = 6$, $\overline{m} = -104\,dBm$, $A_5 = -96\,dBm$, find the value of δ_h during a handoff? (See Fig.11.11.)*
Based on the 40 dB/dec rule, we can obtain $A_4 = -92\,dBm$, $A_3 = -87\,dBm$, $A_2 = -80\,dBm$, $A_1 = -68\,dBm$, $A_6 = -99\,dBm$ and also

$$
p_5 \left(x < \frac{-96 - (-104)}{6} \right) = 0.9082,\ p_4 = 0.948,\ p_3 = 0.9977,
$$

$$
p_2 = 1,\ p_1 = 1,\ p_5 = 0.7967
$$

Then applied to Eq. (11.12-7), we obtain

$$
\delta_h = \frac{(1 - p_5)^2 a_5 + (1 - p_4)(1 - p_6)a_4 + (1 - p_3)a_3 + (1 - p_2)a_2 + (1 - p_1)a_1}{\pi R^2}
$$

$$
= 0.64\%
$$

EXAMPLE 11.2   *Given $\sigma = 6$, $I = -104\,dBm$, $C/I = 12\,dB$, and the signal received is requested to be 8 dB above the average C/I, find the value of μ_h during a handoff? Based on the 40 dB/dec rule, $C = -92\,dBm$ and $A_5 = -84\,dBm$, we obtain $A_1 = -50\,dBm$, $A_2 = -62\,dBm$, $A_3 = -75\,dBm$, and $A_4 = -80\,dBm$, $A_6 = -87\,dBm$. Then applying Eq. (11.12-7), we find:*

$$
\mu_h = \frac{(1 - p_5)^2 a_5 + (1 - p_4)(1 - p_6)a_4 + (1 - p_3)a_3 + (1 - p_2)a_2 + (1 - p_1)a_1}{\pi R^2}
$$

$$
= 1.45\%
$$

11.13   SOFT HANDOFFS

A hard handoff needs to handoff a call from one frequency carrier to another frequency carrier. In CDMA systems, we cannot use hard handoffs, because the traffic channels are the coded channels which are sharing the same frequency carrier. A soft handover is make-before-break, whereby communication exists between the UE and more than one cell (or sector) for a period of time. There are two variations: soft handoff and softer handoff.

A. Occurrence of a soft handoff

A soft handoff occurs between two cells or sectors that are supported by different base stations. The two base stations send the same information to a UE that combines them. In the uplink, the information sent from the UE is relayed from each of two base stations to the RNC where the combination takes place. During the soft handoff, each base station is sending power control commands to the UE.

The overlapped region between two cells is the soft handoff region. The overlapped region should not be kept large as long as the voice/data quality is maintained in the region. The smaller the overlapped region, the higher the capacity. Therefore, one way of adjusting the overlapped region is to maintain the required C/I level at the cell boundary. If the power increases more, the overlapped region becomes bigger and the capacity reduces. If the power reduces more, the overlapped region disappears, and the call drop occurs.

B. The call drop situation

In the overlapped region, *the call drop rate* depends on the situation where the C/I of a combined signal (which is higher than a single signal) is lower than the required level at the home cell, and the C/I level of a new cell is also lower than the required level. The probability of this event is much smaller if a CDMA system is designed properly.

1. If the UE has picked and dropped many weak signals and missed a strong signal, in the soft handoff region, the call can be dropped.

2. At the beginning, the combined signal received by the UE is strong in the soft handoff region. But when the UE went into an area with many other UEs, interference increases and the C/I reduces. In this situation, the overlapped region was exited and disappeared.

C. Capacity issues

A call can be in a soft handoff for an extended period of time. Therefore, the soft handoff is an ongoing process, whereas the hard handoffs are events that happen instantly.

During the soft handoff process in general, there are no call drop problems but capacity problems. If a call starts on Sector A and sees the other sectors (at the same base station or other base stations) then the two or more signals of the same call are beginning added and dropped, it is a softer handoff. It can be a two-way handoff or a three-way handoff.

Typically, about one-half of all calls are in the soft handoff state. Because one-half of the calls use exactly two channels each, assuming a two-way soft handoff, the capacity cost of soft handoff traffic would be one-third of total. Some soft handoff calls use three or more forward channels. If we do not design the system properly, we may end up losing half of the total capacity.

For keeping a call without dropping, cdmaOne supports up to six simultaneous signals. In the soft handoff region, the signals come from different sectors carrying the same message, but different power control commands are used for reversing link connection. It is up to UE to make a decision whether the connection of one signal is needed or not in the soft handoff region. When one signal among the rest of the signal levels is above the required signal level, then the handoff is complete.

REFERENCES

1. "Advanced Mobile Phone Services," Special Issue, *Bell System Technical Journal*, Vol. 58, January 1979.

2. F. H. Blecher, "Advanced Mobile Phone Service," *IEEE Transactions on Vehicular Technology*, Vol. ST-29, May 1980, pp. 238–244.

3. J. Oetting, "Cellular Mobile Radio—an Emerging Technology," *IEEE Communications Magazine*, Vol. 21, No. 8, November 1983, pp. 10–15.

4. V. H. MacDonald, "The Cellular Concept," *Bell System Technical Journal*, Vol. 58, January 1979, pp. 15–43.

5. W. C. Y. Lee, "Elements of Cellular Mobile Radio Systems," *IEEE Transactions on Vehicular Technology*, Vol. VT-35, May 1986, pp. 48–56.

6. W. C. Y. Lee and H. Smith, "A Computer Simulation Model for the Evaluation of Mobile Radio Systems in the Miltary Tactical Environment," *IEEE Transactions on Vehicular Technology*, Vol. VT-32, May 1983, pp. 177–190.

7. W. C. Y. Lee, *Mobile Communications Design Fundamentals*, John Wiley & Sons, 1993, p. 104.

8. D. R. Cox and W. L. Smith, *Queues*, Chapman & Hall Book Co., 1961, Chap. 2.

CHAPTER 12

OPERATIONAL TECHNIQUES AND TECHNOLOGIES

12.1 ADJUSTING THE PARAMETERS OF A SYSTEM

12.1.1 Increasing the Coverage for a Noise-Limited System

In a noise-limited system, there is no cochannel interference or adjacent-channel interference. This means that either (1) no cochannels and adjacent channels are used in the system or (2) channel reuse distance is so large that the interference would be negligible. The following approaches are used at the cell site to increase the coverage.

12.1.1.1 Increasing the Transmitted Power. Usually, increasing the transmitted power of each channel results in coverage of a larger area. When the power level is doubled, the gain increases by 3 dB. Increase in covered area can be found as follows. The received power P_r can be obtained from the transmitted power P_t (see Chap. 8), where P_r is a function of the cell radius. Let the received power P_r be the power received in an original cell of a radius of r_1

$$P_{r_1} = \alpha P_{t_1} r_1^{-4} \tag{12.1-1}$$

Area covered then is

$$A_1 = \pi r_1^2$$

where α is a constant and P_{r_1} can be obtained from P_{t_1}.

Case 1. The transmitted power remains unchanged but the received power changes. If the received power is to be strong, the cell radius should be smaller. The relation is

$$\frac{P_{r_1}}{P_{r_2}} = \frac{r_1^{-4}}{r_2^{-4}} = \frac{r_2^4}{r_1^4} \tag{12.1-2}$$

or

$$r_2 = \left(\frac{P_{r_1}}{P_{r_2}}\right)^{1/4} r_1 \tag{12.1-3}$$

If $P_{r_2} = 2P_{r_1}$, and the transmitted power remains the same, the radius reduces to

$$r_2 = (0.5)^{1/4} \quad r_1 = 0.84r_1$$

and the area reduces to

$$\frac{A_2}{A_1} = \frac{\pi r_2^2}{\pi r_1^2} = \frac{r_2^2}{r_1^2} = \frac{(0.84r_1)^2}{r_1^2} = 0.71 \tag{12.1-4}$$

Case 2. The transmitted power changes but the received power doesn't; then the 1-mi reception level changes if the transmitted power changes. From Eq. (12.1-1) we obtain

$$P_{r_1} = \alpha P_{t_1} r_1^{-4} \quad P_{r_2} = \alpha P_{t_2} r_2^{-4}$$

In this case, because $P_{r_1} = P_{r_2}$, it follows that

$$r_2 = \left(\frac{P_{t_2}}{P_{t_1}}\right)^{1/4} r_1 \tag{12.1-5}$$

If the transmitted power P_{t_2} is 3 dB higher than P_{t_1}, then

$$r_2 = (2)^{1/4} \quad r_1 = 1.19r_1$$

and the area increase is

$$\frac{A_2}{A_1} = \frac{r_2^2}{r_1^2} = (1.19)^2 = 1.42 \tag{12.1-6}$$

A general equation should be expressed as

$$r_2 = \left(\frac{P_{r_1} P_{t_2}}{P_{r_2} P_{t_1}}\right)^{1/4} r_1 \tag{12.1-7}$$

or

$$A_2 = \left(\frac{P_{r_1} P_{t_2}}{P_{r_2} P_{t_1}}\right)^{1/2} A_1 \tag{12.1-8}$$

12.1.1.2 Increasing Cell-Site Antenna Height. In general, the 6 dB/oct rule applies to the cell-site antenna height in a flat terrain, that is, doubling the antenna height causes a gain increase of 6 dB. If the terrain contour is hilly, then an effective antenna height should be used, depending on the location of the mobile unit. Sometimes, doubling the actual antenna height results in a gain increase of less than 6 dB and sometimes more. This phenomenon was described in Chap. 8.

12.1.1.3 Using a High-Gain or a Directional Antenna at the Cell Site. The gain and directivity of an antenna increase with the received level—the same effect seen with an increase of transmitted power.

12.1.1.4 Lowering the Threshold Level of a Received Signal. When the threshold level is lowered, the acceptable received power is lower and the radius of the cell increases [Eq. (12.1-3) applies]. The increase in service area due to a lower received level can be obtained from Eq. (12.1-8). Let $P_{t_2} = P_{t_1}$, and $P_{r_2} = 0.25P_{r_1}$ (i.e., −6 dB). Then $A_2 = 2A_1$. The received level is reduced by 6 dB, and the service area is doubled.

12.1.1.5   A Low-Noise Receiver.   The thermal noise kTB level (see Sec. 10.6.6) is -129 dBm. In a noise-limited environment, if the front-end noise of the receiver is low and the received power level remains the same, the carrier-to-noise ratio becomes large in comparison to a receiver with a high front-end noise. This low-noise receiver can receive a signal from a farther distance than can a high-noise receiver.

12.1.1.6   Diversity Receiver.   A diversity receiver is very useful in reducing the multipath fading. When the fading reduces, the reception level can be increased. Diversity receiver performance is discussed in further detail in Sec. 12.4.3.

12.1.1.7   Selecting Cell-Site Locations.   With a given actual antenna height and a given transmitted power, coverage area can be increased if we can select a proper site. Of course, in principle, for coverage purposes, we always select a high site if there is no risk of interference. However, sometimes we need to cover an important area within the coverage area; in such cases it is necessary to move around the site location.

12.1.1.8   Using Repeaters and Enhancers to Enlarge the Coverage Area or to Fill in Holes.   This is discussed in Sec. 12.4.

12.1.1.9   Engineering the Antenna Patterns.   The technique of engineering the antenna patterns mentioned in Sec. 8.13 can be used to cover a desired service area.

12.1.2   Reducing the Interference

In most situations, the methods mentioned in Sec. 12.1.1 for increasing the coverage area would cause interference if cochannels or adjacent channels were used in the system. Methods for reducing the interference are as follows.

1. *A good frequency-management chart.* From the total channels of an AMPS system shown in Fig. 12.1 as an example, there are 21 sets of channels in the chart. In each channel set, the neighboring frequency is 21 channels away. No interference can be caused within a set of 16 channels.

2. *An intelligent frequency assignment.* In order to assign the 21 sets in a $K = 7$ frequency reuse pattern and to avoid the interference problems from adjacent-channel or cochannel interference, an intelligent frequency assignment in real time is needed.

3. *A proper frequency among a set assigned to a particular mobile unit.* Depending on the current situation, some idle channels may be noisy, some may be quiet, and some may be vulnerable to channel interference. These factors should be considered in assignment of frequency channels.

4. *Design of an antenna pattern on the basis of direction.* In some directions, a strong signal may be needed; in other directions no signal may be needed. The design tool should include the findings of signal requirements on the basis of antenna direction.

5. *Tilting-antenna patterns.* To confine the energy within a small area, we may use an umbrella-pattern omnidirectional antenna or downward tilting directional antenna.

6. *Reducing the antenna height.* We can use this method because reducing interference is more important than radio coverage.

7. *Reducing the transmitted power.* In certain circumstances, reducing transmitted power can be more effective in eliminating interference than reducing the height of the antenna.

8. *Choosing the cell-site location.* The propagation prediction model described in Chap. 8 can be used to select cell-site locations for eliminating interference.

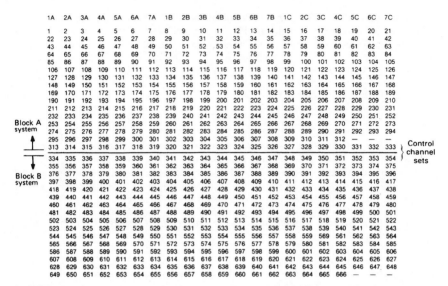

1A	2A	3A	4A	5A	6A	7A	1B	2B	3B	4B	5B	6B	7B	1C	2C	3C	4C	5C	6C	7C
1	2	3	4	5	6	7	8	9	10	11	12	13	14	15	16	17	18	19	20	21
22	23	24	25	26	27	28	29	30	31	32	33	34	35	36	37	38	39	40	41	42
43	44	45	46	47	48	49	50	51	52	53	54	55	56	57	58	59	60	61	62	63
64	65	66	67	68	69	70	71	72	73	74	75	76	77	78	79	80	81	82	83	84
85	86	87	88	89	90	91	92	93	94	95	96	97	98	99	100	101	102	103	104	105
106	107	108	109	110	111	112	113	114	115	116	117	118	119	120	121	122	123	124	125	126
127	128	129	130	131	132	133	134	135	136	137	138	139	140	141	142	143	144	145	146	147
148	149	150	151	152	153	154	155	156	157	158	159	160	161	162	163	164	165	166	167	168
169	170	171	172	173	174	175	176	177	178	179	180	181	182	183	184	185	186	187	188	189
190	191	192	193	194	195	196	197	198	199	200	201	202	203	204	205	206	207	208	209	210
211	212	213	214	215	216	217	218	219	220	221	222	223	224	225	226	227	228	229	230	231
232	233	234	235	236	237	238	239	240	241	242	243	244	245	246	247	248	249	250	251	252
253	254	255	256	257	258	259	260	261	262	263	264	265	266	267	268	269	270	271	272	273
274	275	276	277	278	279	280	281	282	283	284	285	286	287	288	289	290	291	292	293	294
295	296	297	298	299	300	301	302	303	304	305	306	307	308	309	310	311	312	—	—	—
313	314	315	316	317	318	319	320	321	322	323	324	325	326	327	328	329	330	331	332	333
334	335	336	337	338	339	340	341	342	343	344	345	346	347	348	349	350	351	352	353	354
355	356	357	358	359	360	361	362	363	364	365	366	367	368	369	370	371	372	373	374	375
376	377	378	379	380	381	382	383	384	385	386	387	388	389	390	391	392	393	394	395	396
397	398	399	400	401	402	403	404	405	406	407	408	409	410	411	412	413	414	415	416	417
418	419	420	421	422	423	424	425	426	427	428	429	430	431	432	433	434	435	436	437	438
439	440	441	442	443	444	445	446	447	448	449	450	451	452	453	454	455	456	457	458	459
460	461	462	463	464	465	466	467	468	469	470	471	472	473	474	475	476	477	478	479	480
481	482	483	484	485	486	487	488	489	490	491	492	493	494	495	496	497	498	499	500	501
502	503	504	505	506	507	508	509	510	511	512	513	514	515	516	517	518	519	520	521	522
523	524	525	526	527	528	529	530	531	532	533	534	535	536	537	538	539	540	541	542	543
544	545	546	547	548	549	550	551	552	553	554	555	556	557	558	559	560	561	562	563	564
565	566	567	568	569	570	571	572	573	574	575	576	577	578	579	580	581	582	583	584	585
586	587	588	589	590	591	592	593	594	595	596	597	598	599	600	601	602	603	604	605	606
607	608	609	610	611	612	613	614	615	616	617	618	619	620	621	622	623	624	625	626	627
628	629	630	631	632	633	634	635	636	637	638	639	640	641	642	643	644	645	646	647	648
649	650	651	652	653	654	655	656	657	658	659	660	661	662	663	664	665	666	—	—	—

Block A system (rows 253–333) ↕

Rows 313–333 } Control channel sets

Block B system (rows 334–666)

FIGURE 12.1 Frequency-management chart of AMPS system (used for illustration of system Design)

12.1.3 Increasing the Traffic Capacity

12.1.3.1 Small Cell Size. If we can control the radiation pattern, we can reduce the size of the cell and increase the traffic capacity. This approach is based on the assumption that all the mobile units are identical, including the mobile antennas and their mounting.

12.1.3.2 Increasing the Number of Radio Channels in Each Cell. Either omnidirectional or directional antennas can be used in each cell. Sometimes the channel combiner can process only 16 channels. Thus, if we need 96 channels, we need six transmitted antennas. Also, if 6 frequency sets are used, then the total of 21 sets is divided by 6. The closest neighboring channels would be only four channels away. A good channel assignment method is needed (see Sec. 12.2).

12.1.3.3 Enhanced Frequency Spectrum. Cellular mobile industries have been allocated an additional 166 voice channels. With an enhanced frequency spectrum, traffic capacity is increased.

12.1.3.4 Queuing. Queuing of handoff calls can increase traffic capacity, as discussed in Chap. 11.

12.1.3.5 Fixed Channel Assignment Schemes. It can reduce the interference among channels as described in Sec. 12.2.

12.1.3.6 Dynamic Channel Assignment. Dynamic, rather than fixed, channel assignment is another means of increasing traffic capacity. The external environmental factors, such as traffic volume, are considered in dynamic channel assignment (sec. 12.3).

12.2 FIXED CHANNEL ASSIGNMENT SCHEMES

12.2.1 Adjacent-Channel Assignment

Adjacent-channel assignment includes neighboring-channel assignment and next-channel assignment. The near-end–far-end (ratio) interference, as mentioned in Sec. 10.3.1, can occur among the neighboring channels (four channels on each side of the desired channel). Therefore, within a cell we have to be sure to assign neighboring channels in an omnidirectional-cell system and in a directional-antenna-cell system properly. In an omnidirectional-cell system, if one channel is assigned to the middle cell of seven cells, next channels cannot be assigned in the same cell. Also, no next channel (preferably including neighboring channels) should be assigned in the six neighboring sites in the same cell system area (Fig. 12.2a). In a directional-antenna-cell system, if one channel is assigned to a face, next channels cannot be assigned to the same face or to the other two faces in the same cell. Also, next channels cannot be assigned to the other two faces at the same cell site (Fig. 12.2b). Sometimes the next channels are assigned in the next sector of the same cell in order to increase capacity. Then performance can still be in the tolerance range if the design is proper.

12.2.2 Channel Sharing and Borrowing[1,2]

12.2.2.1 Channel Sharing. Channel sharing is a short-term traffic-relief scheme. A scheme used for a seven-cell three-face system is shown in Fig. 12.3. There are 21 channel sets, with each set consisting of about 16 channels. Figure 12.3 shows the channel set numbers. When a cell needs more channels, the channels of another face at the same cell site can be shared to handle the short-term overload. To obey the adjacent-channel assignment algorithm, the sharing is always cyclic. Sharing always increases the trunking efficiency of channels. Since we cannot allow adjacent channels to share with the nominal channels in

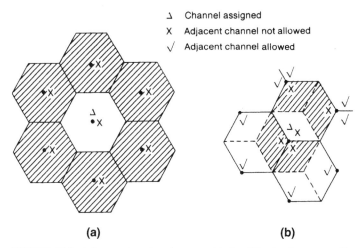

    ⅃   Channel assigned

    X   Adjacent channel not allowed

    √   Adjacent channel allowed

    (a)   **(b)**

FIGURE 12.2 Adjacent channel assignment. (*a*) Omnidirectional-antenna cells; (*b*) directional-antenna cells.

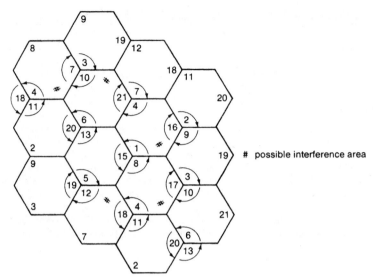

FIGURE 12.3   Channel-sharing algorithm.

the same cell, channel sets 4 and 5 cannot both be shared with channel sets 12 and 18, as indicated by the grid mark. Many grid marks are indicated in Fig. 12.3 for the same reason. However, the upper subset of set 4 can be shared with the lower subset of set 5 with no interference.

In channel-sharing systems, the channel combiner should be flexible in order to combine up to 32 channels in one face in real time. An alternative method is to install a standby antenna.

12.2.2.2   Channel Borrowing.   Channel borrowing is usually handled on a long-term basis. The extent of borrowing more available channels from other cells depends on the traffic density in the area. Channel borrowing can be implemented from one cell-site face to another face at the same cell site.

In addition, the central cell site can borrow channels from neighboring cells. The channel-borrowing scheme is used primarily for slowly-growing systems. It is often helpful in delaying cell splitting in peak traffic areas. Since cell splitting is costly, it should be implemented only as a last resort.

12.2.3   Sectorization

12.2.3.1   Advantage of Sectorization.   The total number of available channels can be divided into sets (subgroups) depending on the sectorization of the cell configuration: the 120°-sector system, the 60°-sector system, and the 45°-sector system. A seven-cell system usually uses three 120° sectors per cell, with the total number of channel sets being 21. In certain locations and special situations, the sector angle can be reduced (narrowed) in order to assign more channels in one sector without increasing neighboring-channel interference. This point is discussed in Sec. 12.8. Sectorization serves the same purpose as the channel-borrowing scheme in delaying cell splitting. In addition, channel coordination to avoid cochannel interference is much easier in sectorization than in cell splitting. Given the same number of channels, trunking efficiency decreases in sectorization.

12.2.3.2   Comparison of Omnicells (Nonsectorized Cells) and Sectorized Cells

Omnicells.   If a $K = 7$ frequency-reuse pattern is used, the frequency sets assigned in each cell can be followed by the frequency-management chart shown in Fig. 12.1. However, terrain is seldom flat; therefore, $K = 12$ is sometimes needed for reducing cochannel interference. For $K = 12$, the channel-reuse distance is $D = 6R$, or the cochannel reduction factor $q = 6$.

Sectorized Cells.   There are three basic types.

1. The $120°$-sector cell is used for both transmitting and receiving sectorization. Each sector has an assigned a number of frequencies. Changing sectors during a call requires handoffs.
2. The $60°$-sector cell is used for both transmitting and receiving sectorization. Changing sectors during a call requires handoffs. More handoffs are expected for a $60°$ sector than a $120°$ sector in areas close to cell sites (close-in areas).
3. The $120°$- or $60°$-sector cell is used for receiving sectorization only. In this case, the transmitting antenna is omnidirectional. The number of channels in this cell is not subdivided for each sector. Therefore, no handoffs are required when changing sectors. This receiving-sectorization-only configuration does not decrease interference or increase the D/R ratio; it only allows for a more accurate decision regarding handing off the calls to neighboring cells.

12.2.4   Underlay-Overlay Arrangement[3]

In actual cellular systems cell grids are seldom uniform because of varying traffic conditions in different areas and cell-site locations.

12.2.4.1   Overlaid Cells.   To permit the two groups to reuse the channels in two different cell-reuse patterns of the same size, an "underlaid" small cell is sometimes established at the same cell site as the large cell (see Fig. 12.4a). The "doughnut" (large) and "hole" (small) cells are treated as two different cells. They are usually considered as "neighboring cells."

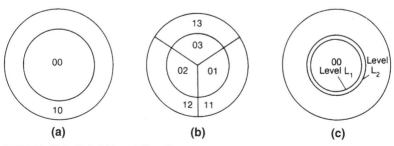

(a)   **(b)**   **(c)**

FIGURE   12.4   Underlaid-overlaid cell arrangements. (*a*) Underlay-overlay in omnicell; (*b*) underlay-overlay in sectorized cells; (*c*) two-level handoff scheme.

The use of either an omnidirectional antenna at one site to create two subring areas or three directional antennas to create six subareas is illustrated in Fig. 12.4b. As seen in Fig. 12.4, a set of frequencies used in an overlay area will differ from a set of frequencies used in an underlay area in order to avoid adjacent-channel and cochannel interference. The channels assigned to one combiner—say, 16 channels—can be used for overlay, and another combiner can be used for underlay.

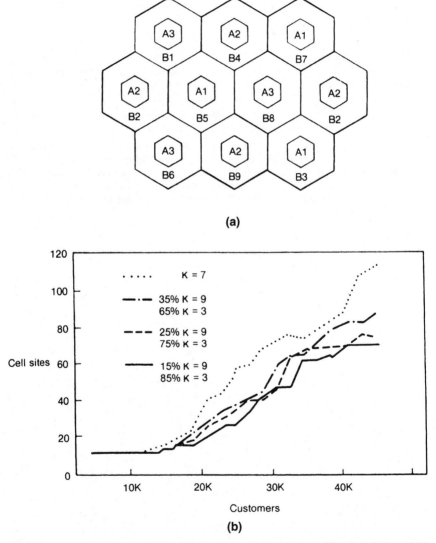

(a)

(b)

FIGURE 12.5   Reuse-partition scheme. (*After Whitehead, Ref. 1.*) (*a*) Reuse partition $K_A = 3$; $K_B = 9$. (*b*) Reuse-partitioning performance.

12.2.4.2 Implementation. The antenna of a set-up channel is usually omnidirectional. When an incoming call is received by the set-up channel and its signal strength is higher than a level L, the underlaid cell is assigned; otherwise, the overlaid cell is assigned. The handoffs are implemented between the underlaid and overlaid cells. In order to avoid the unnecessary handoffs, we may choose two levels L_1 and L_2 and $L_1 > L_2$ as shown in Fig. 12.4c.

When a mobile signal is higher than a level L_1 the call is handed off to the underlaid cell. When a signal is lower than a level L_2 the call is handed off to the overlaid cell. The channels assigned in the underlaid cell have more protection against cochannel interference.

12.2.4.3 Reuse Partition. Through implementation of the overlaid-cell concept, one possible operation is to apply a multiple-K system operation, where K is the number of frequency-reuse cells. The conventional system uses $K = 7$. But if one K is used for the underlaid cells, then this multiple-K system can have an additional 20 percent more spectrum efficiency than the single K system with an equivalent voice quality. In Fig. 12.5a, the $K = 9$ pattern is assigned to overlaid cells and the $K = 3$ pattern is assigned to underlaid cells. Based on this arrangement the number of cell sites can be reduced, while maintaining the same traffic capacity. The decrease in the number of cell sites which results from implementation of the multiple K systems is shown in Fig. 12.5b. The advantages of using this partition based on the range of K are

1. The K range is 3 to 9; the operational call quality can be adjusted and more reuse patterns are available if needed.
2. Each channel set of old $K = 9$ systems is the subset of new $K = 3$ systems. Therefore, the amount of radio retuning in each cell in this arrangement is minimal.
3. When cell splitting is implemented, all present channel assignments can be retained.

12.3 NONFIXED CHANNEL ASSIGNMENT ALGORITHMS

12.3.1 Description of Different Algorithms[4-9]

12.3.1.1 Fixed Channel Algorithm. The fixed channel assignment (FCA) algorithm is the most common algorithm adopted in many cellular systems. In this algorithm, each cell assigns its own radio channels to the vehicles within its cell.

12.3.1.2 Dynamic Channel Assignment. In dynamic channel assignment (DCA), no fixed channels are assigned to each cell. Therefore, any channel in a composite of N radio channels can be assigned to the mobile unit. This means that a channel is assigned directly to a mobile unit. On the basis of overall system performance, DCA can also be used during a call.

12.3.1.3 Hybrid Channel Assignment. Hybrid channel assignment (HCA) is a combination of FCA and DCA. A portion of the total frequency channels will use FCA and the rest will use DCA.

12.3.1.4 Borrowing Channel Assignment. Borrowing channel assignment (BCA) uses FCA as a normal assignment condition. When all the fixed channels are occupied, then the cell borrows channels from the neighboring cells.

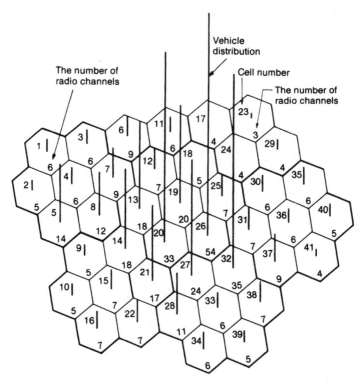

FIGURE 12.6   Cellular system. Vehicle and radio-channel distribution in the busy rush hour. (*After Sekiguchi et al., Ref. 9.*)

12.3.1.5   *Forcible-Borrowing Channel Assignment.*[9]

In forcible-borrowing channel assignment (FBCA), if a channel is in operation and the situation warrants it, channels must be borrowed from the neighboring cells and at the same time, another voice channel will be assigned to continue the call in the neighboring cell.

There are many different ways of implementing FBCA. In a general sense, FBCA can also be applied while accounting for the forcible borrowing of the channels within a fixed channel set to reduce the chance of cochannel assignment in a reuse cell pattern.

The FBCA algorithm is based on assigning a channel dynamically but obeying the rule of reuse distance. The distance between the two cells is *reuse distance*, which is the minimum distance at which no cochannel interference would occur.

Very infrequently, no channel can be borrowed in the neighboring cells. Even those channels currently in operation can be forcibly borrowed and will be replaced by a new channel in the neighboring cell or the neighboring cell of the neighboring cell. If all the channels in the neighboring cells cannot be borrowed because of interference problems, the FBCA stops.

12.3.2   Simulation Process and Results

On the basis of the FBCA, FCA, and BCA algorithms, a seven-cell reuse pattern with an average blocking of 3 percent is assumed and the total traffic service in an area in 250 erlangs. The traffic distributions are (1) uniform traffic distribution—11 channels per cell; (2) a nonuniform traffic distribution—the number of channels in each cell is dependent on the vehicle distribution (Fig. 12.6). The simulation model is described as follows:

1. Randomly select the cell (among 41 cells).
2. Determine the state of the vehicle in the cell (idle, off-hook, on-hook, handoff).

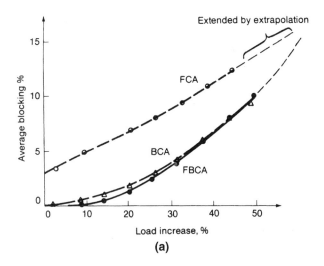

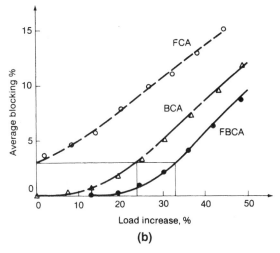

FIGURE 12.7 Comparison of average blockings from three different schemes. (*After Sekguchi et al., Ref. 9.*) (*a*) Average blocking in spatially uniform traffic distribution; (*b*) average blocking in spatially nonuniform traffic distribution.

3. In off-hook or handoff state, search for an idle channel. The average number of handoffs is assumed to be 0.2 times per call. However, FBCA will increase the number of handoffs.

12.3.2.1 Average Blocking. Two average blocking cases illustrating this simulation are shown in Fig. 12.7. In a uniform traffic condition (Fig. 12.7*a*), the 3 percent blocking of both BCA and FBCA will result in a load increase of 28 percent, compared to 3 percent blocking of FCA. There is no difference between BCA and FBCA when a uniform traffic condition exists.

In a nonuniform traffic distribution (Fig. 12.7*b*), the load increase in BCA drops to 23 percent and that of FBCA increases to 33 percent, as at an average blocking of 3 percent.

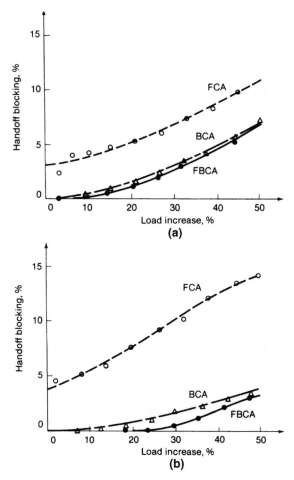

FIGURE 12.8 Comparison of handoff blocking from three different schemes. (*After Sekguchi et al., Ref. 9.*) (*a*) Handoff blocking in spatially uniform traffic distribution; (*b*) handoff blocking in spatially nonuniform traffic distribution.

The load increase can be utilized in another way by reducing the number of channels. The percent increase in load is the same as the percent reduction in the number of channels.

12.3.2.2 Handoff Blocking. Blocking calls from all handoff calls occurring in all cells is shown in Fig. 12.8. Handoff blocking is not considered as the regular cell blocking which can only occur at the call setup stage. In both BCA and FBCA, load is increased almost equally to 30 percent, as compared to FCA at 3 percent handoff blocking in uniform traffic (Fig. 12.8*a*). For a nonuniform traffic distribution, the load increase of both BCA and FBCA at 4 percent blocking is about 50 percent (Fig. 12.8*b*), which is a big improvement, considering the reduction in interference and blocking. Otherwise, there would be multiple effects from interference in several neighboring cells.

12.4 COVERAGE-HOLE FILLER

Because the ground is not flat, many water puddles form during a rainstorm; for the same reason, many holes (weak spots) are created in a general area during antenna radiation. There are several methods for filling these holes.

12.4.1 Enhancers (Repeaters)[10]

An enhancer is used in an area that is a hole (weak spot) in the serving cell site. There are two types of enhancer: wideband and channelized enhancers.

The wideband enhancer is a repeater. It is designed for either block A or block B channel implementation. All the signals received will be amplified. Sometimes it can create intermodulation products; therefore, implementation of an enhancer in an appropriate place to fill the hole without creating interference is a challenging job. One application is shown in Fig. 12.9. The amplifier requires only low amplification. The signal is transmitted from the cell site and received at the enhancer site by a higher directional antenna which is mounted at a high altitude. The signal received in the forward channel will be radiated by the lower antenna, which is either an omnidirectional or a directional antenna at the enhancer. The mobile units in the vicinity of the enhancer site will receive the signal. The mobile unit uses the reverse channel to respond to calls (or originate calls) through the enhancer to the cell site.

However, the amplifier amplifies both the signal and the noise, as discussed in Sec. 10.4.2. Therefore, the enhancer cannot improve the signal-to-noise (S/N) ratio. The function of

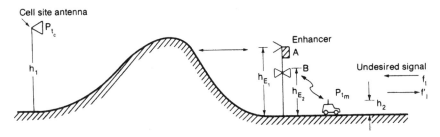

FIGURE 12.9 Enhancer.

enhancers is actually a relay, receiving at a lower height h_2 and transmitting to a higher height h_1 or vice versa. The gain of the enhancer can be adjusted from 10 to 70 dB, and the range is from 0.5 to 3 km.[10] The received signal at the mobile units and at the cell site with an enhancer placed in the middle can be expressed as

$$P_{Rm} = P_{t_r} + g_c - L_a + (G + g_{E_1} + g_{E_2}) - L_b + g_m \qquad (12.4\text{-}1)$$

and

$$P_{R_c} = P_{t_m} + g_m - L_b + (G + g_{E_1} + g_{E_2}) - L_a + g_c \qquad (12.4\text{-}2)$$

where

P_{t_c} = transmitted power at cell site
P_{t_m} = transmitted power at mobile unit
g_c = antenna gain at cell site
g_m = antenna gain at mobile unit
g_{E_1}, g_{E_2} = antenna gain at enhancer
G = amplification gain at enhancer
P_{R_c}, P_{R_m} = received power at cell site and at mobile unit, respectively
h_1 = antenna height at cell site
h_2 = antenna height at mobile unit
h_{E_1}, h_{E_2} = antenna heights at enhancer
L_a = path loss between cell site and enhancer
L_b = path loss between enhancer and mobile unit

The general formula of path loss in a mobile radio environment [see Eq. (8.2-18)] can be used to calculate both L_a and L_b. Equation (8.2-18) contains an expression of a function of antenna height that would vary in different situations.

If the undesired signal received by the antenna at height h_{E_1} is transmitted back to the cell site, cochannel or adjacent-channel interference may result. This could also occur when an undesired signal is received by the antenna at height h_{E_1} because of poor design and is repeatedly transmitted by the antenna at height h_{E_2}, causing interference in a region in which undesired signal enhancement should not occur.

The channelized enhancer should amplify only the channels that it selected previously with a good design. Therefore, it is a useful apparatus for filling the holes.

12.4.1.1 Caution.   Three points should be noted in the installation of an enhancer.

1. Ring oscillation might easily occur. The separation between two (upper and lower) antennas at the enhancer is very critical. If this separation is inadequate, the signal from the lower antenna can be received by the upper antenna or vice versa and create a ring oscillation, thus jamming the system instead of filling the hole.
2. The distance between the enhancer and the serving cell site should be as small as possible to avoid spread of power into a large area in the vicinity of the serving site and beyond.
3. Geographic (terrain) contour should be considered in enhancer installation.

12.4.2 Passive Reflector

In order to redirect the incident energy, the reflector system should be installed in a field far from both the transmitting antenna and the receiving antenna.[11] The approximate separation between the antenna and the reflector is

$$d_1 > \frac{2A_T}{\lambda} + \frac{2A_1}{\lambda} \quad \text{and} \quad d_2 > \frac{2A_1}{\lambda} + \frac{2A_R}{\lambda} \qquad (12.4\text{-}3)$$

where A_T, A_R = effective aperture of transmitting antenna and receiving antennas, respectively

d_1, d_2 = distance from reflector to transmitting antenna and receiving antenna, respectively

λ = wavelength

If the transmitting and receiving antennas are linear elements, then

$$d_1 > \frac{2L_T^2}{\lambda} + \frac{2A_1}{\lambda} \quad \text{and} \quad d_2 > \frac{2A_1}{\lambda} + \frac{2L_R^2}{\lambda} \qquad (12.4\text{-}4)$$

where L_T and L_R are, respectively, the transmitted and received lengths of the elements. The incident angle in this case would be less than 70° in order to deflect the energy in another direction (see Fig. 12.10).

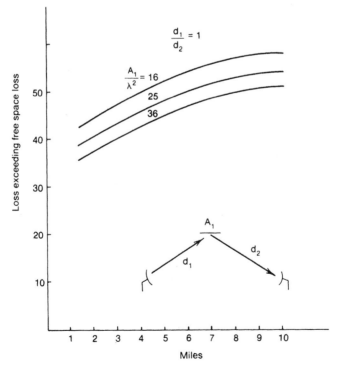

FIGURE 12.10   Effective use of Reflectors, $d_1/d_2 = 1$.

The dimension of the reflector should be many wavelengths. Assume that 100 percent of the incident power is reflected; then

$$P_R = P_T \frac{A_T A_R A_1^2}{\lambda^4 d_1^2 d_2^2} \tag{12.4-5}$$

where P_T, P_R = transmitted and received power, respectively, and

$$A_T = \frac{G_T \lambda^2}{4\pi} \tag{12.4-6}$$

$$A_R = \frac{G_R \lambda^2}{4\pi}$$

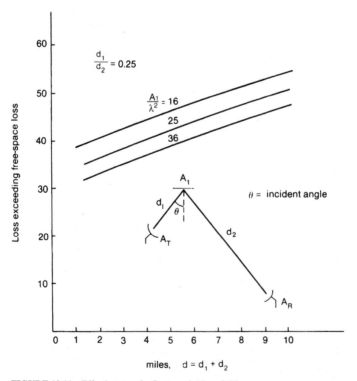

FIGURE 12.11 Effective use of reflectors, $d_1/d_2 = 0.25$.

Then, Eq. (12.4-5) becomes

$$P_R = P_T G_T G_R \frac{A_1^2}{(4\pi)^2 d_1^2 d_2^2}$$

$$= P_T G_T G_R \left[\left(4\pi \frac{d}{\lambda} \right)^2 \right]^{-1} \cdot \left(\frac{d^2 \lambda^2 (A_1/\lambda^2)^2}{d_1^2 d_2^2} \right)$$

free-space loss (FSL)   excessive loss   (12.4-7)

where $d = d_1 + d_2$ and

$$P_R/(P_T G_T G_R) = 10 \log(\text{FSL}) + 10 \log \left[\left(\frac{d^2 \lambda^2}{d_1^2 d_2^2} \right) \left(\frac{A_1}{\lambda^2} \right)^2 \right] \qquad (12.4\text{-}8)$$

The excessive loss in Eq. (12.4-9) is plotted in Fig. 12.10 for the case of $d_1/d_2 = 1.0$ and in Fig. 12.11 for $d_1/d_2 = 0.25$ at 850 MHz.

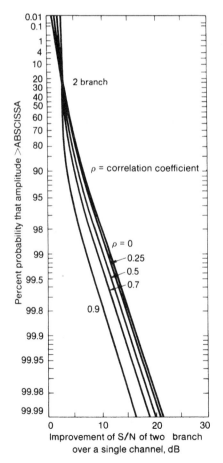

FIGURE 12.12 Improvement of signal-to-noise ratio of a two-branch signal over a single channel signal. (*After Lee, Ref. 12.*)

In a mobile radio environment, d_1 can be considered to be in a free space and d_2 to be a mobile radio path from the reflector to the mobile unit. Then Eq. (12.4-5) can be modified as

$$P_R = P_T \frac{A_T A_R A_1^2}{\lambda^2 d_1^2 d_2^4}$$

$$= P_T G_T G_R \left[\left(4\pi \frac{d_1}{\lambda} \right)^2 \frac{d_2^4}{\lambda^4} \right]^{-1} \cdot \frac{(A_1/\lambda^2)^2}{1} \qquad (12.4\text{-}9)$$

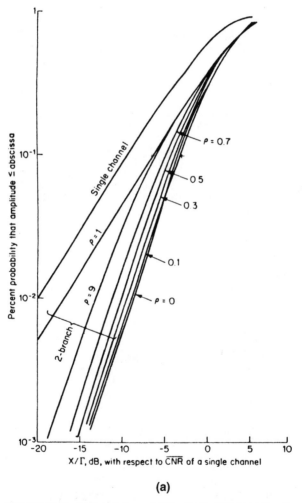

(a)

FIGURE 12.13 (*a*) Cumulative probability distribution of a two-branch correlated equal-gain-combining signal. (*After Lee, Ref. 18.*)

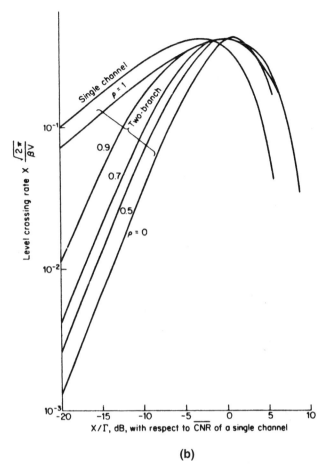

(b)

FIGURE 12.13 (*Continued*) (*b*) Level-crossing rate of a two-branch equal-gain-combining signal. (*After Lee, Ref. 18.*)

or

$$P_R = 10 \log (\text{FSL}) + 10 \, \log \left[\frac{d^2 A_1^2 \lambda^2}{d_1^2 d_2^4} \right] \qquad (12.4\text{-}10)$$

excessive loss

Comparing Eq. (12.4-11) with Eq. (12.4-9), we realize that the excessive loss from a reflector is greater in a mobile radio environment.

12.4.3 Diversity

The diversity receiver can be used to fill the holes. Because the diversity receiver can receive a lower signal level, the hole that existed in a normal receiver reception case now becomes a no-hole (or lesser hole) situation with the use of the diversity receiver. An improvement in the signal-to-noise ratio of a two-branch diversity receiver[12] is shown in Fig. 12.12. The diversity schemes can be classified as[13] (1) polarization diversity,[14] (2) field component-energy density,[15–16] (3) space diversity, (4) frequency diversity, (5) time diversity, and (6) angle diversity.

For any two independent branches the performance obtained from any of the diversity schemes listed above is the same; that is, the correlation coefficient of the two received signals becomes zero. The performance can be degraded if the two signals obtained from the two branches are dependent on a correlation coefficient, as shown in Fig. 12.12. The performance can also vary with different diversity-combiner techniques.[17] The maximal-ratio combiner is the best performance combiner. The equal-gain combiner has a 0.5-dB degradation as compared with the maximal-ratio combiner. The selective combiner has a 2-dB degradation as compared with the maximal-ratio combiner.

The performance increase based on a diversity scheme for a two-branch equal-gain diversity combiner is shown in Fig. 12.13*a* for the cumulative probability distribution (CPD) and in Fig. 12.13*b* for the level-crossing rate (LCR). The average duration of fades $\bar{t}$ can be obtained by calculating $\bar{t} = \text{CPD/LCR}$ as shown in Eq. (2.3-19). Also, we can plot the performance of the diversity combined signal with different correlation coefficients

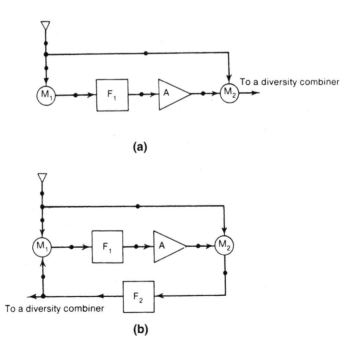

FIGURE 12.14 Two cophase techniques, feedforward and feedback ($F = $ the filter, $M = $ the mixer, and $A = $ the limiting amplifier, as shown in the figure). (*a*) Feedforward combiner; (*b*) feedback (Granlund) combiner.

between two branches. For example, at the cell site, the correlation coefficient ρ between branches is set to be 0.7 for the reality of physical antenna separation. At the mobile unit, however, the signal correlation of two branches is almost zero with a separation of $d = 0.5$). Reductions in fading and in level-crossing rate are shown in Fig. 12.13a and b, respectively. The improvement in the signal-to-noise ratio of a two-branch signal over a single branch with different values of correlation coefficients between channel signals is shown in Fig. 12.12. The maximum improvement occurs when $\rho = 0$.

12.4.4   Cophase Technique

The cophase technique is used to bring all signal phases from different branches to a common phase point. Here, the common phase point is the point at which the random phase in each branch is reduced. There are two kinds of cophase techniques: feedforward and feedback[18] (these circuits are shown in Fig. 12.14a and b, respectively).

The feedforward cophase technique has been used for satellite communication applications. It is simpler than the phase-locked loop. The latter is also called the *Granlund combiner.* The outcome of the feedback technique is always better than that of the feedforward technique provided the two filters in the circuit have been properly designed to avoid any significant time delay.

12.5   LEAKY FEEDER

12.5.1   Leaky Waveguides

Typically, the velocity of propagation of an electromagnetic wave V_g in the waveguide is greater than the speed of light V_c. However, the carrier frequency in hertz should be the same as in the waveguide and in free space. Thus, if two waves have the same frequency, their wavelengths will be longer in the waveguide than in free space, as seen from the following equation.

$$\lambda_g = \frac{V_g}{f} \tag{12.5-1}$$

Therefore,

$$\lambda_g > \lambda_c \tag{12.5-2}$$

If the waveguide structure supporting this mode is properly opened up, then the energy will leak into the exterior region.[19] The opening slots (apertures) will usually be placed along the waveguide periodically. This leaky waveguide is different from a slot antenna. The slot antenna is designed to radiate all the energy into the space at the slot, whereas in the leaky waveguide, fractional energy will be leaking constantly. Because V_g is greater than V_c, the leaky waveguide may sometimes be categorized as a fast-wave antenna.

The general field expression can be written for the interior and exterior regions of the waveguide and matched across the slot boundary. For a circular-shaped waveguide,[20] the internal field is TE_{11}. The attenuation, or the leakage energy, is shown in Fig. 12.15a. Figure 12.15b shows the dimensions of the circular waveguide. The leakage rate is a function of position in the waveguide, where $\alpha = 0.1$ is the fraction of the input power absorbed in the load, that is, the amount of energy that leaks out.

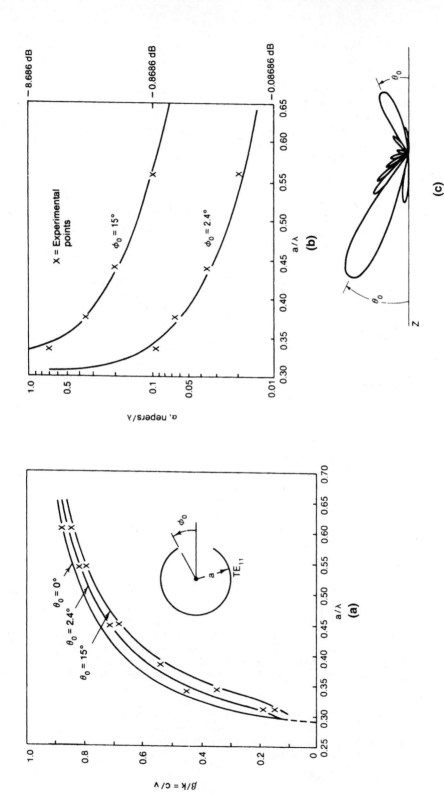

FIGURE 12.15 Complex propagation constant for a TE_{11} slotted cylinder. (*After Harrington, Ref. 9.*) (*a*) Leaky energy due to slot size; (*b*) wave velocity in a slotted cylinder; (*c*) principal plane pattern of a leaky wave slot; showing forward and backward main beams.

12.5.1.1   The Leaky Waveguide Pattern.   Pattern is also a very important factor in the application of leaky waveguides. We would like the pattern to be similar to that in Fig. 12.15c, which can serve a larger area along the waveguide.

12.5.1.2   The Coaxial Cable or Leaky Coaxial.   The phase velocity V of a wave traveling on the line is given by

$$V = \frac{\omega}{\beta} = \frac{1}{\sqrt{LC}} \qquad (12.5\text{-}3)$$

At frequencies below 1000 MHz, the use of coaxial cable is universal because the attenuation per unit length is reasonable and the dimensions are practical for passing the principal modes of leaky waves. At higher frequencies, since the dimensions of coaxial cable cannot be physically reduced in order to suppress the high modes of leaky waves in the coaxial cable, excessively high attenuation might occur. Consequently, for frequencies above 3000 MHz, waveguides are generally used.

12.5.2   Leaky-Feeder Radio Communication

In some areas, such as in tunnels or in other confined spaces such as underground garages or a cell of less than 1-mi radius, leaky-feeder techniques become increasingly important to provide adequate coverage and reduce interference.

In 1956 a "guided radio" was introduced.[21] This "radio" is actually a low-frequency inductive communication device. The proposal included utilization of existing conductors such as power cables and telephone lines to transmit the signal.

Also in 1956, the leaky-feeder principle for propagation of VHF and UHF signals through a tunnel or a confined area was presented.[22] The open-braided type (i.e., containing zigzag slots) of coaxial cable is used in most applications for suppressing any resulting surface-wave interference (Fig. 10.16). However, in this design, if the cable slots are all the same size, then there is nonuniform energy leakage along the cable. A great deal of energy may leak out at the slots which are arrived at first. For instance, a leaky cable can have a loss of 2 dB per 100 ft at 1000 MHz. The "daisy chain" system patented in 1971 avoids the complications and shortcomings of two-way signal boosters along the cable.[23] Therefore, the radiation signal level can be within a specified range.

Because of "intrinsic safety" considerations, in order to prevent any incendiary sparks (e.g., as in a coal mine), the RF powers cannot exceed a maximum of 500 mW, and any line-fed power passed over leaky feeders used for boosters (power amplification along the cable) should be limited to a few watts. In urban applications, a 0.25-mi-long leaky cable can be used without the power amplifying stage.

The leaky feeder is characterized by transmission and coupling losses. Transmission loss is expressed in decibels per unit length. Coupling loss is defined by the ratio of power received by a dipole antenna at a distance s equal to 1.5 m away from the cable to the transmitted power in the cable at a given point. The smaller the ratio, the greater the loss. If the distance is other than 1.5 m, the coupling loss (or free-space loss from a leaky cable) L increases as d increases.

$$L \,(s \text{ at } d) = (\text{coupling loss at } 1.5 \text{ m}) + 10 \log\left(\frac{d}{1.5}\right) \qquad (12.5\text{-}4)$$

The free-space loss from a leaky cable is described later. The coupling loss can be controlled by size and slot angle, whereas the transmission loss L_t varies with the coupling loss L_{co} and

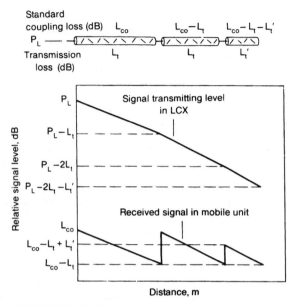

FIGURE 12.16   Grading technique.

cannot be chosen independently of the coupling loss. The principal of leaky-cable operation is

1. Use high-coupling-loss (little energy will leak out) cables near the transmitter end. Usually high-coupling-loss cables have a low-transmission loss and are of greater length in use. We can arrange the lengths of cables due to different coupling losses as shown in Fig. 12.16.

2. The intensive radiation pointing to a specific direction is caused by periodic spacing of slots along the cable. Radiation can be distributed through joint points or boosters and by adjusting the signal phases around boosters as needed.

3. Leaky cables are open fields. Leaky cables in the tunnels are easily implemented because their energy is confined to the tunnel. However, in an open field, if no obstacle blocks the path between the cable and the mobile receiver, the signal should be less varied. The electric field leaking out from the leaky cable is reciprocally proportional to the square of the distance from the leaky cable.

$$L_r = 20 \log s \qquad \text{dB} \qquad (12.5\text{-}5)$$

4. Low temperature affects leaky cable. Transmission-loss levels change with change in temperature. The lower the temperature, the less the transmission loss.

5. Snow accumulation around slots causes an increase in transmission loss. Reflection and path loss due to snow on leaky cable cause an increase of coupling loss.

6. The boosters are power amplifiers. Therefore, many narrowband-modulated carriers passing through common broadband amplifiers generate intermodulation (IM) product power. In order to reduce the IM product to a specified level, the linear amplifiers should

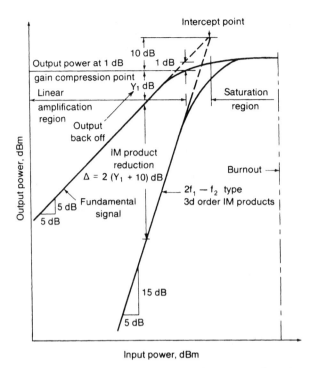

FIGURE 12.17   Input-output characteristics of a linear amplifier. (*After Suzuki et al., Ref. 23.*)

be operated at a reduced output level by backing them off from the 1-dB-gain compression point.

The amplification of a fundamental signal and its most dominant IM (i.e., third-order IM) is illustrated in Fig. 12.17. Because the slopes of curves for fundamental signal and third-order IM are always fixed, the higher the intercept point, the lower the IM product interference. Also, we can find the output backoff level from a given IM product suppression, Y_1, as

$$2(Y_1 + Y_0) = \Delta$$

$$Y_1 = \frac{\Delta}{2} - Y_0 \qquad (12.5\text{-}6)$$

where Y_0 is the power difference between the intercept point and the 1-dB-gain compression point. The IM product levels and numbers are given in Ref. 24. Other literature references can be found in Ref. 25 and 26.

12.6   CELL SPLITTING

When the call traffic in an area increases, we must split the cell so that we can reuse frequency more often, as we have mentioned in Chap. 2. This involves reducing the radius of a cell by half and splitting an old cell into four new small cells. The traffic is then increased fourfold.[27]

12.6.1 Transmitted Power After Splitting

The transmitted power P_{t_1} for a new cell, because of its reduced size, can be determined from the transmitted power P_{t_0}, of the old cell.

If we assume that the received power at the cell boundary is P_r, then the following equations (where α is a constant) can be deduced from Eq. (12.1-1).

$$P_r = \alpha P_{t_0} R_0^{-\gamma} \tag{12.6-1}$$

$$P_r = \alpha P_{t_1} \left(\frac{R_0}{2} \right)^{-\gamma} \tag{12.6-2}$$

Equation (12.6-1) expresses the received power at the boundary of the old cell and Eq. (12.6-2), the received power at the boundary of the new cell $R_1 = (R_0/2)$. To set up an identical received power P_r at the boundaries of two different-sized cells, and dropping the parameter P_r by combining Eqs. (12.6-1) and (12.6-2), we find

$$P_{t_1} = P_{t_0} \left(\frac{1}{2} \right)^{-\gamma} \tag{12.6-3}$$

For a typical mobile radio environment, $\gamma = 4$, Eq. (12.6-3) becomes

$$P_{t_1} = \frac{P_{t_0}}{16} \tag{12.6-4}$$

or

$$P_{t_1} = P_{t_0} - 12 \quad \text{dB} \tag{12.6-5}$$

The new transmitted power must be 12 dB less than the old transmitted power. The new cochannel interference reduction factor q_2 after cell splitting is still equal to the value of q (see Eq. 2.6-1) since both D and R were split in half. A general formula is for a new cell which is split repeatedly n times, and every time the new radius is one-half of the old one; then $R_n = R_0/2^n$.

$$P_{t_n} = P_{t_0} - n(12) \quad \text{dB} \tag{12.6-6}$$

When cell splitting occurs, the value of the frequency-reuse distance q is always held constant. The traffic load can increase four times in the same area after the original cell is split into four subcells. Each subcell can again be split into four subcells, which would allow traffic to increase 16 times. As the cell splitting continues, the general formula can be expressed as

$$\text{New traffic load} = (4)^n \times \text{(the traffic load of start-up cell)} \tag{12.6-7}$$

where n is the number of splittings. For $n = 4$, this means that an original start-up cell has split four times. The traffic load is 256 times larger than the traffic load of the start-up cell.

12.6.2 Cell-Splitting Technique

The two techniques of cell splitting are described below.

12.6.2.1 Permanent Splitting. Selecting small cell sites is a tough job. The antenna can be mounted on a monopole or erected by a mastless arrangement, which will be described later. However, these splittings can be easy to handle as long as the cutover from large cells to small cells takes place during a low traffic period. The frequency assignment should follow the rule (see Sec. 2.6) based on the frequency-reuse distance ratio q with the power adjusted.

12.6.2.2 Real-Time Splitting (Dynamic Splitting). In many situations, such as traffic jams at football stadiums after a game, in traffic jams resulting from automobile accidents, and so on, the idle small cell sites (inactive ones) may be rendered operative in order to increase the cell's traffic capacity.

Cell splitting should proceed gradually over a cellular operating system to prevent dropped calls. Suppose that the area exactly midway between two old $2A$ sectors requires increased traffic capacity as indicated in Fig. 12.18. We can take the midpoint between two old $2A$ sectors and name it "new $2A$." The new $1A$ sector can be found by rotating the old $1A–2A$ line (shown in Fig. 12.18) clockwise[28] $120°$. Then the orientation of the new set of seven split cells is determined. To maintain service for ongoing calls while doing the cell splitting, we let the channels assigned in the old $2A$ sector separate into two groups.

$$2A = (2A)' + (2A)'' \tag{12.6-8}$$

where $(2A)'$ represents the frequency channels used in both new and old cells, but in the small sectors, and $(2A)''$ represents the frequency channels used only in the old cells.

At the early splitting stage, only a few channels are in $(2A)'$. Gradually, more channels will be transferred from $(2A)''$ to $(2A)'$. When no channels remain in $(2A)''$, the

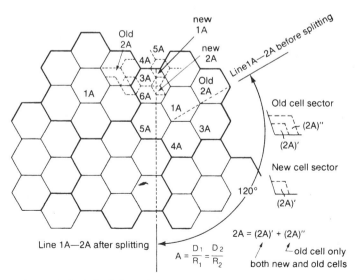

FIGURE 12.18 Cell-splitting techniques.

cell-splitting procedure will be completed. With a software algorithm program, the cell-splitting procedure should be easy to handle.

12.6.3 Splitting Size Limitations and Traffic Handling

The size of splitting cells is dependent on two factors.

The radio aspect. The size of a small cell is dependent on how well the coverage pattern can be controlled and how accurately vehicle locations would be known.

The capacity of the switching processor. The smaller the cells, the more handoffs will occur, and the more the cell-splitting processing power is needed. This factor, the capacity of a switching processor, is a larger factor than the handling of coverage areas of small cells.

12.6.4 Effect on Splitting

When the cell splitting is occurring, in order to maintain the frequency-reuse distance ratio q in a system, there are two considerations.

1. Cells splitting affects the neighboring cells. Splitting cells causes an unbalanced situation in transmit power and frequency-reuse distance, and makes it necessary to split small cells in the neighboring cells. This phenomenon is the same as a ripple effect.
2. Certain channels should be used as barriers. To the same extent, large and small cells can be isolated by selecting a group of frequencies which will be used only in the cells located between the large cells on one side and the small cells on the other side, in order to eliminate the interference being transmitted from the large cells to the small cells.

12.7 SMALL CELLS (MICROCELLS)

As we mentioned in Sec. 12.6, the limitation of a small cell is based on the accuracy of vehicle locations and control of the radiation patterns of the antennas. In this section, we try to find the means of control, the radiation power. The intelligent cell concept and application to microcells are described in Chap. 16.

12.7.1 Installation of a Mastless Antenna

12.7.1.1 Use of Existing Building Structures. Building structures can be used to mount cell-site antennas. In such cases the rooftop usually is flat. There should be enough clearance around the antenna post mounted in the middle of the building to avoid blockage of the beam pattern from the edge of the roof (see Fig. 12.19). A formula may be applied for this situation. Given the vertical beamwidth of antenna ϕ and the distance from the antenna post to the edge of the roof d, the height of the post can be determined by

$$h = d \tan\left(\frac{\phi}{2}\right) \tag{12.7-1}$$

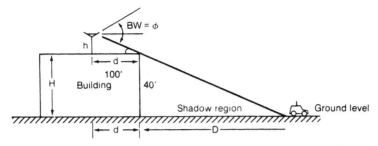

FIGURE 12.19   Rooftop-mounted antennas.

If a 6-dB-gain antenna has a vertical beamwidth of about 28° and the distance from the antenna post to the roof edge is 31 m (100 ft), then the required antenna height is 7.5 m (25 ft). The shaded region around the building depends on the height of the building.

$$D = \frac{H + h}{\tan(\phi/2)} - d \qquad (12.7\text{-}2)$$

If $H = 12$ m (40 ft), $h = 7.5$ m (25 ft), $\phi/2 = 14°$, then Eq. (12.7-2) becomes $D = 49$ m (160 ft).

The shadow region is calculated for a single building only. If there are adjacent buildings, multipath scattered waves are generated, and the shadow region is reduced.

12.7.1.2   Use of the Antenna Structures.   The panel-type antennas[29] are ideal antenna structures for hanging on each side of the wall. For an omnidirectional configuration, the four-panel antennas mounted on the four sides of the building can be combined as in an omnidirectional antenna.

For a sectorized configuration, each antenna occupies one sector. If a three-sector configuration is used, two panel antennas should be mounted close to the two corners of the building and one panel mounted on a flat wall of the building as shown in Fig. 12.20.

12.7.2   Tailoring a Uniform-Coverage Cell

We will develop a lightweight, fold-up, portable directional antenna with adjustable beamwidth capability. It can be in the form of a corner reflector or an n-element array. This kind of antenna can be attached to the outer walls of the building in different directions. Perhaps we can attach such antennas to different buildings and form a desired coverage. The transmitted power of the antenna in each direction is also adjusted so that the coverage becomes uniformly distributed around the cell boundary. These antennas may be called *coverage sectored antennas*. The "coverage sectors" and the "frequency sectors" are not necessarily the same. Usually, several coverage sectors represent a frequency sector when the cell size becomes small. Since the power coverage is based on the coverage sectors and the frequency assignment is based on the frequency sectors, the existing software should be modified to incorporate this feature.

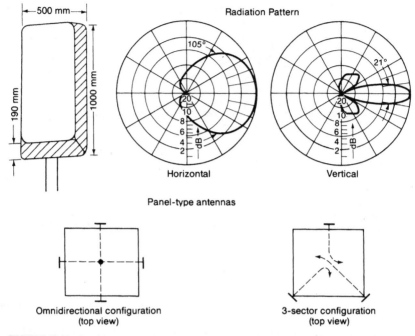

FIGURE 12.20 Panel-type antennas and their applications. (*After Kathrein, Ref. 29.*)

12.7.3 Vehicle-Locating Methods

By locating the vehicle and calculating the distance to it, we can obtain information useful for assigning proper frequency channels.

There are many vehicle-locating methods. In general, we can divide these into two categories: installation of equipment (1) in the vehicles and (2) at the cell site.

12.7.3.1 Installing Equipment in the Vehicles

Triangulation. Three or more transmitting antennas are used at different cell sites. Because the locations of the sites are known, the vehicle's location can be based on identification of three or more sites. However, the accuracy is limited by the multipath phenomenon.

In certain areas of the United States, especially near the coasts, Loran-C transmitters are used by the U.S. Coast Guard. These transmitters operate at 500 kHz. A Loran-C receiver installed in a vehicle can facilitate locating the vehicle.

Fifth-Wheel and Gyroscope Equipment. A gyroscope and a fifth wheel are used for determining the direction and distance a vehicle has traveled from a predetermined point at any given time.

The Global-Position Satellite (GPS). There are seven active GPSs, each of them circling the earth roughly twice a day at an altitude of 1840 km (11,500 mi) and transmitting at a frequency of approximately 1.7 GHz. There are two codes, the C code and the P code. The C code is the coarse code, which can be used by the civilian services. The P code is the precision code, which is used only by the military forces. At least three or more GPS satellites should be seen in space at any time, so that a GPS receiver can locate its position according to the known positions of the GPS satellites. Today, 18 GPSs and six spaces are in the orbit. The GPS location is very accurate, generally within 6 m (20 ft). When four GPSs are in space, we can measure three dimensons (i.e., latitude, longitude, and altitude). The cost of a GPS receiver is very inexpensive at present for commercial cellular mobile systems. Most handsets will equip GPS receivers for location finding and E911 emergency-needs.

A GPS receiver also can be used as a Universal Time clock for a synchronization system such as used in the cdmaOne system.

12.7.3.2 Installing Equipment at the Cell Site.
In general, either of the following three methods alone cannot provide sufficient accuracy for locating vehicles; a combination of two or all three methods is recommended.

Triangulation Based on Signal Strength. Record the signal strength received from the mobile unit at each cell site and then apply the triangulation method to find the location of the mobile unit. The degree of accuracy is very poor because of the multipath phenomenon.

Triangulation Based on Angular Arrival. Record the direction of signal arrival at each cell site and then apply the triangulation method to find the location of the mobile unit.

Triangulation Based on Response-Time Arrival. Send a signal to the mobile unit. It will return with a time delay or a phase change. Measurement of the time delay or the phase change at each site can indicate the distance from that site.

Two or more distances from different sites can help us determine the location of the vehicle. However, the delay spread in the mobile environment can be 0.5 μs in suburban areas to 3 μs in urban areas. We may need ingenuity to solve this problem if the locating method is based on the response-time arrival.

12.7.3.3 Present Cellular Locating Receiver.
Each cell site is equipped with a locating receiver which can both scan and measure the signal strengths of all channels. This receiver can be used to continuously scan the frequencies, or to scan on request.

Continuous-Scanning Scheme. In continuous scanning of all 333 channels in AMPs as an example, assume that scanning each channel takes 20 ms. Thus, the time interval between two consecutive measurements of any single channel is 333×20 ms = 6.6 s.

If a car is driven at 30 mi/h (= 44 ft/s), the interval between two different measurements on one frequency will be 6.6 s or 290 ft, so we would not expect a drastic change in this interval. However, the time interval of 20 ms for measuring the signal strength on a frequency is too short—only about 1 ft in distance (about 1 wavelength). As discussed in Chap. 2, we need 40 wavelengths to obtain good measurement data.[30] Therefore, if we are using the continuous-scanning scheme, the running mean $M(N)$ at the Nth sample based on the average of N samples should be tracked.

$$M(N) = \frac{\sum_{i=1}^{N} x_i}{N}$$

$$M(N + 1) = \frac{\sum\limits_{i=2}^{N+1} x_i}{N}$$

The advantage of this scheme it that

1. Each cell site "knows" the signal-plus-interference levels ($S + I$) of all active channels. The cell site can respond without delay to the mobile switching office (MSO) regarding the $S + I$ level of any one channel for measuring.
2. Each cell site knows the interference (or noise) levels of all idle channels. The cell site can choose a prospective (candidate) channel on the basis of its low interference level.

The selected channel mentioned in item 2 must not only generate a better signal-to-interference ratio but also less interference that affects the other cells. The argument for this is that if no interference is received by a channel, this channel will not cause interference in others. Use of a high-interference channel will not only cause deterioration in voice quality but also generate more interference in other cells.

Scan-Under-Request Scheme. When measurement of a channel's signal strength is requested, the cell site must have enough time to measure it with a locating receiver; there is usually one locating receiver per cell site. Each locating receiver is capable of tuning and measuring all channels. Therefore, actual amount of time spent measuring the signal strength of each individual channel upon request can afford to be relative long for high accuracy. The disadvantages of the continuous-scanning scheme are compensated for by its advantages and vice versa.

12.7.4 Portable Cell Sites

For rapid addition of new cell sites to an existing system, portable cell sites are used to serve the traffic temporarily while the permanent site is under construction. In other situations, when it has not been determined whether the prospective site will be appropriate, the portable cell site can be used for a short period of time so that real operational data can be collected to determine whether this site will be suitable for a permanent site installation. Construction of a cell site normally requires three primary activities: (1) site acquisition, (2) building and tower construction, and (3) equipment installation and testing. A fair amount of time is needed for each activity. The portable cell site consists of buildings, equipment, and antennas, and all three of these items should be transportable.[31]

12.7.5 Different Antenna Mountings on the Mobile Unit

The different antenna mountings used on the mobile units affect system performance. The rooftop-mounted antenna, because of the great antenna height above the ground and the roughly uniform coverage, provides maximum coverage.

On the other hand, antennas mounted on windows, car bumpers, or trunks provide less coverage than do those mounted on roofs. However, more than 70 percent of the cars in cellular systems use glass-mounted antennas in 90's. Now the most handsets are used inside the cars. The system operator must decide whether the available cellular system has to tune for glass-mounted mobile units or handset units.

If the system is tuned for glass-mounted mobile antennas, that is, if the $q = D/R$ ratio is based on the reception of $C/I \geq 18$ dB of the glass-mounted antennas, then the cell coverages for glass-mounted units provides for no holes. However, the cell coverage for handset units does create holes in cell coverages because of the weaker signals around all cell boundaries, which in turn results in excessive call drops.

If the system is tuned for all mobile units with handset units, then coverage of all cells will be suitable for these units. But the mobile units with glass-mounted antennas will travel deeply into the neighboring cells because of a still adequate signal at the cell boundaries and the delay of handoffs taking place. Thus the units with glass-mounted antennas will experience channel interference such as cross talk and dropped calls.

Because the system tuning mentioned above cannot satisfy both kinds of mobile antenna usage, the author recommends that if the handoff is based on signal strength level a system should be tuned for those mobile units which have glass-mounted antennas. Then for the handset units, the weak reception can be solved by the power control features and the enhanced coverage due to the close-in microcells.

If the handoff is based on power-difference schemes (Sec. 11.6), the effect of this scheme on different mobile antenna mountings becomes much less. The handoff occurrence areas for the mobile units with different antennas and different mountings are very much the same.

12.8 NARROWBEAM CONCEPT

The narrowbeam-sector concept is another method for increasing the traffic capacity (see Fig. 12.21). For a $K = 7$ frequency-reuse pattern with $120°$ sectors as a conventional

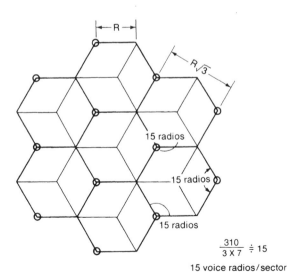

$$\frac{310}{3 \times 7} \doteq 15$$

15 voice radios / sector

FIGURE 12.21   Ideally located cell sites over a flat terrain ($K = 7$).

configuration, each sector will contain approximately 15 voice channels, a number that is derived from the total 310 voice channels as an example.

$$\frac{310}{3 \times 7} = 15 \text{ channels per } 120° \text{ sector}$$

For a $K = 4$ frequency-reuse pattern[32] with 60° sectors (Fig. 12.22a), the number of channels in each 60° sector is

$$\frac{310}{4 \times 6} = 13 \text{ channels per } 60° \text{ sector}$$

In the $K = 7$ pattern there is a total of 21 sectors with 15 channels in each sector; in the $K = 4$ pattern there is a total of 24 sectors with 13 channels in each sector. The spectrum efficiency of using these two patterns can be calculated using the Erlang B table in Appendix A. With a blocking probability of 2 percent, the results are: an offer load of 189 erlangs for $K = 7$ and 177 erlangs for $K = 4$. This means that the $K = 7$ pattern offers a 7 percent higher spectrum efficiency than the $K = 4$ pattern does. As seen in Fig. 12.22a a number of cell sites have been eliminated for $K = 4$ as compared with $K = 7$, assuming the same coverage area. However, the $K = 4$ arrangement[32] results in increased handoff processing. Also the antennas erected in each site with a $K = 4$ pattern should be relatively higher than those with a $K = 7$ pattern. Otherwise, channel interference among channels will be increased because the wrong frequency channels will be assigned to the mobile units due to the low antenna height in the system. As a result, the actual location of the mobile units in smaller sectors may be incorrect.

Here we could use the scheme in Fig. 12.22b for customizing channel distribution; that is, usage of the 120° and 60° sectors can be mixed. Some 120° sectors can be replaced by two 60° sectors in a $K = 7$ pattern. The number of channels can then be increased from 15 to 26 as shown in Fig. 12.22b. This scheme would be suitable for small-cell systems. The antenna-height requirement for 60° sectors in small cells is relatively higher than that for 120° sectors. Besides, the 24 subgroups (each containing 13 channels) are used as needed in certain areas. These sector-mixed systems follow a $K = 7$ frequency-reuse pattern, and the traffic capacity is dramatically increased as a result of customizing the channel distribution according to the real traffic condition.

12.8.1 Comparison of Narrowbeam Sectors with Underlay-Overlay Arrangement

In certain situations, the narrowbeam sector scheme is better in a small cell than the underlay-overlay scheme. In a small cell, it is very difficult to control power in order to make underlay-overlay schemes work effectively. For 60° sectors, the 60° narrowbeam antennas would easily delineate the area for operation of the assigned radio channels. However, choosing the correct narrowbeam sector where the mobile unit is located is hard. As a result, many unnecessary handoffs may take place.

In a 1-mi cell, if the traffic density is not uniformly distributed throughout the cell, the choice of using narrowbeam sectors or an underlay-overlay scheme is as follows; use the former for the angularly nonuniform cells, and use the latter for the radially nonuniform cells.

12.9 SEPARATION BETWEEN HIGHWAY CELL SITES

In generally light-traffic areas, signal-strength coverage is a major concern, especially the coverage along the highways. There are two potential conditions to be considered in highway coverage: (1) relatively heavy traffic and (2) light traffic. In condition 1 there would be a high to average human-made noise level and in condition 2, a relatively to very low human-made noise level. Under these conditions, we recommend that the new highway cell-site separation should be much greater than that used for a normal cell site.

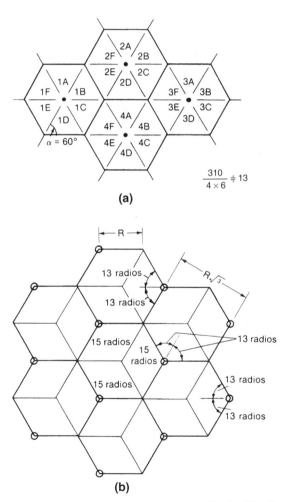

$$\frac{310}{4 \times 6} \doteq 13$$

(a)

(b)

FIGURE 12.22 60°-sector cell sites. (*a*) Motorola's plan ($K = 4$): 13 voice radios per sector in every 60° sector; (*b*) ideally located cell sites ($K = 7$) (mixed 120° and 60° sectors as needed).

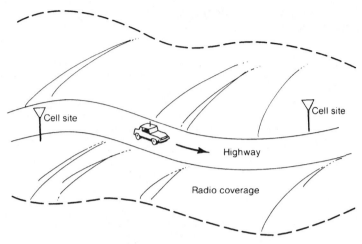

FIGURE 12.23   Highway cell sites.

12.9.1   Omnidirectional Antenna

As it is necessary to cover not only the highway but also areas in the vicinity of the highway, the omnidirectional antenna is used. When the cell sites are chosen and put up along the highway (see Fig. 12.23), the line-of-sight situation is usually assumed.

Although the general area around the highway could be suburban, because of the line-of-sight situation the path loss should be calculated using an open-area curve instead of the suburban-area curve shown in Fig. 8.3c.

The differences between highway cell-site separation and normal cell-site separation using path-loss values from the suburban and the open-area curves (see Fig. 8.3c), respectively, are plotted in Fig. 12.24. The curve is labeled "Noise condition of human origin."

Traffic along highways away from densely populated areas is usually light and the level of automotive noise is low, perhaps 2 dB lower than the average human-made noise-level condition. Based on the 2-dB noise quieting assumption, another curve labeled "Low noise condition of human origin" is also shown in Fig. 12.24.

From Fig. 12.24 we can obtain the following data.

Average Cell-Site Separation, mi; Normal Human-Made Noise Condition	Highway Cell-Site Separation, mi	
	Normal Human-Made Noise Condition	Low Human-Made Noise Condition
6	9.5	11
10	15	17

The purpose of using the omnidirectional antenna at the cell sites along the highway is to cover the area in the vicinity of the highway where residential areas are usually located.

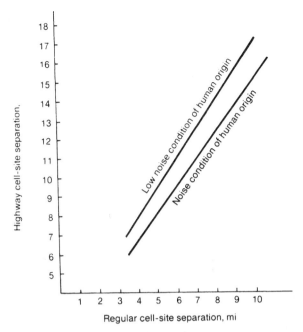

FIGURE 12.24   Highway cell-site separation.

12.9.2 Two-Directional Antennas

In certain areas where only highway coverage is needed, two-directional antennas, such as horns or a pair of Yagi antennas placed back to back at the cell site along the highway, could be installed. The directivity can result in a further increase in separation between the sites. Equation (12.9-1) shows the relation between an increase in directivity ΔG in decibels and the increase in the additional separation Δd.

$$\Delta d = d[10\Delta G/20 - 1] \tag{12.9-1}$$

This equation can easily be derived from a free-space path-loss condition.

12.10 LOW-DENSITY SMALL-MARKET DESIGN

In a small market (city) one of the primary concerns is cost, since the low-density subcriber environment is basically suburban. Here, antennas can be lower but cover the same area as would a higher antenna in an urban area. In a noise-limited environment such as a suburban, there are no problems in frequency assignment. The antenna tower can be constructed according to the following four considerations.

1. Use an existing high tower if available to obtain the maximum coverage in a given area. Because no frequency-reuse scheme will be applied, cochannel interference is of no concern.

2. Use a low-cost antenna tower. If there is no existing tower, then construct a low-cost tower in a farm area, using chicken wire to fasten the structure at a height of 15 to 24 m (50 to 80 ft).

3. Use portable sites. Portable sites can be moved around to serve the best interests of the system. Downtown call traffic and highway call traffic usually occur at different times of the day. One or two portable sites can be moved around to cover two traffic patterns at two different times if needed.

4. Apply enhancers (repeaters). This is an economical way to extend coverage to peripheral fringe areas.

REFERENCES

1. S. W. Halpern, "Reuse Partitioning in Cellular Systems," *Conference Record of the 33rd IEEE VTS Conference*, May 1983.

2. D. L. Huff, "AT&T Cellular Technology Review," *Conference Record of 1985 IEEE Military Communications Conference*, October 1985, Boston, pp. 490-494.

3. J. F. Whitehead, "Cellular Spectrum Efficiency Via Reuse Planning," *35th IEEE Vehicular Technology Conference Record*, May 21–23, 1985, Boulder, Colorado, pp. 16–20.

4. V. H. MacDonald, "The Cellular Concept," *Bell System Technical Journal*, Vol. 58, No. 1, January 1979, pp. 15–42.

5. D. C. Cox and D. O. Reudink, "Increasing Channel Occupancy in Large-Scale Mobile Radio Systems: Dynamic Channel Reassignment," *IEEE Transactions on Vehicular Technology*, Vol. VT-22, November 2 1973, pp. 218–222.

6. L. G. Anderson, "A Simulation Study of Some Dynamic Channel Assignment Algorithms in a High Capacity Mobile Telecommunications System," *IEEE Transactions on Vehicular Technology*, Vol. VT-22, November 1973, pp. 210–217.

7. T. J. Kahwa and N. D. Georganas, "A Hybrid Channel Assignment Scheme in Large-Scale, Cellular-Structured Mobile Communication Systems," *IEEE Transactions on Communication*, Vol, COM-26, April, 1978, pp. 432–438.

8. G. Nehme and N. D. Georganas, "A Simulation Study of High-Capacity Cellular Land-Mobile Radio-Communication Systems." *Canadian Electrical Engineering Journal*, Vol. 7, No. 1, 1982, pp. 36–39.

9. H. Sekiguchi, H. Ishikawa, M. Koyama, and H. Sawada, "Techniques for Increasing Frequency Spectrum Utilization in Mobile Radio Communication Systems," *35th IEEE Vehicular Technology Conference Record*, Boulder, Colorado, May 21–23, 1985, pp. 26–31.

10. Astronet Corporation, *"Cellular Coverage Enhancers,"* Issue 3, Astronet Co., April 1985.

11. H. Jasik (ed.), *Antenna Engineering Handbook*, McGraw-Hill Book Co., 1961, p. 13-2.

12. W. C. Y. Lee, "Antenna Spacing Requirement for a Mobile Radio Base-Station Diversity," *Bell System Technical Journal*, Vol. 50, July-August 1971, pp. 1850–1876.

13. W. C. Y. Lee, *Mobile Communication Design Fundamentals*, John Wiley & Sons, 1993, p. 116.

14. W. C. Y. Lee and Y. S. Yeh, "Polarization Diversity System for Mobile Radio," *IEEE Transactions on Communications*, Vol. COM 20, No. 5, October 1972, pp. 912–923.

15. W. C. Y. Lee, "Statistical Analysis of the Level Crossings and Duration of Fades of the Signal from an Energy Density Mobile Radio Antenna," *Bell System Technical Journal*, Vol. 46, February 1967, pp. 417–448.

16. W. C. Y. Lee, "An Energy Diversity Antenna for Independent Measurement of the Electric and Magnetic Field," *Bell System Technical Journal*, Vol. 46, September 1967, pp. 1587–1599.

17. M. Schwartz, W. R. Bennett, and S. Stein, *Communication Systems and Techniques*, McGraw-Hill Book Co., 1966, Chap. 10.

18. W. C. Y. Lee, *Mobile Communication Engineering*, McGraw-Hill Book Co., 1998, pp. 372–378, pp. 381–386.

19. E. A. Wolff, *Antenna Analysis*, John Wiley & Sons, 1967, p. 423.

20. R. F. Harrington, "Complex Propagation Constant for a TE_{11} Slotted Cylinder," *Journal of Applied Physics*, Vol. 24, 1953, p. 1368.

21. P. N. Wyke and R. Gill, "Applications of Radio Type Mining Equipment at Collieries," *Proceedings of the Institution of Electrical and Mechanical Engineers*, Vol. 36, November, 1955, pp. 128–137.

22. Q. V. Davis, D. J. R. Martin, and R. W. Haining, "Microwave Radio in Mines and Tunnels," *34th IEEE Vehicular Technology Conference Record*, Pittsburgh, May 21–23, 1984, pp. 31–36.

23. T. Suzuki, T. Hanazawa, and S. Kozono, "Design of a Tunnel Relay System with a Leaky Cable Coaxial Cable in an 800-MHz Band Land Mobile Telephone System," *IEEE Transactions on Vehicular Technology*, Vol. 29, August 1980, pp. 305–306.

24. W. C. Y. Lee, *Mobile Communications Design Fundamentals*, 2nd Ed. John Wiley & Sons, 1993, p. 147.

25. R. A. Isberg and D. Turrell, "Applying CATV Technology and Equipment in Guided Radio Systems," *34th IEEE Vehicular Technology Conference Record*, Pittsburgh, May 21–23, 1984, pp. 37–42.

26. T. Yuge and S. Sakaki, "Train Radio System Using Leaky Coaxial Cable," *34th IEEE Vehicular Technology Conference Record*, Pittsburgh, May 21–23, 1984, pp. 43–48.

27. V. H. MacDonald, "The Cellular Concept," *Bell System Technical Journal*, Vol. 58, January 1979, pp. 15–42.

28. W. C. Y. Lee, "Elements of Cellular Mobile Radio Systems," *IEEE Transactions on Vehicular Technology*, Vol. VT-35, May 1986, pp. 48–56.

29. Kathrein, "Directional Antennas (a family of Model 740), Kathrein, Inc., Cleveland, Ohio.

30. W. C. Y. Lee, *Mobile Communications Design Fundamentals*, 2nd Ed. John Wiley & Sons, 1993, p. 49.

31. J. Proffitt, "Portable Cell Site," *36th IEEE Vehicular Technology Conference*, Dallas, Texas, May 1986, *Conference Record*, p. 291.

32. Motorola proposal to FCC, 1977.

CHAPTER 13
SWITCHING AND TRAFFIC

13.1 GENERAL DESCRIPTION

13.1.1 General Introduction

Switching equipment is the brain of the cellular system. It consists of two parts: the switch and the processor. The switch is no different from that used in the telephone central office. The processor used in cellular systems is a special-purpose computer. It controls all the functions that are specific for cellular systems, such as frequency assignment, decisions regarding handoff (including decisions regarding new cells for handoff), and monitoring of traffic. The smaller the cell, the more handoffs involved, and the greater the traffic load required. The processor can be programmed to correct its own errors and to optimize system performance. General (noncellular) telephone switching equipment is described first, and then cellular switching equipment is discussed in detail.

In the AMPS system, the MTSO is able to handle all the cellular network functions. When the digital systems were developed, the MTSO became less sufficient to handle all the newly developed functions. Thus, the base station controller (BSC) was born. BSC is a part of the wireless system's infrastructure that controls one or multiple cell sites' radio signals, thus reducing the load of switch. It performs radio signal management functions for base transceiver stations, managing functions such as frequency assignment and handoffs. Because BSC's functions are a part of switching systems, we may include it in the switching systems. In this book, MSO (mobile switching office) is a general term for any switch: MTSO, BSC, MSC or packet switch.

The history and the trend of the switches is depicted in Fig. 13.1. The manual switches started in 1878. Then, the step-by-step selector was the first automatic telephone exchange in 1923. SPC (Stored Program Controlled) switches also called ESS (Electronic Switching System) started in 1964 as No. 1 ESS. Digital multiplexing based on PCM was introduced around 1970.

The strong growth in data traffic and in the number of users of data communication has resulted in the development of separate data networks and data switches. In many cases, these can meet users' increasingly stringent quality requirements and the need for higher transmission rates in a better and less expensive way. Packet mode and frame relay, for example, provide efficient network utilization, enable packets to be retransmitted when errors occur on a link (applies to packet mode only), and allow for sorting, routing, and buffering.

Development of switches for providing service-integrated networks required both public and private N-ISDN (narrow band integrated services digital network) notes. The technology named ATM, a cell-switching technique, forms the basis of B-ISDN, a broadband ISDN, as the switching equipment has limits in the bandwidth of a connection.

Today, we can make use of very high bit rates, up to tens of billions of bits per second (tens of Gbit/s) in optical transmission systems. However, in switching equipment, we must change over from optical signals to electrical signals and considerably lower bit rates.

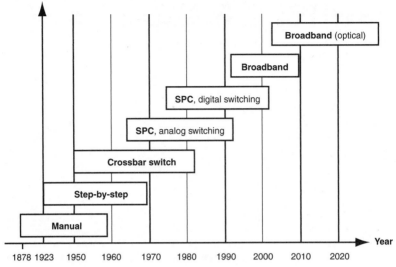

FIGURE 13.1   History and trend of switching equipment.

The next step is to use optical switching with electronic switch control. And in time, we will most assuredly have fully optical switching systems. Indeed, in view of the intensive research and development that is being carried out in this area, it should not be long before the first optical space switches are commercially available.

13.1.2   Basic Switching[1]

In circuit switching (analog switching), a dedicated connection is made between input and output lines or trunks at the switching office and physical switching begins. Space-division switches have been generally used in circuit switching, but they can also be used for digital switching. However, time-division switches can be used only for digital switching. In large digital switches, both time- and space-division switching are used.

13.1.2.1   Space-Division Switching.   A rectangular coordinate switch interconnects n inputs from n lines to k outputs of other lines. When interconnection is possible at every cross-point, the switch is nonblocking.

$$\text{Number of cross-points} = nk \qquad (13.1\text{-}1)$$

These switches are laid out in space as shown in Fig. 13.2.

For simplicity in analyzing the following nonblocking system, let the total number of input lines N equal the total number of output lines. An N-input group is fed into N/n switch arrays, and each switching network has an nk switch as shown in Fig. 13.3a. The three-stage switching network (S-S-S) is shown in Fig. 13.3b with N outputs. The total number of cross-points is[2]

$$C = 2\left(\frac{N}{n}\right)(nk) + k\left(\frac{N}{n}\right)^2 = 2Nk + k\left(\frac{N}{n}\right)^2 \qquad (13.1\text{-}2)$$

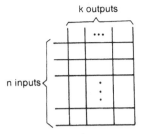

FIGURE 13.2 Number of crosspoints in space-division switches.

If $k = 2n - 1$, the nonblocking rule, then the number of cross-points C can be obtained from Eq. (13.1-2).

13.1.2.2 Time-Division Switching. For time switching to be carried out, all call messages must be first slotted into time samples, such as in pulse-code modulation (PCM) for the digital form of voice transmission. Voice quality is sampled at 8000 samples per second. Each sample (125-μs frame) must have eight levels (2^3); then each voice channel requires 64 kbps (kilobits per second) of transmission.

The time-slot switchings limit the number of channels per frame that may be multiplexed. Multiplexing of more channels requires more memory storage. Take a t_f-microsecond frame and let t_c be the memory cycle time in microseconds required for both write-in

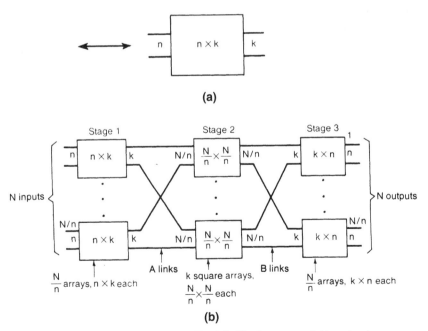

FIGURE 13.3 A switching network. (*a*) An *nK* switch; (*b*) a three-stage switching network.

and readout of a memory sample. Then the maximum number of channels that can be supported is

$$N = \frac{t_f}{2t_c} \qquad (13.1\text{-}3)$$

For $t_c = 50$-nsec logic (write-in-readout time) and $t_f = 125 \ \mu s$, the number N is 1250.

13.1.2.3 Blocking Probability Analysis of Multistage Switching.[3] In three-stage switching, the assumption of an S-S-S case (traversing two links) is the same as that of a T-S-T case. In the latter case, time division and space division are combined. The blocking probability that no free path from input channel to output channel is available is

$$P_B = [1 - (1 - p)^2]^h \qquad (13.1\text{-}4)$$

where

$$p = \frac{An}{k} \qquad (13.1\text{-}5)$$

where k = number of slot frames or number of outputs of each stage
     n = number of input time slots or input lines of each stage
     $A = \lambda/(\lambda + \mu)$ is the inlet channel utilization

We may also treat A as the probability that a typical channel is busy. The parameters λ and μ are explained in Sec. 11.5. If $n = 120$, $k = 128$, and

$$A = \begin{cases} 0.7, \\ 0.9, \\ 0.95, \end{cases} \quad \text{then} \quad P_b = \begin{cases} 10^{-7} \\ 0.042 \\ 0.214 \end{cases}$$

This indicates the sensitivity of the blocking probability to the input utilization. However, when the input utilization reaches a certain level, the blocking probability must increase very rapidly.

13.1.2.4 Dimensions of Switching Equipment. Switching equipment must be designed to meet the projected growth rate of the system. The probability of loss P_b is

$$P_b \ (\text{calls lost}) = \frac{(a^N/N!)}{\sum\limits_{n=1}^{N} (a^n/n!)} \qquad (13.1\text{-}6)$$

$$P_b \ (\text{lost calls held}) = \frac{(a^N/N!)[N/(N-a)]}{\sum\limits_{n=1}^{N} (a^n/n!)} \qquad (13.1\text{-}7)$$

where N is number of trunks and a represents the traffic load, as in Sec. 11.6. Using either Eq. (13.1-6) or Eq. (13.1-7), we can find the number of trunks needed in a given demanding situation.

13.1.3 System Congestion[4,5]

13.1.3.1 Time Congestion. Consider a generic model in a circuit-switched exchange with a simple output trunk group. Each M input either is idle for an exponential length of time $1/\lambda$ or generates a call with a holding time of $1/\mu$. Each arriving call will be assigned to one of the outgoing trunks. For the probability of the number of calls in progress P_n, we obtain

$$P_n = \frac{(\lambda/\mu)^n \binom{M}{n}}{\sum_{n=0}^{N} (\lambda/\mu)^n \binom{M}{N}} \qquad 0 \le n \le N \qquad (13.1\text{-}8)$$

If the system is fully occupied, then

$$P_B = P_N \qquad (13.1\text{-}9)$$

This is called "time congestion."

13.1.3.2 Call Congestion. The other way to measure congestion is to count the total number of calls arriving during a long time interval and record those calls that are lost because of a lack of resources, such as busy trunks.

The probability of call loss is P_L. Let $p(a)$ be the unconditional probability of arrival of a call, P_B be the probability that the system is blocked, and $p_N(a)$ be the probability that a call arrives when the system is blocked. Then

$$P_L = \frac{p_N(a)}{p(a)} P_B \qquad (13.1\text{-}10)$$

If the conditional probability $p_N(a)$ is independent of the state of system blocking, then $p_N(a) = p(a)$, Eq. (13.1-10) becomes $P_L = P_B$, and the two measurements—time congestion and call congestion—are the same.

13.1.4 Ultimate System Capacity

There are two limits on system capacity: (1) the amount of traffic that the switches can carry and (2) the amount of control that the processor can exercise without the occurrence of unacceptable losses. Limit 2, the amount of control that the processor can exercise without excessive losses, can be broken down as follows.

1. *Ultimate capacity due to traffic load.* Traffic capacity consists of two parameters, the number of calls per hour λ and their duration $1/\mu$. The average call duration is about 100 s (i.e., $1/\mu = 100$ s). The physical limits of switching capacity are reflected in the number of trunk interfaces N and the traffic load a.

2. *Ultimate capacity due to control.* Processor control operates on a delayed basis when requests are queued or scanned at regular intervals. There are two levels of control. At level 1, processor control is involved in scanning and interfacing with customers. At level 2, central processors are involved when all the data for a call request are received. The delay on the processor can be calculated as

$$\text{Average call delay (s)} = \frac{1/\mu}{2(1 - a')} \qquad (13.1\text{-}11)$$

where a' is the traffic load on the processor and $1/\mu$ is the holding time that the processor takes to handle a call.

Ultimate system capacity limitations are reflected in limits on control, such as the number of calls that the system can handle, including handoffs, scanning and locating, paging, and assigning a voice channel. Therefore, the processing capacity for cellular mobile systems is much greater than that for noncellular telephone systems. In noncellular telephone switching the duration of the call is irrelevant, but in a cellular system it is a function of frequency management and the number of handoffs.

13.1.4.1 Assigning a Value to the Processor Traffic

Level 2 Control Only (Centralized System). It is extremely difficult to estimate accurately how a system will perform under real traffic conditions. A traffic simulation can be used. For total capacity, let

	$P, \%$	$1 - P, \%$
For eventualities	5	95
For false traffic (i.e., call abandoned before completion)	30	70
For peak traffic	30	70

Thus, $(1 - 0.05)(1 - 0.3)(1 - 0.3) = 0.465$ or a total capacity of 46.5 percent (or in this case 0.465 erlangs) for call processing.

It is assumed that no level 1 control is operating in the processor. Assume that the processor holding time is 100 ms; then applying this to Eq. (13.1-11), we find that the average call delay is

$$t_d = \frac{100 \text{ ms}}{2(1 - 0.465)} = 93.46 \text{ ms}$$

The average delay on call processing during the busy call equals

$$93.46 \times 0.465 = 43.46 \text{ ms}$$

Level 1 and Level 2 Control (Decentralized System). Assume that level 1 control in a system reduces the load on level 2 control by absorbing most of the false traffic at level 1 control. Then at level 2 control the call-processing occupancy rate is $(1 - 0.05)(1 - 0.3) = 0.665$ (or 66.5 percent).

Assume that the total processor holding time is less than 100 ms for the average call (the total time taken to handle a call is the sum of the total number of instructions required during the call); then

$$t_d = \text{average call delays} = \frac{100 \text{ ms}}{2(1 - 0.665)} = 150 \text{ ms}$$

The average delay on call processing during the busy call equals $150 \text{ ms} \times 0.665 = 100 \text{ ms}$.

When comparing the centralized system with the decentralized system, we find that in the centralized system the average call delay time is much shorter but its processing capacity is much less. However, the decentralized system is more flexible, is easier to install, and has a greater potential for expansion.

13.1.5 Call Drops

Call drops are caused by factors such as (1) unsuccessful completion from set-up channel to voice channel, (2) blocking of handoffs (switching capacity), (3) unsuccessful handoffs (processor delay), (4) interference (foreign source), and (5) improper setting of system parameters.

The percentage of call drops is expressed as

$$P_{cd} = \frac{\text{number of call drops before completion}}{\text{total number of accepted calls handled by set-up channels}}$$

$$= \frac{\sum_{i=1}^{5} C_{d_i}}{C_t}$$

Because this percentage is based on many parameters, there is no analytic equation. But when the number of call drops increases, we have to find out why and take corrective action. The general rule is that unless an abnormal situation prevails, call drops usually should be less than 5 percent.

13.2 CELLULAR ANALOG SWITCHING EQUIPMENT

13.2.1 Description of Analog Switching Equipment

Most analog switching equipment consists of processors, memory, switching network, trunk circuitry and miscellaneous service circuitry. The control is usually centralized, and there is always some degree of redundancy. A common control system is shown in Fig. 13.4. The

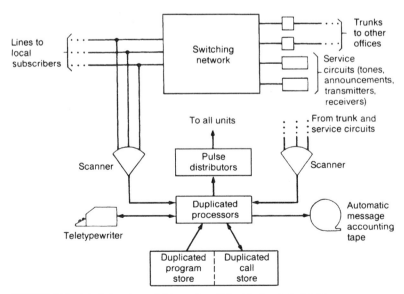

FIGURE 13.4   A typical analog switching system. (*After Chadha et al., Ref. 6.*)

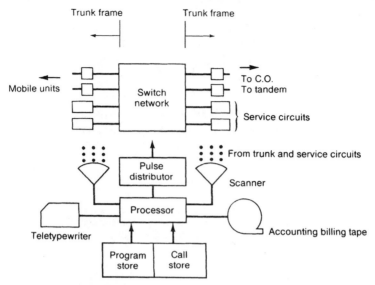

FIGURE 13.5 A modified analog switching system for cellular mobile systems.

programs are stored in the memory that provides the logic for controlling telephone calls. The processor and the memory for programming and calls are duplicated. The switching network provides a means for interconnecting the local lines and trunks. The scanners are read under the control of the central processor. The changes in every connection at the line side and at the trunk side are also controlled by the processor. The central processor sends the order to all the units (switching network, trunk, service circuits) through pulse distributions. The automatic message accounting (AMA) tapes are used for recording the call usage. Three programs are stored in most switching equipment: (1) call processing (set up, hand off, or disconnect a call), (2) hardware maintenance (diagnose failed or suspected failed units), and (3) administration (collect customer records, trunk records, billing data, and traffic count).

13.2.2 Modification of Analog Switching Equipment

The local line side has to change to the trunk side as shown in Fig. 13.5 because the mobile unit does not have a fixed frequency channel. Therefore, the mobile unit itself acts as a trunk line. In addition, the processors have to be modified to handle cellular call processing, the locating algorithm, the handoff algorithm, the special disconnect algorithm, billing (air time and wire line), and diagnosis (radio, switching, and other hardware failure).

13.2.3 Cell-Site Controllers and Hardware

Mobile telephone switching office (MTSO) system manufacturers designed their own cell-site controllers and transceivers (radios). Cell-site equipment is shown in Fig. 13.6. The

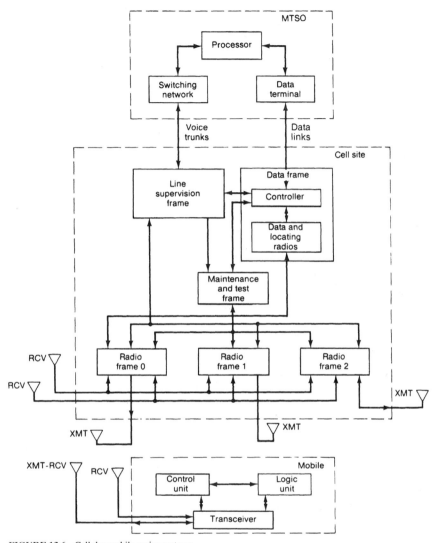

FIGURE 13.6   Cellular mobile major systems.

cell site can be rendered "smarter," that is, programmed to handle many semiautonomous functions under the direction of the MTSO. Cell-site equipment consists of two basic frames.

1. Data frame: consists of controller and both data and locating radios

   a. Providing RF radiation, reception, and distribution

   b. Providing data communication with MTSO and with the mobile units

   c. Locating mobile units

   d. Data communication over voice channels

2. Maintenance and test frame

   a. Testing each transmitting channel for

      i. Incident and reflected power to and from the antenna

      ii. Transmitter frequency and its deviation

      iii. Modulation quality

   b. Testing each receiving channel for

      i. Sensitivity

      ii. Audio quality

In GSM, a BSC (Base Station Controller) is created to handle the function of a number of cell site controllers. MTSO gives up its handoff functions to BSC and is called MSC (Mobile Switching Center). The cell sites without controller are called BTS (Base Transceiver Station). Today the acronyms MSC, BSC and BTS are used in all the new digital cellular systems.

13.3 CELLULAR DIGITAL SWITCHING EQUIPMENT

13.3.1 General Concept

The digital switch, which is usually the message switch, handles the digitized message. The analog switch, which is the circuit switch, must hold a call throughout the entire duration of the call. The digital (message) switch can send the message or transmit the voice in digital form; therefore, it can break a message into small pieces and send it at a fast rate. Thus, the digital switch can alternate between ON and OFF modes periodically during a call. During the OFF mode, the switch can handle other calls. Hence, the call-processing efficiency of digital switching is higher than that of analog switching.

The future digital switch could be a switching packet which would send digital information in a nonperiodic fashion on request. There are other advantages to digital switching besides its greater efficiency. Digital switches are always small, consume less power, require less human effort to operate, and are easier to maintain. Digital switching is flexible and can grow modularly. Digital switching equipment can be either centralized[7,8] (Fig. 13-7a) or decentralized[9,10] (Fig. 13.7b). A centralized system of a digital system has an architecture similar to that of an analog system. Motorola's EMX2500, Ericsson's AXE-10, and Northern Telecom International's DMS-MTXM are large centralized digital systems. A decentralized system is described here.

A decentralized system is slightly different from a remote-control switching system. In the remote-control switching system, a main switch is used to control a remote secondary switch as shown in Fig. 13.6c. In a decentralized system, all the switches are treated equally; there is no main switch.

13.3.2 Elements of Switching

One decentralized switching system is introduced here and one modulized switching system will be introduced in the next section. The first one is the Lucent Autoplex 1000,[9] which consists of an executive cellular processor (ECP), digital cellular switches (DCS), an interprocess message switch (IMS), RPC (ring peripheral control), and nodes

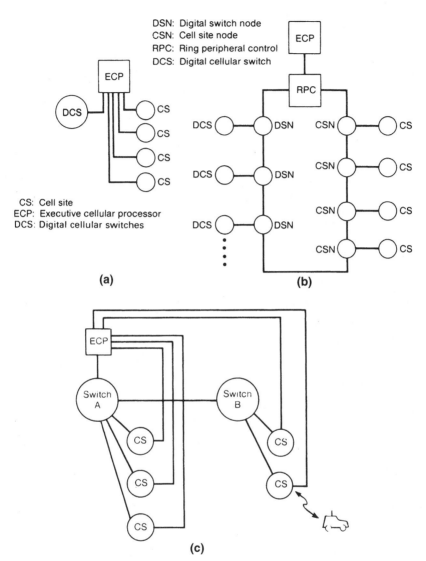

FIGURE 13.7 Cellular switching equipment. (*a*) A centralized system; (*b*) a decentralized system; (*c*) remote-controlled switching.

1. ECP transports messages from one processor to another.

2. IMS attached to a token ring (IMS uses a token ring technology) provides interfaces between ECP, DCS, cell sites, and other networks. The RPC attached to the ring permits direct communication among all the elements through the ring.

3. DCS, which are digital cellular switches, also called MSC (mobile switch center), function as modules to allow the system to grow.

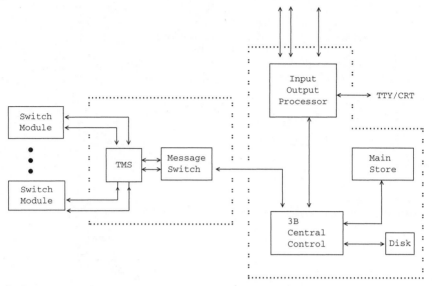

FIGURE 13.8   5ESS system architecture.

4. RPC forms a ring that connects two types of nodes: CSN (cell-site node) and DSN (digital switch nodes).

5. Nodes are RPC nodes for connecting the ECP to the ring, CSN nodes for connecting cell-site data to the ring, and DSN nodes for connecting data links to the ring.

13.3.3   5ESS (No. 5 Electronic Switching System)[11,12]

The 5ESS switch is Lucent's multiservice software-based digital switching system designed to evolve with changing needs. The 5EEE can deploy all types and combinations of services from a single platform, including wireline, wireless, voice, and data. Together with a packet driver called 7R/E Packet Driver, the 5ESS switch integrates IP/ATM network and circuit switching. Actually, 7R/E Packet Driver converts a 5ESS switch into a packet switch. The attributes are as follows:

A. Modular Design: The intelligence is distributed into modules. This unique architecture allows growth in increments simply by adding modules as shown in Fig. 13.8.

B. Supports Wireless: Provides advanced wireless services such as FDMA/TDMA/CDMA on the 5ESS switch Very Compact Digital Exchange (VCDX) that offers all the features and functionality of the large switch.

C. Other Switch Functionality

1. The tandem switch: A high-capacity, high-speed trunk switch that provides communication links between multiple regions and networks.

2. The gateway switch: A specialized network node that connects a national network to an international network.

3. 5ESS Remote Switching: The distributed architecture and modular design of 5ESS enables the operator to locate a remote switching module (RSM) from up to 3200 km from a host 5ESS switch without interrupted services.

13.3.4 Comparison Between Centralized and Decentralized Systems

The analysis of overall system capacity given in Sec. 13.1.4 can be used here for comparison. In general, a centralized system has only one control level, whereas the decentralized system has more than one. In a one-level control system, the utilization of call processing is less than that in a multilevel control system. Moreover, the delay time for a central control system is always shorter than that for a decentralized system; thus, the more levels of control, the greater the call-processing utilization and the longer the delay time. However, in principle, decentralized systems always have room to grow and are flexible in dealing with increasing capacity. Centralized systems deal with large traffic loads.

13.4 PACKET SWITCHING

13.4.1 General Description[13,14]

Switching is used within provider and private networks as a way to maximize use of network resources by sharing bandwidth with multiple clients, most of who do not require access to the network at the same time. Data traffic is intermittent and "bursty" in nature, allowing the network to be sized much smaller than if it were designed to support a constant peak traffic volume with all users active simultaneously.

Packet switching involves the division of application or file transfer traffic into packets and sending them individually to their destination. Because the packets can take many different paths to reach the destination system, they may arrive at any given time. All packets originating from different applications can be mixed, and the circuits or lines, which carry the information, can be shared. Each packet has a specific address and contains the information needed to enable final delivery. This information, contained within the packet header, allows for the reassembly and proper sequencing when delivered to the destination device.

TCP/IP, frame relay, and ATM are all protocols and platforms based on packet switching. Traffic is sent on a variable rate, and network resources are assigned as needed to accommodate the traffic flow. Because these resources are assigned on a "first come, first served" basis, data traffic of a less time-sensitive nature is best handled within a packet switched environment. However, there are two types of packet switched network protocols: connection-oriented and connectionless.

In a connectionless architecture, routers or nodes store each packet, process the information contained within the header, and then send it along to its next destination device. The connection state between these network routers or switches is not contained in any component, so the packets may follow different paths and arrive in a different order from which they were sent. IP or the Internet Protocol alone is an example of connectionless transport, as each packet is independently routed and delivered on a "best effort" basis. For this reason, QoS or quality of service is difficult to enforce, leaving the connectionless network design with enough excess capacity to ensure optimal service for all users. Although TCP is the "connection oriented" piece often used with IP, it should not be confused with a connection-oriented packet switched network architecture.

13.4.2 Packet Switches in Mobile Tandem Switching

13.4.2.1 General Description. A second way that packet systems can reduce costs for mobile operators is in mobile-to-mobile calls. In a typical mobile network, each MSC must

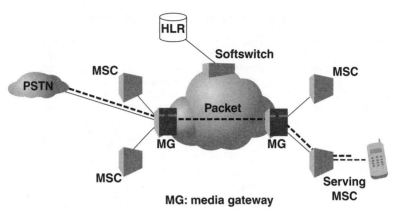

FIGURE 13.9   Packet gateway MSC.

be connected directly to every other MSC. The mesh of trunks interconnecting the MSCs in sizeable markets introduces significant management and other costs.

PSTN carriers, who have had to deal with such issues for some time, routinely deploy tandem switches to optimize such configurations. Tandem switching can provide the same benefits for mobile operators.

The packet switch configuration shown in Fig. 13.9 for gateway MSCs can also provide mobile tandem services. Rather than connecting via small trunk group to every other MSC, each MSC has one larger trunk group to a media gateway. The MSC simply routes any mobile-to-mobile call over that trunk group.

The addition of packet switching can provide significant improvements in efficiency, with a second level of switching, provided by a packet gateway MSC streamlining PSTN-to-mobile call handling. Fig. 13.9 illustrates the same scenario as above, but with the addition of a packet gateway MSC, which consists of media gateways and a mobile softswitch also shown in Fig. 13.9.

In this case, the PSTN routes all PSTN-to-mobile calls to the packet gateway MSC. The mobile softswitch handles the call signaling (SS7) while the media gateway handles the voice stream. The softswitch queries the HLR and routes the call directly to the serving MSC. As shown in Fig. 13.9, the MSCs no longer have to act as transit switches for roaming subscribers. This frees up a significant number of ports and other resources on the MSCs, so they can handle new subscribers or additional subscriber minutes of use without requiring an upgrade.

13.4.2.2   Benefits of Packet Switches

Acquisition (capital) cost savings: Packet switching systems are often less expensive to purchase than circuit switches.

Operating cost savings: Packet solutions typically have much lower facilities costs (space, power, cooling, etc.) and can be operated with a smaller operations staff.

Transport cost savings: Transporting voice traffic over a packet network is substantially less expensive than transporting the same traffic over a circuit network.

Mobile operators, like PSTN carriers, are finding that the economic benefits of deploying next-generation solutions are quite compelling. Additionally, deploying packet-based systems for these applications offers carriers a smooth migration path to third-generation (3G) mobile, as well as the all-IP networks of the future.

13.4.3 Packet Switching Protocols and Hardware

A. Protocols
Ethernet is the de facto standard to connect computers, printers, terminals, and other devices on LANs. It operates over twisted pair, fiber, or coax and accounts for about 80 percent of traffic today on corporate intranets. The most commonly installed Ethernet systems are 10Base-T providing speeds up to 10 Mbps. For LAN backbone systems as well as workstations, Fast Ethernet provides 100 Mbps (100Base-T) while Gigabit Ethernet delivers speeds up to one gigabit per second (1000Base-T).

Frame Relay is a service commonly used for discontinuous data transmission between LANs and between end points in a WAN. This technology puts data in variable-size units called frames that can be as large as 1000 bytes or more. It gains speed by depending on end points to detect errors, drop frames with errors, and retransmit dropped frames. Frame Relay requires a dedicated virtual connection even though individual frames are sent through the network over various routes. Based on older X.25 packet-switching technology, Frame Relay is a widely deployed data service today on fractional TI or full T-carrier systems.

ATM (Asynchronous Transfer Mode) offers much higher speeds than Frame Relay, either 155 Mbps or 622 Mbps, with speeds up to 10 Gbps over SONET. This technology requires a dedicated connection, organizing data into 53-byte cell units. ATM earns its name because each cell is processed and transmitted at a different clock rate than related cells in a communication before being multiplexed over the transmission path. This high-bandwidth, low-delay service is suited for voice, data, and video.

IP, internet protocol, delivers data from one host computer to another, each with its own unique IP address. This protocol divides messages into data packets and affixes the IP address of both the sender and receiver to each packet. Packets are then sent across the network through various gateways by different routes and are often received in a different order than originally sent. This addressing and forwarding protocol only delivers packets; it is up to another protocol, TCP (Transmission Control Protocol), for reassembly of packets into the original message. While perfect for data, IP shows its weakness time-sensitive voice and video transmission due to litter and latency that are introduced as packets traverse the network.

B. Hardware
A hub is a point where data converges from multiple directions and is forwarded out in multiple directions. In many ways, a hub is like a splitter. It is a work-group level device that allows a large, logical Ethernet to be subdivided into multiple physical segments. This is a layer 1 element that offers no intelligent congestion control for data packets.

Bridges connects multiple elements in layers 1 and 2. These devices are used to connect network segments, such as different LANs, and forward packets between them. There is limited congestion control with simple filters that may keep certain packets within a LAN or region.

A switch establishes a transmission path between incoming and outgoing connections, taking an incoming signal and routing it to the proper channel going out. Switches are layer 1 and layer 2 devices that offer no congestion control or intelligence for routing packets. As such, a switch 15 a simpler and faster mechanism than a router and is perfectly suited for moving packets rapidly through the network.

Routers are highly intelligence data switches that serve as the interface between two networks. Routers look at the network as a whole and makes decisions to route data packets based on destination, address, packet priority, least-cost, delay, congestion level, and other factors. Routers use headers and forwarding tables to determine the best path for forwarding the packets, and they use protocols such as ICMP (Internet control message protocol) to communicate with each other and configure the best route between any two hosts. There is very little filtering of data being done through routers. These layer 3 devices are the workhorses of the data network.

13.5 PACKET RELATED NETWORKS

13.5.1 ATM Networks

ATM, or the Asynchronous Transfer Mode platform,[15] is based on connection-oriented packet switching and allows for true QoS. In ATM, a connection between switches is established through a signaling protocol or by operator action. Because connection state information is maintained, bandwidth guarantees can be enabled. In addition, whereas other platforms use packets of varying sizes, ATM breaks all information into uniform packets (or cells) of 53 bytes each. Because each cell is the same size, delay at each switch can be predicted and is easy to manage.

Each of these cells contains a 5-byte header, which has the destination address of where the cell is to be delivered along with a priority designation. This header also contains a priority specification for the data carried in the remaining 48 bytes.

ATM also permits the assignment of traffic priority to different types of application traffic. For example, high delays can degrade the quality of video traffic, while electronic mall and Internet traffic is far less time-sensitive. To ensure video images can be viewed while e-mail flows through the network, a higher priority is assigned to the video stream.

The switches within an ATM network establish connections in one of two ways. Within a PVC, or Permanent Virtual Circuit, a network administrator or operator creates paths between switches ahead of time. These virtual circuits remain up and active at all times, with specific state information stored within each switch.

In an SVC, or Switched Virtual Circuit, each cell travels along a path that is set up in real-time and then torn down again after a designated period of time. These switched circuit connections have an advantage over permanent ones, since they only consume network capacity when they are established.

In either case, when a network router has information to send into an ATM network, it must request a virtual circuit. This circuit request is then passed from the initial switch to other switches within the same network, allowing each switch to see if it can handle the request. If a complete switching path is available, the request is accepted and the cells are then delivered. If the request is denied (due to a network failure or capacity issue), it may be repeated after a specific interval before timing out.

Whether permanent or switched, each virtual circuit has the ability to support a specific quality of service as configured at the switch. These classes of service are listed below.

1. CBR, or Committed Bit Rate: CBR is very similar to a private or dedicated line, in that it has affixed capacity and does not allow for bursting. However, it offers the best guarantee of traffic delivery.

2. VBR, or Variable Bit Rate: VBR adds the ability to burst and oversubscribe user traffic on the circuit. An SCR, or Sustained Cell Rate, is the guaranteed capacity, while the

PCR, or Peak Cell Rate, is the maximum burst size. VBR is also available in real-time and non-real-time varieties.

3. ABR, or Available Bit Rate: ABR is a combination of CBR and VBR, in that some capacity is guaranteed but only within the limitations of the ABR protocol. Resource management cells are used to continuously monitor the amount of bandwidth within each connection.

4. UBR, or Unspecified Bit Rate: UBR is a class that offers no guarantees on capacity or delay, allowing for "best effort" data delivery only.

13.5.2 Soft Switching: Next-Generation Voice Infrastructure

A. Solutions for next-generation voice infrastructure
The two solutions for the next-generation voice infrastructure:

1. Packetization of voice.[13]

2. The separation of call-control intelligence from underlying switching system.

Most of today's local exchange service depends on circuit-switched networks with integrated call control. Next-generation phone network architectures differ from today's public switched telephone network in two key ways.

1. The transport and switching of voice will be performed in the packet domain—a VoIP. The infrastructure efficiencies that can be achieved with VoIP.

2. Computing platforms physically separate from the switching systems—known as the softswitch—will provide the intelligence powering voice services. The service flexibility offered by soft switching is not dependent on VoIP.

But together, VoIP and soft switching bring different, complementary advantages to voice networks.

Soft switching allows industry-standard computing platforms and software tools to be leveraged to deliver new voice services that are difficult or impossible to provide with legacy switching systems.

B. Separation of service and call-control intelligence
In addition, by separating service and call-control intelligence *from* the underlying voice-switching infrastructure, soft switching enables new thinking to be applied to the nature of voice services and the way they are implemented. Soft switching encourages the use of industry-standard computing platforms and operating systems, as well as the use of the same tools that have permitted rapid innovation in the Web space: Hypertext Transfer Protocol, Extensible Markup Language, Java, open databases and object-oriented software design, among others. With these tools, the most commonly used calling features can be easily replicated *for* voice telephony, but more important, new calling features can be quickly created and empowered with Web-based interaction between subscribers and their telephony environment.

Soft switching enables interesting possibilities *for* next-generation voice services with Web-based Interaction. For example, subscribers can visit a Web site to activate and configure calling features. Lists of features such as selective call forwarding and distinctive ringing can be viewed and edited via a browser-based interface, a far more, appealing prospect than trying to use a phone keypad. Click-to-dial applications can launch calls directly from a personal computer-based address book, without the need *for* a local connection between the PC and the phone.

By separating service intelligence from the underlying switching infrastructure, soft switches enable the delivery of new services. Thus, a soft switch that can deliver new services over both traditional circuit-switched networks and new VoIP networks.

C. The functions of soft switches

The soft-switch should implement as a minimum the following functions:

- Routing (e.g., the switch should be able to find out if the callee is connected to a different switch).

- Signaling (e.g., if the callee is connected to another switch, the switch should be able to request the other switch to establish the call).

- Generation/handling of basic Megaco commands for call establishment/tearing down and notifications.

13.6 SPECIAL FEATURES FOR HANDLING TRAFFIC

The switching equipment of each cellular system has different features associated with the radios (transceivers) installed at the cell sites.

13.6.1 Underlay-Overlay Arrangement

The switching equipment treats two areas as two cells, but at a co-cell site (i.e., two cells sharing the same cell site). Therefore, the algorithms have to be worked out for this configuration. In Sec. 12.2.4 we discussed the underlay-overlay arrangement in terms of channel assignment. Here, we discuss this arrangement in terms of MSO control (or as a BSC in digital systems).

To initiate a call, the MSO must know whether the mobile unit is in an overlay or an underlay area. The MSO obtains this information from the received signal strength transmitted by the mobile unit. To hand off a call, the MSO must know whether this is a case of handoff from (1) an overlay area to an underlay area or (2) vice versa. In case 1, the signal strengthens and exceeds a specific level, and then the unconventional handoff takes place. In case 2, the signal strength weakens and falls below a specific level, and then the conventional handoff takes place.

13.6.2 Direct Call Retry

Direct call retry is applied only at the set-up channel. When all the voice channels of a cell are occupied, the set-up channel at that cell can redirect the mobile unit to a neighboring-cell set-up channel. This is the order used by the original set-up channel to override the "pick the strongest signal" algorithm. In this scheme, the MSO received all the call traffic information from all the cells and thus can distribute the call capacity evenly to all the cell sites.

13.6.3 Hybrid Systems Using High Sites and Low Sites

The high site is always used for coverage, and it can also be used to fill many holes that may be created by the low site. Therefore, if in some areas the mobile unit cannot communicate through the low site, the high site will take over, and as soon as the signal reception gets better at the low site, the call will hand off to the low site. The algorithms include computation of the following configuration.

1. When the signal strength received at the cell site weakens, the handoff is requested and the high site picks it up.
2. The MSO continues to check the signal of this particular mobile unit from all the neighboring low sites. If one site receives an acceptable signal from the mobile unit, the handoff will be forwarded to that site.

13.6.4 Intersystem Handoffs

Intersystem handoffs were described in Chap. 11. The processor requires particular software to use this feature. There are four conditions of intersystem handoff, as shown in Fig. 13.10.

1. A long-distance call becomes a local call while a home mobile unit becomes a roamer (Fig. 13.10*a*).

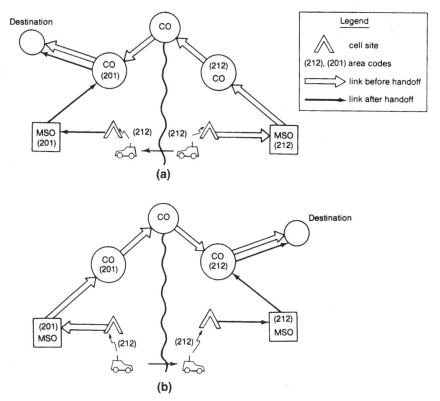

FIGURE 13.10 Four conditions of intersystem handoffs. (*a*) A toll call becomes a local call and the home mobile unit becomes a roamer; (*b*) a toll call becomes a local call and a roamer becomes a home mobile unit.

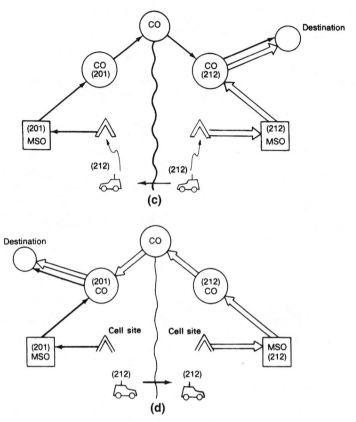

FIGURE 13.10 (*Continued*) (*c*) a local call becomes a toll call and the home mobile unit becomes a roamer; (*d*) a local call becomes a toll call and a roamer becomes a home mobile unit.

2. A long-distance call becomes a local call while a roamer becomes a home mobile unit (Fig. 13.10*b*).

3. A local call becomes a long-distance call while a home mobile unit becomes a roamer (Fig. 13.10*c*).

4. A local call becomes a long-distance call while a roamer becomes a home mobile unit (Fig. 13.10*d*).

All four cases have to be implemented.

13.6.5 Queuing Feature

When a nonuniform traffic pattern prevails and the call volume is moderate, the queuing feature can help to reduce the blocking probability. The improvement in call origination and handoffs as a result of queuing is described in Chap. 11. The switching system has to provide memory or buffers to queue the incoming calls if the channels are busy. The number of queue spaces does not need to be large. There is a finite number beyond which the improvement due to queuing is diminished, as described in Chap. 11.

13.6.6 Roamers

13.6.6.1 Initiating the Call. If two adjacent cellular systems are compatible, a home mobile unit in system A can travel into system B and become a "roamer." The switching MSO can identify a valid roamer and offer the required service. The validation can be the mobile unit's MIN or ESN (see Chap. 3).

13.6.6.2 Handing Off the Call. The feature of intersystem handoffs can be applied in order to continue the call. Intersystem handoffs are described in Sec. 13.6.4.

13.6.6.3 Clearinghouse Concept. Because of the increase of roamers in each system, checking the validation of each roamer in the roamer's own system becomes a complex problem for an automatic roaming system. The cellular system "clearinghouses" (several nationwide companies) provide a central file of the validation of all users' MIN and ESN in every system. There are two files, positive and negative validation. Positive validation is done by checking whether the user's number is on the active customer list. The negative validation file lists the numbers of users whose calls should be rejected from the automatic roaming system. The payment for transmitting validation data to and from the clearinghouse plus the service charge has to be justified against the revenue lost through delinquent users (those who do not pay on time).

13.7 MSO INTERCONNECTION

13.7.1 Connection to Wire-Line Network

The MSO operates on a trunk-to-trunk basis. The MSO interconnection arrangement is similar to a private-branch exchange (PBX) or a class 5 central office (a tandem connection) (see Fig. 13.11). The MSO has three types of interconnection links.

Type 1: interconnects a MSO to a local-exchange carrier (LEC) end office.

Type 2A: interconnects an LEC tandem office.

Type 2B: interconnects to an LEC end office in conjunction with type 2A on a high-usage alternate-routing basis.

The three-level hierarchy of a public telephone network is shown in Fig. 13.12. With this diagram, we can illustrate the three types of calls: (1) a local call, (2) an intra-LATA (local access and transport area) call, and (3) an inter-LATA call. In digital systems, MSC takes these MTSO's functions.

13.7.2 Connection to a Cell Site

Two types of facility are used.

1. Cell-site *trunks* provide a voice communication path. Each trunk is physically connected to a cell-site voice radio. The number of trunks is decided on the basis of the traffic and the desired blocking probability (grade of service).

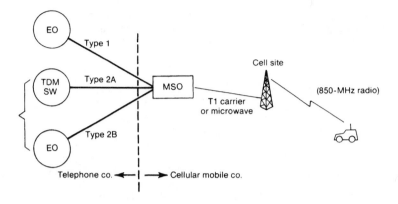

Type 1 interconnects an MSO to an LEC end office

Type 2A interconnects an MSO to an LEC tandem office

Type 2B interconnects to an LEC end office in conjunction with type 2A on a high-usage alternate-routing basis.

FIGURE 13.11   Three types of interconnection linkage.

2. The cell site acts as a *traffic concentrator* for the MSO. For instance, we may design an average busy-hour radio channel occupancy of at least 60 to 70 percent for high-traffic cells.

Both T1-carrier cables and microwave links are used. The duplication is needed for reliability. In digital systems, BSC takes these MTSO's functions.

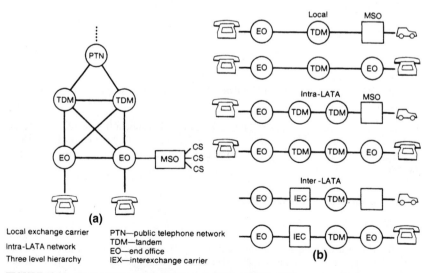

FIGURE 13.12   Three-level hierarchy. (*a*) Interconnection of MSO; (*b*) three types of call.

13.8 SMALL SWITCHING SYSTEMS

Small switching equipment[16-18] can be used in a small market (city). This switching equipment can usually be developed modularly. It consists of (1) a transmitter and a receiver, (2) a cell-site controller, (3) a local switch (a modified PABX should be used), (4) a channel combiner, and (5) a demultiplexer.

Small switches should be low-cost items. A high existing tower can be used for a cell-site antenna to cover a large area.

13.9 SYSTEM ENHANCEMENT

Consider the following scenarios.

1. Each trunk is now physically connected to each voice radio as mentioned previously. But if the trunk can be switched to different radios, then the dynamic frequency assignment scheme can be accomplished.

2. Let a cell site pick up a switch in a decentralized multiple switching equipment system. This is a different concept than usual. Normally the switching equipment controls a cell site. For the land-initiated calls, the switching equipment picks up a cell site through paging. For mobile-originated calls, the cell site handling the call can select the appropriate switching equipment (DCS) from among the two or three units of switching equipment, assuming the cell site can detect the traffic conditions.

We can construct an analogy here. In a supermarket, everyone is waiting in line to pay the cashier for their merchandise. In order to reduce the waiting time, the store manager (central switching office) can direct the customer to the cashier (switching equipment) with the shortest line or the customer (cell site) can select the cashier with the shortest line. Both methods can work equally well assuming both the manager and the customer have the ability to choose well.

This system enhancement may be made in the future to all systems when artifical intelligence techniques become fully developed and can be used to implement the enhancements.

REFERENCES

1. N. Schwartz, *Telecommunication Network*, Addison-Wesley, 1987, Chap. 10.

2. C. Y. Lee, "Analysis of Switching Network," *Bell System Technical Journal*, Vol. 34, November 1955, pp. 1287–1315.

3. J. G. Pearce, *Telecommunications Switching*, Plenum Press, 1981, Chap. 5.

4. M. J. Hills, *Telecommunications Switching Principles*, MIT Press, 1979.

5. C. Clos, "A Study of Non-Blocking Switching Network," *Bell System Technical Journal*, Vol. 32, No. 2, March 1953, pp. 406–424.

6. K. J. S. Chadha, C. F. Hunnicutt, S. R. Peck, and J. Tebes, Jr., "Mobile Telephone Switching Office," *Bell System Technical Journal*, Vol. 58, January 1979, pp. 71–96.

7. Northern Telecom Cellular Switches MTX/MTXCX.

8. Ericsson Cellular Switches AXE 10 and CMS 8800.

9. AT&T Cellular Switches Autoplex 10 and Autoplex 1000.

10. Motorola Cellular Switches DMX 500 and DMX 2500.

11. K. A. Radike, "The AT&T 5ESS Hardware Design Environment: A Large System's Hardware Design Process," 31st Annual ACM IEEE Design Automation Conference Proceedings, San Diego, California, 1994, pp. 527–531.

12. Lucent Technologies "5ESS (5ESS-2000) Switch," A 5E-XC High Capacity Switch.

13. D. J. Wright, "Voice over Packet Networks," Wiley & Son, 2001.

14. V. G. Cerf, P. T. Kirstein, "Issues in Packet Network Interconnection," IEEE Proceedings, Vol. 66, Nov. 1978, pp. 1386–1408.

15. L. L. Peterson, B. S. Davie, "Computer Network: A System Approach," 3rd ed., Morgan Kaufmann Publisher, 2003.

16. Astronet Small Cellular Switches, Astronet Corp., Lake Mary, Florida.

17. Quintron Small Cellular Switches, "Vision Series Cellular System," Quintron Corp., Quincy, Illinois.

18. CRC Freedom-2000 (small cellular switches), Cellular Radio Corp., Vienna, Virginia.

CHAPTER 14
DATA LINKS AND MICROWAVES

14.1 DATA LINKS

Implementation of data links is an integral part of cellular mobile system design, and the performance of data links significantly affects overall cellular system performance.

The cell site receives the data from the MSO* to control the call process of mobile units. It also collects data from the reverse set-up channel from active mobile units and attempts to send it to the MSO. There are four types of data links available: (1) wire line, (2) 800-MHz radios, (3) microwaves, and (4) optical link. The following discussion describes each alternative and its advantages and disadvantages. The wireline connection[1] uses the telephone company's T1 carrier. Regular telephone wire can transmit only at a low rate (2.4 kbps); therefore, a high-data-rate cable must be leased. The T1 carrier has a wideband transmission (1.5 Mbps) that consists of 24 channels, and each channel can transmit at a rate of 64 kbps. The T1 carrier is also called DS1, a standard data link used in North America, Japan, and Korea. It is a TDM (Time Division Multiplexing) Hierarchy. There are different rates of carriers as shown below:

Designation	Channels	Data Rate (Mb/s)	Comments
DS-0	1	0.064	8 kHz × 8 bits PCM voice channel
DS-1	24	1.544	T-1 1 timing bit/frame
DS-1c	48	3.152	T-1c
DS-2	96	6.312	T-2
DS-3	672	44.736	T-3
DS-4	4032	274.176	T-4

The E1 Carrier has a wideband transmission (2.048 Mbps) that consists of 32 channels, and each channel can transmit at a rate of 64 kbps. E1 is a European and ITU standard. There are different rates of carriers as shown below:

Designation	Channels	Data Rate (Mb/s)
E1	30	2.048
E2	120	8.448
E3	480	34.368
E4	1920	139.264
E5	7680	565.148

---

*MSO is a general term for MTSO in AMPS systems and for MSC in digital systems.

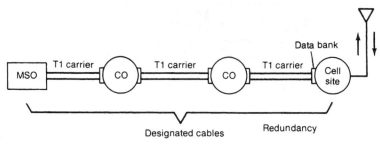

FIGURE 14.1   Data-link connection through cable.

For handling the data, a digital terminal converts the incoming analog signals to a digital form suitable for application in a digital transmission facility. Many digital terminals are multiplexed to form a single digital line called a *digital channel bank*.

In T1 carrier, digital channel banks multiplex many voice-frequency signals and code them into digital form. The sampling rate is 8 kHz. Each channel is coded into 7-bit words. A signaling bit indicates the end of each 7-bit sample. After 24 samples, one sample for each channel, a frame bit is sent again. The total number of bits per frame is

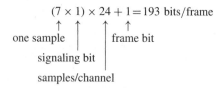

Because 8000 frames per second and 193 bits per frame are specified, a digital capacity of 1.54 Mbps is required for T1 carrier.

The data link has to have a data bank at each end of the T1 carrier cable. The data bank has to convert all the information into the 1.54 Mbps before sending it out through the cable. The number of T1 carriers required is determined by the number of radios installed at the cell site, for example, if 60 radios are installed, then three T1-carrier cables are needed. The T1 carrier cables are installed in duplicate to provide redundancy (see Fig. 14.1). A major disadvantage to using wire-line data links is that the T1-carrier route may be rearranged by the telephone company at any time without notice. Therefore, it is not totally under the user's control. In addition, the leasing cost should be compared to the long-run cost of using the microwave link if owned by the cellular operator.

The data could also be sent by 800-MHz radios. However, this would cause interference among all the channels, and since every radio channel can handle a signaling rate of only 10 kbps, we would need an additional 666 channels just to handle this data link from the cell sites to the MSO. This can be a good idea for low-capacity systems.

Microwave links seem to be most economical and least problematical. Details of their installation are given below. However in a rural area, capacity is not a problem. We can use half of the cellular channels for data-link use.

14.2   AVAILABLE FREQUENCIES FOR MICROWAVE LINKS

The microwave system is used to cover a large area; it should also be used as the "backbone." Before designing it, we must consider (1) system reliability, (2) economical design, (3)

present and future frequency selection, (4) minimization of the number of new microwave sites, and (5) flexible and multilevel systems. The microwave frequencies can be grouped as follows.

Frequency, GHz	Allowed Bandwidth, MHz	5-Year Channel Loading	Minimum Path Length, km
2	3.5	None	5
4	20	900	17
6	30	900	17
11	40	900	5
18	220	None	None
23	100	None	None

As can be seen from this tabular analysis, for the higher frequencies there are fewer restrictions, thus allowing greater flexibility in system design.

The 2-GHz band. The minimum path length of 5 km (3.1 mi) and the limited 3.5-MHz radio-frequency (RF) bandwidth place several restrictions on the use of the 2-GHz band. Capacity is probably limited to eight T1 span lines. Installation of a 6- or 8-ft dish is required. Because of the limited path length, the limited traffic capacity, larger antennas at cell sites, and the difficulty in obtaining frequency coordination, 2 GHz is not desirable.

The 4- and 6-GHz bands. The minimum path length of 17 km (10.5 mi) and the minimum channel load of 900 channels for 6 GHz along with the 4-GHz frequency present a restriction.

The 11-GHz band. The minimum path length of 5 km (3.1 mi) and the minimum channel loadings of 900 voice channels would make this band a poor choice for the final path to the cell sites. However, the greater bandwidth availability and lower frequency congestion would make this an ideal band for high-density routes between the collection points and the MSO.

The 18- and 23-GHz bands. The lack of FCC restrictions on minimum path length and the minimum channel loadings would appear to make these two frequency bands ideal for paths to the cell site. These frequency bands are not characterized by the presence of the RF congestion at lower frequencies. Cell sites can be implemented with 2- or 4-ft dishes, compared to the larger 6- or 8-ft dishes needed at lower frequencies.

14.3 MICROWAVE LINK DESIGN AND DIVERSITY REQUIREMENT

There are three basic considerations here. First, the microwave propagation path length is always longer than the cellular propagation path, say, 25 mi or longer. Second, the path is always 100 or 200 ft above the ground. Third, the microwave transmission is a line-of-sight radio-relay link. Figure 14.2 shows the replacement of T1 carrier cable by microwave radios.

However, microwave links will render the system susceptible to one kind of multipath fading, in which the microwave transmission is affected by changes in the lower atmosphere, where atmospheric conditions permit multipath propagation.

Although deep fades are rare, they are sufficient to cause outage problems in high-performance communications systems.[2,3] A signal is said to be in a fade of depth 20 log L dB; that is, the envelope (20 log l) of the signal is below the level L.

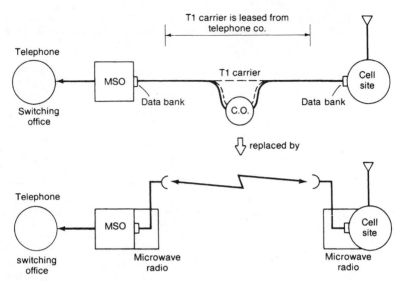

FIGURE 14.2   Replacement of T1 carrier cables by microwave radios.

$$20 \log l \leq 20 \log L$$

Usually, we are interested only in fades deeper than -20 dB.

$$20 \log L < -20 \text{ dB} \qquad \text{or} \qquad L < 0.1$$

From the experimental data, the number of fades can be formulated as

$$N = \begin{cases} 6410L/60.88 \text{ days} = 105.29L/\text{day} & \text{(in the 6-GHz band)} \\ 3670L/60.88 \text{ days} = 60.28L/\text{day} & \text{(in the 4-GHz band)} \end{cases} \qquad (14.3\text{-}1)$$

The average deviation of fades is

$$\bar{t} = \begin{cases} 490L \text{ s} & \text{(in the 6-GHz band)} \\ 408L \text{ s} & \text{(in the 4-GHz band)} \end{cases} \qquad (14.3\text{-}2)$$

In order to reduce the fades, two methods can be used: a spaced diversity and a frequency diversity. In order to use diversity schemes, we have to gather some additional data. The two signals obtained individually from two channels can be used to measure the number of simultaneous fades, as shown in Fig. 14.3.

If the frequency separation or the spaced separation is very large, the number of simultaneous fades can be drastically reduced. Therefore, it follows that the number of simultaneous fades of two signals must be small to obtain good diversity reception.

A parameter F_N is defined as the ratio of N_i to N_{ij}, where N is the number of fades from a single channel and N_{ij} is the number of simultaneous fades from two individual channels.

$$F_N = \frac{N_i}{N_{ij}} \qquad (14.3\text{-}3)$$

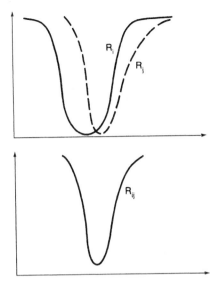

FIGURE 14.3 Formation of a simultaneous fade from two overlapped fades.

The ratio F_N should be large. For deep fades, F_N is

$$F_N = \tfrac{1}{2} q L^{-2} \quad \text{for} \quad L < 0.1 \quad (14.3\text{-}4)$$

The q is a parameter defined by the following equations.

1. For separations in frequency,

$$q = \frac{1}{4} \left(\frac{\Delta f}{f} \right) \quad \text{(in the 6-GHz band)} \quad (14.3\text{-}5)$$

$$q = \frac{1}{2} \left(\frac{\Delta f}{f} \right) \quad \text{(in the 4-GHz band)} \quad (14.3\text{-}6)$$

where Δf is the frequency separation and f is the operational frequency.

2. For separation in space,

$$q = (2.75)^{-1} \left(\frac{s^2}{\lambda d} \right) \quad (14.3\text{-}7)$$

where s is the vertical antenna separation, λ is the wavelength, and d is the path length. All values are measured in the same units.

The term improvement F has been used to describe the ratio of the total time T_i spent in fades to the total time T_{ij} spent in simultaneous fades. For deep fades

$$F = \frac{T_i}{T_{ij}} \approx 2 F_N \qquad L < 0.1 \quad (14.3\text{-}8)$$

The total fading time T_i in a year in a 6-GHz propagation can be obtained from Eqs. (14.3-1) and (14.3-2) as

$$T_i = N\bar{t} = \begin{cases} (37904.4L/\text{year})\,(490L \text{ s}) \\ 1857 \text{ s/year} \quad\quad \text{at} \quad\quad L = 0.01\,(\text{or} - 40\,\text{dB}) \\ 31\,\text{min/year} \quad\quad \text{at} \quad\quad L = 0.01\,(\text{or} - 40\,\text{dB}) \end{cases}$$

We can use the same step to obtain the total fading time T_i in 4-GHz propagation.

$$T_i = N\bar{t} = \begin{cases} (22002L/\text{year})\,(408L \text{ s}) \\ 897.68 \text{ s/year} \quad\quad \text{at} \quad\quad L = 0.01\,(\text{or} - 40\,\text{dB}) \\ 15\,\text{min/year} \quad\quad \text{at} \quad\quad L = 0.01\,(\text{or} - 40\,\text{dB}) \end{cases}$$

The values of F_N at -40 dB are shown along the curves in Fig. 14.4 for 4 and 6 GHz, respectively. To achieve $F_N = 5$ in 4 GHz, we must use a separation in vertical spacing of *10 ft*, or the frequency separation should be *8 MHz*.

To achieve $F_N = 5$ in 6 GHz, we must use a vertical antenna separation of 9 ft, or the frequency separation should be 25 MHz. The improvement F can be obtained from Eq. 14.3-8 as $F = 2 \times 5 = 10$, or the total fading time after a diversity scheme at $L = 0.01$ is reduced to

$$T_{ij} = \begin{cases} 3.1\,\text{min/year} \quad\quad \text{(in the 6-GHz band)} \\ 1.5\,\text{min/year} \quad\quad \text{(in the 4-GHz band)} \end{cases}$$

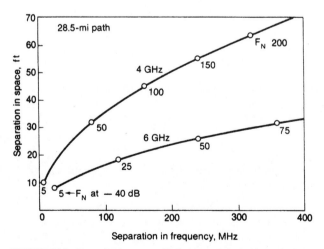

FIGURE 14.4 Separation in space and in frequency that provide equal values of F_N, the ratio of the number of fades to the number of simultaneous fades. (*After Vigants, Ref. 2.*)

14.4 RAY-BENDING PHENOMENON

This phenomenon occurs because air is denser at lower levels than at higher levels.[4] Starting with Snell's law for two layers with different refractive indices n_1 and n_2, we obtain

$$\frac{\sin \theta_1}{\sin \theta_2} = \frac{n_2}{n_1} = \frac{\sqrt{\mu_2 \epsilon_2}}{\sqrt{\mu_1 \epsilon_1}} = \frac{C_1}{C_2} \qquad (14.4\text{-}1)$$

The other parameters are explained as follows.

1. If θ_2 is the reflection angle (Fig. 14.5) and $n_1 = n_2$, then

$$\sin \theta_1 = \sin \theta_2 \qquad (14.4\text{-}2)$$

Snell's law indicates that the incident angle θ_1 is equal to the reflected angle θ_2. Also assume that there are no conductivity effects in the atmosphere and that the troposphere is not magnetic: $\mu_1 = \mu_2 = \mu_0$. For layer 1, the dielectric constant is ϵ_1 and the corresponding velocity C_1 of wave propagation is

$$C_1 = \frac{1}{\sqrt{\mu_0 \epsilon_1}}$$

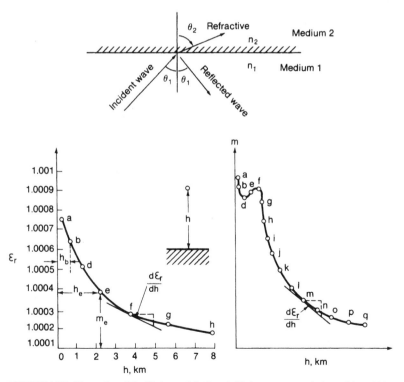

FIGURE 14.5 Illustration of Snell's law and finding dn/dh from a measured piece of data. (*After Hund, Ref. 4.*)

and for layer 2, the dielectric constant is ϵ_2 and the velocity of wave propagation is C_2.

2. If the θ_2 is the refraction angle (see Fig. 14.5) for the wave transmission into medium 2, then

$$n_1 \sin \theta_1 = n_2 \sin \theta_2 \tag{14.4-3}$$

Assume that the refraction indexes n_1, n_2, n_3 decrease as the altitude h_1, h_2, h_3 increases. Then

$$\frac{\sin \theta_1}{\sin \theta_2} = \frac{n_2}{n_1} \tag{14.4-4}$$

$$\frac{\sin \theta_2}{\sin \theta_3} = \frac{n_2}{n_3} \tag{14.4-5}$$

for a gradient dn/dh of n, and $n \sin \theta = $ constant. Then at a certain altitude h, the index of refraction is

$$n = \sqrt{\epsilon_r} \tag{14.4-6}$$

At the altitude $h + dh$

$$n + \left(\frac{dn}{dh}\right) dh = \sqrt{\epsilon_r + \left(\frac{d\epsilon_r}{dh}\right) dh} \tag{14.4-7}$$

The $d\epsilon_r/dh$ can be found from a measured (or statistically predicted) curve at a given location (see Fig. 14.5). Then dn/dh can be found. The equation for ray bending is expressed as

$$\frac{1}{\rho} = -\frac{1}{n}\frac{dn}{dh} \tag{14.4-8}$$

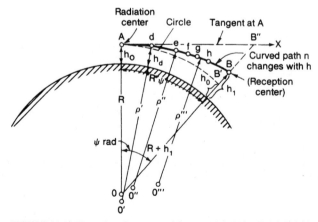

FIGURE 14.6   The radius of curvature of the wave path. (*After Hund, Ref. 4.*) Curved path AB requires the least time to move electromagnetic wave energy from a through angle ψ to line OB''.

Now ρ is the radius of curvature which can be calculated as dn/dh changes as a result of $d\epsilon_r/dh$. The radius ρ can be plotted by computer as shown in Fig. 14.6.

14.5 SYSTEM RELIABILITY

The microwave radio link is a stand-alone system. A typical system layout is shown in Fig. 14.7 for a transmitter and in Fig. 14.8, for a receiver.

14.5.1 Equipment Reliability

All radio equipment should be redundant (i.e., equipped with duplicates) with a standby and automatic switchover in case of failure. An alarm system is available for reporting an emergency condition at any microwave site to the central alarm station at the MSO. Redundant power converters have been included at each cell site. A space diversity can be implemented for further increasing system reliability.

14.5.2 Path Reliability

The microwave path should be a clear line-of-sight path between two points. Each path should be calculated and studied by field survey. Sometimes larger antenna size, higher tower, shorter distance, more diversity, or greater capacity are required to increase the path reliability. An important consideration is elimination or reduction of the multipath reception at the receiver as a result of the reflection along the path. The reflected energy would be negligible if the reflector were out of the first Fresnel zone, which is H

$$H \geq \sqrt{\frac{\lambda d_1(d - d_1)}{d}} \qquad (14.5\text{-}1)$$

where d_1 and d_2 are as shown in Fig. 14.9 and λ is the operating wavelength. Five special cases are as follows.

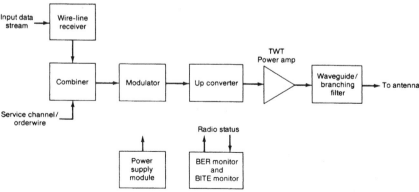

FIGURE 14.7 Microwave radio transmit block diagram.

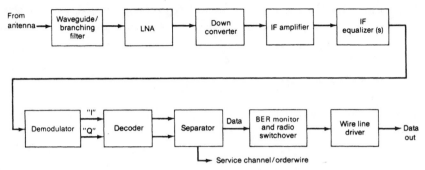

FIGURE 14.8   Microwave radio receive block diagram.

14.5.2.1   Hyperreflectivity.   Hyperreflectivity may occur, such as in wave propagation over water, metal objects, and large flat surfaces. In these cases, additional path clearance is recommended.

14.5.2.2   Bending.   Because the earth is curved and because dielective permittivity varies with height, bending occurs. On the average, the radio wave is bent downward, i.e., the earth radio wave acts as if the earth's radius were four-thirds of its real value (see Fig. 14.10). The effective radius for K (ratio of effective earth radius to true earth radius) can be any value other then $K = \frac{4}{3}$ and can be treated as a function of atmospheric conditions. Sometimes it can be as low as one-half for a small percentage of time. If we base our calculations on $K = \frac{4}{3}$, then the ray is curved downward. This is called an "earth bulge" condition. It will cause the path loss to increase over a wide range of frequencies unless adequate path

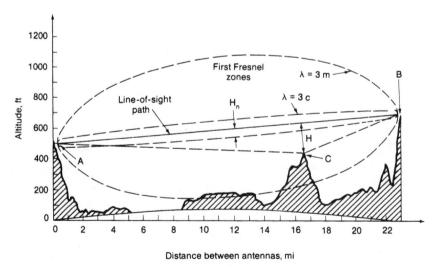

Distance between antennas, mi

FIGURE 14.9   The clearance distance from the closest objects. (*From Ref. 5, p. 439.*) Typical profile plot showing first Fresnel zones for 100 MHz and 10 GHz.

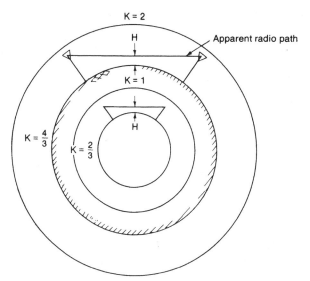

FIGURE 14.10 Illustration of earth bulge conditions.

clearance is provided. A value of $K = 1$ would indicate that the earth is completely flat or the ray travels in a straight line. On the other hand, the wave based on $K = \frac{2}{3}$ will tilt upward and may cause interference over a long distance. An earth bulge factor of $\frac{2}{3}$ or $\frac{4}{3}$ is used to provide a clear area.

$$H \geq \frac{d_1 d_2}{2} \quad \text{(for a factor of } \tfrac{4}{3}) \tag{14.5-2}$$

$$H \geq d_1 d_2 \quad \text{(for a factor of } \tfrac{2}{3}) \tag{14.5-3}$$

where d_1 and d_2 are in miles and H is in feet.

14.5.2.3 High Microwave Frequencies. For a microwave frequency above 10 GHz, the oxygen, water vapor, and rain attenuate (or scatter) the microwave beam. To determine the total path attenuation, we must add the free-space loss (FSL) to the rain loss while considering the anticipated rain rates. The rain rate is measured by millimeters per hour. Usually, a rain rate of 15 mm/h or greater will be considered as heavy rain. Some areas, such as Florida, may have a great deal of precipitation. Some areas, such as southern California, are arid. The history of rain-rate data can be obtained from the U.S. Weather Bureau's annually accumulated rain statistics collected since 1953 in 263 cities. The author was the first to suggest this method at Bell Laboratories in 1972. (Several rain-rate models are given in Refs. 6, 7, and 8.) Once the rain statistics of each city are known, the decibels per kilometer for different rain rates can be found at each operating frequency as shown in Fig. 14.11. The rain rate is governed by the size and shape of the raindrops. The path loss varies with both the raindrop size and rain rate.

The effects of haze, fog, snow, and dust are insignificant. The size of the rain cell (a rain-occupied area) will be considered along the microwave link. The heavier the rain, the smaller the rain cell. Also, the rain-rate profile will be nonuniform. To calculate a microwave link, we need to know the (1) link gain—power, antenna size, antenna height,

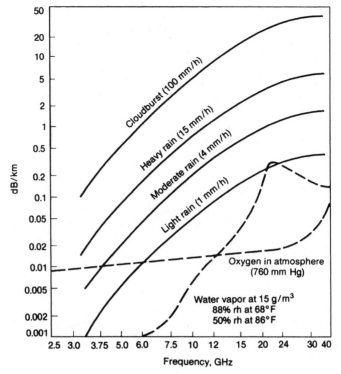

FIGURE 14.11   Estimated atmospheric absorption. (*From Ref. 5, p. 443.*)

and receiver sensitivity; (2) free-space loss; (3) attenuation due to a predicted rain rate; and (4) given availability—allowable downtime, such as 1 h in a year or 10^{-4}.

The transmission rate of a signal over a microwave link is limited to the time-delay spread, and the time-delay spread is based on the distance. Usually we design the link primarily on the basis of the rain effect; therefore, the link is usually short because of the rain attenuation, and the time-delay spread at the shorter distance is not considered.

14.5.2.4   Power System Reliability.   Battery systems or power generators are needed for the microwave systems in case of power failure. Usually a 24-V dc battery system will be installed with 8 to 10 h of reserve capacity.

14.5.2.5   Microwave Antenna Location.   Sometimes the reception is poor after the microwave antenna has been mounted on the antenna tower. A quick way to check the installation before making any other changes is to move the microwave antenna around within a 2 to 4 ft radius of the previous position and check the reception level. Surprisingly favorable results can be obtained immediately because multipath cancellation is avoided as a result of changing reflected paths at the receiving antenna.

Also, at any fixed microwave antenna location, the received signal level over a 24-h time period varies.

14.6 MICROWAVE ANTENNAS

14.6.1 Characteristics of Microwave Antennas[5,9]

Microwave antennas can afford to concentrate their radiated power in a narrowbeam because of the size of the antenna in comparison to the wavelength of the operating frequency; thus, high antenna gain is obviously desirable. Some of the more significant characteristics are discussed in the following paragraphs.

14.6.1.1 Beamwidth. The greater the size of the antenna, the narrower the beamwidth. Usually the beamwidth is specified by a half-power (3-dB) beamwidth and is less than 10° at higher microwave frequencies. The beamwidth sometimes can be less than 1°. The narrowbeam can reduce the chances of interference from adjacent sources or objects such as adjacent antennas. However, a narrowbeam antenna requires a fair amount of mechanical stability for the beam to be aimed at a particular direction. Also, the problem of antenna alignment due to the raybending problems discussed earlier restricts the narrowbeam antenna to a certain degree. The relationship between gain and beamwidth is depicted in Fig. 14.12.

14.6.1.2 Sidelobes. The sidelobes of an antenna pattern would be the potential source of interference to other microwave paths or would render the antenna vulnerable to receiving interference from other microwave paths.

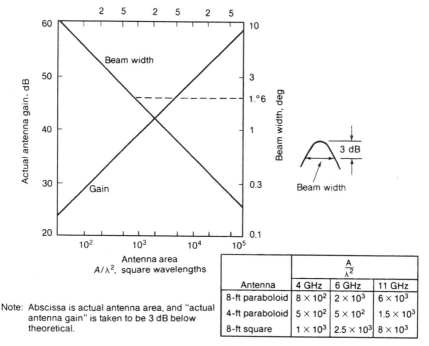

FIGURE 14.12   Approximate antenna gain and beamwidth. (*From Ref. 5, p. 445.*)

14.6.1.3   Front-to-Back Ratio. This is defined as the ratio of the maximum gain in the forward direction to the maximum gain in the backward direction. The front-to-back ratio is usually in the range of 20 to 30 dB because of the requirement for isolating or protecting the main transmission beam from interference.

14.6.1.4   Repeater Requirement. The front-to-back ratio is very critical in repeaters because the same signal frequencies are used in both directions at one site. An improper design can cause a ping-pong ringing type of oscillation from a low front-to-back ratio or from poor isolation between the transmitting port and receiving port of the repeater.

14.6.1.5   Side-to-Side Coupling Loss. The coupling loss, in decibels, should be designed to be high as a result of the transmitting antenna carrying only the output signal and the receiving antenna receiving only the incoming signal. If the transmitting and receiving antennas are installed side by side, the typical transmitter outputs are usually 60 dB higher than the receiver input level. Longer link distance results in increased values. Therefore, the coupling losses must be high in order to avoid internal system interference. The space separation between two antennas and the filter characteristics in the receiver can be combined with a given antenna pattern to achieve the high coupling loss.

14.6.1.6   Back-to-Back Coupling. The back-to-back coupling loss also should be high (e.g., 60 dB) between two antennas. Two antennas are installed back to back, one transmitting and one receiving. However, it is much easier to reach a high back-to-back coupling loss than a side-to-side coupling loss.

14.6.2   Polarization and Space Diversity in Microwave Antennas

14.6.2.1   Polarization. To reduce adjacent-channel interference, microwave relay systems can interleave alternate radio-channel frequencies from a horizontal polarized wave to a vertical polarized wave.

The same approach can be applied to the left- and right-handed circularly polarized waves, but the beamwidths of antennas for this orthogonal system are relatively large and therefore are not attractive.

In the polarization system, the *cross-coupling loss* is specified. This loss is defined as the ratio of the power received in the desired polarization to the power coupling into other polarization. The cross-coupling loss (isolation) should be as high as possible. Usually 25 to 30 dB is required for one hop.

14.6.2.2   Space Diversity. The two antennas separated vertically or horizontally as described in Sec. 14.3 can be used for a two-branch space-diversity arrangement. In a space-diversity receiver, the required reception level is relatively low so that the transmitted power on the other end of the link can be reduced. This is also an effective method for increasing the coupling loss between the transmitting antenna and receiving antenna.

14.6.3   Types of Microwave-Link Antenna

Two kinds of antenna are used for microwave links.

1. A parabolic dish, used for short-haul systems. Antennas sizes range from 1.5 m (5 ft) to 3 m (10 ft) in diameter.

TABLE 14.1. Horn-Reflector Antenna Characteristics

	4 GHz		6 GHz		11 GHz	
Frequency Polarization	Vertical	Horizontal	Vertical	Horizontal	Vertical	Horizontal
Midband gain, dB	39.6	39.4	43.2	43.0	48.0	47.4
Front-to-back ratio, dB	71	77	71	71	78	71
Beamwidth (azimuth), degrees	2.5	1.6	1.5	1.25	1.0	0.8
Beamwidth (elevation), degrees	2.0	2.13	1.25	1.38	0.75	0.88
Sidelobes, dB below main beam	49	54	49	57	54	61
Side-to-side coupling, dB	81	89	120	122	94	112
Back-to-back coupling, dB	140	122	140	127	139	140

2. A horn-reflector antenna, to trap the energy outward from the focal point. The advantages of using this antenna are

   a. Good match: return loss 40–50 dB.

   b. Broadband: a horn antenna can work at 4, 6, and 11 GHz.

   c. One horn can be used for two polarizations with high cross-coupling loss.

   d. Small sidelobes: high back-to-back coupling loss.

The gains, coupling losses, and beamwidths are listed in Table 14.1 for different frequencies and different polarizations.

14.6.4 Installation of Microwave Antennas

A microwave antenna cannot be installed at any arbitrary location. Selection of an optimum position is very important. In many situations if we cannot move horizontally, we can move vertically. In a microwave-link setup, there are two fixed effective antenna heights, one at each end based on each reflection plane where the reflection point is incident on it. The gain of the received signal also relates to the two effective antenna heights if they are low. The antenna location can be moved around to find the best reception level. Sometimes it is worthwhile to take time to search for the location that gives the best reception.

14.7 OPTICAL DATA LINK

14.7.1 Introduction

Prior to the development of the Fiber Cable and Gigabit Ethernet[10] standards in the mid-1990s, multimode fiber link design was based on the use of light-emitting diodes (LEDs). Their use permitted easy characterization of the fiber's major property and its minimum bandwidth. The low data rates of 125 Mb/s [Fiber Distributed Data Interface (FDDI) data rate] and 200 Mb/s [Enterprise Systems Connection (ESCON*) data rate][11] permitted the assumption that all worst-case conditions could occur simultaneously and the link would still work with an adequate margin. With the need for data rates greater than 1 Gb/s, continued use of minimum fiber bandwidth and simultaneous worst-case conditions would have resulted in links with distance limits so short (e.g., 125 m), which was once proposed as the maximum distance for the Gigabit Ethernet 62.5-μm fiber solution, as to render the solution useless or at least unmarketable. Improved link modeling and the use of statistics were needed to restore the multimode fiber solution.

The design of communication links for LAN applications, such as Ethernet and Fiber Channel, differs significantly from the design of long-haul telecommunication links. The long-haul data transmission is usually over a repeater single-mode optical fiber. The primary factor for LAN affecting their design is the overall cost of the components of the links. The multimode fiber is used for the vast majority of the LAN links. Although multimode fiber is unable to reach the distances achieved with single-mode fiber, it offers significant savings in the design of the transmitter and the receiver. Because of the size of the multimode fiber core, the placement tolerances of the laser and the lens relative to fiber in the transmitter are greatly relaxed, permitting passive alignment and resulting in reduced assembly costs. Furthermore, inexpensive materials such as plastics can be used for some of the components, further reducing the cost. In addition, 850-nm vertical-cavity surface-emitting lasers (VCSELs) are used in the vast majority of newly installed LAN links because of their cost advantage.

14.7.2   Optical Communication Systems

Optical communication systems are synchronous systems. The digital signal will convert from electronic to optical before transmitting. Then, the optical waveforms send over the optical fiber and convert back to digital waveform after receiving as shown in Fig. 14.13.

The SONET (Synchronous Optical NETwork) and SDH (Synchronous Digital Hierarchy) are a set of standards for synchronous data transmission over fiber optic networks.

SONET is the United States version of the standard published by the American National Standards Institute (ANSI). SDH is the international version of the standard published by the International Telecommunications Union (ITU). Because SONET and SDH have the same electrical levels, often we name them SONET/SDH. The following table lists the hierarchy of the most common SONET/SDH data rate.

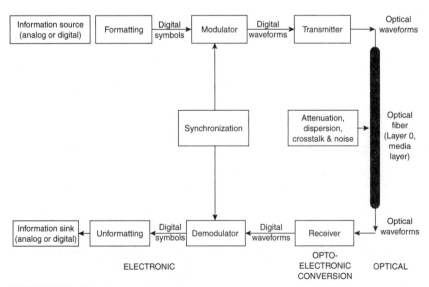

FIGURE 14.13   Optical communication system.

SONET Designation	SDH Designation	Data Rate (Mb/s)	Payload Rate (Mb/s)
STS-1/OC-1		51.84	50.112
STS-3/OC-3	STM-1	155.52	150.336
STS-9/OC-9	STM-3	466.56	451.008
STS-12/OC-12	STM-4	622.08	601.344
STS-18/OC-18	STM-6	933.12	902.016
STS-24/OC-24	STM-8	1244.16	1202.688
STS-36/OC-36	STM-12	1866.24	1804.032
STS-48/OC-48	STM-16	2488.32	2405.376
STS-96/OC-96	STM-32	4976.64	4810.752
STS-192/OC-192	STM-64	9953.28	9621.504
STS-768/OC-768	STM-256	39,813.120	38,486.016

Some rates (OC-9, OC-18, OC-24, OC-36, OC-96) are referenced in some of the standards documents but were never widely implemented. The "data" refers to the raw bit rate carried over the optical fiber.

Sometimes the SONET/SDH level designations include a "c" suffix (such as "OC-48c"). The "c" suffix indicates a "concatenated" or "clear" channel. This implies that the entire payload rate is available as a single channel of communications (i.e., the entire payload rate may be used by a single flow of cells or packets). The opposite of concatenated or clear channel is "channelized." In a channelized link, the payload rate is subdivided into multiple fixed rate channels. For example, the payload of an OC-48 link may be subdivided into four OC-12 channels. In this case, the data rate of a single cell or packet flow is limited by the bandwidth of an individual channel.

14.7.3 Optical Multiplexing Technique: WDM

A. WDM (Wavelength Division Multiplexing) is equivalent to an optical FDMA. Multiple channels of information are carried over the same fiber, each using an individual wavelength. The simple diagram of WDM is shown in Fig. 14.14. The attributes of WDM are

- Can achieve high aggregate bit rate without high speed electronics or modulation.
- Can receive low dispersion penalty for aggregate bit rate.
- Can be very useful for upgrades to installed fibers.
- Can be realized using commercial components, unlike OTDM (optical TDM).

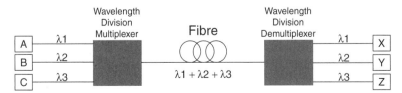

FIGURE 14.14 The diagram of WDM.

The potential problems are loss, cross talk, and nonlinear effects. A possible bottleneck in a WDM system is the need of electronic conversion whenever a light path is terminated in a node. Data must be converted to the electronic domain; packets must be reassembled, processed, forwarded, and then eventually converted again to the optical domain if the current node is not the final destination of the data (hence is implementing a multihop routing strategy for the considered traffic flow). Although the current optical technology allows transmitting data at very high speed, the electronic conversion and elaboration is more speed limited and very costly at high speeds.

B. DWDM (Dense WDM)

DWDM uses closely spaced channels in which channel spacing reduces to 1.6 nm and less. It is cost effective for increasing capacity without replacing fiber. It can use OTDM approach and move to STM-64 data rate. Joint use of DWDM and OTDM technologies can offer a means of splitting the bandwidth of a light path into fixed number of subchannels, using a Time Division Multiplexing (TDM) scheme directly in the optical domain. Because SONET/SDH network management systems are not well equipped to handle DWDM topologies, its performance monitoring and protection methodologies are still in their infancy.

C. Comparison between electrical channels and optical channels:

- Electrons interact strongly with one another in the electrical channels.

  Electrons are good for switching, but not so good for transmission.

  Electrons make the transistors for switches.

  Electrons cause lossy transmission lines.

- Photons interact very weakly with one another in the optical channels.

  Photons are good for transmission but not for switching.

  Photons make good transmission as optical fiber.

  Photons cannot make optical transistor.

  Most optical switching systems are optoelectronic (i.e., using electrical control over the optical data path).

  It is hard to make a fast WDM switch, to switch from λ, λ_2 on incoming interface to outgoing interface.

14.7.4 High-Speed Optical Data Link Modules

High-speed optical data link modules are used in enterprise or premises data communications applications. The term "high-speed" refers to data rates of 1 Gb/s and above. Enterprise and premises applications include networks or point-to-point data links that are confined to a single building or campus. They are usually specified as having link distances of 2 km or less. Table 14.2 shows the universe of communications protocols, data rates, and link distances for optical communications. The link distance categories roughly correspond to those used by various optical communications standards bodies. The vast majority of optical communications applications are included in the table. An "X" entered into a cell in the table means that there is an applicable protocol and/or transmitter/receiver product for that distance and data rate combination.

The data link modules are usually supplied in the form of transceivers; that is, transmitters (850-nm VCSELs or 1310-nm Fabry-Perot lasers) and receivers (detectors) combined in a single package with fiberoptic receptacles (multimode and single-mode, respectively). A laser driver and a transimpedance amplifier are usually also included in the package. An

TABLE 14.2. Application Space for High-Speed Optical Data Link Modules

Data Rate/Protocol	Very Short Reach (<300 m)	Short Reach 1 (0.3–2 km)	Short Reach 2 (2–10 km)	Intermediate Reach (10–40 km)	Long Reach (>40 km)
100 Mb/s FDDI	x	x	x	—	—
10/100 Mb/s Ethernet	x	x	x	—	—
Gigabit Ethernet	x	x	x	x	—
10 Gigabit Ethernet	x	x	x	x	—
1-2 Gb/s Fiber Channel	x	x	x	—	—
10 Gb/s Fiber Channel	x	x	x	—	—
1 Gb/s iSCSI	x	x	x	—	—
10 Gb/s iSCSI	x	x	x	—	—
2.5 Gb/s InfiniBand	x	x	x	—	—
10 Gb/s InfiniBand	x	—	—	—	—
30 Gb/s InfiniBand	x	—	—	—	—
155 Mb/s SONET (OC-3)	x	x	x	x	x
622 Mb/s SONET (OC-12)	x	x	x	x	x
2.5 Gb/s SONET (OC-48)	—	x	x	x	x
10 Gb/s SONET (OC-192)	x	—	x	x	x
40 Gb/s SONET (OC-768)	x	—	—	—	x
Proprietary Parallel Interconnect, 10-40 Gb/s	x	—	—	—	—

exception is parallel optical interconnects, in which multichannel transmitter and receiver packages are most often supplied separately, although there are some exceptions (e.g., a 4-channel transceiver). An emerging packaging format for higher data rates (10 Gb/s)[11] is widely termed a *transponder*. This product incorporates the normal transceiver components, plus a clock and data recovery chip and a mux/demus chipset that multiplexes lower data rate streams up to 10 Gb/s and vice versa.

14.8 POINT-TO-MULTIPOINT (PMP) WIRELESS ACCESS

The point-to-multipoint (PMP) fixed wireless access networks enable service operators to make choices about service and band of operation. PMP solutions connect users to a base station to share the common resource of the transmission capacity available.

A. Service sites

The service sites can be classified into four groups:

1. For large business sites (1 percent of all sites have 250 or more employees).

2. For medium business sites (10 percent of all sites have 10 to 250 employees).

3. For small offices (90 percent of all sites have 1 to 10 employees).

4. Corporate employees, telecommuting employees, and home offices.

B. Frequency bands of operation[12]

1. Below 6 GHz band

  a. 2.4–2.435 GHz: Bluetooth and Wi-Fi (IEEE 802.16) are short-range nomadic systems.

  b. 3.4–3.6 GHz: This band is a preferred band for FWA (Fixed Wireless Access) throughout European countries. The latest generation 3.5-GHz FWA systems have been considered for a standard system. Individual or combined use of adaptive modulation techniques, adaptive access schemes, multiple-carrier, and multiple antenna beam techniques have led to potential base-station capacities in the region of hundreds of Mbit/s. Together with non-line-of-sight capability and quality of service mechanisms, these 3.5-GHz systems can support high-speed IP traffic, multiple E1/T1 circuits, and offer a credible alternative to leased line Mbit/s.

  c. 5.725–5.875 GHz, 150-MHz bandwidth: IEEE. 802.11a (LAN) standard equipment, IEEE 802.16 (MAN) standard equipment, and ETSI HiPERMAN equipment.

2. Above 6 GHz band

  a. 11.7–12.5 GHz: European band for terrestrial fixed service.

  b. 12.2–12.7 GHz: U.S. band for Multichannel Video Distribution and Data Services (MVDDS).

  c. 24.5–26.5 GHz, 27.5–29.5 GHz: for LMDS.

  d. 40 GHz: European band for multimedia wireless systems (MWS); U.S. band for LMDS.

14.9 LMDS (LOCAL MULTIPOINT DISTRIBUTION SERVICES)

LMDS is one solution for bringing high bandwidth services to homes and offices within the "last mile" of connectivity, an area where cable or optical fiber may not be convenient or economical.

LMDS operates in 28 GHz band to provide digital two-way voice, data, Internet, and video services via high-speed dedicated links between high-density nodes in a network.

The majority of system operators will be using PMP wireless access designs. The LMDS network architecture primarily consists of four parts:

1. Network operation center (NOC)—contains network management system (NMS) equipment that manages large regions of the customer network. All the NOCs are interconnected.

2. Fiber-based infrastructure—consists of:

a. synchronous optical network (SONET) operating on optical carrier (OC-1, OC-2, OC-3), and DS-3 links

b. central office (CO) equipment

c. ATM and IP switching systems

d. interconnections with PSTN

3. Base station—where the conversion from fibered infrastructure to wireless infrastructure occurs. Its equipment includes:

a. interface for fiber termination

b. modulation and demodulation functions

c. microwave Tx/Rv equipment, with antenna located atop a roof or a pole.

d. a local switching provides channel access management, billing, registration, and authentication. Those functions also can be performed centrally.

4. Customer premise equipment (CPE)—the microwave equipment can be outdoor mounted and indoor mounted. The CPE may attach to the network using TDMA, FDMA, or CDMA. The customer premise interfaces will run the full range from the different kinds of digital signals—level 0 (DSO), POTS, 10BaseT, DS1, frame relay, ATM25, serial ATM over T1, DS-3, OC-3, and OC-1.

14.10 MMDS (MULTIPOINT MICROWAVE DISTRIBUTION SYSTEM)

Operating frequency and channel bandwidth:

A. Usage of MMDS

MMDS is a wireless broadband technology for Internet access. Signals broadcast at the transmitter site originating from a variety of sources—such as satellite, terrestrial, and cable delivered programs—and local baseband services, makeup the material to be delivered over MMDS.

B. MMDS frequency range and power

• Operating frequency: only 200 MHz (between 2.5 and 2.7 GHz).

• Channel bandwidth is 6 MHz.

• Number of channels is 33 channels.

• Range: 35 miles.

• Transmit power is in the 1–100 W range.

C. An MMDS consists of three parts:

1. Transmit head-end equipment, such as satellite signal reception equipment, radio transmitter, broadcast equipment, and transmit antennas.

• Satellite-delivered baseband programs are remodulated and subsequently up-converted to microwave frequencies.

• Terrestrial delivered signals are usually passed through a hetrodyne processor prior to up-conversion to the desired MMDS frequencies.

2. Repeater stations: Used to redirect MMDS signals to screened areas and to boost power to provide extended range.

3. At receiving site (user's premises)—A rectangular parabolic-shaped antenna is conditioned to receive vertically polarized, horizontally polarized signals, or both at each end user's premises. The microwave signals are then passed through a downconverter, which converts the signal frequencies to standard cable VHF or UHF channel frequencies. TV signals can subsequently be fed directly to a TV set or a set-top converter (i.e., descrambler decoder) box.

14.11 CABLE (WIRE) REPLACEMENT DEVICES

There are five cable (wire) replacement devices for data transmission in short distance. Bluetooth, ZigBee, UWB, IrDA, and RFID are described in this section.

14.11.1 Bluetooth (BT)

A. Introduction
Bluetooth is a radio frequency (RF) specification for short-range, point-to-point and point-to-multipoint voice and data transfer.[13-17] Bluetooth will enable users to connect to a wide range of computing and telecommunications devices without the need for proprietary cables that often fall short in terms of case of use.

B. Bluetooth terminology

Piconet:	a collection of devices connected via Bluetooth wireless technology
Master unit:	the device in a piconet whose clock and hopping sequence are used to synchronize all other devices in the piconet
Slave unit:	all the devices in the piconet that are not the master
Scatter mode:	a collection of piconets joined by a Bluetooth device that is a master in one piconet and a slave in another piconet
Multipoint:	the ability for a Bluetooth device (master) to broadcast information to the other devices (slaves) in the piconet

C. Bluetooth technologies

• System transmission:	FHSS (Frequency Hopping Spread Spectrum)
• Frequency:	2.402–2.480 GHz (in ISM unlicensed band)
• Modulation:	GFSK (Gaussian Frequency Shift Keying)–the carrier is shifted by $+/-160$ KHz (one or zero bit)
• Channels:	79 channels
• Frequency hopping:	1600 hops/sec.
• Power:	Three classes:
	–Class 1—$+20$ dBm (100 milliwatts)
	–Class 2—$+4$ dBm (2.5 milliwatts)
	–Class 3—0 dBm (1 milliwatts)
• Duplexing:	TDD
• Security:	Four basic keys in its security mechanism:

(1) a 48-bit fixed public address that is unique for each device
(2) a 128-bit random number generated for each transaction
(3) a secret key—a 128-bit private user authentication key
(4) a secret key—a 128-bit private user encryption key

- Range: 10 meters
- Voice communications: For up to three synchronous voice channels of 64 kbps
- Bubble of connectivity: Connected in an ad hoc fashion into small Bluetooth
                                  networks called piconets

D. Technical features

Bluetooth technology provides a 10-meter personal bubble that supports simultaneous transmission of both voice and data for multiple devices. Up to eight data devices can be connected in a piconet, and up to ten piconets can exist within the 10-meter bubble. Each piconet supports up to three simultaneous full duplex voice devices (CVSD).

The gross data rate is 1 Mb/s, but the actual data rates are 432 Kbps for full-duplex transmission, and 721/56 Kbps for asymmetric transmission. A time-division duplex scheme is used for full-duplex transmission.

Bluetooth wireless technology is designed to be as secure as a wire with up to 128-bit public/private key authentication and streaming cipher up to 64-bit based on A5 security. The encryption strength can be very robust, which is good for establishing a secure link, but there may be export problems when shipping from the United States. Different hardware with small encryption key lengths may be required to meet United States export controls.

14.11.2 ZigBee

A. Introduction

ZigBee technology is a low-power wireless technology for sensor and control systems. ZigBee technology[18-20] takes full advantages of the IEEE 802.15.4 standard (MAC layer and PHY layer) and adds the logical network, security, and application software. ZigBee technology provides static and dynamic star, cluster tree, and mesh networking structures that allow large area network coverage, scalable networks, and single point of failure avoidance.

B. Technologies

- System transmission: DSSS (Direct-Sequence Spread Spectrum), which has
                                  used less power than FHSS
- Data rate: 20 kpbs–250 kbps
- Frequency: 2.4 GHz, 868 MHz, 915 MHz
- Range: 30 meters
- Channels: 16 channels
- Power: 0 dBm (1 mw)
- Nodes: 64,000 nodes on one network
- Sleep mode: Transition from sleep mode to active mode in 15 msec or
                                  less
- Beacon mode: Normal sleeping network slave nodes wake up periodically
                                  to receive a synchronizing "beacon" from the network's
                                  control mode

C. Technical features

To save as much power as possible, ZigBee employs a talk-when-ready communication strategy, simply sending data when it has data ready to send and then waiting for an automatic acknowledgment. Fortunately, this talk-when-ready leads to very little RF interference. That is largely because ZigBee nodes have very low duty cycles transmitting only occasionally and sending only small amounts of data. Besides ZigBee nodes, as well as Wi-Fi and Bluetooth modules, can easily handle such small, infrequent bursts.

Although contention for airwave access isn't generally a problem for ZigBee, it can be. Each ZigBee device needs to contend for airspace with its neighbors. To avoid

ZigBee's access contention, contention-free TDMA (time division multiple access) technology can be implemented. ZigBee, through the 802.15.4 MAC layer, provides guaranteed time slots in a scheme that somewhat resembles TDMA but is more complex and less power efficient than TDMA.

ZigBee has still more power-saving devices, reducing consumption in ZigBee components by providing for power-saving reduced-function devices (RFDs) in addition to more capable full-function devices (FFDs). Each ZigBee network needs at least one FFD as a controller, but most network nodes can be RFDs. RFDs can only network with FFDs, not to other RFDs, but they contain less circuitry than FFDs and little or no power-consuming memory.

ZigBee is the wireless technology for lower-power sensor networks. ZigBee promises to put wireless sensors in factory automation systems, home security, and consumer electronics.

14.11.3   UWB (Ultrawideband)[21–22]

A. Introduction

Although it began as a military application dating from the 1960s, UWB has been redefined as a high-data-rate (480+ Mbps), short-range (up to 20 meters) technology that specifically addresses emerging applications in the consumer electronics, personal computing, and mobile device markets.

B. Technology overview

The origins of UWB technology stem from work begun in 1962 that was generally referred to as impulse radio, baseband, or carrier-free communications. The term *ultrawideband* was first coined by the U.S. Department of Defense in 1989, and early applications leveraged the technology's properties as ground-penetrating radar.

Today, the definition for ultrawideband, according to the FCC, is any radio technology with a spectrum that occupies greater than 20 percent of the center frequency or a minimum of 500 MHz. In 2002, the FCC allocated unlicensed radio spectrum from 3.1 GHz to 10.6 GHz expressly for UWB. Additional spectrum is also available for use by medical, scientific, law enforcement, and fire and rescue organizations.

Rather than requiring a UWB radio to use the entire 7.5 GHz band to transmit information or even a substantive portion of it, the FCC defined a specific minimum bandwidth of 500 MHz at a 10 dB level. UWB systems can still maintain the same low transmit power as if they were using the entire bandwidth by interleaving the symbols across these subbands. There are three USB technologies being used:

1. Pulse-based single-carrier method

Given this option for a multiband system, information can either be transmitted by the traditional pulse-based single-carrier method or by more advanced multicarrier techniques. Pulse-based single-carrier systems transmit signals by modulating the phase of a very narrow pulse. Although this is a proven technology that only requires a very simple transmitter design, several inherent disadvantages exist:

a. It is difficult to collect enough signal energy in a typical usage environment (with many reflecting surfaces) using a single RF chain.

b. Switching time requirements can be very stringent at both the transmitter and receiver.

c. The receiver signal processing is very sensitive to group delay variations introduced by analog front-end components.

d. Spectral resources are potentially wasted to avoid narrowband interference.

2. MB-OFDM (MultiBand Orthogonal Frequency Division Multiplexing)

This is one of two IEEE 802.15.3a's technology proposed by MBOA (Multiband OFDM Alliance) led by T1/Intel.

3. DS-USB (Direct Sequency—UWB

This is the other IEEE 802.15.3a's technology proposed by UWB Motorola/Freescale.

C. Description of MB-OFDM technology

Frequency allocation:	Three sub-bands: 3168–3696, 3696–4224, and 4224–4752 MHz
Spectral flexibility:	Capable of dynamically turning off certain tones or sub-channels in software.
System transmission:	OFDM
Modulation:	QPSK
Data rate:	110 Mbps and 200 Mbps
Transmit power:	93 mw
Receiver power:	155 μw (110 Mbps)
	169 μw (200 Mbps)
Deep sleep power:	15 μw (always "on")
Security and privacy:	Implemented at several levels of protocol stack as Bluetooth
Range:	Up to 20 meters

D. Technical features

1. The ability to display, edit, listen, share, and download content between devices in the home; also convergence of data, entertainment, and mobile communications within the home.

2. Technologies adopting the UWB radio platform

a. Native IP-based application that is based on the WiMedia Convergence Platform.

b. Wireless USB (universal serial bus)—the Wireless USBS Promoters Group has defined WUSB specification with a data rate of 480 Mbps using the MB UWB (MegaBit UWB) radio.

c. Wireless IEEE 1394 will support up to 400 Mbps and be backward compatible to legacy-wired devices. The 1394 Trade Association approved a protocol adaptation layer.

3. The ecosystem (MB-OFDM UWB) supports high-speed, short-range, point-to-point wireless communications that look to liberate consumers from the other wired PCs, home entertainment, and offices.

14.11.4   IrDA (Infrared Data Association)

A. Introduction

IrDA is based on infrared technology and has the potential to expand use as a cable replacement. Primary use for IrDA is to link notebooks, various personal communications, or video cameras.

B. Technologies

- Transmission: Infrared LED

- Wavelength: 875 nm ($\pm$30 nm tolerance)

- Receivers: PIN photodiodes

- Range: 1.0 m

- BER: 10^{-9}

- Maximum level of surrounding illumination: 10 klux (daylight)

- Deflection (off-alignment) between Tx and Rv: 15°

- Modulation (A): Pulse modulation
  - Data Speed: 2,400–115,200 bps
  - Pulse width: 3/16 of the length of the original duration of a bit
  - Duration of pulse: 1.63 μs (correspond to 115 kbps)
  - Signal waveform: NRZ
  - Correction code: CRC-16
- Modulation (B): 4 PPM modulation
  - Data speed: 4 Mbps
  - Pulse width: 1/4 mark-to-space ratio; two bits are encoded in a pulse
  - Correction code: CRC-32
- Power: Transmit power 40–500 mW/Sr (Sr: Steradiation)
  - Receiving power 4–500 mW/cm^2
- Low power: IrDA device
  - Range: 20 cm
  - Data speed: 115 kbps

C. Issues on device

1. If speed is decreased four times, distance can be increased two times.
2. For greater distances, additional optics is needed.
3. Alignment of the link is critical.

14.11.5 RFID (Radio Frequency Identification)

RFID is a means of storing and retrieving data through electromagnetic transmission to an RF compatible integrated circuit and is now being seen as a radical means of enhancing data-handling processes.[25]

A. History of RFID

The first type of a RFID device was an espionage tool. The related technology, the IFF (Identification of Friend or Foe) transponder went into operation in 1939 and was used by the British in World War II. The Russian government used a passive covert listening device as an espionage tool. The early exploration of RFID was by Harry Stockman in his paper, "Communication by Means of Reflected Power," published in *IRE* in October 1948.

B. System components

RFID systems have several basic components:

1. A reader, including an antenna—a device used to read and/or write data to RFID tags
2. A tag—a device that transmits data to a reader
3. The communication means—RFID uses a defined radio frequency and protocol to transmit and receive data from tags

C. Types of RFID tags

1. Active tag—contain both a radio transceiver and battery. It can have a range of 100 meters. The range can be in the near field or far field depending on the frequencies and the size of antennas.
2. Passive tags—reflect the RF signal transmitted to them from a reader or transceiver and add information by modulating the reflected signal. A passive tag does not use

a battery to boost the energy of the reflected signal. It may use a battery to maintain memory in the tag or power the electronics that enable the tag to modulate the reflected signal. Therefore, there are two kinds of passive tags: batteryless and with a battery.

D. Memory types in the tags

  1. Read/write memory—its data can be dynamically altered.

  2. Read only (chipless)—a factory programmed memory. It cannot be altered after the manufacturing process.

E. Types of communication

  • Two types of wireless signal distinguished RFID systems

  1. Close proximity electromagnetic or inductive coupling (passive tags)

  2. Propagation electromagnetic waves (active tags)

  • Channel encoding schemes are used, such as NRZ (Non-Return to Zero), Differential Biphase, and Biphase L (Manchester).

  • Modulations—the three modulations are used: ASK, FSK, and PSK.

F. Radio frequency and range
Different RFID frequencies have different RF effective ranges. Also, the range can be in the near field or far field depending on the frequencies and the size of antennas.

Frequency Band			Characteristics	Typical Applications
Low 100–500 kHz			Short to medium read range Inexpensive Low reading speed	Access control Animal identification Inventory control Car immobilizer
Intermediate 10–15 MHz			Short to medium read range Potentially inexpensive medium reading speed	Access control Smart cards
Medium-High 420–450 MHz			Frequency is usable globally	Widely used for active RFID
High 850–950 MHz 2.4–5.8 GHz	865.6–867.6 867.6–868 865–865.5	2W (ERP) 0.5w 0.1w	Long read range High reading speed Line of sight required Expensive	Railroad car monitoring Toll collection systems

G. Date rate:

  <u>At 13.56 MHz</u>
  • Low-speed data rate
    • Reader (interrogator) → tag 1.65 kbps or 26.48 kbps
    • tag → Reader (interrogator) 26.48 kbps
  • High-speed data rate
    • Reader → tag   423.75 kbps
    • Tag → reader   105.9375 kbps on each of eight channels

  <u>At 2.45 GHz</u>
  • For read/write tag 384 kbps
  • For read only tag   76.8 kbps

TABLE 14.3. Comparison of Cable Replacement Devices. WiFi, and Cellular Systems

	ZigBee 802.15.4	Bluetooth 802.15.1	UWB	IrDA	RFID	WiFi 802.11 b/a	GPRS/GSM (1) IXRTT/CDMA (2)
Market	WPAN	WPAN	WPAN	WPAN	WSN (Wireless Sensor Network)	WLAN	Cellular system
Application focus	Monitoring & control	Cable replacement	Cable replacement	Cable replacement	Monitoring & sensor	Web, Video, Email	WAN, voice data
Nodes Per network	255/65K+	7	N/A	N/A	1,000	1-100	1,000+
Data rate	20–250 kbps	1 Mbps	110 Mbps	115 kbps/4Mbps	2.48 kbps (slow-speed data at 13.56 MHz) 423 kbps (high-speed data at 13.56 MHz)	11 Mbps (b) 54 Mbps (a)	64-128 kbps (1) 2 Mbps (2)
Range (meters)	1-75+	1-10+	20	0.02-1	1.5m-100m		Reach quality
Key attributes	Reliable low power, cost effective	Cost, convenience	Speed, convenience	Speed, convenience	Cost, low power, convenience	Speed, flexibility	
Frequency	Radio frequency 2.4 GHz, 868 MHz, 915 MHz	Radio frequency 2.4 GHz	Radio frequency 3.1-10.6 GHz	Optical 875 nm	Radio frequency	Radio frequency 2.4 GHz	900/1800 MHz (1) 800/1900 MHz (2)
Transmission technology	DSSS	FHSS	OFDM	Pulse modulation	ASK (bi-phase modulation) FSK PSK	FHSS, DSSS	TDMA (1) CDMA (2)
Power	0 dbm	0/20 dBm	19.68 dBm (93 mw)	40-500 (mW/Sr) (transmit) 4-500 (mW/cm^2) (received)	0.1 w-2w (800 MHz)	20dBm	(see Chapter 6)
Topology	64000 devices (nodes) Point-to-multipoint	8 devices Point-to-multipoint	Point-to-point	Point-to-point	Point-to-multipoint	128 devices CSMA	System configuration

H. Materials of tags

The compositions of materials for RFID tags need to be considered. The different materials can affect RF signals in different ways, such as reflection, cancellation, and absorption.

In some applications, the RFID tag's antenna can be tuned to reduce the material detuning effects.

I. Design aspects

1. The simultaneous reading of several tags in the same RF field is absolute critical. The tags thus will all backscatter the carrier at the same time, and the modulated signal would be garbled. Therefore the tag and reader need to be designed to detect the condition that more than one tag is active.

2. The tag/reader interface is a serial bus traveling through the air, The RFID interface requires arbitration so that only one tag transmits data over the bus at one time.

14.11.6 Comparison of the Cable Replacement Devices

In this section; a table of five cable replacement devices—ZigBee, Bluetooth, UWB, IrDA, and RFID—compared with WiFi and cellular systems is shown in Table 14.3.

REFERENCES

1. Bell Telephone Laboratories, *Engineering and Operations in the Bell System*, 1977, Bell Telephone Labs, Inc., Chap. 10.

2. A. Vigants, "Number and Duration of Fades at 6 and 4 GHz," *Bell System Technical Journal*, Vol. 50, March, 1971, pp. 815–842.

3. A. Vigants, "The Number of Fades in Space-Diversity Reception," *Bell System Technical Journal*, Vol. 49, September 1970, pp. 1513–1554.

4. A. Hund, *Short-Wave Radiation Phenomenon*, Vol. 2, McGraw-Hill Book Co., 1952, pp. 980–985.

5. Bell Telephone Laboratories, *Transmission Systems for Communications*, 4th ed., Western Electric Company, 1970, Chap. 18.

6. W. C. Y. Lee, "No-Cost and Fast Time in Obtaining the Signal Attenuation Statistics due to Rainfall in Major U.S. Cities," Bell Labs Internal Report, May 10, 1974.

7. S. H. Lin, "More on Rain Rate Distributions and Extreme Value Statistics," *Bell System Technical Journal*, Vol. 57, May–June, 1978, pp. 1545–1568.

8. W. C. Y. Lee, "An Approximate Method for Obtaining Rain Rate Statistics for use in Signal Attenuation Estimating," *IEEE Transactions on Antenna and Propagation*, Vol. AP-27, May 1979, pp. 407–413.

9. H. Yamamoto, "Future Trends in Microwave Digital Radio," *IEEE Communications*, Vol. 25, February 1987, pp. 40–52.

10. P. K. Pepeljugoski, D. M. Kuchta, "Design of Optical Communications Data Link," IBM J. Research & Development, Vol. 47, No. 2/3, March/May 2003.

11. Z. A. Matni, W. Chang, C. Neagoy, "Demonstrating a Fiber Optic Link for 10 Gbps Data Communications," A White Paper by Inphi/Broadcom/JDS Uniphase, 12/12/2002, Ver. 1.2.

12. Air Interface for Fixed Broadband Wireless Access Systems, Part A: System Between 2–11 GHz, 802. 16ab-01/01rl, July 2001.

13. J. C. Haartsen, "The Bluetooth Radio System," IEEE Personal Communications, Feb. 2000, pp. 28–36.

14. "Bluetooth Technology Overview,: Smart Handheld Group, Hewlett-Packard Company, 5th Ed., April 2003.

15. J. C. Haartsen, "The Bluetooth radio system," IEEE Personal Communications, pp. 28–36, Feb. 2000.

16. B. A. Miller and C. Bisdikian, Bluetooth Revealed, Englewood Cliffs, NJ: Prentice-Hall, 2001.

17. (1999, Dec.) Specification of the Bluetooth system, Version 1.0 B, www.bluetooth.com

18. S. C. Ergen "ZigBee/IEEE 802.15.4 Summary," September 10, 2004, csinem@eecs.berkeley.edu.

19. ZigBee Alliance, "IEEE 802.15.4 Specification," http//www.caba.org/standard/zigbee.html.

20. E. Callaway, P. Gorday, L. Hester, J. A. Guiterrez, M. Naeve, B. Heile and V. Bahl, "Home Networking with IEEE 802.15.4: A Developing Standard for Low-Power Low-Cost Wireless Personal Area Networks," IEEE Communications, Vol. 40, No. 8, Aug. 2002, pp. 70–77.

21. J. Balakrisnan, A. Batra, and Dabak, "Multi-Band OFDM System for UWB Communication," Proc. 2003, IEEE Conf. UWB Sys. and Tech., Nov. 2003.

22. S. Roy et al., "Ultra-Wideband Radio Design: The Promise of High-Speed, Short Range Wireless Connectivity," Proc. IEEE, Vol. 92, No. 2, Feb. 2004, pp. 295–311.

23. Infrared Data Association, Serial Infrared Physical Layer Link Specification, Version 1.1e, Oct. 1995.

24. R. Ananth, M. Noll, K. Phang, "Low-Voltage Infrared Transceiver Design," Communication Systems Design, Miller Freeman, Inc., Oct. 1997.

25. Z. Li, R. Gadh, B. S. Prabhu, "Applications of RFID Technology and Smart Parts in Manufacturing," Proc. of DETC'04: ASME 2004 Design Engineering Technical Conferences, Sept. 28–Oct. 2, 2004, Salt Lake City, Utah, USA.

CHAPTER 15
SYSTEM EVALUATIONS

15.1 PERFORMANCE EVALUATION

15.1.1 Blockage

There are two kinds of blockage; set-up channel blockage and voice-channel blockage.

15.1.1.1 Set-Up Channel Blockage B_1. Information regarding set-up channel blockage cannot be obtained at the cell site because the mobile unit will be searching for the busy/idle bit of a forward set-up channel in order to set up its call. If the busy bit does not change after 10 call attempts in 1 s, a busy tone is generated, and no mobile transmit takes place. In another case, the mobile transmit takes place as soon as the idle bit is shown. Several initiating cells can intercollide at the same time. When it occurs, the mobile unit counts it as one seizure attempt. If the number of seizure attempts exceeds 10, then the call is blocked. This kind of blockage can be detected only by mobile phone users. If the occurrence of blockage of the system is in doubt, each of the three specified set-up channels can be assigned in each of the three sectors of a cell, and the total number of incoming calls among the three sectors can be compared with that from a single set-up channel (omni). It should be determined whether there is a difference between two call-completion numbers, one from a single set-up channel and the other from three set-up channels. This is one way to check the blockage if the single set-up channel seems too busy. The set-up channel blockage should be at least less than half of the specified blockage (usually 0.02) in the mobile cellular system.

If all the call-attempt repeats are independent events, then the resultant blocking probability B_1 after n attempts is related to the blocking probability of the single call attempt B, as

$$B_1 = 1 - (1 - B) \sum_{i=0}^{N} B^i = B^n \qquad (15.1\text{-}1)$$

EXAMPLE 15.1 *Assume that the blocking probability of a set-up channel is .005, and the holding time at the set-up channel is 175 ms per call. There is only one channel; then the offered load (from Appendix A) A is .005. Thus the number of set-up calls being handled is*

$$C = \frac{.005 \times 3600 \times 1000}{175} = 120 \, calls \qquad \text{(one call attempt)}$$

EXAMPLE 15.2 *All parameters are the same as in Example 15.1, except that the offered load α changes to A = 0.02. Then the number of set-up calls is*

$$C = \frac{.02 \times 3600 \times 1000}{175} = 480 \, calls \qquad \text{(one call attempt)}$$

EXAMPLE 15.3   *Given the number of set-up calls per hour, find the blocking probability B_t after 10 call attempts in 1 s.*

Consider the following cases.

Case 1. Assume that there are two set-up calls per second or 7200 calls per hour. Because each set-up call takes 175 ms, the offered load A is

$$A = \frac{175 \times 2}{1000} = .35$$

The blocking probability B (see Appendix A) is $B = .25$ (assuming one call attempt). Because the average interval for each attempt is 100 ms, 10 attempts have to be completed in 1 s. It is a kind of conditional probability problem. In the worst case, a mobile unit has to fail the tenth call attempt before giving up. During this period, because of the failure of all call attempts, the two set-up calls from other mobile units should have been successful with a probability of 1. The length of two set-up calls is 350 ms, which is roughly the time interval required for four attempts; i.e., these four attempts are definitely blocked with a blocking probability of 1 and should not be counted as attempts. Therefore, only six attempts count. Using Eq. (15.1-1), we obtain

$$B_t = (.25)^6 = .00012$$

which is quite low and, of course, acceptable.

Case 2. Assume that there are three set-up calls per second or 10,800 calls per hour. Then

$$A = \frac{175 \times 3}{1000} = .525 \qquad \text{(offered load)}$$

$$B = .342 \qquad \text{(blocking probability; see Appendix A)}$$

Because three set-up calls take 525 ms, roughly six out of ten attempts are definitely blocked following the same argument stated in case 1. Only four attempts count, then the resultant blocking probability is

$$B_t = (.342)^4 = .013$$

which is too high for the set-up channel.

15.1.1.2   *Voice-Channel Blockage* B_2.   Voice-channel blockage can be evaluated at the cell site. When all calls come in, some are refused for service because there are no available voice channels. Suppose that we are designing a voice channel blockage to be .02. On this basis, $B_2 = .02$, and after determining the holding time per call[1] and roughly estimating the total number of calls per hour at the site,[2] we can find the number of radios required.

EXAMPLE 15.4   *Assume that 2000 calls per hour are anticipated. The average holding time is 100 s per call, and the blocking probability is .02 (2 percent). Then the offered load is*

$$A = \frac{2000 \times 1000 \, s}{60 \times 60 \, s} = 55.5 \, erlangs$$

Use $A = 55.5$ and $B_2 = 0.02$ to find $N = 66$ channels required (refer to Appendix A).

The actual blocking probability data must be used to check the outcome from the Erlang B model (Appendix A). Although the difference can be up to 15 percent, the Erlang B model is still considered as a good model for obtaining useful estimates.

15.1.1.3   End-Office Trunk Blockage $\mathbf{B_3}$**.**   The trunks connecting from the MSO to the end office can be blocked. This usually occurs when the call traffic starts to build up and the number of trunks connected to the end office becomes inadequate. Unless this corrective action is taken, the blockage during busy periods increases. An additional number of trunks could be provided at the end office when needed.

15.1.1.4   The Total Blockage $\mathbf{B_t}$**.**   As the total call blockage is the result of all three kinds of blockage, the total blockage is

$$B_t = B_1 + B_2(1 - B_1) + B_3(1 - B_1)(1 - B_2)$$

$$= 1 - (1 - B_1)(1 - B_2)(1 - B_3) \qquad (15.1\text{-}2)$$

EXAMPLE 15.5   *Assume that $B_1 = .01$ and $B_2 = B_3 = .02$. Then the total blockage is*

$$B_t = .01 + .0198 + .0194 = .0492 = 5\%$$

The result in Example 15.5 indicates that even when each individual blockage (i.e., B_1, B_2, and B_3) is small, the total blockage becomes very large. Therefore, the resultant blockage is what we are determining.

15.1.2   Call Drops (Dropped-Call Rate)

Call drops are defined as calls dropped for any reason after the voice channel has been assigned. Sometimes call drops due to weak signals are called *lost calls*. The dropped-call rate is partially based on the handoff-traffic model and partially based on signal coverage. The calculation of dropped call rate is shown in Sec. 11.10 through Sec. 11.12. The evaluation of call drops is stated in this section.

15.1.2.1   The Handoff Traffic Model.   A new handoff cell site treats handoffs the same way as it would an incoming call. Therefore, the blockage for handoff calls is also $B = .02$. Some MSO (or MSC) systems may give priority to handoff calls rather than to incoming calls. In this case the blocking probability will be less than .02.

A warning feature can be implemented when the call cannot be handed off and may be dropped with high probability, enabling the customer to finish the call before it is dropped. Then the dropped-call rate can be reduced.

15.1.2.2   The Loss of SAT Calls in AMPS System (See Chapter 3).   If the mobile unit does not receive a correct SAT in 5 s, the mobile-unit transmitter is shut down. If the mobile unit does not send back a SAT in 5 s, the transmitter at the cell site is shut down. In both cases the call is dropped. If the correct SAT cannot be detected at the cell site, as in cases of strong interference, then (1) the SAT can be offset by more than 15 Hz (see section entitled "The total dropped-call rate," below) or (2) the SAT tone generator in the mobile unit may not produce the desired tone.

15.1.2.3   Calculation of SAT Interference Conditions.   The desired SAT is $\cos w_1 t$, and the undesired SAT is $\rho \cos w_2 t$. When $\rho \ll 1$, the SAT detector at the cell site can easily detect w_1. When ρ is greater and starts to approach 1, SAT interference occurs. The following analysis shows the degree of the interference due to the value of ρ.

$$\cos w_1 t + \rho \cos w_2 t = A(t) \cos \theta(t) \tag{15.1-3}$$

where

$$A(t) = \sqrt{1 - \rho^2 + 2\rho \cos (w_1 - w_2)t} \tag{15.1-4}$$

$$\psi(t) = w_2 t - w_1 t$$

$$\theta = w_1 t + \tan^{-1} \frac{\rho \sin \psi(t)}{1 + \rho \cos \psi(t)} \tag{15.1-5}$$

$$w = \frac{d\theta}{dt} = w_1 + \frac{w_2 - w_1}{([1 + \rho \cos \psi(t)]/\{\rho[\rho + \cos \psi(t)]\}) + 1} \tag{15.1-6}$$

Let $\cos \psi(t) = 1$ in Eq. (15.1-6), the extreme condition of w which is the offset frequency from a desired SAT.

$$w = w_1 + \left(1 + \frac{1}{\rho}\right)^{-1} (w_2 - w_1) \tag{15.1-7}$$

For

$$\rho = \begin{cases} .3 & w = w_1 + .22(w_2 - w_1) \\ .5 & w = w_1 + .333(w_2 - w_1) \\ .75 & w = w_1 + .45(w_2 - w_1) \end{cases} \tag{15.1-8}$$

If $w_2 - w_1 = 30$ Hz, for two adjacent SATs

$$\rho = \begin{cases} .5 & w = w_1 \pm 9.95 & \text{(acceptable)} \\ .75 & w = w_1 \pm 12.9 & \text{(marginal)} \end{cases}$$

If $w_2 - w_1 = 60$ Hz, for two ends of SATs

$$\rho = \begin{cases} .3 & w = w_1 \pm 13.8 & \text{(marginal)} \\ .5 & w = w_1 \pm 19.9 & \text{(unacceptable)} \\ .75 & w = w_1 \pm 25.8 & \text{(unacceptable)} \end{cases}$$

Adjacent SATs cannot interfere with the desired SAT for an undesired SAT level below $\rho = .75$ (meaning a level of -2.5 dB). However, when two SATs are not adjacent to each other, the undesired SAT level should at least be lower than $\rho = 0.3$ (-10.5 dB) in order for no interference to occur.

15.1.2.4 Unsuccessful Complete Handoffs. Because of the limitations in processor capacity, the duration of the handoff process may occasionally be too long, and the mobile unit may not be informed of a new channel to be handed off.

15.1.2.5 The Total Dropped-Call Rate. Assume that the handoff blocking is B_4, the probability of lost SAT calls is B_5, and the probability of an unsuccessful complete handoff is B_6. Then the total drop call rate is

$$B_d = B_4 + B_5(1 - B_4) + B_6(1 - B_4)(1 - B_5) \tag{15.1-9}$$

Usually, the dropped-call rate should be less than 5 percent.

15.1.3   Voice Quality

It is very important that the voice quality of a channel be tested by subjective means. Some engineers try to use the signal-to-noise-plus-distortion ratio (SINAD) to evaluate voice quality. Although SINAD is an objective test, using it to test voice quality may result in misleading conclusions. Worst of all, engineers are always proud of the apparatus they have designed, and they tend to ignore others' opinions. To serve the public interest, we must survey consumers for their opinions.

Evaluation of system performance based on a subjective test can be used to set performance criteria. As was discussed in Chap. 2, 75 percent of cellular phone users report that voice quality is good (CM4; i.e., circuit merit 4) or excellent (CM5) over 90 percent of the service area.[1] These numbers can vary depending on how well the service is performed—in other words, the cost. First we must know what kind of service we are providing to the public. We should then let the customers judge the voice quality.

A typical curve of subjective tests was shown in Fig. 10.1*b* for different conditions. For this particular run, the mobile speed is 56 km/h (35 mi/h).

15.1.4   Performance Evaluation

Often we encounter a situation where two systems are being installed in two different areas; one system is deployed in a flat area where the average measured bit error rate (BER) is low at the cell site on the basis of bit-stream data received from mobile-units, and the other system is deployed in a hilly area where BER is relatively high. Of course, if the same degree of skill was used to install both systems, the system in the hilly area would otherwise be inferior and would provide the poorer performance. But if each system claims to be better than the other, how can we judge these two systems fairly? One way is to compensate for variations in performance due to geographic location.[2] Assume that system A is deployed in a flat terrain and system B, in a hilly area. Both systems use the same kind of antennas and run the measured data with the same kind of mobile units. Then the handicap of building a system in a hilly area can be compensated for before comparing this system's performance with others.

Another way is to set the BER to, say, 10^{-3} and find the percentage of areas where the measured BER is greater than 10^{-3} in relation to the area of the whole system, then compare the percentages from the two different systems in two different areas.

Here the two pieces of raw field-strength recorded data in the area should be received from two mobile units moving around in two systems, respectively. From these data, the two local means (the envelope of the raw field-strength data) can be obtained. Then the two cumulative probability distributions (CPD), $P(x < X)$ of two local means, can be plotted. Let us first normalize the average power at a 50 percent level because the local means have a log-normal distribution, and the differences in transmitted power in the two systems are factored out. There will be two straight lines on log-normal scale paper (see Fig. 15.1). The standard deviations of two log-normal curves can be found from Fig. 15.1 by determining a level X where $P(x \le X) = 90$ percent.

$$X = \begin{cases} 5\,\text{dB} & \text{for system A} \\ 15\,\text{dB} & \text{for system B} \end{cases}$$

A normal distribution can be found from published mathematical tables indicating that $P(x \le 1.29) = 90$ percent, where

$$x \le \frac{X - m}{\sigma} = \frac{X}{\sigma} = 1.29 \qquad (15.1\text{-}10)$$

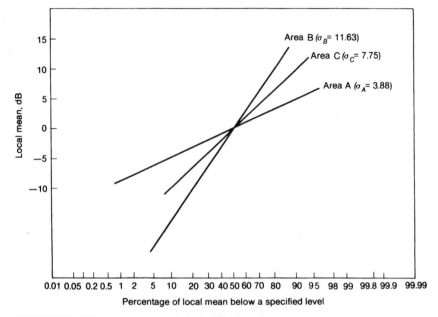

FIGURE 15.1 Different local mean statistics in different areas.

where $m = 0$ dB and σ is the standard deviation. For

$$
X = \begin{cases} 5\,\text{dB} & \sigma_A = \dfrac{5}{1.29} = 3.88\,\text{dB} \\[2ex] 15\,\text{dB} & \sigma_B = \dfrac{15}{1.29} = 11.6\,\text{dB} \end{cases}
$$

The standard deviations of A and B indicate that system B covers a relatively hillier area than system A.

EXAMPLE 15.6 *From these measurements we find that the BER in 10 percent of area A in system A is greater than 10^{-3}. The BER in 25 percent of area B in system B is greater than 10^{-3}. The local means of two systems are shown in Fig. 15.1. We would like to judge which system has a better performance. From Fig. 15.1, 10 percent of the area in system A corresponds to 10 percent of the total signal below -5 dB. If system A is deployed in area C ($\sigma_c = 7.75$ dB), 25 percent of area C will have a BER greater than 10^{-3} below the -5-dB level. Now the variance σ_B of area B is greater than the variance σ_c of area C; thus, area B is more difficult to serve than area C. However, the measurement shows that 25 percent of area B in system B is greater than 10^{-3} below the -9-dB level. Therefore, according to the criterion BER $\geq 10^{-3}$, system B proves to be a better system than system A.*

15.2 SIGNALING EVALUATION

The signaling protocols of AMPS systems are evaluated in the first 3 sub-sections as an example. The signaling format of the forward control channel (FOCC) as deduced from a

BCH code (63, 51) becomes a short code of (40, 28) or that of the reverse control channel (RECC) from a BCH becomes a short code of (48, 36), as described in Chap. 3. The 12 parity-check bits always remain unchanged. This BCH code can correct one error and detect two errors.

15.2.1 False-Alarm Rate

The false-alarm rate is the rate of occurrence of a false recognizable word that would cause a malfunction in a system. The false-alarm rate should be less than 10^{-7}. Now we would like to verify that the BCH code (40, 28) can meet this requirement. The Hamming distance d of BCH (40, 28) is 5. This means that in every different code word at least 5 out of 40 bits are different. Then the false-alarm rate FAR can be calculated as

$$FAR = p_e^d (1 - p_e)^{L-d} \qquad (15.2\text{-}1)$$

where p_e is the BER and d is the length of a word in bits.

Assume that in a noncoherent frequency-shift-keying (FSK) modulation system, the average BER of a data stream in a Rayleigh fading environment is

$$\langle p_e \rangle = \frac{1}{2 + \Gamma} \qquad \text{(noncoherent FSK)} \qquad (15.2\text{-}2a)$$

and the average BER of a data stream received by a differential phase-shift-keying (DPSK) modulation system in the same environment is

$$\langle p_e \rangle = \tfrac{1}{2} \left(\frac{1}{\Gamma + 1} \right) \qquad \text{(DPSK)} \qquad (15.2\text{-}2b)$$

where Γ is the carrier-to-noise ratio. Let[*] $\Gamma = 15$ dB; then we obtain BER from Eq. (15.2-2) as

$$\langle p_e \rangle = .08 \qquad \text{(noncoherent FSK)}$$

$$\langle p_e \rangle = .015 \qquad \text{(DPSK)}$$

Substituting $p_e = .03$, which is the higher BER, into Eq. (15.2-1), we obtain

$$FAR = (.03)^5 = 2.43 \times 10^{-8} \le 10^{-7}$$

This meets the requirement that $FAR < 10^{-7}$.

15.2.2 Word Error Rate Consideration

The word error rate (WER), also called frame error rate (FER), plays an important role in a Rayleigh fading environment. The length of a word of an FOCC is $L = 40$ and the transmission rate is 10 kbps. Then the transmission time for a 40-bit word is

$$T = \frac{40}{10,000} = 4 \, \text{ms}$$

From Sec. 2.3.3, the average duration of fades can be obtained from the following assumptions: frequency = 850 MHz, vehicle speed = 15 mi/h, and threshold level = -10 dB (10 dB

---

[*]The C/N ratio of a data channel can be lower than 18 dB of a voice channel.

below the average power level); then the average duration of fades is

$$\bar{t} = 0.33 \times \left(\sqrt{2\pi} \frac{V}{\lambda} \right)^{-1} = 7\,\text{ms} \qquad (15.2\text{-}3)$$

Equation (15.2-3) shows that the transmission time of one word is shorter than the average duration of fades while the vehicle speed is 15 mi/h; that is, the whole word can disappear under the fade. Therefore, redundancy schemes are introduced. From Chap. 3, the FOCC format is

200 bits	word A (40 bits $\times$ 5 times), 28 information bits
200 bits	word B (40 bits $\times$ 5 times), 28 information bits
10 bits	bit synchronization
11 bits	word synchronization
42 bits	Busy/Idle-status bits
463 bits	56 information bits

The throughput can be obtained from

$$\frac{56}{463} = \frac{1200\,\text{bps}}{10{,}000\,\text{bps}}$$

Therefore, the throughput is 1200 bps (baseband rate).

15.2.3 Word Error Rate Calculation

The WER can be calculated as follows. We may use a DPSK system because it has a general but simple analytic formula, more general than Eq. (15.2-2b)

$$\langle p_e \rangle = \tfrac{1}{2} \left(\frac{1}{\Gamma + 1} \right)^M \qquad (15.2\text{-}4)$$

where M is the number of diversity branches. It is difficult to obtain the WER from the correlation coefficient in the bit stream at a specific vehicle speed because the correlation coefficients of any two bits among all the bits in a word at that particular speed form a correlation coefficient matrix which is difficult to handle. Fortunately, we can find two extreme values, one at the speed $V \to \infty$ and the other at the speed $V \to 0$. The calculations are described in detail in Ref. 3. Here we are simply illustrating the results.[4]

The performance of word error rates is shown in Fig. 15.2 for two cases: (1) no error correction and (2) one error correction. We have noticed that without redundancy (no repeat), the WER of a fast-fading case is worse than that of a slow-fading case. The WER obtained from a finite speed will lie between these two curves.

When a redundancy scheme is applied (Fig. 15.2a), that is, repeating K times and making a majority voting on each bit, the WER of a slow-fading case becomes worse than that of a fast-fading case. This change in WER provides a great improvement in performance. Therefore, a redundancy scheme is of value in a mobile radio environment with a variable vehicle speed. This phenomenon is also illustrated in Fig. 15.2b for a 1-bit error correction code. Figure 15.3a and b shows the WER for two-branch diversity. Figure 15.3a is WER with no error correction code, and Fig. 15.3b is WER with one error correction code. Further

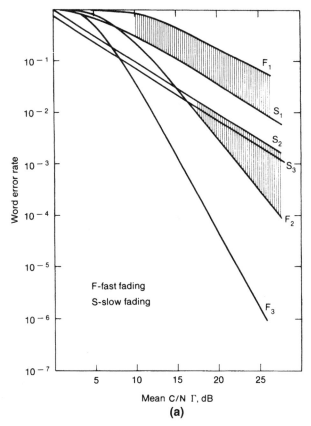

FIGURE 15.2 Word error rate for $N = 40$ bits. Number of branches $M = 1$; S_1, F_1, no repeat ($K = 1$); S_2, F_2 two-thirds voting ($K = 3$); S_3, F_3 three-fifths voting ($K = 5$). (*a*) Case 1: $M = 1$, $t = 0$. No error correction.

improvements are seen in the figure. The error correction code and the diversity plus the redundancy provide a desired signaling performance.

15.2.4 Parity Check Bits

In this section, we illustrate the generation of parity check bits in a word. Let a word of (7, 4) be generated with 4 bits of information and a 3-bit parity check. The word matrix $[C]$ can be expressed as

$$[C] = [x_m][G] \qquad (15.2\text{-}5)$$

where $[x_m]$ is the information matrix and $[G]$ is the generation matrix. Let $[G]$ have the following form.

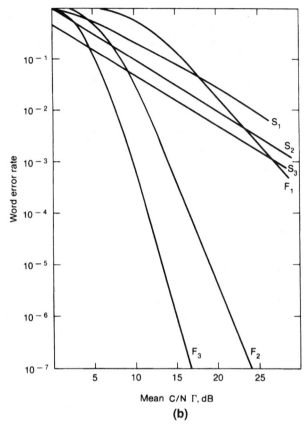

Word error rate

Mean C/N Γ, dB

(b)

FIGURE 15.2 *(Continued)* (*b*) Case 2: $M = 1$, $t = 1$. One-bit error correction.

$$[G] = \begin{bmatrix} 1000 & 101 \\ 0100 & 111 \\ 0010 & 110 \\ 0001 & 001 \end{bmatrix} = [IP] \qquad (15.2\text{-}6)$$

Identity   Parity

The parity matrix of three bits can be arranged in any order and have any combination of 0s and 1s. For example, let $[x_m] = 1001$, then substituting $[x_m]$ and Eq. (15.2-6) into Eq. (15.2-5) yields

5th 6th 7th

$$[G] = [1001] \begin{bmatrix} 1000 & 1 & 0 & 1 \\ 0100 & 1 & 1 & 1 \\ 0010 & 1 & 1 & 0 \\ 0001 & 0 & 1 & 1 \end{bmatrix} = [1001\ C_5 C_6 C_7]$$

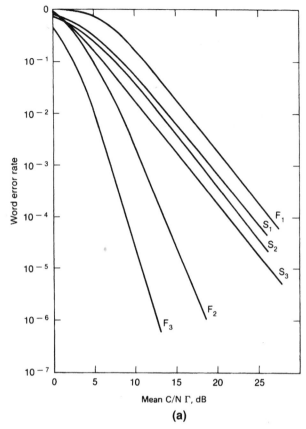

(a)

FIGURE 15.3 Word error rate for $N = 40$ bits. Number of branches $M = 2$; S_1, F_1, no repeat ($K = 1$); S_2, F_2 two-thirds voting ($K = 3$); S_3, F_3 three-fifths voting ($K = 5$). (*a*) Case 3: $M = 2$, $t = 0$. No error correction.

Then C_5 can be obtained by multiplying the fifth column by $[x_m]$ and applying modulo 2 addition* as

$$C_5 = 1 \cdot 1 + 0 \cdot 1 + 0 \cdot 1 + 1 \cdot 0 = 1 + 0 + 0 + 0 = 1$$

The same process is applied to C_6 and C_7 as

$$C_6 = 0 + 0 + 0 + 1 = 1 \qquad C_7 = 1 + 0 + 0 + 1 = 0$$

Therefore the information fits (1001), along with the three parity check bits, become a word (1001110).

---

*Modulo 2 additions;

$$1 + 1 = 0 \qquad 1 + 0 = 1 \qquad 0 + 0 = 0 \qquad 0 + 1 = 1$$

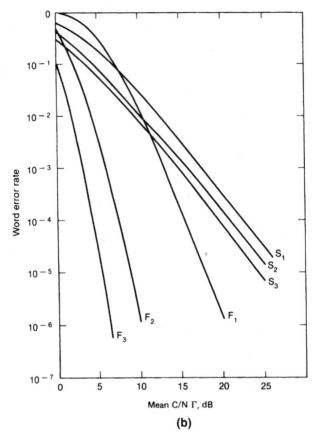

FIGURE 15.3   (*Continued*) (*b*) Case 4: $M = 2$, $t = 1$. One-bit error correction.

15.3   MEASUREMENT OF AVERAGE RECEIVED LEVEL AND LEVEL CROSSINGS

15.3.1   Calculating Average Signal Strength[5,6]

The signal strength can be averaged properly to represent a true local mean $m(x)$ to eliminate the Rayleigh fluctuation and retain the longterm fading information due to the terrain configuration. Let $\hat{m}(x)$ be the estimated local mean. If a length of data L is chosen properly, $\hat{m}(x)$ will approach $m(x)$ as

$$\hat{m}(x) = \frac{1}{2L} \int_{x-L}^{x+L} r(y)\, dy = \frac{1}{2L} \int_{x-L}^{x+L} m(y) r_0(y)\, dy$$

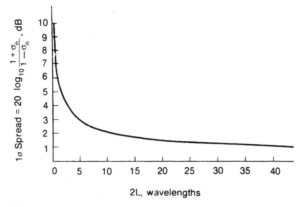

FIGURE 15.4 The value of $1\sigma_{\hat{m}}$ spread.

$$= m(x) \left[\frac{1}{2L} \int_{x-L}^{x+L} r_0(y) \, dy \right] = m(x) \tag{15.3-1}$$

or

$$\frac{1}{2L} \int_{x-L}^{x+L} r_0(y) \, dy \rightarrow 1 \tag{15.3-2}$$

where $r_0(y)$ is a Rayleigh distributed variable. If the value of Eq. (15.3-2) is close to 1, then $\hat{m}(x)$ is close to $m(x)$. The spread of $\hat{m}(x)$, denoted as $\sigma_{\hat{m}}$, can be expressed as

$$1\sigma_{\hat{m}} \text{ spread} = 20 \log \frac{m(x) + \sigma_{\hat{m}}}{m(x) - \sigma_{\hat{m}}} \quad \text{in dB} \tag{15.3-3}$$

Equation (15.3-3) is plotted in Fig. 15.4. The $1\sigma_{\hat{m}}$ spread is used to indicate the uncertainty range of a measured mean value from a true mean value if the length of the data record is inadequate.

***15.3.1.1 The Proper Length* 2L.** If we are willing to tolerate $1\sigma_{\hat{m}}$ spread in a range of 1.56 dB, then $2L = 20\lambda$. If the tolerated spread is in a range of 1 dB, then $2L = 40\lambda$.

For length $2L$ less than 20 wavelengths, the $1\sigma_{\hat{m}}$ spread begins to increase quickly. When length $2L$ is greater than 40λ, the $1\sigma_{\hat{m}}$ spread decreases very slowly.

In addition, the mobile radio signal contains two kinds of statistical distributions: $m(y)$ and $r_0(y)$. If a piece of signal data $r(y)$ is averaged, we find that if the length is shorter than 40λ, the unwanted $r_0(y)$ may be retained whereas at lengths above 40λ smoothing out of long-term fading $m(y)$ information may result. Therefore, 20 to 40λ is the proper length for averaging the Rayleigh fading signal $r(y)$.

15.3.1.2 Sampling Average. As mentioned previously, when using the averaging process with a filter, it is difficult to control bandwidth even when the length of the data to be integrated is appropriate. Therefore, the sample values of $r(t)$ are used for sampling

---

*The detailed derivation is shown in W. C. Y. Lee, *Mobile Communications Design Fundamentals*, John Wiley & Sons, 1993, Sec. 2.2.2.

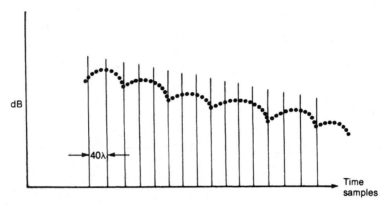

FIGURE 15.5   Sample average over $2L = 40\ \lambda$ of data.

averaging instead of analog (continuous waveform) averaging. Then we must determine how many samples need to be digitized across a signal length of $2L$ (see Fig. 15.5). The number of samples taken for averaging should be as small as possible. However, we have to calculate how many sample points are needed for adequate results. We set a confidence level of 90 percent and determine the number of samples required for the sampling average. The general formula is

$$P\left(-1.65 \le \frac{\bar{r}_j - \hat{m}_j}{\hat{\sigma}_j} \le 1.65\right) = 90\%\qquad(15.3\text{-}4)$$

Let $\hat{m}_j$ and $\hat{\sigma}_j$ be the mean and the standard deviation of ensemble average* $\bar{r}_j$ of jth interval $(2L)$ and r_j be a Gaussian variable

$$\hat{\sigma} = \frac{\sigma_r}{N}\qquad \hat{m} = m$$

where m and σ_r are the mean and the standard deviation of a Rayleigh sample r. N is the number of samples. Therefore,[5]

$$m = \frac{\sqrt{\pi}}{2}\sqrt{\bar{r}^2}\qquad(15.3\text{-}5)$$

$$\sigma_r = \frac{\sqrt{4-\pi}}{2}\sqrt{\bar{r}^2}\qquad(15.3\text{-}6)$$

$$\frac{\sigma_r}{m} = \frac{\sqrt{4-\pi}}{\pi}\qquad(15.3\text{-}7)$$

Substitution of Eqs. (15.3-5) to (15.3-7) into Eq. (15.3-4) yields

$$P\left[\left(1 - \frac{0.8625}{\sqrt{N}}\right)m \le \bar{r}_j \le \left(1 + \frac{0.8625}{\sqrt{N}}\right)m\right] = 90\%\qquad(15.3\text{-}8)$$

---

*Time average in a mobile radio environment is an ergodic process in statistics. Therefore, the values from a time average with a proper interval and an ensemble average are the same.

Then, the 90 percent confidence interval CI expressed in decibels is

$$90\% CI = 20 \log \left(1 + \frac{0.8625}{\sqrt{N}} \right) \tag{15.3-9}$$

$$N = \begin{cases} 50 & 90\% CI = 1\,\text{dB} \\ 36 & 90\% CI = 1.17\,\text{dB} \end{cases}$$

In an interval of 40 wavelengths using between 36 and 50 samples is adequate for obtaining the local means. For frequencies lower than 850 MHz, we may have to use an interval of 20λ to obtain the local means because the terrain contour may change at distances greater than 20λ when the wavelength increases.

15.3.2 Estimating Unbiased Average Noise Levels[6]

Usually, the sampled noise in a mobile environment contains high-level impulses that are generated by the ignition noise of the gasoline engine. Although the level of these impulses is high, the pulse width of each impulse generally is very narrow (see Fig. 15.6). As a result, the energy contained in each impulse is very small and should not have any noticeable effect on changing the average power in a 0.5 s interval.

However, in a normal situation averaging a sampled noise is done by adding up the power values of all samples, including the impulse samples, and dividing the sum by the number of samples. This is called the *conventionally averaged noise power* and is denoted n_c. In this case, these impulse samples dominate the average noise calculation and result in a mean value that is not representative of the actual noise power. Use of this value affects the design requirements of the system (signaling and voice). Hence, before the following new technique was introduced, it was not known why there was no correlation between BER and signal-to-noise ratio measured in certain geographic areas. In a new statistical method

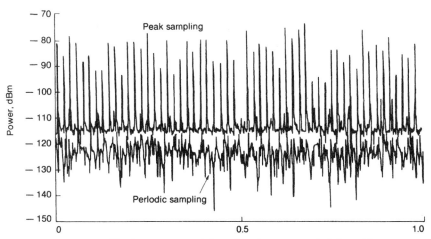

RF noise measurements form Newark—one second of elapsed time

FIGURE 15.6 Environmental noise traces.

the average noise is estimated by excluding the noise impulses while retaining other forms of interference. This technique is compatible with real-time processing constraints.

15.3.2.1 Description of the Method. A counter in the mobile unit counts the instantaneous noise measurements which fall below a preset threshold level X_t and sends a message containing the number of counts n to the database for recording. From the database data, we can calculate the percentage of noise samples x_i below the present level X_t

$$P(x_i \leq X_t) = \frac{n}{N} \tag{15.3-10}$$

where in our case N is the total number of samples. Once we know the percentage of noise samples below level X_t, we can obtain the average "noise" X_0 exclusive of the noise spikes from the Rayleigh model. Furthermore the level X_t can be appropriately selected for both noise and signal measurements, because both band-limited noise and mobile radio fading follow the same Rayleigh statistics.

15.3.2.2 Estimating the Average Noise X_0. For a Rayleigh distribution (band-limited noise), the average noise power exclusive of the noise spikes X_0 can be obtained from

$$X_0 = 10 \log \left\{ -\frac{1}{\ln\left[1 - P(x_i \leq X_t)\right]} \right\} + X_t \quad \text{dBm} \tag{15.3-11}$$

This technique can be illustrated graphically using Rayleigh paper. Because $P(x_i \leq X_t)$ is known for a given X_t, we can find a point P_t on the paper as illustrated in Fig. 15.7. Through that point, we draw a line parallel to the slope of the Rayleigh curve and meet the line of $P = 63$ percent. This crossing point corresponds to the X_0 level (unbiased average power in decibels over 1 mW, dBm).

EXAMPLE 15.7 *If a total number of samples is 256 and 38 samples are below a level -119 dBm, then the percentage is*

$$\frac{38}{256} = 15\%$$

Draw a line at 15 percent and meet at Q on the Rayleigh curve (see Fig. 15.7). Assume that the X_t is -119 dBm. The X_0 is the average power because 63 percent of the sample is below that level. Then

$$X_0 = X_t + 4 \, \text{dB} = -119 + 4 = -115 \, \text{dBm}$$

EXAMPLE 15.8 *The total number of samples is 256. Three noise spikes are 20 dB above the normal average. Find the errors, using the following two methods. Compare the results.*

Use geometric average method: *Let the power value of each sample (of 253 samples) after normalization be 1, that is, the average is 1. Then the measured average of 256 samples, including three spikes, is*

$$\textit{Measured average} = \frac{\sum_1^{253} x_i + 100 \sum_1^3 x_i}{256} = 2.16 \quad \textit{(assume } x_i = 1\textit{)}$$

$$= 3.3 \, \text{dB} \quad \textit{above the true average}$$

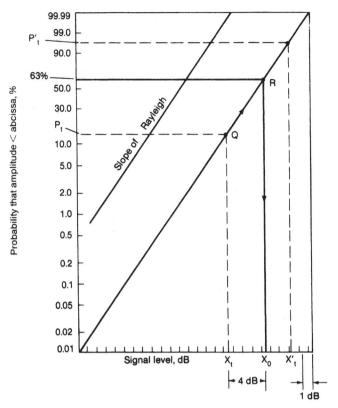

FIGURE 15.7 Technique of estimating average noise.

Statistical average method:

$$63\% \text{ of samples} = 256 \times 0.63 = 161 \text{ samples}$$

This means that 161 samples should be under the average power level. Now three noise spikes added to the 161 samples increases the number of samples to 164.

$$\frac{164}{256} = 64\%$$

The power levels at 63 and 64 percent show almost no change (see Fig. 15.7). Typical data averaging using the geometric and statistical average methods is illustrated in Fig. 15.8. The corrected value is approximately -118 to -119 dBm. The geometric average method biases the average value and causes an unacceptable error as shown in the figure.

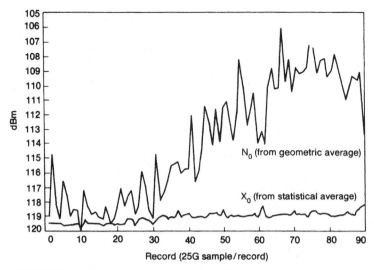

FIGURE 15.8 An illustration of comparison of n_e with x_e.

15.3.3 Signal-Strength Conversion

Confusion arises because the field strength (in decibels above 1 μV, dBμ) is measured in free space, and the power level in decibels above 1 mW (dBm) is measured at the terminal impedance of a given receiving antenna. Furthermore, the dimensions of the two units are different. The signal field strength measured on a linear scale is in microvolts per meter (μV/m), and the power level measured on a linear scale is in milliwatts (or watts).

Further confusion arises because of the notation "dBμ." Sometimes dBμ means the number of decibels above 1 μV at a given voltage. Sometimes, it represents the number of decibels referred to microvolts per meter when field strength is being measured.

The conversion from decibels (microvolts per meter, dBμ) to decibels above 1 mW (dBm) at 850 MHz is shown in Appendix D, Eq. (D-9) using the relationship between induced voltage and effective antenna length.[7] The conversion at a frequency other than 850 MHz can be obtained as follows.[8]

$$P_{\max}(\text{in dBm at} f_1 \text{MHz}) = P_{\max}(\text{in dBm at 850 MHz}) + 20 \log \left(\frac{850}{f_1} \right) \quad (15.3\text{-}12)$$

where f_1 is in megahertz. The details of this conversion are given in Appendix D.

15.3.4 Receiver Sensitivity

The sensitivity of a radio receiver is a measure of its ability to receive weak signals. The sensitivity can be expressed in microvolts or in decibels above 1 μV.

$$Y \quad \text{dB}\mu\text{V} = 20 \log (x \quad \mu\text{V}) \quad (15.3\text{-}13)$$

Also, the sensitivity can be expressed in milliwatts or dBm.

$$y \quad \text{dBm} = 10 \log (x \quad \text{mW}) \qquad (15.3\text{-}14)$$

The conversion from microvolts to decibels above 1 mW, assuming a 50-Ω terminal, has been shown in Appendix D, Eq. (D-15) as

$$0 \, \text{dB}\mu\text{V} = 10 \log \frac{(1 \times 10^{-6})^2}{50}$$

$$= -137 \, \text{dBW} = -107 \, \text{dBm} \qquad (15.3\text{-}15)$$

EXAMPLE 15.9   *A receiver has a sensitivity of 0.7 μV. What is the equivalent level in decibels above 1 mW?*

$$20 \log 0.7 = -3$$

Then 0.7 μV equals -107 dBm $-3 = -110$ dBm.

15.3.5   Level-Crossing Counter[9]

A signal fading level crossing counter will face a false-count problem as a result of the granular noise as shown in Fig. 15.9. The positive slope crossing count should be 3, but the false counts may be 12. A proposed level-crossing counter can eliminate the false counts. First, by sampling the fading signal at an interval of T seconds, we can choose the interval T such that $1/T$ is small in comparison to the fading rate. The duration of stay τ_i is measured for every sample time which is above level L and the time span until the signal drops below level L. We can also use a device for measuring the percentage of time that $y(t)$ is above L. This device may be called a level crossing counter.

Let us define

$$p = P_r[y(t) \geq L] \qquad (15.3\text{-}16)$$

and

$$q = 1 - p = P[y(t) < L] \qquad (15.3\text{-}17)$$

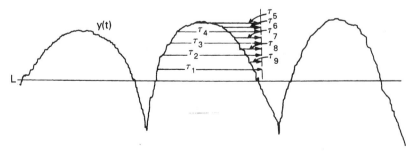

FIGURE 15.9   An algorithm for a level-crossing counter.

We count the number of times M that τ_i is above L and then sum the duration of total stays $T_s(T_s = \sum_{i=1}^{M} \tau_i)$ above L. The average duration of upward fading is

$$\tau_p = \frac{2T_s}{M} \tag{15.3-18}$$

The average duration of fades τ_q where $y(t)$ is below L is

$$\tau_q = \tau_p \frac{1-p}{p} \tag{15.3-19}$$

and the level crossing rate n at level L is

$$n = \frac{1}{\tau_p + \tau_q} = \frac{p}{\tau_p} \tag{15.3-20}$$

The advantage of this method is that we stop our time count whenever $y(t)$ crosses L, thus avoiding false counts due to noise when $y(t)$ is close to level L. Obviously noise can give an incorrect measure of the "duration of stay" for a single interval; however, noise shortens many intervals while it lengthens others, and thus, when averaged over many cycles, the "duration of stay" is an accurate number.

15.4 SPECTRUM EFFICIENCY EVALUATION

15.4.1 Spectrum Efficiency for Analog Cellular Systems[10]

Because the frequency spectrum is a limited resource, we should utilize it very effectively. In order to approach this goal, spectrum efficiency should be clearly defined from either a total system point of view or a fixed point-to-point link perspective. For most radio systems, spectrum efficiency is the same as channel efficiency, the maximum number of channels that can be provided in a given frequency band. This is true for a point-to-point system that does not reuse frequency channels such as a cellular mobile radio. An appropriate definition of spectrum efficiency for cellular mobile radio is the number of channels per cell. Therefore, in cellular mobile radio systems:

Spectrum efficiency $\neq$ channel efficiency

The system capacity is directly related to spectrum efficiency but not to channel efficiency.

In 1985, there was a dispute on whether FM or SSB should be the choice of modulation for analog cellular systems.[10] Because in analog cellular systems, the spectrum efficiency can be achieved by applying frequency reuse scheme, then cochannel interference due to assigning the same frequency for two users arises. The reduction of cochannel interference in analog system can only be resolved by making the geographical separation of two cochannels.

Based on this argument, we found that FM is superior to SSB as described in the following section. This analysis does not apply to digital systems. In Sec. 15.5, we will evaluate the spectrum efficiency between CDMA and OFDMA.

15.4.2 Advantages and Impact of FM

In 1936, E. H. Armstrong published a paper entitled "*A Method of Reducing Disturbance in Radio Signaling by a System of Frequency Modulation.*"[11] This paper explored the trade-offs between noise and bandwidth in FM radio. Since then, engineers have understood the concept of reducing noise by increasing bandwidth in system design.

The parameters for system comparison are *voice quality, transmitted power*, and *cell size*. Satisfactory voice quality is generally accepted as governed by the carrier-to-noise ratio $C/N_{FM} = 18$ dB.* This is the level at which 75 percent of the users state that voice quality is either good or excellent in 90 percent of the service area on a 30-kHz FM channel in a multipath fading environment.[12] For point-to-point radio links, the wider the channel bandwidth, the lower the required level of transmitted power.

To maintain voice quality when channel bandwidth is reduced, it is necessary to increase the signal-to-noise ratio in order to improve the reception. Transmission power is then also increased.

Every time power is increased, interference problems are created. For point-to-point radio links, these problems are manageable because no frequency reuse is involved. This is not the case, however, for a frequency-reuse system such as a cellular radio. A cellular radio telephone system includes many mobile-unit customers and, depending on demand at any given time in a given system, identical channels will be operating simultaneously in different geographic locations. As the number of cells increases in a given area, interference may appear in one of several forms: cochannel, adjacent-channel, or multichannel at colocations; thus the probability of its occurrence increases. Interference may also result from received power-level differences. In a frequency-reuse system, however, cochannel separation is more critical to the system than adjacent-channel interference because adjacent-channel interference may be eliminated by the use of sharp filters.

15.4.3 Number of Frequency-Reuse Cells K

The formula for determining the number of frequency-reuse cells in a standard cellular configuration is derived by combining Eqs. (2.7-3) and (2.7-5) with $\gamma = 4$ based on the 40 dB/dec path-loss rule.[13]

$$\frac{C}{I} = \frac{1}{6}\left(\frac{D}{R}\right)^4 = \frac{(3K)^2}{6} = \frac{3K^2}{2} \tag{15.4-1}$$

or

$$K = \sqrt{\frac{2}{3}\frac{C}{I}} \tag{15.4-2}$$

The number of frequency-reuse cells is a function of the required carrier-to-interference ratio.

A higher required carrier-to-interference ratio at the boundary of a cell results in the need for more frequency-reuse cells. The pattern of reuse cells can then be determined.

---

* If we use values other than 18 dB, the analysis used in this section remains the same.

15.4.4 Number of Channels per Cell *m*

The next factor to be determined is the number of channels per cell, which is a function of the total number of channels available (amount of available spectrum divided by channel bandwidth) and the required carrier-to-interference ratio. The formula for this factor is[10]

$$m = \frac{B_t}{B_c K} = \frac{B_t}{B_c \sqrt{(2/3)(C/I)}} \tag{15.4-3}$$

for $M = mK$ total number of channels,

where m = number of channels per cell, also called radio capacity by Lee[10]
  K = number of frequency-reuse cells (see Eq. 15.4-2)
  B_t = total bandwidth (transmitted or received)
  B_c = channel bandwidth

15.4.5 Rayleigh Fading Environment

The Rayleigh fading environment is the mobile radio environment caused by multipath fading, which is the cellular system environment. Therefore, it is more realistic to determine the spectrum efficiency of a cellular mobile radio in a Rayleigh fading environment.

In a multipath fading environment, a simple FM system that may not have either preemphasis-deemphasis or diversity schemes would receive its baseband signal-to-noise ratio (S/N), which is converted from the carrier-to-interference ratio (C/I) but S/N is 3 dB lower than C/I.[14]

15.4.5.1 System Advantages.   The FCC has released specifications that result in advantages vis à vis the signal-to-noise ratio for transceivers in the existing FM cellular system. The first advantage is preemphasis-deemphasis, which equalizes the baseband signal-to-noise ratio over the entire voice band (f_1 to f_2). We make the assumption of Gaussian noise because the interference obtained from all six cochannel interferers behaves in a noiselike manner. The improvement factor ρ_{FM}, that is, the improvement of FM with preemphasis or deemphasis over FM without them, can be calculated as follows.[15,16]

$$\rho_{FM} = \frac{(f_2/f_1)^2}{3} = \frac{(3000 \, hZ/300 \, Hz)^2}{3} = 33.3 \, (=) \, 15.2 \, dB \tag{15.4-4}$$

Another advantage is the two-branch diversity combining receiver, which is very suitable for FM and reduces multipath fading. The advantage of the two-branch diversity receiver is that the baseband signal-to-noise ratio S/N of a two-branch FM receiver shows a 8-dB improvement over the signal-to-noise ratio of a signal FM channel.

$$\left(\frac{S}{N}\right)_{2brFM} = 8 \, dB + \left(\frac{S}{N}\right)_{FM} \tag{15.4-5}$$

The existence of compandors is assumed for compressing the signal bandwidth and taking advantage of the quieting factor during pauses. However, the voice quality improvement due to the quieting factor cannot be expressed mathematically. It is understood that all the analog modulation systems use compandors.

15.4.5.2 *Present FM System.* The subjective required carrier-to-interference ratio for FM is

$$\left(\frac{C}{I}\right)_{FM} = 18\,dB\,(=)\,63.1 \tag{15.4-6}$$

The baseband signal-to-noise ratio can be obtained from the previous analysis as follows.

$$\left(\frac{S}{N}\right)_{2brFM} = -3\,dB + deemphasis\ gain + diversity\ gain + \left(\frac{C}{I}\right)_{FM}$$

$$= 38.23\,dB\,(=)\,6652.73 \tag{15.4-7}$$

The signal-to-noise value $S/N = 38$ dB is a reasonable figure for obtaining good quality at the baseband.[17] The notation (=) means a conversion between decibels and a linear ratio.

15.4.5.3 *SSB Systems.* Single-sideband receivers, best case, have a carrier-to-interference ratio equal to the signal-to-noise ratio at baseband since SSB is a linear modulation.[17] The term "best case" means that the signal fades are completely removed, that is, the environment approaches a Gaussian.* There is no advantage in using diversity schemes in a Gaussian environment. If the environment is Rayleigh, the carrier-to-interference ratio must always be higher than that in a Gaussian environment in order to obtain the same voice quality at the baseband. An explanation is given in Sec. 15.4.7. To obtain a similar voice quality, the signal-to-noise ratio of both FM and SSB systems at the baseband should be the same.[18] The formula used to determine the required C/I of SSB is

$$\left(\frac{C}{I}\right)_{SSB} = \left(\frac{S}{N}\right)_{SSB} = \left(\frac{S}{N}\right)_{2brFM} = 38.23\,dB\,(=)\,6652.73$$

This means that the required 38.23-dB carrier-to-interference ratio of 38.23 dB for an SSB system (see Sec. 15.4.7) is equivalent to the required carrier-to-interference ratio of 18 dB for an FM system for equivalent voice quality. The number of channels per cell and the number of channels per square mile for the system can then be calculated.

15.4.5.4 *Number of Channels per Cell* **m.** The preceding analysis gives us the information needed to determine the number of channels per cell. Assuming $B_t = 10$ MHz, the formula in [from Eq. (15.4-3)]

$$m = \frac{B_t}{B_c K} = \frac{10\ MHz}{B_c\sqrt{(2/3)(C/I)}} \tag{15.4-8}$$

Given a total bandwidth (B_t) of 10 MHz, $C/I = 18$ dB for FM, and $C/I = 38.23$ dB for SSB, it is possible to determine the number of channels per cell m by the substitution of the above values in Eq. (15.4-8) and shown in Table 15.1. As this table shows, FM cellular systems need fewer cells than do SSB systems to provide quality voice service.

There is a dispute as to whether at 800 MHz, an SSB system needs a C/N of 38 dB or less to provide an S/N of 38 dB at the baseband.[19-22] Because there is no commercial 800-MHz SSB system, no subjective test can be used for SSB voice quality. Comparing the performance of an existing FM system to that of a nonexisting SSB system is difficult. Also, it is not proper to use the results from a 150-MHz SSB system without making a

---

* SSB systems at 800 MHz have not been commercially available because of technical difficulties. It is assumed here that an ideal SSB at 800 MHz can be built for mobile radios.

TABLE 15.1   Channels per Cell (Rayleigh Fading Environment)

System	Bandwidth B_c, kHz	Cells per Set, K	Total Number of Channels, B_t/B_c	Channels per Cell, m
FM	30.0	7	333	47.57
SSB	7.5	68	1333	20.00
SSB	5.0	66	2000	30.0
SSB	3.0	66	3333	50.05

thorough subjective test in a Rayleigh fading environment* and applying it to a 800-MHz SSB system.

15.4.6 Determination of Cell Size

It is possible to determine the size of comparable cells for 30-kHz FM, 3-kHz SSB, 5-kHz SSB, and 7.5-kHz SSB once the number of frequency-reuse cells and the number of channels per cell have been calculated. These values are related to the level of carrier power required at reception to maintain similar voice quality. Because SSB has a relatively narrow bandwidth, the noise level is also lower. The SSB noise level must be adjusted to the FM noise level in order to determine the power required for SSB.

15.4.6.1   Required Power in Each SSB System.   The SSB required carrier-to-interference ratio must be 38.23 dB. Therefore, the power required by the SSB system after the noise level (including interference) has been adjusted can then be determined. The voice quality of an SSB system having a carrier-to-interference ratio of 38.23 dB is equivalent to an FM system having a carrier-to-interference ratio of 18 dB. This assumes that in-band pilot tones can smooth out the fading signal and causes no distortion in SSB reception. The noise levels of different SSB bandwidths can be shown as follows.

$$\left(\frac{C}{I}\right)_{SSB} = 38.23 \text{ dB}$$

$$\left(\frac{C}{I}\right)_{SSB\,3kHz} = 10.23 \text{ dB} + 18 \text{ dB} + 10 \text{ dB}$$

$$\left(\frac{C}{I}\right)_{SSB\,5kHz} = 12.45 \text{ dB} + 18 \text{ dB} + 7.74 \text{ dB}$$

$$\left(\frac{C}{I}\right)_{SSB\,7.5kHz} = 14.21 \text{ dB} + 18 \text{ dB} + 6.02 \text{ dB}$$

These figures are illustrated clearly in Fig. 15.10.

---

* Air-to-ground communications media do not exhibit Rayleigh fading behavior. Also, the required C/I of SSB at 800 MHz would be different from that at 150 MHz.

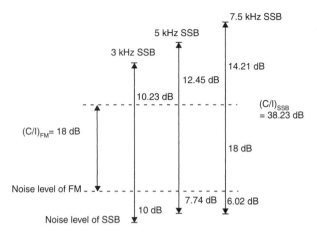

FIGURE 15.10 The interference-plus-noise levels for 30-kHz FM and different bandwidths of SSB.

15.4.6.2 SSB Cell Size Determined for the Required Additional Power.
For a given transmitted power, the cell size can be determined. Assuming an FM cell radius of 10 mi and applying the 40 dB/dec path-loss rule, the cell sizes for an SSB system may be determined as follows.

For 3-kHz SSB system

$$10 \log \left(\frac{10^{-4}}{R^{-4}} \right) = -10.23 \text{ dB} \qquad R = 5.55 \text{ mi}$$

For a 5-kHz SSB system

$$10 \log \left(\frac{10^{-4}}{R^{-4}} \right) = -12.45 \text{ dB} \qquad R = 4.88 \text{ mi}$$

For a 7.5-kHz SSB system

$$10 \log \left(\frac{10^{-4}}{R^{-4}} \right) = -14.21 \text{ dB} \qquad R = 4.41 \text{ mi}$$

The higher the carrier-to-interference ratio for a given power, the closer the mobile unit is to the cell. Assuming the same voice quality at the boundary of the cell, a 10-mi-radius FM 30-kHz cell is equivalent to a 5.5-mi 3-kHz SSB cell, a 4.88-mi 5-kHz SSB cell, or a 4.41-mi 7.5-kHz SSB cell. Therefore, an FM system permits larger cells and an SSB system requires smaller cells to provide for the same voice quality in the same area.

15.4.6.3 Comparison of Cochannel Cell Separation and Radius of FM and SSB Systems in a Rayleigh Fading Environment.
The cochannel cell separations and the radii of both FM and SSB cells in a Rayleigh fading environment are summarized in Table 15.2 and expressed in Fig. 15.11. Therefore, in a cellular mobile radio environment, a FM system *permits* larger cells with less separation between cochannel cells and a SSB system requires smaller cells with greater separation between cochannel cells.

TABLE 15.2 Comparison of Cochannel Cell Separation and Radius of FM and SSB Systems in a Rayleigh Fading Environment

System	Cells per Set K	Radius R, mi	Diameter D, mi	D/R	Bandwidth, kHz
FM	7	10	46	4.6	30
SSB	66.6	5.6	77.77	14.14	3
		4.88	69	14.14	5
		4.41	62.36	14.14	7.5

15.4.6.4 Channels per Square Mile. Table 15.3 shows a comparison of the channels per square mile and the spectrum efficiency of each system in the Rayleigh fading environment based on equivalent voice quality and a given transmitted power. This comparison shows that the existing 30-kHz FM cellular system is about as spectrally efficient as the hypothetical 3-kHz SSB system and much more efficient than either of the two SSB (5- or 7.5-kHz) systems offering a voice quality similar to that proposed for commercial service.

15.4.7 Considerations of SSB Systems in a Rayleigh Fading Mobile Radio Environment

The voice signal requires about a S/N ratio of 40-dB output at the baseband for high quality.[23] Our baseband S/N ratio is calculated to be 38 dB, which is very close to 40 dB.

In a Gaussian environment, if the output S/N of a SSB signal at the baseband is 38 dB, then the S/N at the RF is also 38 dB because SSB is linearly modulated.[17] Now, in a Rayleigh fading environment, the received signal can be further degraded as a result of the multipath fading. Therefore, in order to maintain the baseband S/N at 38 dB, we may need to receive a signal much higher than 38 dB if no diversity scheme is implemented. How high the C/I level at RF should be cannot be determined unless the SSB mobile radio at 800 MHz is realized and a subjective test is done. Because a single-branch SSB cannot be used in a mobile radio environment at 800 MHz because of rapid fading,[24] the value

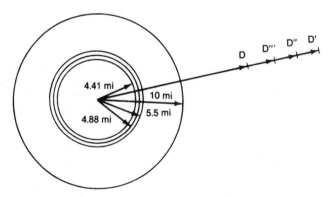

FIGURE 15.11 Cochannel cell separations and radii of FM and SSB systems in a Rayleigh fading environment.

TABLE 15.3 Comparison of System Efficiency and Spectrum Efficiency in an Area of 10-mi Radius

System	Bandwidth, mhz	Cell Radius, mi	No. of Cells Required	Channels per Cell, m	No. of Channels per Square Mile
			System Efficiency	Spectrum Efficiency	
FM	30	10	1.0	47.5	0.15
SSB	7.5	4.4	$\left(\dfrac{10}{4.4}\right)^2 = 5.17$	20.0	0.06
SSB	5	4.8	$\left(\dfrac{10}{4.8}\right)^2 = 4.34$	30.0	0.10
SSB	3	5.5	$\left(\dfrac{10}{5.5}\right)^2 = 3.31$	50.0	0.16

of applying a two-branch diversity to the SSB at 800 MHz also must be questioned. Our reasoning is as follows.

Let S_0 be a voice signal, r_1 and r_2 the envelopes of the fading, θ_1 and θ_2 the random phases received by two spaced antennas, and ω_0 the carrier angular frequency. Where an equal-gain combined receiver is considered, in an SSB system the combined signal envelope is

$$r = \left| r_1 S_0 e^{j(\omega_0 t + \theta_1)} \right| + \left| r_2 S_0 e^{j(\omega_0 t + \theta_2)} \right|$$

$$= r_1 S_0 + r_2 S_0 = (r_1 + r_2) S_0 \qquad (15.4\text{-}9)$$

which is the same as the baseband signal representation. The term $(r_1 + r_2)$ does reduce the fading as compared to either individual r_1 or r_2 to a certain degree, but it also acts as a distortion term to S_0. The distortion of voice S_0 on $(r_1 + r_2)$ received by a two-branch diversity receiver for SSB in a ground mobile radio (Rayleigh) environment is still quite high at 800 MHz. This is because the effect of fading is multiplicative and produces intermodulation products with the signal modulation that cannot be eliminated by filtering.[25] In air-to-ground transmission, the direct-wave path dominates, the fading phenomenon (rician) is not severe, and a two-branch diversity does help in improving the voice quality at the reception.

An amplitude companding single sideband (ACSB) with an in-band pilot tone is considered[26] under the assumption that this kind of SSB can in principle completely remove the Rayleigh fading; therefore, no diversity scheme* is needed. Then we do not require an increase in the received power level at the RF, but rather simply retain the same level as the baseband S/N ratio of 38.23 dB.

Preemphasis and deemphasis are not widely used in SSB systems. The disadvantage of the use for SSB systems in a nonfading environment is discussed by Schwartz[27] and Gregg.[28]

In a mobile radio environment, in order to transmit a predistorted SSB signal using preemphasis to suppress the noise level, the signal cannot be completely restored because the effect of fading is multiplicative and it produces intermodulation products in the voice

---

*The diversity scheme is used to eliminate fading.

band that cannot be eliminated by filtering as mentioned before. Therefore, the use of preemphasis and deemphasis in an 800-MHz SSB mobile radio system is questionable.

Reference 18 shows that an RF signal with required $C/I = 38$ dB received by a SSB system through a Gaussian environment results in a baseband signal where $S/N = 38$ dB also. In a Rayleigh fading environment, the C/I must definitely be higher than 38 dB for S/N to be 38 dB. How high is not known because 800-MHz SSB equipment has not been manufactured. We may use the information obtained from a FM system for maintaining the same voice quality in different environments.

$$\text{Required for FM in a Gaussian environment} \qquad \frac{C}{I} \geq \begin{cases} 10\ \text{dB} \\ 18\ \text{dB} \end{cases}$$
Required for FM in a Rayleigh fading environment

The difference in C/I for the FM system between the two kinds of environment is 8 dB. We may use the 8-dB difference and add it to $C/I = 38$ dB for an SSB system. Then

$$\text{For SSB in a Rayleigh fading environment} \qquad \frac{C}{I} = 46\ \text{dB}$$

Suppose that a diversity scheme is used in SSB as Shivley[21] suggested. Then, C/I for SSB in a less-fading (or no-fading) environment is

$$\frac{C}{I} - 8\ \text{dB} = 38\ \text{dB}$$

The same result is obtained if we assume that the fading is completely removed, $C/I = S/I$, and that the environment becomes Gaussian. In a Gaussian environment, we cannot, reduce C/I below 38 dB, because S/N is 38 dB. Also, in a Gaussian environment, the diversity scheme does not apply and adds no value.

Of course, the analysis shown here remains to be proved if and when an 800-MHz SSB mobile unit is developed in the future. After all, the methodology of solving this problem remains unchanged.

15.4.8   Narrowbanding in FM

*15.4.8.1   Relationship between **C/I** at IF and **S/N** at Baseband.*   In Ref. 12, we defined acceptable voice quality as existing when 75 percent of customers say that the voice quality is good or excellent in a 90 percent coverage area. When these numbers change, voice quality changes accordingly. The changes reflect the cost of deploying a cellular system. As the percentages specified above increase, the cost of designing the system to meet these requirements also increases. For now, we will use the numbers specified above as our criteria.

We let the customer listen to the voice quality of a 30-kHz FM two-branch diversity receiver with preemphasis-deemphasis and companding (compressing and expanding) features at the cell site while the mobile transmitter is traveling at speeds ranging from 0 to 60 mi/h in a Rayleigh environment. Judging by the preceding subjective criterion, the C/I level at the input of the receiver is 18 dB.

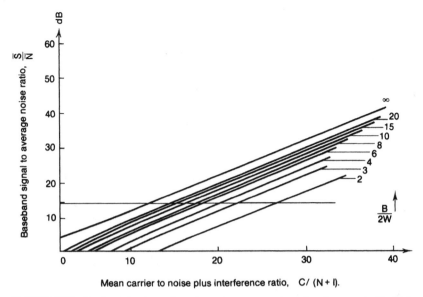

FIGURE 15.12 Baseband signal-to-noise ratio versus average carrier-to-interference ratio (Rayleigh fading). (*From Ref. 29.*)

The baseband signal-to-noise ratio (S/N) has been calculated in Eq. (15.4-7).

$$S/N = \underbrace{18 - 3}_{\text{Rayleigh environment}} + \underbrace{15.23}_{\text{deemphasis advantage}} + \overset{\text{diversity advantage}}{8} = 38.24 \text{ dB}$$

For a 15-kHz FM channel, the bandwidth is half as broad and affects the S/N; the other features, such as diversity and preemphasis-deemphasis, remain the same. We can find from Fig. 15.12 (Ref. 29) that in order to maintain the same voice quality of $(C/I)_{30\,\text{kHz}} = 18$ db, then

$$\left(\frac{C}{I}\right)_{15\,\text{kHz}} = 24 \text{ dB}$$

We may follow the same steps used in Sec. 15.4.6 along with the diagram shown in Fig. 2.16.

$$\frac{C}{N+1} = \frac{C}{(kTB + NF) + \sum_{i=1}^{6} I_i}$$

$$= 24 \text{ dB (15-kHz FM) or 18 dB (30-kHz FM)} \qquad (15.4\text{-}10)$$

Using the techniques from previous sections, we can perform further calculations.

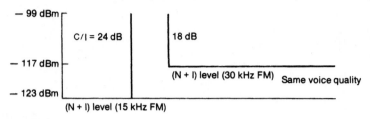

FIGURE 15.13 The interference-plus-noise levels for 30- and 15-kHz FM channels.

15.4.8.2 The Interference-Plus-Noise Levels.
From the preceding calculations Eq. (15.4-10), we can obtain the interference-plus-noise levels $(N + I)$ at the boundary of a 10-mi-radius cell as follows.

$$\text{For 30-kHz FM system} \quad N + I = -117 \text{ dBm}$$
$$\text{For 15-kHz FM system} \quad N + I = -123 \text{ dBm}$$

Because the received signal strength is -99 dBm for both 30- and 15-kHz, the $C/(N + I)$ ratio must be 18 dB and 24 dB for 30- and 15-kHz FM, respectively, in order to maintain the same voice quality. This relationship is shown in Fig. 15.13.

15.4.8.3 The Number of Cells in a Frequency-Reuse Pattern.
Let K be the number of cells in a frequency-reuse pattern; then in 30-kHz systems,

$$q = \frac{D}{R} \overset{\Delta}{=} \sqrt{3K} = 4.6$$

$$K = 7 \qquad \text{(for both noise-neglected and noise-included cases)}$$

For a seven-cell reuse pattern operating in 15-kHz systems,

$$K = \frac{q^2}{3} \begin{cases} = 13 & (q = 6.23) & \text{(noise-neglected case)} \\ = 16 & (q = 7.08) & \text{(noise-included case)} \end{cases}$$

A 13- to 16-cell reuse pattern is needed.

15.4.8.4 Intersystem Comparison of Spectrum Efficiency.
If both the noise-included and the noise-neglected cases are considered, then

$$K = \begin{cases} 7 & \text{(30-kHz FM system, both noise-included and} \\ & \text{noise-neglected cases)} \\ 16 & \text{(15-kHz FM system, noise-included case)} \\ 13 & \text{(15-kHz FM system, noise-neglected case)} \end{cases}$$

The spectrum efficiency for both systems can be shown to be about the same as follows:

$$\frac{333}{7} = 47.5 \text{ channels per cell} \qquad \text{(30-kHz FM)}$$

$$\frac{666}{16} = 41.63 \text{ channels per cell} \qquad \text{(15-kHz FM, noise-included case)}$$

$$\frac{666}{13} = 51.2 \text{ channels per cell} \quad (15 \text{ kHz FM, noise-neglected})$$

15.4.8.5   Increasing Spectrum Efficiency by Degrading Voice Quality. If we accept $C/I = 18$ dB for 15-kHz FM, this means that voice quality is degraded by 6 dB. Then the cochannel interference reduction factor q becomes approximately 4.6, corresponding to a frequency-reuse pattern of $K = 7$. Because the frequency channel is doubled, in a 10-MHz system (666 channels)

$$\frac{666}{7} = 2 \times \text{(number of 30-kHz FM channels per cell)}$$

Therefore, voice quality is sacrificed to gain spectrum efficiency.

Another approach is to increase the transmitted power of the 15-kHz FM system by 6 dB. Then, the C/I remains the same because the interference is also increased by 6 dB. Therefore, no advantage to spectrum efficiency can be obtained by either increasing or reducing power.

15.5   EVALUATION OF SPECTRUM EFFICIENCY BETWEEN CDMA AND OFDMA

In Section 15.4, we have evaluated the spectrum efficiency between FM and SSB used for cellular systems. In an analog system, the effectiveness of reducing cochannel interference can only be achieved by increasing the geographical separations with section antennas. However, the less the separation, the higher the spectrum efficiency. There is always a struggle between the quality of the calls (increasing separation) and the capacity of system (reducing separation). In digital systems, the cochannel interference can be reduced by other means, such as codes, time, as well as frequency.

A. CDMA system

All the CDMA code-channels are shared with one broadband carrier as shown in Fig. 15.14*a*. Every cell can operate on the same CDMA carrier, that is, a $K = 1$ system. In a 1.25-MHz CDMA carrier, cdmaOne can provide 20–25 code channels per cell or per sector for voice communications because of its $K = 1$ advantage. In an AMPS system, a spectrum of 1.25 MHz can provide 42 30-KHz channels for voice. Using a frequency reuse of $K = 7$ and three sectors/cell, the number of channels per cell is two. Therefore, cdmaOne has ten times the capacity of AMPS. The CDMA voice channels are based on the 8 kbps or 13 kbps vocoder. As the transmission rate of CDMA is concerned, the EVDO can have 2.4 Mbps.

In CDMA system, the Walsh code is used for the code-spreading channel. A code length of 128 chips can have 128 codes to be used. However, the Walsh code is not a perfect code, as will be shown in Section 18.2. The multiuser interference is very high in a multipath environment. Therefore, a code length of 128 chips can only provide 20–25 code channels. Besides, in CDMA systems, only the soft handoff can be implemented.

B. OFDMA

OFDMA is subdividing a broadband carrier into many subcarriers as shown in Fig. 15.14*b*. Each subcarrier transmits a portion of data. Because the slow data rate does not cause ISI, the maximum transmission rate can be achieved using a simple equalizer.

Moreover, the orthogonality in the OFDM can increase the spectrum efficiency by doubling it, and the frequency hopping can make the OFDMA from a $K = 3$ system to a $K \to 1$ system. Also, the hard handoff can be applied in OFDMA.

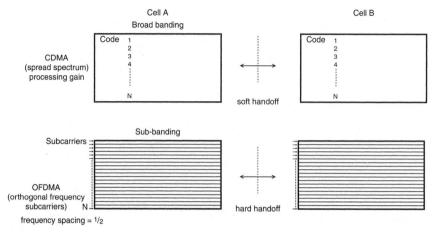

FIGURE 15.14 Comparison of CDMA and OFDMA.

C. Comparison of two systems

Assume that the two systems are using the same modulation and same smart antenna, the maximum spectrum efficiency of both systems is A.

1. If all the 128 code channels can be used in a CDMA system, the maximum spectrum efficiency (SE_1) should be denoted by A. However, the cdmaOne is suffering:

   - Due to the multiuser interference, only 30 channels can be used, $(30/128) \cdot A = 0.2344A$.
   - Due to the soft handoff is implemented, the capacity is dropped 70 percent, $(02344A) \times 0.70 = 0.164A$.

2. Because all the subcarriers of an OFDMA are used, the spectrum efficiency (SE_2) is

   - Due to the orthogonality, $2 \times A = 2A$.
   - Due to hard handoff is implemented $2A \times 1 = 2A$

3. The ratio of two systems' spectrum efficiencies (in theory) is

$$\text{Ratio of spectrum efficiency} = \frac{SE_2}{SE_1} = \frac{2A}{0.164A} = 12$$

D. Logical conclusion

We can go back to study analog signals. In Section 15.4, we realize a 2.5-kHz SSB channel can be used as a voice channel, but we use a 30-kHz FM channel as a voice channel in analog cellular systems despite that the ratio of the two channel bandwidths is 12.

In digital cellular system, when the inverse of the data rate of a narrow band digital channel is lower than the multipath delay time, then the sum of the entire narrow band channels, a broad channel, can provide the maximum data rate of the broad band channel.

15.6 HANDSETS (PORTABLE UNITS)

In the 80's, the portable units for mobile stations (MS) were very heavy to carry. They were called bag phones and used in buildings or on boats. Therefore, at the time all of the system design tools[30] were designed to improve the performance of cellular mobile units (car phones). The portable units were a secondary by-product of the cellular system. Today, the portable units are handsets due to the advanced technology. They are small in size and light in weight and used everywhere.

Due to the mobile environment changes, we have to study the interference caused by the handsets (portable units). There are two parts that need to be calculated; one is loss due to building penetration, and the other is building height effect. Before illustrating the two calculations below, the technology of handsets is described first. However, in the following sections we are using the term "portable unit" instead of the term "handset." In general, "mobile unit" means "car phone." The standard term "mobile station" covers both car phones and handsets.

15.6.1 Technology of Handsets (Portable Units)

In the 80's, the mobile stations (MS) operating in cellular systems were car phones. In the 90's, the handset phones were developed; the mobile station can either be a car phone or a handset. In the 2000's, handsets were not only used as portable units, but also to replace car phones used in a car.

To drive the MS to a small-size handset unit due to two chip technologies: RF chip and base band chip.

RF Chip Technology: Over the past two decades, microwave active circuits have evolved from individual solid-state transistors and passive elements to fully integrated planar assemblies, including active and passive components and interconnections, generically referred to as a microwave integrated circuit (MIC). In the solid state monolithic microwave integrated circuit (MMIC), all interconnections and components, both active and passive, are fabricated simultaneously on a semi-insulating semiconductor substrate (usually gallium arsenate, GaAs) using deposition and etching processes, thereby eliminating discrete components and wire bond interconnects.

Base Band Chip: It belongs to an IC (Integrated Circuit) logic family, and carries out the protocols in physical layer, MAC layer and upper layers. It is based on CMOS (Complementary Metal-Oxide Semiconductor) technology fabrications on a single chip, sometimes also called ASIC (Application Specific Integrated Circuit) chip.

15.6.2 Loss Due to Building Penetration

The loss (attenuation) when propagating an 800-MHz wave due to building penetration is very high.[31-36] Also, the structure-related attenuation varies, depending on the geographic area. In Tokyo, the path-loss difference inside and outside buildings at first-floor level is about 26 dB. But in Chicago, the path-loss difference under the same conditions is 15 dB as shown in Fig. 15.15.

These variations are attributable to differences in building construction. In Tokyo, many supporting metal frames (mesh configuration) are used in the building structures to allow the buildings to withstand earthquakes. In Chicago, fewer supporting metal frames are needed as there is less risk of earthquakes. Therefore, the *building penetration* is far less severe in Chicago than in Tokyo.

The same would apply to buildings in California. For instance, the loss due to building penetration in Los Angeles would be higher than that in Chicago but lower than that in Tokyo, because Los Angeles has only a few high-rise buildings. In Los Angeles the penetration at the first-floor level would be around −20 dB, as compared with the received signals at mobile units outside at street level.

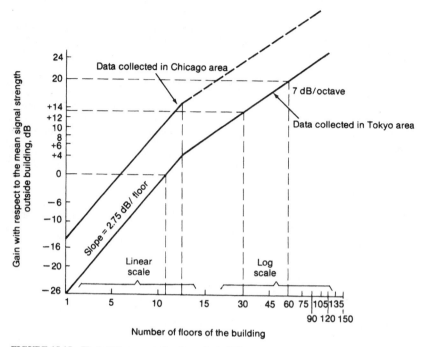

FIGURE 15.15   The building penetration losses in the Tokyo area and in the Chicago area.

Signal attenuation at the building basement level in Chicago is 30 dB below the signal received from the street-level mobile unit. This indicates that the signals do not penetrate basement structures easily. There are two ways to solve this problem.

1. Select the cell site closest to those downtown buildings used for conventions. Then calculate the received power for the portable units. Let the cell coverage be at a radial distance R, with the receiving level of $C/I = 18$ dB at the cell boundary as designed. The same site will be used for portable units. The receiving level of portable units is $C/I = 10$ dB because of the slow-motion or no-motion environment. At the basement, the reception level of a portable unit is $-30 + (18 - 10) = -22$ dB, that is, 22 dB weaker than that received at the cell boundary R. Applying Eq. (8.2-10a), we obtain

$$40 \log \frac{R_1}{R} = -22 \text{ dB} \quad \text{or} \quad R_1 = R(10^{-(22/40)}) = 0.28R \quad (15.6\text{-}1)$$

From this calculation, the region in which the portable unit can be used in the basement is confined to an area of $0.28R$.

2. Install the repeaters (or enhancers) or leaky feeders to enhance the signal strength inside the building.

15.6.3 Building Height Effect

Usually, the signal reception level increases as the height of the building where the antenna is located increases. Comparing the two measurements from Chicago and Tokyo, we find that the slope (gain increase) of 2.7 dB per floor (i.e., 2.7 dB gain per each floor-level increment) can be a good value on which to base calculations regarding suitability of portable unit usage. However, this value is valid only up to the thirteenth floor. After that, a logarithmic 7 dB/oct scale is used. Now we start at the first floor.

15.6.3.1 First-Floor Region. Following the same procedure as when calculating the signal strength in the basement region, we find the signal strength requirements at the first floor inside the building for the portable unit to be

$$-15 + (18 - 10) = -7 \text{ dB} \qquad \text{(Chicago)}$$

$$-26 + (18 - 10) = -18 \text{ dB} \qquad \text{(Tokyo)}$$

$$-20 + (18 - 10) = -12 \text{ dB} \qquad \text{(Intermediate value)}$$

Applying these findings to Eq. (15.6-1), we obtain

$$40 \log \frac{R_1}{R} = \begin{cases} -7 \text{ dB} \\ -18 \text{ dB} \\ -12 \text{ dB} \end{cases} \qquad R_1 = \begin{cases} 0.668R & \text{(Chicago)} \\ 0.35R & \text{(Tokyo)} \\ 0.5R & \text{(intermediate value)} \end{cases}$$

15.6.3.2 Nth-Floor Region. The area serviced increases as a function of height of 2.7 dB per floor below the thirteenth floor, where we see a gain increase of 2.7 dB per floor, and above the thirteenth floor, 7 dB/oct is used. We can calculate the service area in Chicago as follows.

$$40 \log \frac{R_1}{R} = -7 + N(2.7) \qquad \text{(in Chicago)}$$

where N is the number of floors. The same procedures apply to Los Angeles and Tokyo. In Table 15.4, we see that the service region increases at higher floor levels. However, after the thirteenth floor, the increase in gain is very small. The difference between the

TABLE 15.4. Building Penetration Loss

Condition	Building Penetration Loss	Shadow Loss[*]
Building penetration	+27 dB (Tokyo)	27 dB (Chicago)
	+15 dB (Chicago)	(regardless of floor height)
Window area	+6 dB	
1st–13th floors	2.75 dB/floor (Tokyo)	
	2.67 dB/floor (Chicago)	
13th–30th floors	7 dB/oct (Tokyo and Chicago)	

[*] *Shadow loss* is defined as the loss due to a building standing in the radio-wave path.

two floors from two cities becomes smaller for heights beyond the thirtieth floor (see Fig. 15.15).

15.6.4 Interference Caused by Portable Units

15.6.4.1 Interference to the Other Portable Units. The portable unit has a transmitting power of 600 mW (28 dBm). The interference at the cell site from two different portable units can be determined as follows. We now can consider interference at higher floor levels (see Fig. 15.15). We find that reception at the sixth floor is the same as that at street level in Chicago and that reception at the eleventh floor is the same as that at street level in Tokyo. Reception at the thirtieth floor in Tokyo is 13 dB higher than that at street level.

A portable unit transmitter can transmit a signal to a cell site following line-of-sight propagation. A signal from a portable unit on the thirtieth floor that is received by the cell site could interfere with the reception of a signal from a portable unit on the eleventh floor. The interference level for the portable unit on the eleventh floor is 13 dB. The interference range becomes

$$20 \log \frac{R_1}{R} = -13 \text{ dB} \qquad \text{then} \qquad R_1 = 0.22R$$

Because $R_1 = 0.22R$, the portable unit used on the thirtieth floor at the cell boundary R will not interfere with cell-site reception from a portable unit on the eleventh floor at 0.22 R away. If the power of both units can be controlled at the cell site, the near-end to far-end ratio interference of 13 dB can be reduced. We must be aware of this interference and find ways to eliminate it once we know its cause. A method for this was described in Chap. 12. The selection of a method for eliminating interference is based on environmental factors such as building height and density, which vary from area to area.

15.6.4.2 Interference to the Mobile Units (Car Phone). Now assume that at the cell boundary (the cell radius is R) the mobile unit received a signal at -100 dBm and the reception level of a portable unit at the thirtieth floor is -87 dBm ($-100 + 13$ dB). If the cell site have a 10-W transmitter and a 6-dB-gain antenna, then the transmitting site has an effective radiated power (ERP) of 46 dBm. The path loss on a thirtieth floor of the cell boundary becomes 133 dB ($46 + 87$). Now for calculating a reverse path, the portable unit has a 600-mW (28-dBm) transmitter; and the mobile unit has a 3-W (35-dBm) transmitter. Then the signal received at the 100-ft cell-site antenna is $(28 - 133) = -105$ dBm for the portable unit and $(35 - 133 - 13) = -111$ dBm for the mobile unit. The difference in received levels is 6 dB. This near-end to far-end ratio interference can be eliminated by the frequency assignment and power control of the portable units at the cell site.

15.6.5 Difference Between Mobile Cellular and Portable Cellular Systems

It is very interesting to point out the differences in characteristics, coverage charts, and system design aspects for mobile and portable cellular systems.

15.6.5.1   Different Characteristics

Mobile Units	Portable Units
Two-dimensional system	Three-dimensional system
Needs handoffs	No handoffs
Severe signal fading due to vehicle movement	No fading or mild fading if walking
Gain changes with ground elevation	Gain changes with building height
Loss due to multipath reflection	Loss due to building penetration
Required $C/I \geq 18$ dB	Required $C/I \geq 10$ dB
Power consumption is not an issue	Power consumption is a key issue
Attractive because of various features	Attractive because of their small size and light weight

15.6.5.2   Different Coverage Charts.   Using the Philadelphia path-loss curve shown in Fig. 8.3 with the standard condition parameters listed in Sec. 8.2.1, we can illustrate the differences in the coverage charts of mobile units and portable units in urban areas, as shown in Fig. 15.16. The receiver sensitivity of both units is assumed to be -117 dBm. Also assume that the required C/I of a portable unit is 10 dB, and the required C/I of a

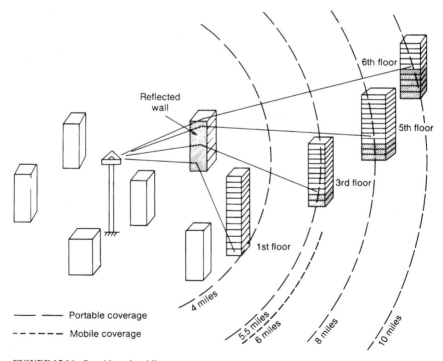

FIGURE 15.16   Portable and mobile coverage.

mobile unit is 18 dB. The mobile-unit coverage is about 6 mi, while the portable coverages differ with building height, as shown in Fig. 15.16. The higher the building, the greater the coverage range.

15.6.5.3 Different Design Concepts.

In mobile cellular systems, we try to cover the area with an adequate signal from a cell site; then transmitted power, antenna height and gain, and location are the parameters involved. Reduction of both multipath fading and cochannel interference is described in Chap. 9.

In a portable cellular system, the coverage range increases with the height of the building. Therefore, no fixed coverage range can be given for the portable units. Also the cochannel interference reduction ratio q [$q = D/R$ see Eq. (2.6-1)] for the portable cellular systems has no meaning since the cell radius R changes with building height. If we try to apply the design techniques for mobile cellular systems to portable cellular systems, the results are not very good. One way to look at this problem is that each building structure offers less interference inside the building. The lower the building, the greater the protection from interference. Therefore, we should not raise the transmitted power and try to penetrate the building; rather we should take advantage of this natural shielding environment. Thus, we should link to each repeater (enhancer) mounted at the top of each building. Because the buildings are tall, reception will be good because of the building's height, and only a small amount of transmitted power is needed at the cell site (see Fig. 15.16). If leaky cables or cables with antennas (shown in Fig. 15.17) from the repeater are connected to each floor, the signal in the whole building will be covered. This is the proper arrangement, but it is also a different concept of designing a portable cellular system.

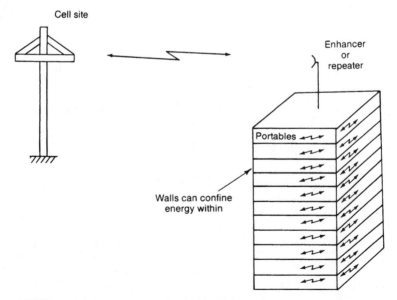

FIGURE 15.17 Proper arrangement for portable cellular system.

15.7 EVALUATION OF DATA SERVICES

15.7.1 Requirement for AMPS System

The data modem used in the current analog system must meet the following requirements.

1. Data transmissions have to use 30-kHz voice channels.
2. The SAT tone must be maintained at around 6000 Hz in voice channels. Then the transmission rate has to be either lower or higher, but it must be clear from the 6000-Hz SAT.
3. The transmission rate cannot be lower than a rate[37] that lies in the dominant random-FM region of $f_{\text{rfm}} < 2(V/\lambda)$. This specification is based on the vehicle speed V and the wavelength of the operating frequency. For instance, if $V = 104$ km/h (65 mi/h), and $\lambda = 1$ ft (at 850 MHz), then $f_{\text{rfm}} = 2(V/\lambda) = 190$ Hz. This means that the data modem transmission rate cannot be below 190 Hz because of the unique random-FM characteristics in the mobile radio environment. When the mobile unit stops, the random FM disappears.
4. The same severe fading requires us to use redundancy, coding, automatic-repeat request (ARQ) scheme, diversity, and so on when transmitting data. The current mobile cellular signaling transmission rate is 10 kbps. Using the BCH code with five repeats, the data throughput is 1200 bits. However, the power spectrum density of a 10-kbps data stream with a Manchester coding (a biphase waveform) is spread out over the 6000-Hz region.[38] If the SAT cannot be detected because of the data modem, then the data modem cannot be used.
5. Mobile unit (vehicular) speed is a significant factor.
   a. Suppose that a car can be driven slowly while approaching a stop but that it never stops. In this case, the average duration of fades is very long. Most of the time, if the word is in the fade, the whole word is undetected.
   b. Suppose that a car can travel at a rate of 104 km/h (65 mi/h). The number of level crossings at -10 dB (10 dB below average power) is 65 crossings per second, and the average duration is 1.54 ms, as mentioned in Sec. 15.2.

   Thus, a word length must be designed to fit in these two cases.
6. Handoff action is another factor in data modem design. Whenever a handoff occurs, a piece of data information is lost. The average would be 200 ms. The ARQ scheme would be useful for this purpose.
7. The data modem must satisfy a specific bit error rate (BER) and word error rate (WER) requirement. The BER is independent of vehicle speed, whereas the WER is not. The higher the throughput rate (baseband transmission rate), the higher the BER and WER. However, there are two data modem markets.
   a. Use of fast data rate: In real-time situations, a customer may need quick access to data but may not need a high degree of accuracy. Examples of such customers are police agencies, real estate agencies, and so forth.
   b. Use of accurate data: For transmitting figures requiring a high degree of accuracy, a slow data transmission rate is needed. These customers need data accuracy more than fast acquisition, as in banking or computer applications.

15.7.2 Digital Data Services

Usually, digital data services support two data service groups: short message services and bearer services. We describe the GSM short message services and GPRS bearer services in this section.

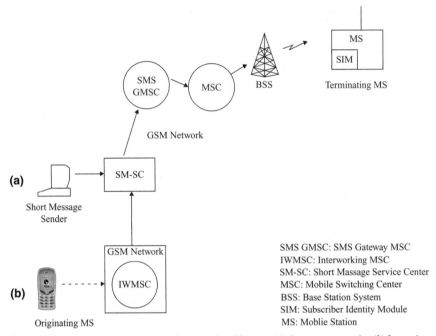

FIGURE 15.18   GSM short message service network architecture: (*a*) short message sender; (*b*) from originating MS.

A. Short message service (SMS)[39]
The GSM short message service network architecture is illustrated in Fig. 15.18.

1. Short message sender origination is shown in Fig. 15.18*a*. In this architecture, the short message is first delivered from the message sender to a short message service center (SM-SC). The SM-SC is connected to the GSM network through a specific GSM MSC called the short message service gateway MSC (SMS GMSC). The SM-SC may connect to several GSM networks and to several SMS GMSCs in a GSM network. Following the GSM roaming protocol, the SMS GMSC locates the current MSC of the message receiver and forwards the message to that MSC. The MSC broadcasts the message to the base station systems, and the base transceiver stations (BTSs) page the destination MS. The MS used for short message services must contain special software to enable the messages to be decoded and stored. Messages can be stored either in the SIM or in the memory of the mobile equipment (ME) for display on the standard screen of the MS.

2. MS origination is shown in Fig. 15.18*b*. An MS may send or reply to a short message. The message is delivered to a short message service interworking MSC (IWMSC) and then to the SM-SC. The recipient of the short message can be an MS, a fax machine, or a PC connected to the Internet. Experience indicates that mobile-originating traffic is around 20 percent of mobile-terminating traffic. Note that SMS is a store-and-forward service. Short messages cannot be sent directly from the sender to the recipient without passing through the SM-SC.

3. Types of short messages.
There are three types of short messages: user-specific, ME-specific, and SIM-specific. A user-specific message is displayed to the user. The mobile equipment,

instead of showing to the user, processes an ME-specific message and SIM-specified message.

B. Bearer services.

The GPRS bearer service architecture is shown in Fig. 15.19. GPRS is a packet-switched protocol for applications such as the Web, where the user spends most of the time reading information, and the bursty data are transferred through the link only when necessary. The GSM circuit-switching architecture cannot satisfy the packet-switching nature of GPRS. Thus, GRPS requires its own transport network as shown in Fig. 15.19.

GPRS introduces two new entities, namely, service GPRS support node (SGSN) and gateway GPRS support node (GGSN), to the GSM architecture. SGSN receives and transmits packets between the MSs and their counterparts in the public-switched data network (PSDN). GGSN interworks with the PSDN using connectionless network protocols, such as the Internet protocol and OSI connectionless network protocol, or connection-oriented protocols such as X.25. SGSN and GGSN interact with the GSM location databases, including the HLR and the VLRs, to track the location of the MSs. The GPRS data units are routed to the destination MSs based on location information. Both SGSN and GGSN may be equipped with caches containing location information to speed up the routing procedure.

GPRS air interface requires a new radio link protocol to guarantee fast call setup procedure and low-bit error rate for data transfer between the MSs and the BSs. Furthermore, GPRS needs to implement a packet radio media access control (MAC) for packet switching (see Sec. 5.1).

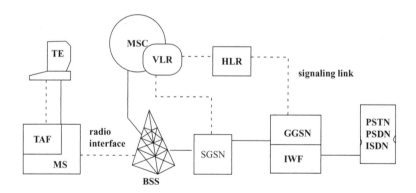

HLR: Home Location Register

VLR: Visitor Location Register

MSC: Mobile Switching Center

MS: Mobile Station (Handset)

BSS: Base Station Subsystem

TAF: Terminal Adaption Functions

SGSN: Serving GPRS Support Node

GGSN: Gateway GPRS Support Node

TE: Terminal Equipment

IWF: Interworking Functions

PSTN: Public Switched Telephone Netwrok

PSDN: Public Switched Data Network

FIGURE 15.19   GPRS architecture.

15.7.3 Testing

Any data modem operating in a cellular mobile unit must demonstrate that its BER and WER satisfy the following conditions.

1. The data modem should be tested while the mobile unit is parked (stationary) at the side of the highway. Because the mobile radio environment is very noisy, the spike noise resulting from ignition-induced combustion and the sharp fades caused by the noise of passing trucks would also affect data transmission.
2. The data modem should be tested while the mobile unit is driven at different speeds, say 5, 10, 45, and 60 mi/h at the boundary of the cell.
3. The data modem should be tested during handoff conditions.

15.8 COMPARING WiMAX AND 3G (HSDPA) FOR MOBILE BROADBAND WIRELESS

The two systems are based on two different technologies—WiMAX is based on OFDM,[40] and HSDPA is based on CDMA.[41] The spectrum efficiency comparison based on the two different technologies is shown in Section 15.5. Here we may compare the performance of the two.[42]

1. Spectrum allocation
   WiMAX can use licensed and unlicensed (2.5, 3.5, 5.8 GHz) bands, whereas HSDPA uses licensed band.
2. In multipath environment
   Since the data rate of OFDMA is slow in each subcarrier, OFDM is better at overcoming ISI (InterSymbol Interference) than CDMA.
3. Under frequency-selective fading
   Since the parallel nature of OFDMA allows errors in subcarriers to be corrected, OFDMA is more resistant to frequency-selective fading.
4. Frequency offset and phase noise
   Although OFDMA uses guard bands to avoid frequency offset, it is still more sensitive to frequency offset that causes phase noise.
5. Impulse noise rejection
   An impulse noise may not cause an increase in the error rate in OFDMA because its symbols are of a longer duration than CDMA symbols. CDMA symbols may be lost because of the impulse noise, and the systems could increase the coded BER.
6. Applying AMC with OFDM
   Using AMC (Adaptive Modulation and Coding) not only achieves higher throughput for OFDMA systems but it also, if applied at the sub-channel level known as SDMA (Space Division Multiple Access), allows the optimization of sub-channel selection based on geographical location.
7. Frequency reuse scheme
   OFDMA needs a frequency reuse of 3, which means the throughput per cell for a specific bandwidth must be divided by 3, CDMA employs interference averaging, which allows it to maintain a frequency reuse of 1.
8. Code limitation
   Sine CDMA employs interference average; most HSDPA clients will be limited to 5 of maximum 15 codes. Each user needs at least one code for voice or data; this could

have an impact on the number of users supported by each system. In OFDMA, there is a high number of sub-carriers to be assigned to the users.

9. Duplexing
WiMAX can take advantage of multiple duplexing modes, including TDD dynamic asymmetry. HSDPA is an FDD system.

10. Voice
Currently, CDMA can better handle mobile voice calls. It supports multiple voice coding schemes, seamless handoffs, and roaming. OFDMA has to use new techniques to make the voice quality better.

REFERENCES

1. S. W. Halpren, "Techniques for Estimating Subjective Opinion in High-Capacity Mobile Radio," *Microwave Mobile Symposium*, Boulder, Colorado, 1976.

2. W. C. Y. Lee, *Mobile Communications Engineering*, 2nd Ed. McGraw-Hill Book Co., 1998, p. 467.

3. W. C. Y. Lee, *Mobile Communications Engineering*, 2nd Ed. McGraw-Hill Book Co., 1988, pp. 473–476.

4. W. C. Y. Lee, "The Advantages of Using Repetition Code in Mobile Radio Communications," *36th IEEE Vehicular Technology Conference Record* (May 1986, Dallas, Texas), pp. 157–161.

5. W. C. Y. Lee, "Estimate of Local Average Power of a Mobile Radio Signal," *IEEE Transactions on Vehicular Technology*, Vol. VT-34, February 1986, pp. 22–27.

6. W. C. Y. Lee, "Estimating Unbiased Average Power of Digital Signal to Presence of High-level Impulses," *IEEE Transactions on Instrumentation and Measurement*, Vol. IM-32, September 1983, pp. 403–409.

7. E. C. Jordan (Ed.), *Reference Data for Engineers, Radio Electronics Computer, and Communications*, 7th Ed., Howard W. Sams & Co., 1986.

8. W. C. Y. Lee, "Convert Field Strength to Received Power for Use in Systems Design," *Mobile Radio Technology*, April 1987.

9. W. C. Y. Lee, D. O. Reudink, and Y. S. Yeh, "A New Level Crossing Counter," *IEEE Transactions on Instrumentation and Measurement*, March 1975, pp. 79–81.

10. W. C. Y. Lee, "Spectrum Efficiency: A Comparison Between FM and SSB in Cellular Mobile Systems," presented at the Office of Science and Technology, Federal Communications Commission, Washington, D.C., August 2, 1985.

11. E. H. Armstrong, "A Method of Reducing Disturbances in Radio Signaling by a System of Frequency Modulation," *Proceedings of the IRE*, Vol. 24, May 1936, pp. 689–740.

12. V. H. MacDonald, "The Cellular Concept," *Bell System Technical Journal*, Vol. 58, January 1979, pp. 15–42.

13. W. C. Y. Lee, *Mobile Communications Design Fundamentals*, John Wiley & Sons, 1993, p. 145.

14. W. C. Y. Lee, *Mobile Communications Engineering*, McGraw-Hill Book Co., 2nd Ed. 1998, p. 121.

15. P. F. Panter, *Modulation Noise, and Spectral Analysis*, McGraw-Hill Book Co., 1965, p. 447.

16. A. B. Carlson, *Communications Systems*, McGraw-Hill Book Co., 1968, p. 279.

17. A. B. Carlson, *Communications Systems*, McGraw-Hill Book Co., 1968, p. 267.

18. A. B. Carlson, *Communications Systems*, McGraw-Hill Book Co., 1968, p. 288.

19. T. L. Dennis, "Mission the Point," *Telephony*, January 20, 1986, p. 18.

20. W. C. Y. Lee, "The Point Is," *Telephony*, January 20, 1986, p. 13.

21. N. R. Shivley, "ACSB vs. FM," *Communications Magazine*, February 1986, p. 10.

22. Joran Hoff, "Digital Mobile," presented at CTLA meeting in Phoenix, Arizona, January 19–21, 1987. (Hoff drew the same conclusion as the author did in Ref. 10.)

23. H. Taub and D. L. Schilling, *Principles of Communication Systems*, McGraw-Hill Book Co., 1971, p. 290.

24. M. J. Gans and Y. S. Yeh, "Modulation, Noise and Interference," in W. C. Jakes (ed.), *Microwave Mobile Communications*, John Wiley & Sons, 1974, Chap. 4, p. 201.

25. M. J. Gans and Y. S. Yeh, "Modulation, Noise and Interference," in W. C. Jakes (ed.), *Microwave Mobile Communications*, John Wiley & Sons, 1974, Chap. 4, p. 207.

26. J. P. McGeeham and A. J. Bateman, "Theoretical and Experimental Investigation of Feed Forward Signal Regeneration as a Means of Combating Multi-Path Propagation Effects in Pilot-base SSB Mobile Radio Systems," *IEEE Transactions on Vehicular Technology*, Vol. 32, February 1983, pp. 106–120.

27. M. Schwartz, *Information Transmission, Modulation, and Noise*, McGraw-Hill Book Co., 1970, p. 486.

28. W. D. Gregg, *Analog and Digital Communications*, John Wiley & Sons, 1977, p. 257.

29. W. C. Y. Lee, *Mobile Communications Engineering*, 2nd Ed. McGraw-Hill Book Co., 1998, p. 285.

30. W. C. Y. Lee, *Mobile Communications Engineering*, 2nd Ed. McGraw-Hill Book Co., 1998, p. 126.

31. S. Kozono and K. Watanabe, "Influence of Environmental Buildings on UHF Land Mobile Radio Propagation," *IEEE Transactions on Communications*, Vol. COM-25, October 1977, pp. 1113–1143.

32. E. H. Walker, "Penetration of Radio Signals into Building in the Cellular Radio Environment," *Bell System Technical Journal*, Vol. 62, No. 9, Part I, November 1983, pp. 2719–2734.

33. M. Sakamoto, S. Kozono, and T. Hattori, "Basic Study on Portable Radio Telephone System Design," *IEEE Vehicular Technology Conference Record* (San Diego, Calif., 1982), pp. 279–284.

34. D. C. Cox, R. R. Murray, A. W. Norris, "Measurements of 800 MHz Radio Transmission into Buildings with Metallic Walls," *Bell System Technical Journal*, Vol. 62, November 1983, pp. 2695–2718.

35. D. Parsons, *The Mobile Cellular Propagation Channel*, Halsted Press, a division of John Wiley & Sons, 1992, Chap. 4.

36. K. Fujimoto and J. R. James (eds.), *Mobile Antenna Systems Handbook*, Artech House, 1994, Chap. 2.

37. W. C. Y. Lee, *Mobile Communications Design Fundamentals*, John Wiley & Sons, 1993, p. 112.

38. W. C. Y. Lee, *Mobile Communications Engineering*, 2nd Ed. McGraw-Hill Book Co., 1998, p. 403.

39. Y. B. Lin; I. Chlamtac, "Wireless and Mobile Network Architectures," John Wiley & Sons, 2001, p. 222.

40. R. vanNee, "A New OFDM Standard for High Rate Wireless LAN in the 5 GHz band," The 50th IEEE VTC Conference Proceedings, Amsterdam, Netherlands, 1999, pp. 258–262.

41. F. Wang, R. Love, A. Ghosh, "System Performance of HSDPA with MMSE Receiver," IEEE Vehicular Technology Conference Proceedings, Vol. 1, May 2004, pp. 580–583.

42. Intel Technical Whitepaper, "Understanding WiMAX and 3G for Portable/Mobile Broadband Wireless," Dec. 2004.

CHAPTER 16
INTELLIGENT CELL CONCEPT AND APPLICATIONS

16.1 INTELLIGENT CELL CONCEPT

16.1.1 What is the Intelligent Cell?

In the cellular industry, system capacity is a great issue. As demand for cellular service grows, system operators try to find ways to increase system capacity. Capacity can be increased by reducing the cell sizes. This is called the *conventional microcell approach*, but it does not provide intelligence. When the cell size becomes smaller, the control of interference among the cells becomes harder. Also, the handoff time from the beginning of the initiation to the action completion sometimes may take around 15 s. If a mobile station is moving at a speed of 25 km/h (7 m/s), then the mobile station will travel 105 m in 15 s; at a speed of 50 km/h, the mobile station travels 205 m in 15 s. Because within a microcell of 0.5-km radius the overlapped region for a handoff is very small, then the mobile station is in the overlapped region too short a time for the handoff action to be complete. As a result, the call drops. In a conventional microcell system, interference is hard to control and the handoffs may not have enough time to complete.

The intelligent cell can solve the two problems. The intelligent cell concept can be used not only in microcells but also in regular cells to bring extra capacity to the system.

There are two definitions to describe an intelligent cell. One definition of intelligent cell is that the cell is able to intelligently monitor where the mobile unit or portable unit is and find a way to deliver confined power to that mobile unit. The other definition of intelligent cell is that signals coexist comfortably and indestructibly with the interference in the cell. From the first definition, the intelligent cell is called the *power-delivery intelligent cell*, and from the second definition, it is called the *processing-gain intelligent cell*. The intelligent cell may be a large cell such as a macrocell or a small cell such as a microcell. The intelligent cell increases capacity and improves performance of voice and data transmission. Because personal communication service (PCS) needs vast capacity and high quality, the intelligent cell concept is well-suited to it. Actually, using any means intelligently in a cell to improve the performance of services is what the intelligent cell stands for.

16.1.2 The Philosophy of Implementing Power-Delivery Intelligent Cells

Many different wireless versions of an intelligent cell can be used as long as they can deliver power to the location of the mobile unit. The easiest explanation is the analogy of a person entering a house (Fig. 16.1). In a conventional macrocell or microcell, when a mobile unit

Conventional macrocell/microcell

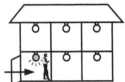

Intelligent microcell

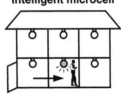
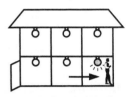

FIGURE 16.1   Microcell philosophy: energy follows the mobile analogy, light follows the person.

enters a cell or a sector, the cell site will cover the power to the entire cell or sector. This is because the cell site does not know where the mobile unit is within the cell or sector. This is just like a house that turns on all the lights when a person enters it.

16.1.2.1 Delivering Power Intelligently.   In an intelligent macrocell or microcell, when a mobile unit enters a cell or a sector, the cell site covers only a local area, which follows the mobile unit. This is just like a house that turns on only the light of the first room a person enters. When the person enters the second room, the light of the first room is turned off and the light of the second room is turned on. Therefore, the light of only one room is on at a time and not the lights in the whole house. When the lights of the entire house A and the lights of the entire house B are on, the two houses should be largely separated in order to avoid the light being seen from one house to the other. If the light of only one room of house A and house B is on, the light that can be seen from one house to the other house is relatively weak. Thus, the distance between the two houses can be much closer.

This same analogy can be applied to a cellular system. In a cellular system, the frequency reuse scheme is implemented for the purpose of increasing spectrum efficiency. If two cochannel cells (cells that use the same frequency) can be placed much closer, then the same frequency channel can be used more frequently in a given geographical area. Thus, the finite number of frequency channels can provide many more traffic channels, and both system capacity and spectrum efficiency can be further increased. In order to reduce the separation between two cochannel cells, the power of each cell should be reduced to cover merely one of numerous local areas in a cell if the cell operator is intelligent enough to know in which local area the mobile unit or handset is. Therefore, there are two required conditions:

1. The cell operator has to know where the mobile unit is located. Different resolution methods can be used to locate the mobile unit.
2. The cell operator has to be able to deliver power to that mobile unit. If the power transmitted from the cell site to the mobile unit can be confined in a small area (analogous to the light of a small room turning on when a person enters it), cochannel interference reduces, and the system capacity increases.

The extreme case of interference reduction is to connect the base transmitter and the mobile receiver by a wire. In this case, the wireless communication system becomes a wire line system, and interference is reduced to a minimum.

16.1.2.2 Radio Capacity. In a frequency-reuse system, such as a cellular system, we always use the term *radio capacity* to measure the traffic capacity. The radio capacity m is defined as[1]

$$m = \frac{M}{K} \quad \text{number of channels/cell} \quad \text{(for omni-cells)} \tag{16.1-1}$$

or

$$m = \frac{M}{K \times S} \quad \text{number of channels/sector} \quad \text{(for sector cells)} \tag{16.1-2}$$

where M is the total number of frequency channels, K is the cell reuse factor, and S is the number of sectors. K can be expressed as[2]

$$K = \frac{1}{3} \left(\frac{D}{R} \right)^2 \tag{16.1-3}$$

D is the cochannel cell separation and R is the cell radius. Also, according to Fig. 16.2*a*, the relationship between the carrier-to-interference ratio C/I and D/R can be expressed[3] as

$$\frac{C}{I} = \frac{(D/R)^4}{6} \tag{16.1-4}$$

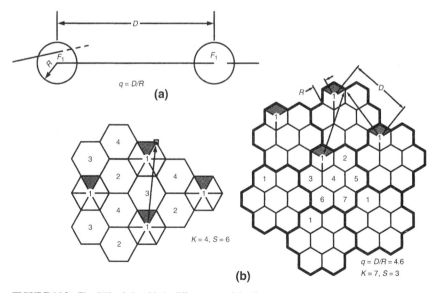

FIGURE 16.2 The D/R relationship in different sectorial cells.

Equation (16.1-4) is based on the propagation path loss of 40 dB/dec and omni cells. The radio capacity of omni-cell systems is[3]

$$m = \frac{M}{\sqrt{\dfrac{2}{3}\left(\dfrac{C}{I}\right)}} \quad \text{channels/cell} \tag{16.1-5}$$

Any other parameters can be derived from the measures of radio capacity such as erlangs/cell, erlangs/Km², and calls/km².

The normalized radio capacity is

$$\hat{m} = m/B_T \quad \text{channel/cell/spectral band} \tag{16.1-6}$$

where B_T is the total spectral band. When two systems operate at two different spectral bands such as B_{T_1} and B_{T_2}, then the radio capacities m_1 and m_2 have to be normalized by first using Eq. (16.1-6) to find m_1/B_{T_1} and m_2/B_{T_2} before comparing their radio capacities $\hat{m}_1$ and $\hat{m}_2$.

In a frequency-division multiple-access (FDMA) system, M is the total number of frequency channels, and in a time-division multiple-access (TDMA) system, M is the total number of slot channels. M is a countable number and is fixed, but K is a variable number and depends on cochannel separation D as shown in Fig. 16.2b. However, because of the reuse of frequency channels, more traffic channels are generated. If one frequency channel is used 50 times, then the traffic channel becomes 50 M. Based on a $K = 7$ system, the number of cells will be $50 \times 7 = 350$ cells. The radio capacity $m = M/7$ is measured by the number of frequency channels per cell, which is determined by the cell reuse factor K only, and not by the number of total cells in the system. The radio capacity m increases if K is reduced, provided that the voice quality and data performance are maintained according to the specification.

Implementation of the intelligent cell concept may involve using multiple zones, multiple antenna beams, multiple isolated spaces, or any means of eliminating interference. There are many kinds of intelligent cells as described in the following sections, where we will compare their radio capacities.

16.1.3 Power-Delivery Intelligent Cells

16.1.3.1 Zone-Divided Cells. In general, there are three kinds of zone-divided cell systems.

Sectorial Cells. Sectorial cells are used to reduce interference. Usually sectorial cells are used when the terrain contour in the cells is not flat, causing unevenly distributed interference from other cells. There are two kinds of sectorial cells.

- 7-cell/3-sector reuse system ($K = 7$, $S = 3$)
- 4-cell/6-sector reuse system ($K = 4$, $S = 6$)

In both systems, each sector has a set of unique designated channels. The mobile unit moving from one sector or one cell to another sector or cell requires an intracell handoff. Based on a cluster of either $K = 7$ cells or $K = 4$ cells (see Fig. 16.2b), the radio capacities of these two systems are

$$m_1 = \frac{M}{7 \times 3} = \frac{M}{21} \quad \text{channels/sector (for a cellular system of } K = 7 \text{ and } S = 3)$$

$$m_2 = \frac{M}{4 \times 6} = \frac{M}{24} \quad \text{channels/sector (for a cellular system of } K = 4 \text{ and } S = 6)$$

Sectorial cells with intracell handoffs do not increase radio capacity, but cochannel interference (Fig. 16.2) can be reduced as shown below:

$$\frac{C}{I} = \frac{R^{-4}}{(D + 0.7R)^{-4} + D^{-4}} = 285 \text{ or } 24.5 \text{ dB} \quad (\text{for } K = 7, S = 3) \quad (16.1\text{-}7)$$

$$\frac{C}{I} = \frac{R^{-4}}{(D + R)^{-4}} = 395 \text{ or } 26 \text{ dB} \quad (\text{for } K = 4, S = 6) \quad (16.1\text{-}8)$$

The above calculation is based on the mobile radio propagation path-loss rule of 40 dB/dec. Because only one or two cochannel interfering sectors are affected, as seen in Fig. 16.2, the C/I will improve by about 7 to 8 dB as compared with $C/I = 18$ dB for a $K = 7$ omni-cell system. When large-size cells are implemented because of the variation of the terrain contour, the sectorial cells should be used to gain this additional margin in decibels to overcome long-term fading. However, more frequent handoffs and larger overlapped regions occur in a $K = 4$ cell than in a $K = 7$ cell.

Intelligent Microcells.[4]   When dividing a cell into many zones as in Fig. 16.3, the cell operator knows which zone the mobile unit is in and delivers the radio signal to that zone. When the mobile unit has been assigned a frequency channel for a call, the frequency channel is always associated with that call within the cell. The cell operator simply turns on the new zone site while the mobile unit is entering and turns off the old zone site when it leaves with the assigned frequency channel to the mobile unit unchanged. With this arrangement, we can find the received C/I value at a mobile unit for a scenario having six cochannel interferers at the first tier surrounding the center cell (Fig. 16.4). It is easy to show that

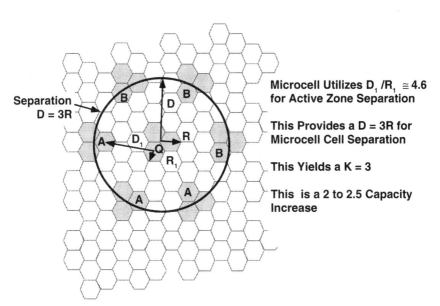

Microcell Utilizes $D_1/R_1 \cong 4.6$ for Active Zone Separation

This Provides a D = 3R for Microcell Cell Separation

This Yields a K = 3

This is a 2 to 2.5 Capacity Increase

Separation D = 3R

FIGURE 16.3   Intelligent microcell capacity application.

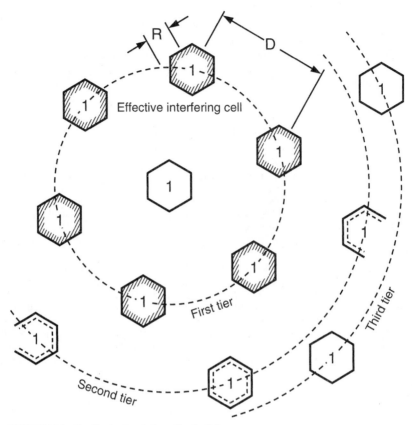

FIGURE 16.4 Six effective interfering cells of cell 1.

the six interferers at the second tier do not contribute any significant interference to the center cell.[4] Assume, as shown in Fig. 16.3, that the desired mobile unit is in zone Q of the center cell and there are three interfering zones marked A and three interfering zones marked B, one in each interfering cell where the six interfering mobile units could be. This is a worst-case scenario. In this case, the voice quality should be maintained at the stated requirement of $C/I \geq 18$ dB in each zone; that is, the ratio of cochannel zone separation D_1 to zone radius R_1 should be $D_1/R_1 = 4.6$. Based on the six worst interfering zones one in each cell, with their minimum D_1/R_1 being 4.6, we can find the resultant C/I received by the desired mobile unit:

$$\frac{C}{I} = \underbrace{\frac{(R_1)^{-4}}{3(4.6R_1)^{-4}}}_{\text{zone A}} + \underbrace{3(5.5R_1)^{-4}}_{\text{zone B}} \approx 100 \text{ or } 20 \text{ db} \qquad \text{(worst case)} \qquad (16.1\text{-}9)$$

The average C/I received by the desired mobile unit can be calculated by taking the probability that each interfering mobile unit would be located in one of its three zones of an interfering cell. Thus:

$$
\frac{C}{I} = \frac{R^{-4}}{2\left[\frac{2}{3}\left(\frac{13}{2}R_1\right)^{-4} + \frac{1}{3}(4.6R_1)^{-4}\right] + \left[\frac{2}{3}(4.6R_1)^{-4} + \frac{1}{3}(6R_1)^{-4}\right]}
$$

$$
+ 2\left[\frac{2}{3}\left(\frac{13}{2}R_1\right)^{-4} + \frac{1}{3}\left(\frac{16}{2}R_1\right)^{-4}\right]
$$

$$
+ \left[\frac{1}{3}\left(\frac{13}{2}R_1\right)^{-4} + \frac{2}{3}\left(\frac{16}{2}R_1\right)^{-4}\right]
$$

$$
= 193.4 \text{ or } 22.8 \text{ db} \quad (\text{average case}) \tag{16.1-10}
$$

As seen from Eq. (16.1-10), the average C/I almost equals 23 dB, which is 5 dB better than the AMPS voice quality specification. By keeping the minimum $D_1/R_1 = 4.6$ in Fig. 16.3, as a result, the cochannel cell separation D equals $3R$. The value of K can be found from Eq. (16.1-3) as $K = 3$. The capacity of intelligent microcells is greater than that of AMPS by a factor of 7/3, or 2.33.

Reuse of Sectorial Beams with Directional Antennas. Applying the same intelligent cell concept, we use antenna beams to confine the energy to individual mobile units in the cell. In a $K = 7$ cellular system, each cell has a set of M/K frequency channels. At a cell site, if six sectorial (directional) antennas are used to cover 360° in that cell and if the whole set of frequency channels assigned to the cell is divided into two subsets which are alternating from sector to sector, then there are three cochannel sectors using each subset in a cell, as shown in Fig. 16.5. In this arrangement, we can increase the capacity by 3 times. If N sector beams are reused alternately, the capacity is increased by $N/2$ times the AMPS capacity. This reuse of the sectorial beam scheme can be used in a small-cell system or a large flat-terrain cell system with much less reduction on trunking efficiency. Of course, in reality, the directional antenna front-to-back ratio should be considered to avoid unnecessary interference in the cochannel sectors.

16.1.3.2 Adaptive Antenna Array.[5] The antenna pattern can be formed by tracking the mobile unit and nulling the interference (see Section 8.14). Therefore, if the same frequency channel x can be used by N mobile units in a cell, the capacity is Nx. Also, because an adaptive antenna array is used, the antenna beam is able to follow the mobile unit, thus reducing interference. The cell reuse configuration may reduce from $K = 7$ to a smaller K depending on the magnitude of N. If N is large, the N antenna beams operating the same frequency to serve N users within a cell can be treated as they are from an omnidirectional antenna. Therefore, $K = 7$ will remain unchanged. If N is confined in a 120° sector, then the required $C/I = 18$ dB can be used to determine the D/R ratio. Since there are only two interfering cells, as shown in Fig. 16.2, the C/I is expressed approximately as

$$
\frac{C}{I} = \frac{R^{-4}}{2D^{-4}} = 63 \text{ or } 18 \text{ dB} \tag{16.1-11}
$$

Solving Eq. (16.1-11) yields

$$
\frac{D}{R} = (126)^{1/4} = 3.35
$$

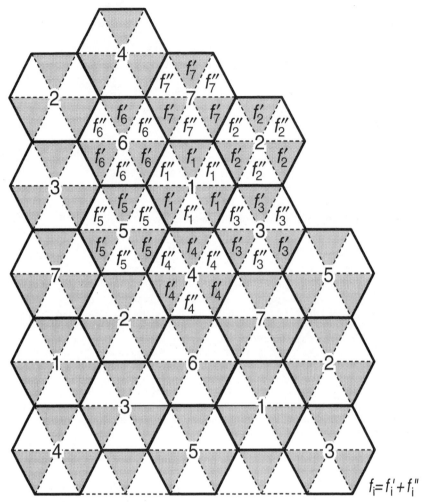

FIGURE 16.5   Reuse of sectorial beams with directional antennas.

The value of K can be obtained from Eq. (16.1-3) as

$$K = \frac{(3.35)^2}{3} = 3.7$$

Because the adaptive antenna beam follows the mobile units, cochannel interference is reduced. Also, because sectorization is used, a system with a frequency reuse factor $K = 4$ can be realized.

   These adaptive antenna patterns provide a good means of generating multiple cochannel mobile calls on the reverse links. Then with the identical antenna patterns for transmitting

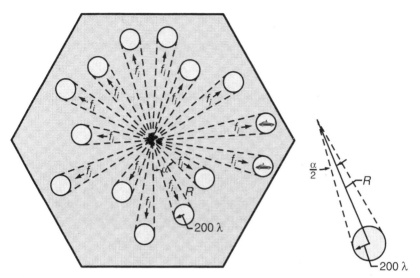

FIGURE 16.6   Intelligent cell with adaptive antenna-array beams.

and receiving at the cell site, the calls are conducted on the forward links as well. This is because the reciprocity principle works based on Lee's Model,[6] the active region around the mobile unit is defined by a radius of about 100 to 200 wavelengths.[7] The beam angle α received at the cell site is a function of distance R, as shown in Fig. 16.6:

$$\alpha = \frac{2 \times 200\lambda}{R} \qquad (16.1\text{-}12)$$

where λ is the wavelength. Usually operating at UHF, the antenna has a beamwidth θ always larger than α. Then the isolation between the two cochannel mobile calls will be measured by θ, not α. Also, the definition of the antenna beamwidth θ is not based on a 3-dB beamwidth but rather on an 18-dB beamwidth. When the two cochannel mobile units move closer within one θ angle, a handoff is initiated. In some proposed systems, the beam nulling is formed between two mobile units. In this case, the nulling angle measured between two mobile units cannot be less than α.

16.1.3.3   In-Building Communication.   In-building communication needs sufficient traffic channels, but the radio spectrum is limited. We may apply the intelligent cell concept to solve this problem. The number of traffic channels can be increased by treating each floor of a building as a cell. The penetration loss of a radio signal through a reinforced concrete building wall is about 20 dB, and the signal isolation between two adjacent floors is also 20 dB. Therefore let a group of frequency channels M_1 be assigned to the inbuilding use, those same M_1 channels will be reused in every floor of the building, and also in every floor of neighboring buildings (i.e., passive intelligence), as shown in Fig. 16.7. Because each floor can be treated as one cell, the radio capacity m_1 of in-building communication can be

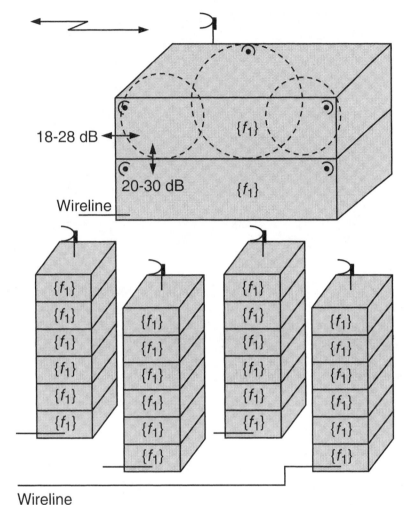

Wireline

FIGURE 16.7   Concept of in-building communication.

obtained by setting $K = 1$. Then:

$$m_1 = \frac{M_1}{K} = M_1 \quad \text{number of channels/floor}$$

Now a 20-floor building has $20 \times M_1$ traffic channels. In case interference occurs between two buildings due to the signal penetration of 4 to 6 dB at the window areas, the intelligent microcell cell with N zones can further reduce the interference. Note that the intelligent cell assumes adequate building shielding. When "active" rather than "passive" intelligence is used, buildings with less isolation can still achieve high efficiency of spectral reuse by self-surveying the amount of signal leakage into the building or between floors.

16.1.4   Processing-Gain Intelligent Cells ($K \rightarrow 1$ system)

16.1.4.1   Philosophy of Implementing Processing-Gain Intelligent Cells.   The concept of the processing-gain intelligent cell can be explained by the analogy of many simultaneous conversations in a big hall (Fig. 16.8). The big hall is just like one big radio channel serving all the traffic in an intelligent cell. The conversations of the different parties are the traffic channels. The processing gain is like the size of the hall, which limits the number of persons, hence, the number of conversations, that can be accommodated. Because all the conversations take place in the hall, the speaker level (power control) of each conversation is the key element in this intelligent cell to keep the interference level in each traffic channel down. Also, if the level of each individual conversation can be controlled intelligently, then we can maintain the total interference level and add more conversations. If the power control is not working, the cell is not an intelligent cell. Then, the cell will face the cocktail-party syndrome in which no parties can talk except by raising their voices. The processing gain calculation will be shown in the next section.

16.1.4.2   Direct-Sequence CDMA.[8–10]   In this code-division multiple-access (CDMA) system, the broadband frequency channel can be reused in every adjacent cell so that K is close to 1, as shown below from our previous definition of Eq. (16.1-3). In a practical sense, D equals $2R$ (i.e., all the same available frequencies are used in each cell). Then

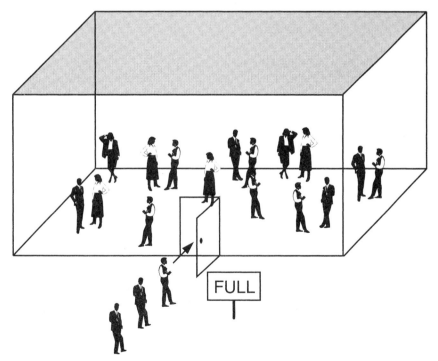

FIGURE 16.8   Analogy to processing-gain intelligent cell.

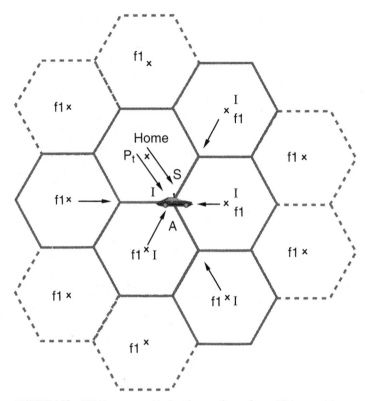

FIGURE 16.9   CDMA system and its interference (from a forward link scenario).

$$K = \frac{(D/R)^2}{3} = 1.33 \tag{16.1-13}$$

Radio capacity is also based on Eq. (16.1-1). However, in direct-sequence CDMA (DS-CDMA), K is fixed but M (the total number of available channels) is a variable and depends on the interference situation. For the scenario shown in Fig. 16.9, the interference comes from the home cell and the adjacent cells and the value of C/I is expressed as

$$\frac{C}{I} = \frac{E_b}{I_0} \times \frac{R_b}{B} = \frac{E_b/I_0}{PG} \tag{16.1-14}$$

where E_b = energy per bit
I_0 = interference per hertz ($I_0 \gg N_0$, where N_0 is thermal noise per hertz)
R_b = information rate
B = bandwidth per channel
PG = processing gain = $10 \log(B/R_b)$ (16.1-15)

In DS-CDMA, because PG is greater than one, C is always smaller than I in Eq. (16.1-14) even if there is only one active user. The processing gain is used to overcome I and determine the number of traffic channels that can be created.

From two sets of given values, E_b/I_0 and R_b/B, we can find the C/I from Eq. (16.1-14). Then, from the scenario of Fig. 16.9, the C/I at the mobile location A can be used to find the number M which is considered a worst case. Assume that the interference level is much higher than the thermal noise level; then

$$\frac{C}{N+1} \to \frac{C}{I}$$

Assume that in a DS-CDMA system,[8] $B = 1.23$ MHz and $R_b = 9.6$ kbps. Then PG $= 1.23$ MHz/9.6 kbps or 21 dB.

In this system, a voice quality is accepted at a frame error rate FER $= 10^{-2}$, which typically corresponds to $E_b/I_0 = 7$ dB. Knowing the values of PG and E_b/I_0, C/I of Eq. (16.1-14) can be obtained:

$$\frac{C}{I} = 7 - 21 = -14 \text{ dB or } 0.03981$$

Find the number of traffic channels m_i in each cell from C/I by:

$$\frac{C}{I} = \frac{\alpha_1(R)^{-4}}{\underbrace{\alpha_1(m_1 - 1) \cdot R^{-4}}_{\text{home cell}} + \underbrace{(\alpha_2 m_2 + \alpha_3 m_3)(R)^{-4}}_{\text{2 adjacent cells}} + \underbrace{\beta \cdot (2R)^{-4}}_{\text{3 interim cells}} + \underbrace{\gamma(2.63R)^{-4}}_{\text{6 distant cells}}}$$

$$= 0.03981 = \frac{1}{25.1} \tag{16.1-16}$$

where

$$\beta = \alpha_4 m_4 + \alpha_5 m_5 + \alpha_6 m_6$$

$$\gamma = \sum_{i=7}^{12} \alpha_i m_i$$

and m_i and α_i are the number of traffic channels and the power level, respectively, in each of the i cells. Solving Eq. (16.1-16), we obtain

$$m_1 = 26.1 - \left[\frac{\alpha_2 m_2 + \alpha_3 m_3}{\alpha_1} \right] - \frac{\beta}{\alpha_1}(2)^{-4} - \frac{\gamma}{\alpha_1}(2.63)^{-4} \tag{16.1-17}$$

Case A. Single cell case ($\alpha_i = 0$ for $i \neq 1$). From Eq. (16.1-17):

$$m_1 = \frac{I}{C} + 1 = 25.1 + 1 = 26.1 \text{ traffic channels/cell}$$

Case B. Identical-cell case. All the cells have the same power and the same number of traffic channels: $m_i = m_j$ and $\alpha_i = \alpha_j$. We may substitute $m_i = m$ and $\alpha_i = \alpha$ into Eq. (16.1-16) or Eq. (16.1-17) and solve for m as follows:

$$26.1 = m[3 + 3 \cdot (2)^{-4} + 6 \cdot (2.633)^{-4}]$$

$$m = 7.85 \text{ traffic channels/cell}$$

Both traffic channels appearing in Case A and Case B include the overhead channels for sync and set-up, but do not take into consideration the voice activity cycle or sector-reuse factor as used in real commercial systems.[8]

16.1.4.3 Frequency Hopping. A frequency-hopping system can be used as a CDMA system (FH-CDMA). The hopping pattern can be formed as a code sequence. Frequency hopping has been used in the past to overcome enemy jammers in military applications. There are two kinds of hopping, fast frequency hopping and slow frequency hopping.

Slow frequency hopping (SFH) is defined as sending multiple bits on a single hop.[11] Depending on the degree of the enemy's quick reaction, the hopping rate would be adjusted. Fast Frequency Hopping (FFH) is defined as sending a bit on a pseudo-random pattern of frequency channels, then sending the next bit on a different pseudo-random pattern of frequency channels. The multiple frequency channels form a code for one bit which is sent out simultaneously or sequentially. The bandwidth of the channel depends on the transmission bit rate. The scheme of simultaneously sending out the same bit on different frequency channels requires a larger bandwidth for sending each bit. This is another wideband CDMA system. Sending bits over frequency channels sequentially is the conventional FH-CDMA system. The fast frequency hopping CDMA system requires a larger bandwidth than the slow frequency hopping CDMA system. This is because in FFH, one bit requires multiple frequency-hopping channels to be sent out sequentially.

In an FH system, there are two kinds of processing gains. One kind of processing gain is used to measure the power of defeating enemy jammers. It is really focused on minimizing collisions of two carriers occupying a frequency channel at the same time. Then if the desired signal has 1000 channels to hop to avoid the jammer, the processing gain is 30 dB. We can derive this processing gain against jamming from $(C/I)_J$ using Eq. (16.1-14):

$$\left(\frac{C}{I}\right)_J = \frac{E_b R_b}{I_0(BN)} \qquad (16.1\text{-}18)$$

where B is the bandwidth of sending R_b through a single channel (assume that $B = R_b$) and N is the number of available frequency channels to be hopped from. Each channel has the same bandwidth B. The processing gain is

$$\text{PG} = \frac{BN}{R_b} = N \qquad (16.1\text{-}19)$$

From Eq. (16.1-19), we may conclude that FFH and SFH can take the advantage of the processing gain in defeating enemies.

The other kind of processing gain is used to increase radio capacity. It is focused on spreading energy channels such that the interference seen by each bit is near the minimum acceptable performance threshold. The carrier-to-interference ratio $(C/I)_F$ of a frequency-hopping system can be expressed differently from Eq. (16.1-14) as

$$\left(\frac{C}{I}\right)_F = \frac{E_b R_b}{I_0(BF)} = \frac{E_c R_c}{I_0(BF)} \qquad (16.1\text{-}20)$$

where E_b = energy per bit
R_b = bits per second
E_c = energy per code bit
R_c = number of code bits per second
F = number of frequency channels per bit ($F \geq 1$)
B = bandwidth of sending a signal of R_b stream

In a non-FH system or an SFH system, R_c and F are always equal to one because there is no spread spectrum using pseudonoise (PN) coding of the data bits. Then $E_c = E_b$, $F = 1$, and Eq. (16.1-20) becomes Eq. (16.1-14). It has been shown that SFH does not experience processing gain in order to increase radio capacity. The SFH system is more like the Aloha multiple access scheme.[12]

In an FFH system, the processing gain for radio capacity depends on F, the number of frequency channels per bit, as

$$PG = \frac{BF}{R_b} = F \tag{16.1-21}$$

Assume that the information rate R_b is 10 kbps and one bit hops among 100 frequencies, $F = 100$, then the total bandwidth required is $BF = 1$ MHz.

16.1.4.4   Impulses in Time Domain.[13,14]   We may create a spread spectrum system based on impulse position modulation in the time domain. The C_p/I can be obtained as

$$\frac{C_p}{I} = \frac{E_p P_b R_s}{I_0 B} \tag{16.1-22}$$

where C_p = carrier power of data stream
E_p = energy per pulse
P_b = number of pulses/bit
R_s = number of bits/s

If $P_b = 1$ then $E_p P_b = E_b$ and Eq. (16.1-22) becomes Eq. (16.1-13). If $P_b > 1$, the impulse position modulation system becomes a spread spectrum system.

The same principle of using DS-CDMA for increasing cellular capacity can be applied to impulse position modulation. When the pulse width of an impulse is less than 1 ns, the advantage of applying impulse position modulation starts to show.

16.1.5   Summary of Intelligent Cell Approaches

The intelligent cell can be described in two ways: (1) it intelligently delivers the signal to the mobile unit; (2) it ensures that the signal indestructibly resides with the interference. Several different methods of increasing traffic capacity by using the intelligent cell concept have been mentioned. These methods are very important for PCSs. Among the methods of forming a power-delivery intelligent cell, the sectorial cells may increase capacity if the cell reuse factor K decreases. Frequency reuse with multiple antenna beams

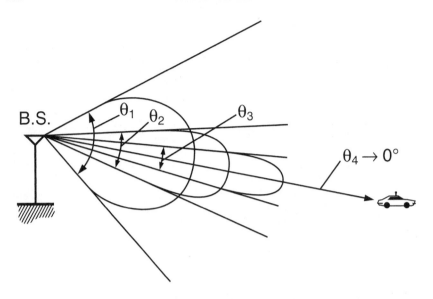

θ-Antenna beamwidth

$$\theta_1 > \theta_2 > \theta_3 > \theta_4 \qquad\qquad \theta_4 \to 0$$

FIGURE 16.10   The best case of delivering power to the mobile unit in space by antenna.

and the microcell with multiple zones apply the intelligent cell concept and can also increase capacity. The method of forming a power delivery intelligent cell can be applied to FDMA and TDMA[15] systems. Among the methods of forming a processing-gain cell, both direct-sequence CDMA[16] and FFH can increase capacity because of their processing gain but SHF cannot.

In a conceptual case, we can narrow the beamwidth θ of an antenna pointing at the mobile unit to a limit; that is, θ becomes narrower and narrower until $\theta \to 0$ (Fig. 16.10). This is the best case for eliminating interference. When $\theta \to 0$, the wireless line is just like a wire line. Therefore, we conclude that the wire line is the least interference link for the wireless link. If a wire line could be replaced by a wireless line with $\theta \to 0°$, then no radio interference exists. As a result, no limitation in increasing the number of channels has imposed by any radio interference among them.

After learning the capacity issues of the three multiple-access schemes, we may present them in three axes, number of frequency channels (x), number of time slots (y), and number of code sequences (z), as shown in Fig. 16.11a. The shaded regions represent the utilization of the spectrum. The larger the region, the higher the spectrum efficiency. Three subcases, FDMA, TDMA, and CDMA, appear in Fig. 16.11b, c, and d, respectively. The shaded regions in each subcase indicate the degree of spectrum efficiency. There is a different representation of spectrum efficiency in each multiple-access scheme.

Therefore, the bottom line of the intelligent cell is either to allow no interference to exist during signal reception or to let the signal tolerate a great deal of interference while it is being received.

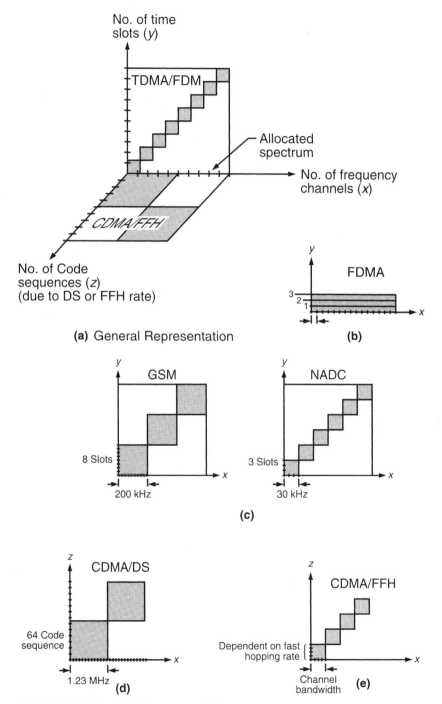

FIGURE 16.11   Spectrum efficiency representation.

16.2 APPLICATIONS OF INTELLIGENT MICROCELL SYSTEMS

16.2.1 Description of the Intelligent Microcell Operation

An intelligent microcell system[17-18] was described in Sec. 16.13. This system can be applied to analog and digital systems. To show the improvement over AMPS provided by intelligent microcells, the voice quality is 2 dB better and the capacity increases more than 2 times. The microcell system is shown in Fig. 16.12. The base-site equipment can be located at one zone site or at any remote place. The base site stores a zone selector, a scanning receiver, and a set of radio channels (Fig. 16.12a). The microcell system can be attached to a regular macrocell site (could be a different cellular vendor's equipment), and can be used without any modification on the base-site controller. Also, the microcell system can operate alone if the controller is replaced with an independent microprocessor. Either has to connect to the MSO.

If the mobile unit is in zone 1, the scanning receiver detects the signal received from zone 1 that is the strongest, then directs the zone selector to switch to zone 1 through a pair of converters (called *translators*). All three zones are receiving the same signal on the same radio channel at any time but only one zone is chosen to transmit the signal. The equipment arrangement for the microcell system at the base site is shown in Fig. 16.12b. In this figure, the new components—zone selector, scanning receiver, and converters—above the dotted line are installed to replace the old components such as power amplifiers, combiner, and 800-MHz antennas.

16.2.1.1 System Elements

Convertors. There are three pairs of converters in the three-zone microcell system. Each pair is used to connect the signals from the base site to the designated zone site. The converter (Fig. 16.12b) is a broadband device that can upconvert signals before transmitting them, then downconvert signals while receiving them. There are two kinds of converters: microwave and optical-fiber. The microwave type can use different upconverting microwave frequencies, such as 18, 23, or 40 GHz. The higher the frequency, the shorter the reception range. The optical-fiber type is used for upconverting the signal to optical frequency and sending it over fiber cable. Every converter is associated with an amplifier for the weak signals after downconverting back to the cellular frequencies. A converter can carry an average of 20 to 30 cellular channels, depending on the linear range of the converter. In this case, on average, if each zone site will take 20 mobile calls, the total of three zones will have 60 mobile calls. The converters[19] can be either analog or digital regardless of whether the system is analog or digital.

At any zone site, only one converter is needed, as shown in Fig. 16.12. The zone site can physically represent a regular cell site. The converter can be mounted on a utility pole or light pole (Fig. 16.13). Therefore, the size of converters becomes a more important factor for the zone site. The smaller, the lighter, the better.

Scanning Receiver. The scanning receiver will scan three zone sites for each frequency. After scanning all the frequencies sequentially, the receiver goes back to the first frequency. The required time of scanning the frequencies and zones is critical. The required time of scanning needs to be short so that more frequencies can be scanned by one scanning receiver.

A scanning receiver for a TDMA system should have the ability to scan not only the frequencies, but also the zones and the time slots. Therefore, a time multiplexing device should be associated with the scanning receiver.

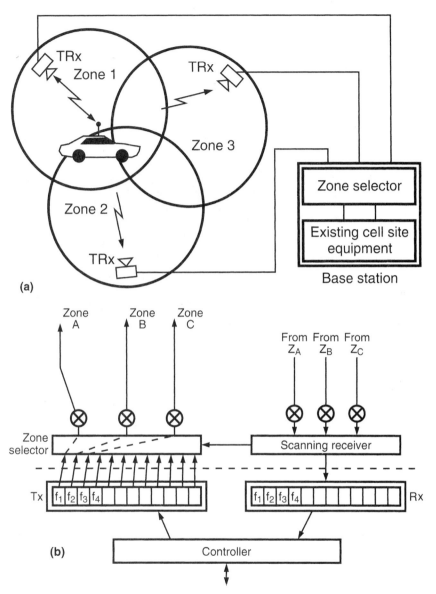

FIGURE 16.12 The structure of the microcell system. *(a)* The basic microcell concept; *(b)* modifying the equipment arrangement for the microcell system at the base station.

FIGURE 16.13   An optical converter (analog conversion) manufactured by
Allen Telecomm.

Zone Selector.   A zone selector is a single switch. It usually switches a signal from one
zone to another zone in less than a microsecond. Therefore, no data stream will be affected
by this fast switch. In TDMA, the zone selector is able to switch a signal in one time slot
of one zone to a designated time slot of another zone.

16.2.1.2   *Areas of Application.*   The intelligent microcell has five applications.

1. *Delivering to extended cells.* Converters can be used to deliver the 800-MHz signal
from the base to an extended cell by upconverting the signal to a new frequency for
transmission through the air, then downconverting to 800 MHz when the signal reaches
a cell where only a converter is installed (Fig. 16.14).

2. *Increasing capacity.* Because the power can be delivered and received intelligently at the
mobile unit, the capacity increases.

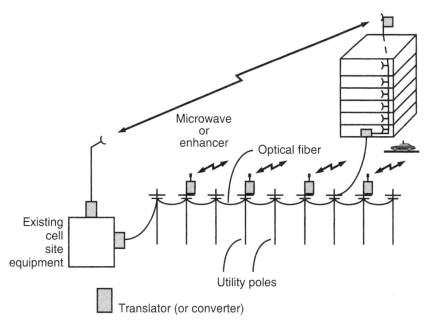

FIGURE 16.14   Microcell delivery system. The translators are used to upconvert an 900-MHz GSM signal to an optical signal (or microwave signal) and downconvert an optical signal (or microwave signal) to 900 MHz.

3. *Coverage.* In some areas, the government will not allow regular cell sites to be installed. Under those circumstances, these invisible zone sites can be used to provide the coverage especially in urban areas.[20–21]

4. *Reducing interference.* At some high cell sites, the generated interference to the other low sites becomes a problem. An intelligent microcell can reduce its unnecessary radiated power and the interference it generates.

5. *In-building communication.* The intelligent cell can increase radio capacity many times. A description of this application will appear later.

16.2.1.3   Advantage of Implementing Intelligent Cells

1. Any number of zones can be included in a microcell. More zones in a microcell can further reduce power and lower the interference.

2. The antennas face inward from the edges of the cell, rather than outward, further reducing the interference.

3. All the zone-site receivers actively receive mobile or portable calls on all frequencies. Because a portable unit's transmit power is usually low, a single cell site receiver has difficulty accepting and maintaining a call, but with three zone sites receiving the same signal from the portable, the reception is much improved. Thus an intelligent microcell is well-suited for PCS terminals.

4. Within a three-zone microcell, no handoff is needed. This arrangement eases the load of switches (MSO) because of fewer handoffs, and the switches can have more capacity

to handle new calls. By reducing handoffs, the intelligent microcell also reduces the number of calls dropped during attempted handoff. In a conventional microcell system, the vehicle often leaves the cell before the handoff action can be completed.

5. The system can be implemented on any existing cellular system. The modification is shown in Fig. 16.12*b*, where a dashed line divides the equipment in a regular cell site from that in a microcell site. Where the power amplifier and channel combiner would be installed in a regular cell site, the scanning receiver, zone selector and the converter are installed instead in a microcell site.

6. The zone site can be moved from one location to another in almost no time. To take an antenna and a converter down from one utility pole and put them up on another utility pole is easy.

7. A fiber-cable network can provide redundancy of connections. If the fiber cable is broken on one end, the signal can be delivered via the network through the other end to the mobile unit.

8. No need to modify the existing cellular subscriber units for the intelligent microcell system.

9. Better voice quality than an analog cellular system.

10. Higher capacity—can be 2.33 times the capacity of the analog system.

16.2.1.4 Cable Cost and Converter Quality.   In high traffic congestion areas, many zone sites will be installed. The major cost of providing the fiber links is the installation of fiber cable. Usually, the initial cost of the fiber links is high. This situation may lead us to recall that in the beginning of this century, many people complained that the initial cost of telephone-wire installation was too high. One hundred years later, we are all benefiting from this telephone network. Because the fiber-cable network will inevitably be the future broadband network, why should we have to be concerned about the initial costs of the installation if it is needed for the future?

The quality of converters is a big challenge. The simplest way of building a converter is to use an analog direct conversion approach. But the required linearity over a broad dynamic range with broadband conversion could make a high-quality analog converter difficult to realize. A digital converter may cost more but may not require linearity, therefore the quality can be better. However, the analog converter would gracefully degrade in performance, but the digital converter would sharply degrade.

16.2.2 Applications to Increasing Capacity

To verify the increased capacity provided by intelligent microcells, four microcells were deployed in West Los Angeles. Each microcell had three zone sites. The cell reuse pattern was $K = 3$ (Fig. 16.15). Cells 1A and 2B were the cochannel microcells. The measured signal strengths at 1A and 2B are shown in Figs. 16.16*a* and 16.16*b*, respectively. From the measured data, we could calculate the C/I at zone 1A and at zone 2B, as shown in Fig. 16.16*c*. The result indicates that C/I at each cochannel microcell (1A or 2B) is about 20 dB, as we have expected. Because the cell reuse factor K reduces from $K = 7$ to $K = 3$ while the C/I improves from 18 dB to 20 dB, both the capacity and the voice quality agree with the theoretical prediction.

16.2.2.1 Deployment Along City Streets.   Deploying intelligent microcells along city streets is depicted in Fig. 16.17. All the zone sites are located at street crossings. They are lined up diagonally, as shown in the figure. Because each zone site transmits low power, only

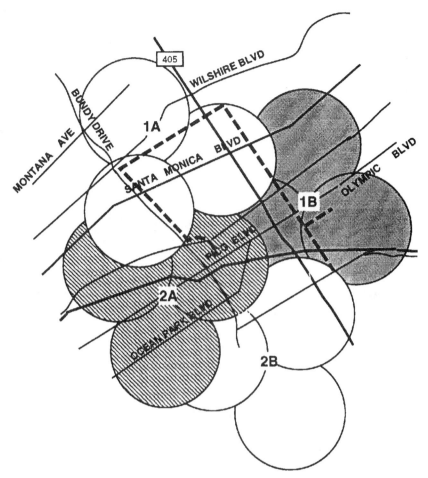

FIGURE 16.15 Four-microcell pattern and fiber-optic backbone.

enough to cover two crossed streets, we may connect the four zone sites to form a microcell using one zone selector. Then, when a vehicle is assigned to one frequency channel f_i, this f_i will be switched from one zone site to another zone site, depending on the zone where the mobile unit is. If the zone selector can serve 20 mobile calls at one time, the same number of calls will be served in this four-zone microcell. For this low-power, intelligent power delivery approach, all the cochannel microcells can be pulled closer. As a result, the capacity is increased.

16.2.3 Applications of Coverage Provision

There are two applications of the coverage provision: coverage along winding roads and coverage under the ground.

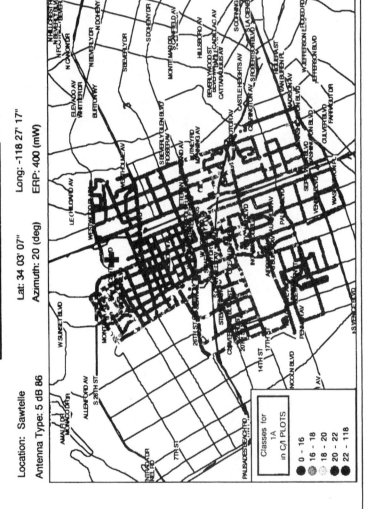

FIGURE 16.16 (*a*) Microcell 1A *C/I* plot (measured).

670

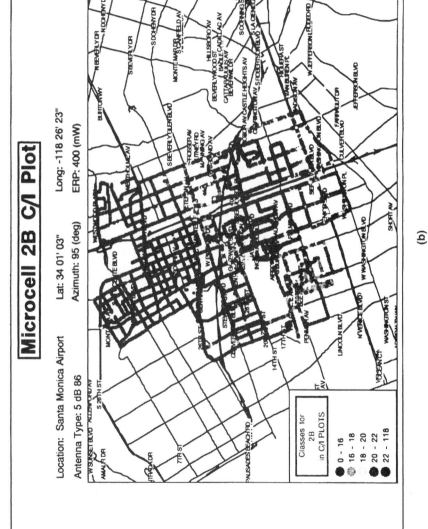

FIGURE 16.16 (*Continued*) (*b*) Microcell 2B *C/I* plot (measured).

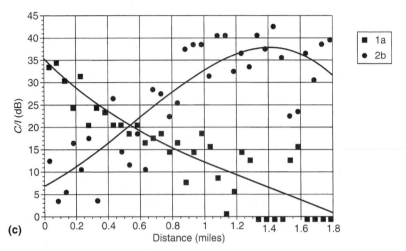

FIGURE 16.16 (*Continued*) (*c*) Microcell *C*/*I* plot (calculated).

16.2.3.1 Coverage Along Winding Roads. Roads like the Pacific Coast Highway, in Malibu, or the road along Santiago Canyon, in Los Angeles, need coverage that stretches up to 15 mi. In Malibu, the zoning regulations prevent the installation of regular cell sites. In Santiago Canyon, the regular cells installed along the winding roads need to be very close for coverage and as a result are very costly. For these reasons, intelligent microcells are a good candidate in both cases. In Fig. 16.18, two directional antennas back-to-back are installed on each zone site. Directional antennas and the converters mounted on utility poles form a zone site. Because the traffic is light along these roads, we may use one zone

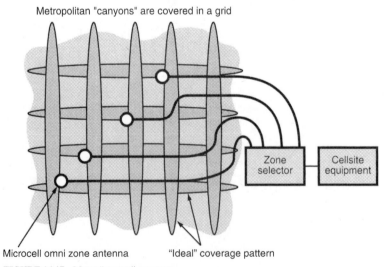

FIGURE 16.17 Metro "canyon" coverage.

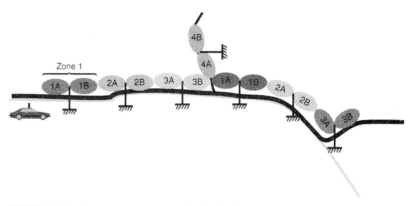

FIGURE 16.18   Linear coverage concept with directional antennas.

selector in the 15-mi microcell system. Along the road, we number the zone sites along the road 1, 2, 3, 1, 2, 3, repeatedly. In the three-zone selector, all zone sites named zone 1 are connected together, all named zone 2 are connected together, and all named zone 3 are connected together. Then, when a vehicle has been assigned a frequency, f_i and starts to travel from the left end of the road, the left directional antenna of zone 1 receives the mobile signal first, then the right directional antenna on zone 1 receives it later. During this period, all zone 1 sites are on. Because the interference caused by the low-power sites is low, interference is not a concern. The mobile call then passes from zone 1 to zone 2 to zone 3, then back to zone 1 to zone 2 to zone 3, and so forth. The frequency f_i always stays with this particular mobile call along the 15-mi-long road. No handoff action is needed. This arrangement is suitable for light traffic road conditions.

16.2.3.2   Coverage Under the Ground (Subway Coverage).   The intelligent microcell also can be used in subways. In a subway, no interference occurs from the ground cell sites. The three-zone selector can be used to cover a microcell with three subway stations when the stations are very closely separated. Each of the three zones is covered in a different shade pattern in Fig. 16.19. The left-bound train (top) and the right-bound train (bottom)

Three station distributed antenna design
Three-zone intelligent cell

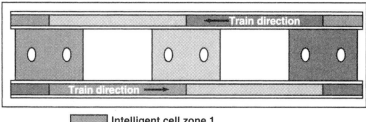

▨ Intelligent cell zone 1
▨ Intelligent cell zone 2
▨ Intelligent cell zone 3

FIGURE 16.19   Underground communication system.

are shared by one zone but covered in different sections. In this case, the two trains stopping at the station will be carried by different zones to ease the traffic.

16.3 IN-BUILDING COMMUNICATION

16.3.1 Differences Between Ground Mobile and In-Building Design

There are many good system design tools that have been developed solely for ground mobile cellular systems. However, no proper design tools have been developed for both ground mobile communications and in-building communications operated within one cellular system. As cellular systems are operated today, in-building communication is provided by transmitting radio signals from cell sites so that they penetrate the building walls to reach portable handsets inside buildings. Several difficulties are raised:

1. The transmitted power for in-building communications has to be about 20 dB stronger than that for the ground mobile communications in order to penetrate into or out from a building. Because the maximum transmit power of a portable handset is 8 dB lower than the maximum power of a ground mobile unit, in-building communication is harder to perform on the reverse link (portable-to-base link) than the forward link.

2. The coverage of portable units is not two-dimensional but three-dimensional. Weak reception of portable units is found on lower floors of a building, but strong reception is found on higher floors. This fact presents a difficult condition for running a system which can serve both ground mobile and in-building communication simultaneously.

3. When a radio channel penetrates from outside into a multifloor building, this particular channel can serve only one user who is located on one floor. The other potential users on different floors cannot use the same channel.

4. In-building communication needs enormous radio channels which the current cellular system cannot provide.

16.3.2 Natural In-Building Radio Environment

16.3.2.1 Building Penetration. The signal penetrating through the building wall is called the *building penetration*. Building penetration studies have shown that penetration loss depends on geographical areas: 22–28 dB in Tokyo, 18–22 dB in Los Angeles, and 13–17 dB in Chicago. The differences are due to the building's construction. Earthquake resistance is the main factor in constructing buildings in some areas. In earthquake areas, the steel frame of a building is built as a mesh-type structure to resist the vibration of the earthquake. The mesh-type structure causes high penetration loss.

16.3.2.2 Building Height Effect. Signal reception is always stronger when the cellular handset is at a higher floor. The floor-height gain is about 2.70 dB/floor, independent of the building construction. In Chicago, the reception on the sixth floor is the same as that on the outside ground level. In Tokyo, with its higher penetration loss because of antiearthquake construction, the reception on the eleventh floor is the same as that on the outside ground level.

16.3.2.3 Building Floor Isolation. The signal isolation between floors in a multifloor building is on the average about 20 dB. Within a floor of 150 × 150 feet, the propagation loss due to interior walls, depending on the wall materials, is about 20 dB between the strong and weak areas.

16.3.3 A New In-Building Communication System

16.3.3.1 Philosophy of Designing a New In-Building Communication System. After studying the natural in-building radio environment, we found that the building structure is a natural radio shield (Fig. 16.20). Therefore, utilizing the shielding advantage is the best policy. This means that a signal should not be forced to penetrate into a building with a high-power radio wave; rather, the signal should be led into the building and distributed onto each floor.

16.3.3.2 Means of Leading the Cellular Signal into the Building. In a cellular system, cellular radios do not need to reside in each building, but rather may be installed in a remote base (Fig. 16.21). This deployment would change the conventional structure of the cell cites and make all the cell sites miniaturized zone sites. There are three methods by which the cellular signal can be led into buildings:

1. Upconvert all cellular signal channels to optical frequency at the base and transmit over optical fibers. When the optical signal reaches the building, downconvert it back to the cellular signals and serve the building users.

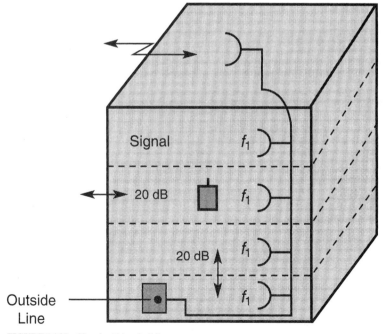

FIGURE 16.20 Signal within a building.

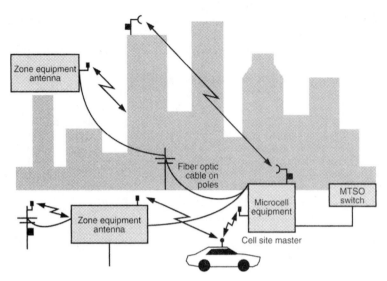

FIGURE 16.21 Microcell installation concept.

2. Upconvert all cellular signal channels to microwave frequency at the base and transmit over a radio link. When the microwave signal reaches the building, downconvert it back to the cellular signals and serve the building users.

3. Downconvert all cellular signal channels to a 200-MHz UHF signal at the base and transmit it over the cable with low path loss. When the 200-MHz UHF signal reaches the building, upconvert it back to the cellular signals and serve the building users.

16.3.4 In-Building System Configuration[22]

An in-building system configuration that uses both the natural shielding of the building structure and a means of leading the cellular signal into the building is illustrated in Fig. 16.7. Calls are sent into the building at upconverted (or downconverted) frequencies to different floors. These lead-in frequencies are converted back to the cellular frequencies as soon as they reach the desired floors.

For a 10-floor building, the same cellular frequency can carry 10 different calls on each of the 10 floors. The capacity is increased 10 times. Also, because of the penetration loss, the same cellular frequencies can be used in neighboring buildings, as shown in Fig. 16.7. Thus, the same cellular frequency is reused many times, and the spectrum utilization is very efficient.

If the building penetration is high, the neighboring buildings will not have cochannel interference. In this case, we can use the intelligent microcell configuration.[23] Each floor will be divided into three or four zones. Only one zone's transmitter is on—the zone where the user is located. Thus, the transmitted power is greatly reduced. Within one floor, the user's assigned cellular frequency does not change during the call. The active zone will change, following the location of the user.

If 30 channels are assigned for the in-building users, then the analog cellular system outside the building can still have 365 cellular channel frequencies. These 30 in-building cellular frequencies can generate thousands of calls in an in-building communication system at any time.

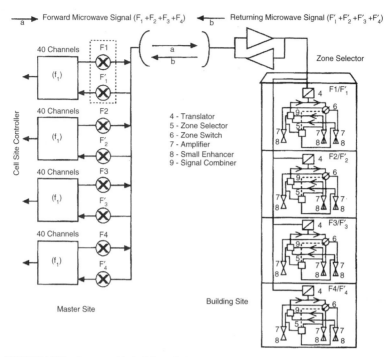

FIGURE 16.22 A proposed in-building wireless system.

Because 30 channel frequencies are designated for the in-building communication only, there is no interference between ground mobile communication and in-building communication. These 30 channel frequencies can be freely reused on each floor in each building without worrying about interference problems with ground mobile communication.

Because the in-building communication in each building can be assigned a station identification (SID) number or the same SID number can be used in all buildings, then the same portable unit can be used for both in-building and the ground mobile communication. The handoff process can be carried out between two communication systems. It would be a benefit to the end user to be able to carry only one portable unit but operate in two systems, the in-building and the ground mobile communication systems.

Handoff between floors can be implemented by assigning a few different channel frequencies from the in-building frequencies to the elevator areas. The handoff will take place by assigning a new elevator area frequency to replace the in-building frequency when the user enters the elevator, and will be handed back to one of the in-building frequencies after the user reaches another floor.

A detailed diagram of an in-building communication system is shown in Fig. 16.22.

16.3.5 A PCS Application

Most wireless operators try to divide the market into many segments. Each segment may have many systems in operation such as cellular, in-building, cordless phones, and many others. Each system has to operate its own subscriber units. Thus, there will be many different types of PCS units on the market. However, users (subscribers) want to carry only one portable unit that is small and lightweight and provides long talk time. In addition, they want a PCS that sends out and delivers calls anywhere, anytime.

The new in-building communication system described in Sec. 16.3.4 can meet the end user's needs. It can be used underground, in subways, and tunnels. It is a complementary system to the ground mobile macrocell system.

16.3.5.1   *The Future PCS Unit.*   The size and weight of today's cellular portable unit are determined by three factors:

1. The size of human fingers is the limiting factor for the size of keypad (or keyboard).
2. The size of the battery is the limiting factor for long radio path communication and long talk time.
3. The length from the mouth to the ear is the limiting factor for the length of the unit.

Today, voice-activated technology is available to replace the dialing process. A memory device in the unit can have the telephone number recorded by voice to correspond to a person's name. Once the person's name is voiced into the memory, the corresponding telephone number will be sent out. In this case, not only is no keypad needed, but also the caller does not have to remember the number.

The transmitted power of a portable unit can be drastically reduced by implementing the new in-building communication system. The antenna (probe) is located in each floor, thus the transmitted power required to reach the floor antenna from the portable unit can be a fraction of a milliwatt. Furthermore, with an intelligent microcell configuration on each floor, the transmitted power can be further reduced. Therefore, only a tiny battery is needed. The length between the ear and the mouth also can be shortened by using acoustic vibration to transfer the voice from the mouth via muscle to the ear area. Thus both the earphone and the microphone can be located at the ear.

All the above-mentioned technologies are in existence now. Therefore, soon the size of PCS subscribers' units could be as small as a mechanical pencil (Fig. 16.23). A short simple message display will be attached to the pencil-like PCS unit, as in today's pager. A pocket-sized miniprinter can be carried for lengthier messages. A long message can be printed out in an office by downloading the information from the unit's memory.

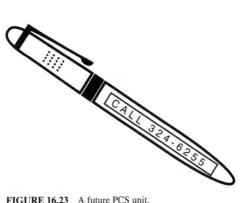

FIGURE 16.23   A future PCS unit.

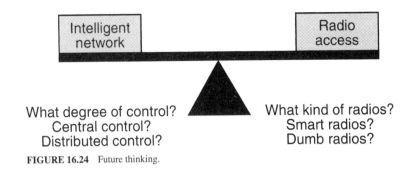

What degree of control?   What kind of radios?
Central control?   Smart radios?
Distributed control?   Dumb radios?

FIGURE 16.24   Future thinking.

16.3.5.2   Future Concerns. We have shown that the building is a natural shield for radio interference. Also, cellular frequency reuse in each floor and in the neighboring buildings has shown great spectral efficiency. The new in-building communication system is compatible with the existing cellular system and could be a PCS system in the future.

As far as the future PCS in concerned, we may have to explore the two areas shown in Fig. 16.24, intelligent network and radio access. We have to decide whether the intelligent network (IN) should be a central control system or distributed control system. As for radio access, what kind of PCS radio should we have, smart or dumb? If the decision is to use a smart radio, what degree of smartness should the radio have?

16.4   CDMA CELLULAR RADIO NETWORK

16.4.1   System Design Philosophy

Deploying CDMA systems is like tuning a sophisticated automobile engine. When proper tuning is done, the engine runs very smoothly. But a sophisticated automobile engine needs a sophisticated, computer-aided tuning device, just as a CDMA system needs a computer-aided design tool. As we know, in analog and TDMA systems, capacity increases are a result of the elimination of interference from the desired signal. The signal level of a desired signal is always much stronger than the interference level, say 18 dB or better, for AMPS. However, in a CDMA system, the capacity increase is based on how much interference the desired signal can tolerate. The signal level of a desired signal is always below the interference level. Also, all the users have to share the same radio channel. If one user takes more power than it needs, then the others will suffer and system capacity will be reduced. This scenario is the same as dining in a formal restaurant. The volume of the conversations at every table is low. Therefore, no walls are needed between tables. The guests never feel their conversations are being interrupted by the next table. Therefore, many conversations can occur in the same dining room. This is the concept of CDMA—that all the voice channels are sharing one big radio channel. If people at one table start to raise their voices, the rest of the tables have to either leave or raise their voices too. The former case destroys CDMA. The latter is the so-called cocktail party syndrome, which reduces the capacity of CDMA. Neither one is desired. This section addresses how to tune the CDMA cellular radio network in order to tolerate interference.

Designing a uniform CDMA system is comparatively simple. Uniform CDMA means all the cells will be assigned the same number of channels. However, in reality, CDMA systems are not uniform. The voice channels of each cell in a CDMA system are not the same. Because of demographic needs, some cells have more voice channels and some have fewer. Since CDMA has only one radio channel, to generate different voice channels on demand from a single CDMA radio is a big challenge. We would like to describe the challenges by illustrating the design aspects of a CDMA system.

16.4.2 Key Elements in Designing[24]a CDMA System

The design of a CDMA system is much more complex than the design of a TDMA system. In analog and TDMA systems, the most important key element is C/I. There are two different kinds of C/I. One is the measured C/I, which is used to indicate the voice quality in the system. The higher the measured value, the better. The other is the specified C/I [$(C/I)_s$], which is a specified value for a specified cellular system. For example, the $(C/I)_s$ in the AMPS system is 18 dB. In analog and TDMA systems, because of spectral and geographical separations, the interference I is much lower than the received signal C, and sometimes we can utilize field strength meters to measure C to determine the coverage of each cell. The field strength meter therefore becomes a useful tool in designing the TDMA system. In CDMA all the traffic channels are served solely by a single radio channel in every cell. Therefore, in an m-voice channel cell, one of the m traffic channels is the desired channel and the remaining $m - 1$ traffic channels are the interference channels. In this case, the interference is much stronger than the desired channel. Then C/I is hard to obtain by using a signal strength meter. Thus, the key elements in designing a CDMA system are different from those in designing a TDMA system.

16.4.2.1 Relationship Between C/I and FER. In CDMA, the key element is E_b/I_o (energy per bit/power per hertz), which is related to the frame error rate. An acceptable speech quality of a specified vocoder would determine the FER which is related to E_b/I_o at a given vehicle speed. From a system design aspect, we consider the system performance with all the vehicle speeds and environmental conditions and come up with a specified E_b/I_o. Now we can design the CDMA system on the basis of the specified E_b/I_o. The following equation is used:

$$\frac{C}{I} = \left(\frac{E_b}{I_o}\right)\left(\frac{R_b}{B}\right)\eta \qquad (16.4\text{-}1)$$

where R_b is the bits per second, B is the CDMA channel bandwidth, and η is the speech activity cycle in percent. From Eq. (16.4-1), B/R_b is the processing gain (PG), which is known in a given CDMA system. E_b/I_0 and η are also known in the system. Then the C/I of each CDMA channel can be obtained. Each coded channel in CDMA can be treated as a frequency channel in FDMA or TDMA. If the coded channels are sent over a cable transmission medium, the interference among the coded channels can be treated as adjacent channel interference. Due to the nature of channel orthogonality, the interference should be very small. But in the mobile radio environment, because of the multipath wave phenomenon, the orthogonality among the channels cannot be held. Therefore, the processing gain is the only interference protection among the channels.

E_b/I_0 always varies in order to meet a specified FER under different conditions. From Eq. (16.4-1) we can find a required $(C/I)_s$ from a specified $(E_b/I_0)_s$ in a worst-case scenario for designing the system. However, the values of $(E_b/I_0)_s$ for the forward link channels and for the reverse-link channels are different because of their different modulation schemes. Therefore, we may have two different requirements for C/I: a $(C/I)_F$ for the forward link channels and a $(C/I)_R$ for the reverse link channels.

16.4.3 Uniform Cell Scenario

Now we try to find the design parameters of each cell for the forward link and the reverse link in a realistic uniform capacity condition.

16.4.3.1 For the Forward Link. A worst-case scenario is used to find the relation among the transmitted powers of all cell sites. First we equation which relates the C/I received at a mobile location A (Fig. 16.25) to the transmitted powers of all cell sites:

$$C/I = \cfrac{1}{\underbrace{m_1 - 1}_{\substack{\text{home cell} \\ (I_1)}} + \underbrace{\frac{\alpha_2 m_2 + \alpha_3 m_3}{\alpha_1}}_{\substack{\text{2 adjacent cells} \\ (I_2, I_3)}} + \underbrace{\frac{\beta \cdot (2)^{-4}}{\alpha_1}}_{\substack{\text{3 interim cells} \\ (I_4, I_5, I_6)}} + \underbrace{\frac{\gamma \cdot (2.633)^{-4}}{\alpha_1}}_{\substack{\text{6 distant cells} \\ (I_7, I_8, I_9, I_{10}, I_{11}, I_{12})}}}$$

(16.4-2)

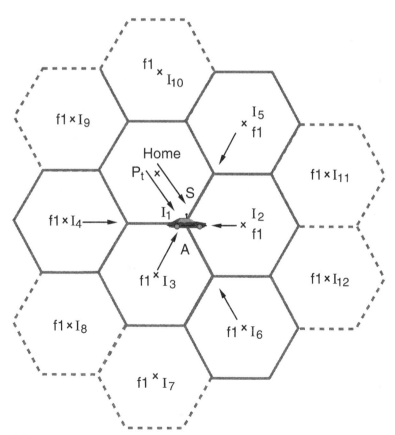

FIGURE 16.25 CDMA system and its interference (from a forward link scenario).

where α_i ($i = 1, 3$) is the transmitted power of each voice channel in the cell and m_i is the number of channels per cell. β and γ are the transmitted powers of the combined adjacent cells at a distance $2R$ and $2.633R$, respectively. By solving Eq. (16.4-2), we can determine m_i as follows:

$$m_1 = \left(\frac{1}{C/I} + 1 \right) - \left[\frac{\alpha_2 m_2 + \alpha_3 m_3}{\alpha_1} \right] - \frac{\beta}{\alpha_1}(2)^{-4} - \frac{\gamma}{\alpha_1}(2.633)^{-4} \qquad (16.4\text{-}3)$$

Case A. No adjacent cell interference. Let $\alpha_2 = \alpha_3 = \beta = \gamma = 0$ in Eq. (16.4-3). Then

$$m_1 = \frac{1}{(C/I)} + 1 \qquad (16.4\text{-}4)$$

If the value of C/I obtained from Eq. (16.4-1) is $C/I = -17$ dB, then $m_1 = 51$, the maximum voice channels in a cell.

Case B. No interference other than from the two close-in interfering cells. In Eq. (16.4-3), the third and fourth terms are much smaller in value than the first two terms and therefore can be neglected. Then

$$\alpha_1 = \frac{\alpha_2 m_2 + \alpha_3 m_3}{\dfrac{1}{C/I} + 1 - m_1} \qquad (16.4\text{-}5)$$

If $C/I = -17$ dB, and the assigned voice channels at three cells are $m_1 = 30, m_2 = 25$, and $m_3 = 15$, respectively, then Eq. (16.4-5) becomes:

$$\alpha_1 = \frac{25\alpha_2 + 15\alpha_3}{51 - 30} = 1.19\alpha_2 + 0.714\alpha_3 \qquad (16.4\text{-}6)$$

Equation (16.4-6) expresses the relationship among α_1, α_2, and α_3.

The total transmitted power P in each cell site is $P_1 = \alpha_1 m_1, P_2 = \alpha_2 m_2, P_3 = \alpha_2 m_3$. Thus, P_1, P_2 and P_3 are the maximum transmitted powers of the three cells. Then, Eq. (16.4-5) can be simplified to:

$$\left(\frac{1}{C/I} + 1 \right) \frac{P_1}{m_1} = P_1 + P_2 + P_3 \qquad (16.4\text{-}7)$$

Following the same derivation steps, we can obtain the following equations:

$$\left(\frac{1}{C/I} + 1 \right) \frac{P_2}{m_2} = P_1 + P_2 + P_3 \qquad (16.4\text{-}8)$$

$$\left(\frac{1}{C/I} + 1 \right) \frac{P_3}{m_3} = P_1 + P_2 + P_3 \qquad (16.4\text{-}9)$$

The relationship of the three maximum transmitted powers of the three cells is

$$\frac{P_1}{m_1} = \frac{P_2}{m_2} = \frac{P_3}{m_3} \qquad (16.4\text{-}10)$$

Deduced from Eq. (16.4-10), a design criterion which we will use in general for a CDMA system of N cells is

$$\frac{P_i}{m_i} = \frac{P_i}{m_i} = \text{constant} \tag{16.4-11}$$

where i indicates the i cell and j indicates the j cell. Equation (16.4-11) indicates that the more voice channels generated, the more transmit power is needed. Therefore, either applying power control to the voice channels in a cell such that more voice channels can be provided with a given transmit power, or using fewer channels in a cell such that the transmit power P will decrease, will reduce interference.

16.4.3.2 For the Reverse Link. The worst-case scenario (shown in Fig. 16.26) is also used in the reverse link analysis. Assume that all the mobile units traveling in the two adjacent cells will be located at the cell boundary of the home cell. From the reverse link, the powers of the m_1 voice signals received at the home site are the same because of the power control implementation to overcome the near-to-far interference.

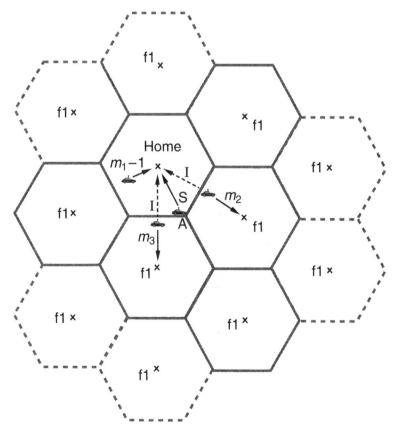

FIGURE 16.26 CDMA system and its interference (from a reverse link scenario).

Let the received signal from a desired mobile unit at the home cell site be C. Assume that each signal of other m_1 channels received at the home site in Fig. 16.26 is also C. Also, assume that the interference of certain mobile units, say $r_{1j}m_1$, from the two adjacent cells ($j = 2,3$) comes from the cell boundary. Because of the power control in each adjacent cell, the interference coming from the adjacent cell for each voice channel would roughly be C as received by the home cell site. The received C/I at the desired voice channel can be expressed as:

$$C/I = \frac{C}{(m_1 - 1) \cdot C + r_{12} \cdot m_2 C + r_{13} \cdot m_3 C} \qquad (16.4\text{-}12)$$

$$= \frac{1}{m_1 - 1 + r_{12}m_2 + r_{13}m_3}$$

where r_{12} and r_{13} are a portion of the total number of voice channels in adjacent cells that will interfere with the desired signal at the home cell, which is cell 1.

From Eq. (16.4-12), the worst-case scenario is when:

$$m_1 + r_{12}m_2 + r_{13}m_3 \leq \frac{1}{C/I} + 1 \qquad (16.4\text{-}13)$$

Following the same steps, we find:

$$r_{21}m_1 + m_2 + r_{23}m_3 \leq \frac{1}{C/I} + 1 \qquad (16.4\text{-}14)$$

$$r_{31}m_1 + r_{32}m_2 + m_3 \leq \frac{1}{C/I} + 1 \qquad (16.4\text{-}15)$$

The value of r_{ij} depends on the size of the overlapped region in the adjacent cell, and can be reasonably assumed as 1/6 (which is 0.166) if the system is properly designed.

If $C/I = -17$ dB, which is 50, and $r_{12} = r_{13} = 0.166$, then Eq. (16.4-13) becomes:

$$m_1 + 0.166(m_2 + m_3) = 51 \qquad (16.4\text{-}13a)$$

The relationships among the numbers of voice channels in each cell, m_1, m_2, and m_3, are expressed in Eqs. (16.4-13), (16.4-14), and (16.4-15).

16.4.3.3 Designing a CDMA System.
From the reverse-link scenario, we can check to see whether all the conditions expressed in Eqs. (16.4-13), (16.4-14), and (16.4-15) can be met. The main elements in these equations are the demanded voice channels, m_1, m_2, and m_3. For representative values of these terms, we can determine the maximum transmitted power of each cell from the forward link equations, Eqs. (16.4-7) to (16.4-10).

EXAMPLE 16.1 *Given $C/I = 17$ dB and all the r's, $r = r_{ij} = 0.3$:*

Case 1. Let the demanded voice channels be $m_1 = 30$, $m_2 = 25$, $m_3 = 15$. Checking the conditions in Eqs. (16.4-13), (16.4-14), and (16.4-15), we find:

$$30 + 0.3\,(25 + 15) = 42 < 51 \quad \text{(OK)}$$

$$25 + 0.3\,(30 + 15) = 38.5 < 51 \quad \text{(OK)}$$

$$15 + 0.3\,(30 + 25) = 31.5 < 51 \quad \text{(OK)}$$

Because the cell sizes of the three cells are the same.

$$\alpha_1 = \alpha_2 = \alpha_3 = CR^{+4}$$

Assume $\alpha_1 = \alpha_2 = \alpha_3 = 100$ mW. Then

$$P_1 = 30 \times 0.1 = 3W$$

$$P_2 = 25 \times 0.1 = 2.5W$$

$$P_3 = 15 \times 0.1 = 1.5W$$

Case 2. Let the demanded voice channels be $m_1 = 40$, $m_2 = 30$, $m_3 = 20$. Checking the conditions in Eqs. (16.4-13), (16.4-14), and (16.4-15), we find:

$$40 + 0.3\,(30 + 20) = 55 > 51 \quad \text{(does not meet the conditions)}$$

$$30 + 0.3\,(40 + 20) = 48 < 51 \quad \text{(OK)}$$

$$20 + 0.3\,(40 + 30) = 41 < 51 \quad \text{(OK)}$$

The number of demanded voice channels should be reduced before the system is designed.

16.4.4 Nonuniform Cell Scenario

16.4.4.1 Transmit Power on the Forward Link Channels. We may first assign the number of voice channels m in each cell according to demographic data. Then we may calculate the total transmit power on the forward link channels in each cell from a worst-case scenario as shown in Fig. 16.27.

All the cell sizes are not the same in a nonuniform CDMA system. We consider only the three cells most affected by the locations of the three vehicles. The vehicles are at the most interference-prone location in each cell.

In this case, the $(C/I)_F$ received at vehicle 1 is

$$(C_1/I_1)_F = \frac{\alpha_1 R_1^{-4}}{(m_1 - 1)\alpha_i R_1^{-4} + \alpha_2 m_2 R_2^{-4} + \alpha_3 m_3 R_3^{-4} + I_{\alpha_1}} \tag{16.4-16}$$

where I_{α_1} is the interference coming from other cells outside the three. I_{α_1} is usually very small compared to the second and third terms in the denominator and can be neglected.

The received $(C/I)_F$ at vehicle 2 is

$$(C_2/I_2)_F = \frac{\alpha_2 R_2^{-4}}{(m_2 - 1)\alpha_2 R_2^{-4} + \alpha_1 m_1 R_1^{-4} + \alpha_3 m_3 R_3^{-4} + I_{\alpha_2}} \tag{16.4-17}$$

The received $(C/I)_F$ at vehicle 3 is

$$(C_3/I_3)_F = \frac{\alpha_2 R_2^{-4}}{(m_3 - 1)\alpha_3 R_3^{-4} + \alpha_1 m_1 R_1^{-4} + \alpha_2 m_2 R_2^{-4} + I_{\alpha_3}} \tag{16.4-18}$$

Let

$$(C_1/I_1)_F = (C_2/I_2)_F = (C_3/I_3)_F = (C/I)_F$$

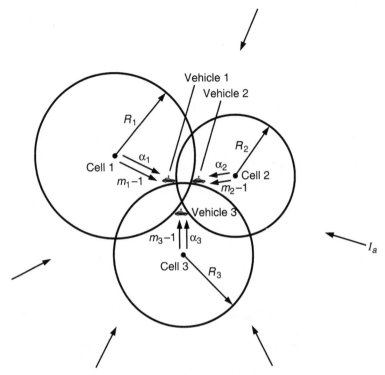

FIGURE 16.27 The worst-case scenario for forward link channel reception in a nonuniform CDMA system.

and

$$I_{\alpha_1} = I_{\alpha_2} = I_{\alpha_3} = 0$$

Simplifying Eqs. (16.4-16), (16.4-17), and (16.4-18), we obtain respectively:

$$\alpha_1 m_1 + \alpha_2 m_2 \left(\frac{R_2}{R_1}\right)^{-4} + \alpha_3 m_3 \left(\frac{R_3}{R_1}\right)^{-4}$$

$$= \alpha_1 \left[\frac{1}{(C/I)_F} + 1\right] = \alpha_1 G \qquad (16.4\text{-}19)$$

$$\alpha_1 m_1 \left(\frac{R_1}{R_2}\right)^{-4} + \alpha_2 m_2 + \alpha_3 m_3 \left(\frac{R_3}{R_2}\right)^{-4} = \alpha_2 G \qquad (16.4\text{-}20)$$

$$\alpha_1 m_1 \left(\frac{R_1}{R_3}\right)^{-4} + \alpha_2 m_2 \left(\frac{R_2}{R_3}\right)^{-4} + \alpha_3 m_3 = \alpha_3 G \qquad (16.4\text{-}21)$$

Solving Eqs. (16.4-19), (16.4-20), and (16.4-21) we come up with the following relation:

$$\alpha_1 R_1^{-4} = \alpha_2 R_2^{-4} = \alpha_3 R_3^{-4} \qquad (16.4\text{-}22)$$

Also, assume that the minimum values of α_1, α_2, and α_3 will be α_1^0, α_2^0, and α_3^0, respectively, which are based purely on the received level of individual voice channels at the vehicle locations:

$$\alpha_1 \geq \alpha_1^0 = C_0 R_1^{+4} + k$$

$$\alpha_2 \geq \alpha_2^0 = C_0 R_2^{+4} + k \qquad (16.4\text{-}23)$$

$$\alpha_3 \geq \alpha_3^0 = C_0 R_3^{+4} + k$$

where C_0 is the required signal level received at the vehicle location and k is a constant related to the antenna heights at the cell sites.

Now the total transmit power of each cell site will be

$$P_1 = m_1 \alpha_1$$

$$P_2 = m_2 \alpha_2 \qquad (16.4\text{-}24)$$

$$P_3 = m_3 \alpha_3$$

16.4.4.2 Transmit Power on the Reverse Link Channels. On the reverse link channels, we use the same worst-case scenario (Fig. 16.28). According to the power control algorithm,

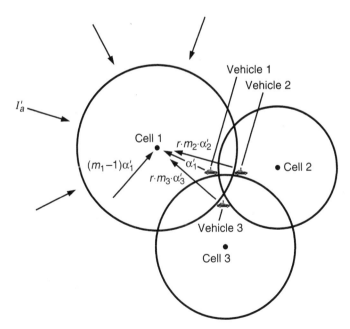

FIGURE 16.28 The worst-case scenario for reverse-link channel reception in a nonuniform CDMA system.

all the signals will be the same when they reach the cell site. The vehicle 1 signal received at cell site 1 is C_1, the rest of the signals are considered interference.

$$(C_1/I_1)_R \geq \frac{\alpha'_1 R_1^{-4}}{(m_1 - 1)\alpha'_1 R_1^{-4} + r_{12} m_2 \alpha'_2 R_1^{-4} + r_{13} m_3 \alpha'_3 R_1^{-4} + I'_{\alpha_1}} \tag{16.4-25}$$

where α'_1, α'_2, and α'_3 are the powers of individual channels transmitted back to their corresponding cell sites, r_{12} and r_{13} are the portion of the total number of voice channels in adjacent cells that will interfere with the desired signal at cell 1, and I'_{α_1} is the interference coming from vehicles in cells other than cell 2 and cell 3. I'_{α_1} is a relatively small value and can be neglected.

Using the same steps, we can derive the following two equations for the two other cases. Cell site 2 receives the vehicle 2 signal:

$$(C_2/I_2)_R \geq \frac{\alpha'_2 R_2^{-4}}{r_{21} m_1 \alpha'_1 R_2^{-4} + (m_2 - 1)\alpha'_2 R_2^{-4} + r_{23} m_3 \alpha'_3 R_2^{-4}} \tag{16.4-26}$$

Cell site 3 receives the vehicle 3 signal:

$$(C_3/I_3)_R \geq \frac{\alpha'_3 R_3^{-4}}{r_{31} m_1 \alpha'_1 R_3^{-4} + r_{32} m_2 \alpha'_2 R_3^{-4} + (m_3 - 1)\alpha'_3 \cdot R_3^{-4}} \tag{16.4-27}$$

where r is the percentage of total channels from the interfering cell that would be received by the cell site. Simplifying Eqs. (16.4-25), (16.4-26), and (16.4-27), we obtain:

$$(I/C)_R \geq (m_1 - 1) + r_{12} m_2 \frac{\alpha'_2}{\alpha'_1} + r_{13} m_3 \frac{\alpha'_3}{\alpha'_1} \tag{16.4-28}$$

$$(I/C)_R \geq r_{21} m_1 \frac{\alpha'_1}{\alpha'_2} + (m_2 - 1) + r_{23} m_3 \frac{\alpha'_3}{\alpha'_2} \tag{16.4-29}$$

$$(I/C)_R \geq r_{31} m_1 \frac{\alpha'_1}{\alpha'_3} + r_{32} m_2 \frac{\alpha'_2}{\alpha'_3} + (m_3 - 1) \tag{16.4-30}$$

where

$$(C/I)_R = (C_1/I_1)_R = (C_2/I_2)_R = (C_3/I_3)_R$$

All the coefficients in Eq. (16.4-28) to Eq. (16.4-30) involve the transmit power of a voice channel in each of the three cells, α'_1, α'_2, and α'_3.

For the same reason stated in the derivation of Eq. (16.4-23), the minimum values of α'_1, α'_2, and α'_3 can be defined as follows:

$$\alpha'_1 \geq \alpha^0_1 = C_0 R_1^4 + k$$

$$\alpha'_2 \geq \alpha^0_2 = C_0 R_2^4 + k \tag{16.4-31}$$

$$\alpha'_3 \geq \alpha^0_3 = C_0 R_3^4 + k$$

where R_1, R_2, and R_3 are the radii of the three cells and k is a constant related to the antenna heights as the cell sites. We may replace all the α' terms in Eqs. (16.4-28), (16.4-29), and

(16.4-30) with the equivalent α^0 terms in Eq. (16.4-31). Equations (16.4-28), (16.4-29), and (16.4-30) become

$$(I/C)_R \geq (m_1 - 1) + r_{12}m_2 \left(\frac{R_2}{R_1}\right)^4 + r_{13}m_3 \left(\frac{R_3}{R_1}\right)^4 \qquad (16.4\text{-}32)$$

$$(I/C)_R \geq r_{21}m_1 \left(\frac{R_1}{R_2}\right)^4 + (m_2 - 1) + r_{23}m_3 \left(\frac{R_3}{R_2}\right)^4 \qquad (16.4\text{-}33)$$

$$(I/C)_R \geq r_{31}m_1 \left(\frac{R_1}{R_3}\right)^4 + r_{32}m_2 \left(\frac{R_2}{R_3}\right)^4 + (m_3 - 1) \qquad (16.4\text{-}34)$$

Under the physical condition, the following relationships have to be held. The values m_1, m_2, and m_3 have to be

$$m_1, m_2, m_3 < \frac{1}{(C/I)_R} + 1 \qquad (16.4\text{-}35)$$

which has been derived in Eq. (16.3-4).

16.4.4.3 Designing a CDMA System. We first have to check whether all the requirements expressed in Eqs. (16.4-32) to (16.4-34) are met with our given conditions. If they are met, then we can find the transmit powers P_1, P_2, and P_3 from Eq. (16.4-24). Usually, among the three equations, only one dominates. If that one meets the given conditions, the other two will meet them also. The following example addresses this point.

EXAMPLE 16.2 *Given: $R_1 = 4$ km, $R_2 = 6$ km, $R_3 = 5$ km, and $(C/I)_R = -17$ dB. Also assume that:*

$$r_{13} = r_{31} = 0.3$$

$$r_{21} = r_{12} = 0.2$$

$$r_{23} = r_{32} = 0.25$$

Then, checking the conditions in Eqs. (16.4-32) through (16.4-34), we obtain:

$$50 \geq m_1 - 1 + 1.0125m_2 + 0.7324m_3 \qquad (16.4\text{-}36)$$

$$50 \geq 0.0395m_1 + m_2 - 1 + 0.1205m_3 \qquad (16.4\text{-}37)$$

$$50 \geq 0.1299m_1 + 0.5184m_2 + m_3 - 1 \qquad (16.4\text{-}38)$$

Among the three equations, Eq. (16.4-36) should be checked first.
Let $m_1 = 20$. Then

$$31 \geq 1.0125m_2 + 0.7324m_3 \qquad (16.4\text{-}39)$$

$$50.21 \geq m_2 + 0.1205m_3 \qquad (16.4\text{-}40)$$

$$48.54 \geq 0.5184m_2 + m_3 \qquad (16.4\text{-}41)$$

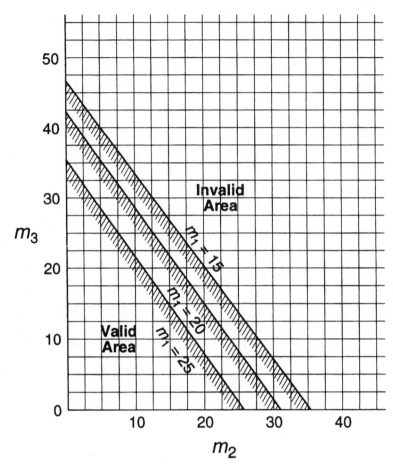

FIGURE 16.29   The limiting conditions of designing a CDMA system.

Among the three equations, the condition of Eq. (16.4-39) is the limiting condition. Also, we may find the conditions for $m_1 = 15$ and $m_2 = 25$ as follows:

$$36 \geq 1.0125m_2 + 0.7324m_3 \qquad (m_1 = 15) \qquad (16.4\text{-}42)$$

$$26 \geq 1.0125m_2 + 0.7324m_3 \qquad (m_1 = 25) \qquad (16.4\text{-}43)$$

The three curves, $m_1 = 15, 20, 25$, are plotted in Fig. 16.29 for various values of m_2 and m_3. From the figure, we may pick three values such as $m_1 = 25, m_2 = 20$, and $m_3 = 7$, and assume that $C = -95$ dBm. Then the transmit power of each voice channel in the respective cell is

$$\alpha_1 = -95\,\text{dBm} + 40\log R_1^4 + k \qquad \text{(for cell 1)}$$

$$\alpha_2 = -95\,\text{dBm} + 40\log R_2^4 + k \qquad \text{(for cell 2)}$$

$$\alpha_3 = -95\,\text{dBm} + 40\log R_3^4 + k \qquad \text{(for cell 3)}$$

where k is a constant depending on the antenna height.
From Eq. (16.4-31), the total power will be

$$P_1 = m_1\alpha_1$$

$$P_2 = m_2\alpha_2$$

$$P_3 = m_3\alpha_3$$

16.5 MIMO
(MULTIPLE INPUT–MULTIPLE OUTPUT)

16.5.1 Introduction

In wireless communications, bandwidth limitations, propagation loss, time variance, noise, interference, and multipath fading make the wireless channel a narrow pipe in which it is difficult to accommodate the flow of data. Further challenges come from power limitations as well as size and speed of wireless portable devices.

In the previous sections, we have introduced the techniques that improve spectral efficiency and combat various types of channel impairments, such as the cellular structure that allows frequency reuse and antenna arrays (smart antennas) that provide spatial diversity and beam forming. These techniques have enormous impact on the extension of improving the wireless communication. Because the request for wireless access to the Internet and future generation wireless systems is leading to a need for much higher capacities than achieved by today's system, the concept of MIMO rises to further improve the channel capacity as mentioned in Sec. 8.14.4. The idea of separating signal transmission in a temporal and spatial domain is not new. The SIMO system, one transmitter and multiple receiver, is known as the receive diversity. It implements with maximum ratio combining scheme to achieve higher capacities. Also, the transmit diversity using two transmit and one receive antenna is a promising technique to increase data rate providing the following requirements:

1. Perfect knowledge of the channel at the receiver.

2. The encoding and transmission sequence of information symbols at the transmitter. The encoding is done in space and time (space-time coding).

3. Maximum ratio combine at the receiver.

4. The decision rule for maximum likelihood detection.

Transmit diversity is an earlier technology moving to the MIMO.

MIMO[24-27] employs multiple transmit and receive antennas, and the transmission capacities can be increased dramatically. Space-time coding and space-time algorithm are necessary in order to ensure an effective approach to the increasing data rate. Space-time coding is a coding technique that is designed for use with multiple transmit antennas. The technique introduces temporal and spatial correlation into signals transmitted from different antennas. The aim is to provide diversity at the receiver and coding gain over an uncoded system without sacrificing the bandwidth. Space-time separation algorithm can be seen as the algorithm that separates the signals transmitted from different antennas on the receive antenna array. With further development of MIMO communication systems, the coding and the space-time separation schemes will more and more tie together. MIMO systems are able to provide the enormous capacity increases that will enable high-speed mobile Internet access, enhanced-capacity wireless local loops, wireless high-definition video transport, and other exciting applications.

16.5.2 Description of Technology [28–30]

MIMO is a dual-antenna system. Consider a wireless communication system with N_t transmit (T) and N_r receive (R) antennas. The idea is to transmit different streams of data on the different transmit antennas, but at the same carrier frequency. The signal on the pth transmit antenna, as function of the time t, will be denoted by $s_p(t)$. When a transmission occurs, the transmitted signal from the pth Tx antenna might find different paths to arrive at the qth Rx antenna, namely, a direct path and indirect paths through a number of reflections. This principle is called multipath. Suppose that the bandwidth B of the system is chosen such that the time delays between the first and last arriving path at the receiver is considerably smaller than $1/B$, then the system is called a flat fading system. For such a system, all the multipath components between the pth Tx and qth Rx antenna can be summed up to one term, say $h_{qp}(t)$. Because the signals from all transmit antennas are sent at the same frequency, the qth receive antenna will not only receive signals from the pth, but from all N_t transmitters. The received signal x_q from the qth antenna is

$$x_q(t) = \sum_{p=1}^{N_t} h_{qp}(t)s_p(t) \tag{16.5-1}$$

h_{qp} must be known at the receiver. Sending a training sequence from each transmitter and receiving it at the receiver to estimate the channel parameters can do it. A schematic representation of a MIMO communication scheme can be found in Figure 16.30.

Mathematically, a MIMO transmission can be seen as a set of equations. The recordings of x_q's in Eq. (16.5-1) on each Rx antenna are obtained with a number of unknowns such as the transmitted signals. If every equation represents a unique combination of the unknown variables and number of equations is equal to the number of unknowns, then there exists a unique solution to the problem. If the number of equations is larger than the number of unknowns, a solution can be found by performing a projection using the least squares

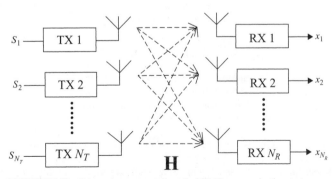

FIGURE 16.30 Schematic representation of a MIMO communication system.

method, also known as the Zero Forcing (ZF) method. For the symmetric case, the ZF solution results in the unique solution.

More detail about the MIMO technology can be found in References 28–30.

16.5.3 MIMO Capacity

A. Idea environment for MIMO system: The analysis of MIMO system is based on the idea that if fades between pairs of transmit-receive antenna are identical independent distributed (i.i.d), then the average channel capacity of a dual-antenna system that uses n antennas at both the transmitter and the receiver is approximately n times higher than that of a single-antenna system for a fixed bandwidth and a fixed overall transmitted power.

In the following, the necessary requirements to obtain these capacities for systems having multiple antennas at both the transmitter and the receiver are described.

- Antenna arrays with sufficient spacing must be deployed at both ends.

- The propagation environment between the transmitter and the receiver must provide numerous propagation paths.

- The link must employ such as frequency- or code-division multiplexing to ensure that the signals sent by different transmitter antennas are orthogonal to each other at the receiver end.

- The receiver must be able to measure or estimate the channel gain, both amplitude and phase shift. To date, the proposed detection techniques require the receiver to apply coherent processing techniques of the received signal.

- The burst duration should be short enough that the channel can be treated essentially as static during a burst but long enough that the standard information-theoretic assumption can be applied.

B. AWGN channel, with bandwidth B, a noise spectral density $N_o/2$ watts/Hz, and a carrier power C can be written as

$$\hat{C} = B \cdot \log_2(1 + \frac{C}{N_o B}) \, \text{bps} \tag{16.5-2}$$

Using a bandwidth of 30 kHz and a CNR of 20 dB, the capacity would be 200 kbps.

The capacity of MIMO can be expressed as

$$\hat{C} = \log_2[\det(I_n + \frac{\rho}{n} HH^\dagger)] = \sum_{k=1}^{N} \log_2(1 + \frac{\rho}{k}\eta^2) \tag{16.5-3}$$

where ρ is CNR, $|H|^2$ is the normalized channel power transfer function, η^2 denotes the eigen values of $HH^\dagger$, $H^\dagger$ is the transposed conjugate, N is denoted by min(N_T, N_R), which is the smaller number of these two, and N channels assumed to be i.i.d flat Rayleigh fading.

From Eq. (16.5-3), we can find that the channel capacity can increase linearly with the min (N_T, N_R). The channel state information (CSI) plays in two types of respect, an important role. The definition of the channel capacity for a MIMO system assumes that the receive side knows the CSI perfectly. On the other side, if the transmit side has the CSI adaptive power allocation, adaptive modulation or/and coding can be applied.

The MIMO link[31-32] is known as rich scattering channels, and with appropriate signal processing, this can bring about an increased data rate of an order of magnitude or more.

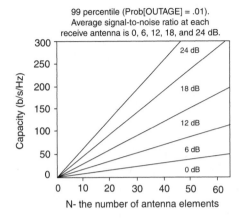

FIGURE 16.31 Capacity vs the number of antenna elements.

C. Simulation

For proving the MIMO technology in the wireless design process, increasingly complex channel models must be used in simulations to realistically assess system performance. These models must take into account the statistical behavior of various phenomena: shadowing (long-term fading), multipath (short-term fading), Doppler spread, angle spread (related to the topology of the scattering region), and in MIMO, correlations between the signal envelopes received/transmitted from different antennas.

D. Implementation of MIMO system: The MIMO can be easily implemented in the wireless systems at an operation frequency over 5 GHz. For a frequency at 5.8 GHz, the wavelength is 5.17 cm. The half-wavelength spacing (λ) is required for achieving independent antenna separation. Then an 8×8 (8 input and 8 output) MIMO planer antenna needs a linear length of 17.5 cm (7×2.5 cm). This size may be suitable for mounting on a PC. If we make the antenna spacing smaller than $\lambda/2$, then the antenna mutual coupling prevails and the performance of MIMO will be deteriorated.

For demonstrating the performance of MIMO for $\eta_T = \eta_R = \eta$ at the 99 percentile, and average carrier-to-noise ratio at each receive antenna is 0, 6, 12, 18, and 24 dB, capacity is b/s/Hz versus the number of antenna elements at each site as shown in Fig. 16.31. The capacity is linearly proportional to the number of antenna elements.

REFERENCES

1. W. C. Y. Lee, *Mobile Communications Engineering*, 2nd ed. McGraw Hill, 1998, p. 520.

2. V. H. MacDonald, "The Cellular Concept," *Bell System Technical Journal*, vol. 58, January 1979, pp. 15–42.

3. W. C. Y. Lee, "Spectrum Efficiency in Cellular," *IEEE Transactions of Vehicular Technology*, May 1989, pp. 69–75.

4. W. C. Y. Lee, "Smaller Cell for Greater Performance," *IEEE Communication Magazine*, November 1991, pp. 19–23.

5. M. Cooper and R. Roy, "SDMA Technology—Overview and Development Status," ArrayComm-ID-010, ArrayComm, Inc., Mountain View, Calif.

6. W. C. Y. Lee, "Lee's Model," *IEEE VTS Conference Record 1992*, Denver, May 11, 1992, pp. 343–348.

7. W. C. Y. Lee, *Mobile Communications Engineering*, 2nd ed. McGraw Hill, 1998, p. 235.

8. K. Gilhousen, I. Jacobs, R. Padovani, A. Viterbi, L. Weaver, C. Wheatley, "On the Capacity of a Cellular CDMA System," *IEEE Transactions on Vehicular Technology*, Vol. 40, May 1991, pp. 303–312.

9. R. Pickholtz, L. Milstein, D. Schilling, "Spread Spectrum for Mobile Communications," *IEEE Transactions on Vehicular Technology*, Vol. 40, May 1991, pp. 313–322.

10. W. C. Y. Lee, "Overview of Cellular CDMA," *IEEE Transactions on Vehicular Technology*, Vol. 40, May 1991, pp. 291–302.

11. ETSI/TC, "Recommendation GSM 01.02," ETSI/PT12, January 1990.

12. R. A. Comroe and D. J. Costello, Jr., "ARQ Schemes for Data Transmission in Mobile Radio Systems," *IEEE Transactions on Vehicular Technology*, vol. VT-33, August 1984, pp. 88–97.

13. F. Anderson, W. Christensen, L. Fullerton, B. Kortegaard, "Ultra-Wideband Beam-forming in Sparse Arrays," *IEEE Proceedings*, vol. 138, no. 4, August 1991, pp. 342–346.

14. R. A. Scholtz, "Multiple Access with Time-Hopping Impulse Modulation," MILCOM 1993, Boston, October 11–14, 1993.

15. K. Raith and J. Uddenfeldt, "Capacity of Digital Cellular TDMA Systems," *IEEE Trans. on Vehicular Technology*, vol. 40, May 1991, pp. 323–332.

16. J. C. Liberti, Jr., and T. S. Rappaport, "Analytical Results for Capacity Improvement in CDMA," *IEEE Trans on VT*, vol. 43, August 1994, pp. 680–690.

17. W. C. Y. Lee, "An Innovative Microcell System," *Cellular Business*, December 1991, pp. 42–44.

18. W. C. Y. Lee, "Applying the Intelligent Cell Concept to PCS," *IEEE Trans. on VT*, vol. 43, August 1994, pp. 672–679.

19. Allen Telecomm Co. and 3dBM Co. manufacture analog converters, ADC Kentron manufacture digital converters.

20. D. Parsons, *The Mobile Radio Propagation Channel*, Pentech Press, London, 1992.

21. H. H. Xia, H. L. Bertoni, L. R. Maciel, A. Lindsay-Stewart, and R. Low, "Microcellular Propagation Characteristics for Personal Communications in Urban and Suburban Environments," *IEEE Transactions on Vehicular Technology*, Part II Special Issue on Future PCS Technologies, vol. 43, August 1994.

22. W. C. Y. Lee, "In-building Telephone Communication System," U.S. patent office number 5,349,631, Sept. 20, 1994.

23. W. C. Y. Lee, Mobile Communications Design Fundamentals, John Wiley & Sons, 1993; Section 2.7 microcell prediction model.

24. W. C. Y. Lee, "Key Elements in Designing a CDMA System," *IEEE VTC '94 Conference Record*, Stockholm, Sweden, June 8–10, 1994, pp. 1547–1550. Also appeared in " Code Division Multiple Access Communications" edited by S. G. Glisic and P.A. Leppanen, Kluwer Acadmic Publishers, 1995, pp. 269–282.

25. Siavash M. Alamouti, "A Simple Transmit Diversity Technique for Wireless Communications" IEEE Journal on Select Area in Communications, vol. 16, no. 8, Oct, 1998, pp. 1451–1458.

26. A. Van Zelst. "Physical Interpretation of MIMO Transmissions," Proceeding Symposium IEEE Belelux Chapter on Communications and Vehicular Technology, 2003, Eindhoven.

27. G. J. Foschini, "Layered space-time architecture for wireless communication in a fading environment when using multi-element antennas," *Bell Labs Tech. J.*, pp. 41–59, autumn 1996. Also G. J. Foschini and M. J. Gans, "On limits of wireless communications in a fading environment when using multiple antennas," *Wireless Personal Communications*, vol. 6, pp. 311–335, 1998.

28. D. Gesbert et al., "From Theory to Practice: An Overview of MIMO Space-Time Coded Wireless Systems," *IEEE JSAC*, vol. 21, no. 3, 2003, pp. 281–302.

29. A. J. Paulraj et al., "An Overview of MIMO Communications–A Key to Gigabit Wireless," *Proc. IEEE*, vol. 92, no. 2, Feb. 2004, pp. 198–218.

30. Special Issue on MIMO Systems and Applications, *IEEE JSAC*, vol. 21, no. 3, Apr. 2003.

31. Special Issue on "Adaptive Antennas and MIMO Systems for Wireless Communications" Part I, *IEEE Communications Magazine*, Nov. 2004, vol. 42, no. 11.

32. Special Issues on Adaptive Antennas and MIMO systems for Wireless Communications Part II, *IEEE Communication Magazine*, Dec. 2004, vol. 42, no. 12.

CHAPTER 17
INTELLIGENT NETWORK FOR WIRELESS COMMUNICATIONS

17.1 ADVANCED INTELLIGENT NETWORK (AIN)

AIN is a network evolving from the intelligent network (IN).[1-3] It has an independent architecture that allows telecommunication service operators to rapidly create and modify services for both network performance and customers' needs.

In the intelligent network concept, the service providers need more control for new service offerings. The IN is able to separate the specification, creation, and control of telecommunication services from the physical switching network such that the HLR (home location register) and the VLR (visitor location register) are no longer integrated in the MSC (mobile switching center).

17.1.1 Intelligent Network Evolution

17.1.1.1 History of Network Evolution. In the 1960s, crossbar switches were developed and demonstrated to be very reliable switches. However, crossbar switches are mechanical and do not provide the intelligence. Then, the No. 1 ESS (electronic switching system) was developed by AT&T and provided stored program control (SPC) capability. In 1965, SPC delivered call waiting and centrex features on No. 1 ESS. In the 1970s, ESSs provided intelligent in-network management and maintenance and offered operations systems (OS) and operation, administration, and maintenance (OA&M). In the 1980s, the intelligent network introduced centralized databases and provided the network database services such as 800 toll-free calls and calling card calls. In 1983, the centralized databases were located at the service control point (SCP) to support alternate billing services (ABS) and 800 calling. The data flow from the physical switches to the SCP is via SS7 (Signaling System No. 7) network. There are several intelligent networks:

IN/1: Functionality is distributed not only at the switches but also at the SS7 network, SCPs, and OSs.

IN/2: To expand the switching and SCP capabilities known as *functional components* (FC), and with these expansions to form a new system called the *intelligent peripheral system* (IPS). It is capable of supporting a wide range of voice and data services.

AIN: The IN evolution began in the 1990s at a forum called Multivendor Interaction (MVI) in which 16 vendors participated. AIN was defined by a series of releases.

Each release contains additional architecture attributes and capabilities of supporting services.

17.1.1.2 AIN's Network Characteristics. AIN is evolving from IN, and its characteristics are as follows:

- Modular: divided into functional entities
- Uniform: became standard architecture
- Service independent
- Programmable network operable by either user or carrier provider, or both
- Supplier transparent: open system architecture (OSA)
- Capable of rapid introduction of new services
- Accessible for other service providers
- Common channel signaling (CCS): using out-of-band signaling
- Service logic: invokes AIN service logic programs (SLPs)

AIN uses CCS to deliver the call set-up signaling and the network information. In this case, the traffic channels are never tied up for signaling. For example, if the called party line is detected as busy by the signaling channel, the network would not assign a traffic channel to the calling party. Thus, the efficient use of the traffic channels increases. Also the use of CCS can increase the speed of process for call process and information delivery. The CCS network uses digital channels with the SS7 protocol at a rate of 56 kbps.

17.1.2 AIN Elements

An AIN (Fig. 17.1) consists of the following elements:

Service control point. The SCP invokes service logic programs. The common channel signaling network allows the SCP to fully interconnect with AIN switching systems through a signaling transport point (STP). The SCP supports 800 toll-free phone calls, area number calling, or personal location services.

Adjunct system. A direct link to the AIN switching system with a high-speed interface.

Service node. Communicates with AIN switch via the integrated services digital network (ISDN) access link and supports user interaction.

Intelligent peripheral. Controls and manages resources such as voice synthesis announcement, speech recognition, and digit collection.

AIN switch. Routes a call to an IPS (IP system) to ask for a function. When the IPS completes the function, it also collects the user's information and sends it to AIN service logic (resides in SCP) via the AIN switch.

Operational system (OS). Provides memory administration, surveillance, network testing, and network traffic management maintenance and operation.

Signaling transport point (STP). The point that interconnects the SCP and AIN switching system.

Service management system (SMS). Provides three functions: (1) provision—creates service order, validation, load record; (2) maintenance—resolves record inconsistency,

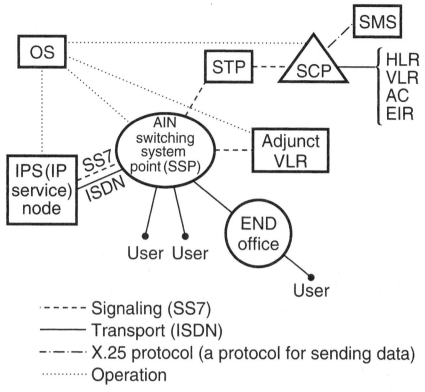

----- Signaling (SS7)
———— Transport (ISDN)
—·—·— X.25 protocol (a protocol for sending data)
············· Operation

FIGURE 17.1   AIN system architecture.

tests call processing logic, performs special studies; (3) administration—creates service logic, maintains service data.

Service switching point (SSP)/Switching point (SP). Functions as a switch.

17.1.3   AIN Interfaces

The interfaces between AIN network elements are

1. Between the switching system and SCPs or adjunct systems using SS7 signaling.

2. Between the switching system and IPS (or service nodes) using ISDN.

3. In AIN, between SCP and SMS using the X.25 protocol.

4. Between end users AIN services; may be either conventional analog or ISDN interface.

The AIN general architecture with the indicated AIN interfaces is shown in Fig. 17.1. In cellular system, the channel link between the mobile switching system and the user does not use ISDN, because a 64 kbps ISDN channel needs a bandwidth of 64 kHz for radio transmission. In cellular systems, the data rate of a channel is 16 kbps or less and needs only a bandwidth of 25 kHz or less. Using less channel bandwidth increases more spectrum efficiency.

17.2 SS7 NETWORK AND ISDN FOR AIN

17.2.1 History of SS7[4]

This is an out-of-band signaling method in which a common data channel is used to convey signaling information related to a large number of trunks (voice and data). Signaling has traditionally supported (1) supervisory functions (e.g., on-hook/off-hook to indicate idle or busy status); (2) addressing function (e.g., called number); and (3) calling information (e.g., dial tone and busy signals). The introduction of electronic processors in switching systems made it possible to provide common channel signaling.

In 1976, common channel interoffice signaling (CCIS) was introduced. (CCIS) is based on the International Consultative Committee on Telegraphy and Telephony (CCITT) Signaling System No. 6 recommendations and called CCS6. The CCS6 protocol structure was not layered. It was a monolithic structure. The signaling efficiency was high.

In 1980 CCITT first recommended SS7, a signaling system for digital trunks. The layered approach to designing SS7 protocols was being developed for open system interconnection (OSI) data transport. Also, the HDLC (higher-level data link control) bit-oriented protocols had an influence on the development of SS7.

17.2.2 SS7 Protocol Model

The inefficiencies of layered protocols are far outweighed by their flexibility in realization and management of complex functions. The protocol becomes more aligned with the seven-layer OSI reference model (Fig. 17.2a). The seven layers are physical, data link, network, transport, session, presentation, and application. The SS7 protocol model is shown in Fig. 17.2b for comparison with the OSI model. In SS7, the message transfer part (MTP) provides the OSI layered protocol model as level 1 data service, level 2 link service, and level 3 network service. The full level 3 service is provided by the signaling connection

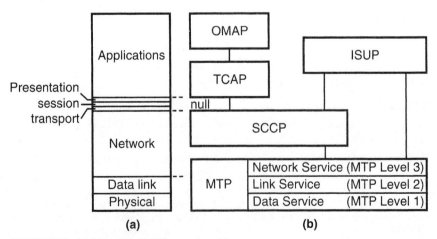

FIGURE 17.2   (a) OSI model. (b) SS7 protocol model.

control part (SCCP). SCCP provides an enhanced addressing capability that may be considered as level 3+ or a level close to level 4. Layers 4 to 6 in the OSI model do not exist in the SS7 protocol model. The transaction capabilities application part (TCAP) level and the operations maintenance and administration part (OMAP) level are considered the same as the application part (level 7) in OSI. The application service element (ASE) is at the same level as OMAP. TCAP includes protocols and services to perform remote operations. The primary use of TCAP in these networks is for invoking remote procedures in supporting IN services like 800 service. OMAP provides the application protocols and procedures to monitor, coordinate, and control all the network resources which make communication based on SS7 possible. ASE is for the MTP routing verification test (MRVT), which uses the connectionless services of TCAP. MRVT is an important function of OMAP.

17.2.3   SS7 Network Link Deployment for AIN

The SS7 links can provide high-speed service because of the common channel signaling. Based on the connection among all the resource elements, there are six links from A to F.

$$
\text{A link:} \quad \begin{cases} \text{STP} \leftrightarrow \text{SCP} \\ \text{STP} \leftrightarrow \text{SP/SSP} \end{cases}
$$

B/D and C links   STP ↔ STP

E link   STP ↔ SP/SSP

F link   SP/SSP ↔ SP/SSP

The SS7 network link deployment chart is shown in Fig. 17.3. The interfaces between any two entities are indicated by the letters from A to F.

17.2.4   ISDN

Signaling has evolved with the technology of the telephone. The integrated services digital network (ISDN)[5] is used to integrate all-digital networks in which the same digital exchanges and digital transmission paths are used for provision of all voice and data services.

Signaling in ISDN has two distinct components:

- Signaling between the user and the network node to which the user is connected (access signaling). The SS7 signaling is not used between the mobile user and network node.

- Signaling between the network nodes (network signaling)

The current set of protocol standards for ISDN signaling is Signaling System No. 7 (SS7).

17.2.4.1   ISDN-UP.   In the SS7 protocol model, functions not covered by the SS7 levels will be provided by the ISDN-UP protocol, such as the signaling functions that are needed to support the basic bearer service and supplementary services for switched voice and data applications in an ISDN environment.

17.2.4.2   B-ISDN.[6]   The broadband ISDN will support a range of voice, video, data, image, and multimedia services using available resources. These resources include transmission, switching and buffer capacity, and control intelligence. The target is to

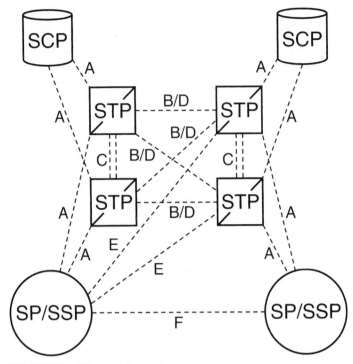

FIGURE 17.3 SS7 network link deployment.

provide switched services over synchronous optical network/asynchronous transfer mode (SONET/ATM) transport using signaling based on the extended ISDN protocol.

17.2.5 SONET and ATM[7,8]

A fiber-optic transport system named SONET was introduced in 1984. By 1988, as a global transmission standard, synchronous digital hierarchy (SDH) became an umbrella standard that allowed local variations. SDH is a set of interface standards that is common to all SONET equipment. The highest rate for SONET is 155 Mbps. Rates above 155 Mbps can be carried by the ATM cells. All services are divided into a series of cells and routed across the ATM network via an ATM switch which is a broad band switch. ATM is a connection-oriented packet-like switching and multiplexing principle. ATM offers flexibility and relative simplicity in network arrangements as a whole. ATM has been chosen by CCITT as the information transfer mode for B-ISDN.

Present SONET rings use STM (synchronous transfer mode). SONET rings can be self-healing rings to provide reliable transport for high-speed switched data services such as SMDS (switched multimegabit data service) and FDDI (fiber distributed data interface interconnection). A four-channel information structure for SONET uses STM, shown in Fig. 17.4a. A frame consists of five time slots; a framing slot and four channel slots. Recently a

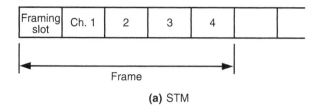

(a) STM

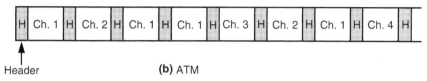

Header   (b) ATM

FIGURE 17.4 The information structures of (*a*) STM and (*b*) ATM.

SONET ring uses ATM is called SONET/ATM ring which architecture using point-to-point virtue paths overcomes the problem of inefficient and expensive use of SONET bandwidth for SMDS services. In an ATM information structure, the information is carried in fixed-size cells that consist of a header and an information field. The header contains a label that uniquely identifies a logical channel and is used for multiplexing, routing, and switching. A four-cell ATM information structure is shown in Fig. 17.4*b*. The physical transport of ATM cells is the SONET or SDH optical network.

17.3 AIN FOR MOBILE COMMUNICATION

The AIN for mobile communication[9–12] has to meet a unique requirement: the call has to reach the mobile station in a required time frame while it is in motion. Therefore, the call processing time or the handoff time has to be within a specific limit, otherwise the mobile station can move out of the coverage area and the call either cannot be connected or will be dropped. Besides, the call has to be delivered to wherever the mobile station is (i.e., the system must have a roaming feature). The system handoff between the two different systems also needs AIN.

Two major directions in AIN for mobile communications are wireless access technology and increased network functionality. Wireless access technology is aiming at low power, light weight, efficiently used spectrum, and low-cost operation and maintenance. The increased network functionality is achieved through the use of SS7 for call control and database transactions. Mobility is the main concern in the connectionless structure of the protocol, which has to be suited to real-time application. The mobile application part (MAP) can be applied to mobile communications. The exchange of data between components of a mobile network to support end user mobility and network call control are taken care of by MAP. The MAP is an application service element. The MAP of CCITT SS7 is shown in Fig. 17.5. TCAP is composed of both the component sublayer and transaction sublayer. The component sublayer provides the exchange of protocol data units, invoking remote

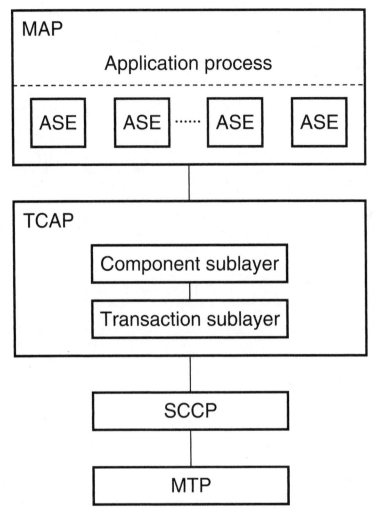

FIGURE 17.5   Map of CCITT SS7.

operations and reporting their results. The transaction sublayer is responsible for establishing a pseudo-association service for exchange of related protocol data units. The interrogations and transfer of information take place by using the ASE of the MAP and the component sublayer of TCAP. A number of MAP procedures relate to (1) location registration and cancellation, (2) handling of supplementary services, (3) retrieval of subscriber information during call establishment, (4) handoff, and (5) subscriber management including location information request and retrieval. The AIN mobile system architecture is shown in Fig. 17.6, which is the same as Fig. 17.1 except that SSP is replaced by MSC, and SMS collocates with the service creation environment (SCE), which defines new features and services.

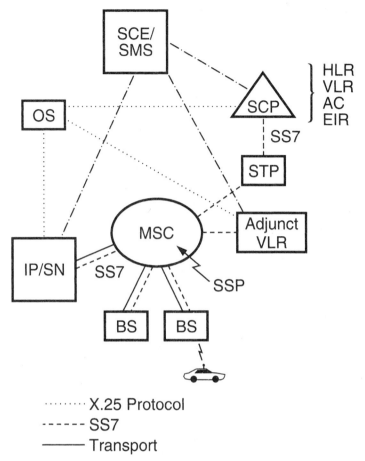

········ X.25 Protocol
------ SS7
—— Transport

FIGURE 17.6 Mobile communication architecture.

17.4 ASYNCHRONOUS TRANSFER MODE (ATM) TECHNOLOGY

ATM technology,[13–22] because of its flexibility and its support of multimedia traffic, draws much interest and attention. In wire line and wireless communications, we are interested in broadband switches as mentioned in Sec. 17.2.5. The ATM switch can meet our needs. The ATM technology will be described in this section.

The interest in ATM first came from carriers and manufacturers of wide-area networking equipment, and now interest is growing in the application of ATM technology to the local and campus area networking environment. ATM is designed to support multimedia traffic and is capable of offering seamless integration with wide-area ATM networks, both public and private. Because it offers the benefit of handling the broadband signal channels needed for the increasing volume of data communications traffic, it has been chosen for the switch of B-ISDN. The ATM network concept is shown in Fig. 17.7.

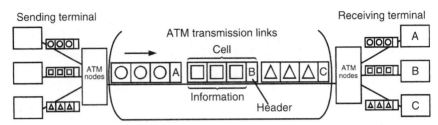

FIGURE 17.7   ATM network concept.

17.4.1   LAN Applications

For bringing ATM technology to the customer premises, it must offer LAN-like service for data traffic and be compatible with the existing data communication protocols, application, and equipment. A local-area network (LAN) offers connectionless (i.e., "best effort"), service for transferring variable size data packets. The term *best effort* means that the lost or corrupted packets are not retransmitted. Users are not required to establish a connection before submitting data for transmission, nor are they required to define the traffic characteristics of their data in advance of transmission.

17.4.2   Connectionless Service

ATM switches are connection-oriented. A connectionless server (a packet switch) attached to an ATM switch can provide connectionless service. The connectionless servers are connected together with virtual paths through the ATM switches to form a "virtual overlay network," the same as is used for narrowband ISDN.

17.4.3   Star Configuration

The physical topology of a LAN has migrated from the ring and multidrop toward the star (hub) configuration. As the bandwidth requirement of LAN approaches the gigabit per second range, switched star topologies are the most likely to be chosen in the commercial environment.

17.4.4   ATM Packet-Switching Techniques

ATM is a high-speed packet-switching technique using short fixed-length packets called *cells*. Fixed-length cells simplify the design of an ATM switch at the high switching speeds involved. The short fixed-length cell reduces the delay, and most significantly the variance of delay, which is *jitter*, for delay-sensitive services such as voice and video. Therefore, short fixed cells are capable of supporting a wide range of traffic types such as voice, video, image, and various classes of data traffic.

17.4.5   ATM Applications

1. ATM multiplexing and switching technologies are used for the B-ISDN.

2. ATM offers LAN, a high-capacity network.

3. ATM's switching technique offers seamless access to private widearea networking.

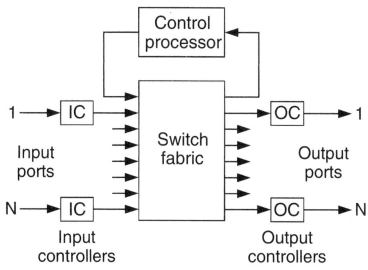

FIGURE 17.8   General structure of an ATM switch.

17.4.6   Connection-Oriented Service

All ATM cells belong to a preestablished virtual connection. All traffic is segmented into cells for transmission across an ATM network. The ATM standard or broadband ISDN defines a cell as having a fixed length of 53 bytes, consisting of a header of 5 bytes and a payload of 48 bytes. Each cell's header contains a virtual channel identifier (VCI) to identify the virtual connection to which the cell belongs. An ATM switch will handle a minimum of several hundred thousand cells per second at every switch port. Each switch port will support a throughput of at least 50 Mbps, while 150 Mbps and 600 Mbps are proposed as standard ports. A switch, if it has more than 100 ports, is considered a large switch. The general structure of an ATM switch is shown in Fig. 17.8. In an ATM switch, cell arrivals are not scheduled. A number of cells from different input ports may simultaneously request the same output port. This event is called *output contention*. A single output port can transmit only one cell at a time. Thus, only one cell can be accepted for transmission and others simultaneously requesting that port must either be buffered or discarded. Therefore, the most significant aspects of the ATM switch design are (1) the topology of the switch fabric, (2) the location of the cell buffers, and (3) the contention resolution mechanism.

17.4.6.1   Switch Fabric.   A switch fabric can be based on time division and space division.

1. *Time division.* All cells flow across a single communication highway shared in common by all input and output ports. The communication highway may be either a shared medium such as a ring or a multidrop bus, or a shared memory as shown in Fig. 17.9. This single shared highway fixes an upper limit on the capacity for a particular implementation.

2. *Space division.* A plurality of paths is provided between the input and output ports. These paths operate concurrently so that many cells may be transmitted across the switch fabric at the same time. Total capacity is measured as follows:

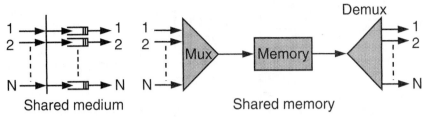

FIGURE 17.9   Time-division ATM switch fabrics.

$$\text{Capacity} = \text{path's bandwidth} \times \text{number of paths.}$$

The upper limit on the total capacity is theoretically unlimited. However, it is restricted by physical implementation constraints, (i.e., device capability, connector restrictions, and synchronization considerations for high capacity). There are two approaches:

a. A single-path, self-routing interconnection network is most often proposed for use in ATM switch design.

b. Multiple-path networks are used to improve the performance of a single-path network or to construct large switches from switch modules. Since multiple paths are available between every input-output pair, an algorithm is required to select one of the paths.

17.4.6.2   Buffering Strategies.   The buffering strategy is based on whether any cell queries are located within the switch fabric (internally buffered) or outside the switch fabric (externally buffered):

1. *Internal buffering.* A single shared memory switch module may be considered internally buffered when it permits a single buffer to be shared by many input and output parts. This sharing of buffers substantially reduces the number of cell buffers required to support a given switch performance.

2. *External buffering.* Allows the cell queries to be located close to the switch ports that they serve. The absence of cell queries within the switch fabric eases the support of multiple levels of priority across the switch fabric for different classes of traffic.

17.4.6.3   Contention Resolution

1. In an internally buffered switch, contention is handled by placing buffers at the point of contention.

2. In an externally buffered switch, a contention resolution mechanism is required. Three basic actions can be taken once contention is detected.

    a. *Backpressure.* Used in the input-buffered switch design. The cell that cannot be handled at the point of contention will be sent back to the input buffers.

    b. *Deflection.* This mechanism will route the cells in contention over a path other than the shortest path to the requested destination.

    c. *Loss.* Pure output-buffered designs use a loss mechanism that discards cells that cannot be handled.

17.5   IP NETWORK

17.5.1   History of the Internet

The Internet began in the late 1960s from the Advanced Research Project Agency's ARPANET project to build a packet-switched network. In 1970, the ARPANET project grew to support the Department of Defense and other government and research organizations. The term *Internet* was first used in 1983 to describe the concept. In 1985, National Science Foundation (NSF) funded several supercomputer centers and used a 56-kbps ARPANET network, called NSFNET, to link them. NSF allowed any regional or university computer centers that could reach this NSFNET network by connecting to it. This was the seed of the Internet, as we know it today. In 1987, NSF awarded a contract to Merit-Network Inc., which is in partnership with MCI, IBM, and University of Michigan, to upgrade and operate the NSFNET backbone by using 1.5-Mpbs T1 leased lines to connect six regional networks, five existing supercomputer centers, and other sites such as university sites. On July 24, 1988, the old 56-kbps network was shut down. From 1989 to 1991 the Merit/IBM/MCI team proposed and upgraded to a higher-speed 45-Mbps backbone, which expanded to 16 regional sites and connected more than 3500 networks. In 1993, NSF decided to get out of the backbone business and solicited bids for building Network Access Points (NAPs), from which the commercial backbone operators could interconnect. In 1994, four NAPs were built. In 1995, NSFNET was essentially shut down and the NAP architecture became the Internet.

17.5.2   Internet Architecture[23]

The Internet is packet-switched network. The packet-switch network has the following attributes.

1. There is no single, unbroken connection between the sender and the receiver.
2. The data stream is split into IP packets, and each packet contains its address. Therefore, the data stream is sent out without establishing a dedicated connection at beginning and each packet is routed independently, possibly over a different route. Thus the packet-switched system is a connectionless system in contrast to a circuit-switched telephone system, which establishes a connection for each call from the sender to the receiver and dedicates network resources to it (see Sec. 7.7). We call the packet-switch network a connectionless network because it does not have a dedicated connection. Connectionless networks as of today cannot offer the quality of service (QoS), such as the latency and throughput.
3. The packets can be lost, duplicated, corrupted, and/or arrive out of order at the destination.

The Internet is made up of hardware, software, and communication links that provide users with a ubiquitous platform from which to run applications and access information. The fundamental entities in the Internet are clients, routers, and gateways, as shown in Fig. 17.10.

1. A client is generally an application on a user device, such as a computer that facilitates setting up either communication or information sessions with other users or applications. Netscape's Web browser is an example of a client.
2. A server is a combination of hardware and software that satisfies a client's request for information or communication. Yahoo's stock and travel quote services are examples of a server application.
3. A router is a device that routes traffic among different networks [e.g., from an enterprise network to an Internet Service Provider (ISP) network].

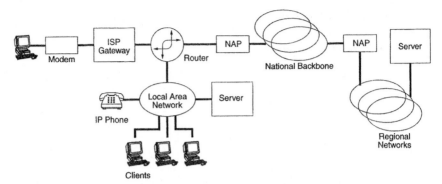

FIGURE 17.10 Structure of the Internet, composed of hardware, software, and communication links.

4. A gateway is an entity that generally transforms traffic from one type of network to another type (e.g., conventional telephone signals to IP packets for Internet telephony). The routing functionality usually handles multiple gateways.

5. Network Access Point (NAP) interconnects the commercial backbone operators.

17.5.3 TCP/IP

TCP/IP is the technology platform for the Internet. The Internet has no single, unbroken connection between the sender and the receiver. The data is split into IP packets, each of which has an address overhead. Each packet is routed independently, possibly over different routes, which is in contrast to a circuit-switched telephone system, which establishes a specific connection and dedicates part of the network to each call. The IP networks are connectionless networks, and circuit-switched networks are connection networks. In the connectionless network, packets can be lost, duplicated, corrupted, and/or arrived out of order at the destination. There are two protocol-handling layers, Layers 3 and 4 (see Fig. 17.11).

The Internet Protocol: The user's data is transformed into IP packets. IP enables routers along the way through the network to send the packets to the right destination. It is a

INTERNET AND WIRELESS FUTURE

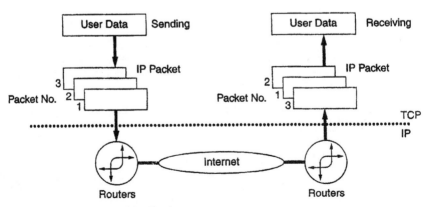

FIGURE 17.11 The protocol-handling layers.

best-effort delivery, and packets may be lost along the way. The wide bandwidth (in the fiber optics) of the network can reduce the loss of packet in the wire-line Internet network. This IP protocol uses Layer 3, the Network Layer.

The Transmission Control Protocol (TCP): A header that includes a packet identifier, a checksum, and source and destination IP address is added to each of the IP packets. TCP is the Application Layer, or Layer 4. At the receiving end, the checksum of each set of data is calculated and the packet identifier tracked. The checksum is a computed value that depends intimately on characteristics of a particular set of data, and the checksum changes if the data changes. The packets will be asked for retransmission if packets are lost or corrupted. In this layer, once they are properly received, the packets are reassembled into the original data format.

TCP Connection: A network application often has to identify the connection end points that are receiving data through some connection over the network. If an application running on a network client needs to send a file to its remote server, the protocols invoked by the application need to be formatted to the data according to specifications. Every data transfer between network end points has to be tightly controlled by conformance to interoperable network protocols such as TCP, the User Datagram Protocol (UDP), or the Real-Time Transport Protocol (RTP). The latter two deal with real-time data such as voice or priority data.

17.5.4 IP Packet Format and IP Addressing

A. IP Packet Format: An IP packet contains 14 fields of information shown in Fig. 17.12. The following description of each IP packet fields is illustrated:

- Version: indicates the version of IP currently used.
- IP Header Length (IHL): indicates the datagram header length in 32-bit words.

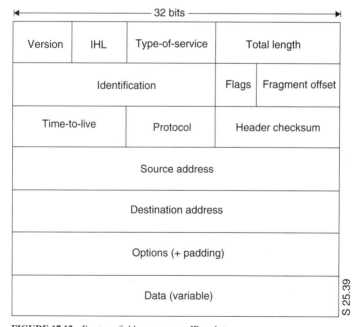

FIGURE 17.12 Fourteen fields compose an IP packet.

- Type-of-service: specifies how an upper-layer protocol would like a current datagram to be handled, and assigns datagrams various levels of importance.
- Total length: specifies the length, in bytes, of the entire IP packet, including the data and header.
- Identification: contains an integer that identifies the current datagram. This field is used to help piece together datagram fragments.
- Flags: consists of a 3-bit field of which the two low-order (least-significant) bits control fragmentation. The low-order bit specifies whether the packet is the last fragment in a series of fragmented packets. The third or high-order bit is not used.
- Fragment offset: indicates the position of the fragment's data relative to the beginning of the data in the original datagram, which allows the destination IP process to properly reconstruct the original datagram.
- Time-to-live: maintains a counter that gradually decrements down to zero, at which point the datagram is discarded. This keeps packets from looping endlessly.
- Protocol: indicates which upper-layer protocol receives incoming packets after IP processing is complete.
- Header checksum: helps ensure IP header integrity.
- Source address: specifies the sending node.
- Destination address: specifies the receiving node.
- Options: allows IP to support various options, such as security.
- Data: contains upper-layer information.

B. IP Address Format
The 32-bit IP address is grouped eight bits at a time, separated by dots, and represented in decimal format (known as dotted decimal notation). Each bit in the octet has a binary weight (2^7, 2^6, 2^5, 2^4, 2^3, 2^2, 2^1, 2^0). The minimum value for an octet is 0, and the maximum value for an octet is 255. Illustrates the basic format of an IP address.

An IP address 216.27.61.137 in binary is

$$11011000.00011011.00111101.10001001.$$

An IP address format consists of 32 bits, grouped into four octets is shown in Fig. 17.13.

C. IP Address Classes
IP addressing supports five different address classes: A, B, C, D, and E. Only classes A, B, and C are available for commercial use. The left-most (high-order) bits indicate the network class. Provides reference information about the five IP address classes as shown in Table 17.1.

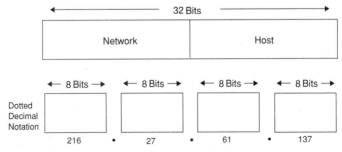

FIGURE 17.13   An IP address consists of 32 bits, grouped into four octets.

TABLE 17.1. Reference Information About the Five IP Address Classes

IP Address Class	Format	Purpose	High-Order Bit(s)	Address Range	No. Bits Network/Host	Max. Hosts	First Octet in Decimal
A	N.H.H.H*	Few large organizations	0	1.0.0.0 to 126.0.0.0	7/24	16,777, 214 $(2^{24} - 2)$	1–126
B	N.N.H.H.	Medium-size organizations	1, 0	128.1.0.0 to 191.254.0.0	14/16	65, 543 $(2^{16}-2)$	128–191
C	N.N.N.H	Relatively small organizations	1, 1, 0	192.0.1.0 to 223.255.254.0	22/8	245 (2^8-2)	192–223
D	N/A	Multicast groups (RFC 1112)	1, 1, 1, 0	224.0.0.0 to 239.255.255.255	N/A (not for commercial use)	N/A	224–239
E	N/A	Experimental	1, 1, 1, 1	240.0.0.0 to 254.255.255.255	N/A	N/A	240–254

*N = network number, H = host number.

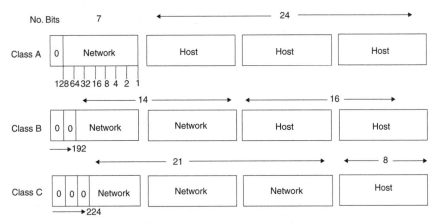

FIGURE 17.14   IP address formats A, B, and C are available for commercial use.

D. IP address formats A, B, C for commercial class use is shown in Fig. 17.14. The class of address can be determined easily by examining the first octet of the address and mapping that value to a class range in Table 17.1. In an IP address of 216.27.61.137, for example, the first octet is 216. Because 216 falls between 192 and 223, 216.27.61.137 is a Class C address. Table 17.1 summarizes the range of possible values for the first octet of each address class.

17.5.5   Addressing in the Internet

Addressing in an Internet network is different from addressing in the telecommunications network. Each device in an Internet network is given an IP address, which is a 32-bit number in the current IP implementation [i.e., Internet Protocol version 4 (IPv4)]. A more abstract textual address, arranged in a hierarchy of domains, is commonly assigned to a device or a user with a name to keep track of the association between the IP addresses and the names (see Fig. 17.15).

The top-level domains in the United States are

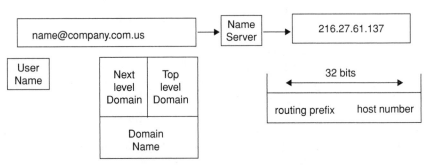

FIGURE 17.15   Addressing in an Internet network.

com for commercial organization
gov for government organizations
edu for educational institutions
net for network (e.g., ISP network)

International domains are

au for Australia
uk for United Kingdom
in for India
us for United States

The next-level domain identifies a specific organization and a host computer within the higher-level domain. The host computer looks up the user name and delivers information to the user. All communicating entities on the Internet must have an IP address. This implies that mobile phones and terminals, when connected to the Internet, also must have IP addresses. For a device that is not permanently attached to the Internet (e.g., a dial-up mobile data device), an IP address is temporarily assigned from a pool of addresses for the duration of the connection.

17.5.6 Security on the Internet

The security of access and transactions performed on the Internet becomes crucial as commercial use on the Internet increases. Corporate networks, banking services, stock services, and so forth, are generally protected from malicious attacks by the use of "firewalls." A firewall is a combination of hardware and software. A typical firewall, shown in Fig. 17.16, includes the following:

1. A secure server is the primary point of contact for connections from the Internet for service authentication and to protect the secrecy and integrity for transactions such as banking and credit card payments, receiving e-mail, and accessing a corporate database. It also processes any requests from the internal corporate network to the Internet, such as browsing the Web or downloading files. It can be used to log the Internet traffic between the internal corporate network and the Internet and downloads to the level of every IP address accessed, data and time of access, number of bytes downloaded, and so forth.

2. A router examines packet headers and allows only certain types of packets to be sent or received and blocks other packets.

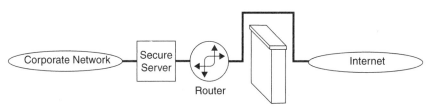

FIGURE 17.16   The concept of a firewall.

3. In addition to the primary point of security check, such as the secure server mentioned in item 1, secure electronic transaction protocols are used to authenticate and protect the secrecy and integrity of transactions such as banking and credit card payments on the Internet.

17.6 FUTURE OF IP NETWORKS

17.6.1 IP Network Standards

IP network standards are evolving to support long-term growth, quality, billing, and mobility. The wireless Internet does not have enough bandwidth (air link) in the system. Therefore, the current Internet connectionless system, with packet transmission, can cause a long latency and packet loss if the system is used for the wireless mobile system. As a result, the IP network standard will need to be modified.

A. Long-Term Growth

1. IP addresses are scarce commodities. The rapid growth of the Internet is quickly exhausting the numerical address space. The new IP version 6 (IPv6) increases the number of bits for addressing from 32 to 128, accommodating a much larger address space. Besides, IPv6 also supports a graceful transition from IPv4 and the autoconfiguration of the network by having plug and play capability. The auto configuration of the network can automatically detect which devices and applications are attached and removed from the network. IPv6 is being promoted in the IP network industry.

2. Because of the fast growth of the Internet, today's Internet may not meet tomorrow's needs. Development of a second generation of the Internet, called Internet 2, has started. The Internet 2 development group consists of major universities and government agents. The goal of Internet 2 is to develop a high-volume, high-usage network.

3. The wireless Internet will become a hot trend. The wireless IP network will replace the current conventional network with limited bandwidth. However, many issues such as nomadic mobility and mobilized mobility, quality of service, and so forth, need to be solved by using mobile IP.

4. The application of mobile networks[24-25] is different from the wireline network and is the weakness of the Internet. When a mobile phone moves from one base station to another, or from one mobile switch to another, the handoff functionality assures the continuity of the voice connection. In the Internet, if a user terminal moves and its connection point to the Internet changes, the numerical IP address of the device also needs to change. Mobile IP uses protocol tunneling to hide a mobile node's home address from two intervening routers between its home network (home agent) and its current network (foreign agent) when away from home. The mobile IP protocol allows movement between different types of networks as long as these networks are IP-based packet networks supporting the protocol. The mobile IP forms the basis for providing packet data services in mobile networks.

B. Quality of Service (QoS)
A variety of QoS techniques are being constantly developed and enhanced to support real-time applications,[26] such as voice over IP and video conferencing over the Internet. These techniques are used to reduce latency and maintain quality. They include (1) assigning different priorities to different types of traffic, (2) reserving bandwidth or processing capacity (a priority for certain types of connections), (3) supporting

policy-oriented schemes for prioritizing different types of users or applications, and (4) improving the Internet protocol header format. A combination of these techniques, along with judicious network design, is already placing Internet telephony quality metrics within the guidelines specified by the ITU.

C. Authentication, Authorized, Accounting (AAA) and Billing
AAA and billing are needed because of the increased use of the Internet for commercial purposes. The Internet community is developing standards for AAA. Several commercially available routers are capable of collecting detailed accounting data for billing purposes. In the wireline Internet, AAA function takes care of the accounting but has no billing function. In the wireless Internet, the accounting function is very complicated and should be separated from AAA. In wireless mobile systems, the billing function needs to be continuously updated according to the marketing strategy demand. Therefore, the accounting and billing should be combined as one utility in the wireless mobile system.

D. Mobility
The recent IP standard supports mobile devices accessing Internet applications. It is generally referred to as mobile IP capability. Although mobile IP is currently targeted to support packet data or nomadic mobility such as laptop computers, it will apply to mobilized mobility such as cellular data transmission. Also, it could conceivably be used to support mobile voice as well.

17.6.2   The Problems of the Internet

The Internet Protocol (IP), the Layer 3 (network layer) protocol used by the Internet, sends information by breaking up messages into packets. The packets are then sent from a source host to a destination host via routers that determine the best path for each packet. This method of storing packets, determining the next router or hop, and then forwarding the packet is often referred to as store-and-forward or hop-by-hop routing. This store-and-forward routing enables a relatively inexpensive, robust, and scalable network. Consequently, IP is connectionless, meaning all the information needed for routing is contained in the packet. These features have allowed for the rapid growth of the Internet, but IP is a best-effort approach, meaning that although the no-delay of the packets is not guaranteed, it can be minimized.

A likely solution is to run IP on a fast Layer 2 (data link layer) technology. Asynchronous Transfer Mode (ATM) has emerged as the leading candidate because of its high speed. However, certain characteristics of ATM make the job of integrating ATM with IP difficult.

ATM uses short, fixed-length packets that allow for fast switching and low latency. This is the main reason for the increasing popularity of ATM. ATM is a connection-oriented technology, meaning that a point-to-point connection is set up for every message sent. The connection remains for the duration of the message and is then torn down. Because the connection, or virtual circuit, is set up prior to the message transfer, a guaranteed bandwidth can be negotiated between the sender and the network. Therefore, an ATM network allows for QoS guarantees, making it useful for real-time applications that, combined with the falling price, make ATM an attractive technology. However, ATM is a complex technology, and network management remains a difficult problem. It cannot be scalable because it is connection oriented.

17.6.3   IP Switch

IP switch consists of IP switch controller and ATM switch. It is a multiplayer switching technology that combines ATM Layer 2 switching and IP Layer 3 routing. The IP switch uses

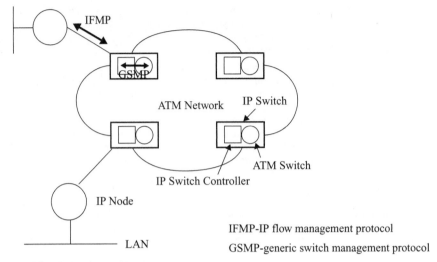

IFMP-IP flow management protocol

GSMP-generic switch management protocol

FIGURE 17.17   IP over ATM topology.

a traffic driven approach in the sense that it dynamically shifts between store-and-forward and cut-through switching based on the IP over ATM topology in Fig. 17.17.

Two protocols are needed for the operation. A Generic Switch Management Protocol (GSMP), which allows the IP Switch Controller to control the ATM hardware, and a Flow Management Protocol (IFMP), which associates IP flows with ATM virtual channels. At system start-up, each IP node sets up a virtual channel on each of its ATM physical links to be used as the default-forwarding channel.

Because the IP switch is a traffic driven approach, the performance gain is dependent on the characteristics of the incident traffic. The gain is higher when more packets can be switched to the network.

The internet employs best-effort methods to reserve capacity in the network in order to reach a certain QoS level by providing Resource Reservation Protocol (RSVP), which is an Internet network end-to-end control protocol that can deliver QoS in a router-based network. Applications can request a QoS from the network that will be guaranteed by all of the routers in the path. RSVP lets the user inform the network about a desired QoS. The network nodes then perform admission control and traffic management to allocate the resources for the traffic flows.

17.6.4   Tag Switching

It is like the IP switch that combines ATM Layer 2 switching with Layer 3 routing, thus avoiding the slow store-and-forward methods of the network layer. The difference between tag switching and IP switch is that tag switch is binding of routes with tags. Tag switching is topology driven. Tags are allocated and changed when the topology of the network changes and can be assigned for any length flow. Therefore, short messages may be routed.

Tag switching does not provide QoS. It depends on information from network layer protocol such as RSVP. However, RSVP is a flow-driven approach to QoS. It negotiates QoS for each flow that requests it. Because Tag Switch is topology driven, the incorporation of RSVP may not apply. Also, because tags are determined from the network layout not each flow, the QoS information is contained.

17.6.5 Summary

IP switch and tag switch attempts to improve the performance of IP networks by integrating ATM switches with IP routers. The IP switch accomplishes this by flow classification while the tag switch sets up direct paths before packets are sent. The traffic-driven approach leads to a number of advantages that have previously been discussed.

Both solutions for IP over ATM have drawbacks. Neither solution provides for efficient multicast and neither addresses the cell-interleaving problem of ATM. Thus, their applicability to extremely large networks, such as the Internet, is limited. Neither tag switching nor the IP switch can provide guaranteed QoS but they do provide substantially reduced delays compared to IP over ATM. Both solutions are "best effort" networks because they still use IP routing protocol to find path for packets. The IP switch needs to label a flow after a certain number of packets have passed. Before a flow is labeled, the network is acting as a store-and-forward network. Therefore, the IP switch has a variable setup delay. In tag switching, every packet is tagged and switched through the network, and therefore there are no setup delays.

Tag switching is not specifically for IP over ATM in contrast to IP switching. This allows for the integration of tag switching in variety of network types. This added dimension could make tag switching the choice for networks of the future, and switching is clearly the choice for today's IP over ATM networks.

17.7 AN INTELLIGENT SYSTEM: FUTURE PUBLIC LAND MOBILE TELECOMMUNICATION SYSTEM (FPLMTS)

The International Radio Consultative Committee (CCIR) has made recommendations for the third generation of land-mobile systems. The overall objectives of FPLMTS[27-28] are to provide all services generally available through the fixed network (e.g., voice, fax, and data) to mobile systems. It is intended to provide these services over a wide range of user densities and geographic coverage areas. The frequency allocations were made by the World Administrative Radio Conference of 1992 (WARC '92) in the 1- to 3-GHz frequency range with an amendment of a worldwide co-primary allocation to mobile services over the frequency range 1700 to 2600 MHz. The 230 MHz of spectrum in the following bands is designated for FPLMTS:

    1800 to 2025 MHz (140 MHz)

    2110 to 2200 MHz (90 MHz)

In addition, the following bands are designated for mobile satellite systems:

    1980 to 2010 MHz

    2170 to 2200 MHz

17.7.1 Future Enhancement

The *land* in FPLMTS refers to the land base station, which can be either a terrestrial or satellite station. Calls within the mobile system are routed to and from the intelligent network, either fixed or mobile via terrestrial or satellite links using at least four kinds of radio interface (R_1, R_2, R_3, R_4). The R_1 interface is used by mobile stations. The R_2

interface is used by indoor and outdoor personal stations (handsets). The R_3 interface is used by mobile stations communicating through a satellite, and the R_4 interface is used by pagers. All mobile calls can be connected either directly to PSTN (public service telephone network) or via a mobile switch. The mobile systems can be either a narrowband or wideband.

The requirement of developing an FPLMT system has been described. Intelligent mobile units, intelligent cells, and the intelligent network will make this intelligent system a reality.

17.8   MESH NETWORK/AD HOC NETWORK

A mesh network/Ad Hoc network[25] is a network that employs one of two connection arrangements: full mesh topology or partial mesh topology. In the full mesh topology, each node is connected directly to each of the others. In the partial mesh topology, nodes are connected to only some, not all, of the other nodes.

Note that these definitions mention no dependency on any time parameter—nothing is necessarily dynamic in a mesh. However, in connection with wireless networks, the term *mesh* is often used as a synonym for *ad hoc* or *mobile* network. Obviously, combining the two characteristics of a mesh topology and ad hoc capabilities is a very attractive proposition.

17.8.1   Radio Structure of Ad Hoc Mesh[29–30]

In Ad Hoc network, the focus is temporary peer-to-peer connectivity on an impromptu basis. The multi-hop mesh network needs repeaters. The name of a repeater can be a device (one radio) or a station.

- 1-Radio Ad Hoc Mesh: In conventional wireless mesh network, there is one radio used as a service radio. Also, as a repeater for all nodes to talk to each other, but all must be talking on the same channel. Therefore, it is a shared service and the radios should be backhaul radios. In this case, the bandwidth is reduced for each hop, as each packet has to be repeated as relayed as shown in Fig. 17.18*a*. The bandwidth loss of up to 50 percent per hop, depending on the mesh topology. Over four hops, the data would be delivered by 1/16 of the bandwidth.

- 2-Radio Ad Hoc Mesh: One radio at each node is used to form a shared backhaul. One is used as service radio as shown in Fig. 17.18*b*. It can be used in a low-density area.

- 3-Radio Ad Hoc Mesh: Two radios simultaneously receive and send, thus form a private backhaul as shown in Fig. 17.18*c*. The backhaul paths do not interfere or contend with service radio. Also, the backhaul radios do not interfere with each other. This 3-radio Ad Hoc mesh provides the maximum bandwidth efficiency.

17.8.2   MAC Layer of Ad Hoc Network[31]

In the Ad Hoc Network, the nodes communicate directly with each other on a peer-to-peer level sharing a given cell coverage area. This type of network is often formed on a temporary basis. Therefore, the radio technology in the PHY layer of Ad Hoc Network should be capable to make multihops among the nodes.[32]

IEEE 802.11 wireless MAC described in Sec. 7.2.8 has a distributed MAC component called distributed coordination function (DCF) and a centralized MC component called point coordination function (PCF).

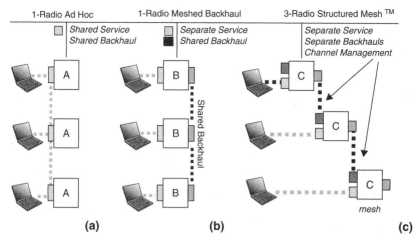

FIGURE 17.18　Competing mesh architectures: (*a*) Ad HOC, (*b*) 1-Radio Meshed Backhaul, (*c*) Multi-radio Mesh.

DCF uses RTS-CTS (request-to-send and clear-to-send) exchange to avoid hidden terminal situation.

- Any node overhearing foreign CTS cannot transmit
- Any node receiving foreign RTS cannot transmit

DCF uses ACK to achieve reliability. The DCF is a Carrier Sense Multiple Access/Collision Avoidance (CSMA/CA) protocol. In the virtual carrier sense, DCF is using network allocation vector (NAV), which is updated, based on the overheard RTS/CTS/DATA/ACK packets, each of which specified duration of a pending transmission.

The PCF function supports time sensitive traffic flow. However, the transmission times are not predictable so this approach has not been widely adopted.

Contention Window (CW) is chosen dynamically depending on collision occurrence. When transmitting a packet, the node chooses a back-off interval in the range [o, CW] and then counts down the back-off interval when medium is idle. When the back-off interval reaches o, transmit RTS.

- *Fairness Issue:* Because all nodes should receive equal bandwidth, the bandwidth used by each node should be proportional to the weight assigned to the node. A fully distributed algorithm for achieving weighed fair queuing is called distributed fair scheduling (DFS).
- *Priority Scheduling Issue*

  1. CTS and ACK have priority over RTS.

  2. If a node wants to send CTS/ACK, it transmits SIFS (Short Interference Space) duration after channel goes idle.

  3. If a node wants to send RTS, it waits for DIFS (distributed interframe space) greater than SIFS.

  4. For high-priority packets, the back-off interval is [o, CWh].

  5. For low-priority packets, the LIFS (Long Interference Space) idle period before counting down is LIFS = DIFS + CWh.

- *Power Save in Ad Hoc Mode*
  If host A has a packet to transmit to B, A must send an ATIM (Announcement Traffic Indication Message) request to B during an ATIM window. ATIM window size is based on observed load. If it is too large, the energy consumption is reduced.

- *Power Control in Ad Hoc Mode*
  1. To avoid interference, transmit RTS/CTS at highest power level, and DATA/ACK at least required power level.
  2. Increase DATA power periodically so distant hosts can sense transmission.

17.8.3 Protocols for Mesh and Ad Hoc Networks

Many protocols are available, each with differing goals and design criteria.

- AODV (Ad Hoc On-Demand Distance Vector Routing) is a routing protocol for Ad Hoc Networks designed with mobile wireless devices in mind.
- Mobile Mesh protocol contains three separate protocols, each addressing a specific function: (1) Link Discovery, (2) Routing, and (3) Border Discovery.
- TBRPF, or Topology Broadcast based on Reverse-Path Forwarding, is a proactive, link-state routing protocol.
- OSPF is a link-state routing protocol.
- GNU Zebra manages TCP/IP-based routing protocols.
- LocustWorld develops a CD solution based on the AODV protocol.

17.8.4 ODMA (Opportunity Driven Multiple Access)[33–34]

ODMA was one of five air interface concepts submitted to UMTS in December 1996. It is a relay technology applicable in principle to all multiple access schemes. Although ODMA was later integrated in the WCDMA and WCDMA/TDMA concept groups, the merit of its technology is worth mentioning. ODMA is an intelligent adaptive multihop system supporting full mobility of calls and relays. An adaptive communication system uses opportunistic peak-mode transmissions to transmit data between originating and destination stations, via one or more intermediate stations. Each station monitors the activity of other stations in the network, storing connectivity information for use in subsequent transmissions. Each station also sends out probe signals from time to time, to establish which other stations are in range. Messages are then sent across the network from station to station, with confirmation data being transmitted back to the originating station, until the destination station is reached. Old messages, which would otherwise clog the network, are timed out and deleted.

ODMA can also be treated as an intelligent protocol that sits on a radio subsystem and supports replaying. A WCMDA cell can use ODMA enhancement as shown in Fig. 17.19. Relaying is used to route packet data services to and from mobiles close to the WCDMA BTS, using a TDD (separate unpaired spectrum) band. The relay nodes in range of the BTS will toggle between ODMA and WCDMA modes. Relaying extends the range of the high rate data services and can be used to provide coverage in dead spots. The final hop to the BTS uses the WCDMA slotted mode. In this way, relaying can brng concentrated traffic near to the WCDMA BTS, which can then work in a spectrally efficient manner over a short range.

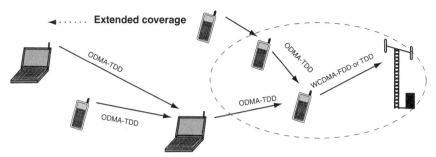

FIGURE 17.19   Scenario for WCDMA with ODMA enhancement.

Because ODMA is an intelligent relay technology, it is applicable as well in operating the advanced mesh network.

17.8.5 Mesh Network Attributes

Traditional wireless systems using point-to-multipoint transmission have generally used cellular radio links.

In contrast, wireless mesh networks[35] are multihop systems in which devices assist each other in transmitting packets through the network, especially in adverse conditions. These Ad Hoc Networks can be deployed into place with minimal preparation, and they provide a reliable, flexible system that can be extended to thousands of devices.

The wireless mesh network topology developed for industrial control and sensing is a point-to-point-to-point, or peer-to-peer, system called an Ad Hoc, multihop network. A node can send and receive messages, and in a mesh network, a node also functions as a router and can relay messages for its neighbors. Through the relaying process, a packet of wireless data will find its way to its destination, passing through intermediate nodes with reliable communication.

- A self-configuring and self-healing network: A mesh network is self-organizing and doesn't require manual configuration. Because of this, adding new gear or relocating existing gear is as simple as plugging it in and turning it on. The network discovers the new node and automatically incorporates it into the existing system.

- Scalability: A mesh network is also scalable and can handle hundreds or thousands of nodes. Because the network's operation doesn't depend on a central control point, adding multiple data collection points or gateways is convenient.

- Adaptability: If point-to-point is too far apart for a solid RF communications link, you just add one or more repeater nodes to fill the gaps in the network.

- Reliability: A network can be deliberately overdesigned for reliability simply by adding extra nodes, so each device has two or more paths for sending data. This is a simpler way of obtaining redundancy.

- Robustness: If the nearest AP is down or there is localized interference, the network will continue to operate router along an alternate path.

- Higher bandwidth: The physics of wireless communication dictate that bandwidth is higher[36] at shorter range, because of interference and other factors that contribute to loss of data as distance increases. One way to get more bandwidth out of the network, then, is to transmit data across multiple short hops. That's what mesh network does.

17.8.6 Wireless Sensor Network (WSN) Attributes[37-38]

A. Introduction
These inexpensive low-power communication devices, such as ZigBee, can be deployed throughout a physical space, providing dense sensing close to physical phenomena, processing and communicating this information, and coordinating actions with other nodes. To minimize energy consumption, most of the device's components, including the radio, will likely be turned off most of the time.

The sensor network applications are in environment monitoring and motion monitoring.

B. Technologies
WSNs merge a wide range of information technology that spans hardware, system software, networking, and programming methodologies.

1. Hardware
A sensor network node's hardware consists of a microprocessor, data storage, sensors, analog-to-digital converters (ADCs), a data transceiver, controllers that tie the pieces together, and an energy source.

2. Microsensors
Sensors give these nodes their eyes and ears. A wide variety of MEMs (microelectromechanical systems) can sense a wide variety of physical phenomena cheaply and efficiently.

3. Microradios
WSN radios consume about 20 mW, and their range is typically in tens of meters. For small devices to cover long distances, the network must route the information hop by hop through nodes.

4. Network functions
The network must allocate limited hardware to multiple concurrent activities, such as sampling sensor processing and streaming data.

C. Self-organized networks
A network consists of many nodes, each with multiple links connecting to other nodes. Information moves hop by hop along a route from the point of production to the point of use.

1. Connectivity: The networking capability of WSNs is built up in layers.

- To avoid contending for the radio channel, the link layer listens on the channel and transmits only when the channel is clear. It transmits a structured series of bits that form a packet encoded in the radio signal.

- The lowest layer controls the physical radio device. When one node transmits, a collection of others can receive the signal unless it is garbled by other transmissions at the same time.

- The packet layer manages buffers, schedules packets onto the radio, detects or even corrects errors, handles packet losses, and dispatches packets to system or application components.

2. Dissemination
The network uses dissemination to issue commands, convey alarms, configure and task the network. It also uses dissemination to establish routes.

3. Data collection for nodes
Communication in sensor network: is usually performed in the aggregate, and participants are identified by attributes, such as physical location or sensor value range.

Tree formation: data can begin following up the tree as soon as a parent node is discovered. Nodes may learn of potential parents by overhearing data messages. *Style of routing:* formulated as directed diffusion, a process in which nodes express interest in data by attitude. It forms a routing gradient.

4. Reliability also follows a different pattern. Increasingly, sensor networks will depoly disruption-tolerant networking approaches in which they transfer bundles of data reliably, hop by hop.

D. Conservation of power and bandwidth
Communication must contend for a share of limited bandwidth and be handled in a most energy-intensive operation.

1. Nodes could process data locally.

2. Performing aggregation within the network can reduce communication.

3. Compression and scheduling also can conserve energy at lower layers.

17.9 WIRELESS INFORMATION SUPERHIGHWAY

In 1993, the United States government asked the communications and computer industry to move ahead on building the information superhighway. The information superhighway will provide the ability for many users to frequently send and receive large volumes of information.

There are two types of information superhighways: wireline and wireless. The wireline information superhighway uses optical fiber. The spectral bandwidth of optical fiber is very broad. There is apparently no limitation on assigning a number of broadband channels to the users in the wireline information superhighway system. Therefore, in developing a wireline information superhighway system, the problem is relatively simple. The most difficult task is how the information will get on and off the information superhighway because of the high volume of call traffic. A future advanced intelligent network will be developed for the information superhighway systems.

However, in developing a wireless information superhighway system, the problem is more difficult. Besides the problem of developing the wireline information superhighway, the major difficulty is how to reach and serve customers over radio waves. In the mobile radio environment there is excessive pathloss, multipath fading, and dispersive time delay spread as stated in Sec. 2.3. Also, video data transmission over the information superhighway requires a large bandwidth (5 MHz or higher) for each wireless channel. The carrier frequency, which can carry multiple wideband channels, has to be in the range of 20 GHz or above. Therefore, a broadband spectrum is required in order to build this information superhighway. The higher the frequency, the more difficult it is for the radio wave to reach the customer. Thus, Mother Nature limits the utilization of wide bandwidths for the information super-highway. Mobility in the information superhighway presents another difficulty in wireless.

The means for deploying the broadband channels for the information superhighway systems are by a microwave link and an infrared link. The spectrum of the radio and infrared bands is illustrated in Fig. 17.20.

The advantages of using a microwave system are

1. The system does not require line-of-sight conditions for reception.

2. Broadband signal provides less fading.

3. The conventional diversity schemes can further reduce fading.

4. Can apply CDMA scheme for long-range transmission.

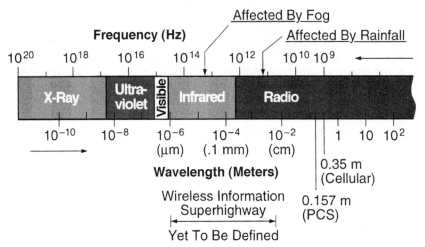

FIGURE 17.20 Radio and infrared bands.

The disadvantages of using a microwave system are

1. The noise floor is relatively high.
2. The propagation loss is high.
3. Attenuation is affected mostly by rainfall.

The advantages of using an infrared link are

1. Eavesdropping can be prevented.
2. It is highly directional.
3. It provides power conservation.
4. No license is required.
5. It is light weight.

The disadvantages of using an infrared link with today's technology are

1. For short distances.
2. For mobile communications within rooms using diffused radiation, which recreates multiple reflection waves to reach the terminals.
3. Most fixed-to-fixed communications are under the line-of-sight condition.
4. The conventional diversity schemes cannot help reduce fading.
5. Attenuation is affected mostly by fog.

The infrared wavelength is roughly between 0.1 mm to 1 μm. It attenuates heavily by the fog. At a half mile, the loss of over 60 dB is due to thick fog, 30 dB due to moderate fog, and 0 dB due to the thin fog. The background noises due to environment illumination are (1) sunlight (daylight)—a high noise level at a wavelength less than 1.2 μm; (2) tungsten lamps; (3) fluorescent lamps; and (4) heaters. These noises can produce DC and low-frequency photocurrents and generate shot noise in the photodetector. Also, the rapidly fluctuating components associated with higher harmonic of the main frequency emitted by some artificial light sources received by the photodetector. The background noise can be reduced by the optical filters. (1) The interference filter (bandpass), the transmission

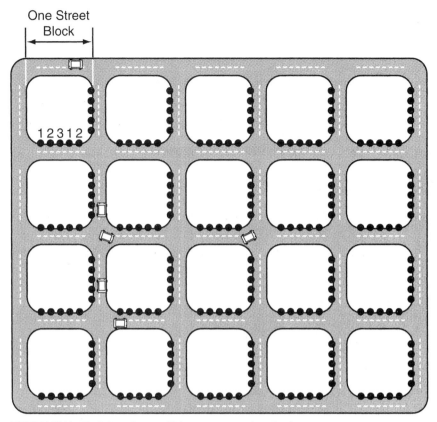

FIGURE 17.21 The information superhighway structure—along the city streets.

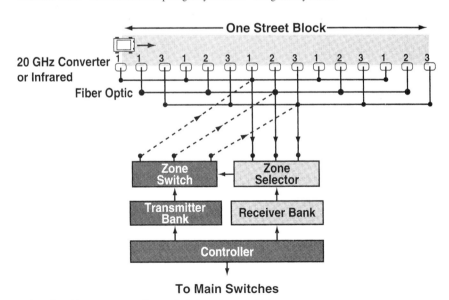

FIGURE 17.22 Microcell application for information superhighway.

coefficient of which is less than 40 percent, optical response changes with angle of incidence of light, and cost is high. (2) Absorption filters, which noise reduction is 54 percent for fluorescent tubes, depend on the choice of absorbing material and cost is low.

In the mobile application, we are using diffuse and quasi-diffuse transmission. In diffuse transmission, use sufficient emitted optical power for covering the multipath dispersion, create reflections, and create multibeams in wireless-transmission configurations. In the quasi-diffuse transmission, the photodetector receives and the laser or LED emits from and the remote station (RS). Then the common node (CN) and RS are in a line-of-sight condition. All the RS are aiming at CN, which is the control center.

Among these difficulties the weather, as mentioned above, introduces undesirable factors to the higher band microwave frequencies or to optical frequencies. Therefore, combining the two systems—the infrared system, which is affected by fog, but not affected by rainfall, and the microwave system, which is affected just the opposite—can achieve multi-propagation-medium diversity. The experiment has been carried out and stated in Sec. 18.4. With that, the airlink for providing the wireless information superhighway system may barely reach 50 meters, which is our goal.

The most difficult part of developing the wireless information superhighway is the last 50 meters. Due to the requirements of the wide bandwidth, future technology for the last 50 meters should use microwave and infrared and intelligent cell technologies to obtain the wireless information superhighway. However, more research needs to be conducted in this area. The future wireless information superhighway, thus, has to be hybrid with the wireline information superhighway whose transmission medium uses noninterference wideband optical fiber. For personal mobility and personal communications, the wireless information superhighway will add great value in the entire information superhighway system. We may illustrate an application of using the last 50 meters.

17.9.1 An Example for Applying the Last 50 Meters

A wireless information superhighway structure along city streets can be provided as shown in Fig. 17.21. In order to only concentrate on the last 50-meter link, the means of delivering the broadband signal from a distant source will lean on the optical fiber. In the last 50 meters, the microwaves or infrared and the intelligent microcell can help provide the link along each street block as shown in Fig. 17.22. The signal is delivered via optical fibers to the zone sites along the street. At the zone sites, the signal can be converted to infrared radiation or microwave transmission. The intelligent microcell technology stated in Sec. 16.2 will be applied to convey the signal from the zone site to the mobile unit. The range is within 50 meters. The three-zone selectors detect the signal at each zone. For instance, if the signal at zone 1 is strong, all the zone 1's are turned on. Because the power is very low, no interference would occur at the other neighboring streets. Then the mobile unit traveling along the whole block of the street will keep the same channel, but the zone sites along the street will turn on and turn off as the location of the mobile unit changes. No handoff takes place along the whole street block. This arrangement can ease the load of mobile switching for handoffs and provide more capacity to receive the new calls. Also, this arrangement can reduce the number of zone selectors to only one. This illustration of the wireless information superhighway system needs a lot of research effort to make it happen.

REFERENCES

1. R. B. Robrock II, "The Intelligent Network," *Proc. IEEE*, vol. 75, no. 1, Jan. 1991, pp. 7–20.

2. R. K. Berman, J. H. Brewster, "Perspective on the AIN Architecture," *IEEE Communications Magazine*, vol. 31, February 1993, pp. 27–33.

3. D. A. Pezzutti, "Operations Issues for Advanced Intelligent Networks," *IEEE Communications Magazine*, Feb. 1992, pp. 58–63.

4. A. R. Modarressi, "Signaling System No. 7: A Tutorial," *IEEE Communications Magazine*, July 1990, pp. 19–35.

5. H. Rarig, "ISDN Signal Distribution Network," *IEEE Communications Magazine*, vol. 32, June 1994, pp. 34–38.

6. K. Murano, K. Murakami, E. Iwabuchi, T. Katsuki, H. Ogasawara, "Technologies Towards Broadband ISDN," *IEEE Communications Magazine*, vol. 28, April 1990, pp. 66–70.

7. T. H. Wee, "Cost-Effective Network Evolution," *IEEE Communications Magazine*, Sept. 1993, pp. 64–73.

8. M. Hibino, F. Kaplan, "User Interface Design for SONET Networks," *IEEE Communications Magazine*, vol. 30, August 1992, pp. 24–27.

9. B. Jabbain, "Intelligent Network Concepts in Mobile Communications," *IEEE Communications Magazine*, vol. 31, February 1992, pp. 64–69.

10. A. S. Acampora and M. Naghshinch, "Control and Quality-of-service Provisioning in High-speed Microcellular Network," *IEEE Personal Communications*, vol. no. 2, April, 1994, pp. 36–43.

11. D. J. Goodman, G. P. Pollini, and K. S. Meier-Hellstern, "Network Control for Wireless Communications," *IEEE Communications Magazine*, Dec. 1992, pp. 116–125. W. T. Webb, "Modulation Methods for PCNs," *IEEE Communications Magazine*, Dec. 1992, pp. 90–95.

12. A. Nakajima, M. Eguchi, T. Arita, and H. Takeda, "Intelligent Mobile Communications Network Architecture," *Proceeding of ISS '90*, Stockholm, Sweden, May 1990.

13. I. W. Habib, T. N. Saadawi, "Controlling Flow and avoiding Congestion in Broadband Networks," *IEEE Communications Magazine*, October 1991, vol. 29, pp. 46–53.

14. A. A. Lazar, G. Pacifici, "Control of Resources in Broadband Networks With Quality of Service Guarantees," *IEEE Communications Magazine*, October 1991, vol. 29, pp. 66–73.

15. Y. Inoue, N. Terada, "Granulated Broadband Network," *IEEE Communications Magazine*, April 1994, pp. 56–63.

16. K. Sato, S. Ohta, I. Tokizawa, "Broadband ATM Network Architecture Based on Virtual Paths," *IEEE Transactions on Communication*, August 1990.

17. P. Newman, "ATM Local Area Networks," *IEEE Communications Magazine*, vol. 32, March 1994, pp. 86–98.

18. S. Isaku, M. Ishikura, "ATM Network Architecture for Supporting the Connectionless Service," *Proc. IEEE Infocom*, vol. 2, pp. 796–802, San Francisco, June 1990.

19. K. Kato, T. Shimoe, K. Hajikano, K. Murakarni, "Experimental Broadband ATM Switching System," *Proc. Globecom '88*, pp. 1288–1292.

20. J. A. McEachern, "Gigabit Networking on the Public Transmission Network," *IEEE Communications Magazine*, vol. 30, April 1992, pp. 70–78.

21. E. W. Zegma, "Architecture for ATM Switching Systems," *IEEE Communications Magazine*, vol. 31, February 1993, pp. 28–37.

22. P. Condreuse, M. Servel, "Prelude: An Asynchronous Time-Division Switched Network," *Proc. Intl. Communication Conference*, June 1987, pp. 769–773.

23. M. Thottan, C. Ji, "Anomaly Detection in IP Network," IEEE Trans. On Signal Proc., Vol. 51, Aug. 2003, pp. 2191–2204.

24. W. C, Y. Lee, *Lee's Essentials of Wireless Communications*, McGraw-Hill Co., 2001, Section 8.4.

25. C. E. Perkins, *Mobile IP, Design Principles and Practices*, Addison-Wesley, 1998, New York.

26. R. Caceres, N. G. Dufield, A. Feldmann, J. Friedmann, A. Greenberg, R. Greer, T. Johnson, C. Kalmanek, B. Krishnamurthy, D. Lavelle, P. Mishra, K. K. Ramakrishnan, J. Resford, F. True, and J. E. van der Merwe "Measurement and analysis of IP network usage and behaviour," IEEE Commun. Mag., pp. 144–151, May 2000.

27. P. Gardenier, M. Shafi, R. B. Vernall, M. Milner, "Sharing Issues Between FPLMTS and Fixed Services," *IEEE Communications Magazine*, vol. 32, June 1994, pp. 74–78.

28. R. Steele, "The Evolution of Personal Communications," *IEEE Personal Communications*, April 1994, pp. 6–11.

29. A. Bruce McDonald, T. Znati, "A Path Availability Model for Wireless Ad-Hoc Network," IEEE WCNC' 99, New Orleans, LA.

30. "Mesh Dynamics "Structured Mesh Technology," Mesh Dynamics Inc., Santa Clara, CA, *www.meshdynamics.com.*

31. N. H. Vaidya, "Mobile Ad Hoc Networking: MAC and Routing Protocols," University of Illinois at Urbana-Champaign, *nhv@uiuc.edu*, 2002.

32. A. Nasipuri and S. Das, "On-Demand Multipath Routing for Mobile Ad Hoc Networks," In Proc. of the 8th Annual IEEE ICCCN, Boston, MA, October 1999.

33. D. V. Larsen, J. D. Larsen, G. W. Van Lochem, M. S. Larsen, "Multi-Hop Packet Radio Network," U. S. Patent 6, 097,703, August 1, 2000. A technology for ODMA systems.

34. T. Ojanpera, R. Prasad "Wideband CDMA for third Generation Mobile Communications," Artech House Publishers, 1998, p. 16.

35. R. Poor, "Wireless Mesh Networks," Sensor Business Digest, Feb. 2003, *www.sensorsmag.com/arataicles/0203/38/main.shtml.*

36. P. H. Ho, J. Tapolcai, T. Cinkler, "Segment Shared Protection in Mesh Communications Networks with Bandwidth Guaranteed Tunnels." *IEEE/ACM Trans. Networking*, 2004;12,1105–1118.

37. J. Hill, et al, "System Architecture Directions for Networked Sensors," Proc. ASPLOS 2000, pp. 93–104.

38. S. Bhatnagar, B. Deb, and B. Nath, "Service Differentiation in Sensor Networks," In Proc. Of the Fourth International Symposium on Wireless Personal Multimedia Communications, September 2001. WPMC 2001.

CHAPTER 18

PERSPECTIVE SYSTEMS OF 4G AND RELATED TOPICS

18.1 PERSPECTIVE SYSTEMS OF 4G

18.1.1 Introduction

As radio spectrum is a primary, but limited, resource for wireless technologies, the main thrust of 4G researches worldwide is directed toward spectrally efficient systems. The requirement of developing 4G systems is stated in Sec. 1.1. New powerful technologies that emerged recently promise a tenfold improvement in spectral efficiency over existing solutions. Also, the 4G systems are considered to be IP-based cellular systems. A number of different 4G air interfaces are now being examined. Also, the 4G systems have to be cost-effective and QoS driven. These potential 4G tools and techniques include:

a. Advanced antenna technologies, such as Antenna Array, can add value to reduce the interference and solve capacity problems.

b. MIMI techniques, combining the array or multiple antennas with advanced coding techniques to form extremely efficient MIMO (multiple input multiple output) systems.

c. Adaptive and reconfigurable systems, such as SDR (software defined radio), can optimize the modulation, coding power control, and so forth, to the varying transmission conditions. The high-order modulation, turbo coding, and LDPC (low-density parity-check codes) are the tools for easy implementation.

d. Wireless access technologies such as OFDMA (orthogonal frequency-division multiple access) and MC-CDMA (multiple carrier code-division multiple access) are the main contenders for future systems. A single scheduling packet-based system also is a more radical access scheme for the downlink.

e. Broadcast and cellular network hybrid, such as using some broadcast technologies to carry high-bandwidth downlink multicast data, leads to improved spectral efficiency.

Up to today, there is no single technology that can be used to achieve ITU 4G's requirement. Therefore, the trend of combining many technologies for 4G systems is underway.

18.1.2 Different Proposed 4G Systems

All major international wireless companies are engaging in 4G developments today. The core technology in most proposed 4G systems is MIMO-OFDMA. Besides, each company has its own thought in applying different technologies.

731

On August 24–25, 2004, Samsung hosted the 2nd 4G Forum in Jeju Island, Korea.[1] All major international wireless companies presented their proposed 4G systems or technologies. In this section, a brief description of each company's proposal is carried out. Some good attributes of their systems may be found in Reference 1.

- Ericsson's proposed 4G technologies:
  1. In broadband transmission
     - Broadband RF
     - Multicarrier transmission
  2. Advanced antenna transmission
     - Multiple antennas
  3. Advanced radio-network structures
     - Cross-layer interaction
- Nokia's proposed 4G technologies: dual bandwidth approach
  1. Using a 100-MHz wideband (WB) carrier and a 10-MHz narrowband (NB) carrier as a dual bandwidth approach.
  2. Using a NB carrier for certain situations
     - Low-bit rate connections
     - Terminals on cell edges

  Therefore, a dual bandwidth system with flexible inter-bandwidth channel allocation provides an implementable solution for the future system.
- Siemens proposed 4G Radio Interface
  The system uses MIMO multiplexing, Tx/Rx diversity, and beam forming technologies. A trial of OFDM-TDMA was held in Munich, Germany. It is a TDD system and operates at 5.18–5.32 GHz (7 carriers). Each carrier has a bandwidth of 20 MHz and has 64 subcarriers. The maximum data rate is 72 Mbps (uncoded) and 54 Mbps (coded).
- Motorola proposed 4G Systems
  A full duplex OFDM experimental link was trialed in Chicago. It is a TDD system and operates at 3.675 GHz with a bandwidth of 20 MHz and 751 subcarriers. The maximum data rate is 90 MHz.
- NTT DoCoMo's broadband packet wireless access for future cellular systems.
  1. Wireless access scheme in forward link is based on VSF-OFCDM (variable spread factor–orthogonal frequency and code division multiplexing).
     - Adaptive control of spreading factor (SF) in both time and frequency domains based on cell structure, channel load, radio link condition, and modulation parameters.
     - Maintain higher system capacity by using the same air interface.
  2. Wireless access scheme in reverse link is based on DS-CDMA. It can lower the transmission power and apply the one-cell frequency.
  3. Uses multiple-antenna transmission techniques for 1 Gbps data transmission in local areas (i.e., isolated-cell or indoor environment).
  4. A field trial has been carried out in Tokyo.
     In forward link, the carrier frequency is 4.635 GHz with a bandwidth of 101.5 MHz and 768 subcarriers. The data rate (throughput) is 300 Mbps. In reverse link, the carrier frequency is 4.9 GHz with a bandwidth of 40 MHz and a chip rate of 16.384 Mcps.

- Samsung's new air interface is called TOPAZ (Terrestrial OFDM Packet Access System for Zillion). The key features are as follows:

   1. Using FH-OFDMA/CDM (frequency hopping–OFDMA/Code Division Multiplexing) as the multiple access schemes.

   2. Dynamic channel allocation (DCA)

   3. Adaptive modulations and coding (AMC)

   4. Using HARQ (hybrid ARQ) in physical layer

   5. The gain from multiuser diversity is traded off with that from frequency diversity.

   6. System parameter: The operating carrier is 5 GHz. The bandwidth for both downlink and uplink is 2 MHz. The subcarrier spacing is 15 kHz. The peak data rate for downlink is 60 Mbps and for uplink is 30 Mbps.

- WiBro (Wireless Broadband)[2]
  WiBro is the Korean standard based on IEEE 16-2004 and 802.16e draft 3. The physical and MAC specs. are listed as follows:

A. PHY Spec.

- Frequency Band   : 2.3 GHz (Korea)
- Channel Bandwidth   : 9 MHz
- Duplex   : TDD/5 msec frame
- Multiple Access   : OFDMA
- Modulation   : QPSK, 16 QAM, 64 QAM
- Channel Coding   : CTC (Convolution Turbo Codes)
- Cell Coverage   : ~1 km
- Maximum Data Rate
   Sector throughput   : DL : 18 Mbps, UL : 6 Mbps
   User throughput   : DL : 3 Mbps, UL : 1 Mbps
- Optional Adaptive Antenna System
- H-ARQ (Hybrid Automatic Response Request)
- Band selection AMC (Adaptive Modulation and Coding) and diversity sub-channel
- Support 60 km/h mobile speed

B. MAC Spec.

- Flexible BW Allocation by MAP
   Frame by Frame
- Supports flexible QoS offering
   RTPS: real-time Polling Service,
   NRTPS: (non real-time Polling Service)
   Fine granularity
- Efficient MAC PDU construction
   Variable size MAC PDU
   MAC-level framing (No PPP)
   Fragmentation, packing, concatenation

- Payload header suppression support
- Security support
- Sleep mode support
- H-ARQ/ARQ support
- Handoff: Break before make
- AMC support

18.2   A CDD SYSTEM: CS-OFDMA

In this section, a perspective new wireless CDD (Code Division Duplexing)[3-5] physical layer scheme for 4G access technologies called CS-OFDMA (code spread–orthogonal frequency division multiple access) is introduced to take advantage of both attributes of CDMA and OFDMA toward a simpler and more spectral-efficient system. This system also can be improved in its spectral efficiency by adding other 4G technologies as mentioned in Chapter 16. CS-OFDMA technology is very suitable for a CDD system and will emphasize a further explicit claim of its advantages.

18.2.1   Realization of a CDD System

Up to the present, only FDD (frequency division duplexing) and TDD (time division duplexing) are used in the wireless communication systems. Now after many kinds of smart codes[6-11] are found, their explicit merits can be used to realize a Code Division Duplexing (CDD) system.[4] The characteristics of a smart code x can be expressed as follows:

The properties of auto-correlation of the code x itself are

$$\rho_{xx}(\tau = 0) = 1$$

$$\rho_{xx}(\tau \neq 0) = 0 \qquad \tau \leq \tau_a \qquad (18.2\text{-}1)$$

where τ_a is called the autocorrelation zero window. Within the window, the multipaths of the signal (i.e., Code x) itself can be eliminated due to the code property shown in Eq. (18.2-1). Usually the window τ_a can be large if the arrangement of the code structure can be handled properly.

The property of cross-correlation of any two different codes in the set of smart codes:

$$\rho_{xy}(\tau) = 0 \qquad \textit{for all } \tau, \qquad \tau \leq \tau_c \qquad (18.2\text{-}2)$$

where τ_c is the cross-correlation zero window generated from the smart code structure. Within the window τ_c, the multiuser interference due to the multipaths can be eliminated by the code property.

Strictly speaking, CDD system should be realized by continuously transmitting on a single frequency with a set of smart codes to provide two-way communications:

In reality, within the cross-correlation zero windows τ_c of the two current smart codes, one for downlink and one for uplink, the cross-correlation value of two codes is not exactly zero when the signal (UL or DL) arrives at the other terminal over a communication link. It is due to the imperfection from the current smart code properties. Therefore, at any T/R terminal of communications, the strong transmit power at one terminal would mask the weak signal arrival from the other end along a communication link, although the signal traveling time can be adjusted such that the arriving time falls within the window τ_c. Thus, CDD cannot be used by continuously transmitting on a single frequency. These transmit-receiving signal ratio situations and the near-far ratio situations in cellular systems face the same difficulty in receiving signals. Therefore, the FDD is a solution to resolve the transmit-receiving signal ratio situation, just as the power control is a solution to resolve the near-far ratio situation.

Then, we try to apply a set of smart codes on a single frequency while transmitting and receiving alternately.

The smart codes used in a CDD system (or strictly speaking, a TDD setup coupled with a CDD system) can avoid both the multiuser interference and the neighboring cell interference, which the conventional TDD system, without the smart codes, cannot.

18.2.2 Code Attributes

There are many smart codes in the literature.[6-11]

Assume that a smart code is a complementary orthogonal code, such as LS code,[9-10] with a length of L bits, and then there are L numbers of different combinations of code sequences.

A. A complementary orthogonal code with a length of L chips consists of C and S codes. The lengths of both C and S codes are L/2 chips. The correlations between C and S codes possess the following properties. The sum of the autocorrelation coefficients of code C_1 and code S_1 equals one for $\tau = 0$. The sum of autocorrelation coefficients of code C_1 and code S_1 equals zero for $\tau \neq 0$ where $\tau \leq \tau_a$. This property is the same as CCK codes described in Sec. 18.3. The sum of the cross-correlation coefficients of code C_1 and code S_1 are always zero under the condition of $\tau \leq \tau_c$. Thus, the properties of a smart code shown in Section 18.2.1 can be achieved by using a complementary orthogonal code with properties shown above.

B. If all L codes are used, then there is no cross-correlation zero windows between any two codes. If only L/2 number of codes is used, the minimum cross-correlation zero window is $-1c \leq \tau_c \leq 1c$, where c is the chip interval in time. If L/4 number of codes are used, the minimum cross-correlation zero window is $-3c \leq \tau_c \leq 3c$. It can also be seen that among the L/2 number of codes used, one half of them (i.e., L/4) can have a cross-correlation zero window of $-3c \leq \tau_c \leq 3c$. A quarter of L/2 number of codes (i.e., L/8) can have a cross-correlation window of $-5c \leq \tau_c \leq 5c$; however, we always apply the minimum cross-correlation zero window $-1c \leq \tau_c \leq 1c$ when all L/2 number of codes is used.

C. By using code spreading, we can obtain the Processing Gain (P.G.) in dB $= 10 \log L$, and carrier-to-interference ratio $C/I = E_b/I_0/P.G.$, where $I = I_0 B$, $C = E_b R_b$; B is the channel bandwidth, E_b is the energy per bit, and R_b is bit per second. Thus,[8] we have $P.G. = B/R_b = L$ and R_c (chip rate) $= R_b L$.

D. The autocorrelation zero windows τ_a can be counted by the number of inserted blank bits separated between C and S. As long as there is no overlap in time τ_a between C and S codes, the autocorrelation of the smart code is zero.

Due to the autocorrelation properties of the smart code, the Rayleigh fading and random FM generated by the multipaths while the mobile station[9] is moving would not be observed at the received signal. Thus, the moving speed of the mobile station should not affect the received signal. Using smart codes in a mobile radio system achieves great value.

E. The time spread τ due to the multipath in the terrestrial medium, in most cases, is less than 10 μs. For a data rate of 100 kbps, the time interval between neighboring bits is 1b = 10 μs. It means $\tau < 1b$ in most cases, and then the cross-correlation zero window $\tau_c = 1b$ can be set if a data rate of 100 kbps is transmitted. When a code spreading modulation is applied, a chip rate R_c of 100 kcps is transmitted, the time interval between neighboring chips is 1c, then the time spread τ is less than 1c, $\tau < 1c$ or $\tau_c = 1c = 10$ μs.

18.2.3 CS-OFDMA System

Because the code spreading (CS)[9–10] can only use a limited number of smart codes, it is not an ideal set of codes for a conventional CDMA system.[12] In a conventional CDMA system, a single wideband spectral channel is used to transmit as many codes as possible. Each code acts as a traffic channel. However, the number of smart codes is inversely proportional to the size of the zero-correlation window. It is not desirable for a CDMA system. Nevertheless, the limited number of smart codes can be used repeatedly in different subcarriers of an OFDMA system. Therefore, the smart codes are suitably applied on an OFDMA system.

OFDMA[13] signal splits a high-rate data stream transmitted over a carrier-frequency into a number of low-rate data streams transmitted over a number of subcarrier channels (Schs.). In each subcarrier, we may use code spreading on the low-rate data stream to benefit the attributes of CDMA system.[14] The limited number of codes applied on each subcarrier of an OFDMA system is a good choice.

In OFDMA, the subcarrier spacing is a multiple of 1/T instead of normally 2/T where T is the symbol (or chip) period. These orthogonal-frequency subcarriers shown in Fig. 18.1 depict that reducing the subcarriers spacing by half produces no cross talk. It is a highly efficient multicarrier transmission scheme.

However, in mobile radio system, the phenomenon of the multipath fading and time delay spread can destroy the orthogonality and create intersymbol interference (ISI) and intercarrier interference (ICI) which result in cross talk as shown in Fig. 18.1b. These issues have been resolved in OFDMA with special treatment such as adding guard time and cyclic extension to maintain the orthogonal property among the subcarriers and eliminate both

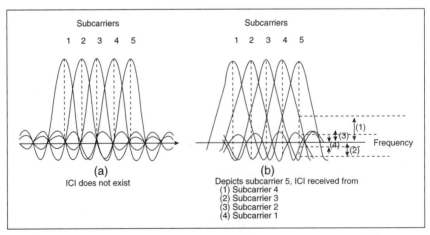

FIGURE 18.1 Spectra of an OFDM symbol: (*a*) orthogonality is kept among all subcarriers; (*b*) orthogonality is distorted, and ICI is created in all subcarriers.

TABLE 18.1. C Codes Assignment of Each Sch_p in Four Subgroups and Four Corresponding Cells

Subchannels	Subgroups of C Codes
(in Sch_p) $Cell_1$	$CS_1: C_1 \quad C_1 \quad C_1 \quad C_1 \quad .....$ $CS_2: C_2 \quad C_2 \quad C_2 \quad C_2 \quad .....$ $CS_3: C_3 \quad C_3 \quad C_3 \quad C_3 \quad .....$ ... ... $CS_{N/4}: C_{N/4} \quad C_{N/4} \quad C_{N/4} \quad C_{N/4} \quad .....$
(in Sch_p) $Cell_2$	$CS_{N/4+1}: C_{N/4+1} \quad C_{N/4+1} \quad C_{N/4+1} \quad C_{N/4+1} \quad ....$ ... ... $CS_{N/2}: C_{N/2} \quad C_{N/2} \quad C_{N/2} \quad C_{N/2} \quad .....$
(in Sch_p) $Cell_3$	$CS_{N/2+1}: C_{N/2+1} \quad C_{N/2+1} \quad C_{N/2+1} \quad .....$ ... ... $CS_{3N/4}: C_{3N/4} \quad C_{3N/4} \quad C_{3N/4} \quad .....$
(in Sch_p) $Cell_4$	$CS_{3N/4+1}: C_{3N/4+1} \quad C_{3N/4+1} \quad C_{3N/4+1} \quad .....$ ... ... $CS_N: C_N \quad C_N \quad C_N \quad ....$

ISI and ICI. In CS-OFDMA system, we try to take advantage of the smart code property to do the same thing instead of using guard time and cyclic extension. In this case, the orthogonality among the subcarriers is no longer held as supposed to be shown in Fig. 18.1b. Due to the low rate of parallel subcarriers, the properties of smart codes can help to eliminate ISI and ICI with a careful engineering design.

Assume that a carrier channel Ch has been subbanded into M subcarrier channels (Schs), and Δf_i is the subcarrier spacing. The carrier bandwidth Δf is the summation of M subcarrier spacing.

Each Sch_i can have code spreading (CS) by N codes with a code length L. Each code consists of C and S codes, and the length of each C and S is L/2. Thus, each Sch_i in M Schs contains the number of N of CS channels, $Sch_i = \sum_{j=1}^{N} CS_j$. Each Sch_i (i = 1, M) of M subcarriers can transmit the same number N of CS_j channels. The maximum number of N is L; thus, $N \leq L$.

Each CS_j is treated as a traffic channel. In a normal arrangement, there are gaps (blank bits) between C's and S's as $CS_j = C_j$ (gap) S_j (gap) C_j (gap) S_j (gap)....

This arrangement can be used when the rate of data stream is very low, so that C_j and S_j can only overlap each other in a small portion. However, when the rate of data stream is not very low, C and S need a big gap separation or to be separated in different ways.

Now, a new approach of eliminating gaps between C and S is proposed, and each CS_j will be arranged with C's and S's on different Sch_i, respectively. Also, the number N of C codes and S codes are divided into four subgroups, and each subgroup has a number N/4 of C and S codes to be assigned to one of four cells.

In this system, the number M of total subcarriers is an odd number. Each of the first half of M Schs, denoted by p (p = 1, (M − 1)/2), are used for C codes. Also, in each Sch_p there are N of C codes divided into four subgroups and assigned in four corresponding cells as shown in Table 18.1. Therefore, each Sch_p is used in all four cells with different subgroups of C codes.

Each of the second half M Schs, denoted by q (q = (M + 3)/2, M), is used for S codes. Also, in each Sch_q there are N of S codes divided into four subgroups and assigned in four

TABLE 18.2. S Codes Assignment of Each Sch_q in Four Subgroups and Four Corresponding Cells

Subchannels	Subgroups of C Codes				
(in Sch_q) $Cell_1$	$CS_1: S_1$	S_1	S_1	S_1	.....
	$CS_2: S_2$	S_2	S_2	S_2	.....
	$CS_3: S_3$	S_3	S_3	S_3	.....
	... ...				
	$CS_{N/4}: S_{N/4}$	$S_{N/4}$	$S_{N/4}$	$S_{N/4}$	.....
(in Sch_q) $Cell_2$	$CS_{N/4+1}: S_{N/4+1}$	$S_{N/4+1}$	$S_{N/4+1}$	$S_{N/4+1}$	....
	... ...				
	$CS_{N/2}: S_{N/2}$	$S_{N/2}$	$S_{N/2}$	$S_{N/2}$	.....
(in Sch_q) $Cell_3$	$CS_{N/2+1}: S_{N/2}$	$S_{N/2}$	$S_{N/2}$	.....	
	... ...				
	$CS_{3N/4}: S_{3N/4}$	$S_{3N/4}$	$S_{3N/4}$	.....	
(in Sch_q) $Cell_4$	$CS_{3N/4+1}: S_{3N/4+1}$	$S_{3N/4+1}$	$S_{3N/4+1}$	.....	
	... ...				
	$CS_N: S_N$	S_N	S_N	.....	

corresponding cells, as shown in Table 18.2. Therefore, each Sch_q is used in all four cells with different subgroups of S codes.

In Sch_p (p = 1, (M − 1)/2), only C code is transmitted in every CS code. Each subgroup has a number N/4 of C codes to be assigned to one of four cells. In Sch_q (q = (M + 3)/2, M), only S code is transmitted in every CS code. Each subgroup has a number N/4 of S codes to be assigned to one of four cells.

A particular subcarrier at the number (M + 1)/2 is designated as a special training signal for synchronization. This arrangement can effectively reduce the frequency jitter and phase noise, which is needed the most in a CS-OFDMA system. Also, it can be used as the broadcast channel of the system.

All four cells are using the same M subcarriers. It is a CDMA system also. Because one of the four subgroups of codes is assigned to one of four cells, the codes reuse factor K = 4 is applied to reuse the four subgroups of CS codes.[15] As a result, each individual cell can be identified by one of the subgroups of CS codes (see Fig. 18.2). Therefore, CS-OFDMA is a high spectral efficient system, as we only reuse the codes.

In each cell, there are N/4 CS codes transmitting in each pair of subcarriers, one for C codes and one for S codes, and the processing gain of each Sch due to code CS_j spreading is 10 log L/2 (in dB).

The N smart codes spreading in each Sch are like the N Walsh codes spreading in a CDMA carrier channel. If the code length is L, the processing gain is 10 log L/2 in each Sch channel due to the CS code. There are M subcarriers in CS-OFDM, half of M − 1 is used for C codes and half of M − 1 is used for S codes. Therefore, the total number of traffic channels in each cell is (M − 1)/2 × N/4.

To make a workable CS-OFDMA system, we may use LS codes[9–10] and assume the code length L = 32 chips (i.e., C has 16 chips and S has 16 chips). For having a transmit rate of 100 kcps, the time interval between two adjacent chips is 10 μs, (i.e., 1c = 10 μs), the total number of the CS-OFDMA channels (4 × 4 (M − 1)/2) are eight times that of (M − 1) of the conventional OFDMA channels.

Here is a new concept in appreciation of CS-OFDMA. In every CS-OFDMA subcarrier, there are 16 CS channels. Every one of the 16 CS channels possesses 12-dB processing

In all cells:

M/2 *Sch$_i$* (*i* = even) transmit C codes

M/2 *Sch$_i$* (*i* = odd) transmit S codes

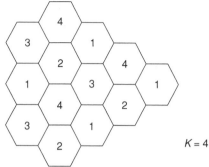

CS codes in each cell:

Cell 1: CS codes (1–4)
Cell 2: CS codes (5–8)
Cell 3: CS codes (9–12)
Cell 4: CS codes (13–16)

K = 4

FIGURE 18.2   The reuse of CS codes in a four-cell configuration.

gain. The 12-dB processing gain can be translated as an increase of its C/I by 12 dB as compared to an OFDMA subcarrier, whereas the throughput of its subcarrier is one-half of a conventional OFDMA subcarrier. We may use the formula shown in Section 18.2.2 that C/I is a function of data rate R$_b$. Reducing a throughput by half will only gain 3 dB in its C/I ratio. Based on the same throughput in two systems, C/I of a CS/OFDMA subcarrier can have 9-dB gain over that of an OFDMA subcarrier. By taking advantage of 9 dB of C/I and lowering it to gain an increased data rate, CS-OFDMA subcarrier can have eight times of throughput over the OFDMA subcarrier, or R$_b$ (CS-OFDMA subcarrier) = 8 × R$_b$ (OFDMA subcarrier). Thus, the CS-OFDMA has much higher spectrum efficiency than the OFDMA.

18.3 COMPLEMENTARY CODE KEYING (CCK) CODES AND MODULATION

The new high rate modulation scheme called CCK[16] is used for 5.5 and 11 Mbps data rates in 2.4-GHz band. A binary complementary code was found by Golay[16] and represents subsets of the more general class of codes known as poly phase codes. The CCK codes are poly phase complementary.

A. Binary complementary code

Binary complementary codes comprise a pair of equal finite length sequences, sequence *x* and a sequence *y* with a length *n* bits of both sequences, which are also called code words.

Then, the autocorrelations of two sequences {x$_i$} and {y$_i$} with a shift of *j* bits can be expressed as

$$\rho_{xx}(j) = \sum_{i=1}^{n-j} x_i x_{i+j} + \sum_{i=1}^{j} x_i \cdot x_{n-j+i} \qquad (18.3\text{-}1)$$

$$\rho_{yy}(j) = \sum_{i=1}^{n-j} y_i y_{i+j} + \sum_{i=1}^{j} y_i \cdot y_{n-j+i} \tag{18.3-2}$$

The two sequences $\{x_i\}$ and $\{y_i\}$ are complementary if their correlations

$$\rho_{xx}(j) + \rho_{yy}(j) = o \qquad \text{when } j \neq o \tag{18.3-3}$$

$$\rho_{xx}(o) + \rho_{yy}(o) = 2n \qquad \text{when } j = o \tag{18.3-4}$$

For example, two sequences x and y have a length of 8 bits, $n = 8$, shown as follows:

sequence $\{x_i\}$ $-1, -1, -1, 1, 1, 1, -1, 1$

sequence $\{y_i\}$ $-1, -1, -1, 1, -1 - 1, 1, -1$

When $j = 0$, $\rho_{xx}(0)$ of sequence $\{x_j\}$ can be found from Eq. (18.3-1) as

$$\rho_{xx}(0) = \sum_{i \times 1}^{8} x_i^2 = 8$$

and $\rho_{yy}(0)$ of sequence $\{y_i\}$ can be found from Eq. (18.3-2) as

$$\rho_{yy}(0) = \sum_{i=1}^{8} y_i^2 = 8$$

when $j = 3$, the correlation $\rho_{xx}(3)$ from Eq. (18.3-1) for $\{x_i\}$ is

$$\rho_{xx}(3) = \sum_{i=1}^{5} x_i x_{i+3} + \sum_{i=1}^{3} x_i x_{5+i} = (-1 - 1 - 1 - 1 + 1) + (-1 + 1 - 1)$$

$$= -3 - 1 = -4$$

The correlation $\rho_{yy}(3)$ from Eq. (18.3-2) for $\{y_i\}$ is

$$\rho_{yy}(3) = \sum_{i=1}^{5} y_i y_{i+3} + \sum_{i=1}^{3} y_i y_{5+i} = (-1 + 1 + 1 + 1 + 1) + (+1 - 1 + 1)$$

$$= +3 + 1 = 4$$

Substituting $\rho_{xx}(3)$ and $\rho_{yy}(3)$ into Eq. (18.3-3) and $\rho_{xx}(0)$ and $\rho_{yy}(0)$ into Eq. (18.3-4) proves that $\{x_i\}$ and $\{y_i\}$ are complementary. The tabulation of autocorrelation functions for a pair of complementary codes is shown in Table 18.3.

The property shown in Eq. (18.3-3) and Eq. (18.3-4) makes complementary codes useful in digital communications systems.

B. Polyphase codes
A polyphase code could contain elements having four different phases. It is a complex complementary code set. Its elements x_i are a number from a set of complex numbers $\{1, -1, j, -j\}$ and the code set is characterized by the autocorrelation property described in Eq. (18.3-3) and Eq. (18.3-4) for binary codes.

C. CCK Modulation
The polyphase codes can be used to modulate a digital waveform. Because the direct sequence spread spectrum (DSSS) technique is used for the high-rate modulation scheme,

TABLE 18.3. Tabulation of Autocorrelation Functions for a Pair of Complementary Codes

Shift	Sequence $\{x_i\}$ Code								$\rho_{xx}(j)$	Sequence $\{y_i\}$ Code								$\rho_{yy}(j)$	Complementary $\rho_{xx}(j) + \rho_{yy}(j)$
0	−1	−1	−1	1	1	1	−1	1	8	−1	−1	−1	1	−1	−1	1	−1	8	16
	−1	−1	−1	1	1	1	−1	1		−1	−1	−1	1	−1	−1	1	−1		
1	−1	−1	−1	1	1	1	−1	1	0	−1	−1	−1	1	−1	−1	1	−1	0	0
	1	−1	−1	−1	1	1	1	−1		−1	−1	−1	−1	1	−1	−1	1		
2	−1	−1	−1	1	1	1	−1	1	0	−1	−1	−1	1	−1	−1	1	−1	0	0
	−1	1	−1	−1	−1	1	1	1		1	−1	−1	−1	−1	1	−1	−1		
3	−1	−1	−1	1	1	1	−1	1	−4	−1	−1	−1	1	−1	−1	1	−1	+4	0
	1	−1	1	−1	−1	−1	1	1		−1	1	−1	−1	−1	−1	1	−1		
4	−1	−1	−1	1	1	1	−1	1	0	−1	−1	−1	1	−1	−1	1	−1	0	0
	1	1	−1	1	−1	−1	−1	1		−1	−1	1	−1	−1	−1	−1	1		
5	−1	−1	−1	1	1	1	−1	1	−4	−1	−1	−1	1	−1	−1	1	−1	+4	0
	1	1	1	−1	1	−1	−1	−1		1	−1	−1	1	−1	−1	−1	−1		
6	−1	−1	−1	1	1	1	−1	1	0	−1	−1	−1	1	−1	−1	1	−1	0	0
	−1	1	1	1	−1	1	−1	−1		−1	1	−1	−1	1	−1	−1	−1		
7	−1	−1	−1	1	1	1	−1	1	0	−1	−1	−1	1	−1	−1	1	−1	0	0
	−1	−1	1	1	1	−1	1	−1		−1	−1	1	−1	−1	1	−1	−1		

TABLE 18.4. Phase Parameter Encoding Scheme

Dibit	Phase Parameter
(d1, d0)	$\varphi 1$
(d3, d2)	$\varphi 2$
(d5, d4)	$\varphi 3$
(d7, d6)	$\varphi 4$

the CCK can be the spreading codes. The IEEE 802.11 CCK codes have a code length 8 and a chipping rate of 11 Mcps. The 8 complex chips comprise a single symbol. By making a symbol rate 1.375 MSps, the 11 Mbps waveform ends up occupying the same approximate bandwidth as that for the 2 Mbps of 802.11 QPSK waveform.

The 8-bit CCK words are derived from the following formula:

$$\{xi\} = \{e^{j(\varphi_1+\varphi_2+\varphi_3+\varphi_4)}, e^{j(\varphi_1+\varphi_3+\phi_4)}, e^{j(\varphi_1+\varphi_2+\varphi_4)}, -e^{j(\varphi_1+\varphi_4)},$$

$$e^{j(\varphi_1+\varphi_2+\varphi_3)}, e^{j(\varphi_1+\varphi_3)}, -e^{j(\varphi_1+\varphi_2)}, e^{j(\varphi_1)}\} \tag{18.3-5}$$

The parameters from φ_1 to φ_4 determine the phase values of the complex code set. For the 11 Mbps data rate, each symbol represents 8 bits of information. At 5.5 Mbps, 4 bits per symbol are transmitted. In here, the 11 Mbps mode is described as follows:

The data bit stream is partitioned into bytes as $(x_7, x_6, x_5, \cdots x_o)$, where x_o is first in time. The 8 bits are used to encode the phase parameters φ_1 *and* φ_4 according to scheme shown in Table 18.4. The encoding is based on differential QPSK modulation shown in Table 18.5. For example, the 11 Mbps made has a data bit stream as

$$d_7, d_6, d_5, d_4, d_3, d_2, d_1, d_0 = 10110101$$

which is an 8-bit symbol. From Table 18.4, we can find that

$$d_1, d_0 = 01 \rightarrow \varphi_1 = \pi$$

$$d_3, d_2 = 01 \rightarrow \varphi_2 = \pi$$

$$d_5, d_4 = 11 \rightarrow \varphi_3 = \pi/2$$

$$d_2, d_6 = 10 \rightarrow \varphi_4 = \pi/2$$

TABLE 18.5. DQPSK Modulation of Phase Parameters

Dibit (d_{I+1}, d_I)	Phase
00	0
01	π
10	$\pi/2$
11	$-\pi/2$

Substituting the phase parameter values into the code word formula shown in Eq. (18.3-5)

$$\{x_i\} = \{e^{j(\pi+\pi-\pi/2+\pi/2)}, e^{j(\pi-\pi/2+\pi/2)}, e^{j(\pi+\pi+\pi/2)},$$

$$-e^{j(\pi+\pi/2)}, e^{j(\pi+\pi-\pi/2)}, e^{j(\pi-\pi/2)}, -e^{j(\pi+\pi)}, e^{j\pi}\}$$

$$= \{e^{j2\pi}, e^{j\pi}, e^{j\frac{5\pi}{2}}, -e^{j\frac{3\pi}{2}}, e^{j\frac{3\pi}{2}}, +e^{j\pi/2}, -e^{j2\pi}, e^{j\pi}\} \qquad (18.3\text{-}6)$$

Because

$$e^{j\theta} = \cos\theta + j\sin\theta \qquad (18.3\text{-}7)$$

Substituting Eq. (18.3-7) into Eq. (18.3-6) yields

$$\{x_i\} = \{\cos 2\pi + j\sin 2\pi, \ \cos\pi + j\sin\pi, \cos\frac{5\pi}{2} + j\sin\frac{5\pi}{2}, -\cos\frac{3\pi}{2}$$

$$- j\sin\frac{3\pi}{2}, \cos\frac{3\pi}{2} + j\sin\frac{3\pi}{2}, \cos\frac{\pi}{2} + j\sin\frac{\pi}{2}, -\cos 2\pi - j\sin 2\pi, \cos\pi$$

$$+ j\sin\pi\} = \{1, -1, j, j, -j, j, -1, -1, \}$$

Any 8 bits of data stream can obtain a complex CCK code word.

18.4 TURBO CODES AND LDPC

The challenge of developing new coding solutions is to provide performance gains closer to the channel capacity while not limiting throughput or adding latency. Claude Shannon showed that it is possible to optimize the energy and time transmitting data across a communications channel if you have the right coding scheme.

In the mid-1990s, turbo code was chosen for 3G system, and in year 2000, LDPC has been discovered and may be used for WiMAX systems.

18.4.1 Turbo Code

In 1993, a significant breakthrough occurred when two French electrical engineers, Claude Berou and Alain Glavieux,[17] discovered turbo codes. Their claim was that their turbo coding scheme would result in a 3-dB performance improvement over the best competing FEC coding solutions in existence. The claims were so unbelievable that many coding experts refused to even read the IEEE paper presenting the codes at the conference on Communications in Geneva, Switzerland. Later, other researchers began to replicate the results and realized the significance of this discovery.[18]

Turbo codes come in two flavors that are very different in structure: convolutional turbo codes (CTCs) and turbo product codes (TPCs). CTCs is also called turbo convolutional codes (TCCs) which use parallel convolutional encoders and an interleaver to generate the parity bits. TPCs are also called BTC (Block Turbo Codes) which use block structures. These are the Turbo Codes discovered by Berrou and Glavieux.

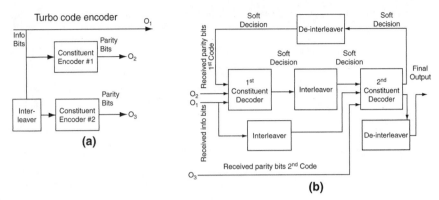

FIGURE 18.3 (*a*) Basic turbo code encoder. (*b*) Basic turbo code decoder.

A. CTC (Convolutional Turbo Codes)
CTC encoder is situated at the sending end, and the CTC decoder is situated at the receiving end.

- CTC Encoder: The CTC encoder consists of two systematical recursive convolutional codes, first and second constituent codes, running in parallel. An interleaver proceeds at the second recursive convolutional encoder, as shown in Fig. 18.3*a*. The mappings of interleaving for 3G two modes, WCDM and cdma2000, are different.

- CTC Decoder: This first decoder receives the systematic bits and parity bits from the first constituent code, as shown in Fig. 18.3*b*. The second decoder receives the parity bits from the second constituent and improves the performance on the soft-decision likelihood values. The process can be iterated many times, as shown in the returning path in Fig. 18.3*b*. The iteration process improves the performance. It is simplistic in decoding due to the algorithm but the trade-off is in the delayed response.

B. TPC (Turbo Product Codes)
In contrast to CTCs, TPCs use extended Hamming codes and parity codes as constituent codes to build 2D and 3D block structures. CTC results in a coding scheme that is far less complex to decode than the CTCs and is scalable to easily support the full range of data rate requirements up to gigabits per second. It is simplistic in decoding due to the product code type of structure and in implementation due to the use of simple row/column interleaving. It has a high energy efficiency. The benefit of this is smaller, less expensive decoders for cost-sensitive applications.

Turbo code is accepted to be used in the 3G standard because high-speed data are a requirement of the wireless information age, and the turbo code can meet this requirement to a great extent.

18.4.2 LDPC (Low Density Parity Check) Code[19]

After the turbo codes started to gain attention in the communications sector, designers turned their FEC research efforts toward the area of soft decision iterative decoders and toward searching for lower complexity codes. These efforts led to a rediscovery of LDPC codes, first proposed by Robert Gallagher[20] in his 1960 doctoral dissertation. Robert Tanner,[21] in 1981, generalized LDPC codes and developed a graphical method of representing these codes, now called Tanner graphs or bipartite graphs. Other than Tanner's important work, little was done with LDPC codes until David MacKay,[22] Michael Luby,[23] and others resurrected them in the mid-1990s. The LDPC codes have resulted in FEC solutions that perform even closer to the Shannon Limit and could replace turbo codes.[24]

An LDPC code is a linear error-correcting code that has a parity check matrix H with a small number of nonzero elements in each row and column. Although LDPC codes can be defined over any finite field, the majority of research is focused on LDPC codes over GF(2), in which "1" is the only nonzero element.

First, the generator G is found by Gaussian elimination

$$G = [I : P] \qquad (18.4\text{-}1)$$

I is the identity matrix. P is the matrix that can be turned to H matrix.

$$H = [P^T : I] \qquad (18.4\text{-}2)$$

P^T is the transpose matrix of P.

For example, a matrix G can be generated by Eq. (18.41-1)

$$G = \begin{bmatrix} 1\,0\,0\,0 : 1\,1\,1 \\ 0\,1\,0\,0 : 1\,1\,0 \\ 0\,0\,1\,0 : 1\,0\,1 \\ 0\,0\,0\,1 : 0\,1\,1 \end{bmatrix}$$

Where P can be identified as

$$P = \begin{bmatrix} 1\,1\,1 \\ 1\,1\,0 \\ 1\,0\,1 \\ 0\,1\,1 \end{bmatrix}$$

Then, H can be found from Eq. (18.4-2)

$$H = \begin{bmatrix} 1\,1\,1\,0 : 1\,0\,0 \\ 1\,1\,0\,1 : 0\,1\,0 \\ 1\,0\,1\,1 : 0\,0\,1 \end{bmatrix}$$

The LDPC codes is generated by taking the data block x

$$c = xG = [x : xp] \qquad (18.4\text{-}3)$$

If C is a valid code word, then

$$CH^T = 0$$

And sum of the 1's in each row should be zero by Mod-2 addition.

Gauss-elimination is in linear algebra a process for finding the solutions of a system of simultaneous linear equations. Using this method of encoding eliminates the need to explicitly determine the generator matrix and subsequently using the generator matrix equations to encode the data.

With the flexibility of LDPCs, codes can be constructed to exactly match a particular block size or code rate, though practical implementations may impose certain constraints on block sizes and/or obtainable code rates. After the block size and code rate are established, an H matrix is constructed that is n columns wide by $(n - k)$ rows high and contains a sparse number of ones.

A properly designed H matrix should have a large minimum distance (dmin). This is a result of having a low number of ones in the H matrix, and as such the number of columns of H required to sum to zero tends to be high even for randomly constructed codes.

EXAMPLE 18.1 *A simple LDPC encoder can be demonstrated using a simple (16,9) code with the following H matrix. Parameters for this example are*

$$n = 16$$

$$k \text{ message bits} = 9$$

$$n - k \text{ parity bits} = 7$$

$$\text{Code Rate} = k/n = 9/16$$

$$H = \begin{array}{cccccccccccccccc} n0 & n1 & n2 & n3 & n4 & n5 & n6 & n7 & n8 & n9 & n10 & n11 & n12 & n13 & n14 & n15 \\ 1 & 1 & 1 & 0 & 0 & 0 & 0 & 0 & 0 & 1 & 0 & 0 & 0 & 0 & 0 & 0 \\ 0 & 0 & 0 & 1 & 1 & 1 & 0 & 0 & 0 & 0 & 1 & 0 & 0 & 0 & 0 & 0 \\ 0 & 0 & 0 & 0 & 0 & 0 & 1 & 1 & 1 & 0 & 0 & 1 & 0 & 0 & 0 & 0 \\ 1 & 0 & 0 & 1 & 0 & 0 & 1 & 0 & 0 & 0 & 0 & 0 & 1 & 0 & 0 & 0 \\ 0 & 1 & 0 & 0 & 1 & 0 & 0 & 1 & 0 & 0 & 0 & 0 & 0 & 1 & 0 & 0 \\ 0 & 0 & 1 & 0 & 0 & 1 & 0 & 0 & 1 & 0 & 0 & 0 & 0 & 0 & 1 & 0 \\ 0 & 0 & 0 & 0 & 0 & 0 & 0 & 0 & 0 & 0 & 0 & 1 & 1 & 1 & 1 \end{array}$$

In the code example above, columns n0 through n8 represent the message part of the encoded block, while columns n9 through n15 represent the $(n - k)$ parity bits and form a submatrix that is lower triangular in nature, further simplifying the encoding process.

A data block $x = 101110110$ can become a code word c as

$$c = 101110110000100$$

Using equations derived from the H matrix to generate the parity check bits does encoding. Decoding is accomplished using "soft-inputs" with these equations to generate new estimates of the sent values. This process is repeated in an iterative manner resulting in a very powerful decoder. LDPC codes can be subject to error floors, as is common with CTCs. To address the error floor, an error floor is a region in which the error probability does not approach 0 as fast as it might be expected to. An outer code, such as Bose-Bhaudhuri-Hocquenghem (BCH), can be added to LDPC technology. The BCH outer code has the effect of lowering the error floor. Digital Video Broadcast (DVB) has chosen this method of FEC.

Comparing LDPC code with TPCs and Shannon limit depicted in Fig. 18.4 shows gains of more than 0.5 dB from a low code rate TPC and up to 2 dB from a high code rate. The modulation used in this comparison is BPSK and the channel is AWGN as shown in Fig. 18.4.

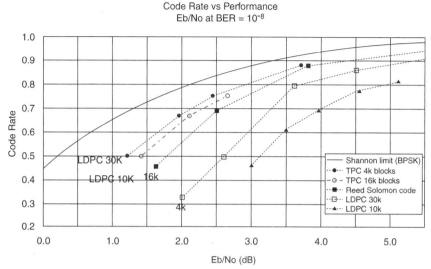

FIGURE 18.4   Comparing LDPC with TPC and other coding schemes.

18.5   STUDY OF A 60-GHz CELLULAR SYSTEM

A series of studies[25,26] have explored the implementation of a 60-GHz mobile telephone system using direct line-of-sight transmission along urban streets. Use of the 60-GHz band is encouraged for the following reasons.

1. The 60-GHz band is in the oxygen-absorption range. In this range, the attenuation of radio signals in the oxygen-absorption band is two orders of magnitude greater than the attenuation outside the oxygen-absorption band over a 1-km distance. Therefore, the 60-GHz band cannot be used by many applications; however, if it is properly implemented, it can be allocated to a cellular mobile radio system. The FCC may be glad to give this band away.

2. The characteristics of this high-attenuation signal over the propagation path create a natural barrier to cochannel or adjacent-channel interference in the cellular mobile system.

18.5.1   Propagation in the Scattered Environment

In the UHF range or at X band, multipath signal scattering from vehicles and buildings in the mobile radio environment has frequently caused deep and rapid fading of the received signals. Sometimes, the signal can be received by propagation through scattered or reflected signals, a natural phenomenon. However, when a 60-GHz band is used, line-of-sight propagation is required. A series of experiments at 59.5 GHz were carried out in 1972 in urban areas.[26]

The average output power at the mobile antenna was 40 mW (16 dBm), and the parabola antenna beamwidths were 3° at both the base station and mobile ends. The data were collected on three streets in Red Bank, New Jersey. The streets were chosen because they were representative of the urban mobile environment and were at least 0.5 mi long.

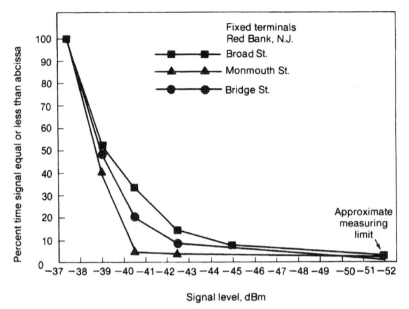

Signal level, dBm

FIGURE 18.5   Fading statistics from fixed terminals, Red Bank, N.J. (*From Ref. 26.*)

18.5.2 Fixed Terminals

The mobile transmitter and the mobile receiver were parked about 0.56 km (0.35 mi) apart on opposite sides of a street. The results for each street are plotted in Fig. 18.5. Fades exceeding 3 dB occurred 5 percent of the time on Monmouth Street, 20 percent of the time on Bridge Street, and 34 percent of the time on Broad Street. The measuring limit was at −52 dBm, which presents a signal fade of 15 dB. Fades exceeding this limit occurred 1 percent of the time on Bridge Street, 2 percent of the time on Monmouth Street, and 3 percent of the time on Broad Street. Fades exceeding 15 dB were caused by large trucks or buses completely blocking the path within 30 m (100 ft) of the transmitter or receiver.

18.5.3 Moving Terminal

The mobile receiver was parked at the side of the street, and the mobile transmitter started at least 0.8 km (0.5 mi) from the receiver and proceeded toward and past the receiver at a constant speed of 24 km/h (15 mi/h). The results are plotted in Fig. 18.6. The fading statistics of all three streets are roughly the same. The fades exceeded 3 dB about 70 percent of the time. The fades exceeding the −52-dBm measuring limit (15 dB fades) occurred 9 percent of the time on Broad and Monmouth Streets but only 5 percent on Bridge Street because the line-of-sight signal was blocked by large trucks or buses. The Doppler frequencies ranged from a few hertz to 170 Hz. When vehicle speed was 15 mi/h the fading rate was 25 Hz. Fades exceeding 10 dB occurred 20 percent of the time. A typical run measured on Monmouth Street is shown in Fig. 18.7.

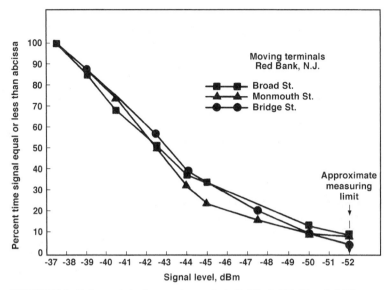

FIGURE 18.6   Fading statistics from moving terminals, Red Bank, N.J. (*From Ref. 26.*)

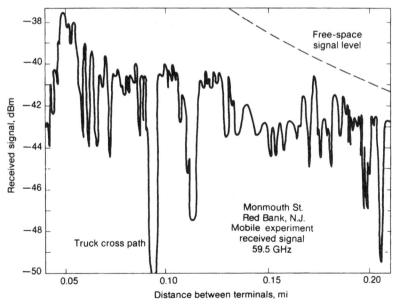

FIGURE 18.7   Received signal at Monmouth Street, Red Bank, N.J. (*From Ref. 26.*)

The experiments at 60 GHz reveal that the amplitude of the scattered signal was small in comparison to the direct signal. The effect of the scattered signal is small. The fading observed was neither deep nor rapid.

18.5.4 System Consideration

From the preceding data, we may note the following problems in a 60-GHz mobile radio system: (1) the excessive propagation loss, (2) the pointing mechanism of the antennas, (3) the small separation between repeaters, and (4) the ways of avoiding line-of-sight blockage from large trucks and buses.

18.6 DIVERSITY MEDIA SYSTEM WITH MILLIMETER-WAVE LINK AND OPTICAL-WAVE LINK

18.6.1 Introduction

A diversity system with millimeter-wave and optical-wave links can be achieved.[27] The idea is based on the fact that the optical wave is primarily attenuated by fog[28] and the millimeter wave primarily by rain.[29] Because fog and rain usually do not occur at the same time, a diversity advantage using an optical-wave signal and a millimeter-wave signal may be realized.

For investigating the diversity advantage on these two links (optical wave and millimeter wave) in a metropolitan area, data on the signal attenuation by fog on an optical-wave link and data on the signal attenuation by rain on a millimeter-wave link over the same path simultaneously in that area was collected.

In 1973, an optical-wave (0.9 μm) link between the 88th floor of the Empire State Building and the 58th floor of the Pan American building (a distance of about 0.55 mi) was installed.[30] The data on signal attenuation by fog has been converted to a probability distribution curve (PDC), shown in Fig. 18.8. In addition, there are three other curves, one obtained at Holmdel, New Jersey, and two at the AT&T building in New York City, with different floor heights, also shown in Fig. 18.8 for comparison. We may note that the signal attenuation by fog is drastically changed by the height of the link.

A 3-mm link between the Empire State and Pan Am buildings, using a 15-mW IMPATT diode as a source, two 30-in parabolic dish antennas (one transmitting and one receiving) for a link gain of 106 dB, and a Schottky-barrier diode for detection, was installed.[31] Limited data were collected to demonstrate that the link was clearly established. The 3-mm signal attenuation caused by rainfall in New York City should be acquired from other sources.

First, we assume that the effect on millimeter-wave signal attenuation of rainfall is small where the link is short. Using this assumption, we can then obtain the 3-mm-wave signal attenuation caused by rainfall over the Empire State–Pan Am link in New York City from some other nearby sources, such as the data collected at Central Park, Manhattan, or New York City.

Now there are two pieces of data: the optical-wave attenuation over the Empire State–Pan Am link and the millimeter-wave attenuation, which is based on the rainfall statistics at Central Park, Manhattan, and New York City. From these two pieces of data, a study of a diversity system consisting of a millimeter-wave link and an optical-wave link will be carried out.

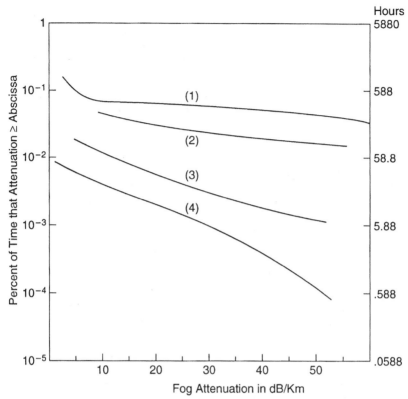

FIGURE 18.8   Optical signal attenuation by fog at various places: (1) 88th floor of Empire State Building–58th floor of Pan Am Building, New York City, 0.55 mi in distance (one-way transmission); (2) Radio Range Building, Bell Laboratories, Holmdel, N.J., round-trip path is 300 ft; (3) 21st floor of AT&T Building–19th floor of Western Electric Building, New York City, round-trip path is 240 ft; (4) 4th floor of AT&T Building–3rd floor of Western Electric Building, New York City, round-trip path is 240 ft. (*From Ref. 33.*)

18.6.2   Comparison of Two Signal Attenuations From Their PDC Curves

At first, we have to obtain an annual PDC of millimeter-wave attenuation caused by rainfall from a nearby location of the Empire State–Pan Am link. We know that the rain accumulation data at Central Park can be obtained from U.S. climatological data.[32] From the cumulative rain data, a distribution curve of rain rate versus time for each rainfall event can be generated.[33] The conversion from rain rate to signal attenuation has been obtained by several methods;[28,33,34] Oguchi's approximate method[34] provides a table that can easily be used. The PDC curves of 3-mm-wave attenuation (dB/km) in New York City calculated annually for three consecutive years are shown in Fig. 18.9. The details of how Fig. 18.9 was obtained are described in Ref. 33. In Fig. 18.9, we find that rainfall was slightly more frequent in 1971 and 1972 than in 1970. The rainfall statistics in all three years, 1970 to 1972, are similar. The PDC curve of signal attenuation caused by rain in 1972 was picked and compared with the PDC curve of signal attenuation caused by fog in our analysis.

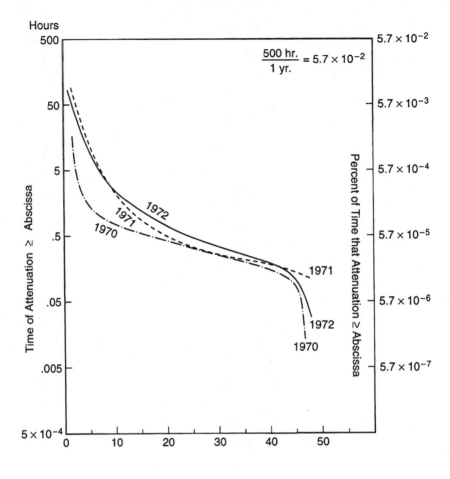

Rainfall Attenuation in dB/Km

FIGURE 18.9   100-GHz signal attenuation by rain at Central Park, New York City. (*From Ref. 33.*)

Comparing Fig. 18.8 with Fig. 18.9, we find that the optical wave is attenuated by fog more frequently than the millimeter wave is attenuated by rain.

Assuming that fog and rain do not occur simultaneously, then the PDC obtained from a selection-combining diversity signal between the millimeter and the optical wave is

$$P_c = P_r P_f \tag{18.6-1}$$

where P_r and P_f are PDC curves of signal attenuation caused by rainfall and fog, respectively. P_r was obtained from Central Park and used for representing the signal attenuation by rain in the Manhattan area. Three selection-combining diversity signals can be obtained from Equation (18.6-1), one at Empire State–Pan Am, one at Empire State-AT&T 21st floor, and one at Empire State-AT&T 4th floor (Fig. 18.10). All three links are in the Manhattan area. The most advantageous outcome of using this millimeter wave–optical

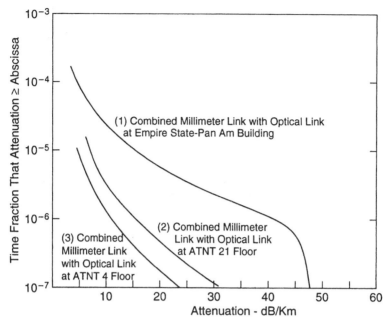

FIGURE 18.10   A predicted selection-combining signal between two frequencies in New York City. (*From Ref. 33.*)

wave diversity scheme can be seen from the selection-combining diversity signal at AT&T 4th floor. We may conclude that a diversity system consisting of a millimeter-wave link and an optical-wave link is suitable for a site at a lower height above the ground.

18.7   MVNO AND MVNE

18.7.1   MVNO (Mobile Virtual Network Operator)

Because the host network operators will have plenty of capacity in their 4G systems and want to sell their unused capacity, many MVNO's will be formed to fulfill the needs.

MVNO is a mobile operator that does not own its own spectrum and usually does not have its own network infrastructure. Many are familar with simple resellers who buy minutes of use (MOU) from the host network operator and provide services such as long distance, local exchange, and mobile network services. The MVNO's do the same but add value such as brand appeal, distribution channels, and other affinities to the resale of mobile services.

Successful MVNO's are those that position their operations so that customers do not distinguish any significant differences in service or network performance yet offer some special affinity to their customers. MVNO's are typically well-known, well-positioned companies. For example, Virgin Atlantic Airlines is a MVNO in the UK that uses its market recognition to position itself for selling directly to its airline customers and others.

MVNO's have full control over the SIM card, branding, marketing, billing, and customer care operations. While sometimes offering operational support systems (OSS) and business support systems (BSS) to support the MVNO, the incumbent mobile operators mainly keep their own OSS/BSS processes and procedures separate and distinct from those of the MVNO.

18.7.2   MVNE (Mobile Virtual Network Enabler)

Whereas a MVNO is a Mobile Virtual Network Operator, an MVNE is a Mobile Virtual Network Enabler. A MVNE does not have a relationship with end-user customers. Instead, a MVNE provides infrastructure and services to enable MVNO's to offer services and to have a relationship with end-user customers.

An MVNE offers infrastructure and related services ranging from network element provisioning, administration and operations to OSS/BSS support. MVNE's often provide the "middle-ground" between MVNO's that do not want to have any control over network elements and those that want complete control.

Some MVNO's wanted to completely rely on the underlying wireless network infrastruture of the host mobile network operators whereas other MVNO's wanted to own and/or control their own network elements. MVNE's provide the middle ground in the sense that they can provide options to MVNO's for what they bring in-house versus what they rely on the host carrier. For example, a MVNE can provide HLR, SMSC, MMSC, as well as more advanced network elements such as GGSN, OSS/BSS, and other systems.

Since the host operator is satisfied to sell unused capacity, but is not interested in helping the MVNO differentiate itself, this could cannibalize host carrier customers.

With a MVNE, a MVNO could literally use the host mobile network for only radio and switching infrastructure, outsourcing everything else to the MVNE.

REFERENCES

1. "Samsung 4G Forum", held at Jiju Island, Korea, August 25–26, 2004.

2. S. Y. Yoon, "Introduction to WiBro Technology," Telecom R&D Center, Samsung Electronics Co., Sept. 10, 2004.

3. W. C. Y. Lee, "CS-OFDMA: A New Wireless CDD Physical Layer Scheme," *IEEE Communications Magazine*, Vol. 43, Feb. 2005, pp. 74–79.

4. W. C. Y. Lee, "The Most Spectrum-Efficient Duplexing System: CDD," *IEEE Communications Magazine*, Mar. 2002, Vol. 40, No. 3, pp. 163–166.

5. W. C. Y. Lee, "Analysis and Realization of a Physical CDD System," Wireless Communication and Mobile Comp., 2003, Vol. 3, pp. 571–583.

6. F. S. Gutleber, Spread spectrum multiplexed noise codes. IEEE Milcom '82 Boston, MA, 1982; pp. 15.1.1.–15.1.10.

7. Z. Li, Q. Zhang., Introduction to bridge functions. IEEE Transactions on Electromagnetic Compatibility 25 (4) 1983: EMC-25(4): 459–464.

8. P. Z. Fan and M. Darnell, Sequence Design for Communications Applications, Wiley, 1996.

9. P. Z. Fan and L. Hao, "Generalized Orthogonal Sequences and their Applications in Synchronous CDMA Systems," IEICE Trans. Fundamentals 2000, Vol. E83-A, No. 11, pp. 1–16.

10. D. Li, "A High Spectrum Efficient Multiple Access Code," Chinese J. Elect. Vol. 8 July 1999, pp. 221–226; also, WG-1, CWTS, LAS-CDMA presented at 3GPP2 RAN WG-1, Seoul, Korea, Apr. 10, 2000.

11. H. Chen, J. Yeh, and N. Suehiro, "A Multicarrier CDMA Architecture Based on Orthogonal Complementry Codes for New Generations of Wideband Wireless Communications," *IEEE Communications Magazine*, Oct. 2001, Vol. 30, No. 10, pp. 126–135.

12. W. C. Y. Lee, Overview of cellular CDMA. IEEE Transactions on Vehicular Technology 1991; 40(2): 291–302.

13. R. VanNee, R. Prasad, OFDM for Wireless Multimedia Communications, Artech House, Boston, 2000, Chapter 9.

14. L. Hanzo, L. L. Yang, E. L. Kuan, K. Yen, Single and Multi-carrier DS-CDMA, IEEE Press and Wiley, 2003, Chapter 19.

15. W. C. Y. Lee, Mobile Cellular Telecommunications System, McGraw-Hill, 1995, p. 58.

16. R. Sivaswamy, "Multiphase Complementary Codes," IEEE Trans. On Information Theory, Vol. IT-24, Sept. 1978, pp. 546–552.

17. C. Berrou, A. Glavieux, P. Thitimajshima, "Near Shannon limit error correcting coding and decoding: turbo-codes," Proceedings of ICC '93, Geneva, pp. 1064–1070, May 1993.

18. S. S. Pietrobon, "Implementation and Performance of a Turbo/Map decoder" International Journal of Satellite Communications, pp. 4–17, 1998.

19. A. Shokrollahi, "LDPC Codes: An Introduction," Digital Fountain, Inc., Fremont, CA, April 2, 2003.

20. R. G. Gallager, "Low Density Parity-Check Codes," MIT Press, Cambridge, MA 1963.

21. Robert M. Tanner, "A recursive approach to low complexity," IEEE Trans. Inf. Theory, pp. 533–547, Sept. 1981.

22. David MacKay, et al. "Comparison of constructions of irregular Gallager codes," IEEE Trans. Comm. October 1999.

23. Michael Luby et al. "Improved low-density parity-check codes using irregular graphs," IEEE Trans. Inf. Theory, Feb. 2001.

24. T. Richardson, R. Urbanke, "Efficient Encoding of Low-Density Parity-Check Codes," IEEE Trans. Inform. Theory, Vol. 47, pp. 638–656, 2001.

25. C. L. Ruthruff, "A 60 GHz Cellular System," Microwave Mobile Symposium, Boulder, Colorado, 1974.

26. L. U. Kibler, "A 60 Propagation Measurement," Microwave Mobile Symposium, Boulder, Colorado, 1974.

27. L. C. Tillotson, "Customer-to-Customer via Millimeter Wave," private communication, June 26, 1972.

28. C. L. Ruthroff, "Rain Attenuation and Radio Path Design," *Bell System Technical Journal*, Vol. 49, pp. 121–136, January 1970.

29. T. S. Chu and D. C. Hogg, "Effects of Precipitation on Propagation at 0.63, 3.5, 10.6 Microns," *Bell System Technical Journal*, May–June 1968, pp. 723–759.

30. H. J. Schulte, "Optical-Wave Link Setup," private communication, 1973.

31. W. C. Y. Lee, "Milimeter-Wave Link Setup," private communication, 1973.

32. U.S. Dept. of Commerce, "Climatological Data, Annual," published once a year.

33. W. C. Y. Lee, "An Approximate Method for Obtaining Rain Rate Statistics for Use in Signal Attenuation Estimating," *IEEE Trans. On Antennas and Propagation*, Vol. AP-27, May 1979, pp. 407–413.

34. T. Oguchi, "Attenuation of Electromagnetic Wave Due to Rain with Distorted Raindrops (Part II)," *Journal of Radio Research Lab*, Tokyo, Vol. II, pp. 19–44, January 1964.

APPENDIX A
BLOCKED-CALLS-CLEARED (ERLANG *B*)

Blocked-Calls-Cleared (Erlang *B*)

						A, Erlangs							
						B							
N	1.0%	1.2%	1.5%	2%	3%	5%	7%	10%	15%	20%	30%	40%	50%
1	.0101	.0121	.0152	.0204	.0309	.0526	.0753	.111	.176	.250	.429	.667	1.00
2	.153	.168	.190	.223	.282	.381	.470	.595	.796	1.00	1.45	2.00	2.73
3	.455	.489	.535	.602	.715	.899	1.06	1.27	1.60	1.93	2.63	3.48	4.59
4	.869	.922	.992	1.09	1.26	1.52	1.75	2.05	2.50	2.95	3.39	5.02	6.50
5	1.36	1.43	1.52	1.66	1.88	2.22	2.50	2.88	3.45	4.01	5.19	6.60	8.44
6	1.91	2.00	2.11	2.28	2.54	2.96	3.30	3.76	4.44	5.11	6.51	8.19	10.4
7	2.50	2.60	2.74	2.94	3.25	3.74	4.14	4.67	5.46	6.23	7.86	9.80	12.4
8	3.13	3.25	3.40	3.63	3.99	4.54	5.00	5.60	6.50	7.37	9.21	11.4	14.3
9	3.78	3.92	4.09	4.34	4.75	5.37	5.88	6.55	7.55	8.52	10.6	13.0	16.3
10	4.46	4.61	4.81	5.08	5.53	6.22	6.78	7.51	8.62	9.68	12.0	14.7	18.3
11	5.16	5.32	5.54	5.84	6.33	7.08	7.69	8.49	9.69	10.9	13.3	16.3	20.3
12	5.88	6.05	6.29	6.61	7.14	7.95	8.61	9.47	10.8	12.0	14.7	18.0	22.2
13	6.61	6.80	7.05	7.40	7.97	8.83	9.54	10.5	11.9	13.2	16.1	19.6	24.2
14	7.35	7.56	7.82	8.20	8.80	9.73	10.5	11.5	13.0	14.4	17.5	21.2	26.2
15	8.11	8.33	8.61	9.01	9.65	10.6	11.4	12.5	14.1	15.6	18.9	22.9	28.2
16	8.88	9.11	9.41	9.83	10.5	11.5	12.4	13.5	15.2	16.8	20.3	24.5	30.2
17	9.65	9.89	10.2	10.7	11.4	12.5	13.4	14.5	16.3	18.0	21.7	26.2	32.2
18	10.4	10.7	11.0	11.5	12.2	13.4	14.3	15.5	17.4	19.2	23.1	27.8	34.2
19	11.2	11.5	11.8	12.3	13.1	14.3	15.3	16.6	18.5	20.4	24.5	29.5	36.2
20	12.0	12.3	12.7	13.2	14.0	15.2	16.3	17.6	19.6	21.6	25.9	31.2	38.2
21	12.8	13.1	13.5	14.0	14.9	16.2	17.3	18.7	20.8	22.8	27.3	32.8	40.2
22	13.7	14.0	14.3	14.9	15.8	17.1	18.2	19.7	21.9	24.1	28.7	34.5	42.1
23	14.5	14.8	15.2	15.8	16.7	18.1	19.2	20.7	23.0	25.3	30.1	36.1	44.1
24	15.3	15.6	16.0	16.6	17.6	19.0	20.2	21.8	24.2	26.5	31.6	37.8	46.1
25	16.1	16.5	16.9	17.5	18.5	20.0	21.2	22.8	25.3	27.7	33.0	39.4	48.1
26	17.0	17.3	17.8	18.4	19.4	20.9	22.2	23.9	26.4	28.9	34.4	41.1	50.1
27	17.8	18.2	18.6	19.3	20.3	21.9	23.2	24.9	27.6	30.2	35.8	42.8	52.1

28	18.6	19.0	19.5	20.2	21.2	22.9	24.2	26.0	28.7	31.4	37.2	44.4	54.1
29	19.5	19.9	20.4	21.0	22.1	23.8	25.2	27.1	29.9	32.6	38.6	46.1	56.1
30	20.3	20.7	21.2	21.9	23.1	24.8	26.2	28.1	31.0	33.8	40.0	47.7	58.1
31	21.2	21.6	22.1	22.8	24.0	25.8	27.2	29.2	32.1	35.1	41.5	49.4	60.1
32	22.0	22.5	23.0	23.7	24.9	26.7	28.2	30.2	33.3	36.3	42.9	51.1	62.1
33	22.9	23.3	23.9	24.6	25.8	27.7	29.3	31.3	34.4	37.5	44.3	52.7	64.1
34	23.8	24.2	24.8	25.5	26.8	28.7	30.3	32.4	35.6	38.8	45.7	54.4	66.1
35	24.6	25.1	25.6	26.4	27.7	29.7	31.3	33.4	36.7	40.0	47.1	56.0	68.1
36	25.5	26.0	26.5	27.3	28.6	30.7	32.3	34.5	37.9	41.2	48.6	57.7	70.1
37	26.4	26.8	27.4	28.3	29.6	31.6	33.3	35.6	39.0	42.4	50.0	59.4	72.1
38	27.3	27.7	28.3	29.2	30.5	32.6	34.4	36.6	40.2	43.7	51.4	61.0	74.1
39	28.1	28.6	29.2	30.1	31.5	33.6	35.4	37.7	41.3	44.9	52.8	62.7	76.1
40	29.0	29.5	30.1	31.0	32.4	34.6	36.4	38.8	42.5	46.1	54.2	64.4	78.1
41	29.9	30.4	31.0	31.9	33.4	35.6	37.4	39.9	43.6	47.4	55.7	66.0	80.1
42	30.8	31.3	31.9	32.8	34.3	36.6	38.4	40.9	44.8	48.6	57.1	67.7	82.1
43	31.7	32.2	32.8	33.8	35.3	37.6	39.5	42.0	45.9	49.9	58.5	69.3	84.1
44	32.5	33.1	33.7	34.7	36.2	38.6	40.5	43.1	47.1	51.1	59.9	71.0	86.1
45	33.4	34.0	34.6	35.6	37.2	39.6	41.5	44.2	48.2	52.3	61.3	72.7	88.1
46	34.3	34.9	35.6	36.5	38.1	40.5	42.6	45.2	49.4	53.6	62.8	74.3	90.1
47	35.2	35.8	36.5	37.5	39.1	41.5	43.6	46.3	50.6	54.8	64.2	76.0	92.1
48	36.1	36.7	37.4	38.4	40.0	42.5	44.6	47.4	51.7	56.0	65.6	77.7	94.1
49	37.0	37.6	38.3	39.3	41.0	43.5	45.7	48.5	52.9	57.3	67.0	79.3	96.1
50	37.9	38.5	39.2	40.3	41.9	44.5	46.7	49.6	54.0	58.5	68.5	81.0	98.1
51	38.8	39.4	40.1	41.2	42.9	45.5	47.7	50.6	55.2	59.7	69.9	82.7	100.1
52	39.7	40.3	41.0	42.1	43.9	46.5	48.8	51.7	56.3	61.0	71.3	84.3	102.1
53	40.6	41.2	42.0	43.1	44.8	47.5	49.8	52.8	57.5	62.2	72.7	86.0	104.1
54	41.5	42.1	42.9	44.0	45.8	48.5	50.8	53.9	58.7	63.5	74.2	87.6	106.1
55	42.4	43.0	43.8	44.9	46.7	49.5	51.9	55.0	59.8	64.7	75.6	89.3	108.1
56	43.3	43.9	44.7	45.9	47.7	50.5	52.9	56.1	61.0	65.9	77.0	91.0	110.1
57	44.2	44.8	45.7	46.8	48.7	51.5	53.9	57.1	62.1	67.2	78.4	92.6	112.1
58	45.1	45.8	46.6	47.8	49.6	52.6	55.0	58.2	63.3	68.4	79.8	94.3	114.1

(cont.)

Blocked-Calls-Cleared (Erlang B) (Continued)

A, Erlangs

B

N	1.0%	1.2%	1.5%	2%	3%	5%	7%	10%	15%	20%	30%	40%	50%
59	46.0	46.7	47.5	48.7	50.6	53.6	56.0	59.3	64.5	69.7	81.3	96.0	116.1
60	46.9	47.6	48.4	49.6	51.6	54.6	57.1	60.4	65.6	70.9	82.7	97.6	118.1
61	47.9	48.5	49.4	50.6	52.5	55.6	58.1	61.5	66.8	72.1	84.1	99.3	120.1
62	48.8	49.4	50.3	51.5	53.5	56.6	59.1	62.6	68.0	73.4	85.5	101.0	122.1
63	49.7	50.4	51.2	52.5	54.5	57.6	60.2	63.7	69.1	74.6	87.0	102.6	124.1
64	50.6	51.3	52.2	53.4	55.4	58.6	61.2	64.8	70.3	75.9	88.4	104.3	126.1
65	51.5	52.2	53.1	54.4	56.4	59.6	62.3	65.8	71.4	77.1	89.8	106.0	128.1
66	52.4	53.1	54.0	55.3	57.4	60.6	63.3	66.9	72.6	78.3	91.2	107.6	130.1
67	53.4	54.1	55.0	56.3	58.4	61.6	64.4	68.0	73.8	79.6	92.7	109.3	132.1
68	54.3	55.0	55.9	57.2	59.3	62.6	65.4	69.1	74.9	80.8	94.1	111.0	134.1
69	55.2	55.9	56.9	58.2	60.3	63.7	66.4	70.2	76.1	82.1	95.5	112.6	136.1
70	56.1	56.8	57.8	59.1	61.3	64.7	67.5	71.3	77.3	83.3	96.9	114.3	138.1
71	57.0	57.8	58.7	60.1	62.3	65.7	68.5	72.4	78.4	84.6	98.4	115.9	140.1
72	58.0	58.7	59.7	61.0	63.2	66.7	69.6	73.5	79.6	85.8	99.8	117.6	142.1
73	58.9	59.6	60.6	62.0	64.2	67.7	70.6	74.6	80.8	87.0	101.2	119.3	144.1
74	59.8	60.6	61.6	62.9	65.2	68.7	71.7	75.6	81.9	88.3	102.7	120.9	146.1
75	60.7	61.5	62.5	63.9	66.2	69.7	72.7	76.7	83.1	89.5	104.1	122.6	148.0
76	61.7	62.4	63.4	64.9	67.2	70.8	73.8	77.8	84.2	90.8	105.5	124.3	150.0
77	62.6	63.4	64.4	65.8	68.1	71.8	74.8	78.9	85.4	92.0	106.9	125.9	152.0
78	63.5	64.3	65.3	66.8	69.1	72.8	75.9	80.0	86.6	93.3	108.4	127.6	154.0
79	64.4	65.2	66.3	67.7	70.1	73.8	76.9	81.1	87.7	94.5	109.8	129.3	156.0
80	65.4	66.2	67.2	68.7	71.1	74.8	78.0	82.2	88.9	95.7	111.2	130.9	158.0
81	66.3	67.1	68.2	69.6	72.1	75.8	79.0	83.3	90.1	97.0	112.6	132.6	160.0
82	67.2	68.0	69.1	70.6	73.0	76.9	80.1	84.4	91.2	98.2	114.1	134.3	162.0
83	68.2	69.0	70.1	71.6	74.0	77.9	81.1	85.5	92.4	99.5	115.5	135.9	164.0
84	69.1	69.9	71.0	72.5	75.0	78.9	82.2	86.6	93.6	100.7	116.9	137.6	166.0
85	70.0	70.9	71.9	73.5	76.0	79.9	83.2	87.7	94.7	102.0	118.3	139.3	168.0

86	70.9	71.8	72.9	74.5	77.0	80.9	84.3	88.8	95.9	103.2	119.8	140.9	170.0
87	71.9	72.7	73.8	75.4	78.0	82.0	85.3	89.9	97.1	104.5	121.2	142.6	172.0
88	72.8	73.7	74.8	76.4	78.9	83.0	86.4	91.0	98.2	105.7	122.6	144.3	174.0
89	73.7	74.6	75.7	77.3	79.9	84.0	87.4	92.1	99.4	106.9	124.0	145.9	176.0
90	74.7	75.6	76.7	78.3	80.9	85.0	88.5	93.1	100.6	108.2	125.5	147.6	178.0
91	75.6	76.5	77.6	79.3	81.9	86.0	89.5	94.2	101.7	109.4	126.9	149.3	180.0
92	76.6	77.4	78.6	80.2	82.9	87.1	90.6	95.3	102.9	110.7	128.3	150.9	182.0
93	77.5	78.4	79.6	81.2	83.9	88.1	91.6	96.4	104.1	111.9	129.7	152.6	184.0
94	78.4	79.3	80.5	82.2	84.9	89.1	92.7	97.5	105.3	113.2	131.2	154.3	186.0
95	79.4	80.3	81.5	83.1	85.8	90.1	93.7	98.6	106.4	114.4	132.6	155.9	188.0
96	80.3	81.2	82.4	84.1	86.8	91.1	94.8	99.7	107.6	115.7	134.0	157.6	190.0
97	81.2	82.2	83.4	85.1	87.8	92.2	95.8	100.8	108.8	116.9	135.5	159.3	192.0
98	82.2	83.1	84.3	86.0	88.8	93.2	96.9	101.9	109.9	118.2	136.9	160.9	194.0
99	83.1	84.1	85.3	87.0	89.8	94.2	97.9	103.0	111.1	119.4	138.3	162.6	196.0
100	84.1	85.0	86.2	88.0	90.8	95.2	99.0	104.1	112.3	120.6	139.7	164.3	198.0
102	85.9	86.9	88.1	89.9	92.8	97.3	101.1	106.3	114.6	123.1	142.6	167.6	202.0
104	87.8	88.8	90.1	91.9	94.8	99.3	103.2	108.5	116.9	125.6	145.4	170.9	206.0
106	89.7	90.7	92.0	93.8	96.7	101.4	105.3	110.7	119.3	128.1	148.3	174.2	210.0
108	91.6	92.6	93.9	95.7	98.7	103.4	107.4	112.9	121.6	130.6	151.1	177.6	214.0
110	93.5	94.5	95.8	97.7	100.7	105.5	109.5	115.1	124.0	133.1	154.0	180.9	218.0
112	95.4	96.4	97.7	99.6	102.7	107.5	111.7	117.3	126.3	135.6	156.9	184.2	222.0
114	97.3	98.3	99.7	101.6	104.7	109.6	113.8	119.5	128.6	138.1	159.7	187.6	226.0
116	99.2	100.2	101.6	103.5	106.7	111.7	115.9	121.7	131.0	140.6	162.6	190.9	230.0
118	101.1	102.1	103.5	105.5	108.7	113.7	118.0	123.9	133.3	143.1	165.4	194.2	234.0
120	103.0	104.0	105.4	107.4	110.7	115.8	120.1	126.1	135.7	145.6	168.3	197.6	238.0
122	104.9	105.9	107.4	109.4	112.6	117.8	122.2	128.3	138.0	148.1	171.1	200.9	242.0
124	106.8	107.9	109.3	111.3	114.6	119.9	124.4	130.5	140.3	150.6	174.0	204.2	246.0
126	108.7	109.8	111.2	113.3	116.6	121.9	126.5	132.7	142.7	153.0	176.8	207.6	250.0
128	110.6	111.7	113.2	115.2	118.6	124.0	128.6	134.9	145.0	155.5	179.7	210.9	254.0
130	112.5	113.6	115.1	117.2	120.6	126.1	130.7	137.1	147.4	158.0	182.5	214.2	258.0
132	114.4	115.5	117.0	119.1	122.6	128.1	132.8	139.3	149.7	160.5	185.4	217.6	262.0
134	116.3	117.4	119.0	121.1	124.6	130.2	134.9	141.5	152.0	163.0	188.3	220.9	266.0

(cont.)

Blocked-Calls-Cleared (Erlang B) (Continued)

N	A, Erlangs												
	B												
	1.0%	1.2%	1.5%	2%	3%	5%	7%	10%	15%	20%	30%	40%	50%
136	118.2	119.4	120.9	123.1	126.6	132.3	137.1	143.7	154.4	165.5	191.1	224.2	270.0
138	120.1	121.3	122.8	125.0	128.6	134.3	139.2	145.9	156.7	168.0	194.0	227.6	274.0
140	122.0	123.2	124.8	127.0	130.6	136.4	141.3	148.1	159.1	170.5	196.8	230.9	278.0
142	123.9	125.1	126.7	128.9	132.6	138.4	143.4	150.3	161.4	173.0	199.7	234.2	282.0
144	125.8	127.0	128.6	130.9	134.6	140.5	145.6	152.5	163.8	175.5	202.5	237.6	286.0
146	127.7	129.0	130.6	132.9	136.6	142.6	147.7	154.7	166.1	178.0	205.4	240.9	290.0
148	129.7	130.9	132.5	134.8	138.6	144.6	149.8	156.9	168.5	180.5	208.2	244.2	294.0
150	131.6	132.8	134.5	136.8	140.6	146.7	151.9	159.1	170.8	183.0	211.1	247.6	298.0
152	133.5	134.8	136.4	138.8	142.6	148.8	154.0	161.3	173.1	185.5	214.0	250.9	302.0
154	135.4	136.7	138.4	140.7	144.6	150.8	156.2	163.5	175.5	188.0	216.8	254.2	306.0
156	137.3	138.6	140.3	142.7	146.6	152.9	158.3	165.7	177.8	190.5	219.7	257.6	310.0
158	139.2	140.5	142.3	144.7	148.6	155.0	160.4	167.9	180.2	193.0	222.5	260.9	314.0
160	141.2	142.5	144.2	146.6	150.6	157.0	162.5	170.2	182.5	195.5	225.4	264.2	318.0
162	143.1	144.4	146.1	148.6	152.7	159.1	164.7	172.4	184.9	198.0	228.2	267.6	322.0
164	145.0	146.3	148.1	150.6	154.7	161.2	166.8	174.6	187.2	200.4	231.1	270.9	326.0
166	146.9	148.3	150.0	152.6	156.7	163.3	168.9	176.8	189.6	202.9	233.9	274.2	330.0
168	148.9	150.2	152.0	154.5	158.7	165.3	171.0	179.0	191.9	205.4	236.8	277.6	334.0
170	150.8	152.1	153.9	156.5	160.7	167.4	173.2	181.2	194.2	207.9	239.7	280.9	338.0
172	152.7	154.1	155.9	158.5	162.7	169.5	175.3	183.4	196.6	210.4	242.5	284.2	342.0
174	154.6	156.0	157.8	160.4	164.7	171.5	177.4	185.6	198.9	212.9	245.4	287.6	346.0
176	156.6	158.0	159.8	162.4	166.7	173.6	179.6	187.8	201.3	215.4	248.2	290.9	350.0
178	158.5	159.9	161.8	164.4	168.7	175.7	181.7	190.0	203.6	217.9	251.1	294.2	354.0
180	160.4	161.8	163.7	166.4	170.7	177.8	183.8	192.2	206.0	220.4	253.9	297.5	358.0
182	162.3	163.8	165.7	168.3	172.8	179.8	185.9	194.4	208.3	222.9	256.8	300.9	362.0
184	164.3	165.7	167.6	170.3	174.8	181.9	188.1	196.6	210.7	225.4	259.6	304.2	366.0

186	166.2	167.7	169.6	172.3	176.8	184.0	190.2	198.9	213.0	227.9	262.5	307.5	370.0
188	168.1	169.6	171.5	174.3	178.8	186.1	192.3	201.1	215.4	230.4	265.2	310.9	374.0
190	170.1	171.5	173.5	176.3	180.8	188.1	194.5	203.3	217.7	232.9	268.2	314.2	378.0
192	172.0	173.5	175.4	178.2	182.8	190.2	196.6	205.5	220.1	235.4	271.1	317.5	382.0
194	173.9	175.4	177.4	180.2	184.8	192.3	198.7	207.7	222.4	237.9	273.9	320.9	386.0
196	175.9	177.4	179.4	182.2	186.9	194.4	200.8	209.9	224.8	240.4	276.8	324.2	390.0
198	177.8	179.3	181.3	184.2	188.9	196.4	203.0	212.1	227.1	242.9	279.6	327.5	394.0
200	179.7	181.3	183.3	186.2	190.9	198.5	205.1	214.3	229.4	245.4	282.5	330.9	398.0
202	181.7	183.2	185.2	188.1	192.9	200.6	207.2	216.5	231.8	247.9	285.4	334.2	402.0
204	183.6	185.2	187.2	190.1	194.9	202.7	209.4	218.7	234.1	250.4	288.2	337.5	406.0
206	185.5	187.1	189.2	192.1	196.9	204.7	211.5	221.0	236.5	252.9	291.1	340.9	410.0
208	187.5	189.1	191.1	194.1	199.0	206.8	213.6	223.2	238.8	255.4	293.9	344.2	414.0
210	189.4	191.0	193.1	196.1	201.0	208.9	215.8	225.4	241.2	257.9	296.8	347.5	418.0
212	191.4	193.0	195.1	198.1	203.0	211.0	217.9	227.6	243.5	260.4	299.6	350.9	422.0
214	193.3	194.9	197.0	200.0	205.0	213.0	220.0	229.8	245.9	262.9	302.5	354.2	426.0
216	195.2	196.9	199.0	202.0	207.0	215.1	222.2	232.0	248.2	265.4	305.3	357.5	430.0
218	197.2	198.8	201.0	204.0	209.1	217.2	224.3	234.2	250.6	267.9	308.2	360.9	434.0
220	199.1	200.8	202.9	206.0	211.1	219.3	226.4	236.4	252.9	270.4	311.1	364.2	438.0
222	201.1	202.7	204.9	208.0	213.1	221.4	228.6	238.6	255.3	272.9	313.9	367.5	442.0
224	203.0	204.7	206.8	210.0	215.1	223.4	230.7	240.9	257.6	275.4	316.8	370.9	446.0
226	204.9	206.6	208.8	212.0	217.1	225.5	232.8	243.1	260.0	277.8	319.6	374.2	450.0
228	206.9	208.6	210.8	213.9	219.2	227.6	235.0	245.3	262.3	280.3	322.5	377.5	454.0
230	208.8	210.5	212.8	215.9	221.2	229.7	237.1	247.5	264.7	282.8	325.3	380.9	458.0
232	210.8	212.5	214.7	217.9	223.2	231.8	239.2	249.7	267.0	285.3	328.2	384.2	462.0
234	212.7	214.4	216.7	219.9	225.2	233.8	241.4	251.9	269.4	287.8	331.1	387.5	466.0
236	214.7	216.4	218.7	221.9	227.2	235.9	243.5	254.1	271.7	290.3	333.9	390.9	470.0
238	216.6	218.3	220.6	223.9	229.3	238.0	245.6	256.3	274.1	292.8	336.8	394.2	474.0
240	218.6	220.3	222.6	225.9	231.3	240.1	247.8	258.6	276.4	295.3	339.6	397.5	478.0
242	220.5	222.3	224.6	227.9	233.3	242.2	249.9	260.8	278.8	297.8	342.5	400.9	482.0
244	222.5	224.2	226.5	229.9	235.3	244.3	252.0	263.0	281.1	300.3	345.3	404.2	486.0
246	224.4	226.2	228.5	231.8	237.4	246.3	254.2	265.2	283.4	302.8	348.2	407.5	490.0
248	226.3	228.1	230.5	233.8	239.4	248.4	256.3	267.4	285.8	305.3	351.0	410.9	494.0

(cont.)

Blocked-Calls-Cleared (Erlang B) (*Continued*)

A, Erlangs

N	1.0%	1.2%	1.5%	2%	3%	5%	7%	10%	15%	20%	30%	40%	50%
250	228.3	230.1	232.5	235.8	241.4	250.5	258.4	269.6	288.1	307.8	353.9	414.2	498.0
	.976	*.982*	*.988*	*.998*	*1.014*	*1.042*	*1.070*	*1.108*	*1.176*	*1.250*	*1.428*	*1.666*	*2.000*
300	277.1	279.2	281.9	285.7	292.1	302.6	311.9	325.0	346.9	370.3	425.3	497.5	598.0
	.982	*.984*	*.990*	*1.000*	*1.016*	*1.044*	*1.070*	*1.108*	*1.174*	*1.248*	*1.428*	*1.668*	*2.000*
350	326.2	328.4	331.4	335.7	342.9	354.8	365.4	380.4	405.6	432.7	496.7	580.9	698.0
	.982	*.988*	*.994*	*1.004*	*1.020*	*1.046*	*1.070*	*1.108*	*1.176*	*1.250*	*1.430*	*1.666*	*2.000*
400	375.3	377.8	381.1	385.9	393.9	407.1	418.9	435.8	464.4	495.2	568.2	664.2	798.0
	.986	*.990*	*.996*	*1.004*	*1.018*	*1.046*	*1.072*	*1.110*	*1.176*	*1.250*	*1.428*	*1.666*	*2.000*
450	424.6	427.3	430.9	436.1	444.8	459.4	472.5	491.3	523.2	557.7	639.6	747.5	898.0
	.988	*.994*	*.998*	*1.006*	*1.022*	*1.048*	*1.070*	*1.108*	*1.176*	*1.250*	*1.428*	*1.668*	*2.000*
500	474.0	477.0	480.8	486.4	495.9	511.8	526.0	546.7	582.0	620.2	711.0	830.9	998.0
	.991	*.994*	*1.000*	*1.008*	*1.022*	*1.047*	*1.073*	*1.110*	*1.176*	*1.249*	*1.429*	*1.666*	*2.000*
600	573.1	576.4	580.8	587.2	598.1	616.5	633.3	657.7	699.6	745.1	853.9	997.5	1198.
	.993	*.997*	*1.002*	*1.010*	*1.024*	*1.049*	*1.073*	*1.110*	*1.176*	*1.250*	*1.428*	*1.665*	*2.00*
700	672.4	676.1	681.0	688.2	700.5	721.4	740.6	768.7	817.2	870.1	996.7	1164.	1398.
	.994	*.998*	*1.004*	*1.011*	*1.025*	*1.050*	*1.073*	*1.110*	*1.176*	*1.250*	*1.433*	*1.67*	*2.00*
800	771.8	775.9	781.4	789.3	803.0	826.4	847.9	879.7	934.8	995.1	1140.	1331.	1598.
	.997	*1.000*	*1.004*	*1.013*	*1.025*	*1.050*	*1.074*	*1.111*	*1.172*	*1.249*	*1.42*	*1.67*	*2.00*
900	871.5	875.9	881.8	890.6	905.5	931.4	955.3	990.8	1052.	1120.	1282.	1498.	1798.
	.997	*1.001*	*1.006*	*1.013*	*1.025*	*1.046*	*1.077*	*1.112*	*1.18*	*1.25*	*1.43*	*1.66*	*2.00*
1000	971.2	976.0	982.4	991.9	1008.	1036.	1063.	1102.	1170.	1245.	1425.	1664.	1998.
	.998	*1.000*	*1.006*	*1.011*	*1.03*	*1.05*	*1.07*	*1.11*	*1.18*	*1.25*	*1.43*	*1.67*	*2.00*
1100	1071.	1076.	1083.	1093.	1111.	1141.	1170.	1213.	1288.	1370.	1568.	1831.	2198.

Source: After Lee, chapter 2 Ref. 5, pp. 265–275.

APPENDIX B
LIST OF MSAs AND RSAs

1. New York, NY	39. Salt Lake City, UT	77. Tucson, AZ	115. Utica-Rome, NY
2. Los Angeles, CA	40. Dayton, OH	78. Lansing, MI	116. Lexington-Fayette, KY
3. Chicago, IL	41. Birmingham, AL	79. Knoxville, TN	117. Colorado Springs, CO
4. Philadelphia, PA	42. Bridgeport, CT	80. Baton Rouge, LA	118. Reading, PA
5. Detroit, MI	43. Norfolk, VA	81. El Paso, TX	119. Evansville, IN
6. Boston, MA-NH	44. Albany, NY	82. Tacoma, WA	120. Huntsville, AL
7. San Francisco, CA	45. Oklahoma City, OK	83. Mobile, AL	121. Trenton, NJ
8. Washington, DC	46. Nashville, TN	84. Harrisburg, PA	122. Binghamton, NY
9. Dallas, TX	47. Greensboro, NC	85. Johnson City, TN-VA	123. Santa Rosa-Petaluma, CA
10. Houston, TX	48. Toledo, OH	86. Albuquerque, NM	124. Santa Barbara, CA
11. St. Louis, MO	49. New Haven, CT	87. Canton, OH	125. Appleton, WI
12. Miami, FL	50. Honolulu, HI	88. Chattanooga, TN	126. Salinas, CA
13. Pittsburgh, PA	51. Jacksonville, FL	89. Wichita, KS	127. Pensacola, FL
14. Baltimore, MD	52. Akron, OH	90. Charleston, SC	128. McAllen, TX
15. Minneapolis, MN-WI	53. Syracuse, NY	91. San Juan, PR	129. South Bend, IN
16. Cleveland, OH	54. Gary, IN	92. Little Rock, AR	130. Erie, PA
17. Atlanta, GA	55. Worcester, MA	93. Las Vegas, NV	131. Rockford, IL
18. San Diego, CA	56. Northeast, PA	94. Saginaw Bay-Midland, MI	132. Kalamazoo, MI
19. Denver, CO	57. Tulsa, OK	95. Columbia, SC	133. Manchester-Nashua, NH
20. Seattle, WA	58. Allentown, PA-NJ	96. Fort Wayne, IN	134. Atlantic City, NJ
21. Milwaukee, WI	59. Richmond, VA	97. Bakersfield, CA	135. Eugene-Springfield, OR
22. Tampa, FL	60. Orlando, FL	98. Davenport, IA-Mol., IL	136. Lorain-Elyria, OH
23. Cincinnati, OH	61. Charlotte, NC	99. York, PA	137. Melbourne, FL
24. Kansas City, MO	62. New Brunswick, NJ	100. Shreveport, LA	138. Macon, GA
25. Buffalo, NY	63. Springfield, MA	101. Beaumont, TX	139. Montgomery, AL
26. Phoenix, AZ	64. Grand Rapids, MI	102. Des Moines, IA	140. Charleston, WV
27. San Jose, CA	65. Omaha, NE	103. Peoria, IL	141. Duluth, MN
28. Indianapolis, IN	66. Youngstown, OH	104. Newport News, VA	142. Modesto, CA
29. New Orleans, LA	67. Greenville, SC	105. Lancaster, PA	143. Johnstown, PA
30. Portland, OR-WA	68. Flint, MI	106. Jackson, MS	144. Orange County, NY
31. Columbus, OH	69. Wilmington, DE-NJ-MD	107. Stockton, CA	145. Hamilton, OH
32. Hartford, CT	70. Long Branch, NJ	108. Augusta, GA-SC	146. Daytona Beach, FL
33. San Antonio, TX	71. Raleigh-Durham, NC	109. Spokane, WA	147. Ponce, PR
34. Rochester, NY	72. W. Palm Beach, FL	110. Huntington-Ashland, WV	148. Salem, OR
35. Sacramento, CA	73. Oxnard, CA	111. Vallejo, CA	149. Fayetteville, NC
36. Memphis, TN	74. Fresno, CA	112. Corpus Christi, TX	150. Visalia-Tulare, CA
37. Louisville, KY	75. Austin, TX	113. Madison, WI	151. Poughkeepsie, NY
38. Providence, RI	76. New Bedford, MA	114. Lakeland, FL	152. Portland, ME

(Continued)

153. Columbus, GA	205. Alexandria, LA	257. Hagerstown, MD	310. Bib, AL-4
154. New London-Norwich, CT	206. Longview-Marshall, TX	258. Jacksonville, NC	311. Cleburne, AL-5
155. Savannah, GA	207. Jackson, MI	259. State College, PA	312. Washington, AL-6
156. Portsmouth, NH	208. Fort Pierce, FL	260. Lawton, OK	313. Butler, AL-7
157. Roanoke, VA	209. Clarksville, TN-KY	261. Albany, GA	314. Lee, AL-8
158. Lima, OH	210. Fort Collins-Loveland, CO	262. Danville, VA	315. Wade Hampton, AK-1
159. Provo-Orem, UT	211. Bradenton, FL	263. Wausau, WI	316. Bethel, AK-2
160. Killeen-Temple, TX	212. Bremerton, WA	264. Florence, SC	317. Haines, AK-3
161. Lubbock, TX	213. Pittsfield, MA	265. Fort Walton Beach, FL	318. Mohave, AZ-1
162. Brownsville, TX	214. Richland-Kennewick, WA	266. Glens Falls, NY	319. Coconino, AZ-2
163. Springfield, MO	215. Chico, CA	267. Sioux Falls, SD	320. Navajo, AZ-3
164. Fort Myers, FL	216. Janesville-Beloit, WI	268. Billings, MT	321. Yuma, AZ-4
165. Fort Smith, AR-OK	217. Anderson, IN	269. Cumberland, MD-WV	322. Gila, AZ-5
166. Hickory, NC	218. Wilmington, NC	270. Bellingham, WA	323. Graham, AZ-6
167. Sarasota, FL	219. Monroe, LA	271. Kokomo, IN	324. Madison, AR-1
168. Tallahassee, FL	220. Abilene, TX	272. Gadsden, AL	325. Marion, AR-2
169. Mayaguez, PR	221. Fargo-Moorhead, ND-MN	273. Kankakee, IL	326. Sharp, AR-3
170. Galveston, TX	222. Tuscaloosa, AL	274. Yuba City, CA	327. Clay, AR-4
171. Reno, NV	223. Elkhart-Goshen, IN	275. St. Joseph, MO	328. Cross, AR-5
172. Lincoln, NE	224. Bangor, ME	276. Grand Forks, ND	329. Cleburne, AR-6
173. Biloxi-Gulfport, MS	225. Altoona, PA	277. Sheboygan, WI	330. Pope, AR-7
174. Lafayette, LA	226. Florence, AL	278. Columbia, MO	331. Franklin, AR-8
175. Santa Cruz, CA	227. Anderson, SC	279. Lewiston-Auburn, ME	332. Polk, AR-9
176. Springfield, IL	228. Vineland-Millville, NJ	280. Burlington, NC	333. Garland, AR-10
177. Battle Creek, MI	229. Medford, OR	281. Laredo, TX	334. Hempstead, AR-11
178. Wheeling, WV-OH	230. Decatur, IL	282. Bloomington, IN	335. Quachita, AR-12
179. Topeka, KS	231. Mansfield, OH	283. Panama City, FL	336. Del Norte, CA-1
180. Springfield, OH	232. Eau Claire, WI	284. Elmira, NY	337. Modoc, CA-2
181. Muskegon, MI	233. Wichita Falls, TX	285. Las Cruces, NM	338. Alpine, CA-3
182. Fayetteville-Sprngdl., AR	234. Athens, GA	286. Dubuque, IA	339. Madera, CA-4
183. Asheville, NC	235. Petersburg, VA	287. Bryan-College Station, TX	340. San Luis Obispo, CA-5
184. Houma-Thibodaux, LA	236. Muncie, IN	288. Rochester, MN	341. Mono, CA-6
185. Terre Haute, IN	237. Tyler, TX	289. Rapid City, SD	342. Imperial, CA-7
186. Green Bay, WI	238. Sharon, PA	290. La Crosse, WI	343. Tehama, CA-8
187. Anchorage, AK	239. Joplin, MO	291. Pine Bluff, AR	344. Mendocino, CA-9
188. Amarillo, TX	240. Texarkana, TX-AR	292. Sherman-Denison, TX	345. Sierra, CA-10
189. Racine, WI	241. Pueblo, CO	293. Owensboro, KY	346. El Dorado, CA-11
190. Boise City, ID	242. Olympia, WA	294. San Angelo, TX	347. Kings, CA-12
191. Yakima, WA	243. Greeley, CO	295. Midland, TX	348. Moffat, CO-1
192. Gainesville, FL	244. Kenosha, WI	296. Iowa City, IA	349. Logan, CO-2
193. Benton Harbor, MI	245. Ocala, FL	297. Great Falls, MT	350. Garfield, CO-3
194. Waco, TX	246. Dothan, AL	298. Bismarck, ND	351. Park, CO-4
195. Cedar Rapids, IA	247. Lafayette, IN	299. Casper, WY	352. Elbert, CO-5
196. Champaign-Urbana, IL	248. Burlington, VT	300. Victoria, TX	353. San Miguel, CO-6
197. Lake Charles, LA	249. Anniston, AL	301. Lawrence, KS	354. Saguache, CO-7
198. St. Cloud, MN	250. Bloomington-Normal, IL	302. Enid, OK	355. Kiowa, CO-8
199. Steubenville-Werton, OH	251. Williamsport, PA	303. Aurora-Elgin, IL	356. Costilla, CO-9
200. Parkersburg-Marietta, WV	252. Pascagoula, MS	304. Joliet, IL	357. Litchfield, CT-1
201. Waterloo-Cedar Falls, IA	253. Sioux City, IA-NE	305. Alton-Granite City, IL	358. Windham, CT-2
202. Arecibo, PR	254. Redding, CA	307. Franklin, AL-1	359. Kent, DE-1
203. Lynchburg, VA	255. Odessa, TX	308. Jackson, AL-2	360. Collier, FL-1
204. Aguadilla, PR	256. Charlottesville, VA	309. Lamar, AL-3	361. Glades, FL-2

(Continued)

362. Hardee, FL-3	414. Monroe, IA-3	466. Washington, ME-4	518. Stone, MO-15
363. Citrus, FL-4	415. Muscatine, IA-4	467. Garrett, MD-1	519. Laclede, MO-16
364. Putnam, FL-5	416. Jackson, IA-5	468. Kent, MD-2	520. Shannon, MO-17
365. Dixie, FL-6	417. Iowa, IA-6	469. Frederick, MD-3	521. Perry, MO-18
366. Hamilton, FL-7	418. Audubon, IA-7	470. Franklin, MA-1	522. Stoddard, MO-19
367. Jefferson, FL-8	419. Monona, IA-8	471. Barnstable, MA-2	523. Lincoln, MT-1
368. Calhoun, FL-9	420. Ida, IA-9	472. Gogebic, MI-1	524. Toole, MT-2
369. Walton, FL-10	421. Humboldt, IA-10	473. Alger, MI-2	525. Phillips, MT-3
370. Monroe, FL-11	422. Hardin, IA-11	474. Emmet, MI-3	526. Daniels, MT-4
371. Whitfield, GA-1	423. Winneshiek, IA-12	475. Cheboygan, MI-4	527. Mineral, MT-5
372. Dawson, GA-2	424. Mitchell, IA-13	476. Manistee, MI-5	528. Deer Lodge, MT-6
373. Chattooga, GA-3	425. Kossuth, IA-14	477. Roscommon, MI-6	529. Fergus, MT-7
374. Jasper, GA-4	426. Dickinson, IA-15	478. Newaygo, MI-7	530. Beaverhead, MT-8
375. Haralson, GA-5	427. Lyon, IA-16	479. Allegan, MI-8	531. Carbon, MT-9
376. Spalding, GA-6	428. Cheyenne, KS-1	480. Cass, MI-9	532. Prairie, MT-10
377. Hancock, GA-7	429. Norton, KS-2	481. Tuscola, MI-10	533. Sioux, NE-1
378. Warren, GA-8	430. Jewell, KS-3	482. Kittson, MN-1	534. Cherry, NE-2
379. Marion, GA-9	431. Marshall, KS-4	483. Lake of the Woods, MN-2	535. Knox, NE-3
380. Bleckley, GA-10	432. Brown, KS-5	484. Koochiching, MN-3	536. Grant, NE-4
381. Toombs, GA-11	433. Wallace, KS-6	485. Lake, MN-4	537. Boone, NE-5
382. Liberty, GA-12	434. Trego, KS-7	486. Wilkin, MN-5	538. Keith, NE-6
383. Early, GA-13	435. Ellsworth, KS-8	487. Hubbard, MN-6	539. Hall, NE-7
384. Worth, GA-14	436. Morris, KS-9	488. Chippewa, MN-7	540. Chase, NE-8
385. Kauai, HI-1	437. Franklin, KS-10	489. Lac qui Parle, MN-8	541. Adams, NE-9
386. Maui, HI-2	438. Hamilton, KS-11	490. Pipestone, MN-9	542. Cass, NE-10
387. Hawaii, HI-3	439. Hodgeman, KS-12	491. Le Sueur, MN-10	543. Humboldt, NV-1
388. Boundary, ID-1	440. Edwards, KS-13	492. Goodhue, MN-11	544. Lander, NV-2
389. Idaho, ID-2	441. Reno, KS-14	493. Tunica, MS-1	545. Storey, NV-3
390. Lemhi, ID-3	442. Elk, KS-15	494. Benton, MS-2	546. Mineral, NV-4
391. Elmore, ID-4	443. Fulton, KY-1	495. Bolivar, MS-3	547. White Pine, NV-5
392. Butte, ID-5	444. Union, KY-2	496. Yalobusha, MS-4	548. Coos, NH-1
393. Clark, ID-6	445. Meade, KY-3	497. Washington, MS-5	549. Carroll, NH-2
394. Jo Daviess, IL-1	446. Spencer, KY-4	498. Montgomery, MS-6	550. Hunterdon, NJ-1
395. Bureau, IL-2	447. Barren, KY-5	499. Leake, MS-7	551. Ocean, NJ-2
396. Mercer, IL-3	448. Madison, KY-6	500. Claiborne, MS-8	552. Sussex, NJ-3
397. Adams, IL-4	449. Trimble, KY-7	501. Copiah, MS-9	553. San Juan, NM-1
398. Mason, IL-5	450. Mason, KY-8	502. Smith, MS-10	554. Colfax, NM-2
399. Montgomery, IL-6	451. Elliott, KY-9	503. Lamar, MS-11	555. Catron, NM-3
400. Vermilion, IL-7	452. Powell, KY-10	504. Atchison, MO-1	556. Santa Fe, NM-4
401. Washington, IL-8	453. Clay, KY-11	505. Harrison, MO-2	557. Grant, NM-5
402. Clay, IL-9	454. Claiborne, LA-1	506. Schuyler, MO-3	558. Lincoln, NM-6
403. Newton, IN-1	455. Morehouse, LA-2	507. De Kalb, MO-4	559. Jefferson, NY-1
404. Kosciusko, IN-2	456. De Soto, LA-3	508. Linn, MO-5	560. Franklin, NY-2
405. Huntington, IN-3	457. Caldwell, LA-4	509. Marion, MO-6	561. Chautauqua, NY-3
406. Miami, IN-4	458. Beauregard, LA-5	510. Saline, MO-7	562. Yates, NY-4
407. Warren, IN-5	459. Iberville, LA-6	511. Callaway, MO-8	563. Otsego, NY-5
408. Randolph, IN-6	460. West Feliciana, LA-7	512. Bates, MO-9	564. Columbia, NY-6
409. Owen, IN-7	461. St. James, LA-8	513. Benton, MO-10	565. Cherokee, NC-1
410. Brown, IN-8	462. Plaquemines, LA-9	514. Moniteau, MO-11	566. Yancey, NC-2
411. Decatur, IN-9	463. Oxford, ME-1	515. Maries, MO-12	567. Ashe, NC-3
412. Mills, IA-1	464. Somerset, ME-2	516. Washington, MO-13	568. Henderson, NC-4
413. Union, IA-2	465. Kennebec, ME-3	517. Barton, MO-14	569. Anson, NC-5

(Continued)

570. Chatham, NC-6	612. Crawford, PA-1	654. Parmer, TX-3	696. Grays Harbon, WA-4
571. Rockingham, NC-7	613. McKean, PA-2	655. Briscoe, TX-4	697. Kittitas, WA-5
572. Northampton, NC-8	614. Potter, PA-3	656. Hardeman, TX-5	698. Pacific, WA-6
573. Camden, NC-9	615. Bradford, PA-4	657. Jack, TX-6	699. Skamania, WA-7
574. Harnett, NC-10	616. Wayne, PA-5	658. Fannin, TX-7	700. Whitman, WA-8
575. Hoke, NC-11	617. Lawrence, PA-6	659. Gaines, TX-8	701. Mason, WV-1
576. Sampson, NC-12	618. Jefferson, PA-7	660. Runnels, TX-9	702. Wetzel, WV-2
577. Greene, NC-13	619. Union, PA-8	661. Navarro, TX-10	703. Monongalia, WV-3
578. Pitt, NC-14	620. Greene, PA-9	662. Cherokee, TX-11	704. Grant, WV-4
579. Cabarrus, NC-15	621. Bedford, PA-10	663. Hudspeth, TX-12	705. Tucker, WV-5
580. Divide, ND-1	622. Huntingdon, PA-11	664. Reeves, TX-13	706. Lincoln, WV-6
581. Bottineau, ND-2	623. Lebanon, PA-12	665. Loving, TX-14	707. Raleigh, WV-7
582. Barnes, ND-3	624. Newport, RI-1	666. Concho, TX-15	708. Burnett, WI-1
583. McKenzie, ND-4	625. Oconee, SC-1	667. Burleson, TX-16	709. Bayfield, WI-2
584. Kidder, ND-5	626. Laurens, SC-2	668. Newton, TX-17	710. Vilas, WI-3
585. Williams, OH-1	627. Cherokee, SC-3	669. Edwards, TX-18	711. Marinette, WI-4
586. Sandusky, OH-2	628. Chesterfield, SC-4	670. Atascosa, TX-19	712. Pierce, WI-5
587. Ashtabula, OH-3	629. Georgetown, SC-5	671. Wilson, TX-20	713. Trempealeau, WI-6
588. Mercer, OH-4	630. Clarendon, SC-6	672. Chambers, TX-21	714. Wood, WI-7
589. Hancock, OH-5	631. Calhoun, SC-7	673. Box Elder, UT-1	715. Vernon, WI-8
590. Morrow, OH-6	632. Hampton, SC-8	674. Morgan, UT-2	716. Columbia, WI-9
591. Tuscarawas, OH-7	633. Lancaster, SC-9	675. Juab, UT-3	717. Door, WI-10
592. Clinton, OH-8	634. Harding, SD-1	676. Beaver, UT-4	718. Park, WY-1
593. Ross, OH-9	635. Corson, SD-2	677. Carbon, UT-5	719. Sheridan, WY-2
594. Perry, OH-10	636. McPherson, SD-3	678. Piute, UT-6	720. Lincoln, WY-3
595. Columbiana, OH-11	637. Marshall, SD-4	679. Franklin, VT-1	721. Niobrara, WY-4
596. Cimarron, OK-1	638. Custer, SD-5	680. Addison, VT-2	722. Converse, WY-5
597. Harper, OK-2	639. Haakon, SD-6	681. Lee, VA-1	723. Rincon, PR-1
598. Grant, OK-3	640. Sully, SD-7	682. Tazewell, VA-2	724. Adjuntas, PR-2
599. Nowata, OK-4	641. Kingsbury, SD-8	683. Giles, VA-3	725. Ciales, PR-3
600. Roger Mills, OK-5	642. Hanson, SD-9	684. Bedford, VA-4	726. Aibonito, PR-4
601. Seminole, OK-6	643. Lake, TN-1	685. Bath, VA-5	727. Ceiba, PH-5
602. Beckham, OK-7	644. Cannon, TN-2	686. Highland, VA-6	728. Culebra-7
603. Jackson, OK-8	645. Macon, TN-3	687. Buckingham, VA-7	729. Viegues, PR-6
604. Garvin, OK-9	646. Hamblen, TN-4	688. Amelia, VA-8	730. St. Thomas, VI-1
605. Haskell, OK-10	647. Fayette, TN-5	689. Greensville, VA-9	731. St. Croix, VI-2
606. Clatsop, OR-1	648. Giles, TN-6	690. Frederick, VA-10	732. Guam
607. Hood River, OR-2	649. Bledsoe, TN-7	691. Madison, VA-11	733. American Samoa
608. Umatilla, OR-3	650. Johnson, TN-8	692. Caroline, VA-12	734. N. Marianas
609. Lincoln, OR-4	651. Maury, TN-9	693. Clallam, WA-1	
610. Coos, OR-5	652. Dallam, TX-1	694. Okanogan, WA-2	
611. Crook, OR-6	653. Hansford, TX-2	695. Ferry, WA-3	

APPENDIX C
MAJOR TRADING AREAS AND BASIC TRADING AREA IN THE UNITED STATES

Part 1: Broadband PCS Major Trading Area Designations (*From FCC*)

Market No.	Major Trading Area	Market No.	Major Trading Area
M 001	New York	M 027	Phoenix
M 002	Los Angeles-San Diego	M 028	Memphis-Jackson
M 003	Chicago	M 029	Birmingham
M 004	San Francisco-Oakland-San Jose	M 030	Portland
M 005	Detroit	M 031	Indianapolis
M 006	Charlotte-Greensboro-Greenville- Raleigh	M 032	Des Moines-Quad Cities
M 007	Dallas-Fort Worth	M 033	San Antonio
M 008	Boston-Providence	M 034	Kansas City
M 009	Philadelphia	M 035	Buffalo-Rochester
M 010	Washington-Baltimore	M 036	Salt Lake City
M 011	Atlanta	M 037	Jacksonville
M 012	Minneapolis-St. Paul	M 038	Columbus
M 013	Tampa-St. Petersburg-Orlando	M 039	El Paso-Albuquerque
M 014	Houston	M 040	Little Rock
M 015	Miami-Fort Lauderdale	M 041	Oklahoma City
M 016	Cleveland	M 042	Spokane-Billings
M 017	New Orleans-Baton Rouge	M 043	Nashville
M 018	Cincinnati-Dayton	M 044	Knoxville
M 019	St. Louis	M 045	Omaha
M 020	Milwaukee	M 046	Wichita
M 021	Pittsburgh	M 047	Honolulu
M 022	Denver	M 048	Tulsa
M 023	Richmond-Norfolk	M 049	Alaska
M 024	Seattle (Excluding Alaska)	M 050	Guam-Northern Mariana Islands
M 025	Puerto Rico-U.S. Virgin Islands	M 051	American Samoa
M 026	Louisville-Lexington-Evansville		

Part 2: Basic Trading Areas in the United States

No.	Basic Trading Area	No.	Basic Trading Area	No.	Basic Trading Area
001	Aberdeen, SD	056	Brownsville-Harlingen, TX	111	Des Moines, IA
002	Aberdeen, WA	057	Brownwood, TX	112	Detroit, MI
003	Abilene, TX	058	Brunswick, GA	113	Dickinson, ND
004	Ada, OK	059	Bryan-College Station, TX	114	Dodge City, KS
005	Adrian, MI	060	Buffalo-Niagara Falls, NY	115	Dothan-Enterprise, AL
006	Albany-Tifton, GA	061	Burlington, IA	116	Dover, DE
007	Albany-Schenectady, NY	062	Burlington, NC	117	Du Bois-Clearfield, PA
008	Albuquerque, NM	063	Burlington, VT	118	Dubuque, IA
009	Alexandria, LA	064	Butte, MT	119	Duluth, MN
010	Allentown-Bethlehem-Easton, PA	065	Canton-New Philadelphia, OH	120	Dyersburg-Union City, TN
011	Alpena, MI	066	Cape Girardeau-Sikeston, MO	121	Eagle Pass-Del Rio, TX
012	Altoona, PA	067	Carbondale-Marion, IL	122	East Liverpool-Salem, OH
013	Amarillo, TX	068	Carlsbad, NM	123	Eau Claire, WI
014	Anchorage, AK	069	Casper-Gillette, WY	124	El Centro-Calexico, CA
015	Anderson, IN	070	Cedar Rapids, IA	125	El Dorado-Magnolia-Camden, AR
016	Anderson, SC	071	Champaign-Urbana, IL	126	Elkhart, IN
017	Anniston, AL	072	Charleston, SC	127	Elmira-Corning-Hornell, NY
018	Appleton-Oshkosh, WI	073	Charleston, WV	128	El Paso, TX
019	Ardmore, OK	074	Charlotte-Gastonia, NC	129	Emporia, KS
020	Asheville-Hendersonville, NC	075	Charlottesville, VA	130	Enid, OK
021	Ashtabula, OH	076	Chattanooga, TN	131	Erie, PA
022	Athens, GA	077	Cheyenne, WY	132	Escanaba, MI
023	Athens, OH	078	Chicago, IL	133	Eugene-Springfield, OR
024	Atlanta, GA	079	Chico-Oroville, CA	134	Eureka, CA
025	Atlantic City, NJ	080	Chillicothe, OH	135	Evansville, IN
026	Augusta, GA	081	Cincinnati, OH	136	Fairbanks, AK
027	Austin, TX	082	Clarksburg-Elkins, WV	137	Fairmont, WV
028	Bakersfield, CA	083	Clarksville, TN-Hopkinsville, KY	138	Fargo, ND
029	Baltimore, MD	084	Cleveland-Akron, OH	139	Farmington, NM-Durango, CO
030	Bangor, ME	085	Cleveland, TN	140	Fayetteville-Springdale-Rogers, AR
031	Bartlesville, OK	086	Clinton, IA-Sterling, IL	141	Fayetteville-Lumberton, NC
032	Baton Rouge, LA	087	Clovis, NM	142	Fergus Falls, MN
033	Battle Creek, MI	088	Coffeyville, KS	143	Findlay-Tiffin, OH
034	Beaumont-Port Arthur, TX	089	Colorado Springs, CO	144	Flagstaff, AZ
035	Beckley, WV	090	Columbia, MO	145	Flint, MI
036	Bellingham, WA	091	Columbia, SC	146	Florence, AL
037	Bemidji, MN	092	Columbus, GA	147	Florence, SC
038	Bend, OR	093	Columbus, IN	148	Fond du Lac, WI
039	Benton Harbor, MI	094	Columbus-Starkville, MS	149	Fort Collins-Loveland, CO
040	Big Spring, TX	095	Columbus, OH	150	Fort Dodge, IA
041	Billings, MT	096	Cookeville, TN	151	Fort Myers, FL
042	Biloxi-Gulfport-Pascagoula, MS	097	Coos Bay-North Bend, OR	152	Fort Pierce-Vero Beach-Stuart, FL
043	Binghamton, NY	098	Corbin, KY	153	Fort Smith, AR
044	Birmingham, AL	099	Corpus Christi, TX	154	Fort Walton Beach, FL
045	Bismarck, ND	100	Cumberland, MD	155	Fort Wayne, IN
046	Bloomington, IL	101	Dallas-Fort Worth, TX	156	Fredericksburg, VA
047	Bloomington-Bedford, IN	102	Dalton, GA	157	Fresno, CA
048	Bluefield, WV	103	Danville, IL	158	Gadsden, AL
049	Blytheville, AR	104	Danville, VA	159	Gainesville, FL
050	Boise-Nampa, ID	105	Davenport, IA-Moline, IL	160	Gainesville, GA
051	Boston, MA	106	Dayton-Springfield, OH	161	Galesburg, IL
052	Bowling Green-Glasgow, KY	107	Daytona Beach, FL	162	Gallup, NM
053	Bozeman, MT	108	Decatur, AL	163	Garden City, KS
054	Brainerd, MN	109	Decatur-Effingham, IL	164	Glens Falls, NY
055	Bremerton, WA	110	Denver, CO	165	Goldsboro-Kinston, NC

Part 2: (*Continued*) Basic Trading Areas in the United States

No.	Basic Trading Area	No.	Basic Trading Area	No.	Basic Trading Area
166	Grand Forks, ND	216	Janesville-Beloit, WI	270	Mccook, NE
167	Grand Island-Kearney, NE	217	Jefferson City, MO	271	Macon-Warner Robins, GA
168	Grand Junction, CO	218	Johnstown, PA	272	Madison, WI
169	Grand Rapids, MI	219	Jonesboro-Paragould, AR	273	Madisonville, KY
170	Great Bend, KS	220	Joplin, MO-Miami, OK	274	Manchester-Nashua-Concord, NH
171	Great Falls, MT	221	Juneau-Ketchikan, AK	275	Manhattan-Junction City, KS
172	Greeley, CO	222	Kahului-Wailuku-Lahaina, HI	276	Manitowoc, WI
173	Green Bay, WI	223	Kalamazoo, MI	277	Mankato-Fairmont, MN
174	Greensboro-Winston-Salem-High Point, NC	224	Kallspell, MT	278	Mansfield, OH
		225	Kankakee, IL	279	Marinette, WI-Menominee, MI
175	Greenville-Greenwood, MS	226	Kansas City, MO	280	Marion, IN
176	Greenville-Washington, NC	227	Keene, NH	281	Marion, OH
177	Greenville-Spartanburg, SC	228	Kennewick-Pasco-Richland, WA	282	Marquette, MI
178	Greenwood, SC	229	Kingsport, TN-Johnson City, TN-Bristol, VA-TN	283	Marshalltown, IA
179	Hagerstown, MD-Chambersburg, PA-Martinsburg, WV			284	Martinsville, VA
		230	Kirksville, MO	285	Mason City, IA
180	Hammond, LA	231	Klamath Falls, OR	286	Mattoon, IL
		232	Knoxville, TN	287	Meadville, PA
181	Harrisburg, PA	233	Kokomo-Logansport, IN	288	Medford-Grants Pass, OR
182	Harrison, AR	234	La Crosse, WI-Winona, MN	289	Melbourne-Titusville, FL
183	Harrisonburg, VA	235	Lafayette, IN	290	Memphis, TN
184	Hartford, CT	236	Lafayette-New Iberia, LA	291	Merced, CA
185	Hastings, NE	237	La Grange, GA	292	Meridian, MS
186	Hattiesburg, MS	238	Lake Charles, LA	293	Miami-Fort Lauderdale, FL
187	Hays, KS	239	Lakeland-Winter Haven, FL	294	Michigan City-La Porte, IN
188	Helena, MT	240	Lancaster, PA	295	Middlesboro-Harlan, KY
189	Hickory-Lenoir-Morganton, NC	241	Lansing, MI	296	Midland, TX
		242	Laredo, TX	297	Milwaukee, WI
190	Hilo, HI	243	La Salle-Peru-Ottawa-Streator, IL	298	Minneapolis-St. Paul, MN
191	Hobbs, NM	244	Las Crucea, NM	299	Minot, ID
192	Honolulu, HI	245	Las Vegas, NV	300	Missoula, MT
193	Hot Springs, AR	246	Laurel, MS	301	Mitchell, SD
194	Houghton, MI	247	Lawrence, KS	302	Mobile, AL
195	Houma-Thibodaux, LA	248	Lawton-Duncan, OK	303	Modesto, CA
196	Houston, TX	249	Lebanon-Claremont, NH	304	Monroe, LA
197	Huntington, WV-Ashland, KY	250	Lewiston-Moscow, ID	305	Montgomery, AL
198	Huntsville, AL	251	Lewiston-Auburn, ME	306	Morgantown, WV
199	Huron, SD	252	Lexington, KY	307	Mount Pleasant, MI
200	Hutchinson, KS	253	Liberal, KS	308	Mount Vernon-Centralia, IL
201	Hyannis, MA	254	Lihue, HI	309	Muncie, IN
202	Idaho Falls, ID	255	Lima, OH	310	Muskegon, MI
203	Indiana, PA	256	Lincoln, NE	311	Muskogee, OK
204	Indianapolis, IN	257	Little Rock, AR	312	Myrtle Beach, SC
205	Iowa City, IA	258	Logan, UT	313	Naples, FL
206	Iron Mountain, MI	259	Logan, WV	314	Nashville, TN
207	Ironwood, MI	260	Longview-Marshall, TX	315	Natchez, MS
208	Ithaca, NY	261	Longview, WA	316	New Bern, NC
209	Jackson, MI	262	Los Angeles, CA	317	New Castle, PA
210	Jackson, MS	263	Louisville, KY	318	New Haven-Waterbury-Meriden, CT
211	Jackson, TN	264	Lubbock, TX		
212	Jacksonville, FL	265	Lufkin-Nacogdoches, TX	319	New London-Norwich, CT
213	Jacksonville, IL	266	Lynchburg, VA	320	New Orleans, LA
214	Jacksonville, NC	267	McAlester, OK	321	New York, NY
215	Jamestown, NY-Warren, PA-Dunkirk, NY	268	McAllen, TX	322	Nogales, AZ
		269	McComb-Brookhaven, MS	323	Norfolk, NE

Part 2: *(Continued)* Basic Trading Areas in the United States

No.	Basic Trading Area	No.	Basic Trading Area	No.	Basic Trading Area
324	Norfolk-Virginia Beach -Newport News- Hampton, VA	370	Reading, PA	421	Sioux City, IA
		371	Redding, CA	422	Sioux Falls, SD
		372	Reno, NV	423	Somerset, KY
325	North Platte, NE	373	Richmond, IN	424	South Bend-Mishawaka, IN
326	Ocala, FL	374	Richmond-Petersburg, VA	425	Spokane, WA
327	Odessa, TX	375	Riverton, WY	426	Springfield, IL
328	Oil City-Franklin, PA	376	Roanoke, VA	427	Springfield-Holyoke, MA
329	Oklahoma City, OK	377	Roanoke Rapids, NC	428	Springfield, MO
330	Olean, NY-Bradford, PA	378	Rochester-Austin-Albert Lea, MN	429	State College, PA
331	Olympia-Centralia, WA			430	Staunton-Waynesboro, VA
332	Omaha, NE	379	Rochester, NY	431	Steubenville, OH-Weirton, WV
333	Oneonta, NY	380	Rockford, IL	432	Stevens Point-Marshfield-Wisconsin Rapids, WI
334	Opelika-Auburn, AL	381	Rock Springs, WY		
335	Orangeburg, SC	382	Rocky Mount-Wilson, NC	433	Stillwater, OK
336	Orlando, FL	383	Rolla, MO	434	Stockton, CA
337	Ottumwa, IA	384	Rome, GA	435	Stroudsburg, PA
338	Owensboro, KY	385	Roseburg, OR	436	Sumter, SC
339	Paducah-Murray-Mayfield, KY	386	Roswell, NM	437	Sunbury-Shamokin, PA
		387	Russellville, AR	438	Syracuse, NY
340	Panama City, FL	388	Rutland-Bennington, VT	439	Tallahassee, FL
341	Paris, TX	389	Sacramento, CA	440	Tampa-St. Petersburg-Clearwater, FL
342	Parkersburg, WV-Marietta, OH	390	Saginaw-Bay City, MI		
		391	St. Cloud, MN	441	Temple-Killeen, TX
343	Pensacola, FL	392	St. George, UT	442	Terre Haute, IN
344	Peoria, IL	393	St. Joseph, MO	443	Texarkana, TX-AR
345	Petoskey, MI	394	St. Louis, MO	444	Toledo, OH
346	Philadelphia, PA-Wilmington, DE-Trenton, NJ	395	Salem-Albany-Corvallis, OR	445	Topeka, KS
		396	Salina, KS	446	Traverse City, MI
347	Phoenix, AZ	397	Salinas-Monterey, CA	447	Tucson, AZ
348	Pine Bluff, AR	398	Salisbury, MD	448	Tulsa, OK
349	Pittsburgh-Parsons, KS	399	Salt Lake City-Ogden, UT	449	Tupelo-Corinth, MS
350	Pittsburgh, PA	400	San Angelo, TX	450	Tuscaloosa, AL
351	Pittsfield, MA	401	San Antonio, TX	451	Twin Falls, ID
352	Plattsburgh, NY	402	San Diego, CA	452	Tyler, TX
353	Pocatello, ID	403	Sandusky, OH	453	Utica-Rome, NY
354	Ponca City, OK	404	San Francisco-Oakland-San Jose, CA	454	Valdosta, GA
355	Poplar Bluff, MO			455	Vicksburg, MS
356	Port Angeles, WA	405	San Luis Obispo, CA	456	Victoria, TX
357	Portland-Brunswick, ME	406	Santa Barbara-Santa Maria, CA	457	Vincennes-Washington, IN
358	Portland, OR	407	Santa Fe, NM	458	Visalia-Porterville-Hanford, CA
359	Portsmouth, OH	408	Sarasota-Bradenton, FL	459	Waco, TX
360	Pottsville, PA	409	Sault Ste. Marie, MI	460	Walla Walla, WA-Pendleton, OR
361	Poughkeepsie-Kingston, NY	410	Savannah, GA	461	Washington, DC
362	Prescott, AZ	411	Scottsbluff, NE	462	Waterloo-Cedar Falls, IA
363	Presque Isle, ME	412	Scranton-Wilkes-Barre-Hazleton, PA	463	Watertown, NY
364	Providence-Pawtucket, RI-New Bedford-Fall River, MA	413	Seattle-Tacoma, WA	464	Watertown, SD
		414	Sedalia, MO	465	Waterville-Augusta, ME
		415	Selma, AL	466	Wausau-Rhinelander, WI
365	Provo-Orem, UT	416	Sharon, PA	467	Waycross, GA
366	Pueblo, CO	417	Sheboygan, WI	468	Wenatchee, WA
367	Quincy, IL-Hannibal, MO	418	Sherman-Denison, TX	469	West Palm Beach-Boca Raton, FL
368	Raleigh-Durham, NC	419	Shreveport, LA	470	West Plains, MO
369	Rapid City, SD	420	Sierra Vista-Douglas, AZ	471	Wheeling, WV
				472	Wichita, KS
				473	Wichita Falls, TX

Part 2: (*Continued*) Basic Trading Areas in the United States

No.	Basic Trading Area	No.	Basic Trading Area	No.	Basic Trading Area
474	Williamson, WV-Pikeville, KY	479	Winchester, VA	483	York-Hanover, PA
475	Williamsport, PA	480	Worcester-Fitchburgh-Leominster,	484	Youngstown-Warren, OH
476	Williston, MD		MA	485	Yuba City-Marysville, CA
477	Willmar-Marshall, MN	481	Worthington, MN	486	Yuma, AZ
478	Wilmington, NC	482	Yakima, WA	487	Zanesville-Cambridge, OH

CONVERSION BETWEEN dBμV AND dBm

I. At the receiving end, dBμV $\leftrightarrow$ dBm (decibels above 1 μV $\leftrightarrow$ decibels above 1 mW)

A receiving antenna at a distance r from the transmitting antenna with an aperture A will receive power P_r

$$P_r = \rho \cdot A = \frac{P_t A}{4\pi r^2} \qquad Watt \qquad \text{(D-1)}$$

where ρ is the Poynting vector.
We can also obtain the received power from Fig. D.1c

$$P_r = \frac{V^2 Z_L}{(Z_L + Z_a)^2} \qquad \text{(D-2)}$$

where V is the induced voltage in volts. For a maximum power delivery $Z_L = Z_a^*$, where the notation $*$ indicates complex conjugate. Then, we obtain $Z_L + Z_a = 2R_L$, where R_L is the real-load resistance. Equation (D-2) becomes

$$P_r = \frac{V^2}{4R_L} \qquad \text{(D-3)}$$

Assume that a dipole or a monopole is used as a receiving antenna. The induced voltage V can be related to field strength E as[*]

$$V = \frac{E\lambda}{\pi} \qquad \text{(D-4)}$$

Where E is expressed in volts or microvolts per meter. Substitution of Eq. (D-3) into Eq. (D-4) yields

$$P_r = \frac{E^2 \lambda^2}{4\pi^2 R_L} \qquad \text{(D-5)}$$

If we set $R_L = 50\,\Omega$, P_r in decibels above 1 m, and E in decibels (microvolts per meter), Eq. (D-5) becomes

$$P_r\,(\text{dBm}) = E\,(\text{dB}\mu V) - 113\,\text{dBm} + 10\log\left(\frac{\lambda}{\pi}\right)^2 \qquad \text{(D-6)}$$

---

[*] E. C. Jordan (ed.). *Reference Data for Engineers*, 8th ed. Howard W. Sams & Co., 1993, p.32–33.

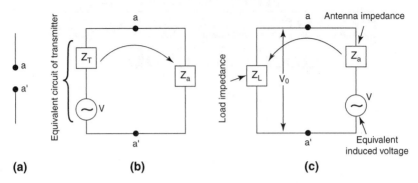

(a)   **(b)**   **(c)**

FIGURE D.1   An actual antenna and its equivalent circuit. (*a*) An actual antenna; (*b*) equivalent circuit of a transmitting antenna; (*c*) equivalent circuit of a receiving antenna.

The notation "dBμV" in Eq. (D-6) is a simplification of decibels above 1 μV/m and has been accepted by the Institute of Radio Engineers. We can find the equivalent aperture A of Eq. (D-1) because of the Poynting vector

$$\rho = \frac{E^2}{Z_0} \tag{D-7}$$

where Z_0 is the intrinsic impedance of the space ($= 120\,\pi$). By substituting Eq. (D-7) into Eq. (D-1) and comparing it with Eq. (D-5), we obtain the equivalent aperture A.

$$A = \frac{\lambda^2 Z_0}{4\pi^2 R_L} \tag{D-8}$$

Equation (D-8) is the same as that given in Eq. (3.11) in Ref. 2 of Chapter 3.

II. Practical use of field-strength-received-power conversions. There is always confusion between the following two conversions.

    A. Measuring field strength and converting it to received power. From Eq. (D-6), converting field strength in decibels above 1 μV/m to power received in decibels above 1 mW at 850 MHz by a dipole with a 50-Ω load is -132 dB.

$$P_r \ \ \text{dBm} = E \ \ \text{dB}\,(\mu\text{V/m}) - 132\,\text{dB} \tag{D-9}$$

$$\text{at 850 MHz}$$

$$39\,\text{dB}\,(\mu\text{V/m}) = -93\,\text{dBm} \tag{D-10}$$

The notation "39-dB μV contour" is commonly used to mean 39 dB (μV/m) in cellular system design. Equation (D-9) is valid only at a given frequency (850 MHz), for a given antenna (monopole or dipole antenna), and for a given antenna load (50 Ω). Otherwise, the field strength and the power have to be adjusted accordingly.

B. Measuring the voltage V_0 at the load terminal (Fig. D.1c) and converting to received power. Given $P_r = (V_0^2/R_L)$, where $R_L = 50\,\Omega$, we can obtain a relationship

$$0\,dB\mu V \langle = \rangle - 107\,dBm \qquad \text{(D-11)}$$

For example, if a voltage meter at V_0 is 7 $dB\mu V$, then the received power is -100 dBm. Equation (D-11) expresses a voltage-to-power ratio that varies with the load impedance but is independent of the frequency and the type of antenna.

APPENDIX E

DEFINITIONS OF FUNCTIONS IN LAN AND MAN

- association: The service used to establish access point/station (AP/STA) mapping and enable STA invocation of the distribution system services (DSSs).
- basic service set (BSS): A set of stations controlled by a single coordination function.
- basic service set (BSS) basic rate set: The set of data transfer rates that all the stations in a BSS will be capable of using to receive frames from the wireless medium (WM). The BSS basic rate set data rates are preset for all stations in the BSS.
- broadcast address: A unique multicast address that specifies all stations.
- clear channel assessment (CCA) function: That logical function is the physical layer (PHY) that determines the current state of use of the wireless medium (WM).
- coordination function: The logical function that determines when a station operating within a basic service set (BSS) is permitted to transmit and may be able to receive protocol data units (PDUs) via the wireless medium (WM).
- elements of coordination function: coordination function. The coordination function within a BSS may have one point coordination function (PCF) and will have one distributed coordination function (DCF).
- coordination function pollable: A station able to (1) respond to a coordination function poll with a data frame, if such a frame is queued and able to be generated, and (2) interpret acknowledgments in frames sent to or from the point coordinator.
- disassociation: The service that removes an existing association.
- distributed coordination function (DCF): A class of coordination function where the same coordination function logic is active in every station in the basic service set (BSS) whenever the network is in operation.
- distribution: The service that, by using association information, delivers medium access control (MAC) service data units (MSDUs) within the distribution system (DS).
- distribution system (DS): A system used to interconnect a set of basic service sets (BSSs) and integrated local area networks (LANs) to create an extended service set (ESS).
- distribution system medium (DSM): The medium or set of media used by a distribution system (DS) for communications between access points (APs) and portals of an extended service set (ESS).

- distribution system service (DSS): The set of services provided by the distribution system (DS) that enable the medium access control (MAC) to transport MAC service data units (MSDUs) between stations.

- extended rate set (ERS): The set of data transfer rates supported by a station (if any) beyond the extended service set (ESS) basic rate set. This set may include data transfer rates that will be defined in future physical layer (PHY) standards.

- extended service area (ESA): The conceptual area within which members of an extended service set (ESS) may communicate. An ESA is larger than or equal to a basic service area (BSA) and may involve several basic service sets (BSSs) in overlapping, disjointed, or both configurations.

- extended service set (ESS): A set of one or more interconnected basic service sets (BSSs) and integrated local area networks (LANs) that appears as a single BSS to the logical link control layer at any station associated with one of these BSSs.

- independent basic service set (IBSS): A BSS that forms a self-contained network, and in which no access to a distribution system (DS) is available.

- medium access control (MAC) management protocol data unit (MMPDU): The unit of data exchanged between two peer MAC entities to implement the MAC management protocol.

- medium access control (MAC) protocol data unit (MPDU): The unit of data exchanged between two peer MAC entities using the services of the physical layer (PHY).

- medium access control (MAC) service data unit (MSDU): Information that is delivered as a unit between MAC service access points (SAPs).

- network allocation vector (NAV): An indicator, maintained by each station, of time periods when transmission onto the wireless medium (WM) will not be initiated by the station whether or not the station's clear channel assessment (CCA) function senses that the WM is busy.

- point coordination function (PCF): A class of possible coordination functions in which the coordination function logic is active in only one station in a basic service set (BSS) at any given time that the network is in operation.

- portal: The logical point at which medium access control (MAC) service data units (MSDUs) from a non-IEEE 802.11 local area network (LAN) enter the distribution system (DS) of an extended service set (ESS).

- reassociation: The service that enables an established association [between access point (AP) and station (STA)] to be transferred from one AP to another (or the same) AP.

- station (STA): Any device that contains an IEEE 802.11 conformant medium access control (MAC) and physical layer (PHY) interface to the wireless medium (WM).

- station basic rate: A data transfer rate belonging to the extended service set (ESS) basic rate set that is used by a station for specific transmissions. The station basic rate may change dynamically as frequently as

- unicast frame: A frame that is addressed to a single recipient, not a broadcast or multicast frame. *Syn:* directed address.

- wired equivalent privacy (WEP): The optional cryptographic confidentiality algorithm specified by IEEE 802.11 used to provide data confidentiality that is subjectively equivalent to the confidentiality of a wired local area network (LAN) medium that does not employ cryptographic techniques to enhance privacy.

- wireless medium (WM): The medium used to implement the transfer of protocol data units (PDUs) between peer physical layer (PHY) entities of a wireless local area network (LAN).

ABBREVIATIONS AND ACRONYMS

1) ABBREVIATIONS AND ACRONYMS FOR WORLDWIDE PERSONAL COMMUNICATIONS

Acronym	Definition
AIN	Advanced Intelligent Network
AMPS	Advanced Mobile Phone Service
ANSI	American National Standards Institute
BCF	Base Station Control Function
BSS	Base Station System
CAI	Common Air Interface
CAPCODE	The electronic address of a radio pager and telephone number in a paging terminal
CC	Country Code
CCITT	Consultive Committee for Internation Telephony & Telegraphy
CCS	Communications Call Seconds-a measure of traffic density
CCIR	International Radio Consultative Committee
CCIS	Common Channel Interoffice Signaling
CCIS7	Common Channel Interoffice Signaling System #7, a CCITT standard
CDMA	Code Division Multiple Access
CEEC	Commission of the European Economic Community
CEPT	Conference of European Posts and Telecommunications
CGSA	Cellular Geographic Service Area
CO	Central Office
COAM	Customer Owned And Maintained equipment
CP	Construction Permit
CT-1	Cordless Telephone first generation (Current Cordless)
CT-2	Cordless Telephone second generation-outbound public and in/outbound home service (A United Kingdom standard)
CT-3	Cordless Telephone third generation (standards still formative)
CTIA	Cellular Telecommunications Industry Association
CU	Carrier Unit
DCA	Dynamic Channel Allocation
DCC	Digital Cross Connection
DCT	Dynamic Digital Cordless Telephone
DCU	Digital Control Unit

DDS	Digital Data System
DECT	Digital European Cordless Telephony (standard)
DREA	Digital Radio Exchange Access
DSP	Digital Signal Processing
DSS	Direct Sequence Spread Spectrum
E-TDMA	Enhanced TDMA Access
EAMPS	Expanded Advanced Mobile Phone Service
ECSA	Exchange Carriers Standards Association
EDI	Electronic Data Interchange
EOC	Embedded Operations Channel
ERMES	European Radio Messaging Services
ESN	Electronic Serial Number
ESP	Enhanced Service Provider
ETSI	European Telecommunications Standards Institute
FCC	Federal Communications Commission (U.S.)
FDD	Frequency Division Duplexing
FDDI	Fiber Distributed Data Interface
FDMA	Frequency Division Multiple Access
FHSS	Frequency Hopping Spread Spectrum
FM	Frequency Modulation
FPLMTS	Future Public Land Mobile Telecommunications System
FSK	Frequency Shift Keying
GPS	Global Positioning System
GSM	Groupe Speciale Mobile-the Pan European digital cellular standard
High Band	Radio Frequencies in the 150–160 MHz Band
IDLC	Integrated Digital Loop Carrier
IETF	Internet Engineering Task Force (Internet standard organization)
IILC	Information Industry Liason Committee
IMTS	Improved Mobile Telephone Service
IN	Intelligent Network
IS-41	Interim Standard 41-the cellular intersystem handoff and call delivery standard
ISDN	Integrated Services Digital Network
ISM	Industrial, Scientific & Medical Applications (freq. allocation 902–928 MHZ and other bands)
ISO	International Standards Organization
ITU	International Telecommunications Union
LAN	Local Area Network
LEC	Local Exchange Carrier
LEO	Low Earth Orbit
Low Band	Radio Frequencies in the 30–50 MHz VHF Band
MAN	Metropolitan Area Network
MCTV	Merlin Cordless Voice Terminal (1989 by AT&T)
MIN	Mobile Identification Number, the cellular telephone number
MM	Mobility Management
MPU	Main Processing Unit
MS	Mobile Station
MSA	Metropolitan Statistical Area
MTSO	Mobile Telephone Switching Office
N-AMPS	Narrowband Advanced Mobile Phone Service
NAM	Number Assignment Module

NMT	Nordic Mobile Telephone
NOI	Notice of Inquiry
NPA	Numbering Plan Area
PCI	Peripherial Channel Interface
PCM	Pulse Code Modulation
PCN	Personal Communications Network
PCN	Prior Coordination Notice
PCP	Private Carrier Paging
PCS	Personal Communications System or Service
PIN	Personal Identification Number
POCSAG	Post Office Code Standards Advisory Group
POTS	Plain Old Telephone Service
PPSN	Public Packet Switched Network
PSDS	Packet Switch Digital Service
PSTN	Public, Switched, Telephone Network (wireline)
PTN	Personal Telephone Number
RABC	Radio Advisory Board of Canada
RCC	Radio Common Carrier
RF	Radio Frequency
RSA	Rural Service Area
SAP	Service Access Point
SAT	Supervisory Audio Tone
SCP	Service Control Point
SID	System Identification
SMR	Specialized Mobile Radio
SS7	Signaling System 7 protocol
ST	Signaling Terminal
SWR	Standing Wave Ratio
TA	Terminal Adaptor
TACS	Total Access Communications
TAS	Telephone Answering Service
TCU	Terminal Control Unit
TDD	Time Division Duplexing
TDMA	Time Division Multiple Access
TIA	Telecommunications Industry Association
TR45.3	Cellular Digital Standard Committee under TIA
TUP	Telephony User Part
TXU	Transmitter Unit
Type 2	An Architecture whereby the RCC serves as a central office with the network
UHF	Ultra-High Frequency
VHF	Very-High Frequency
VLSI	Very Large Scale Integration
VME	Voice Messaging Equipment
WAN	Wide Area Network
WCA	Wireless Communications Association
WCC	Wireline Common Carrier
X.25	CCITT Specification & Protocol for Public Packet-Switching Networks—Layer 3

2) ABBREVIATIONS AND ACRONYMS FOR MOBILE AND CELLULAR SYSTEMS

Acronym	Definition
1G	First generation of cellular system, analog systems
2G	Second generation of cellular system, digital systems
3GPP	Third generation partnership project (produces WCDMA standard)
3GPP2	Third generation partnership project 2 (produced cdma2000 standard)
AAA	Authentication, Authorization, and Accounting
AAL2	ATM Adaptation Layer type 2
AAL5	ATM Adaptation Layer type 5
ACELP	Algebraic code excitation linear prediction
ACG	Access control gateway
ACIR	Adjacent channel interference ratio, caused by the transmitter non-idealities and imperfect receiver filtering
ACLR	Adjacent channel leakage ratio, caused by the transmitter non-idealities, the effect of receiver filtering is not included
ACM	Admission confirm
ACTS	Advanced communication technologies and systems, EU research projects framework
AICH	Acquisition indication channel
ALCAP	Access link control application part
AM	Acknowledged mode
AMC	Adaptive modulation and coding
AMD	Acknowledged mode data
AMPS	Advance mobile plane service
AMR	Adaptive multirate (speech codec)
AN	Advanced network
ANSI	American National Standard Institute
APN	Access point name
ARIB	Association of radio industries and businesses (Japan)
ARQ	Automatic repeat request
ART	Admission request
ASC	Access service class
ASE	Application service element
ASN, 1	Abstract syntax notation one
AT	Access terminal
ATM	Asynchronous transfer mode
AUC	Authentication center
AWGN	Additive white Gaussian noise
BB SS7	Broad band signalling system #7
BCA	Borrowing channel assignment
BCCH	Broadcast control channel (logical channel)
BCFE	Broadcast control functional entity
BCH	Broadcast channel (transport channel)
BER	Bit error ratio
BLER	Block error ratio
BMC	Broadcast/multicast control protocol
BoD	Bandwidth on demand
BP	Burst period (time slot)

BPSK	Binary phase shift keying
BR	Base Radio
BS	Base station
BSC	Base station controller
BSS	Base station subsystem
BTS	Base transceiver station
CA-ICH	Channel assignment indication channel
CB	Cell broadcast
CBC	Cell broadcast center
CBS	Cell broadcast service
CCCH	Common control channel (logical channel)
CCH	Common transport channel
CCH	Control channel
CD-ICH	Collision detection indication channel
CDF	Cumulative distribution function
CDMA	Code division multiple access
CFN	Connection frame number
CGF	Charging gateway function
CIR	Carrier to interference ratio
CLC	Close logical channel
CM	Connection management
CN	Core network
C-NBAP	Common NBAP
CODIT	Code division test bed, EU research project
CPCH	Common packet channel
CPICH	Common pilot channel
CRC	Cyclic redundancy check
CRNC	Controlling RNC
C-RNTI	Cell-RNTI, radio network temporary identity
CS	Cell site
CS	Circuit switched
CSI	Channel state information
CSICH	CPCH status indication channel
CTC	Convolutional turbo codes
CTCH	Common traffic channel
CVSD	Continuously variable step delta
CWTS	China wireless telecommunications standard group
DAP	Dispatch application processor
DCA	Dynamic channel allocation
DCCH	Dedicated control channel (logical channel)
DCFE	Dedicated control functional entity
DCH	Dedicated channel (transport channel)
DECT	Digital enhanced cordless telephone
DF	Decision feedback
DL	Downlink
D-NBAP	Dedicated NBAP
DPCCH	Dedicated physical control channel
DPDCH	Dedicated physical data channel
DRNC	Drift RNC
DRT	Diagnostic rhyme test
DRX	Discontinuous reception

DS-CDMA	Direct spread code division multiple access
DSCH	Downlink shared channel
DTCH	Dedicated traffic channel
DTX	Discontinuous transmission
DVB	Digital video broadcast
DWDM	Dense WDM
EDGE	Enhanced data rates for GSM evolution
EFR	Enhanced full rate speech codec
EIR	Equipment Identity Register
EIRP	Equivalent isotropic radiated power
EP	Elementary procedure
ESN	Electronic serial number
ETSI	European Telecommunications Standards Institute
EUDCH	Enchanced uplink for dedicated channel
FA	Foreign agent
FACCH	Fast associated control channel
FACH	Forward access channel
FBCA	Force-borrowing channel assignment
FBI	Feedback information
FC	Forward channel
FCA	Fixed channel assignment
FDD	Frequency division duplex
FDDI	Fiber distributed data interface
FDMA	Frequency division multiple access
FER	Frame error ratio
FL	Forward link
FNE	Fixed network equipment
FOCC	Forward control channel
FOMA	Freedom of mobile multimedia access
FP	Frame protocol
FPLMTS	Future public land mobile telecommunications system
FRAMES	Future radio wideband multiple access system, EU research project
FTP	File transfer protocol
GGSN	Gateway GPRS support node
GMM/SM	GPRS mobility management and session management
GMSC	Gateway MSC
GPRS	General packet radio system
GPS	Global positioning system
GSIC	Groupwise serial interference cancellation
GSM	Global system for mobile communications
GTP-U	User plane part of GPRS tunnelling protocol
HA	Home agent
HARQ	Hybrid ARQ
HLR	Home location register
IC	Interference cancellation
ID	Identity
IETF	Internet Engineering Task Force
IM	Intermodulation
IM	IP multimedia (domain)
IMSI	International mobile subscriber identity
IMT-2000	International mobile telephony, third generation networks are referred as IMT-2000 within ITU

IN	Intelligent network
IOS	Interoperability specification
IOT	Interoperability testing
IP	Internet protocol
IPI	Inter-path interference
IPS	Intelligent peripheral system
IPS	IP service
IRC	Interference rejection combining
IS-41	A cellular standard signaling protocol
IS-2000	IS-95 evolution standard (cdma2000)
IS-136	US-TDMA, one of the second generation systems, mainly in Americas
IS-95	cdmaOne, one of the second generation systems, mainly in Americas and in Korea
ISDN	Integrated services digital network
ISI	Intersymbol interference
ISM	Industrial, scientific, medical (band)
ISO	International Organization for Standard
ISUP	ISDN user part
ITU	International telecommunications union
ITUN	SS7 ISUP Tunnelling
L2	Layer 2
LAI	Location area identity
LAN	Local area network
LCS	Location services
LDPC	Low density parity check
LEC	Local exchange company
LEO	Low earth orbit satellite
LP	Low pass
MA	Midamble
MAC	Medium access control
MAHO	Mobile assistance handoff
MAI	Multiple access interference
MAP	Maximum a posteriori
MAP	Mobile application part
MBMS	Multimedia broadcast multicast service
MCU	Multipoint control unit
ME	Mobile equipment
MF	Matched filter
MIN	Mobile Identification Number
MLSD	Maximum likelihood sequence detection
MM	Mobility management
MMSE	Minimum mean square error
MPEG	Motion picture experts group
MPS	Metro packet switch
MR-ACELP	Multirate ACELP
MS	Mobile station
MSC/VLR	Mobile services switching centre/visitor location register
MSC	Mobile switching center, a general term for both digital and analog switches.
MSO	Mobile switching office
MT	Mobile termination
MTP	Message transfer part (broadband)

MTSO	Mobile telephone switching office
MUD	Multiuser detection
N-AMPS	Narrowband AMPS
NAP	Network access point
NAS	Non access stratum
NBAP	Node B application part
NRT	Non-real-time
NSF	National science foundation
ODMA	Opportunity driven multiple access
O&M	Operation and maintenance
OLC	Open logical channel
OS	Operational system
OSA	Open system architectural
OTDM	Optical TDM
OVSF	Orthogonal variable spreading factor
PACCH	Packet associated control channel
PAD	Padding
PAGCH	Packet Access Grant Channel
PBCCH	Packet Broadcast Control Channel
PC	Power control
PCCC	Parallel concatenated convolutional coder
PCCCH	Physical common control channel
PCCH	Paging channel (logical channel)
PCCPCH	Primary common control physical channel
PCH	Paging channel (transport channel)
PCN	Personal communication network
PCPCH	Physical common packet channel
PCS	Personal communication systems, second generation cellular systems mainly in Americas, operating partly on IMT-2000 band
PCU	Packet control unit
PDC	Personal digital cellular, second generation system in Japan
PDCH	Packet data channel
PDCCH	Packet Dedicated Control Channel
PDCP	Packet data converge protocol
PDP	Packet data protocol
PDSCH	Physical downlink shared channel
PDTCH	Packet Data Traffic Channel
PDU	Protocol data unit
PER	Packed encoding rules
PHS	Personal handy phone system
PHY	Physical layer
PI	Page indicator
PIC	Parallel interference cancellation
PICH	Paging indicator channel
PLMN	Public land mobile network
PNCH	Packet notification in channel
PNFE	Paging and notification control function entity
PoC	Push to talk over cellular
PPCH	Physical PCH
PPP	Point to point protocol
PRACH	Physical random access channel

PRACH	Packet random access channel
PS	Packet switched
PSCH	Physical shared channel
PSTN	Public switched telephone network
PTCCH	Packet timing control channel
P-TMSI	Packet-TMSI
PTT	Push to talk
PU	Payload unit
PVC	Predefined virtual connection
QoS	Quality of service
QPSK	Quadrature phase shift keying
RA	Routing area
RA	Rate-adapted (Box)
RAB	Radio access bearer
RACH	Random access channel
RAI	Routing area identity
RAN	Radio access network
RANAP	RAN application part
RAS	Registration Admission status
RB	Radio bearer
RC	Reversed channel
RC	Radio Configuration
RECC	Reverse control channel
RF	Radio frequency
RL	Reverse Link
RLC	Radio link control
RLP	Radio Link Protocol
RNC	Radio network controller
RNS	Radio network subsystem
RNSAP	RNS application part
RNTI	Radio network temporary identity
RPC	Remote procedure call
RRC	Radio resource control
RRM	Radio resource management
RSSI	Received signal strength indicator
RSVP	Resource reservation protocol
RT	Real-time
RTCP	Real-time transport control protocol
RTP	Real-time protocol
RTSP	Real-time streaming protocol
RU	Resource unit
SAAL-NNI	Signaling ATM adaptation layer for network to network interfaces
SAAL-UNI	Signaling ATM adaptation layer for user to network interfaces
SACCH	Slow associated control channel
SAP	Service access point
SAP	Session announcement protocol
SAPI	Service access point identifier
SCCP	Signaling connection control part
SCCPCH	Secondary common control physical channel
SCE	Service creation environment
SCH	Synchronization channel

SCP	Service control point
SCTP	Simple control transmission protocol
SDCCH	Stand-alone dedicated control channel
SDD	Space division duplex
SDH	Synchronous digital hierarchy
SDMA	Space division multiple access
SDP	Session description protocol
SDU	Service data unit
SF	Spreading factor
SFN	System frame number
SGSN	Serving GPRS support node
SGW	Signaling gateway
SHO	Soft handover
SIB	System information block
SIC	Successive interference cancellation
SID	Silence indicator
SID	System ID
SINR	Signal-to-noise ratio where noise includes both thermal noise and interference
SIP	Session initiation protocol
SIR	Signal to interference ratio
SM	Session management
SMDS	Switch multimegabit data service
SMS	Service management system
SMS	Short message service
SMSC	SMS center
SN	Sequence number
SNDCP	Subnetwork dependent convergence protocol
SNR	Signal-to-noise ratio
SONET	Synchronous optical network
SP	Switching point
SR	Spread rate
SRB	Signaling radio bearer
SRNC	Serving RNC
SRNS	Serving RNS
SS7	Signaling system #7
SSP	Service switching point
SSCF	Service specific coordination function
SSCOP	Service specific connection oriented protocol
STD	Switched transmit diversity
STM	Synchronous transfer mode
STP	Signaling transport point
STTD	Space time transmit diversity
TCAP	Transaction capabilities application parts
TCC	Turbo convolutional codes (also called CTC)
TCH	Traffic channel
TCP	Transport control protocol
TCTF	Target channel type field
TD/CDMA	Time division CDMA, combined TDMA and CDMA
TDD	Time division duplex
TDMA	Time division multiple access

TE	Terminal equipment
TF	Transport format
TFCI	Transport format combination indicator
TFCS	Transport format combination set
TFI	Transport format indicator
TMSI	Temporary mobile subscriber identity
TPC	Transmission power control
TPC	Turbo product codes
TR	Transparent mode
TRAU	Transcoder Rate Adaption Unit
TRCD	Transcoder
TS	Technical specification
TSTD	Time switched transmit diversity
TTA	Telecommunications technology association (Korea)
TTC	Telecommunication technology commission (Japan)
TTI	Transmission time interval
TxAA	Transmit adaptive antennas
UDP	User datagram protocol
UE	User equipment
UL	Uplink
UM	Unacknowledged mode
UMTS	Universal mobile telecommunication system
URA	UTRAN registration area
URL	Universal resource locator
U-RNTI	UTRAN RNTI
USCH	Uplink shared channel
USF	Uplink state flag
USIM	UMTS Subscriber identity module
US-TDMA	IS-136, one of the second generation systems mainly in USA
UTRA	UMTS Terrestrial radio access (ETSI)
UTRA	Universal Terrestrial radio access (3GPP)
UTRAN	UMTS Terrestrial radio access network
VAD	Voice activation detection
VCI	Virtual channel identifier
VLR	Visitor Location Register
VoIP	Voice over IP
WARC	World administrative radio conference
WBLA	Wireless broadband local access
WCDMA	Wideband CDMA, Code division multiple access
WDM	Wavelength division multiplexing
WER	Word-error rate
WLL	Wireless local loop
WWW	World Wide Web

3) ABBREVIATIONS AND ACRONYMS
FOR LAN AND MAN

Acronym	Definition
AAA	Authentication, Authorization and Accounting
ACK	acknowledgment
AI	air interface
AID	association identifier
AP	access point
API	Application programming interface
ATIM	announcement traffic indication message
AZR	assign zone restriction
BE	best effort
BSA	basic service area
BSS	basic service set
BSSID	basic service set identification
BWA	broadband wireless access
CC	convolutional coding
CCA	clear channel assessment
CCK	complementary code keying
CF	contention free
CFP	contention-free period
CID	connection identifier
CP	contention period
CPS	contention period sublayer
CRC	cyclic redundancy code
CS	carrier sense
CS	convergence sublayer
CTS	clear to send
CW	contention window
DA	destination address
DBPSK	differential binary phase shift keying
DCE	data communication equipment
DCF	distributed coordination function
DCLA	direct current level adjustment
DI	dwell interval
DIFS	distributed (coordination function) interframe space
DIUC	downlink interval usage code
DFS	dynamic frequency selection
DL	downlink
DLL	data link layer
Dp	desensitization
DQPSK	differential quadrature phase shift keying
DRQ	disengage request
DS	distribution system
DS	distribution service
DSAP	destination service access point
DSM	distribution system medium
DSS	distribution system service
DSSS	direct sequence spread spectrum
DTIM	delivery traffic indication message

ED	energy detection
EDCF	extended DCF
EIFS	extended interframe space
EIRP	equivalent isotropically radiated power
EMEA	Europe, Middle East, and Africa
ERS	extended rate set
ESA	extended service area
ESS	extended service set
FC	frame control
FCH	frame control header
FCS	frame check sequence
FER	frame error ratio
FH	frequency hopping
FHDC	frequency hopping diversity coding
FHSS	frequency-hopping spread spectrum
FIFO	first in first out
GFSK	Gaussian frequency shift keying
IBSS	independent basic service set
ICV	integrity check value
IDU	interface data unit
IE	information element
IFS	interframe space
IMp	intermodulation protection
IOT	interoperability testing
IR	infrared
ITP	IP transfer point
ISM	industrial, scientific, and medical
IV	initialization vector
LAN	local area network
LFS	link frame structure
LLC	logical link control
LME	layer management entity
LRC	long retry count
lsb	least significant bit
MAC	medium access control
MAN	metropolitan area network
MDF	management-defined field
MIB	management information base
MLME	MAC sublayer management entity
MMPDU	MAC management protocol data unit
MMS	multimedia messaging service
MPDU	MAC protocol data unit
MS	mobile station
msb	most significant bit
MSDU	MAC service data unit
MSS	mobile subscriber station
N/A	not applicable
NAV	network allocation vector
NMS	network management system
NRTPS	non-real-time polling service
OFDM	orthogonal frequency division multiplexing

PAN	personal access network
PAPR	peak average power ratio
PAR	project authorization request
PC	point coordinator
PCF	point coordination function
PDU	protocol data unit
PHY	physical (layer)
PHY-SAP	physical layer service access point
PIFS	point (coordination function) interframe space
PLCP	physical layer convergence protocol
PLME	physical layer management entity
PMD	physical medium dependent
PMD-SAP	physical medium dependent service access point
PMP	point to multiple point
PPP	point-to-point protocol
PN	pseudo-noise (code sequence)
PPDU	PLCP protocol data unit
ppm	parts per million
PPM	pulse position modulation
PPP	point-to-point protocol
PRNG	pseudo-random number generator
PS	power save (mode)
PS	privacy sublayer
PSDU	PLCP SDU
PTP	point to point
PWLAN	public WLAN
RA	receiver address
RF	radio frequency
RSSI	received signal strength indication
RSVP	resource reservation protocol
RTPS	reel time polling service
RTS	request to send
RX	receive or receiver
SA	source address
SAP	service access point
SDU	service data unit
SFD	start frame delimiter
SIFS	short interframe space
SLRC	station long retry count
SME	station management entity
SMI	structure of management information
SMP	symmetric multiprocessing
SMS	short messaging service
SMT	station management
SNMP	simple network management protocol
SOP	start of packet
SQ	signal quality (PN code correlation strength)
SRC	short retry count
SS	station service
SSAP	source service access point
SSCS	service specific convergence sublayer
SSID	service set identifier

SSRC	station short retry count
STA	station
STC	time space coding
TA	transmitter address
TBTT	target beacon transmission time
TIM	traffic indication map
TLV	type-length-value coding
TPC	transmit power control
TSF	timing synchronization function
TU	time unit
TX	transmit or transmitter
TXE	transmit enable
UCT	unconditional transition
UIUC	uplink interval usage code
UL	uplink
VAS	value added service
VLAN	virtual LAN
WAN	wide area network
WDM	wireless distribution media
WDS	wireless distribution system
WECA	wireless ethernet compatibility alliance
WEP	wired equivalent privacy
Wi-Fi	wireless fidelity (forum)
WiMAX	worldwide interoperability for microwave access (forum)
WLAN	Wireless LAN
WM	wireless medium
WPA	WiFi protected access
WPA2	2nd generation of WPA

INDEX

ABOUT THE AUTHOR

Dr. William C.Y. Lee is Chairman of Treyspan, Inc., and was formerly Vice President and Chief Scientist of Vodafone Airtouch PLC, and Chairman of LinkAir Communications, Inc. Dr. Lee was one of the original pioneers who developed wireless technology at Bell Labs. World-renowned for his development of commercial AMPS and CDMA technologies, Dr. Lee is a technologist, innovator, teacher, and writer. He is a distinguished Alumni of The Ohio State University, Life Fellow of IEEE, and California Council on Science and Technology Fellow. He is an Honorable Professor at three universities: Beijing University of Aeronautics and Aero Astronautics, Southwest Jiaotong University (Chengdu), and Taiwan National Chiao Tung University. He taught 3-day mobile communication courses internationally, sponsored by George Washington University (1982 to 1998), the first cellular and mobile communications courses offered to the industry. He is the author of the previous two editions of this book (then called *Mobile and Cellular Telecommunications*) as well as four other books.